C0-ATS-006

JUDAISM IN THE FIRST CENTURIES
OF THE CHRISTIAN ERA
THE AGE OF THE TANNAIM

VOLUME I

.LONDON : HUMPHREY MILFORD

OXFORD UNIVERSITY PRESS

JUDAISM

IN THE FIRST CENTURIES OF THE CHRISTIAN ERA
THE AGE OF THE TANNAIM

BY

GEORGE FOOT MOORE

PROFESSOR OF THE HISTORY OF RELIGION
IN HARVARD UNIVERSITY

VOLUME I

CAMBRIDGE
HARVARD UNIVERSITY PRESS
1944

IN MEMORIAM

𝔐. 𝔥. 𝔐.

OBIIT MDCCCCXXIV

A

PREFACE

The aim of these volumes is to represent Judaism in the centuries in which it assumed definitive form as it presents itself in the tradition which it has always regarded as authentic. These primary sources come to us as they were compiled and set in order in the second century of the Christian era, embodying the interpretation of the legislative parts of the Pentateuch and the definition and formulation of the Law, written and unwritten, in the schools, in the century and a half between the reorganization at Jamnia under Johanan ben Zakkai and his associates, after the fall of Jerusalem in the year 70, and the promulgation of the Mishnah of the Patriarch Judah. About the schools of the preceding century, especially about the two great masters, Hillel and Shammai, and the distinctive differences of their disciples, our knowledge comes incidentally through their successors. The whole period, from the time of Herod to that of the Patriarch Judah is the age of the "Tannaim," the representatives of authoritative tradition.

The learned study of the two-fold law is, however, much older, and other sources of various kinds disclose not only the continuity of development in the direction of the normative Judaism of the second century, but many divergent trends — the conflict of parties over fundamental issues, the idiosyncrasies of sects, the rise of apocalyptic with its exorbitant interest in eschatology — a knowledge of all of which is necessary to a historical understanding of the Judaism which it is the principal object of this work to describe.

In the Introduction I have sketched the external and internal history of the centuries with which we are concerned so far as religion was affected by it, and have given a summary account of the sources on which the presentation is based. The chapters on Revealed Religion are meant to make plain at the outset the fundamental principle of Judaism and some of the ways in which it was applied. The succeeding parts treat of the Idea of God; the Nature of Man, and his relation to God; the Observances of Religion; Morals; Piety; and the Hereafter.

I have avoided imposing on the matter a systematic disposition which is foreign to it and to the Jewish thought of the times. The few comprehensive divisions under which it is arranged are not sharply bounded, and the same subject often naturally belongs in more than one of them. In such cases repetition has seemed preferable to cross-references.

The nature of the sources makes simple citation insufficient, and large room has therefore been given to quotations from them or paraphrases of them, thus, so far as possible, letting Judaism speak for itself in its own way. The translations keep as close as may be to the expression of the original, even at some sacrifice of English idiom. A peculiar difficulty arises in the biblical quotations, which rabbinical exegesis, following its own rules or giving rein to the ingenuity of the interpreter, frequently takes in a way quite different from the familiar versions of the Bible or our philological commentators. But when the meaning or the application hinges on the turn given — at least for the nonce — to the words, the translation must try to convey the peculiar interpretation, however strange it may be.

References are given in the footnotes to the sources from which the quotations are taken or on which the statements in the text are based. In many cases these references are a selection from a large array of different age, character, and authority. It has seemed desirable to represent this range and variety of attestation even by what might otherwise appear a superfluity of learning. The homiletical Midrashim, for example, illustrate the popularization of the teaching of the schools as well as the fertility of the homilists, and give evidence of the perpetuation of the tradition in later centuries.

For the rest, I have confined the footnotes to things necessary to immediate understanding, reserving all discussions for an eventual volume of detached notes and excursuses. In the first volume anticipatory references to such detached notes are made in full-faced type; in order not unduly to delay the publication of the work itself, similar references are not made in the second volume.

The transliteration of Hebrew words and names follows, with slight adaptation, the simplified system adopted in the Jewish Encyclopedia. Proper names familiar to English readers are left as they are in the Authorized Version.

These volumes are the outcome of studies which have extended over more than thirty years and ranged over a wide variety of sources. The plan of the present work was conceived ten years since; the execution has taken much more time than I foresaw, but I venture to hope that the presentation has gained thereby in maturity as well as in completness. When I projected it, I contemplated a similar work on Hellenistic Judaism; the occasional parallels and comparisons in these volumes may serve at least to illustrate the fundamental unity of Judaism, as well as to indicate the influence of Greek thought on the religious conceptions of men like Philo.

The material in these volumes is drawn in great part from extensive collections made in the course of my own reading, but it will be evident on every page that I have availed myself largely of the work of others, especially of the mustering and critical sifting of tradition in Wilhelm Bacher's *Agada der Tannaiten*.

Exhaustiveness I have not aimed at; inerrancy is the last thing I should pretend to; but I trust that no essential point has been altogether overlooked, and I am confident that those who know the material best will be the most considerate in their judgment.

My colleague, Professor Harry A. Wolfson, has taken upon him the onerous task of verifying in the proof-sheets the thousands of references to the Talmuds and Midrashim, and by his painstaking examination of the passages quoted or cited has contributed much to the accuracy of the text as well as to the correctness of the references.

A work like the present is made possible by the labors of generations of scholars who have given their lives to the study of this literature; an enumeration even of those from whom I have learned much would read like a bibliography. Special obligations are acknowledged in the notes. The living repositories of this learning of whom I have made inquiry on particular points have been most generous in their response. If among them I name especially Professor Louis Ginzberg, of the Jewish Theological Seminary in New York, it is in acknowledgment not only of his ready helpfulness, but of the constant encouragement I have derived from his interest in my undertaking.

CONTENTS

INTRODUCTION

I. HISTORICAL

CONTENTS

PART II

THE IDEA OF GOD

PART III

MAN, SIN, ATONEMENT

INTRODUCTION

I

HISTORICAL

CHAPTER I

THE FOUNDATIONS OF JUDAISM

THE centuries which we designate politically by the names of the dominant powers of the age successively as the Persian, Greek, and Roman periods of Jewish history constitute as a whole an epoch in the religious history of Judaism.[1] In these centuries, past the middle of which the Christian era falls, Judaism brought to complete development its characteristic institutions, the school and the synagogue, in which it possessed not only a unique instrument for the education and edification of all classes of the people in religion and morality, but the centre of its religious life, and to no small extent also of its intellectual and social life. Through the study of the Scriptures and the discussions of generations of scholars it defined its religious conceptions, its moral principles, its forms of worship, and its distinctive type of piety, as well as the rules of law and observance which became authoritative for all succeeding time. In the light of subsequent history the great achievement of these centuries was the creation of a normative type of Judaism and its establishment in undisputed supremacy throughout the wide Jewish world. This goal was not reached without many conflicts of parties and sects and more than one grave political and religious crisis, but in the end the tendency which most truly represented the historical character and spirit of the religion prevailed, and accomplished the unification of Judaism.

The definitive stage of this development was reached in the latter half of the second century of our era and the beginning of

[1] The name Judaism is now generally appropriated to the religion of this period and what came after it, in distinction from that of the preceding centuries down to the fall of the Kingdom of Judah (586 B.C.), which is called the religion of Israel.

3

the third. The terminus is formally marked by the completion and general acceptance of the body of traditional law (Mishnah) redacted by the Patriarch Judah and promulgated with his authority.[1] The recognized Palestinian scholars of the preceding generations from about the beginning of the Christian era, as transmitters of the unwritten law, are called *Tannaim*, "Traditioners," or, more generally, "Teachers." Their successors are the *Amoraim*, — we might say, "Expositors," — a name given in both Palestine and Babylonia to the professors who taught the law as formulated in the Mishnah and discussed its provisions with their colleagues and pupils. This branch, or stage, of study was called *Talmud*, "Learning,"[2] and eventually gave its name to the great compilations in which the discussions of the schools through many generations are reported, the Palestinian and the Babylonian Talmuds.[3] The former reached substantially the shape in which it has come down to us in the schools of Galilee in the last quarter of the fourth century; the latter in Babylonia about a century later.[4]

The beginning of the period is connected by both Jewish tradition and modern criticism with the name of Ezra, a priest and scribe[5] who came from Babylonia, bringing the Book of the Law of Moses, as a royal commissioner to investigate conditions in Judaea, with authority to promulgate and administer this law among the Jews in the province west of the Euphrates.[6]

According to the Book of Ezra, the company of Jews who returned from Babylonia to the land of their fathers under the lead of Ezra arrived in Jerusalem in the seventh year of Arta-

[1] The date of his death is put, on probable grounds, about 219 A.D.

[2] Both the method and the name come from the age of the Tannaim.

[3] The name Jerusalem Talmud commonly given to the former is a misnomer.

[4] On the Mishnah and the Talmuds, see further below, pp. 150 ff.

[5] *Sofer* was in earlier times a scrivener or secretary. In the present instance, and generally in later usage, it is a man learned in the Scriptures. Ezra 7, 6, 11, 12, 21; Neh. 8, 1, 4, 9, etc.; 12, 26, 36. So γραμματεύς in the Gospels. See W. Bacher, Die älteste Terminologie der jüdischen Schriftauslegung, p. 134.

[6] Ezra 7, 14, 25 f.

xerxes.[1] The proclamation of the law[2] did not take place, however, according to the present order of the narrative, until more than a dozen years later,[3] after Nehemiah had come, in the twentieth year of Artaxerxes,[4] as governor [5] of the district of Judaea, and had restored the fortifications of Jerusalem.[6]

The Artaxerxes of Ezra and Nehemiah has generally been identified with the first of the name, who reigned from 465 to 424, on which assumption Ezra's advent in Jerusalem falls in the year 458 and Nehemiah's in 445. The reading of the Law before the assembled people is commonly put in the autumn of the latter year, at the beginning of the month Tishri.[7] These are the dates adopted by the majority of historians, and the documents of the colony at Elephantine brought to light in 1907–1908 lend additional probability to this interpretation. Others have dated the events under Artaxerxes II, Mnemon (reigned 404–359), which would bring Ezra to Jerusalem in 397 and Nehemiah in 384.[8] The internal difficulties of the account in Ezra-Nehemiah are the same in either case. In the attempt to relieve them it has been proposed to introduce Ezra's mission in Nehemiah's *second* governorship, shortly after 432, by transposing Ezra 7–10 to a place between Neh. 13, 4–36, and Neh. 9–10 (followed by Neh. 8);[9] or even thirty-five years later, in

---

[1] Ezra 7, 8.   [2] Neh. 8.

[3] Hitzig, Geschichte des Volkes Israel, 1869, pp. 283 f. (cf. 287), cancelling on critical grounds the cross-connections of Ezra and Nehemiah in Neh. 8, 9; 10, 2, 12, 26, 36, puts the reading of the Law two months after Ezra's arrival in Jerusalem. In Hitzig's view Ezra was the redactor of our Pentateuch (ibid., p. 288 f.), which he brought with him complete from Babylonia.

[4] Neh. 2, 1.

[5] פחה, Neh. 5, 14; 12, 26, and elsewhere; תרשתא, Neh. 8, 9; 10, 2.

[6] Neh. 3–6.

[7] Neh. 7, 73b. No year is named in the account of the reading of the Law; it is inferred that the leaders would have proceeded to the introduction of the Law as soon as possible after the defences of the city were restored (Neh. 6, 15).

[8] J. Elhorst; Marquart, Fundamente israelitischer und jüdischer Geschichte, p. 31. See C. C. Torrey, Composition and Historical Value of Ezra-Nehemiah (Giessen, 1896), p. 65; cf. Ezra Studies, 1910, pp. 333–335.

[9] W. H. Kosters, Herstel van Israël in het Persische Tijdvak, 1894. German translation, Die Wiederherstellung Israels, u. s. w. 1895.

the seventh year of Artaxerxes II (398/7).[1] Nehemiah 8 is obviously misplaced where it stands. It belongs to the story of Ezra, the chief actor in it, not to that of Nehemiah, who is brought in (harmonistically) only in 8, 9; and the appropriate place for it, on all the presumptions of the narrative,[2] is after Ezra 8.[3]

These critical questions were quite foreign to the Jewish notions of Ezra and his work. As for the dates, they had not the Canon of Ptolemy to operate with, but only four names of Persian kings in the confusing disorder in which they occur in the Books of Ezra, Nehemiah, and Daniel, and they were consequently always far out of the way in their chronology of the Persian period. The oldest rabbinical manual of chronology, the Seder 'Olam Rabbah, allows for the dominion of the Medes and Persians but fifty-two years in all, and from the rebuilding of the temple to the overthrow of the Persian monarchy by Alexander only thirty-four.[4] This compression of the history brought Ezra into the same generation with Zerubbabel and Joshua, who rebuilt the temple in Jerusalem.[5] With this generation he is consistently associated in Jewish tradition. He was, it is said, a student of the law in Babylonia under Baruch son of Neriah, the disciple and amanuensis of Jeremiah,[6] and went up to Jerusalem only after the death of his master; this explains why he did not accompany Zerubbabel and Joshua in their return.[7] According to the Seder 'Olam, Ezra and his party

---

[1] Van Hoonacker, Néhémie et Esdras, 1890; Néhémie en l'an 20 d'Artaxerxes II, 1892.

[2] See especially Ezra 7, 14, 25 f.

[3] C. C. Torrey, Ezra Studies, 1910, pp. 252 ff. His order is: Ezra 8; Neh. 7, 70–73a; 7, 73b–8, 18; Ezra 9, 1–10, 44; Neh. 9, 1–10, 40.

[4] Seder 'Olam Rabbah c. 30 (ed. Ratner, f. 71a; cf. f. 69a and note 15); 'Abodah Zarah 8b–9a (R. Jose bar Ḥalafta, a special authority in chronology). Leaving the Medes ("Darius the Mede" in Daniel) out of the reckoning, our chronology (after Ptolemy) gives, from the first year of Cyrus as king of Babylon (538) to the end of Darius III (332), 206 years, and from the completion of the second temple (516) to the same terminus, 184 years. On the names of the Persian kings see also Rosh ha-Shanah 3b, bottom; Seder 'Olam c. 30 (Ratner, p. 68b, and notes). See Note 1.

[5] Ezra 1–6. See Haggai; Zechariah 1–8.   [6] Jer. 36 and 43.

[7] Megillah 16b, bottom. They did not find his name in Ezra 2, 2.

arrived in Jerusalem the year following the completion of the temple.[1] Others, however, have him go up with Zerubbabel and Joshua and begin with them the building of the temple,[2] finding his name in Neh. 7, 7, Azariah (of which Ezra is an abridged form; cf. Neh. 12, 1).[3] The most probable conjecture about the three "sheep" who, at the opening of a new epoch, began to build up the ruinous house in Enoch 89, 72, is that Zerubbabel, Joshua, and Ezra are meant.

These differences do not touch the main agreement, which associates Ezra with the men of the restoration. His great part in it was the restoration of the law. He had brought the Book of the Law of Moses with him from Babylonia, and, as the Jews presumably combined the dates,[4] a few months after the completion of the temple, made it public by reading it aloud in a great assembly of the people, as narrated in Neh. 8. The light in which this transaction appeared to later generations is expressed in the sentence: When the law had been forgotten in Israel, Ezra came up from Babylonia and established it.[5] Ezra was qualified to have given the law originally, if it had not already been given by Moses.[6]

To the observance of this law the people, after a solemn day of fasting and humiliation, with confession of the sins of their forefathers and their own, bound themselves by a covenant

---

[1] Seder 'Olam Rabbah c. 29 (ed. Ratner, f. 67b); cf. Seder 'Olam Zuṭa, where it is added that Zerubbabel returned to Babylon and died there.

[2] Pirkè de-R. Eliezer c. 38, near the end.

[3] The list of members of the Great Synagogue in a commentary on Abot by R. Jacob ben Samson, a pupil of Rashi, begins: "Azariah, who is Ezra." Maḥzor Vitry, p. 463; cf. p. 481.

[4] Ezra 6, 15–22; Neh. 7, 73b. See Rosh ha-Shanah 3b, below; 'Arakin 13a (Baraita): Ezra came to Jerusalem in the year following the completion of the temple.

[5] Sukkah 20a, below. It is not implied that the law was altogether unknown in Judaea, as is clear from the sequel, in which it is said that when it had been again forgotten Hillel came from Babylonia and did the same thing, and later still R. Ḥiyya and his sons. The words are attributed to R. Simeon ben Laḳish, a Palestinian teacher of the third century. Cf. Sifrè Deut. § 48 (ed. Friedmann, f. 84b, above): Shaphan, Ezra, Akiba.

[6] Sanhedrin 21b, end; Tos. Sanhedrin 4, 7.

under the signature and seal of the notables, and for the whole community by an oath and curse.[1]

The restoration of the law by Ezra is the theme of 4 Esdras 14, 18–48.[2] The date of the first vision is given as the thirtieth year after the destruction of Jerusalem; the seer is in exile in Babylon.[3] The situation in c. 14 is the same. The Law of God has been destroyed (so also 4, 23), not only the legislation but history and prophecy (14, 21). Ezra prays that he may be inspired to reproduce it and "write everything that has happened in the world from the beginning, the things that were written in Thy Law, that men may be able to find the way, and that those who would live in the last days may live." His prayer is granted, and in mantic ecstasy he dictates day and night to five stenographers for forty days the sum of ninety-four books, the twenty-four of the Hebrew Bible and seventy others. The former are to be made public, to be read by worthy and unworthy alike; the latter Ezra is to reserve to transmit them only to the wise (sapientibus de populo tuo), "in his enim est vena intellectus et sapientiae fons et scientiae flumen."[4] He is imagined as the restorer, not of the Law alone but of the whole

[1] Neh. 9–10. Compare the ratification of the Book of the Law in the reign of Josiah, 2 Kings 23, 1–3. The significance of this parallel struck Lagarde and Kuenen simultaneously in 1870.

[2] This apocalypse was written toward the close of the first century of the Christian era.

[3] G. A. Box (The Ezra-Apocalypse, p. 1 f.), following Kabisch, is so sure that "no Jewish writer could have made such a blunder as to transfer Ezra to a time so remote from his true situation," that he strikes out the name Esdras in 3, 1, and thus obtains a "Salathiel Apocalypse." That the Jews did make precisely this "blunder" and maintained it consistently has been shown above. See Note 2.

[4] The esoteric seventy are commonly taken to be apocalyptic books like his own. It is much more probable, however, that these books, which are to be entrusted to the learned (חכמים) only, are the traditional law (F. Rosenthal, Vier Apokryphische Bücher aus der Zeit und Schule R. Akiba's, 1885, pp. 41, 57 f.). L. Ginzberg, 'Tamid. The Oldest Treatise of the Mishnah,' Journal of Jewish Lore and Philosophy, 1919 (and separately 1920), thinks that seventy is not a round number, but a summation of the number of the books which constituted the entire halakic literature of the Tannaim (58 Parts of the Mishnah, 9 of Sifra, Mekilta, Sifrè Num. and Deut. = 70).

Bible, and reproduces by revelation the post-exilic literature before it had been produced, to say nothing of the seventy other books. This autobiographic account of the restitution of the sacred books was taken as authentic by many Christian writers from Irenaeus down.[1] Jerome had it in mind when he wrote, in reference to the phrase "unto this day" in the Pentateuch (Gen. 35, 4; Deut. 34, 6):[2] Certe hodiernus dies illius temporis aestimandus est, quo historia ipsa contexta est, sive Moysen dicere volueris auctorem Pentateuchi, sive Ezram eiusdem instauratorem operis, non recuso.[3]

Ezra has been a great figure in modern biblical criticism also. The surmise that Ezra was the compiler or editor of the Pentateuch was enounced in one form or another by several scholars in the sixteenth and seventeenth centuries.[4] The leading critics of the middle of the nineteenth century were agreed, however, that all the sources into which they divided the Pentateuch were older than the Babylonian exile, and the prevailing opinion was that they had been united in the composite whole as we now have it[5] in the generation between the introduction of Deuteronomy (621) and the fall of Jerusalem (586), or that, at the latest, it was completed in Babylonia in the following generation. They were agreed also that the source which begins in Genesis 1 and includes the bulk of the legislation in Exodus, Leviticus, and Numbers, though not all of the same origin or age, was the oldest stratum of narrative and law in the Pentateuch, and Deuteronomy the latest.[6] Ezra was, as in the traditional view,

---

[1] Fabricius, Codex Pseudepigraphus Veteris Testamenti, pp. 1156–1160.

[2] These words played a prominent part in the beginnings of doubt about the Mosaic authorship of the whole Pentateuch.

[3] Adversus Helvidium c. 7 (ed. Vallarsi, II, 211 f.).

[4] Andreas Masius (1574); Spinoza (1670); Richard Simon (1685); van Dale (1696), and others.

[5] More or less extensive reserve being made for minor additions, glosses, textual changes, and the like.

[6] It is sufficient here to name Ewald, Geschichte des Volkes Israel, 3 ed., IV (1864), 173, cf. I, 190 f.; and Kuenen, Historisch-kritisch Onderzoek, enz., I (1865), 165 f. According to Kuenen, the redactor of the Pentateuch,

the restorer of the law. He brought up the Pentateuch from
Babylonia, and was chiefly instrumental in getting it put in
force as the law of the returned exiles in Judaea.[1]

A radically different theory of the age of the constituent elements of the Pentateuch had been put forward a generation
earlier, namely, that the Levitical law as we find it in Exodus,
Leviticus, and Numbers was not the earliest stratum, but the
latest: it originated among the exiles in Babylonia, in priestly
circles under the influence of the ruling ideas of Ezekiel. That
the redaction of the Pentateuch as a whole was completed by
Ezra was regarded as probable; but no material part in it was
attributed to him.[2] The ruling critics of the day promptly and
emphatically rejected this construction based on the history of
the religion and its institutions, pronouncing on it the veto of
the critical analysis and of the language, and the episode was
almost forgotten.

Conclusions substantially agreeing with those of Vatke and
George were reached independently of them by K. H. Graf
in 1866,[3] with whom the modern period of criticism may be said
to begin. By an exhaustive comparison of the three strata of
legislation among themselves and with the historical books and
the prophets he argued that the ritual and ceremonial laws in
the three middle books of the Pentateuch, in the form in which
we have them, represent a development in general character as
well as in many particulars posterior to Deuteronomy and beyond Ezekiel. To this mass of laws many authors in the course
of a century or more had contributed. Graf surmised that Ezra

a member of the priesthood of Jerusalem, completed his task between 600
and 590 B.C.

[1] See Ewald, Geschichte des Volkes Israel, 3 ed., IV (1864), 173 ff.,
213 ff.

[2] W. Vatke, Die Religion des Alten Testaments, 1835. A similar result
was reached independently, through a different approach, by G. F. L. George,
Die älteren jüdischen Feste, 1835.

[3] Die geschichtlichen Bücher des Alten Testaments. Graf had been a
pupil of Eduard Reuss at Strasbourg, who had propounded a similar theory
in a series of unpublished theses as early as 1834.

collected these various writings and brought them with him to Jerusalem, where in the fifteen years or so that elapsed between his arrival and the promulgation of his Book of the Law of Moses he compiled and redacted them, perhaps with additions of his own. The account of the introduction of the law shows that the community in Jerusalem till then had possessed no copy of this book and had no definite knowledge about it.[1]

Kuenen, whose earlier position has been referred to above, was led by Graf's presentation of the evidence to revise his opinion about the general priority of the levitical legislation. Graf had detached the laws from the corresponding narrative in Genesis and the beginning of Exodus, the early date of which he did not question; Kuenen made the theory consistent by bringing this strand of the narrative also down to the exile, and reuniting it with the legislation.[2]

The hypothesis with which Kuenen's name is properly associated goes, however, very much further than Graf. It was, in brief, that both the history and the laws in what is called the Priests' Code were composed in Babylonia in circles of which Ezra, at once priest and scholar, is representative. "It was not laws long in existence which, after having been for a time forgotten, were now proclaimed anew and adopted by the people. The priestly ordinances were *then for the first time* made known and imposed on the Jewish nation." [3] The introduction of Ezra's new lawbook, the Priests' Code, made an epoch in the history of the religion comparable to that made by Hilkiah's Book of the Law (Deuteronomy) [4] in the reign of Josiah, and, like the latter, was composed for the end which it accomplished.

Kuenen is inclined to conjecture that Ezra found it advisable

---

[1] Graf, op. cit., pp. 70–72.

[2] Colenso and Popper had prepared the way for this step, in which Graf himself eventually followed Kuenen.

[3] De Godsdienst van Israël, II (1870), 136. He is speaking of the promulgation of the law (444 B.C.), as narrated in Neh. 8–10.

[4] The correspondence between the rôle of Shaphan (2 Kings 22, 8 ff.) and that of Ezra had not escaped Jewish observation. Sifrè Deut. § 48 (ed. Friedmann, p. 84 b, above).

to adapt some provisions of the book he brought from Babylonia to the established usage of the priesthood in Jerusalem
whose support it was necessary to ensure, and to actual conditions of other kinds; and that he did so in the years that intervened between his arrival and the promulgation of the law; but
to this accessory hypothesis he attaches no great importance.[1]

In Kuenen's construction the Book of the Law of Moses which
Ezra, with the support of Nehemiah, introduced was the so-
called Priests' Code *only*.[2] At a later time the older historical
and legal sources were worked into the scheme of the Priests'
Code by an unknown editor in such a way as to give a semblance
of unity and continuity to the whole, and Deuteronomy appended.   Thus was eventually formed the composite work
which we call the Five Books of Moses.[3]

To the wide acceptance of the new conception of the nature
and significance of Ezra's work Wellhausen contributed equally
with Kuenen, and the modern critical school is often named
after him. Graf's transposition of the sources solved for him
at one stroke difficulties for which he had seen no solution, and
he found the evidence Graf adduced of the exilic origin of the
levitical law completely convincing. In regard to the introduction of the law and its effect on religion he was in accord with
Kuenen, with one important exception: in his opinion the
Priests' Code which had been drawn up in Babylonia was already
united with the older historical and legal literature that was
in the hands of the Jews in Jerusalem, presumably by Ezra

[1] Godsdienst, II, 137 f.
[2] Historisch-kritisch Onderzoek, 2 ed., I, 294 f. So also E. Reuss, Geschichte der Heiligen Schriften Alten Testaments, pp. 460 ff., 474; B. Stade,
Geschichte des Volkes Israel, II, 183, and others. All these critics recognized that more or less extensive additions to the laws in the original Priests'
Code were made after Ezra.
[3] The most complete development of Kuenen's theory is Eduard Meyer's
Die Entstehung des Judenthums, 1896, in which the trustworthiness of the
account of the introduction of the law in Neh. 8 (from Ezra's Memoirs
through an intermediate source) and the authenticity of the documents in
the Book of Ezra are maintained. With Stade he lays weight on the interest
of the Persian government in the ordering of affairs in Judaea.

himself, before the transactions recorded in Neh. 8–10, so that the book to the observance of which the people then covenanted themselves was not the Priests' Code alone but the Pentateuch, minus later additions.[1]

Wellhausen recognized also that the Law made no abrupt break in the development of the religion. It choked it only gradually. A long time passed before the kernel turned wooden inside the shell. Until Pharisaism prevailed, the freer impulses emanating from the prophets remain in living force. The older Judaism is the forecourt of Christianity. The greater part of what in the Old Testament still exerts an influence today and can be relished without previous historical training is a product of the post-exilic age.[2] In general, Wellhausen had a much juster estimate of the character of Judaism than many of those who came after him.[3]

For the history of Judaism the radical thing in the theory of Kuenen is not the chronological order of the sources discovered by criticism in the Pentateuch, nor the date assigned to the Priests' Law and the narrative that goes with it, but the thesis that the introduction of Ezra's lawbook changed the whole character of the religion. It was, in the words of Kuenen, the origin of Judaism. The nature of the change is set out by him in pointed antitheses: There (i.e., before Ezra) the spirit ruled, here (after him) the letter; there the free word, here the scripture. The outstanding figure of the preceding centuries was the prophet; after Ezra his place was taken by the scribe.[4] The reform was anti-prophetic and anti-universalistic;[5] inevitably the law extinguished the remnants of prophecy, and it fastened exclusiveness on the religion for all time to come.

[1] Israelitische und jüdische Geschichte, 7 ed., p. 167.
[2] Ibid., p. 193 f.
[3] See the chapters, Die jüdische Frömmigkeit, and Die Ausbildung des Judaismus, — in the latter, particularly p. 285.
[4] De Godsdienst van Israel, II, 152. See the foregoing and following pages, 146–156.
[5] Ibid., p. 146.

It is evident in this contrast that when Kuenen speaks of
the age before Ezra what he has in mind is not the actual religion
of Judah under the kingdom or after the restoration, but the
ideal of religion propounded by the prophets from Amos down
to the author of Isa. 40 ff.; and when he speaks of the age after
Ezra he has at least in the background of his mind the Judaism
of the Scribes and Pharisees in the New Testament, and in the
remote distance the Talmud. Kuenen is aware that his antitheses are too categorical, but they do not exaggerate the change
in the character of the Jewish religion which he believed to have
been wrought by the introduction and ratification of the Priests'
Code, nor misrepresent its nature as he conceived it.

That there are many and great differences between Judaism
in the centuries with which the present volumes have chiefly to
do and the religion of the kingdom of Judah needs no words;
the differences, as we shall see, are in fact much profounder than
those which Kuenen emphasizes. The question is whether the
adoption of Ezra's lawbook as related in Neh. 8 is the prime
cause of these differences, or, as he puts it, the origin of Judaism.

Antecedently, nothing would seem less likely to bring about
such a revolutionary result than a book like the Priests' Code,
which, as the name imports, is a law for the priests, chiefly occupied with the ritual of sacrifice and festivals; the interdictions
(sacred and abhorred) with the proper purifications or expiations, about which laymen had always had to go to the priests
for expert advice; and the rights and privileges of the sacerdotal
caste. These things belong in themselves to the most primitive
elements of religion, and neither enrichment of the cultus, nor
more minute rules about interdictions and expiations, nor increase of priestly revenues and prerogatives, affect their essential
character. Nor can it easily be imagined that a compact to fulfil their obligations under such a lawbook made a thorough and
permanent change in the attitude of the Jews toward the institutions of their religion. Nehemiah 13, 4–31, which Kuenen
derives from the Memoirs of Nehemiah, Malachi, which he puts

in his second governorship, Joel, and the various prophetic writings which critics date in the later Persian and Greek periods, are strong testimony to the contrary.

On the other hand, the Jews in the Persian period, before the days of the supposed reforms of Ezra as well as after them, had all that we possess of the pre-exilic and exilic literature, with the increments it received in the age of the restoration. What had been preserved and collected of the words of the prophets had acquired, through the fulfilment of their predictions of doom, an estimation and authority such as their contemporaries had never accorded to their spoken words. The whole history of the people was recast to impress upon it the moral of prophecy in what is often called a deuteronomic pragmatism. The influence of the prophets on the religion of the people was in fact the greatest in the age in which it is supposed to have been finally suffocated by the law.

The revolutionary changes in the cultus which Josiah made in 621 on the authority of the book produced by Hilkiah (2 Kings 22–23) can hardly have lasted long after his death; in any case it was less than half a century to the end of the kingdom and cultus together. The opinion of most critics is that Hilkiah's Book of the Law was expanded into the book we call Deuteronomy after the fall of the kingdom. It is presumable that it was the law of the community which rebuilt the temple at the urgency of the prophets Haggai and Zechariah, and thereafter.[1] Deuteronomy is, however, much more than a book of laws; it is the quintessence of the prophets, a monument of Hebrew religious genius, and a chief cornerstone of Judaism. Of other foundation stones, such as the stories of the patriarchs and God's dealing with them in Genesis,[2] the lawgiving at Sinai in the older narratives, with the revelation of God's character in Exod. 33, 17–23; 34, 5–7, on which the Jewish conception of God is

---

[1] Always assuming that in details it was supplemented by the tradition of the priesthood (see, e.g., Deut. 17, 9; 24, 8).

[2] Think, for example, of the ideal of faith in Abraham.

based, and the idea of holiness in Lev. 17–26, it is unnecessary here to do more than make passing mention.

The writings which critics assign to the Persian and Greek periods — many of the finest Psalms, the Proverbs, Job, the later additions to the prophetic scriptures — prove that the achievement of those centuries and their legacy to succeeding generations was the appropriation and assimilation of the religious and moral teachings of the writings that have been named. That Ezra's lawbook turned Judaism into an arid ritualism and legalism is refuted by the whole literature of the following time.

This is equally manifest in the Palestinian literature outside the canon, particularly in the Book of Sirach (Ecclesiasticus), whose author was himself a Scribe. The predominance of this element in the Judaism of a later age is attested by the juristic exegesis (Tannaite Midrash) [1] of the second century of the Christian era, and by the influence of the highest religious and moral teaching of the Pentateuch and the Prophets on the legal norms (Halakah) defined in the Mishnah and kindred works.

It cannot be too strongly emphasized that, whatever part Babylonian Jews returning to Jerusalem may have had in the restoration or subsequently, the Judaism which is the subject of our present study was not a new kind of religion introduced from Babylonia, but a normal and fruitful growth on Palestinian soil.

The definition and administration of the levitical law was in the hands of the priests. Various practical modifications of the laws to adapt them to changing conditions in Judaea in the Persian period are recognized by critics. The permissive substitution, for example, of a pair of doves or pigeons for a lamb in several species of sacrifice, which is a manifest appendix to the older provision, is taken as a concession to poverty, and seems to contemplate an urban population. Besides such natural

[1] See Note 3.

accommodation to circumstances, there are supplements of a different kind, such as the cumulative scheme of sacrifices at the festivals in Num. 28 f., or the scale of sin offerings in Lev. 4 for the high priest, the whole congregation, the ruler, one of the common people, which seem to represent an ideal — like the whole of Ezekiel's programme in chapters 40–48 — rather than an actuality. In fact, criticism since 1870 has by degrees come to regard so large a part of these laws as "secondary," that is, of Palestinian origin and of the later Persian period, that the supposed original Babylonian Priests' Code threatens to become a superfluous hypothesis, and it would not be surprising if the next phase of criticism should maintain that the whole development of the Law took place in Judaea.

In matters of ritual and of permissions and interdictions, clean and unclean, purifications and expiations, it must be understood that the great bulk of the law was always the traditional practice and rule of the priesthood; what is set down in writing, primarily as a manual for the priests themselves, is in general a bare outline which at every step requires the interpretation of usage and technical tradition. And the vastly more extensive unwritten law was a living and growing thing.

Of the development of civil and criminal law we have no information. The Jews possessed a few fragmentary pages from a code of the kingdom, preserved in Exod. 21–23. From the first section — the solitary one that remains intact — and the surviving parts of others, it is evident that the code was ordered and formulated with a precision that testifies to juristic experience and skill; it was plainly laid out on a large scale, and must have made a considerable volume. The loss of this code cannot be too greatly regretted; it would have given a survey of the civilization of the age such as nothing else can give. Some of the lacunae in the text have been filled by matter of similar content, but in a preceptive form. The Book of Deuteronomy also preserves remnants of ancient laws (e.g., in chap. 22). But these survivals are clearly not sufficient for the administration of justice. Here also it must be assumed that the elders of the town or village — the heads of the families or family groups that made up the community — administered the law in accordance with custom and precedent, a consuetudinary law in essence older than the written law and underlying it. Like all such common law it adapted itself to new situations by judicial interpretation and application without the aid of legislation.

Under Persian rule the Jews were doubtless left, as in the succeeding empires, to live under their own laws and judicial procedure in matters that involved Jews only. The principle of all ancient law was not uniformity for all within the territorial limits of a state, but different laws and jurisdictions determined by the status or nationalities of the persons.

Deuteronomy 17, 8–13, provides for a reference to the priests in Jerusalem and "the judge that shall be in those days" of cases too hard for local adjudication, and binds the local judges to accept and enforce the decision.[1] Through a central court of this kind, a sufficient uniformity would be secured. In later times the Senate or Sanhedrin in Jerusalem performed this function.

There was no conflict between this legal development, priestly or judicial, and the appropriation and assimilation of the great principles of religion of which we have spoken above. In a religion which had inherited, as Judaism did, sacred scriptures of various kinds which were all believed to embody divine revelation (Torah), in which God made known his own character and his will for the whole conduct of life, there is no incompatibility between the most minute attention to rites and observances, or to the rules of civil and criminal law, and the cultivation of the worthiest conceptions of God and the highest principles of morality, not only in the same age, but, as we see in the literature of the schools and the synagogue, by the same men. On the contrary, the seriously religious man could not be indifferent to any part of the revealed law of God. The same rabbis who

---

[1] This probably belongs to the programme of the Deuteronomic reforms. Cf. the account of Jehoshaphat's judicial institutions, 2 Chron. 19, 5–11.

extended the law of tithing to garden herbs paraphrased the principle, Thou shalt love thy neighbor as thyself, as Let thy neighbor's property be as dear to thee as thine own, and thy neighbor's honor as thine own, and developed the prohibition of interest ('usury') into laws of bargain and sale and definitions of unfair competition which to modern ideas of business seem utopian.   They made love to God the one supremely worthy motive of obedience to his law; and found in Exodus 34, 6 f., not only the character of God revealed — "God merciful and gracious, long-suffering, and abundant in loving-kindness and truth; keeping mercy unto the thousandth generation, forgiving iniquity and transgression and sin" — but in the imitation of these traits the ideal of human character.

In the conditions that existed in Judaea in the age of the restoration and afterwards, an urgent part of the task of the religious leaders was to resist the admixture of heathenism and lapses from Judaism through the intimate relations between Jews and the surrounding peoples, and especially through intermarriage. The Books of Ezra and Nehemiah represent those worthies as greatly concerned by the frequency of such connections in all classes, even in the priesthood, and describe the drastic measures they resorted to to abate the evil.[1]   In their attitude the origin of Jewish exclusiveness, or, in Kuenen's phrase, the "anti-universalistic" character of the reform, is sought.

The opposition to intermarriage with other peoples was, however, no new thing; it is categorically prohibited in earlier laws (Exod. 34, 16; Deut. 7, 3 f.); [2] Ezra's prayer puts the prohibition into the mouth of "the prophets" (Ezra 9, 11 f.). Nor is there anything peculiarly Jewish in the restriction of marriage to the members of a people, citizens of a state, or even to a class of citizens in the state.   In Rome marriage was confined to members of the patrician families; the offspring of a

---

[1] Ezra 9–10; Neh. 10, 28–30; 13, 23 ff.

[2] It is to be noted that there is no corresponding law in the Priests' Code, though the patriarchal story makes plain enough the feeling of its author.

patrician by any other connection could not be Roman citizens, nor represent either family or state in any capacity.[1] The Canuleian law of 445 B.C.,[2] legitimizing intermarriage between patricians and plebeians, was violently opposed by the former, on the ground that it would contaminate their blood and throw into confusion the laws concerning the *gentes*.[3]

In Athens, Pericles put through a law [4] that only those both of whose parents were Athenian citizens should be reckoned Athenians. The law was not immediately enforced and seems to have been generally regarded as a dead letter; but when occasion later arose, the consequences, as recounted by Plutarch, make the proceedings in Ezra 10 appear tame by comparison. Nearly five thousand were proved to be the offspring of such illegitimate alliances, and were not only struck from the register of citizens but sold into slavery.[5] The text of a law of similar effect is quoted in the prosecution of Neaera,[6] which provides that an alien who cohabits with an Athenian woman under any pretext whatever shall, on conviction, be sold into slavery; his property also was sold, one third of the proceeds going to the man who instituted the prosecution. In the converse case of an Athenian citizen and an alien woman, she was to be sold into slavery, and the man fined ten thousand drachmae. The motive of such legislation is to perpetuate a pure-bred race, especially to keep unmixed the blood of the citizen body; it is a measure of self-preservation, and nothing more. There is no equity in judging it otherwise in the case of the Jews under the prejudicial title of exclusiveness.

Among the Jews, however, the preservation of the purity of

[1] W. Warde Fowler, Encyclopaedia of Religion and Ethics, VIII, 463.

[2] The date curiously coincides with that generally taken for the adoption of Ezra's lawbook.

[3] Livy, iv. 1 ff.; Cicero, De republica, ii. 37.

[4] In 451/50. The date is again to be noted.

[5] Plutarch, Pericles, c. 37.

[6] Among the orations of Demosthenes, lix. 16. The speech is assigned by critics to ca. 340 B.C.

the national religion is emphasized both in the laws and in the account of Ezra's reform. This consideration comes out strongly in the argument of the Roman patricians; [1] and, in consequence of the relation of the citizen body to the religion of the city, is implicit in the Athenian example. But the Jews under Persian rule had no political existence; they had only a national religion, and in its preservation lay their self-preservation.[2] That the religious leaders had the insight to perceive this and the loyalty to contend with all their might against the dissolution of both nationality and religion, whether in the age of the restoration or in the crisis of Hellenism, or after the destruction of the temple and the war under Hadrian, is certainly not to their discredit. The separateness of the Jews, their ἀμιξία, was one of the prime causes of the animosity toward them, especially in the miscellaneous fusion of peoples and syncretism of religions in the Hellenistic kingdoms and the Roman world; but it accomplished its end in the survival of Judaism, and therein history has vindicated it.

It seems still sometimes to be imagined that the laws about clean and unclean in the Priests' Code, including the interdictions of various kinds of food and the prescription of a peculiar mode of slaughtering animals, not only had the effect of putting hindrances in the way of intercourse with the heathen, especially at table, but that they were invented or revived on purpose to accomplish this end. Of this there is neither internal nor external evidence. They were ancient customs, the origin and reason of which had long since been forgotten. Some of them are found among other Semites, or more widely; some were, so far as we know, peculiar to Israel; but as a whole, or, we may say, as a system, they were the distinctive customs which the Jews had inherited from their ancestors with a religious sanction in the two categories of holy and polluted. Other peoples had

---

[1] Livy, iv. 2; cf. vi. 41, 4 ff.
[2] Converts to the religion (proselytes) were naturalized in the race.

their own, some of them for all classes, some, as among the
Jews, specifically for the priests, and these systems also were
distinctive.[1]

The interdictions, which in the Pentateuch fall into a few
general classes, were, no doubt, as among other peoples, known
to everybody as part of the tradition of custom in which all
grew up. Haggai 2, 11–13, shows that responses were asked of
the priests in cases of clean and unclean; but the priests' Torah
was principally concerned with the appropriate remedies for the
inadvertent or accidental transgression of the interdictions, the
piacula and purifications prescribed or performed by them,
whereby the incommensurate consequences of intrusion into the
sphere of the holy or contact with the unclean might be nullified.
This is a salient feature of the treatment of this subject everywhere in the Pentateuch, not peculiarly in the Priests' Code.

The idea of one only God has for its corollary one religion.
That this God would one day be acknowledged and served by
all mankind was proclaimed by the prophets from Isaiah 40 ff.
on, and became the faith of the following centuries.[2] It was
self-evident that the universal religion of the future would be
that which God had revealed, immutable as himself, and entrusted meanwhile to one people, that it might be his prophet
to the nations. The Jews were the only people in their world
who conceived the idea of a universal religion,[3] and labored to
realize it by a propaganda often more zealous than discreet,
which made them many enemies; and precisely in the age when

[1] See Frazer, Golden Bough, III, chapters iii–vii (pp. 100–418); X, chap.
ii (pp. 22–100, passim). Priests, in Greece, P. Stengel, Griechische Kultus-
altertümer, §§ 20–22; at Rome, G. Wissowa, Religion und Kultus der Römer,
§ 67; Samter, in Real-Encyclopaedie der classischen Altertumswissenschaft,
VI, col. 2486 ff.—Anyone who will take the trouble to compare Aulus Gellius,
x. 15, on the restrictions to which the Flamen Dialis was subject with the
corresponding laws for the Jewish high priest will find that the latter are few
and simple by contrast.

[2] See Zech. 8, 20–23; Zech. 14, 16–21; 14, 9; etc.

[3] On Nationality and Universality, see below, Part I, chapter i, and
Vol. II, pp. 371 ff.

the "anti-universalistic" law was enthroned in the completest authority was the expansion of Judaism at its height.[1]

Of the history of the Jews in Palestine under Persian rule there is no record. The prophets Haggai and Zechariah give a glimpse of the internal situation at the time of the rebuilding of the temple (520–516 B.C.) and let us divine the flaring up of the hope of national restoration which attached to the person of Zerubbabel. The fragmentary Memoirs of Nehemiah, eighty years or more later, show that Jerusalem had recently passed through a crisis — we do not know what — in which its fortifications had been dismantled, and tells how he restored them, and of the domestic and foreign difficulties of his task as governor.

The discovery a few years ago of a series of documents from a Jewish military colony on the upper Nile, ranging over the greater part of the fifth century, gives a surprising picture of the religion of this remote and isolated community, and reveals something of their relations to the authorities in Palestine. Bagohi, the governor of Judaea, and Johanan the high priest in Jerusalem, to whom the Jews of Elephantine write in 408, are doubtless the Bagoses and Johannes of the story in Josephus, Antt. xi. 7, 1. Sanballat, the governor of Samaria, named in the same letter, is generally taken to be identical with the Sanballat with whom Nehemiah had so much trouble.[2] With the conquest of Alexander (333 B.C.) the Jews come at least casually within the view of the Greek historians.

With the expulsion of one of the sons of Joiada the son of Eliashib the high priest, who had married a daughter of Sanballat (Neh. 13, 28 f.), is commonly connected the so-called Samaritan schism, with its rival temple at Shechem. There is, indeed, nothing of this in the text cited, but it is thought to furnish the true date for events which Josephus narrates as oc-

[1] See Part I, chapter vii.

[2] If this identification is right, it would settle the question about the Artaxerxes of Nehemiah in favor of Artaxerxes I.

curring in the times of the last Darius and Alexander the Great.[1] The Alexander part of the story in Josephus is not embellished legend but pure fiction of a species very familiar in the Hellenistic literature of the Jews. The romance of Manasseh and Nikaso, which puts the brand of illegitimacy on the whole succession of Samaritan high priests, the founding of the temple on Gerizim by a heathen, the accession to the Shechemites of reprobates who fled from Jerusalem under charges of eating the unclean or violation of the sabbath, and the like,[2] are from the same hand and display the same motive. A historian may properly decline to admit such testimony as to either fact or date.[3]

It is probable that Shechem, one of the most venerable religious sites in the land, had all along been a place of worship, with a priesthood of its own and a cultus not unlike that in Jerusalem, though, of course, lacking the *sacra publica* — in rabbinical phrase, a public high place. As such there was no reason why the Jews should concern themselves particularly about it. All this took an entirely different complexion when the claim was set up that Gerizim, and not Zion, was the place which God had chosen for his habitation, or "to put his Name there" (Deut. 12, 5, and often), the only place in the land where sacrifice was legitimately offered, vows absolved, festivals observed, and the rest.[4] It is this claim, not the mere building of the Shechemite temple, that constitutes the Samaritan schism. Jews and Samaritans [5] worshipped the same God with the same rites; they

[1] Antt. xi. 7, 2; 8, 2–7. Josephus' source, as appears from internal evidence, was a historical work by an Alexandrian Jew whose ambition it was to magnify his own nation in the eyes of Greek readers, and who lost no occasion to vilify the "Samaritans" of Shechem. See, besides the present passage, his account of the disputation before Ptolemy Philometor, Antt. xiii. 3, 4, and the next note.

[2] Antt. xi. 8, 7.

[3] As to date he may take warning from the story of Bagoses and the high priest John

[4] See John 4, 20; cf. Josephus, Antt. xiii. 3, 4.

[5] It is to be observed that, as the name of a religious body, Samaritans does not mean the people of the city of Samaria, or of the old kingdom of Israel, but only those who worshipped on Mt. Gerizim.

had the same law, the complete Pentateuch. The differences between them in the interpretation and application of this law, when we begin to know about them, are not fundamental. But on the sole place where God had ordained that he should be worshipped the breach was irremediable.

The Samaritans, as has been said, had the entire Pentateuch, which they have preserved to this day in an archaic script, a peculiar variety of the old Hebrew alphabet, while the Jews before the Christian era adopted for the Scriptures the new "Syrian" style of letters.[1] They had their own interpretation of the laws, which often coincided with that of the Jews, and we have Jewish testimony to the strictness with which they observed such as they accepted.[2] The date of the schism was formerly debated in its bearing on the introduction of the Law among the Samaritans, as a terminus *post quem non* for the final redaction of the Pentateuch. The nature of the testimony, as we have seen, does not warrant any chronological decision. All other considerations, however, incline the scales of probability to the fourth century, rather than the fifth.

For the rest, if we had no testimony, we should infer from the following history that the elevation of Shechem from provincial obscurity to a religious capital of high pretensions was more likely to have come about through an abrupt change than by the slow growth of local ambitions. The temple may have been built and a high priest of indisputable legitimacy installed, and a complete copy of the Judaean lawbook, the Pentateuch, procured, with no further intention than to match Jerusalem. The idea of supplanting Jerusalem came from the law itself. In it they found that Moses had enjoined the people, as soon as they came into the land, to put the blessing on Mt. Gerizim and the curse on Mt. Ebal (Deut. 11, 29; cf. 27, 11–26; Josh. 8, 33 f.). In Deut. 27, 4, the Jewish text has "Mount Ebal,"

---

[1] They ascribed this exchange to Ezra; see below, p. 29. Cf. 4 Esdras 14, 42: scripserunt quae dicebantur successione notis quas non sciebant.

[2] Berakot 47b, and repeatedly; Ḥullin 4a; Niddah 56b. (Matters of tithes, etc., slaughtering of animals, uncleanness, tombs.)

where the whole tenor of the context demands "Gerizim," as the Samaritan Hebrew reads; the same change has been made in the Jewish text in Josh. 8, 30. At Shechem, also, Joshua, at the end of the complete conquest, made the final covenant with the people and set up a memorial of it by the sanctuary of the Lord.[1] Shechem-Gerizim was therefore manifestly the place so often spoken of in Deuteronomy where God would put his name; Jerusalem had usurped a precedence never meant for it. So far as the letter of Scripture went, the Shechemites could make out an embarrassingly good case; but it was worthless against prescriptive possession.

The hostility of Jerusalemites and Shechemites was deep and lasting; it was carried into the Diaspora, especially in Egypt. Sirach relieves himself: "Two peoples my soul abhors, and the third is no people: The inhabitants of Seir, the Philistines, and that fool nation that dwells in Shechem."[2] Antiochus Epiphanes made no fine distinctions of locality among worshippers of the God of the Jews, and dedicated the temple on Gerizim to Zeus Xenios,[3] as he converted that of their rivals in Jerusalem into a temple of Zeus Olympios. John Hyrcanus destroyed it when he took Shechem in 128 B.C., but a religion that has no idol to house has no real need of a temple, and the Samaritans were as much of a thorn in the side of the Jews afterwards as before. The durable animosity of the two parties appears in the Gospels and the Tannaite literature, and in many later testimonies.

---

[1] On the passages cited see Eduard Meyer, Die Israeliten und ihre Nachbarstämme, pp. 542 ff., and on the whole subject, C. C. Torrey, Ezra Studies, pp. 321 ff.

[2] Ecclus. 50, 25 f.; cf. Deut. 32, 21.

[3] 2 Macc. 6, 2. The letter of the Samaritans to the king in Josephus (Antt. xii. 5, 5), in which they disclaim any kinship or sympathy with the Jews and ask the king to name their "anonymous temple," temple of "Zeus Hellanios," to which Antiochus graciously accedes, comes from the same source with xi. 7, 2; 8, 2–7; xiii. 3, 4, and is on the face of it fraudulent. In the revolt of the Jews under Nero, the Samaritans (in 67 B.C.) assembled under arms on Mt. Gerizim, evidently to attempt on their own account to throw

The Samaritans took over only the Pentateuch, and later expressly rejected the Prophets and the rest of the Jewish Scriptures. They thus excluded themselves from the religious and intellectual progress of Judaism to which that literature contributed so much. Of a learned study even of the Law, like that of the Scribes and their successors, there is no trace. Their reactionary conservatism meant stagnation from the beginning.

Through the Persian and into the Macedonian period a good deal was written which got into the final collection of Jewish Scriptures. Chronicles (of which Ezra-Nehemiah was once a part) was probably written somewhere between 300 and 250 B.C. In the Psalter there are psalms from the heat of the Maccabaean struggle.[1] The collection of prophetical writings contains oracles for which a situation and occasion can be found only in the Persian age or later. In our ignorance of the history of those centuries, the attempt to assign more definite dates to these compositions by what seem to be allusions to events of the time is unprofitable guesswork which frequently moves in a circle. What is more important is the character of this late prophecy, particularly the large place taken in it by what in the wider sense may be called eschatological motives — the final crisis and deliverance — the foreshadowing of apocalyptic without the mechanism of visions or the fiction of ancient seers, for which anonymity as yet suffices.[2]

A striking feature of many psalms is the note of intestine strife. Society is divided into two classes, the righteous, pious, lowly, on the one side, and the rich and powerful, the wicked and ungodly, on the other — in the phrase of more modern puritans and pietists, the godly and the worldly. What is new here is not the condemnation of the wicked but the self-con-

off the Roman yoke. Vespasian's prompt offensive extinguished the rising in blood. Josephus, Bell. Jud. iii. 7, 32.

[1] This was noted by Theodore of Mopsuestia in the fourth century and in the Reformation age by Calvin and others.

[2] Isa. 24–27 is a striking example. See also Zech. 9–14.

sciousness of the righteous and the outcry of personal grievance. The same note is heard in the Hellenistic Wisdom of Solomon and in the Judaean Psalms of Solomon.

Of the active intellectual life of this period, the discussion of the problem of theodicy in the Book of Job is conclusive proof,[1] as it is the most conspicuous achievement in Hebrew literature.

[1] It is worth noting incidentally that the problem of the Book of Job does not arise from the Law, but from the doctrine of retribution in Ezekiel, pushed to the end of its logic by what was evidently the current orthodoxy of the times.

CHAPTER II

EZRA AND THE GREAT SYNAGOGUE

FROM this critical and historical survey it is time to return to the point of view of the Jews themselves, from which all their notions of this period were formed. As we have seen, Ezra was for them the restorer of the law received in its entirety by Moses from the mouth of God, and delivered by him at various times to the Israelites, from Sinai to the Plains of Moab. Neither Ezra nor any other had ever added a word to this law or subtracted a word from it. They found in Neh. 8 that Ezra had not only read the law in the Hebrew in which it was given, but taken pains that it should be understood by having it rendered orally into the vernacular Aramaic as it was read; hence the institution of the Targum was referred to him.

To Ezra is ascribed the substitution, in the copying of the Scriptures, of the "Assyrian" (Syrian) characters, with which we are familiar in manuscripts and printed books, for the old Hebrew alphabet which was retained by the Samaritans.[1] Ten ordinances (*takkanot*) of his are enumerated, some of which have to do with the service of the synagogue,[2] the rest with domestic and personal matters, most of them, from our point of view, of a somewhat trivial character. It appears that in this case, as in others noted below, customs the origin of which was lost in antiquity were carried back to the beginning of the new era. What is of importance, however, is that the exercise of legislative authority is ascribed to Ezra and his contemporaries and succes-

[1] Sanhedrin 21b–22a; Jer. Megillah 71b–c. Origen on Psalm, 2, 2; Jerome, Prologus Galeatus.

[2] Synagogue service on Sabbath afternoon, and on Monday and Thursday mornings (market days), on which days the courts should be open. Megillah 31b adds that the comminations in Lev. 26 should be read before Pentecost and those in Deut. 28 before New Year's. See Note 3.

sors. The Book of the Law of Moses might be a final law, but it was not a finished law. Many things which had, from a time when the memory of man ran not to the contrary, been generally observed and were regarded as necessary and binding were not contained in it at all. Some of these figure in later times as "traditions of Moses from Sinai";[1] others as ordinances of Ezra, or of the prophets of his time, or the men of the Great Synagogue, or more indefinitely of the Soferim, or the Early Elders.[2]

Nehemiah 10, 29–40, which is the conclusion of the history of Ezra, records the compact which the notables and the people entered into 'to walk in God's law which was given by Moses, the servant of God, and to observe and do all the commandments of the Lord our lord, and his statutes and ordinances,' pledging themselves particularly not to intermarry with the people of the land, not to trade with them on a sabbath or a holy day; to leave (the produce of) the seventh year[3] free to all, and in that year to cancel all loans.[4] Then follow obligations[5] which they imposed on themselves for which there was no prescription in the law: a poll-tax of one third of a shekel for the maintenance of the public cultus, an arrangement for purveying the wood for the altar by families in turn through the year;[6] and, in connection with a pledge faithfully to bring to the temple the various *primitiae* assigned for the support of the priests and to let the Levites have their tithes, a regulation for the supervision by a priest of the Levites in their collection of tithes, to make sure that the priests got the tithe of the tithe that was coming to them. Here was an example of ordinances supple-

---

[1] See p. 256.
[2] *Zeḳenim ha-rishonim.*
[3] Cf. Exod. 23, 10 f.; Lev. 25, 3–7.
[4] Deut. 15, 1–3.
[5] *Miṣwot,* the usual word for the particular commandments of the law.
[6] According to M. Ta'anit 4, 5, in the Herodian temple wood was brought in by the families who had this privilege on nine days in the year. The fifteenth of Ab was a general festival of wood-offering. Megillat Ta'anit 5; cf. Josephus, Bell. Jud. ii. 17, 6.

Ezra The Great Synagogue

mentary to the law, framed, it would be assumed, by the leading men, whom Ezra associates with himself when he says, "We imposed on ourselves obligations."

It is probably from this precedent that the idea of the body commonly called the Great Synagogue arose.[1] It was imagined as a kind of council which in that generation made ordinances and regulations as they found necessary, and promulgated them with authority.

In tracing the continuous tradition of the Law from Moses to the days of Shammai and Hillel — Moses, Joshua, the elders, the prophets, — the Pirkè Abot has, "The prophets transmitted it to the men of the Great Synagogue." The last in the prophetic succession were Haggai and Zechariah, who had a leading part in the rebuilding of the temple, and Malachi,[2] whom the Jews made a contemporary of the other two. These were the link between their predecessors in the prophetic tradition and the Great Synagogue. In the Abot de-R. Nathan, these prophets of the restoration have a place by themselves: "Haggai, Zechariah, and Malachi received the tradition from the prophets; the men of the Great Synagogue received it from Haggai, Zechariah, and Malachi."[3] They are doubtless reckoned among the prophets in that body.[4] Ezra was one of the leading members, and, in the light of Neh. 8–10, was naturally thought of as presiding over the body. Nehemiah was associated with him, as in those chapters. Others were Zerubbabel and Joshua; also Mordecai. In a commentary on Abot in the Maḥzor Vitry [5]

---

[1] *Keneset ha-Gedolah.* It was not, in our use of the word, a synagogue at all; a better rendering is Great Assembly, or Convention. In Hebrew this distinction is indicated by the epithet 'Great,' for which a far-fetched explanation is given in Yoma 69b. See Note 4.

[2] Some identified Malachi with Ezra. Megillah 15a; Targum on Mal. 1, 1; Jerome, Preface to Malachi. Nehemiah was similarly identified with Zerubbabel.

[3] Abot de-R. Nathan 1, 3.

[4] Megillah 17b. In M. Peah 2, 6 (Gamaliel II) the Pairs receive the tradition from the Prophets.

[5] Page 463. To harmonize Neh. 10, 3, with 12, 1.

the following list is given: "Azariah (that is Ezra, who came up
from Babylon with his company of returning exiles), Zerubbabel, Joshua, Nehemiah, Mordecai-Bilshan." [1] In older texts the
Great Synagogue is represented as a large body, numbering one
hundred and twenty members, and including other prophets
besides those named.[2]

To the Men of the Great Synagogue is ascribed the completion
of the collection of sacred books,[3] adding to it the books of
Ezekiel, Daniel, and Esther, and the Twelve Prophets, in which
group Haggai, Zechariah, and Malachi were appended to the
earlier prophets. Ezra wrote his own book (of which our Nehemiah was a part), and Chronicles as far as his own genealogy.[4]
A number of slight alterations of the text from motives of reverence are sometimes called corrections of Ezra,[5] sometimes corrections of the Soferim,[6] who are identified with the men of the
Great Synagogue. They are also said to have prescribed the
benedictions and prayers (in the daily prayer), and the benedictions ushering in holy time or marking its close (Ḳiddush and
Habdalah).[7] They authorized the observance of the Feast of
Purim, and fixed the days that were to be kept.[8] Some thought
that they prescribed the curriculum of study in the three chief
branches of Jewish learning, Midrash, Halakah, and Haggadah.[9]

[1] After Neh. 7, 7. The identification of Mordecai with the Bilshan of
that verse, Menaḥot 65b; Targum Cant. 7, 3; cf. 6, 4. Another list (Maḥzor
Vitry, p. 481, from Seder Tannaim we-Amoraim) makes Azariah (Ezra)
the intermediary between Zechariah and the Great Synagogue, viz., Zerubbabel, Joshua, Nehemiah, and Mordecai-Bilshan, Mispar, Bigvai, Rehum,
Baanah (Ezra 2, 2).

[2] Cf. Berakot 33a with Megillah 17b and Jer. Berakot 4d; Megillah 2a
with Jer. Megillah 7od. On the discrepancies in these statements see W.
Bacher, 'Synagogue, The Great,' Jewish Encyclopedia, XI, 640 f.

[3] Baba Batra 15a. This must be what is meant when it is said that they
"wrote" these books, as when it is said in the preceding context that Hezekiah and his associates "wrote" Isaiah, Proverbs, Canticles, and Ecclesiastes.

[4] Ibid.   [5] תקוני עזרא.

[6] תקוני סופרים. Tanhuma, Beshallaḥ § 16 (on Exod. 15, 7). See Bacher,
Tannaiten, II, 205 n.; Terminologie, I, 83 f.

[7] Berakot 33a.

[8] Megillah 2a. See below, p. 319.   [9] Jer. Sheḳalim 48c.

Thus the distinctive religious institutions of Judaism as it was in the first centuries of our era were carried back to its beginnings. Ezra and the Men of the Great Synagogue were believed to have introduced these institutions and regulations by ordinances (*takkanot*) having the force of law, as their successors, the Soferim, and the Rabbis who succeeded them did.[1]

The motto of the Men of the Great Synagogue in Abot 1, 1, is: "Be deliberate in giving judgment, and raise up many disciples, and make a barrier about the law." The first two clauses contemplate the learned, to whom these hortatory counsels are directed, as judges and as teachers of the law; the third is addressed to them as makers of law. We have seen how the ordinances (*takkanot*) attributed to the leaders of the restoration and of the authorities in later generations formed in reality a body of legislation supplementary to the written law in the Pentateuch. Another side of the law-making of the same authorities was enactments meant to guard against any possible infringement of the divine statute.[2] This is what is here meant by making a barrier around the law. Thus — to take an example from the first page of the Mishnah — things which by the letter of the law must be completed before morning,[3] by rabbinical rule must be done before midnight, "to keep a man far removed from transgression."[4]

The distinction between the ordinances and decrees of the Scribes (Soferim) and the biblical law is constantly made in the juristic literature, but the authority of the Scribes or the Learned to make such regulations was not questioned, nor was the transgression or neglect of their rules a venial offense. On the con-

---

[1] E.g., Simeon ben Shaṭaḥ, Hillel, Johanan ben Zakkai; the Synod at Usha, etc.

[2] Authority for such an extension of the law was found in Lev. 18, 30, interpreted, "Ye shall make an injunction additional to my injunction." Sifra Aḥarè, end; Yebamot 21a. Perpetuity; annulment, Giṭṭin 36b.

[3] See, e.g., Lev. 7, 15; 22, 30.

[4] M. Berakot 1, 1. The technical name for such prohibitions is *gezerot*, which we might render 'decrees.' On the whole subject see Weiss, Dor, II, 50 ff.; Jewish Encyclopedia, 'Gezerah' and 'Takkanah.'

trary, a more serious matter is made of the words of the Scribes than of the words of the (written) law.[1]

It is clear that the Jews in the early centuries of our era had no other knowledge of the restoration or of Ezra and the Great Synagogue than what they gathered from the sources we possess,[2] combined in an artificial and erroneous chronological scheme.[3] They imagined that body in the likeness of a rabbinical council, legislating like one by ordinance and decree, and thus founding the distinctive institutions of Judaism. Its individual members were, like the rabbis in their time, both teachers in the law schools and judges in the courts, and, in a way, law-makers. The maxim attributed to them embodies the ideal of Jewish scholars in all after time.

One of the last survivors of the Great Synagogue was Simeon the Righteous,[4] and it is in conformity to the rabbinical chronology, which has room for but one generation (thirty-four years) between the rebuilding of the temple [5] and the fall of the Persian Empire,[6] that Simeon is the high priest who, arrayed in full pontificals, went out to meet Alexander the Great.[7] Historically, this Simeon the Righteous is probably the high priest Simeon son of Onias, contemporary of Jesus son of Sirach,[8] with an eloquent eulogy of whom (50, 1–24) that author brings his Praise of the Forefathers (41, 1–50, 24) to a close. The public works for which Simeon is here lauded, the repairs on the temple and the strengthening of its fortifications and those of the city,

[1] A collection of utterances to the same effect in Jer. Berakot 3b, apropos of the instance in M. Berakot 1, 3.
[2] The prophecies of Haggai and Zechariah, and the Books of Ezra and Nehemiah.
[3] See Note 4.
[4] Abot 1, 2. See Note 5.
[5] Completed, by our dates, in 516 B.C.
[6] Above, p. 6.
[7] In our chronology, 332 B.C. Yoma 69a. Josephus (Antt. xi. 8, 4 §§ 325 ff.) tells the story of Jaddua (Neh. 12, 11, 22), who in his succession of high priests is Simeon's grandfather.
[8] Ca. 200 B.C.

would fit very well with this date when Jerusalem had recently been taken and retaken in the struggle between Syria and Egypt.[1] It will be observed that in his catalogue of worthies Sirach passes at once from Zerubbabel and Joshua and Nehemiah,[2] who rebuilt the temple or restored the walls of Jerusalem, to his contemporary Simeon, who did the like. He apparently knew no notable name between. No more did the author of Abot 1, 1–2; and inasmuch as to be of any use such a chain of tradition must possess unbroken continuity, it followed of necessity that Simeon must have been associated with the men of the Great Synagogue. He is, however, not only one of the last survivors of that group, but the beginning of a new succession of teachers, singly or in pairs, who are known by name, and who by degrees come into historical light.

Simeon's memorable word was: "The world rests on three pillars, on the Torah, on the cultus, and on works of charity"[3]— we may paraphrase, knowledge of divine revelation, the worship of God, and deeds of lovingkindness to men. Antigonus of Socho, who received the traditional law from Simeon, said: "Be not like slaves who serve their masters with the expectation of receiving a gratuity; but be like slaves who serve their master without expectation of receiving a gratuity, and let the fear of Heaven be upon you," [4] the often repeated principle that duty should be done for God's sake, or for its own sake (because it is duty),[5] not for the reward of obedience. 'The man who fears the Lord delights greatly in His commandments' (Psalm 112, 1): "In His *commandments*, not in the reward of His commandments." [6]

---

[1] It is a tempting conjecture that, in the story from which Yoma 69 was derived, the king whom Simeon went out to make his peace with was not originally Alexander, but one of these contending monarchs, most likely Antiochus III. See Note 5.

[2] Ezra is nowhere named.

[3] Abot 1, 2.   [4] Ibid. 1, 3.

[5] See Vol. II, pp. 95 ff.

[6] 'Abodah Zarah 19a. R. Eleazar (ben Shammua'), quoting the words of Antigonus.

These sayings are set down at the beginning of the Sentences of the Fathers as recognized fundamentals of Judaism. They have so many counterparts in the Tannaite literature that they might be called Maxims of the Pharisees.[1]

[1] See the Catena on Abot by Noah Kobryn (Wilna, 1868).

CHAPTER III

THE SCRIBES

THE book of Jesus son of Sirach, commonly cited by the abbreviated title, Sirach,[1] is a landmark in the history of the Jewish religious literature of this age. It is the work of a single author who has put his own name to it (50, 27),[2] and who makes his individuality felt throughout. It was plainly not composed as a whole on a preconceived plan, and may perhaps be described as a collection of short essays, written probably at intervals of time. The situation, however, is the same in them all, and the external and internal evidence coincide to fix the date in the vicinity of 200 B.C.

The author makes it abundantly evident that he was a teacher, and we may imagine that he set down from time to time in writing such lessons as he was accustomed to give to young men of the upper classes in Jerusalem, or that he worked up his notes for the purpose of publication. The subject of his instruction was "wisdom" ($\sigma o \phi \iota a$)[3] in the sense of that word which the Book of Proverbs made familiar. Another common term is $\pi a \iota \delta \epsilon \iota a$, for which "education" is perhaps our nearest equivalent, with the understanding that, like the Hebrew *musar* which it commonly represents, it is primarily moral instruction and discipline. The wisdom which he aimed to impart was not theoretical philosophy or ethics but a practical guide for the conduct of life in the various stations and relations in which those who frequented his instruction might find themselves.

Jewish wisdom was, however, fundamentally a religious ethic. Its first principle, its mainspring and motive, was "the fear of

---

[1] In the Latin Bible, Ecclesiasticus.
[2] The case is unique.
[3] In Hebrew, *Ḥokmah*.

the Lord," and its normative principle was the law of God revealed in the Scriptures. Sirach explicitly identifies Wisdom, which has just sung its own high praises (24, 1–22), with "the law which Moses commanded, an inheritance to the congregation of Jacob."[1] Judaism is the only true wisdom, as it is the only true religion.

The emphasis on this uniqueness is explained by the circumstances of the times. The inclination to adopt the Hellenic civilization, which was fast becoming oecumenic, was not far from its climax in Jerusalem in his day, and was nowhere stronger, we may be sure, than among the young aristocrats who were sent to school to him. Sirach was himself a cultivated man of their own class; he had broadened his mind by travel, and perhaps been in the service of one or another of the Hellenistic rulers. That he knew Greek may fairly be presumed. There was all the more force in his words when such a man declared his conviction that whatever there was in the wisdom of the Greeks, however excellent their science, art, and letters, — their culture, in a word, — the wisdom of the Jews, even in the classic Greek definition, "knowledge of things divine and human," was vastly superior, because it came from God himself.

It is upon this axiomatic premise that he treats every subject. Wisdom is the condition of well-being and happiness, and wisdom is conformity to the will of God as He has revealed it. Man is accountable for his own conduct, he cannot shift the responsibility upon God (15, 11 ff.); His judgment is inescapable (16, 17 ff.). The evils which experience shows to be the consequence of misdoing are retributive. The religious point of view prevails throughout,[2] and is emphasized at points where it evidently encountered skepticism. Significant also is the prominence of the national note. The Praise of the Forefathers is a swift summary of the great things God did for them and through

---

[1] Ecclus. 24, 23 (32); cf. 1, 1–15. On this identification in rabbinical sources see pp. 263 ff.

[2] A comparison with Proverbs on this point is instructive.

them, well fitted to inspire the loyalty of Jews to their religion and their people. Sirach has faith also in the national future, his conception of which is set forth in a prayer for the speedy realization of this hope.[1]

What makes the Book of Sirach of peculiar importance in our present inquiry is not only that he was a teacher of religious morals to young men in a critical age, but that in his primary calling he was a biblical scholar and a teacher of the Law, a representative of the class of Soferim. His eminent attainments in the Scriptures are commemorated by his grandson and translator in his preface, and the book itself fully confirms this estimate. Sirach himself calls his school, to attendance on which he invites the unlearned, by a name which is later appropriated to the seat of more advanced biblical studies.[2] It may fairly be presumed that besides such instruction in religion and morals as we have in the Book of Sirach, law in the narrower sense was in his time studied in schools. On matters of ritual, and in questions of clean and unclean with the proper purifications and expiations, the priests were the recognized authorities; but a knowledge of the civil and criminal law was necessary for the judges before whom such cases were brought, and that competence in this field could be acquired only by what we should call the professional studies of the Scribe, Sirach strongly reiterates.[3] It involved not only the juristic interpretation of the laws in the Pentateuch, but knowledge of the common law that went beside it and supplemented it, and of the ordinances and decrees of earlier or contemporary authorities. We need not assume that didactic lectures were given on these subjects; it may be that students acquired their knowledge by frequenting the sessions of the learned and listening to their discussions;[4] but whatever

---

[1] Ecclus. 33, 1–22 (Swete). Here also the contrast to Proverbs is to be noted.

[2] Ecclus. 51, 23: αὐλίσθητε ἐν οἴκῳ παιδείας, for which the recently discovered Hebrew has ולינו בבית מדרשי. Cf. also 51, 29, בישיבתי.

[3] Ecclus. 38, 33; 39, 1; cf. 39, 8.

[4] See Abot 1, 4, and below, p. 46.

the method may have been, there was an effective provision for legal education.

That small matters as well as great received attention is illustrated in Ecclus. 42, where the author exhorts his reader not to be ashamed to conform to the "law and covenant of the Most High" because others (Gentiles or hellenized Jews) ridiculed such scrupulousness. Such matters are care for the accuracy of weights and measures, and in buying and selling. The Hebrew Sirach is more explicit. It speaks of dusting scales and balances and of wiping off measures and weights, on which the Mishnah lays down the rule: "A shopkeeper must wipe his measures twice a week and wipe off his weights once a week and wipe his scales every time he uses them." [1]

An attentive reading of Sirach shows many striking parallels not only to religious and moral sentences such as are collected in the Pirkè Abot or are scattered through the rabbinical literature,[2] but to the rules and regulations which are finally formulated in the Mishnah and kindred lawbooks.

In a memorable passage Sirach draws the portrait of the ideal Scribe:[3]

Learning is the privilege of leisure. Husbandmen and artisans are the support of the social structure, but, wholly occupied as they must be in their several callings and often highly expert in them, they have no time for the wide-ranging studies that make the scholar. They are therefore not qualified to be called to the council or to take the lead in the assembly; they cannot sit on the judge's bench, for they do not understand the principles of the law, and cannot bring out the rights of the case and a just judgment. Different is the case of the man who gives his whole mind to it, and concentrates his thought on the law of the Most High. He will seek out the wisdom of all the ancients, and

[1] M. Baba Batra 5, 10. Compare also the sequel in the Mishnah with Ecclus. 42, 4b–5a.
[2] The schoolmen of the Tannaite period cultivated the art of condensing wisdom into pithy aphorisms which we associate with the class of proverb-makers, and did quite as well in it.
[3] Γραμματεύς, סופר. See Ecclus. 38, 24–39, 11.

occupy himself with the study of prophecies, and pay attention to expositions of famous men, and will penetrate into the elusive turns of parables. He will search out the hidden meaning of proverbs, and will be versed in the enigmas of parables.[1]

He will serve among the magnates and appear in the presence of the ruler. He will travel in foreign countries, for he has experience of good and evil among men. He will resolve to rise early to the service of the Lord his creator, and will make his petition to the Most High; he will open his mouth in prayer, and beseech forgiveness for his sins. If the great Lord please, he will be filled with a spirit of understanding, and will himself pour out like rain his words of wisdom, and praise the Lord in prayer.[2] He will direct aright his counsel and knowledge, and reflect on the hidden things of God. He will make public the instruction he has to impart, and his pride will be in (knowledge of) the law of the covenant of the Lord.

Many will praise his understanding, and his reputation will never be obliterated; the memory of him will not pass away, but his name will live to countless generations. Other nations will talk of his wisdom, and the congregation (of Israel) will tell forth his praise. If he lives he will leave a greater name than the multitude; and if he rests from his labors, it will be greater still.

The Scribes, as Sirach here represents them, were a professional class, with a wide range of learning and activities. Of the previous history of this class little is to be known. Ezra appears in the name and character of a Scribe, and the Men of the Great Synagogue were thought of after the same pattern. In Sirach, however, they are an institution, for which a history must be assumed to bring it to the stage on which we find it there. The biblical scholars, students and teachers of the law written and unwritten, not only have attained great proficiency in their calling, but as a class have taken an independent place alongside

---

[1] His studies embrace all parts of the Scripture. The Praise of the Forefathers (c. 44 ff.) takes us over Sirach's canon, and his familiarity with all parts of it is evident throughout his book.

[2] The Scribe seems here to be thought of as holding discourse and leading the prayers in a religious assembly.

the priesthood, in whose hands in older times was the law and its interpretation.

The importance of this can hardly be overestimated. It is here, and not in the introduction of the Priests' Code, which would presumably have tended in quite the opposite direction, that Judaism as we know it has its antecedents. Many of the early Scribes may have been priests, as some of the most eminent rabbis were in later times; but there is no indication that Sirach was one, or that priests had any precedence, much less prerogative, in the calling of the Scribes.

Manifold as the activities of the Scribes, or of individuals among them, may have been, the field in which their labors had most to do with shaping the future of Judaism was unquestionably what in a wide sense we may call jurisprudence. The development of a lay jurisprudence, not dependent on the priesthood, the hereditary custodians of the law, presumes the publication of a body of written law accessible to any who chose to occupy themselves with the study of it. According to the narrative in Ezra and Nehemiah, an official publication of the Book of the Law of Moses took place in Ezra's time; and, apart from this account, there is evidence in the later books of the Old Testament of the existence of such a work, substantially our Pentateuch, in the Persian period. The history of Roman jurisprudence offers a partial analogy. It was the surreptitious publication about 300 B.C. of a digest of forms of legal procedure which had previously been kept to themselves by the *pontifices* that made possible the rise of professional jurisconsults and of legal education.[1]

It is a natural supposition that the lay Scribes did not concern themselves so much about points of ritual with which the priests alone had to do as about other spheres of the law. Later, however, they extended their research to that field, and at last, relying on popular support, undertook to regulate or reform

[1] See the article, 'Jurisprudentia,' in Pauly-Wissowa, Real-Encyclopädie der classischen Altertumswissenschaft, X, col. 1159 ff.

priestly practice in conformity with the letter of the law or their own exegesis of it. The character and conduct of the priesthood, particularly of the sacerdotal aristocracy, was frequently very remote from such an ideal of the office as would be formed from the study of the Law. After Simeon the Righteous, who perhaps owed the laudatory cognomen to the contrast with his successors,[1] high priests who bought their appointment from the king were willing tools of his hellenizing plans, and turned the Scribes, with all the Jews who were zealous for their own religion (the Ḥasidim), against them. The national high priests, from John Hyrcanus in his later years, went over to the Sadducean party, and the priestly nobility under Herod and the procurators were of the same stripe. The Scribes, on the other hand, had the support of the Pharisaean party, to which many of them belonged. The Pharisees in turn had the people behind them, and with the growing importance of the synagogue, the professionally educated class gained increasing influence as the teachers of the people. Both the scope and the methods of study in the schools of the law changed, as we shall see, with time and changing conditions, and scholars became more and more the dominant factor in the conservation and development of Judaism through all the vicissitudes of the centuries.

The old name, Scribes, was apparently the only one in use in the age from which the Gospels come. In the Tannaite literature scholars are called Ḥakamim, in the sense of "the learned," students are Talmidè Ḥakamim, disciples of the learned,[2] the name Soferim, Scribes, being restricted to the learned of an older time. The sources at our command do not disclose the reason for this change in usage or the date at which the new designation was introduced. It may perhaps be connected with the reorganization of the schools after the destruction of Jerusalem and the

---

[1] The Talmud tells a scandalous story about his own sons. Menaḥot 109b; Jer. Yoma 43c; Tos. Soṭah 13, 6 ff. One of these sons was the founder of the Onias Temple in Egypt.

[2] The latter name, as the more modest, is often used of those who have passed beyond the student stage.

use thereafter of Rabbi as a title for what we might call a diplomaed Doctor of the Law.

In sketching the history of the Scribes we have run ahead of our subject. To return to Sirach, it remains to direct attention to another aspect of his book which is of even greater importance than those which have hitherto engaged us. More completely and more certainly than any other writings of the period the Book of Sirach shows us the extent to which the higher religious and ethical principles of the Law and the Prophets had been selectively appropriated, coördinated, and assimilated by the best learning and thought of his time, and were digested for ends of education. No less clearly does it prove the progress which had been made since the beginning of the Persian period in the direction of later Judaism. The same thing, in different degrees, may be observed in other writings of the Persian and Macedonian centuries when we bring them into parallel with Sirach. The value of the book as a landmark is very great in another respect, because it enables us to assure ourselves that the theology and ethics of the Tannaim in the second century of our era were substantially the same as those of the Soferim at the beginning of the second century before it.

Hardly less instructive in comparison with the rabbinical literature is the silence of the book on some points on which the Tannaim laid great stress, particularly on retribution after death or the revivification of the dead (resurrection of the body). On this account Sirach has been labelled Sadducee. It does not appear that the rabbis entertained any such suspicion.

The book of Ben Sira in Hebrew was well known in the Tannaite period and later, highly esteemed, and not infrequently quoted, sometimes with the formula usual with quotations from the Bible.[1] It was, in fact, found necessary sometime about

---

[1] See Cowley and Neubauer, The Original Hebrew of a Portion of Ecclesiasticus, etc. (1897), p. xix-xxx; I. Levi, Jewish Encyclopedia, XI, 390.

the end of the first century of our era to make a formal deliverance to the effect that it was not sacred Scripture.[1] This did not imply any depreciation of the book itself; it was sufficient that it was written at a time when, with the death of the last prophets, the inspiration of biblical books had ceased.[2]

After Antigonus of Socho the tradition is said to have been carried on by a couple of colleagues in each succeeding generation, beginning with Jose ben Jo'ezer of Seredah and Jose ben Johanan of Jerusalem, and ending with Shammai and Hillel.[3] The first pair fall in the days of Antiochus Epiphanes (175–164 B.C.).[4] Between them and the last, in the time of Herod, three pairs have to fill a space of more than a century and a quarter. What is historically established is that Shemaiah and Abtalion were the most highly reputed teachers of the Law and heads of the Pharisees in the earlier part of Herod's reign (37–4 B.C.); and that Simeon ben Shatah was active under Alexander Jannaeus (103–76) and had great influence with his successor Queen Alexandra (76–67), who is said to have been Simeon's sister. Most of the members of these pairs are hardly more than names; besides the sentences ascribed to them in the Abot, what little is told of them is chiefly legendary. It is evident that the Tannaim had nothing like a continuous historical tradition of the lives and labors of their predecessors.

[1] Tos. Yadaim 2, 13.

[2] Abaye, a Babylonian scholar of the 4th century, in answer to the question why the book was disapproved, quotes utterances that might seem objectionable or foolish. Sanhedrin 100b.

[3] Abot 1, 4 ff. According to M. Hagigah 2, 2, the first named in each pair was the president, the second the vice-president, of the Sanhedrin. This is carrying back into antiquity the organization of the high court after the destruction of Jerusalem.

[4] A midrashic legend makes Jose ben Jo'ezer one of the company of scholars who paid with their lives for their confidence in the high priest Alcimus (162/161 B.C. 1 Macc. 7, 16). Gen. R. 65, 22; Midrash Tehillim on Psalm 11, 7. The death of Jose ben Jo'ezer and his colleague is remembered as a disastrous crisis in the history of the schools. M. Sotah 9, 9; Sotah 47a–b; Temurah 15b.

The maxims of Jose ben Jo'ezer testify to his zeal for the study
of the Law: "Let thy house be a meeting place of the learned,
and sit in the dust at their feet and thirstily drink in their
words." [1] Jose ben Jo'ezer and his colleague Jose ben Johanan
are the first in this series of authorities in whose names decrees
(*gezerot*) [2] are reported. They are said to have pronounced
heathen soil unclean, and also that glass vessels are unclean.[3]

Looking back out of the controversies of schools and conflict
of individual opinions in a later age, scholars idealized a past of
which they had no record, and sometimes went so far as to
imagine that previous to this pair the authorities had always
been in complete accord: the two Jose's differed on a single
point in the ritual of private sacrifice on holy days,[4] and down
to Shammai and Hillel this was the sole controversy.[5] Shammai
and Hillel raised the number of contentions to four, but, "When
their disciples increased in numbers and did not attend their
masters as diligently as they ought, the divisions of opinion
multiplied in Israel. They formed two parties, the one declaring
unclean what the other declared clean; and things will not return to their former state (of unanimity) till the Son of David
comes." [6] From our point of view, the actual tradition of the
disputes of the schools begins in the generation before the
Christian era. The differences of the "houses" of Shammai and
Hillel are in the foreground from that time to the destruction of
Jerusalem in the year 70, and were not wholly composed for a
good while after that.[7]

---

[1] Abot 1, 4. Compare the advice of Joshua ben Peraḥiah (ibid., 1, 6):
"Take to yourself a master (teacher), and get for yourself a comrade (in
studies); and judge every man in the most favorable light."

[2] Widening the scope of prohibitive laws. See p. 33.

[3] Shabbat 14b; the explanations in the Talmud, ibid. 15b. Other deliverances of Jose ben Jo'ezer on questions of clean and unclean are found in
'Eduyot 8, 4; cf. Sifra, Shemini Pereḳ 9, end (ed. Weiss f. 55b).

[4] The דופי של סמיכה, Temurah 16a, top; cf. 15b.

[5] Jer. Ḥagigah 77d; Tos. Ḥagigah 2, 8.

[6] Jer. Ḥagigah l.c.

[7] See below, pp. 80 f., 86.

Simeon ben Shaṭaḥ, the restorer of the Law in the reign of Queen Alexandra,[1] is the first in the series of pairs who stands out with a certain distinctness of character. He was the author of several ordinances (*takkanot*), perhaps the most important of which have to do with the marriage contract (*ketubah*).[2]

[1] Ḳiddushin 66a. See below, p. 58 n. 6.
[2] See below, Vol. II, pp. 122 f.

CHAPTER IV

THE RELIGIOUS CRISIS

WITHIN a few years after the death of Sirach there came a momentous crisis in the history of the Jews in Palestine. He had probably seen Judaea pass finally from the dominion of the Ptolemies to that of the Seleucids by the battle of Panium in 198 B.C., and the restorations of the walls of the temple and city under the high priest Simon [1] may have been made possible by the favor of Antiochus III.[2] But evil times soon followed.

The Seleucids were much more zealous for disseminating the blessings of Hellenic culture among their subjects than the Ptolemies, and in the cities of Syria, long since completely denationalized, the populations displayed a gratifying alacrity in adopting the newest fashion in civilization. Of the finer intellectual and aesthetic influences of Greek culture little is discernible; the difference in this respect between Antioch and Alexandria is salient. The picture which Poseidonios, himself a native of Apameia, paints of the Syrian cities in his day was probably no less true at an earlier time.[3]

In the century of Ptolemaic rule, knowledge of the Greek language must have been common among the upper classes, especially among the higher priesthood in Jerusalem, to whom, indeed, their relations with the government on the one hand, and intercourse with the large Greek-speaking Jewish population of Egypt and the Cyrenaica on the other, made it a necessity. Nor is there any doubt that Greek civilization exercised over many Jews the same fascination it had for other Orientals, and that among them its customs and fashions were imitated, its luxuries

---

[1] Ecclus. 50, 1 ff.
[2] Josephus, Antt. xii. 3, 3 §§ 138 ff.
[3] Frag. 18. C. Muller, Frag. Historicorum Graecorum, III, 258.

eagerly sought after. Some families acquired great wealth in farming the taxes by the usual methods of extortion and oppression, and with riches their power grew and their ambitions rose, as we read in the romance of the Tobiads.[1] They made no effort, so far as we know, to promote the spread of foreign ways among their countrymen otherwise than by setting a bad example.

Shortly after the accession of Antiochus Epiphanes, however, a calculated attempt of this kind was made, and the initiative came from the highest quarters. A brother of the high priest Onias, who hellenized his Jewish name Jesus[2] into Jason, ingratiated himself with the new king by displaying a flattering zeal for civilization and by his willingness to pay well for it. Besides the high price he offered for the appointment to the high priesthood in the room of his brother, he promised other large sums for the privilege of establishing a gymnasium in Jerusalem with the institution of *ephebi*, and for the enrolment of Jews as Antiochian citizens,[3] enterprises which were doubtless quite to the mind of Antiochus, especially when accompanied by tangible considerations. With the Jews the argument for assimilation ran, "Let us go and make alliance with the peoples around us, for since we separated from them many evils have befallen us."[4]

Jason was made high priest in 175/4 B.C. The privileges conferred by Antiochus III were annulled; Jerusalem was given a Greek constitution, with a right for its citizens to acquire — doubtless not gratuitously — Antiochian citizenship also. A gymnasium was built below the citadel; athletic young Jews enrolled as *ephebi* scandalized their pious elders by putting on broad-brimmed Greek hats. Priests hurried through their office in the temple to take part in the sports. Many submitted to a surgical operation to efface the blemish of circumcision, which provoked the ridicule of bystanders when the Jewish youths stripped for gymnastic exercises. When Greek games were being

[1] Josephus, Antt. xii. 4, 1 ff.
[2] Jeshu'a (Joshua). Jason of Cyrene is probably a parallel instance.
[3] 2 Macc. 4, 8 f.   [4] 1 Macc. 1, 11.

held at Tyre in the presence of the king, the Jewish high priest, Jason, sent ambassadors [1] with a contribution for the sacrifices to Hercules.[2]

The hellenization of Jerusalem was thus in full swing. Jason's success encouraged a certain Menelaus[3] to imitate his example, and he supplanted Jason in the high priesthood by larger promises. That he did not get possession without bloodshed may be inferred from 2 Macc. 4, 25, which on this occasion remarks, "He had the passions of a cruel tyrant and the fury of a ferocious wild beast." He prevailed, however, and Jason found a refuge beyond the Jordan, whence later, upon a rumor of Antiochus' death in Egypt, he emerged, took Jerusalem by a *coup de main*, and executed sanguinary vengeance on the defenders, but was unable to maintain his conquest and was soon in flight again.

That the efforts of the king and his creatures to heathenize them ran counter not only to the attachment of the Jews to their religion but to their national sentiment is clear. The high priest and the senate had received Antiochus III as a deliverer from the misgovernment of the recent Ptolemies, and he was politic enough to assume the rôle. But notwithstanding the new political constellation, Judaea was closer in every way to Egypt than to Syria, and the associations of a hundred years were not sundered in a day. Whatever expectations of better times may have been raised by the first acts of Antiochus III were speedily dashed. The chronic financial straits of the Seleucid empire, especially in consequence of the crushing indemnity imposed by

[1] Θεωροί, such as the Athenians sent to the four great Hellenic games. It was a religious function. The ambassadors were not so completely emancipated as the high priest, and asked that the contribution be expended on the fleet. 2 Macc. 4, 18–20.

[2] With whom Melkart, the god of Tyre, was identified.

[3] In good Jewish, Menahem. It has been inferred from 2 Macc. 4, 23 (Menelaus brother of Simon, of the tribe of Benjamin, ibid., 3, 4), that Menelaus was not of priestly extraction. There was, however, an order of priests, *Miniamin* (Neh. 12, 17, cf. 12, 5; 1 Chron. 24, 9), for which some Greek MSS and the Syriac have Benjamin; cf. Ta'anit 12a. See Geiger, Urschrift und Uebersetzungen, pp. 221 f.

the Romans after Magnesia, made the burden of taxation more
onerous than ever; Seleucus IV had tried to rob the temple in
Jerusalem of its treasures and the large private deposits laid up
in it; Menelaus appropriated some of its golden vessels to use
in bribing Syrian officials, and left his brother Lysimachus to get
the rest. To crown all this came the aggressive hellenizing
policy of Antiochus IV. From such an evil and threatening
present it would be strange if the Jews had not looked back to
the good old times of Ptolemaic rule, when, whatever other
grievances they had, at least nobody tried to modernize them,
and they were left to isolate themselves in their national religion
and customs as completely as they liked.

Such was the situation when the war between Antiochus IV
and Egypt opened. That the sympathy of very many Jews
should be on the Egyptian side was inevitable, and Antiochus
was doubtless apprised by Menelaus of their disloyal sentiments.
On his way back from this campaign in the autumn of the year
169 he came up to Jerusalem with a considerable force.[1] Under
the conduct of the high priest, Menelaus, he entered the adytum
of the temple, the Most Holy Place, and when he left carried
off the altar of incense, the candelabra, the table of shewbread,
the golden utensils of the cultus, and everything else he could
lay his hands on, even stripping the gold plating from the front
of the edifice.[2]

In the spring of 168 B.C. Antiochus invaded Egypt a second
time, but in the midst of his operations the Roman senate intervened and peremptorily ordered him out of the country. The
temper in which he returned to Syria may be imagined, nor
would it be strange if he vented it on anything that came in his
way. Whatever vindictiveness there may have been, however,
in his dealing with the Jews, the measures he took in Judaea

---

[1] According to 2 Macc. 5, 11, to punish the city for its supposed connivance
in Jason's raid, construed as a revolt.

[2] 1 Macc. 1, 20–24; 2 Macc. 5, 15 f.; cf. Josephus, Antt. xii. 5, 3. These
accounts speak of much bloodshed in the city, which, according to 2 Macc.,
he turned over to his soldiers to sack.

were themselves justified by political reasons.[1] His promising
scheme for hellenizing the Jews, so to say from within, by the
agency of the high priests and an upper-class minority had had
an effect diametrically opposite to his expectations. It had
created a national opposition which was strengthened by everything he did to accomplish his end. This national opposition
had become an Egyptian party, whose rejoicing in his discomfiture was probably more sincere than discreet. Even if he could
have brought himself to reverse his policy, he could not hope to
regain their allegiance by the sacrifice of the only supporters he
had. On the other hand, elementary strategical considerations
forbade him to leave a stronghold like Jerusalem in the possession of a thoroughly disloyal population so near the frontier of
a hostile empire.

He proceeded therefore to demolish the walls of the city and
pull down or burn many of its houses. On the eastern hill, south
of the temple, he built and strongly fortified a smaller city, and
colonized it with foreigners. What was in his eyes the loyal
remnant of the Jews was also established there under the protection of a mercenary garrison in the citadel which held it
for the king through all vicissitudes until 142 B.C.

When this had been accomplished Antiochus converted the
temple to the worship of the Olympian Zeus.[2] The great altar
in the court became the pedestal of a smaller altar of Greek
fashion ($\beta\omega\mu\acute{o}s$), on which swine were offered in sacrifice.[3] The
whole Jewish cultus was thus superseded.

Antiochus understood perfectly well that the heart of the opposition to him was religious. He resolved to extirpate the
religion. All its observances, particularly circumcision and the

---

[1] The essentially political motive of the religious persecution is evident
from the fact that it was confined to Palestine. There is no evidence that the
Jews in Syria or Babylonia were molested in the observance of their religion.

[2] The Samaritan temple on Gerizim was similarly dedicated to Zeus
Xenios.

[3] The high priest Menelaus remained in office as the political head of the
nation. It is not to be supposed that he officiated in the worship of the new
god who had usurped the temple.

keeping of sabbaths and festivals, were prohibited under pain of death. Copies of the Law were destroyed and the possession of such a volume was made a capital offense. Altars were set up in the towns and villages, and participation in the heathen sacrifices was made a test of loyalty. Many obeyed the king's edict either voluntarily or under duress. Those who refused thus publicly to apostatize were put to death. Many fled and concealed themselves from the king's officers.

This persecution provoked an insurrection headed by Judas Maccabaeus and his brothers. Their bands roved through the country, destroying the altars, circumcising the children, and ruthlessly harrying the "apostates" who had submitted to the royal decree. The Syrian commanders made the mistake of underrating their enemy, and the defeats they suffered in the first encounters led larger numbers to rally to Judas and raised the confidence of his followers. Antiochus himself had greater enterprises, which took him to the far east of his empire never to return. The expeditions successively despatched by the regent Lysias failed to suppress the revolt. In the autumn of the year 165 Judas got possession of the temple, which he restored and reconsecrated.[1] Law-abiding priests were installed and the worship resumed in its ancient forms. The temple was strongly fortified, especially against attack from the side of the citadel. The regent Lysias was by this time convinced that the attempt to root out the religion was a failure. After negotiations with Judas, full liberty was guaranteed to the Jews to worship their own God in their own way and live according to their national law and custom, and an amnesty was offered in the king's name [2] to all who had taken part in the rebellion, on condition that they came in within a month.

This change in the policy of the government did not bring peace. Judas and his brothers did not deem their task accomplished so long as their countrymen beyond Jordan and in

---

[1] Kislev (roughly December) 25, 165 B.C.
[2] Antiochus V, Eupator.

Galilee, or on the seaboard and in Idumaea, were harassed by the heathen, and undertook what are now called punitive expeditions for their relief. Nor were they content to leave the citadel of Jerusalem itself in foreign hands. When Judas laid siege to this fortress, however, it was relieved by a Syrian army, and Judas was in turn besieged in the temple and reduced by famine to the verge of capitulation. Lysias was in a position to dictate terms, and besides requiring Judas to evacuate the temple made it indefensible by breaching its fortifications. But religious liberty was again guaranteed; that phase of the struggle was ended.

The attempt to hellenize Judaea by force aroused, in the act of resistance to it, a violent hostility to heathenism with all its works and ways. The neighboring peoples reciprocated this enmity in full measure and made the Jews settled among them suffer from it on every occasion, partly as a vent to their own feelings and a pretext for violence and rapine, partly perhaps as a demonstration of loyalty. In defense of their outraged countrymen the Maccabees, when they were able, retaliated in kind.

At home they had to reckon with the loyalist party. The revolt was not, as is sometimes imagined, the uprising of the Jewish people with one heart to save its imperilled religion. To say nothing of the high priests and their ilk, what would nowadays be called the solid part of the community, the men of property and position in Jerusalem, would have been unlike their kind if peace and order in which to enjoy their privilege had not seemed to them the condition of all earthly good. Many of them had compromised themselves too deeply by compliance with the king's edict to hope to make their peace with the rebels who were so merciless against all "apostates." After the recovery of the temple and the guarantee of religious liberty by the compact between Lysias and Judas, the cause for which the Maccabaean faction had taken up arms was no longer a living issue, but peace and order were as far away as before. The more evidently the aim of this party now developed into the autonomy of Judaea under one of the rebel chiefs, the more strongly the royalists were opposed to the movement. For a quarter of a century there was always a possibility that in some of the over-turnings of the times they might come into power again.

The subsequent chapters of the political history of Judaea need not be summarized here. Suffice it to say that in the twenty years that followed the death of Judas [1] his brothers Jonathan and Simon by adroit and unscrupulous use of the opportunities political conditions put in their hands achieved the goal of independence. Demetrius II recognized Simon as high priest and the autonomous ruler of a Jewish state. First Maccabees records that in the year 170 [2] the yoke of the heathen was removed from Israel, and the people of Israel began to date documents and contracts, 'In the year (so and so) of Simon, the great high priest and commander-in-chief and ruler of the Jews' (13, 41 f.). [3]

---

[1] In the spring of 160 B.C.
[2] Of the Seleucid era, equivalent to 143/2 B.C.
[3] The use of a native era was the formal attestation of independence.

CHAPTER V

RISE OF THE PHARISEES

SIMON's son and successor, John Hyrcanus (135–104 B.C.), waged aggressive wars on all sides. He made a campaign east of the Jordan in the old territory of Moab; took Shechem and destroyed the temple on Mt. Gerizim which pretended to rival Jerusalem; conquered the Idumaeans in the south and made Jews of them by compulsory circumcision; recovered Joppa and Gazara; and finally, toward the end of his reign, after a long siege conducted by his sons, captured the city of Samaria and totally destroyed it. Aristobulus, who assumed the title King,[1] in his brief reign (104 B.C.), pursued a similar policy in judaizing Galilee. His brother and successor, Alexander Jannaeus (103–76 B.C.), conquered the remaining cities on the coast, including Gaza, and waged war with varying fortunes beyond Jordan. At the height of his success his dominion extended almost to the traditional bounds of the empire of Solomon.

The wars in which the Jews engaged, first for religious liberty, then for the independence of Judaea, and finally for the reconquest of the whole land of Israel, aroused an aggressive national spirit which was reflected in religion. Triumphant Judaism was under no temptation to assimilate itself to the religions of the heathen over whom its God had given it the victory. Some enthusiasts saw in the events of the time the Lord's deliverance foretold in ancient prophecies and the dawning of the yet more glorious day that was to follow. The Jews in other lands shared in this exaltation of spirit. As in older times, the triumphs of the Lord were a revival of religion, in the sense, at least, of enthusiasm for it and heightened loyalty to it.

[1] Josephus, Bell. Jud. i. 3, 1. Jannaeus was the first to put the title in the Greek legend on his bilingual coins.

That otherwise this century was favorable to religious advance can hardly be imagined. Its history is written in a succession of wars at home and abroad which must have wrought wide devastation and, according to all experience, demoralization on a corresponding scale, all the more because they were in some sort wars of religion.

Our sources deal, however, almost exclusively with political history, and tell us nothing about the everyday doings of common men. ʼWe can well believe that in the intervals of peace and even amid the disorders of war scholars stedfastly pursued their studiesʼin Scripture and tradition, and pious men were as scrupulous in the observance of their religious duties as in happier times. In the early years of the period we read of a company of scholars (συναγωγὴ γραμματέων) who presented themselves to the newly appointed high priest Alcimus, and had reason to rue their simplicity; [1] and though we have no other notice of them it is certain from later events that the learned succession was not broken off.

Later we find the guild of scholars (Scribes) with their tradition supported by what may properly be called a party of tradition, the Pharisees. The first mention of the Pharisees in Josephus [2] is in a paragraph injected without relation to the context in the midst of Jonathan's wars with Demetrius II and his negotiations with the Romans and the Spartans,[3] telling that "about this time" there were three schools, or sects (αἱρέσεις), of the Jews, who entertained different notions about fate and free will, the Pharisees, the Sadducees, and the Essenes, for fuller information about which the reader is referred to what he had written previously in the second book of the Jewish War.

A little further on the Pharisees emerge on the historical stage in conflict with John Hyrcanus,[4] and here we find them in their true character as the partisans of the unwritten law. "The Pharisees have delivered to the common people by tradition

---

[1] 1 Macc. 7, 12 ff.   [2] Antt. xiii. 5, 9 §§ 171–173.
[3] In 139 B.C.   [4] Antt.xiii. 10, 5 f.

from a continuous succession of fathers certain legal regulations which are not written in the Law of Moses, on which account the Sadducean sort rejects them, affirming that what is written is to be regarded as law, but what comes from the tradition of the fathers is not to be observed." On this point the Pharisees have the mass of the people on their side, and they have so much influence that anything they say, even against a king or a high priest, finds ready credence.[1] Elsewhere the importance they attach to the exact interpretation and application of the laws is noted.[2]

According to Josephus, John Hyrcanus was a disciple of the Pharisees and highly esteemed by them. Later, however, he broke with them upon a personal grievance, and went over to the Sadducees. In conformity to the Sadducean position that the Bible only is law, he abrogated the ordinances the Pharisees had established,[3] and punished those who observed them. This, it is added, was the cause of the hatred of the commonalty toward him and his sons.[4] What is patently a doublet of this story is told in the Talmud of King Jannai (Alexander Jannaeus);[5] with a sequel which makes it certain that Jannai is not here a confusion of names with Johanan (Hyrcanus),[6] as has sometimes been assumed.[7] That John Hyrcanus went over to the Sadducees is attested by another Baraita: "Do not put confidence in yourself till the day of your death; for there was

[1] Cf. Antt. xvii. 2, 4 § 41.
[2] Bell. Jud. ii. 8, 14 § 162.
[3] The implication is that they had previously been backed by his authority.
[4] The difficulties of Hyrcanus with the Pharisees are elsewhere ascribed to the jealousy of the latter. See Bell. Jud. i. 2, 8 § 67, and Antt. xiii. 10, 5 § 288 (ultimately from the same source); cf. also Antt. xiii. 10, 7.
[5] Jannai is here a nickname for Jonathan, as is proved by his coins.
[6] "They slew all the leading scholars of Israel, and the world was upside down until Simeon ben Shaṭaḥ came and restored the law to its old place." This restoration took place under Queen Alexandra. Ḳiddushin 66a. Cf. Josephus, Antt. xiii. 13, 5 § 372; 14, 2 § 383.
[7] Of which of the two the story was first told is of no great moment. That there was an estrangement between Hyrcanus and the Pharisees seems to be sufficiently attested independently of the legend of its origin.

Johanan the high priest (Hyrcanus), he ministered for eighty years,[1] and became a Sadducee at the last." [2]

It is clear that in the latter part of the second century before our era the Pharisees were already established in a position of great influence, and thenceforward they bore a leading part in the development and triumph of normative Judaism — so prominent, in fact, that the name Pharisaism is sometimes given to it.

Of the origin and the antecedents of the Pharisees there is no record. It is commonly surmised that they were the successors of those who in earlier generations called themselves Ḥasidim,[3] to distinguish themselves as what we call religious men from their worldly and indifferent countrymen. Their temper is illustrated by the fact that, at the beginning of the persecution under Antiochus Epiphanes, a body of refugees of this kind let themselves be slaughtered, with their wives and children, in their retreat in the wilderness, rather than profane the sabbath by raising a hand to defend themselves, saying, "Let us all die together in our innocency." [4] Before long, however, the "Asidaeans" joined forces with the Maccabaean leaders,[5] consenting under the stress of circumstances to a suspension of the sabbath observance to permit fighting in self-defence.[6]

When religious liberty was secured, and a new high priest, Alcimus, was appointed in the room of Menelaus, the Asidaean were the first to seek to make peace with him and the Syria general Bacchides who came to see him installed in his office. Alcimus was not disposed to condone their part in the rebellion, and, as Judas and his brothers declined his treacherous overtures for a conference, executed sixty of the Scribes and the religious

---

[1] Yoma 9a also gives him 80 years.
[2] Berakot 29a.
[3] Literally, the Pious, or the Religious.
[4] The name Asidaean does not occur in this narrative. 1 Macc. 2, 29–38
[5] Ibid. 2, 42–44: τότε συνήχθησαν πρὸς αὐτοὺς συναγωγὴ Ἀσιδαίων ι χυροὶ δυνάμει ἀπὸ Ἰσραήλ, πᾶς ὁ ἑκουσιαζόμενος τῷ νόμῳ. This reading (Cꝍ A. al., Vulg.) is obviously right; see 1 Macc. 7, 13; 2 Macc. 14, 6.
[6] 1 Macc. 2, 40 f.   [7] Cf. 2 Macc. 14, 6.   [8] 1 Macc. 7, 13 ff.

who indiscreetly put themselves in his power, to the disillusionment and consternation of the rest. This is all that our sources tell us about the attitude or the conduct of the Asidaeans in the Maccabaean struggle, and if the connection of the Pharisees with them were established it would add nothing to our knowledge of the latter.

The word Pharisee [1] represents the name in its vernacular form, Pĕrīsha.[2] The derivation from the verb pĕrash (Hebrew parash) is plain; not so the significance and occasion of the name. The interpretation that first suggests itself is 'one who is separated, or, is separate';[3] but from whom or from what — a complement which is necessary to give it meaning — the word contains no intimation; nor does either usage or tradition supply the deficiency.

From the peculiar rules and customs of the Pharisees it is commonly inferred that they were so called because they religiously avoided everything that the law branded as unclean, and for fear of contamination kept aloof from persons who were suspected of negligence in such matters.[4] Definitions in this general sense were current among the Church Fathers.[5] In the 'Aruk [6] the name is defined: "A Pharisee is one who separates himself from all uncleanness and from eating anything unclean," in distinction from the mass of the common people, who were ᴏt so particular. In the Tannaite and Amoraic sources the ᴧme Perushim is used in contrast to 'Am ha-Areṣ, the ignorant ᴧnd negligent vulgus.[7]

---

[1] Φαρισαῖος, Pharisaeus.

[2] In rabbinical texts it appears only in the equivalent Hebrew form, Parūsh.

[3] "Separatist," which is sometimes used as an equivalent, is objectionable, because, through its English associations, it may suggest that the Pharisees separated themselves as a sect from the body of the Jewish church.

[4] So Wellhausen, Pharisäer und Sadducäer, pp. 76 ff. Schürer, Geschichte des jüdischen Volkes, u. s. w., II, 398 f.

[5] See Schürer, l.c.

[6] A lexicon to the Talmud by Nathan ben Jehiel of Rome (died 1106).

[7] And in accounts of controversies, e.g. with Sadducees.

Such an appellation might have been bestowed on them in a derogatory sense by those who resented their pretensions to superior purity or were otherwise prejudiced against them,[1] and, as has happened in similar cases — the Methodists, for instance — been accepted with a favorable implication by the Pharisees themselves. On the other hand, it may have been a name originally assumed by them. In the latter case, it may be observed that in the Tannaite Midrash *parūsh* is frequently associated with *ḳadōsh*, 'holy.' In Lev. 11, at the end of the chapter of unclean beasts, fishes, birds, and vermin with which the Israelites are forbidden to defile themselves, this prohibition is enforced by the motive: 'For I am the Lord thy God. Hallow yourselves therefore and be ye holy; for I am holy.' On this the Sifra: "As I am holy, so be ye also holy; as I am separate (*parūsh*), so be ye also separate (*pĕrūshīm*)." [2] Similarly, on Lev. 19, 2 ('Ye shall be holy, for I, the Lord your God, am holy'): "Be ye separate (*pĕrūshīm*)." Again, in the Mekilta on Exod. 19, 6 ('Ye shall be unto me a kingdom of priests, a holy nation'): "Holy — holy, hallowed, separated from the peoples of the world and their detestable things." [3] Separateness in these contexts is synonymous with holiness in God and in man; the ideal of holiness for Israelites is the ideal of separateness, and it is easy to see how those who made it their end to fulfil this ideal might take its name *Pĕrūshīm* as a less presuming title than *Ḳĕdōshīm*.

Others look for the origin of the name in an historical situation and conjecture that it was originally applied to the Asidaeans who separated from Judas Maccabaeus when freedom of religion was achieved and a legitimate high priest succeeded Menelaus. An alluring parallel is adduced from the early history of Islam, when the ultra-religious faction in his army seceded from Ali

---

[1] It is applied to them by their opponents, the Sadducees.

[2] Shemini Pereḳ 12 (ed. Weiss, f.57 b). Exactly so also on 20, 26 (Ḳedoshim, end, f. 93d, top), in a similar connection.

[3] Ed. Friedmann, f. 63a; ed. Weiss, f. 71a.

in his conflict with Moʻawiya and from this secession were called Kharijites, 'Come-outers.' [1]

In more than one place in Josephus the Pharisees are said to be noted for their precise and minute interpretation of the laws,[2] and it is thought by some that the name may be derived from this activity. The verb *parash*, *pĕrash*, in fact, means not only 'separate' but 'distinguish,' or 'express distinctly,' and so, 'interpret.' The Pharisees would, in this view, be 'the exegetes.' [3] To this theory it is objected that *pĕrūshīm* is not a natural expression in Hebrew for 'exegetes.' Others would take the name in the more general sense, something like 'precisians,' to which this difficulty need not apply.

The foregoing cursory survey of the proposed explanations of the name may suffice to show that etymology has no addition to make to what is known of the Pharisees from historical sources.

The breach between John Hyrcanus and the Pharisees has already been mentioned. In the later years of his rule he had to put down a seditious movement which grew to the proportions of war. The motive of the insurrection is said to have been envy inspired by the king's success.[4] In the corresponding passage in the Antiquities [5] the same motive is alleged, but mention is somewhat inconsequentially introduced of the ill-disposition of the Pharisees toward him, and their influence with the people. We have already seen that the hostility of the masses toward him and his sons is attributed to his abrogation

---

[1] E. Meyer, Ursprung und Anfänge des Christentums, II, 283 f. (1921). The same theory of the origin of the name was propounded by Professor Mary I. Hussey in the Journal of Biblical Literature, XXXIX (1920), 66–69.

[2] Bell. Jud. i. 5, 2 § 110; ii. 8, 14 § 162; Antt. xvii. 2, 4 § 41.

[3] This explanation was, so far as I know, first advanced by Graetz. It has recently found an advocate in Leszynsky, Die Sadduzäer (1912), pp. 27 ff., 105 ff.

[4] Bell. Jud. i. 2, 8 § 67. It is generally recognized that Josephus here reproduces the statements and judgment of his source, presumably Nicolaus of Damascus.

[5] Antt. xiii. 10, 5 § 288

of the ordinances of the Pharisees. If this enmity broke out
in overt act it would give a more intelligible reason for the sedi-
tion than the vague "envy" of Josephus' first source. After the
suppression of the revolt, both accounts relate that Hyrcanus
lived in prosperity and ruled well. Josephus concludes with a
eulogy of him as one whom God had deemed worthy of the three
greatest things, the government of the nation, and the high
priesthood, and the gift of prophecy.[1]

The conflicts of Alexander Jannaeus with his people were
much more serious. The beginning was a riot in the temple at
the Feast of Tabernacles where he was officiating as high priest.
The multitude, incensed by his negligence in a part of the ceremony, threw at him the citrons [2] they carried in the festal procession, and shouted the slander that his mother had been a
captive in war, and that he, therefore, was disqualified for the
priesthood. He turned his Pisidian mercenaries on the mob,[3] and
the disturbance was quelled after six thousand had been killed.

In the sequel of Alexander's disastrous defeat in a war with
the Arabs in which he lost almost the whole of his army, the
malcontents took advantage of his calamity to rebel against
him. The civil war lasted six years, and cost fifty thousand
lives; but, although beaten, his enemies rejected his overtures
of peace — nothing but his death could reconcile them to him.
The implacables called in the Seleucid Demetrios Eukairos to
deliver them from their native king, and joined forces with him.
Despite the gallantry of his mercenaries, who were cut to pieces
in the battle, Alexander was defeated and put to flight. The
very completeness of their success, however, caused a revulsion,
and six thousand of the Jews who had fought under the Syrian
banner decamped from the victorious army and went over to
Alexander, out of pity for him in his fallen fortunes, it is said;
more likely because in the moment of triumph it dawned upon

---

[1] Antt. xiii. 10, 7 § 299. Cf. Jer. Soṭah 24b; Soṭah 33a.
[2] *Etrogim.*
[3] Like all the tyrants of the time, the Asmonaean princes maintained a
guard corps of foreigners, as, for that matter, David had done.

their tardy intelligence that the collapse of the Judaean national kingdom meant inevitable subjection to the Seleucid dominion from which the Asmonaeans had delivered them. Demetrios abandoned such inconstant allies and withdrew.

Left a free hand, Alexander at length completely crushed the rebellion. He celebrated his triumph by the crucifixion of eight hundred of his prisoners [1] at Jerusalem with circumstances of ingenious atrocity, which caused such a panic that eight thousand who had reason to fear a like fate fled the country and did not venture to return till after the king's death. [2]

This intestine strife is frequently represented in modern books as a conflict between Alexander Jannaeus and the Pharisees. This rests, however, on an inference from the character of the two parties rather than on the testimony of the sources. Neither in the primary account of the civil contention in the War nor in the secondary one in the Antiquities do the Pharisees figure at all. In the former they come in only after the events of Alexander's last years, the accession of Queen Alexandra, and a description of the character and conduct which won for her the good-will of the people. [3] "The Pharisees associated themselves with her administration, a body of Jews who profess to be more religious than the rest, and to explain the laws more precisely. Alexandra, being fanatically religious, paid great attention to them. By degrees they insinuated themselves into the confidence of the foolish woman, and soon got the management of affairs, banishing or recalling, liberating or imprisoning, whomsoever they pleased. In a word, the advantages of royalty were theirs, the cost and the troubles were Alexandra's." [4]

[1] Taken at the capture of the rebels' last refuge, the city of Bemeselis (or Bethome; the site is unknown).

[2] Josephus, Bell. Jud. i. 4, 3–6; Antt. xiii. 13, 5–14, 2. However greatly some or all of the numbers may be exaggerated, the ferocity of the long-continued struggle is beyond question.

[3] Bell. Jud. i. 4, 7–5, 1.

[4] Ibid. i. 5, 2 §§ 110 f. This is the first mention of the Pharisees in the War. The characterization and the depreciatory judgment are taken bodily

Nor is there any mention of the Pharisees as agitators, instigators, or belligerents anywhere in the parallel account of the civil war in the Antiquities. They appear only in the melodramatic deathbed scene, where the dying king counsels the weeping queen, as soon as she returns to Jerusalem, to give some measure of power to the Pharisees, who would laud her for this honor, and make the people favorable to her; it was by affronting them that he had come into collision with the nation.[1] Acting on this advice, she let the Pharisees do anything that they pleased, and commanded the populace to obey them. She also restored all the ordinances that the Pharisees had introduced in accordance with ancient tradition and her father-in-law Hyrcanus had annulled.[2] According to the rabbinical sources, this restoration took place under the superintendence of Simeon ben Shaṭaḥ, a brother of the queen.

How they exercised their power when Alexandra let them have their own way in internal affairs is illustrated by their treatment of the counsellors and loyal supporters of the late king. They themselves killed Diogenes, a distinguished man and friend of Alexander, whom they accused of advising him to execute the eight hundred prisoners that he crucified, and they persuaded the queen to put to death the others who had incited him against them. When she yielded to them for religious reasons,[3] they themselves put out of the way whomsoever they wished. The nobles [4] appealed to Aristobulus, who persuaded his mother to spare their lives on account of their rank, but to banish them from the city if she deemed them at fault.

from Josephus' source in this part of the book, the historian Nicolaus of Damascus.

[1] Antt. xiii. 15, 5. Note also the king's directions about what was to be done with his body, and the effect of this stratagem. The historical value of the story of the king's dying counsels in the Antiquities may be zero; but the power of the Pharisees is no less apparent in the account of their relations with Alexandra in the War.

[2] Antt. xiii. 16, 2 § 408; cf. 16, 1 § 405.

[3] ὑπὸ δεισιδαιμονίας in Josephus' source is meant in a derogatory sense, "out of superstition." [4] οἱ δυνατοί.

Amnesty being granted on these terms, they were scattered through the country.[1]

The succinct definition of the Pharisees quoted above, "A body of Jews who profess to be more religious than the rest and to explain the laws more precisely," [2] describes them as they appeared to an outside observer who had ample opportunity of acquaintance with them in the days of Herod. These are exactly the traits that characterize them in the first three Gospels and the Acts of the Apostles. In those writings they are frequently bracketed with the Scribes in the phrase "Scribes and Pharisees." The Scribes, as we have seen, were a learned class whose vocation was the study and exposition of the Law. In the first instance biblical scholars, as the name suggests, they became authorities also in the unwritten branch of the law, in the development of which they had the leading part. The Pharisees were a party whose endeavor it was to live in strict accordance with the law thus interpreted and amplified, and to bring the people to a similar conformity. Most of the Scribes were of this party,[3] but the bulk of the Pharisees were not scholars.

The devotion of the Pharisees to the traditional law, with its manifold regulations or ordinances (νόμιμα), is signalized by Josephus (or his sources) in numerous passages, some of which have previously been cited.[4] This was in fact their distinguishing characteristic — they were the zealous partisans of the unwritten law. The fundamental issue in their controversy with the Sadducees was the obligation of traditional rules and observances

---

[1] Bell. Jud. i. 5, 3 § 114. In the parallel account in Antt. xiii. 16, 2 f. §§ 411–417, they set forth the peril they are in, plead their services to the king and their loyalty to his house, and beg that if the queen was resolved to prefer the Pharisees, she would assign them to garrison duty in the fortresses. It may be observed that the sources on which Josephus draws in both accounts are distinctly hostile to the Pharisees, though from different sides.

[2] Bell. Jud. i. 8, 14 § 162; cf. Antt. xvii. 2, 4 § 41; xviii. 1, 3 § 12.

[3] Note οἱ γραμματεῖς τῶν Φαρισαίων, Mark 2, 16.

[4] Bell. Jud. ii. 8, 14 § 162; Antt. xvii. 2, 4 § 41; Vita c. 38 § 191. How they were abrogated by John Hyrcanus (Antt. xiii. 10, 6 § 296) and reënacted by Alexandra (xiii. 16, 2 § 308) has already been told.

for which there was no direct biblical authority.[1] Herein lies
the historical importance of the Pharisees. They mediated to
the people the knowledge of the law, impressed upon them by
precept its authority, and set them the example of punctilious
observance of its minutiae. They were the better able to do
this because their adherents were drawn from various social
classes, but principally, it appears, from that medium layer of
society in which puritan movements in all religions have found
their chief support.

In opposition to the Pharisees, the Sadducees maintained that
the written law alone was valid, and rejected the additions the
Pharisees made to it on the alleged authority of ancient tradition.[2] The written law, however, requires interpretation, and
in their interpretation the Sadducees were in general more
literal, and in matters of criminal law more severe, than the
Pharisees.[3] These interpretations and the precedents established under them could not fail to constitute what may in a
proper sense be called a Sadducean tradition; but, however
tenaciously they may have adhered to it in practice or in controversy, they did not ascribe to it intrinsic authority as the
Pharisees did to their "tradition of the elders." The Sadducees
were all the more under the necessity of having such a body of
common law because for a long time the actual administration
was in the hands of the classes among whom they were most
numerously represented. In later times, at least, they had
schools of their own; and the different temper of the two parties
is illustrated when we read in Josephus that, while the Pharisees
showed the greatest deference to their seniors and had not the
audacity to contradict their utterances, among the Sadducees
it was counted a virtue to dispute the teachers whom they
frequented.[4]

[1] Antt. xiii. 10, 6 §§ 297 f. This is confirmed by the Mishnah.
[2] Ibid. xviii. 1, 4 § 16. Matt. 15, 1 ff.; Mark 7, 1 ff.
[3] Ibid. xx. 9, 1 § 199; cf. xiii. 10, 6 § 294.
[4] Ibid. xviii. 1, 3 § 12; 1, 4 § 16. Josephus is probably describing things
as they were in his own youth.

The primary cleavage between the Sadducees and the Pharisees was on the doctrine of revelation. Scripture is the only
authority, said the Sadducees; Scripture and Tradition, said
the Pharisees. Next to this the most important doctrinal difference between the two was in the field of eschatology. The
Pharisees believed in the survival of the soul, the revival of the
body, the great judgment, and the life of the world to come. The
Sadducees found nothing in the Scriptures, as they read them
in their plain sense, about the resurrection of the dead or retribution after death, and rejected these new imaginations along
with the subtleties of exegesis by which they were discovered in
the Law.[1]

In Acts 23, 8, the Sadducees are said to deny not only the
revival of the dead but the existence of angels and spirits. That
they consistently rationalized the biblical appearances of angels
into men acting as the messengers of God is unlikely; but it is
in accord with their whole attitude that they should repudiate
as vulgar superstition the exuberant angelology and demonology which flourished in that age and was cultivated in apocalyptic circles.[2] With it would fall the belief in the individual
guardian angel (Acts 12, 15; Matt. 18, 10), as well as in ghosts,
the spirits of dead men (Luke 24, 37, 39).

The statement of several of the Fathers that the Sadducees
(like the Samaritans) acknowledged as Scripture nothing but
the Pentateuch may be a misunderstanding of what Josephus
says about their rejection of everything but the written law,
meaning that they did not admit legal or doctrinal deductions
from the Prophets.

The origin or occasion of the name Sadducee is as obscure
as that of the Pharisees. It is evidently formed from the proper
name which is familiar in the English Old Testament as Zadok,

[1] Bell. Jud. ii. 8, 14 § 175; Antt. xviii. 1, 4 § 16. Cf. Mark 12, 18–27
(Matt. 22, 23–33; Luke 20, 27–40); Acts 23, 6–9. For specimens of the rabbinical proofs see Sanhedrin 90b; cf. also Matt. l.c.
[2] Take the Book of Enoch for an example. For the esoteric lore of the
Essenes about the names of angels see Josephus, Bell. Jud. ii. 8, 7 § 142.

and the derivative would mean 'a follower of Zadok' — in the English 'a Zadokite.' The most widely accepted surmise connects the name with that Zadok whom Solomon installed as chief priest in the room of Abiathar, when he deprived him on account of his participation in Adonijah's attempt to seize the throne.[1] As the priesthood of Jerusalem before the exile, "the sons of Zadok" are, in Ezekiel's ideal of the restoration, to be the only priests of the new temple; the descendants of the old local priesthoods, the priests of the high places, being degraded to a lower order of the clergy, and strictly excluded from all higher sacerdotal functions and privileges.[2] On the testimony of the Chronicler, not all the priests of the second temple traced their lineage to Zadok, but the descendants of Zadok were more numerous among the leading men.[3]

The name Zadokite (Sadducee) may thus first have designated an adherent, or partisan, of the priestly aristocracy, and in time have been extended to all who shared the principles or opinions current in those circles. In Acts 5, 17, we read, "The high priest stood up and those that were with him (which is the sect of the Sadducees)." In Acts 4, 9, also, the high priests and the Sadducees act together, just as elsewhere the Scribes and Pharisees are coupled.

In the Abot de R. Nathan (c. 5) it is narrated how the twin heresies of the Sadducees and the Boethusians about retribution after death started in the schools of two disciples of Antigonus of Socho named respectively Zadok and Boethus.[4] They

---

[1] 1 Kings 2, 35. So A. Geiger, Urschrift und Uebersetzungen der Bibel, 1857; Sadducäer und Pharisäer, 1863; Wellhausen, Pharisäer und Sadducäer, 1874.

[2] Ezek. 44, 10–16; 48, 11; 43, 19; 40, 46. Cf. 2 Kings 23, 8–9; Deut 18, 6–8.

[3] 1 Chron. 24, 1–6. The author, there as elsewhere, makes the conditions existing at his own time an institution of David. See also the Hebrew text of Sirach, 51, 12 (in a psalm-like passage to which there is no Greek or Syriac counterpart), and the writing of the Damascene sect, ed. Schechter, page 4, lines 2 f.

[4] There is a strong probability that the Boethusians really got their name from a high priest of Herod's creation.

reasoned that Antigonus would never have exhorted men to serve God without hope of reward if he had believed that there was another world and a resurrection of the dead. The existence of such an explanation shows that it had not occurred to the Jews to connect the name with the Zadokite priesthood. The possibility remains that the party, or sect, perpetuates the name of some (to us) unknown founder or leader.[1]

The adherents of the Sadducees were found only in the class of the well-to-do; they had no following among the masses, who were on the side of the Pharisees.[2] This item in the characterization of the Sadducees has of late years been greatly emphasized. They were, it is said, not properly a religious party, or sect, as the Pharisees were, but primarily a social class, the aristocracy of the priesthood, together with the wealthy and influential laity whom community of interests and culture attached to the sacerdotal nobility, with whom they were frequently allied also by marriage. Their position on the sole authority of Scripture or on the new eschatology was the instinctive conservatism of the upper classes, clerical and lay, in the face of an aggressive and popular party which threatens their primacy. This representation, closely associated with the first theory of the origin of the name Sadducee reported above, is a reaction from the older notions which made the division between Pharisees and Sadducees purely dogmatic. It gives a good explanation of the fact that the Sadducees were almost exclusively of the upper classes. But in laying the whole stress on the hierarchical and social affiliations of the Sadducees, it runs counter to the unanimous testimony of the sources. Whatever their origin, they were, in contemporary eyes, a religious party in Judaism, characterized by the distinguishing beliefs — or negations — which have been set forth above.

The triumph of the Pharisees under Alexandra was the restora-

---

[1] So most recently Eduard Meyer, Ursprung und Anfänge des Christentums, II, 209 f.

[2] Josephus, Antt. xiii. 10, 6 § 298; xviii. 1, 4 § 17. "Their doctrine reaches only a few men, but those who hold the highest offices."

tion of their regulations, which were in effect a legislation supplementary to the Law in the form of an interpretation of it or a fence about it. Of the particular regulations and ordinances which were then at issue no record has come down to us.[1] The subsequent elaboration in the schools and the ultimate comprehensive and codified collections made in the second century of our era superseded all earlier formulations.

The extra-canonical books illustrate in various ways the existence of an unwritten law scrupulously observed by religious people. Judith, for example, breaks her voluntary fast in mourning for her husband on the Sabbath and the day before it, on the New-Moon and the day before, on the Festivals, and the joyous days of the house of Israel.[2] When she set out for the camp of Holophernes she took with her her own victuals, wine, and oil, in order not to have to eat the unclean food of the heathen.[3] Daniel and his comrades are unwilling to defile themselves with their rations of food and wine from the king's table, and persuade the chief eunuch to give them pulse to eat and water to drink, on which they thrive miraculously.[4] Tobit shows that the unwritten law about the burial of the neglected dead was regarded as a duty of the highest obligation,[5] as it is in rabbinical law.[6] Evidently much which we otherwise know only in the rabbinical sources of the first and second centuries after our era was custom and law in the preceding centuries.

[1] The ordinances of Simeon ben Shaṭaḥ are from the reign of Alexandra. On sectarian Halakah from this age, see below, pp. 198 f., 200–202.

[2] Judith 8, 6. Cf. the prohibition of fasting on the Sabbath, Jubilees 50, 12; and perhaps the Damascus text (p. 11, l. 4), on which see Ginzberg p. 90 f. (reading יתרעב for יתערב). "The day before" seems to be supererogatory.

[3] Judith 10, 5; 12, 1–4, 19.

[4] The reason for the specification of 'pulse' is perhaps that, being dry, it did not contract uncleanness by contact. See M. 'Ukṣin 3, 1; Maimonides, Hilkot Tum'at Okelin 1, 1.

[5] Tobit 1, 17–19; 2, 1–9. The מת מצוה.

[6] It takes precedence even of the study of the Law, the circumcision of a son, or the offering of the paschal lamb. Megillah 3b, et alibi. Priests — even the high priest — and nazirites are allowed to make themselves unclean by burying a מת מצוה. Sifrè Num. § 26; cf. Sifrè Zuṭa on Num. 6, 7.

CHAPTER VI

SHAMMAI AND HILLEL

THE recognition given by Queen Alexandra to the Pharisees doubtless augmented their already dominant influence with the great body of the people, a leadership they never lost. What part they took in the strife between her sons, Hyrcanus and Aristobulus, is not recorded. We have seen that Aristobulus was not in sympathy with her policy of letting the Pharisees have their own way in dealing with those who were obnoxious to them, and pleaded the cause of the officers and friends of Jannaeus who were in fear of their lives from them. It is natural to suppose that this class supported the energetic younger son, who evidently had a good deal of his father about him, rather than his *fainéant* brother Hyrcanus whom Alexandra had made high priest and presumptive successor to the crown. But whether the Pharisees were any better content with the latter, especially when he let himself be managed by the Idumaean Antipater for his own ambitious schemes, is doubtful.

Certain it is that when the two brothers appeared before Pompey in Damascus with their rival claims to the throne, "the nation" (τὸ ἔθνος) protested against them both: By their ancestral constitution the Jews were subject to the priests of the God they worshipped; these men, though descendants of the priests, were trying to change the form of government so as to bring the nation into servitude. Against Aristobulus in particular more than a thousand of the most distinguished of the Jews, "whom Antipater had suborned," testified in support of Hyrcanus' accusations.[1] The protest, it is not superfluous to remark, is against the royal form of government, of which the Asmonaeans had given them all the experience they wanted; not on

[1] Antt. xiv. 3, 2 § 41.

the ground that these priests had usurped the throne of David
and were no legitimate kings — an interpretation sometimes
read into the passage. The supporters of Aristobulus were a lot
of swaggering young bloods whose garb and mien made a bad
impression on the Romans; the cause of Hyrcanus was in the
hands of Antipater.

Pompey talked softly to them both, and postponed a decision
till he should visit Judaea. The suspicious actions of Aristobulus brought him thither sooner than he had planned. The
supporters of Hyrcanus let the Romans into the city; the partisans of Aristobulus occupied the temple and prepared to stand
a siege. The Romans proceeded to a regular investment, in
which labors they had every assistance from Hyrcanus. The
walls were finally breached and the temple taken, with much
slaughter not only of the defenders but of the priests, who went
on unflinching with the routine of their office till their blood was
mingled with that of the sacrificial victims. As a reward for
his other services to the Romans and for keeping the Jews in
the country from fighting on the side of Aristobulus, Pompey
gave the high priesthood to Hyrcanus; the "authors of the
war" he executed.[1]

The inland cities which the Jews in the preceding reign had
subjected were separated from Judaea and put under the administration of a Roman official; those on the coast were made
free cities of the province of Syria. "The nation which a little
while before had been so highly exalted, he shut up in its own
boundaries." The royal authority, which had been a prerogative of the high priest, was done away; the government was
an aristocracy. Aristobulus and his sons, Antigonus and Alexander, made repeated unsuccessful efforts in the next quarter
of a century to regain their dominion by arms. Antipater and
his sons, Phasael and Herod, with their puppet Hyrcanus, were
always on the Roman side, and in the vicissitudes of the civil
wars managed to be always in the end on the winning side.

[1] Josephus, Antt. xiv. 4.

The restoration of Antigonus, son of Aristobulus, by the aid of the Parthians, which drove Herod out of the country and sent him as a suppliant to Rome, proved to be the making of his fortune, for the Senate, at the instance of Mark Antony supported by Octavian, made Herod king, and promised him aid to get possession of his kingdom. Three years elapsed, however, before Jerusalem itself, after a protracted siege ending with the storming of the temple, fell into the hands of the allied forces of the Romans under Sosius and of Herod. Antigonus surrendered himself to the Romans, and shortly after, at Herod's instance, was decapitated by Antony's orders in Antioch.

The sentiment of loyalty to the Asmonaean house, from which had sprung their rulers for a century and a quarter, and with which were connected the memories of the wars of liberation and of conquest that seemed to bring back the glorious times of the old monarchy, was still strong. As often as Aristobulus or his sons raised the standard of revolt they found a following waiting for them. When the Parthians released Hyrcanus, whom they had carried off as a prisoner, and allowed him to go to Babylonia, the Jews in the whole region east of the Euphrates treated him with the honor due to a high priest and king, and urged him to remain with them and not return to Jerusalem, where he could expect no such recognition.[1]

The resistance of the Jews to Herod was to a king imposed on them by the Romans — a king who was not only not of the blood royal, but not even of the Jewish race. Antony caused Antigonus to be beheaded — the first time the Romans had inflicted such ignominy on a king — because he was convinced that in no other way could the Jews be brought to acknowledge Herod; they held their former king in such esteem that not even tortures could force them to give Herod that title.[2] One of Herod's first measures when he had taken Jerusalem was to put to death forty-five prominent men of the party of Antigonus and

[1] Josephus, Antt. xv. 2, 2.
[2] Strabo, quoted in Josephus, Antt. xv. 1, 2 §§ 9 f.

confiscate their property, and to punish many others, while he promoted men of private station who had been well disposed to himself. He especially honored the two leading Pharisees, Pollio and Sameas, because when he besieged Jerusalem they counselled their fellow citizens to surrender the city.[1] Pollio, we are told, had an additional claim on his favor, because, when Herod had been summoned before the Sanhedrin by Hyrcanus for executing the brigands in Galilee without a trial, and that body let itself be intimidated by Herod's defiant mien, he had foretold that if they let Herod off he would be the undoing of them all [2] — a prediction which he fulfilled to the letter.

From the Jewish aristocracy Herod had nothing to expect. His double alliance with the Asmonaean house through his marriage with Mariamne [3] did not legitimate the Idumaean parvenu in their eyes, and his hand in the death of Antigonus, and later of the aged Hyrcanus himself, made reconciliation with the partisans of either branch impossible. Alexandra's ambition was to have her son Aristobulus (III) made high priest in succession to his grandfather Hyrcanus; Herod's interest, after he had been made king by the Romans, was to let no Asmonaean fill that office with its traditions of royalty. When, acting on this policy, he installed a Babylonian Jew named Ananel, of priestly ineage but unrelated to the aristocratic priesthood of Jerusalem,[4]

[1] Josephus, Antt. xv. 1, 1.

[2] Ibid. xiv. 9, 4 § 176.

[3] Her father Alexander was the eldest son of Aristobulus II; her mother, Alexandra, a daughter of Hyrcanus. It is a probable surmise that the initiative in this alliance came from the girl's mother or from Hyrcanus himself. — Mariamne was apparently very young when she was betrothed to Herod (perhaps as early as the year 42). In his flight from Jerusalem before the Parthians (40) he carried off to security in the fortress of Masada, with his own kindred, Alexandra and her daughter. The marriage itself was celebrated at Samaria in 37, on the eve of his siege of Jerusalem. Josephus, Bell. Jud. xiv. 15, 14 § 467.

[4] Josephus, Antt. xv. 2, 4 § 22 (cf. 3, 1 § 39 f.). In M. Parah 3, 5, Hanamael is called an Egyptian. Possibly he was a Jew of Babylonian extraction living in Egypt. The Boethus family, which furnished at least four high priests, came from Alexandria (Antt. xv. 9, 3 § 320). What the

Alexandra secretly besought Cleopatra to use her influence to persuade Antony to have Herod confer the high priesthood on Aristobulus. The intrigue was no secret to Herod; but he yielded to the importunity of Mariamne in behalf of her brother, deprived Ananel, and made Aristobulus high priest in his place, though he was still a youth in his teens. The discovery of a fresh intrigue of Alexandra with Cleopatra, and a demonstration by the people at the Feast of Tabernacles of their attachment to Aristobulus and the memory of his fathers, made plain to Herod that he had not made peace in his family by his concession, but had given a figure-head if not a rallying point to the old loyalties; and he lost no time in arranging a drowning accident at Jericho, followed by a magnificent funeral by which the youth's kindred and friends were not deceived. Ananel was restored to the high priesthood, and thenceforward Herod made and unmade high priests as it pleased him, but raised none to that rank who had any other claim to it than that they were his creatures.

By war and proscriptions the upper classes, among whom the Sadducees were numerous, had been brought to low estate. Herod exerted himself, on the other hand, to put the mass of the people under obligation to him by remission of taxes in bad years,[1] and in a time of famine by distribution of grain which he imported from Egypt, and by using his influence with the Roman authorities to gain exemptions and privileges for the Jews in foreign parts, particularly in Asia Minor and the Greek islands. The rebuilding of the temple in fabulous splendor gratified the passion for such works which he had indulged in many other cities, but it was doubtless meant also to display himself to his subjects as a munificent patron of religion. In this endeavor to win the loyalty of the common people he had every reason to keep on good terms with the Pharisees, and when they refused to take the oath of allegiance which he demanded, he was

religious Jews thought of these priests may be read in Pesaḥim 57a; Tos Menaḥot 13, 21.

[1] On the disaffection of the people and its religious causes, see Antt. xv. 10, 4 § 365.

politic enough to let it pass and to exempt the Essenes also from the requirement.[1]

The Pharisees on their side did not meddle in politics or incite the people against Herod. They were not a dynastic or nationalist party, and were content with the freedom they enjoyed to pursue their religious studies and practices, and to labor with their countrymen for a better observance of the divine law. With this harmless employment of the intellect of the nation Herod was doubtless well pleased, and he had no motive for interfering with regulations and ordinances for the Jewish life. When it came to laws for the kingdom, he made them himself as occasion required, without concern for the ancient legislation, as when in his zeal to suppress crime he enacted a law that housebreakers should be deported from his kingdom — a punishment, as Josephus remarks, unheard of in Jewish law, and very unpleasant for the burglars.[2]

With the reign of Herod coincides roughly the activity of the last of the Pairs, Shammai and Hillel, and the beginning of the Tannaite school tradition. Shammai was a native Judaean, while Hillel came from Babylonia to Jerusalem when already a mature man. There were schools of the Law in Babylonia, as in other centres of Jewish population, and there is good reason to believe that Hillel had been a student in his own country [3] before he migrated to Jerusalem to sit under the most eminent teachers and expositors of the time, Shemaiah and Abṭalion.[4] The name of Hillel is associated with certain hermeneutic norms for juristic deduction and analogy which are called Hillel's Seven Rules.[5]

[1] Antt. xv. 10, 4 §§ 370 f.; cf. xvii. 2, 4 § 42.

[2] Ibid. xvi. 1, 1. For many other examples of Herod's tyrannical disregard of Jewish law, see Juster, Les Juifs dans l'empire romain, II, 127 ff. See also Josephus, Antt. xv. 10, 4 § 365.

[3] Jer. Pesaḥim 33a, below, specifies three problems which he had solved and proved before he went up to Palestine. Cf. also Ḳiddushin 75a.

[4] The story of the privations and hardships he overcame in the pursuit of learning is told in a Baraita (Yoma 35b) to show that poverty is no excuse for neglecting the study of the Law.

[5] *Middot.* They are found in Tos. Sanhedrin 7, 11.

They are obvious principles of interpretation for a divinely revealed law every word of which was significant and authoritative, and had doubtless been thus applied by scholars before his
time; but with Hillel they became a method, defining certain
ways in which logically valid conclusions in the juristic field are
derivable from the written law.

It is a surmise for which some probability may be claimed
that, in germ at least, this method came from the Babylonian
schools. In Jerusalem the doctors of the Law sat at the fountain-
head of tradition and were able to draw directly upon that
source for answer to the questions that arose in practice or in
discussion. In remoter lands this appeal to tradition must often
have been unavailable, and the necessity of arriving at an authoritative conclusion from the biblical text itself must have
been correspondingly more strongly felt.[1]

However this may be, an old Baraita instructively illustrates
the attitude of the strict traditional school toward an attempt to
settle questions of law by reasoning in lieu of authority, and
their low opinion of Babylonian scholarship. The Elders of
Bathyra [2] were in doubt whether, in case the fourteenth of
Nisan fell on a Sabbath, the slaughter and preparation of the
paschal victim was an obligation superior to the sabbatical
prohibition of labor.[3] Hillel was recommended to them as a disciple of Shemaiah and Abṭalion who might know the tradition
on the point. Instead of the tradition they asked, however, he
undertook to demonstrate to them by three distinct arguments
that the Passover took precedence of the Sabbath. They con-
temptuously exclaimed, "How could we expect anything of a

[1] The same difference, as is well known, existed in Moslem jurisprudence
between the traditional school of Medina and the jurists in other lands, who
gave larger scope to logical deductions and analogical inferences (ḳiyās).

[2] The name בתירה is usually thus transliterated on the supposition that it
is the place Βαθύρα in Batanaea where Herod in the last years of his reign
established a small garrison colony of Babylonian Jews. Josephus, Antt.
xvii. 2, 1 f.

[3] For the conflicting opinions on this question, see Chwolson, Das letzte
Passamahl, pp. 18 ff.; Ginzberg, Eine unbekannte jüdische Sekte, pp. 99 f., 204.

Babylonian!" and proceeded to pick his reasoning to pieces. Though he sat and argued to them all day,[1] they did not accept his conclusion, until he said to them, "Thus I heard it from Shemaiah and Abṭalion." As soon as he fell back from argument to recognized authority, they rose from their seats and elected him their president (*Nasi*). He requited them for their previous disrespect with reproaches: If they had used their opportunities for study under the two great scholars who taught in their own country, they would have had no need to call in a Babylonian.[2]

Many anecdotes about Shammai and Hillel illustrate the contrasted temperaments of the two men, and set the rigorousness of the one over against the humanity of the other. In the interpretation and application of the laws Shammai was nearly always more stringent than Hillel, and that not merely from a harsher disposition but in consequence of his traditional principle. It has been remarked above that what has been called the old Halakah, whether exemplified in the schools or the sects, was in general stricter than that which eventually prevailed. In this sphere Shammai was conservative of the letter of tradition and developed its consequences in the same spirit.

Hillel came from another environment. In Babylonia a large part of the legislation, including the ritual of the temple, and many laws which were not in force "outside the Land," had only an academic interest, and the traditions on these matters were not binding rules of practical observance as the Palestinian teachers endeavored to make them. It was natural under these circumstances that the unwritten law should be more largely deduced from the text itself by certain exegetical principles.

[1] In this long debate he had opportunity to exemplify the rest of his rules, which are introduced as "the seven norms that Hillel expounded in the presence of the elders of Bathyra." See above, pp. 77 f., and Sifra, Introduction, end (ed. Weiss, f. 3a).

[2] Jer. Pesaḥim 33a; Pesaḥim 66a, and elsewhere. On the deference of the Bene Bathyra, see Baba Mesi'a 84b–85a. Who the Elders of Bathyra were, and what is meant by their *Nasi*, are curious questions which do not here concern us.

When he came to be the head of a school in Jerusalem, Hillel recognized that the laws must take account of actual conditions. The septennial cancellation of debts in Deut. 15, for example, might have been a benevolent institution in the society for which the law was framed, but in his time it worked great hardship to the necessitous borrower, who in the later years of the period could get no accommodation. To remedy this evil he devised the "Prosbul," which left the law unchanged, but by a legal fiction secured the creditor against the loss of his loan through the coming of the year of release.[1]

More important than such striking adaptations of the law to circumstances was eventually the application of his hermeneutic principles to establish the harmony between tradition and Scripture. It may be conjectured that at least one motive of this endeavor was to silence the Sadducees with their contention that tradition is devoid of authority — only Scripture is law — by proving from Scripture that what is explicit in tradition is implicit in Scripture. From particular instances the schools went on to a consecutive juristic exegesis of the legislative parts of the Pentateuch, the Tannaite Midrash, and by the results amplified the unwritten law. To this phase of the work of the schools, especially in the second century, we shall have occasion to recur further on.

Whatever may have been the relation between the members of the preceding Pairs, there is no intimation that they were the heads of rival schools.[2] Shammai and Hillel, however, represent such different tendencies that a division of this kind was inevitable. It perpetuated itself after the death of the two masters, and the school differences between the "House of Shammai" and the "House of Hillel" fill a large room in what is recorded of Jewish tradition from about the beginning of the Christian era to the war of 66–72. More than three hundred

---

[1] The reason and the legal form of words are given in Sifrè Deut. § 113; M. Shebi'it 10, 2, etc.; cf. Giṭṭin 36a–b.

[2] See above, p. 46.

conflicting deliverances of the two schools on matters of law and observance are reported in one connection or another in the Talmud.[1] In their very zeal for the Law they were fast making of it "two laws." The evil consequences of these dissensions were so obvious that even partisanship could not be blind to them. We hear of what we should call rabbinical conferences, in which members of the two schools came together to discuss their differences and to reach a decision by a majority vote. At one such meeting, in which the Shammaites outnumbered the Hillelites, eighteen restrictive decrees (*gezerot*) were adopted,[2] and there is mention of other meetings later. Some have thought that such conferences were a regular institution with periodical sessions; but the sources give no support to this theory.

It seems that in the middle decades of our first century the Shammaites were the more numerous, as well as the more aggressive, and it was perhaps only after the fall of Jerusalem that the Hillelites gained the ascendency. The rigorist tendencies of the former school were perpetuated in certain leading rabbis of the following generations; and it is possible that some irreconcilable Shammaites were left on one side by the movement of unification, but danger that the differences of the schools would split their adherents into sects was over. The dissidence of these two schools may be regarded as an inner crisis in the history of Pharisaism, from which the more progressive tendency emerged superior.

Hillel, of all the rabbis, is the most familiar name to most Christians. He owes this reputation to the anecdotes which illustrate his genial temper and to the fine religious and moral aphorisms that are quoted from him; but his great significance in the history of Judaism lies not so much in these things as in the new impulse and direction he gave to the study of the Law, the new spirit he infused into Pharisaism.

[1] A classified enumeration of them with references in Weiss, Dor, I, 168 ff. See Jewish Encyclopedia, III, 115 f.

[2] M. Shabbat 1, 4 ff.; cf. Tos. Shabbat 1, 8 ff. (see 1, 16).

Under the procurators the Jews had larger room to manage their own affairs in their own way than under Herod. The Roman administration had need of a representative and responsible intermediary between it and the people, and found such an organ in the Council,[1] or Sanhedrin,[2] which under Herod's autocratic rule had probably cut politically a very small figure. In this body, under the presidency of the high priest, besides the heads of the great priestly families, lay elders, men of rank and authority,[3] had seats; among both, probably, there were legal experts, Scribes. The upper priesthood was prevailingly Sadducean; among the other members of the Sanhedrin the Pharisaean party was represented.[4]

In religious matters the Romans did not interfere at all. Sacrifices for the emperor were regularly offered in the temple according to the Jewish rite; but, except for the project of Caligula to instal an image of himself in the temple and an occasional *faux pas* of a procurator, the peculiarities of the Jews were respected. Cases between Jew and Jew were left to the adjudication of their own tribunals, from the village judges up to the high court in Jerusalem.[5]

[1] In Josephus usually βουλή.

[2] συνέδριον.

[3] δυνατοί.

[4] The composition of the Council, or Senate as it had earlier been called, and the mode of election to it, are nowhere described in our sources.

[5] The nearest modern analogy is the status of the several so-called 'national' churches, *millets* (e.g., the Armenians), in the former Turkish empire. On the power of the Sanhedrin under the procurators to pronounce and execute sentence of death according to Jewish law, see Juster, Les Juifs dans l'empire romain, II, 133 ff.

CHAPTER VII

REORGANIZATION AT JAMNIA

IN the commotions which grew into the rebellion under Nero the most eminent of the Pharisees joined the high priests and the influential men of the city in futile efforts to restrain the people from plunging headlong into war and ruin. After the failure of Cestius Gallus' attempt to take Jerusalem by assault, and his retirement, which pursuit turned into precipitate flight, seeing that there was no more hope of peace, they tried to keep the control of affairs in their own hands, making the high priest Ananus and Joseph ben Gorion governors of the city, and appointing military commanders for the several districts to prepare for the impending war.[1] Their efforts were in vain. One faction outdid another in atrocities, and things took their inevitable course to the fall of Jerusalem and the burning of the temple in 70 A.D.

It is related that in the midst of the internecine strife within the walls in which the Jews were destroying themselves while the Romans looked on, Rabban Johanan ben Zakkai made his escape from the city to the Roman camp, and (in one form of the story) obtained from the commander permission to settle in Jamnia and establish a school there. Thus, even before the final catastrophe, the study of the Law had found refuge in the new seat from which the restoration was to proceed.[2] What is certain is that at Jamnia (Jabneh),[3] under the lead of Johanan

[1] It is a probable view that these measures were taken by the Sanhedrin, which was the only authority left in the city. In support of this opinion it may be noted that the generals appointed seem all to have been members of priestly aristocracy, like Josephus who was sent to organize the defense of Galilee.

[2] Lam. R. on Lam. 1, 5; Abot de-R. Nathan c. 4; Giṭṭin 56a–b.

[3] On the coastal plain a little north of the parallel of Jerusalem, in a region which had been spared the devastation of war.

ben Zakkai in the years immediately following the destruction of Jerusalem, the work of conservation and adaptation was accomplished with such wisdom that Judaism not only was tided over the crisis but entered upon a period of progress which it may well count among the most notable chapters in its history.

In the succession of teachers Johanan ben Zakkai is said to have received the tradition from Shammai and Hillel, and there is a story that Hillel, when his disciples gathered around his sick-bed, declared Johanan, the youngest of them all, to be the greatest, "father of wisdom and father of future generations." [1] Unless we could stretch our imagination to allotting to each of them, like Moses, a hundred and twenty years of life, as the rabbinical scheme does, there is some difficulty in supposing that Johanan was an immediate pupil of Hillel, but that in a larger sense he deserves to rank as the greatest of his disciples may be freely admitted. Before the war he was a man of importance in Jerusalem, and his teaching attracted many students, some of whom were themselves scholars of renown before the migration to Jamnia.[2] It seems that they accompanied him thither or soon followed him. After the fall of the city other scholars and students resorted to the new seat of learning, or established themselves in neighboring places.

The re-opening of the schools was not, however, the only contribution of Johanan to the restoration of Judaism. There was urgent need of a body competent to determine matters of the utmost importance to all Jews, foremost among which was the fixing of the calendar with the correct dates of all the festivals and fasts, for which the law prescribed days certain as of the essence of the observance. Innumerable questions arose also from the cessation of the temple worship, for which there was no rule or precedent, and about which an authoritative decision was necessary if there was not to be endless perplexity of conscience and confusion of practice.

[1] Jer. Nedarim 39b.
[2] Five are named, with the master's estimate of them, in Abot 2, 8.

The doctors of the Law in Jamnia and its vicinity, under the lead of Johanan ben Zakkai, accordingly formed themselves into a council, which assumed such of the functions of the Sanhedrin as did not inevitably lapse with the loss of its political character.

But, however it may have regarded itself as a successor to the Sanhedrin, the Great Bet Din [1] at Jamnia was a very different body from its predecessor. The Sanhedrin, under the procurators, was a national council, having recognized political powers and responsibilities. At its head was the high priest, and the aristocracy of the priesthood constituted a large part of its membership.[2] The lay notables were closely allied to them and shared their Sadducean leanings. In the Sanhedrin the Sadducees were therefore, to the end, a strong, if not the predominating party. Johanan ben Zakkai was a leader of the Pharisees, and anecdotes about him laid in the time before the war tell with satisfaction how he worsted the Sadducees in controversy, and even thwarted a high priest who was going to burn the red heifer according to Sadducean rule and precedent. His disciples and colleagues were from the same party, and his rabbinical council was a purely Pharisaean body.[3] It was the definitive triumph of Pharisaism.

The two tendencies in Pharisaism, represented by the Shammaites and the Hillelites respectively, persisted, but the influence of Johanan ben Zakkai and his disciples contributed much to the ultimate predominance of the Hillelites. The outcome is recorded in legendary form: A voice from heaven (*bat ḳol*) was heard (at Jabneh), saying, The teachings of both schools are words of the Living God, but in practice the Halakah of the school of Hillel is to be followed.[4]

The classes to which the Sadducees chiefly belonged had been reduced to insignificance. Many had perished in the war or by

---

[1] High Court. The name 'Sanhedrin' was not assumed by the Bet Din at Jamnia, nor by the Bet Din, or academy, of the Patriarchs (L. Ginzberg).

[2] Mark 14, 53, 55 (Matt. 26, 57, 59); Acts 4, 5 f.; 5, 27, 34, 41; 6, 12.

[3] See L. Ginzberg, 'Bet Din,' Jewish Encyclopedia, III, 114 f.

[4] Jer. Berakot 3b, end; 'Erubin 13b.

the daggers of assassins, others had been executed by the Romans or carried into slavery. In the new order of things the Sadducees lost the extrinsic importance which the high station of their adherents had given them, and subsided into a sect which, besides preserving memories of controversies the subject of which had ceased to exist, and making itself disagreeable by cavilling at specific rules or dicta of the Pharisees, had for its differential doctrine the rejection of the whole Pharisaean eschatology. The Pharisees made a dogma of the resurrection of the dead, and thus the Sadducees became heretics: the Israelite who denies that the resurrection is revealed in the Torah has no lot in the World to Come.

Before the death of Johanan ben Zakkai, Gamaliel II [1] succeeded him, with the title Nasi, which Greek and Latin writers render "Patriarch," but for which we might use "President." [2] His great endeavor was to secure the recognition of all Jewry for the Bet Din at Jamnia and submission to its authority. His colleagues thought him too arbitrary in asserting his own preeminence, and he was for a time deprived of the presidency of the academy (*yeshibah*). It was probably in his time that the long-standing strife between the schools of Shammai and Hillel was terminated by a general decision in favor of the latter, and the grave evil of conflicting observances, with the possibility of schism about them, overcome.

The controversy between the two schools over the question whether Ecclesiastes and the Song of Songs were holy scripture was decided by a majority vote in favor of both of them, following the opinion of the school of Hillel. Another decision in this period — the time and place are unknown — concerning what we call the canon of Scripture was that the Book of Ben Sira (Ecclesiasticus) was not sacred scripture, nor any other books written from his time on. The passages in the Tosefta which report this

---

[1] Called Gamaliel of Jabneh to distinguish him from his grandfather of the same name.

[2] 'Nasi' is, in Ezekiel 40 ff., the title of the civil head of the Jewish people, and as such the Patriarch was recognized by the Roman government.

decision name specifically "the gospel" (*euangelion*) and the books of the sectarians (or heretics), among which, in the context, it is fair to presume that Christian writings are at least included.[1]

The older and younger contemporaries of Gamaliel II, and their disciples and successors in the next generation,[2] are the fundamental authorities of normative Judaism as we know it in the literature which it has always esteemed authentic. One main division of their learned labors was the definition and exact formulation of the rules of the unwritten law (Halakah), as they had been received through tradition, or were adapted to meet new conditions, or were developed by biblical exegesis or casuistic discussion. Along with this ran the minute study, in course, of the written law in the Pentateuch from Exodus to Deuteronomy, in primary intention a juristic exegesis with constant reference to the Halakah.

In the interpretation of the Law large use was made of the Prophets and the Hagiographa,[3] and the numerous quotations from these writings prove that the Tannaim were no less familiar with them than with the Pentateuch itself. An index to one of the Tannaite Midrashim, such as Friedmann has appended to his edition of the Mekilta, is ample evidence of this. The quotations from Isaiah in the 250 pages of the Mekilta fill three closely printed pages; those from the Psalms take five. Ruth is the only book of the Twenty-Four from which there is no quotation. Hoffmann's index to his Midrash Tannaim is equally to the point.

The two great scholarchs of the generation before the war under Hadrian were R. Akiba ben Joseph and R. Ishmael ben Elisha. To Akiba is commonly attributed the systemization of the Halakah with which we are familiar, distributing the rules by

---

[1] Tos. Yadaim 2, 13; cf. Tos. Shabbat 13 (14), 5.

[2] Say, from 80 to 140 A.D.

[3] These books contained the "tradition" (Ḳabbalah) by the side of the Law (Torah), from which parallels, explanations, and illustrations were drawn

subjects under six capital divisions with numerous subdivisions, thus giving the unwritten law the form of a code.[1] This arrangement greatly facilitated a mastery of its vast and varied contents and the exact transmission of its concise phraseology.

In the interpretation of Scripture, Akiba went on the principle that in a book of divine revelation no smallest peculiarity of expression or even of spelling is accidental or devoid of significance, and evolved certain new hermeneutic rules for the discovery of the meaning thus suggested by the letter.[2] By these methods, and by fabulous acumen and ingenuity in the employment of them, Akiba found in the written law many things for which theretofore it had been possible only to allege tradition.[3] For Greek-speaking Jews the proselyte Aquila, who had imbibed the principles of Akiba, provided a translation in which he endeavored to reproduce in Greek the peculiarities of the Hebrew so literally that the reader might apply to it the Akiban hermeneutics. There was another reason for a new version in the fact that the Gentile Christians had appropriated the Septuagint, and based their apologetic and polemic on its renderings, proving, for example, the conception of Christ by a virgin mother from its ἡ παρθένος in Isa. 7, 14, which Aquila corrected to ἡ νεᾶνις.

Ishmael adhered more closely to the methods of interpretation embodied in the seven norms of Hillel. These he analyzed and subdivided, with some modification, into thirteen, which became the standard principles of juristic hermeneutics.[4] In contradiction to Akiba he held that the Torah speaks ordinary human language;[5] varieties in the mode of expression of which

[1] Topical treatment of parts of the material was older; Akiba carried it through the whole.

[2] In the rules about extension and restriction, of which he made a great deal, he had a predecessor in Nahum of Gimzo.

[3] Attention has been so focussed on these curiosities that Akiba's real merits as an exegete are seldom recognized.

[4] They are prefixed to Sifra. For purposes of homiletic "improvement" the strict logic of legal deduction is not insisted on.

[5] דברה תורה כלשון בני אדם, Sifrè Num. § 112 (ed. Friedmann, p. 33a, end), and in many other places.

in common speech no notice would be taken are not to be forced to yield a hidden significance.

From these schools there is preserved a series of Tannaite Midrash on the books from Exodus to Deuteronomy,[1] which, though incomplete and in part fragmentary, far outrank all other sources in the disclosure they make of the biblical interpretation of the schools and of the religious and moral teachings they based upon the Books of Moses.

This flourishing epoch in the history of the schools was brought to an abrupt end by the war under Hadrian. According to Cassius Dio the Jews rebelled because the emperor, on his visit to Judaea in the spring of 130, gave orders for the rebuilding of Jerusalem, with a temple of Jupiter Capitolinus to be erected on the site of the ruined Jewish temple.[2] The revolt did not actually break out, however, until 132, after Hadrian had left Syria. The Jews had cherished the expectation that in time they would be allowed to rebuild the temple as they had done after its destruction by Nebuchadnezzar. So long as it lay in ruins nothing forbade such hope; but, apart from the profanation of the holy place which renewed the days of Antiochus Epiphanes and his "abomination of desolation," it could not be imagined that the Romans would ever permit a temple of the Jupiter of the Capitol to be razed to make room for the God of the Jews. The conversion of Jerusalem into a heathen city must be prevented or all was lost. The leader of the Jews was acclaimed by Akiba the "Star out of Jacob" of Balaam's prophecy (Num. 24, 17), a militant Messiah, whence the name (preserved in Christian writers) Bar Cocheba, "the Star man."[3] Early in the revolt

---

[1] See below, pp. 135 ff.

[2] Was there a deliberate irony in dedicating this temple to the god to whom, since Vespasian, the Jews had had to pay the didrachm poll tax previously levied for the temple in Jerusalem?

[3] From coins it is learned that his name was Simeon. In Jewish sources he is called Bar Kozibah, probably from the name of his native town. Not all his colleagues shared Akiba's enthusiasm. When he declared Bar Kozibah to be the messianic king, Johanan ben Torta replied, "Akiba, grass will be growing on your cheeks long before the Son of David comes." Jer. Ta'anit 68d.

the Jews got possession of the ruins of Jerusalem and held it for
some time. The war itself lasted three years and a half, and
ended with the fall of Bether, a few miles from Jerusalem, in
134/135.

The war had one incidental result of which mention must be
made briefly here: it brought about the final separation of the
Nazarenes from the rest of the Jews. Hitherto these "disciples
of Jesus the Nazarene" had been a conventicle within the synagogue, rather than a sect. Their peculiarity was the belief that
the Messiah foretold in the Scriptures had appeared in the reign
of Tiberius in the person of Jesus of Nazareth, who had been
executed by the procurator of Judaea, Pontius Pilate, at the
instance of the chief priests, as a prospective revolutionary,
"the king of the Jews." His followers believed that he had come
to life again and been taken up to heaven, whence he would soon
come again in power and glory, to execute the divine judgment
on those who had rejected him and usher in the expected golden
age.[1] For the rest they were pious and observant Jews, who worshipped in the temple and in the synagogues like others. Their
efforts to make converts to their belief, especially at the beginning, when they gathered crowds around them in the courts of
the temple to argue about it, led to the intervention of the authorities to prevent disturbances, but there was no attempt to
put a ban on the belief itself. The Jews had no doctrine about
the Messiah invested with the sanction of orthodoxy, and on the
fundamental articles of Judaism, the unity of God, his peculiar
relation to Israel, the revelation of his character, will, and purpose in Scripture, the Nazarenes were as sound as any Jews
could be. On the doctrine of the resurrection of the dead and
the final judgment they held with the Pharisees, with all the more
tenacity because the resurrection of Jesus was the cornerstone
of their faith, and in their observance of the Law conformed to
tradition as expounded by the Scribes and Pharisees.[2]

[1] Matt. 24, 29 ff. (Dan. 7, 13 f.); Acts 1, 11.
[2] See Matt. 5, 17 ff.; 23, 2.

The destruction of Jerusalem, interpreted as a judgment of
God on the nation which had repudiated the Messiah He had
sent and the precursor of the greater crisis to follow, lent to their
propaganda a revived activity and a new argument; and, to
judge from the acutely hostile utterances of several of the leading rabbis of the two generations after the war,[1] it had considerable success. The commination which Rabban Gamaliel II
caused to be introduced in the daily prayer was presumably
meant to make it impossible for a Nazarene to lead the prayers
in the synagogue or to join in them. What effect this had in
driving them out of the synagogues is unknown.

It was impossible, however, for those who had their own Messiah in Jesus of Nazareth, and saw in the commotions of the times
the signs of his imminent coming from heaven to judgment, to
acknowledge the revolutionary Messiah, Bar Cocheba, and join
their countrymen in the revolt. According to Justin Martyr,
Bar Cocheba took dire vengeance upon them if they refused to
deny Jesus their Messiah.[2] That their disloyalty to the national
cause should have been visited upon them by the revolutionists
is natural enough, without emphasizing the motive of persistent
religious antipathy as Justin does in the context. Probably
those who could sought refuge outside the area of war.

When the war was over, they, as Jews, were forbidden to
enter Aelia equally with the rest. The succession of bishops of
the circumcision in Jerusalem ended; the church that replaced
them was a Gentile church.[3] The Nazarenes and off-shoots from
them are found thenceforth east of the Jordan, and later in the
region of Aleppo. Coincidently, the rabbinical invective subsided when they became a sect outside the synagogue.[4]

Meantime the messianic faith of the disciples of Jesus had

[1] See Tos. Yadaim 2, 13; Tos. Shabbat 13 (14), 5; (Jer. Shabbat 15c;
Shabbat 116a in uncensored texts).
[2] Apology, c. 31. Justin was a native of Neapolis in Palestine (Shechem),
and a contemporary.
[3] Eusebius, Hist. Eccles. iv. 5–6.
[4] Later controversy is with catholic Christians.

spread through Greek-speaking Jews to Gentiles, and in the process had become Christianity, which presently cut loose from Judaism altogether, throwing off the Law, written as well as unwritten, even to the cardinal observances of circumcision and the sabbath, and by its worship of "the Lord Christ," the Son of God, seemed to infringe the principle of monotheism. In Jewish eyes it was not a heretical Judaism, but — whatever it might have owed to Judaism in its origin — was in its nature a wholly different religion. There can be no doubt that the knowledge of this development abroad increased the prejudice against the Nazarenes at home, although they were as averse as the rabbis themselves to its antinomian trend.

Christianity made many converts among Greek-speaking Jews and many more in the Gentile fringe of the synagogue; but neither the Nazarenes in Palestine, whom the church soon branded as heretics for their backwardness in Christology and their adherence to Jewish observances, nor Gentile Christianity made any mark on Judaism. Even reminiscences of controversy are infrequent in the Tannaite literature.[1]

---

[1] More of them are preserved in the Tosefta than in any other source.

CHAPTER VIII

CONSOLIDATION OF JUDAISM

THE reconquest cost the Romans very dear, but it was almost the destruction of the population of Judaea. Hadrian understood the religious motive of the war, and took vengeance on the religion. Jerusalem was rebuilt with many splendid public edifices, and, as Aelia Capitolina, was made a Roman colonia; Jupiter Capitolinus got his temple, in which stood an equestrian statue of Hadrian. Jews were forbidden to enter or even approach the city on pain of death. Circumcision of children and the observance of sabbaths and festivals were prohibited under the same penalty. The edict struck at the root when it made the study and teaching of the Law, and even the possession of a copy of it, a capital crime.

Antoninus Pius relaxed these vindictive enactments, and scholars were at liberty to resume their calling. Some eminent rabbis had perished in the war; others, foremost among them Akiba, had been put to death for defying the edict; the rest had been dispersed. There was danger that the results of the labors of the previous two generations might be lost. The immediate task of the survivors was to recover and complete the work of their predecessors.

Judaea and the adjacent region had been so completely devastated by the war that when it became possible to revive the schools and convene a rabbinical synod Galilee was the seat of this restoration. The first assembly of this kind was held at Usha, only nine or ten miles inland from Haifa.[1] Later, the centre of Jewish learning and authority in Palestine shifted to the eastward into Galilee proper, to Sepphoris and its vicinity,

---

[1] Usha and the neighboring Shefar'am were probably outside the jurisdiction of the governor of Judaea.

and ultimately to Tiberias.[1] The rabbis who are named in the account of the synod at Usha [2] are the most distinguished of the disciples of Akiba, and there is no question that the men who had sat under him had the leading part in the revival.

Scholars set up schools in various places, and soon attracted large numbers of students. Hitherto Galilee had in this respect been behind other parts of Jewry, but now that learning knocked at their doors they responded to its invitation with the zeal for which they were noted.

The branches and methods of study were the same as before the war. In the field of the Halakah the first thing was to make sure that nothing was lost of the accumulated mass of traditional laws, and that they were reproduced in their exact terms, and then to complete the distribution and ordering of these aws upon Akiba's plan. Every head of a notable school did this in his own school, and, where there were diverse traditions or conflicting opinions among his predecessors, exercised his right to choose among them or to add his own opinion. Thus every principal school had its own Mishnah.

The Mishnah of R. Meir was taken by the Patriarch Judah [3] in the next generation as the basis of his own, which soon acquired what may not inaptly be called canonical authority not only in Palestine but in Babylonia, and is always meant when "the Mishnah" is named without other qualification. The filiation is defined in an often cited dictum of R. Johanan (bar Nappaḥa): [4] "In the Mishnah when no authority is specifically named it is understood to be R. Meir; in the Tosefta R. Nehemiah; in Sifra R. Judah (ben Ila'i); in Sifrè R. Simeon (ben Yoḥai); all of them following R. Akiba." [5] Modern criticism

---

[1] Ten successive migrations of the high court are enumerated in Rosh ha-Shanah 31a–b.

[2] Cant. R. on Cant. 2, 5. R. Judah (ben Ila'i), R. Nehemiah, R. Meir, R. Jose (ben Ḥalafta), R. Simeon ben Yoḥai, R. Eliezer son of R. Jose the Galilean, and R. Eliezer ben Jacob. Cf. the lists of his disciples in Gen. R. 61, 3.

[3] Judah ha-Nasi; generally cited simply as "Rabbi."

[4] Third century.   [5] Sanhedrin 86a, and elsewhere.

has its reserves about some of these, and even in the Mishnah
R. Johanan's simplification holds only for the general relation
of our Mishnah to that of R. Meir, and of Meir's to Akiba.

Of all the disciples of Akiba, R. Meir was probably the best
qualified to undertake the redaction of the Mishnah. He had
studied under R. Ishmael also, and not only learned tradition
in his school but became familiar with his method of connecting
Halakah with Scripture.[1] He did not, however, addict himself unreservedly to the hermeneutic principles of either school,
discerning, presumably, that deduction by rule may be as unintelligent as interpretation by guess, and no more conclusive,
inasmuch as the contrary result can in most cases be arrived
at by another rule. On the other hand, his own dialectic, in
which considerations were adduced on both sides of a question,
often left his hearers in doubt what his conclusion was.[2]

R. Meir is said to have died in Asia (probably meaning the
province), and to have been buried, by his own direction,
beside the sea which washed the shores of the Land of Israel.[3]
Other passages speak of missions or visits to Asia on more than
one occasion, and it has been conjectured that he was born
there,[4] in which case it would be supposed that, like Saul of
Tarsus, his mother tongue was Greek. He taught chiefly at
Tiberias and the vicinity, and there are several stories in the
homiletic Midrash about his intercourse with a philosopher,
Abnimos ha-Gardi, in whom it has been proposed to recognize
the cynic Oinomaos of Gadara, whose gibes at the gods and their
oracles would have been much to the liking of a Jew.[5]

---

[1] The third of his masters was Elisha ben Abuyah, with whom, to the scandal of some of his colleagues, he remained in intimate relations even after the
revered teacher became an infidel.

[2] 'Erubin 13b; cf. 53a. This is given as the reason why, although he had
no equal in his generation, it was not decided that the rule (Halakah) is as
defined by R. Meir.

[3] Jer. Kilaim 32c, below. His tomb is now shown in Tiberias.

[4] That he was of proselyte parentage is an independent legend.

[5] "A contemner of all things divine and human." Julian, Orat. vi. (199 A).
— Gadara and Tiberias were within an easy day's journey of each other.

Besides the Mishnah of R. Meir, Judah digested much material not only from other Mishnah collections but from the juristic Midrash. Some important sections had been brought to substantially their present form in earlier generations;[1] others had been especially worked up by individual contemporaries in their schools.[2] It is probable that in this redaction Judah had the coöperation of his Bet Din, and that the preëminence which his Mishnah immediately attained was due to the fact that it represented the deliberations of this body as well as the authority of the patriarch and his right of ordination.

Our Mishnah is frequently concise to an extreme; the Halakah is formulated in a few words, with no indication of the grounds, biblical or logical, for the decision. In the schools the meaning and reason of the rule were expounded and discussed, and it is probable that in some of them the Halakot were not so completely skeletonized as in the Mishnah of the Patriarch Judah; somewhat of the elucidation was included in their Mishnah collections. Three such "Large Mishnahs" are known by reference to them in the Talmud, under the names of R. Ḥiyya, Bar Ḳappara, and R. Hoshaʿya,[3] the first two of whom were disciples of Rabbi, the last a pupil of theirs. These Large Mishnahs amplified, explained, and sometimes corrected our Mishnah.

The Mishnah is often described as a code of rabbinical law. If this expression is used of it, however, it must be understood that it was not meant to be a legal code in the sense those words first suggest to us, a corpus of law systematized for practical use, but an instrument for the study of the law, an apparatus of instruction.

One work of a similar character to the Mishnah has survived,

[1] Those which deal with the worship in the temple were probably composed in the generation following the destruction, from the tradition of priests (of whom there were in the schools a number who had ministered in the temple), to preserve the tradition for the expected restoration.

[2] It is known that certain scholars were regarded as special authorities on particular subjects or fields of the law.

[3] Jer. Horaiyot 48c; Pesiḳta ed. Buber f. 122a; Eccles. R. on 2, 8, etc.

the Tosefta. The (Aramaic) name, which means "Supplement," probably expresses the opinion of a later generation about its relation to the Mishnah rather than the compiler's intention. It is laid out on the same lines as the Mishnah and is in large part parallel to it, but differs in many particulars and contains much additional matter which gave ground for its name.[1]

Other scholars of that generation set themselves to collect and edit the Tannaite Midrash, the juristic interpretation of the Mosaic legislation, as it had been developed on older foundations in the schools of Ishmael and Akiba.

The literature is thus extensive and varied. The writings that have come down to us and those that are known only through extracts or quotations were all redacted in substantially their extant form toward the close of the second century or in the first quarter of the third. They are all compilations, in which the work of previous generations of scholars is preserved, reviewed, and continued to the date of redaction.

The question whether this body of teaching — to avoid for the moment the question-begging word "literature" — was transmitted solely memoriter, and when it was first committed to writing, is acutely controversial. In the Middle Ages, R. Jacob ben R. Nissim on behalf of the Jews of Kairwan addressed the latter question (with others about the Tannaite literature) to Sherira Gaon, head of the Babylonian school at Pumbeditha. Sherira replied that the Mishnah was first reduced to writing and published by Rabbi (the Patriarch Judah), in whose age this became necessary, as it had not been before,[2] and this became the accepted opinion among North African and Spanish scholars.[3]

On the other hand, Rashi[4] maintained that the Mishnah

---

[1] See below, pp. 155 f.

[2] The Response is dated in the Seleucid year 1298, corresponding to 987 A.D. Two recensions exist, which are contradictory on this point. They are printed side by side in Lewin's edition, p. 18; cf. p. 23. Comparison leaves no uncertainty as to the authenticity of the so-called Spanish recension.

[3] Nissim, Samuel ha-Nagid, Abraham ben David, Maimonides, and others. See Strack, Einleitung in Talmud und Midrasch, 5th ed. (1921), p. 15.

[4] Died in 1105.

as well as the Talmud was not reduced to writing till after the age of the Amoraim; through all those centuries the enormous and ever-growing mass of tradition and discussion was deposited solely in the memories of the learned. In this he was followed by the French Talmudists, and the so-called French recension of the Letter of Sherira was made to support the theory that the writing down of Halakah had always been forbidden. When, by virtue of the excellence of his commentary, Rashi became the supreme interpreter through whom all European students were inducted into the Talmud, his appeal to Talmudic tradition itself, and the internal evidence he adduced that in the age that made the Talmud there was no Talmud — no written compilation — were widely accepted and tenaciously held.

The critic who, disregarding this controversy, takes the internal evidence of the literature itself will find in it as much proof as can be had in such matter, that in the compilation of these works written sources were used not only by the final redactors, but in all probability by those predecessors who, in the middle of the second century, revived the schools of the Law after the rescinding of Hadrian's edict. The use of written sources is peculiarly clear in the composition of the Midrash books,[1] but there are whole treatises in the Mishnah which are probably a century or more older in writing than the publication of the Mishnah of the Patriarch Judah.

No doubt in the earlier period, as in Talmudic times, the theory was that tradition was strictly oral. No manuscript was allowed in the school; the teacher quoted from memory, and the students were required to memorize the Halakot. Such manuscripts as existed were, therefore, in the private possession of teachers for use as an aid to memory in preparation or reference.[2] They may frequently have been memoranda on particular topics.[3]

---

[1] See D. Hoffmann, Zur Einleitung in die halachischen Midraschim, 1887.
[2] The history of Moslem tradition is an instructive parallel.
[3] See Maimonides in the Introduction to his Mishneh Torah.

In the oral transmission of tradition in the schools the aim was to secure not only substantial correctness but verbal accuracy, and a comparison of the reports that have reached us through different channels and in works of different character indicate that this aim was in large measure attained not only in individual schools but in the interchange between them. This is especially the case in the Halakah, where it was most important. The exact and concise formulation was adapted to memorizing and memoriter reproduction, and the order frequently seems to be intended to make it easier for the memory by more superficial associations, rather than determined by the logical development of the topic. Such associations are often found in the connection or juxtaposition of biblical laws, which was naturally reflected in the halakic conclusions of the juristic Midrash. This Tannaite Midrash itself was scholastic, and its transmission and reproduction was subject to a kind of control which did not exist in the freer homiletic Midrash that had for its object the instruction and edification of popular audiences in the synagogue.

One further remark may be made about these sources, namely that, notwithstanding all the deference to the "traditions of the elders" attributed to the Pharisees in the New Testament and by Josephus, there is in the Tannaite literature no apparent tendency to attach traditions to the great names of former generations in order to give them the prescription of antiquity or the authority of famous masters. The principle that in defining the law the high court of each generation or the consensus of its scholars had the same authority as those of every other [1] removed the motive for such antedating.

The language of the Tannaite literature is Hebrew, but a Hebrew with characteristic peculiarities of its own which distinguish it sharply from that of even the latest books of the Old Testament. The Jews were fully aware of the difference,

[1] Sifrè Deut. §§ 153–154; Midrash Tannaim, ed. Hoffmann, on Deut. 17, 11.

and call one "the language of the Bible," the other "the language of scholars."[1] The latter is neither simply a degenerate Hebrew whose idiom was disintegrated by the influence of the Aramaic vernacular, nor is it an artificial language, a kind of academic jargon. It is a scholastic language, which has its roots not only in biblical Hebrew but in living speech, and was developed and adapted to serve as a medium for technical definition and discussion. Classical Hebrew owes its charm to the wealth of its diction and the subtlety of its syntax, neither of which excellences is conducive to the juristic precision which the schools of the Law aimed at. Their idiom, on the other hand, is admirably fitted to their purpose, and it may fairly be inferred that it had had a long evolution in the schools before it attained the stage in which we have our first acquaintance with it. There are peculiarities of terminology which distinguish the Midrash of the school of Ishmael from that of Akiba, for example; but the scholastic language was established before their time, and it continued through the whole period unchanged. To have created and perfected such an instrument is a part of the work of the Tannaim not to be underestimated.

Perhaps something similar may be said about the language of the official Targums. The closeness with which they reproduce the Hebrew original trammels the freedom of Aramaic idiom, but apart from this these Targums make the impression of a conventional rather than of a colloquial vehicle, another "language of scholars," one might guess. A learned language it must have been, at least in Babylonia, where the vernacular belonged to a different branch of the Aramaic family.

The method of interpretation employed in the schools, especially in that of Akiba, which deduced rules of law and observance, or religious and moral lessons, from minute peculiarities

---

[1] R. Johanan (3d century) objected to mixing the two by using biblical words or conforming to the biblical gender of nouns instead of following the usage of the school language: לשון תורה לעצמה ולשון חכמים לעצמה. Ḥullin 137b; ʻAbodah Zarah 58b; cf. Jer. Nazir 51a. Both are "the holy language," לשון הקדש.

of expression and even of orthography, presumes a standard text, copies of which consistently agreed in these peculiarities. In earlier centuries there was no such uniformity, as appears not only from a comparison of the Hebrew text used by the early Greek translators with that which we have in manuscripts and printed editions, but from a collation of parallel passages in the Hebrew Bible itself. The later Greek versions, beginning with Aquila, on the other hand, are evidently based on a Hebrew text substantially identical with ours (without our vowel points and accents), and the Tannaite Midrash frequently operates with what we should call its eccentricities. It is a good inference from these facts that the fixing of a standard text was the work of the biblical scholars of this period. The need was greatest in the case of the Pentateuch, and probably this was earliest taken in hand. From the second century of our era the Jews had a standard Hebrew text which was transmitted with great fidelity, and if the fixing of this text is to be attributed to their predecessors in the schools, as seems probable, it must be regarded as in all its consequences one of the most important things they did.

Aquila translated this text with extreme literalness for Greek-speaking Jews; [1] others made more readable versions of it, some keeping closer to the Septuagint, some rendering with more freedom and a literary aim. Christian scholars revised their Septuagint by the aid of these new Jewish translations, to bring it into accord with the Hebrew.

In the lands of Aramaic speech the reading of the Hebrew Scriptures in the synagogue was accompanied by an oral translation into the vernacular. [2] An effort to create a standard

[1] Aquila is said to have made his version under the auspices of R. Eliezer (ben Hyrcanus) and R. Joshua (ben Hananiah), contemporaries of Rabban Gamaliel II (Jer. Megillah 71c); in another place (Jer. Ķiddushin 59a, above) he is associated with Akiba. The version would thus be earlier than the war under Hadrian. The first reference to it by name in a Christian author is in Irenaeus, Adv. haeres. iii. 24 (al. 21).

[2] The custom was believed to go back to the time of Ezra (Neh. 8, 8). Jer. Megillah 74d; Nedarim 37b.

Aramaic version was made in the Tannaite period in the so-
called Targum of Onkelos on the Pentateuch.[1] The dialect of
this version is Palestinian, and it certainly originated in that
country, though the language has suffered some adaptation to
Babylonian usage, and it was in Babylonia that it obtained
official recognition and authority. It is cited in the Babylonian
Talmud as "our Targum," and quotations are introduced with
the words, "as we translate," sometimes over against the rendering of the Palestinians.

The Hebrew text represented by this version is what has been
called above the standard text of the second century. The
translation for the most part follows the text closely, and in its
interpretation agrees with the schools of the period, particularly
with that of Akiba. This is especially evident where the interpreter indicates (generally in an unobtrusive way) the Halakah
implied in the text.[2]

The Babylonian Jews had an authorized Aramaic version of
the Prophets also, which, like that on the Pentateuch, they
got from Palestine. It resembles the latter in its general character, but, as was unavoidable in the interpretation of the
prophecies, paraphrases more freely.

That both these Targums were redacted in writing there is
no more reason to question than that Aquila wrote down his
translation.

The Jews in the region of Nisibis spoke an Aramaic dialect
so different from those of Palestine on the one side and of Babylonia on the other that they must have felt the need of a translation of their own, and it is highly probable that what we call
the Syriac version of the Pentateuch and some of the other books
of the Old Testament was made by Jewish scholars, though it

---

[1] אונקלם is a Babylonian pronunciation of עקילם ('Ακύλας, Aquila), whose
Greek version is repeatedly mentioned in the Talmudic literature. What in
Jer. Megillah 71c (near the top) is said of this version is in the Babylonian
Talmud (Megillah 3a) erroneously transferred to the Aramaic translation
(Targum).

[2] See A. Berliner, Targum Onkelos, Theil 2, pp. 224–245.

has come down to us only as part of the Bible of the Syrian church. It, also, is based on the Hebrew standard text, and shows many traces of Jewish interpretation. This might be accounted for by the hypothesis that the translation was made by Jewish converts to Christianity, but the simpler supposition, especially in view of the antiquity of the version, is that it was appropriated from the Jews. Aphraates and Ephrem show how close was the intercourse between Christians and Jews in that part of the East. The former has a larger and more accurate knowledge of Jewish teaching than any of his contemporaries, and himself utilized a good deal of the Haggadah.

Besides their labors in the fields of Mishnah and Midrash, the Tannaim presumably had their part in the development of worship in the synagogue. The introduction of features of the temple cultus such as the blowing of the horn at New Year's and the festal procession at Tabernacles was older, but it went further after the destruction of the temple, when the erection of the temple of Jupiter Capitolinus on its site, ending all hopes of an early restoration, left the synagogue the one seat of religious worship.

The revision of the old daily prayers under the direction of R. Gamaliel II has already been mentioned, and various other regulations about prayers are ascribed to him, some of which did not meet the approval of all his contemporaries. The discussions in the Mishnah show the importance that the rabbis, particularly after the war under Hadrian, attached to uniformity, and how they endeavored to attain it in many points in which there had previously been variety of usage and about which there were divided opinions. Our sources are more concerned with modalities and circumstances than with the content of the prayers. There is good reason to think, however, that by the end of this period the framework of the liturgy had been fixed substantially as, with much variety in particulars and large expansion, it has remained ever since. Prayer books with fixed forms for all occasions came much later.

The study of the Law was pursued in Babylonia from a time at least before the Christian era, but little beyond the mere fact is known. Students went thence to sit under famous Palestinian doctors, as we have seen in the case of Hillel. Before the war under Hadrian, Hananiah, a nephew of R. Joshua ben Hananiah, migrated to Babylonia and established there a school of great repute. In the suspension of the schools in Palestine he undertook to regulate the calendar independently, a step which, if acquiesced in, would have thrown the observance of the festivals into confusion, and divided the Babylonian Jews from the rest, who took their calendar from Palestine. The remonstrances of the Palestinian authorities when they began to function again did not move him, but he was persuaded by Judah ben Bathyra, head of the school at Nisibis, to desist, and the schism was averted.[1]

Under Simeon ben Gamaliel, R. Nathan — called, from his native land, the Babylonian — came to Palestine, and was appointed by the patriarch vice-president of his Bet Din. He may have owed this elevation to the fact that he was a son of the civil head of Babylonian Jewry, the Resh Galuta, but he could not have filled the post in such company unless he had been a respectable scholar. No mention is made of his teachers, and it is a fair presumption that at least the foundations of his learning were laid in Babylonian schools.

Of much greater consequence for the future of Judaism in Babylonia was the migration to Tiberias of R. Ḥiyya in the days of the Patriarch Judah. With him came two sons, Judah and Hezekiah, who became scholars of note in Palestine. His nephew, Abba Arika, generally called simply Rab, Master, by way of eminence (in the same way that Judah I is called Rabbi), was brought up by R. Ḥiyya as a son. Besides the instruction he received from his uncle, he early became a member of the rabbinical academy over which the Patriarch Judah presided at Sepphoris, where in time he became eminent equally

[1] See Bacher, Tannaiten, I, 385–389.

for erudition and acumen. Thus equipped with all the learning of the Palestinian schools, and with a restricted ordination by the Patriarch,[1] Rab returned to Babylonia before the death of Rabbi,[2] and taught for a time in the school of Rab Shela at Nehardea, but after the death of the latter established at Sura a school of his own which was frequented by a concourse of students from many quarters.[3]

At Nehardea, R. Shela was succeeded by Mar Samuel, a native of that city, whose wide learning in secular as well as religious subjects became famous, and under whom that school also flourished greatly.

In both schools the Mishnah of the Patriarch Judah was made the textbook of instruction in the traditional law, and thus the unity of Judaism was assured. On the other hand, the possession of the Mishnah and the eminence of the heads of the two schools, who were not surpassed in learning and ability by any of their generation in Palestine, made it unnecessary for advanced students to go to Palestine to complete their education, and thus the foundation was laid for the independent development of Talmudic studies in Babylonia. The coming and going of scholars between the two centres of Jewish learning, however, kept up close intercourse, and counteracted any tendency to provincialism. Other parts of the Tannaite literature, especially the Midrash of the school of Akiba, and other Mishnah collections, had a recognized though secondary place in the Babylonian schools.

There was a school at Nisibis before the destruction of the temple, presided over by Judah ben Bathyra. A second of the same name, presumably a grandson or nephew of the first, was head of the school there in the first half of the second century,

---

[1] Sanhedrin 5a–b; Weiss, Dor, III, 133.

[2] In 219 A.D.

[3] Nehardea was the chief centre of Babylonian Jewry, residence of the Exilarch. It was situated not far from ancient Babylon, to the south. Sura was one or two days' journey farther south, in the vicinity of the later city of Kufa. Pumbeditha succeeded Nehardea, in the vicinity of which it was.

as we have seen. In the time of persecution under Hadrian, R. Eleazar ben Shammuaʻ, one of the disciples of Akiba who was ordained by Judah ben Baba, set out to go to Nisibis and hear R. Judah ben Bathyra there, as did also R. Johanan ha-Sandelar.[1] Judah ben Bathyra had himself been a student under R. Eliezer ben Hyrcanus, and discussions between him and Akiba are reported. His intervention to dissuade R. Hananiah, nephew of R. Joshua, from fixing the calendar independently is evidence that his counsel carried much weight.

Rome had long had a considerable Jewish population, partly attracted by trade, partly carried thither as prisoners of war from Pompey on. Many of the latter had been redeemed from slavery by their countrymen or emancipated by their masters. The victory of Titus brought a fresh influx of Jewish captives, among whom were many of high station in their own people,[2] and the war under Hadrian brought others.[3] The leaders of Palestinian Jewry took a great interest in the Roman community, and we read more than once of missions or visitations undertaken by them. Under Domitian, Gamaliel II made a journey thither in company with Eleazar ben Azariah, Joshua ben Hananiah, and Akiba, and it is related that they discoursed in the synagogues and school-houses, and discussed religious subjects with heathen and Christians.[4] After the war under Hadrian we hear of a visit to Rome by R. Simeon ben Yoḥai and R. Eleazar, son of Jose ben Ḥalafta.[5] There was already a school of the Law in Rome, presided over by R. Mathia ben Ḥeresh, whose name is associated with R. Jonathan and R. Josiah, the chief disciples of R. Ishmael. At the same time that Judah ben Bathyra went

---

[1] Sifrè Deut. § 80. See Bacher, Tannaiten, I, 374 f., II, 275.

[2] Ishmael ben Elisha, later famous head of a school, is said to have been one of these; see, however, Bacher, Tannaiten, I, 166.

[3] On the numbers of Jews sold into slavery at different times see Juster, Les Juifs dans l'empire romain, II, 17 f.

[4] The references to this journey and what happened on it are collected by Bacher, Tannaiten, I, 79. See Vogelstein und Rieger, Geschichte der Juden in Rom, I, 28 f.

[5] Yoma 53b–54a; Meʻilah 17a–b.

to Nisibis, R. Mathia ben Ḥeresh went to Rome, and planted there, so far as is known, the first regular rabbinical school.

The relation of these schools to those in Palestine tended to bring the Jews in the Diaspora into line with those of the home land. Not only was the traditional law as formulated and codified in those schools accepted as final authority, but their principles and methods were perpetuated and their work carried on by succeeding generations in the same spirit. In time the Babylonian schools outshone those of Palestine and were aware of it, but they remained true to the type which had been impressed on them at the beginning.

About the relations of the Palestinian schools to the Greek-speaking part of the Jewish world comparatively little is known. The writings of Philo precede our rabbinical sources by a century or more, during which time the schools had been most active in the discussion and definition of the traditional law, and the question how the Alexandrian Halakah of his day was related to contemporary Palestinian teaching cannot be positively answered. Agreement in many points may signify no more than that the Scripture was explicit or the custom ancient and uniform; disagreement, that the Palestinian Halakah had not reached the stage in which we know it. On the whole, however, it seems probable that Alexandrian scholars of his day did not feel themselves bound by the authority of their Palestinian colleagues.

It appears, from the absence of quotations or references in Christian writers like Clement of Alexandria, that the age of a flourishing Hellenistic Jewish literature in Alexandria did not last long after Philo. The war of 66–72 was attended by some commotions in Egypt, which led to the closing of the temple of Onias, but had no other effect of which we are informed. Jewish culture in those regions must have suffered much more severely from the ravages of war in the reign of Trajan. While the emperor was engaged in his Parthian campaign (116–117 A.D.) the Jews in the Cyrenaica and Egypt and in Cyprus rose in a formidable

insurrection. The rebellion was put down with vindictive severity, and the outcome, however large subtractions we may be inclined to make from the numbers in which the narrators in-
dulge, must have been a vast calamity to the Jews of those
countries.

The wars under Nero and Vespasian and under Trajan were
not only revolts against the imperial government but internecine conflicts between the Jewish and Greek (Gentile) civilian
population of the regions affected, with all the atrocities of which
mobs doubly inflamed by enmities of race and religion are
capable.[1] Pagan opinion made the Jews everywhere the ag-
gressors, and the dislike in which they were widely held deepened
into animosity toward these irreconcilable enemies of gods and
men. It is a reasonable inference that this hostile temper had
its natural effect on conversions to Judaism, which in the preceding generations had been numerous. The law prohibiting
circumcision, also, remained in full force for proselytes, the exemption made by Antoninus Pius applying only to the case of
Jews circumcising their own sons.

The new Christian movement drew into itself many of the
looser adherents of the synagogue [2] and some of its proselytes,
and probably a still larger number of the kind of Gentiles from
which these Greek-speaking accessions had come. Jews like
the Alexandrian Apollos and Aquila from Pontus, with his wife
Prisca, were active in spreading the gospel before or with Paul,
and they had numerous successors. Such defections would tend
to stiffen the conservatism of the stricter sort among the Jews
of the dispersion, and lead them to look to Palestine for guidance
and support.

The patriarch, who was recognized both **by the** Jews and by

---

[1] See Josephus, Bell. Jud. ii. 18; Eusebius, Hist. Eccles. iv. 2; Cassius Dio,
lxviii. 32. Juster, Les Juifs dans l'empire romain, II, 182–190.

[2] The 'religious persons' ($\sigma\epsilon\beta\delta\mu\epsilon\nu\omicron\iota$) of the New Testament.

the Roman government as the head of the Jewish nation,[1] maintained intercourse with the communities in the dispersion by
delegates whom he sent periodically to visit them.[2] One object
of these missions was to collect the tax imposed for the support
of the patriarch.[3] Another was doubtless the publication of the
calendar.[4] Eusebius says that they delivered the circular letters
of the patriarch. They may very well have been an effective instrumentality in bringing about uniformity of observance between the Greek Diaspora and Palestine in other matters.[5]

The history of Greek-speaking Jewry in these centuries is extremely obscure; but in the end the triumph of normative
Judaism as it had been developed in the schools of Palestine and
Babylonia seems to have been complete; not only was law and
usage uniform, but the intellectually hellenized Judaism which
flourished in the century or two before our era disappears.

---

[1] The Jews in the Parthian empire (Babylonia, Mesopotamia, etc.) had a
similar civil head, the Resh Galuta, 'Chief of the Exile,' for whom, as for the
patriarchs in Palestine, Davidic ancestry was claimed; but in religious
matters the authority of the Patriarch was recognized.

[2] Shelūḥim, ἀπόστολοι; in Roman law apostoli.

[3] The Theodosian Code calls it aurum coronarium.

[4] See the letter of Rabban Gamaliel II to the Jews in Babylonia, Media,
Greece, etc., announcing the intercalation of a thirteenth month, Jer. San-
hedrin 18d, and the letters of R. Simeon ben Gamaliel and Johanan ben
Zakkai, Midrash Tannaim, pp. 175 f.

[5] Eusebius on Isa. 18, 1.

CHAPTER IX

CHARACTER OF JUDAISM

Of all the religions which at the beginning of the Christian era flourished in the Roman and Parthian empires Judaism alone has survived,[1] and it survived because it succeeded in achieving a unity of belief and observance among Jews in all their wide dispersion then and since. The danger of a widening gulf between Aramaic-speaking Jews and Greek-speaking Jews, which at the beginning of our era was not inconsiderable, was completely overcome. The influential party which we know by the name of Sadducees, who maintained that the Scripture alone was law, denying authority to the traditional law of their opponents, the Pharisees, shrunk after the war of 66–72 A.D. to a heretical sect whose distinguishing mark was the rejection of the doctrine of retribution after death. In the second century Pharisaism was completely triumphant both in establishing the authority of the traditional law and in making its eschatology Jewish orthodoxy. Down to the rise of the Karaites in the eighth century and their revolt against the Talmud there was nothing that deserves the name of schism, and that movement, after a period of vigorous and often violent controversy lasting some four centuries, gradually subsided into an innocuous sect.

The ground of this remarkable unity is to be found not so much in a general agreement in fundamental ideas as in community of observance throughout the whole Jewish world. Wherever a Jew went he found the same system of domestic observance in effect. This was of especial importance in the sphere of what are now called the dietary laws, because it assured him

[1] Zoroastrianism, represented by about 100,000 Parsees in India, chiefly in Bombay and the vicinity, and perhaps 10,000 in Persia, is the sole exception.

against an unwitting violation of their manifold regulations. If he entered the synagogue he found everywhere substantially the same form of service with minor variations. The prayers (Shema' and Tefillah) might legitimately be said in any language,[1] but in the public prayers Hebrew seems to have been generally used wherever Palestinian example was followed. In the same area the lessons were read in Hebrew accompanied by an Aramaic translation. The often cited Novel of Justinian [2] shows that at that time there was a party among the Jews who contended that Hebrew was the only proper language for this purpose, while others, in accordance with the older usage of the Grecian synagogues, maintained that the lessons might also be read in a Greek translation. The decision of the emperor authorizes the use of Greek, commending the Septuagint but permitting the version of Aquila. "The Synagogue of Israel" (*Keneset Israel*) — we should say the Jewish church — might with good right have taken to itself the title catholic (universal) Judaism in an inclusive sense, not, like catholic Christianity, with the implied exclusion of a multitude of sects and heresies.

This unity and universality, as has been said, was not based upon orthodoxy in theology but upon uniformity of observance. But the same authorities which had regulated and systematized the worship and observance had also set forth the fundamental principles of the Jewish religion and its religious ethics and exemplified its characteristic piety, and these also were disseminated through the schools and the synagogues as an integral part of traditional belief and practice.

The character of this catholic Judaism can only be apprehended and appreciated through a detailed exhibition of its authentic teachings, but some of its distinctive features may be briefly summarized here.

[1] M. Soṭah 7, 1; Tos. Soṭah 7, 7; cf. Shabbat 12b. Maimonides, Hilkot Tefillah 1, 4.
[2] Novel. 146 (553 A.D.). See Juster, Les Juifs dans l'empire romain, I, 369 ff.

The foundation of Judaism is the belief that religion is revealed. What man is to believe concerning God and what duty God requires of man, he has made known in one form or another by revelation. Specific commandments had been given to Adam, Noah, Abraham, and Jacob; to Moses the complete revelation was given once for all. The prophets who came after him repeated, explained, emphasized, applied, what was revealed to Moses; they added nothing to it. The revelation to Moses was in part embodied in writing in the Pentateuch, in part transmitted orally from generation to generation in unbroken succession down to the schools of the Law in which tradition was defined, formulated, and systematized. The whole of religion was revealed — "nothing was kept back in heaven" — and the whole content of revelation was religion.

There could be but one religion properly deserving the name, for God is One; and revelation was not only consistent but identical throughout, for God is ever the same. The forefathers had fallen away from the true religion, not only by worshipping other gods and by worshipping their own God in a heathenish way, but by tolerating injustice and immorality. Later generations were far from living up to the acknowledged standard set for them in the twofold Law. But whatever the sins or shortcomings of the people, however negligent or however zealous in the practice of their religion, religion itself was neither impaired nor improved. It was perfect from the beginning, and therefore unalterable.

Modern students approach Judaism with prepossessions of so radically different an order that it requires an effort of imagination to put ourselves at this point of view. The idea of historical development in religion, as in science and in institutions — in civilization as a whole — so dominates us that it is hard to understand a religion to which it is a contradiction in terms. But it is idle to try to comprehend Judaism at all unless we are prepared to accept its own assumptions as principles of interpretation, and not substitute ours for them.

Nevertheless, theory to the contrary notwithstanding, Judaism had made great progress between the days of the last prophets and the end of the age of the Tannaim, and it had made it chiefly through the appropriation and assimilation of the prophetic teaching, including the prophetic element in the Law.

In this process a notable change took place. The mission and the message of the prophets was to the nation. The people in its solidarity was responsible for the evils, individual, social, political, which they denounced, and upon the guilty nation the judgment of God was about to fall. In its ruin the whole people would suffer the doom which collectively they had deserved. The only way of averting the catastrophe or repairing it was a religious and moral reformation in which the whole people should turn from their evil ways to God and the doing of his will, and to the allegiance and obedience of its origins. For this thoroughgoing reformation, our word, coming through the Latin version of the prophetic Scriptures, is Repentance.

The previsions of the prophets were fulfilled in the extinction of the national state and the breaking up of the people. In the dissolution of the political community and the bond of a common cultus, and often in close contact and association with heathen, adherence to the religion of his fathers became for the individual not a matter of course but a matter of choice. Many, doubtless, fell away and were absorbed in the surrounding heathenism. The saving remnant was the true Israel.

Into this situation came an individualizing of the doctrine of sin, retribution, and repentance, such as we find in Ezekiel. That God bestows his favor on those who please him by conformity to his will and visits his displeasure on those who transgress or ignore it was in a general way an old and universal belief. Ezekiel converts it into an inexorable law of retribution, and as a counterpart he makes repentance the sole but all-sufficient ground for the remission of all former offences of the individual, as the earlier prophets from Hosea on had done for those of the nation.[1] The

---

[1] Ezek. 18; Hosea 14, 2–10 (cf. 2, 16–25).

law of retribution, especially when construed quantitatively as
it is by Job's friends, conflicts with experience, and if such retribution in this life is insisted on as a necessary corollary to God's
justice, can only lead to a denial of his justice, as the author of
the book set himself to show by the example of Job. From this
dilemma an escape was ultimately found in the transfer of the
final sphere of retribution to an existence beyond death.

The individualizing of repentance was of vastly greater religious
consequence. It not only became a cardinal doctrine of Judaism — its doctrine of salvation — but it impressed upon the
religion itself its most distinctive character. The piety of the
Psalmists is a testimony to the penetration of this idea. The
interpreters of the Law taught that the promises of divine forgiveness attached to the prescribed sacrifices and expiations, including those of the Day of Atonement, contain the implicit condition of repentance, and when sacrifices and expiations ceased
with the destruction of the temple, that repentance of itself sufficed.[1] Religion thus became a personal relation of the individual
man to God.

Long before the *sacra publica* in behalf of all Jews everywhere
came to an end, the synagogue had become for the vast majority
the real centre of the common religious life, and the cessation of
sacrifice, however deeply it was deplored, caused no crisis. Religion had its seat in the home also, in the domestic rites, the
table blessings, the private prayers, and parental instruction of
children. The personalizing of religion was furthered by the
many observances obligatory on every individual, on the head
of the family, the wife and mother, and gradually on the children
as they grew up.

The synagogue was not in Jewish apprehension primarily a
house of worship, but a place where the common prayers were
said together and individuals offered their private petitions, and
where the Scripture was read, interpreted, and expounded — a

[1] See Encyclopaedia Biblica, IV, cols. 4223–4225 (§§ 50–52).

place of religious instruction and edification. It was a unique institution in the ancient world and it had a unique purpose, to educate a whole people in its religion. In this it was supplemented by the more advanced study of the Bet ha-Midrash, the Lecture-Room, and by what we may call professional schools for the study of the traditional law and the juristic exegesis of the written law.

The idea of God in Judaism is developed from the Scriptures. The influence of contemporary philosophy which is seen in some Hellenistic Jewish writings — the Wisdom of Solomon, 4 Maccabees, and above all in Philo — is not recognizable in normative Judaism,[1] nor is the influence of other religions, among which it is natural to think first of Zoroastrianism, to be discovered. The tendency of Zoroastrianism to exempt God from responsibility for the evil in the world by attributing the latter to another author conflicted so obviously with the fundamental idea of unity and with the explicit teaching of the Scriptures that it was rejected by Jewish religious thinking with all other forms of the heresy of "two powers."

In the development of older conceptions both reflection and selection have a part, especially in regard to the moral character of God. Jewish monotheism was reached neither by postulating the unity of nature nor by speculation on the unity of Being — the physical or the metaphysical approach of science and philosophy — but by way of the unity of the moral order in the history of the world, identified with the will and purpose of God. In it, therefore, the personality of God was as integral as his unity.

Nothing in the universe could resist God's power or thwart his purpose. His knowledge embraced all that was or is or is to be. Though his abode was in the highest heaven, there was no place and no humblest thing on earth devoid of his presence. He was

[1] Superficial acquaintance with Philonic conceptions was apparently mediated in the third century by contact with Christian theologians in centres like Caesarea.

at once above all and in all. He was wholly righteous, and could not abide unrighteousness. But he was at the same time merciful, compassionate, and long-suffering. His two moral attributes were justice and mercy, but it was mercy that best expressed his nature. These ideas are derived from the Law and the Prophets.[1] They were illustrated and confirmed by God's dealing with the patriarchs and by the history of the nation interpreted in the light of prophetic teaching.

The thought of God as father has its antecedents in the same sources, but has a much more prominent place in Judaism. While in Philo the phrase "father and maker," adopted from Plato, is used in the sense of 'author,' in Judaism, "Father in heaven" expresses a personal relation to the people collectively and to the individual. Taking it not as a theological proposition but as the attitude of piety, it is a summary of the whole relation between God and the religious man.

God's love to the forefathers is constant to their descendants also; they may be rebellious and sinful children, but they are his children still. What God demands of men is a responsive love, the love of the whole man, mind, soul, possessions, and effort. This is the sole worthy motive of obedience to God's revealed will, and it gives to right conduct the religious touch of emotion.

The corollary of the law, 'Thou shalt love the Lord thy God,' is 'Thou shalt love thy fellow as thyself,' and, lest we should suppose this to be restricted to the fellow Israelite, the same chapter contains the additional injunction, 'Thou shalt love the stranger (ger) as thyself.' The rabbis defined this obligation, The property and the good name of another should be as precious to you as your own, and applied the principle to the laws of trade and to competition in business, and they made it prohibit injurious gossip as well as slanderous defamation.

Sin, in a revealed religion, is "any want of conformity unto,

---

[1] Especially in such passages as Exod. 34, 5–7; Deuteronomy, *passim*, and among the prophets particularly Hosea and Jeremiah; cf. also 1 Kings 8.

or transgression of, the law of God," [1] equally whether the act or neglect itself is *malum per se*, or is morally indifferent. This conception, whether entertained by Jew or Puritan, is often called "legalism," and many bad things are said about it. The far-reaching religious consequences of the establishment of this relation between sin and law are commonly overlooked. For where sin is the violation or the neglect of a divine law, the only remedy is God's forgiveness. The primitive expiations and purifications are perpetuated in the Mosaic laws, but they no longer possess in themselves a mysterious, or if we choose, a magical, efficacy; they are rites which God has appointed for men to seek pardon through, and are thus conditions of forgiveness. Judaism, as we have seen, made repentance the condition *sine qua non* of them all, and eventually the substitute for them all.

Correspondingly, transgressions of what we call the moral law, for which the Mosaic law has no specific expiations — only the universal riddance by the scapegoat on the Day of Atonement — are not forgiven except upon condition of individual repentance. In other words, the legal conception of sin leads directly to the recognition that the only remedy for sin is God's forgiving grace, having its ground in his mercy, or his love, and its indispensable condition in repentance, a moral renovation of man which is compared to a new creation, with its fruit in works meet for repentance. To the Jewish definition of repentance belong the reparation of injuries done to a fellow man in his person, property, or good name, the confession of sin, prayer for forgiveness, and the genuine resolve and endeavor not to fall into the sin again.

The Jews in their wide dispersion looked forward to the day when they should be gathered again to their own land as the prophets had foretold, and an era of peace and prosperity should follow. The implicit or explicit condition of this restoration was a reformation (repentance) so complete that it amounted to a transformation of the whole character of the people. The mag-

---

[1] Westminster Shorter Catechism, Question 14.

nitude of this change so impressed Jeremiah and Ezekiel that they could conceive it possible only as the work of God himself, who should not only cleanse them but put a new heart and a new spirit — his own spirit — in them and 'cause them to walk in his statutes and keep his judgments and do them.'[1] Repentance itself is a gift of God, for which he is besought in prayer by the congregation and by the individual.

The prophets had depicted the golden age in various forms and frequently with idyllic imagery. The common element which was in the foreground of Jewish religious thought was freedom to live their own life and follow their own religion unhindered by foreign dominion, enjoying the favor of God. Some prophecies foretold a restoration of the monarchy under a prince of the line of David, and greater stress was perhaps laid on the legitimate succession out of antipathy to the Asmonaean kings.[2] The Scion of David, or the Son of David, or the Anointed (Messiah) son of David are titles of the expected king in the Tannaite literature and in the liturgy.[3] The character of this ruler in the golden age to come is set forth in Isaiah 11, 1 ff., which the official Targum closely follows.

In other prophecies, notably in Isaiah 40 ff., there is no mention of an earthly sovereign; God himself is the king of Israel. Borrowing the word from Josephus, we may call this the theocratic, in distinction from the political, type of the national hope. There is in the prophecies no indication of the human instrumentalities through which the will of the divine king is effectuated.[4] In the thought of the makers of normative Judaism we may be sure that it was not a hierocracy, in which God was represented on earth by the priesthood. Rather it was the "learned," the

---

[1] Ezek. 36, 25 ff.; cf. 11, 19 f.; Jer. 31, 31 ff.; 17, 14; Psalm 51, 9, 12. See M. Yoma 8, 9, R. Akiba: Blessed are ye, Israelites. Before whom are ye purified and who purifies you? Your Father who is in heaven. (Ezek. 36, 25 ff., combined with Jer. 17, 14).

[2] Psalms of Solomon 2, and especially 17.

[3] "The Messiah," without anything more, is not found in the older sources.

[4] The Nasi (E.V. "Prince") in Ezek. 40 ff. has no such general commission.

authoritative interpreters of the divine law, who would in that age not only teach the law but as judges apply it. The time when the Messiah should appear, or the rule of God be established in power, was fixed in God's plan, and signs of its approach were given in the prophets, but it was God's secret, into which it was not for men to pry.[1]

The idea of God's rule in his own people widened into the expectation of a day when his sovereignty should be established and acknowledged by all mankind, when 'the Lord shall be King over all the earth; in that day shall the Lord be One and his name One' (Zech. 14, 9). The universality of the true religion is the origin and meaning of the phrase, Malkut Shamaim, "the reign of God," or, in the familiar rendering of our version in the New Testament, "the kingdom of Heaven," for the coming, or in their phrase, the revealing, of which prayer is made.

The utterances of the prophets about the fate of the heathen nations in this consummation were various. In the Books of Isaiah, Jeremiah, and Ezekiel there are collections of vindictive oracles which consign them all and single to destruction, while others foretell only the overthrow of the great powers which successively oppressed Israel. The conversion of the remaining heathen appears in both the royal and the theocratic forms of the expectation.

One of the most salient differences between Judaism and the older religion of Israel is in the beliefs about what is beyond death. The ancient Israelites shared the primitive notions of survival, and imagined the dead, shadows of their living selves, as inhabiting the family tomb or gathered with the great multitude of the dead of all nations in a dismal cavern in the inwards of the earth, the common lot of all.[2] To the end of the Old Testament and beyond, this continued to be the general belief. Other

---

[1] This caution was perhaps accentuated by the disillusion of the Bar Cocheba war. Akiba had deduced in his way that the deliverance was due. See Sanhedrin 97b.

[2] For the latter see Isa. 14, 4 ff.; Ezek. 32, 17 ff.

peoples with whom the Jews were in contact had earlier separated the good from the bad dead — however they discriminated these categories — and their religions and philosophies developed the idea of divine retribution in the hereafter, frequently picturing the wicked there in torments apt to their offence. The prevailing representation was that the soul is by nature imperishable, and at death goes to the place and lot in another sphere of existence which the individual has deserved by his character and conduct in this life. Such conceptions were current in the Hellenistic world, and were appropriated by some of the Greek-speaking Jews, as we see in the Wisdom of Solomon.

In Judaea the belief in retribution after death took a different form. At the end of the present age of the world there was to be a universal judgment. The bodies of the dead would come out of the tomb and be reunited with their souls, that both together, the man entire, might be judged in the great assize. Those who were justified in the judgment would live forever on a transfigured earth, exempt from all the infirmities of flesh and the evils of the present world, while the wicked would be condemned to the unquenchable fire. This new eschatology was not unopposed. The Sadducees, as we have seen, rejected it for want of warrant in Scripture. The Pharisees were zealous for it, and insisted that it could be found in the Law. In the second century, if not earlier, they made a dogma of it by attaching an anathema to the proposition — whoever denies that the revivification of the dead is taught in the Torah has no part in the Future World. Eventually the doctrine triumphed completely.

The transfer of the sphere of final retribution to another existence not only put theodicy beyond the reach of refutation because beyond experience, but — what was of far greater religious consequence — reversed the whole interpretation of the experiences of this life. The afflictions of the upright are no longer punishments, but chastisements of love, evidence of God's favor, not of his displeasure. The prosperity of the wicked is God's way of letting irreclaimable sinners heap up for themselves

greater condemnation. Nowhere is the effect of the individualizing of religion more conspicuous than in this eschatology. In
the universal judgment every man is judged on the ground of
his personal character and conduct.[1]

The new eschatology did not displace the national hope. When
the necessity of an adjustment was felt, it was accomplished by
making the old golden age, the Days of the Messiah, which had
once been final and perpetual, an intermediate and temporary
period of determinate length,[2] after which, with convulsions
among the nations and cataclysms in nature, the last act in the
history of "this world" was ushered in. There was no attempt
to construct a doctrine of the Messianic Age or the Last Things.
The apocalypses in their enthusiastic vagaries make up shifting
combinations of native and alien elements. The sobriety and
reticence of the authentic literature is a testimony to the good
sense of the rabbis. Some of them had their own adventures in
the occult, cosmological or theosophical, but they did not profess
to reveal the secrets of the hereafter. and they evidently had
little taste for such revelations.

Judaism thus made religion in every sphere a personal relation
between the individual man and God, and in bringing this to
clear consciousness and drawing its consequences lies its most
significant advance beyond the older religion of Israel. It was,
however, a relation of the individual to God, not in isolation,
but in the fellowship of the religious community and, ideally, of
the whole Jewish people, the *Keneset Israel*. Not alone the synagogue but the entire communal life — even what we should call
the secular life — knit together by its peculiar beliefs, laws, and
observances was the expression and the bond of this fellowship.
Thus Judaism became in the full sense personal religion without
ceasing to be national religion.

[1] Adherence to the true religion is, as in Zoroastrianism, a weighty factor
in this judgment, but that upright Gentiles have a lot in the Future World
is an opinion frequently expressed.

[2] There were various opinions about its duration, of which the thousand
years (millennium) in the Revelation of John is one.

II

THE SOURCES

CHAPTER I

CRITICAL PRINCIPLES

THE aim of the present work is to exhibit the religious conceptions and moral principles of Judaism, its modes of worship and
observance, and its distinctive piety, in the form in which, by the
end of the second century of the Christian era, they attained
general acceptance and authority. The evolution of this normative Judaism and the causes of its supremacy have been outlined
in the historical part of this Introduction. It remains to give
account briefly here of the sources from which the following
representation of Judaism is derived.

This survey is not intended to serve a bibliographical purpose,
but to put readers who may not be familiar with this literature
in a position to use these volumes understandingly. For more
detailed information recourse may be had to H. Strack, Einleitung in Talmud und Midrasch, 5 ed. (1921); E. Schürer,
Geschichte des jüdischen Volkes im Zeitalter Jesu Christi, 4 ed.
(1901–1909), 3 volumes;[1] J. Juster, Les Juifs dans l'empire
romain (1914), 2 volumes; and to the relevant articles in the
Jewish Encyclopedia (1901–1906), 12 volumes. For the Apocrypha and Pseudepigrapha see also the introductions to the
several books in R. H. Charles, Apocrypha and Pseudepigrapha
of the Old Testament (1913), 2 volumes.

In any such undertaking the primacy is properly given to
those sources which are recognized by the religion itself as authentic. The historian who attempts to set forth the theology
and ethics of the Christian church, say in the Ante-Nicene period,
takes as fundamental the men and the books which the church
has accepted as in the line of the catholic tradition, authentic ex-

[1] Schürer is cited by the pages of the 3d edition, which are carried in the
headlines of the 4th.

ponents of its doctrine and discipline; and especially the consensus of the representative leaders and the official acts of synods and councils. There are many other writings to which no such authority was accorded. Some of them the church at large ignored; some it repudiated as infected with error or as plainly heretical. The interest of much of this material is considerable, and its value to the historian as a whole very great for the insight it gives into the varieties of belief and opinion among Christians, and the way in which the doctrine of the church was formed in conflict with sects and heresies, and ultimately prevailed. The number of Christians who were addicted to one or another of these factions was large; some of them in certain regions were serious rivals of the catholic church, and themselves professed to be the true church. But whatever use the historian may make of their literature, he does not form from it his conception of Christianity or mix it up with the sources which contain the recognized teachings of the church.

The same obvious methodical principle applies to Judaism. It may properly claim to be represented by the teachers and the writings which it has always regarded as in the line of its catholic tradition, all the more because the resulting consensus is authoritative, and is embodied in a corpus of tradition possessing not only universal authority but in some sense finality. Numerous other Jewish writings have come down to us from these centuries,[1] to which neither biblical nor rabbinical authority attached. With the exception of Sirach, they are ignored in the Tannaite literature and in the Talmud, or only included as a class in a prohibition of reading from "extraneous books." Considering the character of the rabbinical literature on the one hand and of these writings on the other, there is nothing particularly significant in this silence. Some of these books are edifying popular tales, such as Judith and Tobit, or moral counsels in a setting of ancient story like the Testaments of the Twelve Patriarchs; Jubilees is bent on a radical reconstruction of the calendar which

---

[1] With a solitary exception, in Christian hands.

would not commend itself to conservatives. From such books the historian gets glimpses of the religion of the times outside the schools, and inasmuch as these writings come chiefly from the centuries preceding the Christian era this evidence is welcome, even when not intrinsically of immense importance.

A singular genus of literature which was in vogue in this period has an especial interest, namely the apocalypses, in which, in fantastic visions demanding angelic interpretations, the time and circumstance of the end of the present order of things, the secrets of nature, the interiors of hell and heaven with their occupants, are revealed to ancient seers and recorded by them for far distant times. Of these compositions we shall have occasion to speak further on. In the present connection it is sufficient to say that not only are the writings themselves ignored in the Tannaite literature, but many of the subjects with which they deal are foreign to it. It may be inferred from their number and volume that they found eager acceptance, particularly in times of tribulation which inspired new ones and caused old ones to be revamped to match a postponement of the date. One of the latest (4 Esdras) was written by a man of genius, and another (the Syriac Baruch) had an author full of haggadic lore. But it may well be doubted whether the exegetical and juristic studies of the rabbis, and under ordinary circumstances the hard realities of life for the people, let them get more excited about the end of the world and afterwards than either scholars or the mass of Christians today over the cabalistic combinations and chronological calculations of our own millenarians.

However that may be, inasmuch as these writings have never been recognized by Judaism,[1] it is a fallacy of method for the historian to make them a primary source for the eschatology of Judaism, much more to contaminate its theology with them.

That Christians set a high value on the apocalypses is natural. The imminent return of Christ, as Daniel had seen the Son of

---

[1] It does not appear that the authorities ever felt it necessary even to repudiate them.

Man in his vision, was a corner-stone of their faith. For Jews it was at most one of various ways in which, with prophetic authority, the deliverance of Israel and the inauguration of a golden age could be conceived;[1] to Christians it was the only one, for it was his own prediction.[2] It is indeed not impossible that the earliest form of this belief accessible to us was influenced by such revelations as are preserved in the Book of Enoch (cc. 37–64).

Christians had, therefore, the strongest motive for appropriating every apocalypse they found in the hands of Jews, besides recasting similar material for themselves as in the Revelation of John. The entire tradition of the Jewish apocalyptic literature (excepting of course the Book of Daniel) is Christian, and the many versions of 4 Esdras show how wide and lasting its influence was. In Judaism nothing of the kind is to be discovered. The eschatological apocalypse, which from the days of Antiochus IV to those of Domitian had apparently revived in every crisis of the history, disappears completely. Personally conducted visits to Paradise and Gehenna were attributed to some favored rabbis, notably to Joshua ben Levi; and much later Enoch reëmerges in a similar rôle with descriptions of the Heavenly Courts and the like, showing that some reminiscence of his journeys through the universe had survived or been revived.[3]

When we come to deal with Jewish teaching concerning the hereafter of the nation, the world, and the individual,[4] we shall have occasion to take the testimony of the apocalypses for a type of eschatology which, at least in some circles, for two or three centuries attracted writers and readers, though, so far as the evidence goes, without countenance from the exponents of what we may call normal Judaism. But upon this, as on other points, normal Judaism must be allowed to speak for itself.

---

[1] The Son of David (Messiah) coming with the clouds of heaven (Dan. 7, 13), or, lowly and riding on an ass (Zech. 9, 9). Sanhedrin 98a. See Part VII.
[2] Mark 13 and parallels; cf. Acts 1, 1–11; 3, 19–23; I Thess. 4, 14–17, etc.
[3] Several pieces of this sort are to be found in Jellinek, Bet ha-Midrasch (1853–1877, six parts). Among these particular mention may be made of that in Part V, pp. 170–190.   [4] Vol. II, pp. 278 ff.

The most mischievous consequence of basing a representation of Judaism upon the apocalypses is not, however, in the sphere of eschatology but of theology — the idea of God. The conception of an extramundane God, remote and inaccessible in his majesty and holiness, — "transcendent" God, as they say, — which is set down in so many modern books as characteristically Jewish, is created in this way. As I have written elsewhere: "Whoever derives the Jewish idea of God chiefly from apocalypses will get the picture of a God enthroned in the highest heaven, remote from the world, a mighty monarch surrounded by a celestial court, with ministers of various ranks of whom only the highest have immediate access to the presence of the sovereign, unapproachable even by angels of less exalted station, to say nothing of mere mortals; and this not because theological reflection has elevated him to transcendence, but because the entire imaginative representation is conditioned by the visionary form. If the prophet has a vision of the throne-room of God's palace, as in Isaiah 6, or the seer is conducted by an angel through one heaven after another to the very threshold of the adytum, what other kind of representation is possible? To extract a dogma from such visions is to misunderstand the origin and nature of the whole apocalyptic literature."[1]

There are several reasons for the precedence given by many modern Christian authors to writings which Judaism does not recognize over those sources which it has always regarded as authentic. The first is that the prime interest of almost all who have written on the subject is in the beginnings of Christianity, to which Judaism serves as a background, an environment, and often, with a more or less conscious apologetic motive, as a contrast. Another, of a more temporary character, is the elation of discovery by which the just proportion of things is dislocated, as may be observed in the recent boom of the mysteries in the re-

[1] 'Christian Writers on Judaism,' Harvard Theological Review, XIV (1921), 247–248. For another source of this error see ibid., pp. 227–228, 233–234.

construction of early Christianity. The apocalypses and kindred writings, the most important of which (except the Latin of 4 Esdras) have come down to us chiefly in Oriental languages (Ethiopic, Syriac, Armenian, etc.), had engaged the attention of philologists well back in the last century, and much excellent work was done on them, not only in the editing and translating of texts and the investigation of the critical problems, but in the discussion of the bearings of these discoveries on the history of Judaism and Christianity, but these labors made little stir outside the circle of the learned. In the present generation, the English scholar R. H. Charles has been indefatigable in editing, translating, and commenting on these books, and in popularizing the whole subject.

These writings are therefore accessible in modern translations; the Apocrypha and such books as the Testaments of the Twelve Patriarchs have long been known in Greek or Latin. Of the rabbinical sources, on the contrary, a great part, including those which are of the first importance for such an investigation, are not available in translation at all; while their nature is such that the best translation is in many cases intelligible only to those who are acquainted with the ways of the original. Quite naturally recent Christian scholars who have written on Judaism have drawn chiefly on the sources they could read rather than on those they knew only through select quotations, and, when they introduce rabbinical parallels, not seldom exemplify the danger of quotation — frequently at several removes — without knowledge of the context or the hermeneutic method.[1]

In justification of the preference for the Apocrypha and Pseudepigrapha over the rabbinical sources it is often urged that the former are considerably the older; with the exception of the two great apocalypses, 4 Esdras and the Syriac Baruch, toward the end of the first century, almost all the rest precede the Christian era, while the oldest books in which the teachings of the Tannaim are preserved date, as such, from the end of the second century.

[1] See Harvard Theological Review, u. s., pp. 235 f.

Here, as not infrequently, the Christian era is taken as if in some way it marked an epoch in the history of Judaism. The point really in mind is that the books assigned to the preceding period were in circulation in the generation in which Jesus appeared and in that which produced the first three Gospels or their sources, and may, therefore, so far as dates go, have had some influence on the beginnings of the religious movement that became Christianity; while on the other hand, it is said, we cannot know how much of the teaching of the Tannaim, which we have only in compilations from the end of the second century, was really current in the time of Jesus and his immediate disciples.[1]

This chronological discrimination of sources has evidently no significance for Judaism itself, but only for the Jewish antecedents of Christianity. Even from the latter point of view it is fallacious. If Jesus and his immediate disciples had any acquaintance with notions such as we find in the apocalypses, say in Enoch 45-58, it may be taken for certain that they did not get them by reading the books, but by hearsay, perhaps remote hearsay. In the same way they had their knowledge of the teachings of the Scribes from the homilies of the synagogue and other religious discourses. With our Gospels the case is antecedently somewhat different. One or more of the writers may have looked up things in books, as they undoubtedly looked up Bible texts and brought in more Scripture.[2] But that even they drew immediately on apocalyptic writings is not demonstrable.

The series of Tannaite sources begins to flow in any volume only with the reëstablishment of the schools at Jamnia after the destruction of Jerusalem, that is, about the time when our trio of Gospels may be supposed to have attained the form in which we know them. But the task of Johanan ben Zakkai and his fellows was one of conservation, not of reformation. The following gen-

---

[1] That in the sphere of religion and morals this skepticism is not justified will be abundantly evident in the sequel.

[2] There are places in the Gospel of Matthew which suggest contributions by a more learned hand. Cf., e.g., Matt. 5, 30, with Niddah 13b (R. Tarfon). See Vol. II, pp. 268 f.

erations made great progress both in the formulation and ordering of the rules of the oral law and in connecting them with the
biblical law, and the interrupted work was taken up again after
the war under Hadrian, but of anything like a new departure or
a new religious attitude there is no indication.

The Gospels themselves are the best witness to the religious
and moral teaching of the synagogue in the middle forty years of
the first century, and the not infrequent references, with approval or dissent, to the current Halakah are evidence of the
rules approved in the schools of the Law and taught to the people.
It is this relation between the Gospels and the teaching of the
rabbis, whether tacitly assumed or criticized and controverted,
which makes them the important source they are for a knowledge
of the Judaism of their time, and on the other hand makes the
rabbinical sources the important instrument they are for the
understanding of the Gospels. The Gospels with the first part
of the Acts of the Apostles are thus witnesses to authentic Jewish
tradition, while the apocalypses (and the kindred element in the
Gospels) represent groups, or at least tendencies, outside the
main current of thought and life.[1]

What may for brevity be called the rabbinical sources divide
themselves into three classes. In the first place there are the
rules of the traditional law (Halakot), succinctly formulated,
generally without citation of the relevant biblical law or reason
for the particular rule, eventually codified in six grand divisions
with many tractates under each. Systematic compilations are
called Mishnah;[2] the individual rules are Mishnayot. The
Midrash of the schools, frequently distinguished by modern
scholars as the Halakic, or Tannaite, Midrash, constitutes the
second class. It is in primary intent the juristic exegesis of the

---

[1] On the opinion that much of this literature comes out of a sectarian
movement, by some identified with the Essenes, see Vol. II, pp. 280 f.

[2] When *Mishnah* in the sense of 'study of tradition' is used in contrast to
Mikra, 'study of the Bible,' it includes Halakah, Midrash, and Haggadah.
See below, p. 319.

biblical laws, by means of which the rules of the traditional law are derived from the written law or connected with it. The third class is the Homiletical Midrash (Midrash Haggadah), which may be roughly described as collections of sermonic material for ends of religious and moral instruction and edification. Like modern compilations made for a similar purpose, the Homiletical Midrash draws largely upon the discourses of favorite preachers in the school or the synagogue, often by name; and these quotations, with or without an author's name, are passed on from one book to another for centuries.

The Homiletic and Expository Midrashim are compilations for practical purposes. Their contents had no place in the school tradition like the Halakah and the Halakic Midrash; for the Haggadah, however highly it was valued, had no such authority. The oldest collections of this kind in our hands are from a time not far removed from the completion of the Palestinian Talmud. Many earlier authors are quoted in them by name, and the attributions are frequently confirmed by other testimony or by internal evidence. The large body of anonymous matter, unless in particular instances it can be otherwise dated, may be of any age down to the final editing of the book — so far as there was such a stage in its history — or may have been introduced in copies of it after that from the Haggadah of the Talmud or from other extant or lost Midrashim. In this state of the case the anonymous Haggadah in these works can be used to any critical purpose for the period with which we are concerned only when it is parallel to known teaching of that time. There is indeed in most of this matter little originality of ideas, but great ingenuity in getting familiar lessons and morals into and out of biblical texts where nobody had ever looked for them, or in illustrating them by exempla, biblical or legendary, or newly invented parables.

For our purpose the second class, the Tannaite Midrash, is first in importance. As has been said above, the books in which we have it all come substantially from the second century, and embody the authoritative teaching of the schools from the rest ation at Jamnia under Johanan ben Zakkai to the generation of the Patriarch Judah. They represent both the great schools of the beginning of that century, those of Akiba and Ishmael, and it may be assumed that where they agree, especially in principles or interpretations for which no authority is named and no dissent recorded, they reproduce the common tradition of the preceding generations, and in many cases, as can often be proved, of a longer past. The Mishnah collections are of the same age, and the established Halakah is in many instances of the highest value as evidence of the way and measure in which great ethical principles have been tacitly impressed on whole fields of the traditional law.[1] The concise technical formulation of the rule requires explanation outside itself,[2] for which recourse must be had to the Talmud, and that in its turn often recurs to the Halakic Midrash.

---

[1] Some striking examples in the laws of bargain and sale are cited in Part V.
[2] Like any code, the Mishnah demands a juristic commentary.

CHAPTER II

COMMENTARIES ON THE LAWS

THE Halakic Midrash is primarily interpretation of the laws in the Pentateuch. It does not, however, confine itself strictly to juristic exegesis even in the laws, and where narrative accompanies the laws sometimes includes the former also. The proportion of legal and non-legal matter (Halakah and Haggadah) differs in the different books of the Pentateuch, but in all of them the latter forms a large, and in some instances even the larger, part of the contents. It is this religious and moral element by the side of the interpretation of the laws, and pervading it as principle, that gives these works their chief value to us.

The Tannaite Midrash on Exodus is known as Mekilta. This Aramaic term (like the Hebrew Middah) means measure, norm, rule. Thus the hermeneutical rules of R. Ishmael are the Thirteen Middot. In the homiletical Midrash on Leviticus the books which a *Bar Mekilan* (Mekilta scholar) is supposed to have mastered (besides the Halakot) are called collectively Middot.[1] Elsewhere we read that the professional reciter of traditions (Tanna) must be able to cite Halakot, Sifra, Sifrè, and Tosefta.[2] The name Mekilta is first found specifically appropriated to the Midrash on Exodus after the close of the Babylonian Talmud.[3]

It begins with the first piece of legislation, the law of the Passover in Exod. 12; goes on with the narrative from 13, 17,

---

[1] Middot (Mekilata) in Lev. R. 3, 8 presumably correspond to the Sifra and Sifrè of Ķiddushin 49b. The Sifrè of the Babylonian schools included Exodus as well as Num. Deut. See Hoffmann, p. 45 ff.

[2] Lev. R. 3, 1.

[3] See D. Hoffmann, Zur Einleitung in die halachischen Midraschim, p. 36. In a Response of one of the Geonim (Harkavy, no. 229, p. 107) it is referred to as the Palestinian Mekilta (דאריץ ישראל). R. Nissim of Kairwan and R. Samuel ha-Nagid (first half of the 11th century) call it the Mekilta of R. Ishmael, by which name it has since been generally known.

through ch. 19 to ch. 20 (Decalogue 20, 2–17), and the laws in 21, 1–23, 19. After this only the sabbath laws in Exod. 31, 12–17, and 35, 1–3, are taken up. The conclusion of the covenant (Exod. 24, 1–11), Moses' ascent of the mount to receive the tables of stone (24, 12–18), with the sequel, the golden calf, the breaking of the tables of the law, etc. (Exod. 32–34), as well as the plans and specifications for the tabernacle and its furnishings (25, 1–31, 11) and the execution of these directions (35, 4–40, 38) are not commented on. There is some reason to think that the original work covered more of Exodus than what is now extant.

The basis of the Mekilta is a Midrash of the school of R. Ishmael, as is especially evident in the legal chapters, but many rabbis of the second century who were not of the school are quoted in it, down to the Patriarch Judah, whose name occurs over fifty times; his great contemporaries appear seldom, and later authorities hardly at all — not even R. Ḥiyya. It may fairly be inferred that the editor had for his additions a parallel second-century source (or sources), the chief authorities in which were Akiba with some of his contemporaries and disciples. On the single verse, Exod. 14, 15, utterances of a score of rabbis are adduced, from Shemaiah and Abṭalion in the time of Herod to the Patriarch Judah at the end of the second century.[1]

Of peculiar interest in the Mekilta are the chapters on the deliverance of Israel at the Red Sea (Exod. 14) and the Song (15, 1–21). The former closes with a eulogy of faith (on 14, 31, 'They had faith in the Lord and in his servant Moses'), in which biblical texts and examples are lavished on the theme, "Great is faith," the Jewish counterpart to Hebrews 11. To the literary beauty of that chapter there is no approach; but in the conception of faith as invincible trust in God, and in recognition of such faith as the fundamental principle of religion, there is a full parallel. "Through faith alone Abraham our father acquired this world and the world to come, as it is written, And

[1] Such profusion, it should be said, is not the rule.

Abraham had faith in the Lord, and He imputed it to him for righteousness" (Gen. 15, 6). 'The righteous shall live through his faith' (Hab. 2, 4).

The Midrash on the Song (Exod. 15) brings together clause by clause in profusion the biblical sentences on the greatness and the majesty of God; his might and his mercy; his relation to his people and his interventions on their behalf throughout their history and in the future; his incomparable godhead, sole in power and knowledge and above all in holiness; his eternal kingship. The hundreds of quotations introduced under these heads, and the lessons drawn from them in a few words scattered through the catena, come nearer than any other passage in this literature to being a connected exhibition of these topics in what may be called the biblical doctrine of God, as that doctrine was interpreted by Jewish scholars. Other aspects of the divine character are treated in the Tannaite Midrash in appropriate contexts. The most fruitful of these for the Jewish conception of God (in Exod. 33–34) is unfortunately not covered by the Mekilta.

The editions of the Mekilta now in common use are: I. H. Weiss, Mechilta. Der älteste halachische und hagadische Commentar zum Zweiten Buche Moses. Vienna, 1865. With an introduction and commentary by the editor (in Hebrew). — M. Friedmann, Mechilta de-Rabbi Ismael, der älteste halachische und hagadische Midrasch zu Exodus. Vienna, 1870. With an introduction, critical and explanatory notes, and indexes (in Hebrew). The latter is the more highly esteemed, and in recent works the Mekilta is prevailingly cited by the pages of Friedmann's edition. Since this volume has become extremely rare, I have regularly given references to the pages of Weiss also, as well as to the chapters and sections of the Midrash itself, and sometimes to chapter and verse of Exodus. — J. Winter und A. Wünsche, Mechiltha. Ein tannaitischer Midrasch zu Exodus. Erstmalig ins Deutsche übersetzt und erläutert. Leipzig, 1909. With introduction, notes, indexes of biblical texts cited in the Mekilta, of the Tannaim whose names appear in it, and to its technical terminology. The volume answers all the purposes which such a translation can be expected to serve. The notes give the most necessary elucidation.

Some mediaeval authors cite a Midrash on Exodus, in which they found both legal and non-legal matter, under the name of Mekilta de-R. Simeon ben Yoḥai,[1] and scholars here and there down to the early sixteenth century show acquaintance with this work. That it was not identical with our Mekilta was demonstrated by Friedmann in the introduction to his edition of the latter (pp. li–lv).

In a conglomerate Midrash on the Pentateuch brought to Europe from Southern Arabia, called Midrash ha-Gadol (The Large Midrash), extracts from a Tannaite Midrash on Exodus different from our Mekilta were observed, and the conjecture was hazarded that they were taken from the lost Mekilta de-R. Simeon ben Yoḥai. A collection of these extracts was made by David Hoffmann, of Berlin, from a manuscript of the Midrash ha-Gadol in the Royal Library there, and published in parts in a periodical, Ha-Peles.[2] In 1905, after further critical study, and with the control put in his hands by the independent tradition of the fragments (twelve scattered leaves) of a manuscript found in the Genizah at Cairo, Hoffmann issued a greatly revised edition of the whole, under the title Mekilta de-R. Simeon ben Yoḥai.[3]

The Midrash ha-Gadol is a compilation of the thirteenth century at the earliest, the author of which drew freely on authors as late as Maimonides (d. 1204). Unlike the comprehensive Midrashic catena on the Bible, the Yalḳuṭ Shim'oni, the Midrash ha-Gadol gives no indication either in general or in particular of the sources from which its materials were taken, nor has the

---

[1] R. Moses ben Naḥman (d. ca. 1270) in his commentary on the Pentateuch in a half-dozen places. See Hoffmann, Einleitung in die halachischen Midraschim, p. 48; Introduction to his edition of Mechilta de-R. Simeon ben Yoḥai (1905), p. vi.

[2] Vols. I–IV (1900–1904).

[3] In justification of this attribution see L. Ginzberg in the Lewy Festschrift, pp. 403 ff.

compiler any conscience about trimming his texts, or mixing up extracts from the dictionary and mediaeval commentators with those from the Talmuds and the ancient Midrashim, and, worse yet, about dressing up passages from Maimonides' Code and other authors in Talmudic style and introducing them by the technical formula for Tannaite tradition.[1] Nor did he take the trouble to mark the place where he dropped one source and went on with another.

The extrication of a single lost source from this medley and the reconstruction of it in continuity is an enterprise in criticism, on the difficulty of which it is unnecessary to expatiate. Two circumstances came to the critic's help. One was that for Exodus the compiler appeared to have had only one source of the kind, so that extensive conflation had not to be reckoned with;[2] the second, that the dozen pages of the Genizah manuscript furnish for several considerable passages an opportunity to test the compiler's method. That there is a large residuum of uncertainty, the editor fully recognizes.

The legal part turns out to be, as was anticipated, a Midrash of the school of Akiba, and here the differences, formal and material, from the Mekilta of R. Ishmael are salient. In the non-legal portions (Haggadah),[3] on the other hand, the differences between the two are few;[4] the greater part of the matter is common to both. It has been surmised with some probability that this Midrash is identical with a collection cited in the Talmuds as Tane Ḥizḳiah, or Tanna de-Be Ḥizḳiah, attributed to R. Hezekiah son of R. Ḥiyya, in the early third century.[5] Among the names of the Tannaim the contemporaries of the Patriarch

---

[1] S. Schechter, Midrash Hag-gadol (Genesis), 1902, p. xiii. The Midrash ha-Gadol on Exodus (to Exod. 20, 21) was edited by D. Hoffmann, Berlin, 1913, and the completion of the book is expected from L. Ginzberg.

[2] Hoffmann, Preface, § 2, p. viii.

[3] Namely, the Parashahs Beshallaḥ and Yitro to the end of Exod. 19.

[4] Hoffmann, Preface, § 3, p. xi. Hoffmann remarks that the same thing is true in the Sifrè of Numbers (school of Ishmael) and the Sifrè Zuṭa: the haggadic parts are almost the same.

[5] Ibid., § 4, p. xii.

Judah are more numerous than in our Mekilta, but there the array ends. It is noteworthy that in Hoffmann's index neither R. Ḥiyya nor his son Hezekiah appears.

The parts of the Book of Exodus over which the Midrash extends are the same as in the extant Mekilta of R. Ishmael, except that the volume edited by Hoffmann begins with Exod. 3, 1 (the call of Moses and his deprecation), followed by 6, 1.[1] In an appendix (pp. 167–173) the editor has collected other pieces on verses here and there in chapters 3, 4, 5, 6, 8, 9, and 10.

The edition is: D. Hoffmann, Mechilta de-Rabbi Simon b. Jochai, ein halakischer und haggadischer Midrasch zu Exodus. 1905. Pp. xvi, 180. With an introduction and notes (in Hebrew), and an index of names.

The Tannaite Midrash on Leviticus was known in the Babylonian schools as Sifra de-Be Rab,[2] The Book of the School,[3] more frequently abridged to Sifra. The old name of the Book of Leviticus was Torat Kohanim,[4] the Priests' Law, and the legal Midrash on the book is known by this name also.

The contents of the Book of Leviticus are almost wholly legal, though there is a slender thread of narrative connection, and the law is sometimes, as in cc. 8–10,[5] precedent instead of formal prescript.[6] It deals not only with ritual but with many of the laws which regulated the religious life of the individual and the family, and with fundamental moral precepts. It was "filled with a multitude of legal rules" (Halakot), and it attached to them great promises on condition of obedience, and denounced the direst woes on unfaithfulness (Lev. 26, 3–45). It was well fitted, therefore, as, so to say, a compendium of the law, to be

[1] The rabbis who contribute on 6, 1, are specially worthy of note.
[2] Berakot 11b, 18b.
[3] Hoffmann, Einleitung, u. s. w., p. 35; cf. 16 f. Others take Rab as a proper name (R. Abba Arika, head of the school at Sura; died in 247), understanding either that he composed the work, or edited it, or that this was the recension used in his school.
[4] M. Megillah 3, 5.
[5] With which 16, 1 f., connects.   [6] See also Lev. 24, 10–23.

the beginning of study in the schools both elementary and advanced.[1]

The Sifra is a continuous legal commentary on Leviticus, following the text almost clause by clause. Where the same law occurs in more than one context the comment also is occasionally repeated, but elsewhere a reference to the place where the subject is treated suffices.

The redaction of Sifra is ascribed on internal evidence to R. Ḥiyya, an associate of the Patriarch Judah, and falls, therefore, in the early decades of the third century.[2] The Talmud attributes that part of the work for which no authority is named to R. Judah (ben Ila'i),[3] and the inference is that R. Ḥiyya took the Midrash of R. Judah as the basis of his work. Another considerable source was a Midrash of R. Simeon ben Yoḥai. Both these scholars were disciples of R. Akiba, and the book as a whole bears all the distinguishing marks of his school. It was redacted after the completion of our Mishnah, which the editor evidently had before him in some places in his work. The rabbis whose names occur most frequently in Sifra, besides Judah and Simeon and their common master Akiba, are Akiba's contemporaries, R. Eliezer (ben Hyrcanus), R. Jose the Galilean, R. Ishmael; his disciples, R. Meir and R. Jose (ben Ḥalafta); and in the following generation, Rabbi himself and, less frequently, some of his distinguished colleagues. Later authorities are not quoted.

The account of the installation of Aaron and his sons, Lev. 8, 1–10, 7, not being properly laws, seem not to have been discussed in the school of Akiba, and the editor had for them no commentary from R. Judah or R. Simeon ben Yoḥai. The gap is filled from other sources which show their different origin by

---

[1] It has been suggested that the earliest schools were for the young priests, whose studies naturally began with this book.

[2] See D. Hoffmann, Zur Einleitung in die halachischen Midraschim, pp. 20 ff.

[3] As the anonymous element in the Mishnah is attributed to R. Meir. 'Erubin 96b; Sanhedrin 86a, etc.

diversities in phraseology as well as substance. The chapters on incest (Lev. 18 and 20) were skipped in the public lectures in Akiba's school,[1] and it is to be presumed that a Midrash of his school would also pass over these laws. Internal evidence supports this inference: the comment on them bears the marks of the Midrash of the school of Ishmael which was taken to fill the gap.[2] From a similar source comes the so-called Baraita de-R. Ishmael prefixed to the Sifra, containing his thirteen hermeneutic rules.

Notwithstanding its predominantly legal character, Sifra is one of the most valuable sources for the religion of the Tannaite period. In it the idea of the holiness of the people as the correlate of the holiness of God has its completest expression.

The editions most in use are: M. L. Malbim,[3] Sifra, i. e., the Book Torat Kohanim, with the commentary (by the editor) Ha-Torah we'ha-Miṣwah. Bucharest, 1860. — I. H. Weiss,[3] Sifra de-Be Rab, i. e., the Book Torat Kohanim, with the commentary of Abraham ben David of Posquières (d. 1198), etc. Vienna, 1862. — M. Friedmann had an edition of Sifra in hand, but his death left it unfinished. A fragment (as far as Lev. 3, 9) was published posthumously: Sifra. Der älteste Midrasch zu Leviticus. 1908.

There is no translation in a modern language, and the Latin translation in Ugolini Thesaurus cannot be depended on.

In my citations from the Sifra the folios and columns of Weiss' edition are given, as well as the name of the current division of the work and number of the section (Pereḳ).[4]

---

[1] M. Ḥagigah 2, 1, and Jer. Ḥagigah 77a.

[2] Aḥarè 13, 3–15; Ḳedoshim 9, 1–7; and 9, 11–11, 14 (Weiss' numeration). These passages are not in the first printed edition (Venice, 1545). See Weiss' notes on f. 85d, 91c. They are commented on, however, by R. Abraham ben David (d. 1198), and were therefore in the manuscripts known to him. See Hoffmann, Zur Einleitung, u. s. w., p. 29 f.

[3] Title in Hebrew.

[4] There was an older division into nine parts, but it is now divided into fourteen:

    1. Wayyiḳra Nedabah (Lev. 1–3); 2. Wayyiḳra Ḥobah (Lev. 4–5); 3. Ṣau (Lev. 6–7); 4. Mekilta de-Millu'im (Lev. 8); 5. Shemini (Lev. 9–

Under the name Sifrè are comprehended two works which, though of diverse origin, have long been treated as one, namely, a Midrash on Numbers and one on Deuteronomy. Sifrè is apparently an abbreviation of Sifrè de-Be Rab,[1] Books of the School, that is, Midrash collections recognized in the Babylonian schools by the side of Sifra on Leviticus. Into the difficult questions that arise about this nomenclature we have here no occasion to go; for us it is only the title of the volume generally known as Sifrè. The Talmud makes R. Simeon (ben Yoḥai) the authority for Sifrè so far as no other is named;[2] but the Talmudic Sifrè cannot be off-hand identified with the work that has reached us under this name; in fact, there are good grounds to the contrary.

Our Sifrè on Numbers begins with 5, 1, the first legal passage, and ends with the next to last chapter in the book (35, 34). On very considerable parts of Numbers, however, there is no Midrash. These vacancies are chiefly in the narrative chapters,[3] but are not confined to them.[4] It would be rash to infer that these large gaps existed in the ancient Midrash; they may result from a subsequent curtailment which cut the book down to the legal part, and there are some indications that this was the case.

Sifrè on Numbers is from the school of R. Ishmael, like the Mekilta on Exodus, to which it has in all respects a close affinity. The disciples of R. Ishmael, R. Josiah and R. Jonathan, and others who hardly figure at all in Sifra, are here frequently quoted. The interpretations of the leaders of the rival school,

---

11); 6. Tazria' (Lev. 12); 7. Tazria' Nega'im (Lev. 13); 8. Meṣora' Nega'im (Lev. 14); 9. Meṣora' Zabim (Lev. 15); 10. Aḥarè Mot (Lev. 16–18); 11. Ḳedoshim (Lev. 19–20); 12. Emor (Lev. 21–24); 13. Behar (Lev. 25); 14. Beḥuḳḳotai (Lev. 26, 3–27, 34).

[1] See above on Sifra. Sifrè de-Be Rab, Alfasi, R. Ḥananel, Rashi.

[2] Sanhedrin 86a.

[3] Solid omissions, ch. 13–14 (the spies, etc.); 16–17 (Korah, Dathan, and Abiram); 20–24 (from the death of Miriam to the death of Aaron); 22–24 (Balak, Balaam); 31, 25–35, 8.

[4] Thus, for instance, the offerings on New Year's and the Day of Atonement, 29, 1–11, and the abbreviation of the rest of the chapter (Tabernacles).

Akiba, Simeon ben Yoḥai, R. Judah (ben Ilaʻi), also are often
given, and those of Rabbi (the Patriarch Judah). As in the other
Tannaite Midrashim, his contemporaries appear rarely, and with
them the list ends. The redaction, therefore, like that of the
others, probably falls in the early third century. Besides his
principal source, the editor seems to have made use of others.
A number of haggadic comments elsewhere ascribed by name to
R. Simeon ben Yoḥai which are found in Sifrè Num. are probably derived from a special source.

The edition generally cited is: M. Friedmann, Sifrè debè Rab,
der älteste halachische und hagadische Midrasch zu Numeri und
Deuteronomium. Vienna, 1864. With an introduction, critical
and explanatory notes, and indexes.—The most recent edition is:
H. S. Horovitz, Siphre d'be Rab, Fasciculus primus: Siphre ad
Numeros adjecto Siphre Zutta, cum variis lectionibus et adno-
tationibus, ed. H. S. Horovitz. Leipzig, 1917. The introduction
(in German) discusses the critical problems.

The Sifrè is cited by the numbered paragraphs, and, when
they are long, by the pages of Friedmann's edition.

As in Exodus the Midrash of the school of Ishmael (Mekilta)
had a parallel from the school of Akiba,[1] so in Numbers also there
was a parallel to Sifrè which is cited by some mediaeval authors
as Sifrè Zuṭa (Minor Sifrè),[2] which name has passed into modern
books. Sifrè Zuṭa is somewhat largely excerpted, by the side of
our Sifrè, in the Yalḳuṭ Shimʻoni, and these extracts have the
unmistakable marks of the school; on the other hand, they present peculiarities which distinguish them from the most familiar
works of that school as we know them in Sifra. It is inferred
that the Midrash came from a less conspicuous branch of the
school. The homiletic Midrash on Numbers, Bemidbar Rabbah,
has drawn upon the Sifrè Zuṭa in numerous places,[3] and in the

[1] Mekilta de-R. Simeon ben Yoḥai.
[2] For other names, see Zunz, Gottesdienstliche Vorträge der Juden, ed. 2,
p. 51, n.d.
[3] For a list see Hoffmann, Zur Einleitung, u.s.w., pp. 61 f. In these compilations there is no indication of the source.

Midrash ha-Gadol on Numbers there are many extracts which are not in our Sifrè, and of which the Sifrè Zuṭa may be surmised to be the source. Where there is no other evidence, the habits of the compiler very often leave the ascription highly dubious. In Horovitz's edition of the Sifrè on Numbers the probable (or possible) remains of the Zuṭa are collected (pp. 227–336), the most doubtful being marked with a °. A fragment of a manuscript from the Cairo Genizah containing Num. 31, 23 f.; 35, 11–20, was printed by Schechter in the Jewish Quarterly Review, VI (1894), 657–663.

The half of our Sifrè containing the Midrash on Deuteronomy is not all of one piece. The legal part (Deut. 12, 1–26, 15) comes from the school of Akiba, resembling Sifra but with minor peculiarities of its own. One of these is the frequent formal deduction of the Halakah from the exegesis of the text. Differences of our text from that of quotations in the Babylonian Talmud suggest that, as in the case of Sifra, the book has come down to us in a Palestinian recension, and Hoffmann, attributing the original redaction to R. Simeon ben Yoḥai, conjectures that this recension represents the school of R. Johanan (bar Nappaḥa). The references to the Halakah seem to point to our Mishnah, and the recension in our hands is evidently later than Rabbi.

The exegesis of the laws, beginning with Deut. 12, is preceded by Midrash on passages in the earlier chapters (1, 1–30; 3, 23–29; 6, 4–9 (Shemaʿ); 11, 10–32 (containing the second paragraph in the recitation of the Shemaʿ, Deut. 11, 13–21). The last two are from the school of Ishmael;[1] the first two are apparently composite, the predominant element being from Simeon ben Yoḥai combined with extracts derived from the school of Ishmael. What follows the legislation (Deut. 31, 14; 32, 1–34, 12) is, like the Midrash on the laws, from the school of Akiba (R. Simeon ben Yoḥai).

The comment on the Deuteronomic legislation (12–26) occupies

---

[1] They contain, however, passages from Simeon ben Yoḥai, e. g., § 31, where he claims that his interpretation of four passages is better than Akiba's

less than half of the Sifrè,[1] and such passages as are named above in Deut. 6 and 11 are peculiarly fruitful sources for religious and moral instruction. Of especial interest in another way is the topographical section on the boundaries of the land at different times, and on its towns and cities (§ 51). From the nature of much of the legislation in Deuteronomy, a great deal in the Midrash on chapters 12–26 is of quite as great value for the religious and moral teaching of Judaism in this period as the parts called haggadic; take for illustration the topic of charity and the relief of the poor, or the principles of justice.

References are made to Friedmann's edition, as on Numbers.

Of the Sifrè on Deuteronomy there is a recent German translation with notes by Gerhard Kittel: Sifrè zu Deuteronomium. Part I. (to § 54, Deut. 11, 28) Stuttgart, 1922.

The Sifrè has evidently not reached us in its original extent, as appears from quotations in the Talmuds and later writings which are no longer found in our copies. The Midrash ha-Gadol on Deuteronomy contains, besides many excerpts which substantially agree with our Sifrè and are doubtless taken from it, much that obviously comes from a different Tannaite source (or sources). D. Hoffmann, whose reconstruction of the Mekilta de-R. Simeon ben Yoḥai (on Exodus) has been described above, has collected from the Midrash ha-Gadol and elsewhere these remains of Tannaite Midrash on Deuteronomy, to which he has properly given the non-committal title, Midrasch Tannaim zum Deuteronomium (two parts, Berlin, 1908, 1909). The preface (in German) sets forth the relation of this material to our Sifrè, and the editor's method. Indexes of the biblical quotations, of the names of the Tannaim and others, and of places, add to the usefulness of the volume.

Three fragments of Tannaite Midrash on Deuteronomy from the Cairo Genizah were printed by S. Schechter in the Jewish Quarterly Review, New Series, IV (1904), 446–452 and 695–

---

[1] Three sevenths, Hoffmann reckons.

697, containing respectively Deut. 11, 31–12, 3, and 12, 27–13, 1; Deut. 11, 26–29; and Deut. 13, 14–19, which Hoffmann reprints (pp. 56–62, and 69–71).[1]

Through the recent additions to our resources (Mekilta de-R. Simeon ben Yoḥai, Sifrè Zuṭa, Midrash Tannaim) we possess large parts of two series of Midrash on Exodus, Numbers, and Deuteronomy, which, though more or less incomplete, supplement one another in such a way as to constitute an amply sufficient source for the religious and moral teaching of the Tannaim, and for the interpretation of the particular laws controlled by the fundamental principles of religion and morals.

The value of these works to the historian is enhanced by the fact that they fall in a sharply circumscribed period, beginning with the associates and disciples of Johanan ben Zakkai and closing a century and a half later with the contemporaries of the Patriarch Judah, while much the larger part of it proceeds from the schools of the great disciples of Akiba, transmitting and developing the teachings of their master, and correspondingly from the immediate disciples of Ishmael. A mean lower limit for the bulk of this Midrash may be set about the year 175. The crisis of the war under Hadrian, and the edicts against the study of the Law, of which Akiba and Ishmael are reputed martyrs,[2] divides the period in the middle.

It is a significant fact that, however much the two schools or individual authorities in them differed about what verse of Scripture a religious conception or a moral principle was to be derived from, or by what exegetical arts it was to be got out of the text, on the ideas and principles themselves there is virtual unanimity. There could be no better proof that this consensus is not an achievement of these generations but their common inheritance by tradition from a time long before the beginning of the rabbinical literature.

---

[1] Cf. Midrasch Tannaim, pp. iv f.

[2] The accounts of the fate of Ishmael are less well attested than those about Akiba.

From the legal Midrash in the narrower sense a long previous development of the Halakah is to be inferred, according with other evidence. But there is every probability that in the exact definition and formulation, and especially the organization, of the Halakah, there was much greater activity in the schools after the crises of 66–72 and 132–134 and much more of new development than there was need or room for in the field of long-established religious ideas and moral principles. The stability of the latter is attested by the Gospels, the Book of Sirach, and the popular writings of the intervening centuries, and by the Scriptures themselves.

In the discussions of the Mishnah in Babylonian schools certain writings containing Midrash on the legislative books of the Pentateuch were cited with formulas [1] which imply that more deference was paid to them than to others of a similar kind from which quotations are also made. That this authentic Midrash of the school represented the tradition of the school of R. Akiba through his eminent disciples, R. Judah ben Ila'i, R. Simeon ben Yoḥai, and others, is unquestioned,[2] though, with the exception of Sifra, their precise relation to the books in our hands is uncertain. The Midrash of the school of R. Ishmael also is very frequently cited in the Babylonian Talmud as well as in the Palestinian Talmud and the homiletical Midrashim.[3]

There are, besides these, very many quotations from Tannaite Midrash without the name of any authority. The same is true in Palestine, where the schools do not seem to have fixed upon any one series of Midrash as in a sense official, just as they had no official Targum such as Onkelos was in Babylonia. Such quotations in the Talmuds from Tannaite sources are called Baraita, 'extraneous' tradition, i. e., outside the authoritative Mishnah; and this name is given both to quotations of formulated rules (Halakah) from our Tosefta and other Mishnah collections,

---

[1] Tanna de-Be Rab; contrast Tanna de-Be R. Ishmael (Tane R. Ishmael).
[2] See the Response of R. Sherira, ed. Lewin, pp. 39–41.
[3] A list of the places is given by Hoffmann, Zur Einleitung, u.s.w., pp. 18 f.

and to those in the form of Midrash, the connection of the rule with Scripture or derivation from it, so that we may distinguish Mishnah Baraita and Midrash Baraita.

A good deal of the matter thus embodied in the Talmud is from the Midrash books described above; but there is also much from lost works of the same character and age. The general accuracy of the quotations which we can verify warrants confidence in those that we cannot. The Baraitas in the Talmuds are of great use in the critical study of the extant Midrash books; and they add not immaterially to the volume of authentic second-century (Tannaite) teaching.

CHAPTER III

FORMULATION AND CODIFICATION

WHEN the name Mishnah is used in contrast to Midrash, as we have already seen, it designates the branch of Jewish learning which has particularly to do with the rules of the traditional law (Halakot) as such.[1] The question which is the older method of study, Midrash or Mishnah,[2] is one of those simplified alternatives to which a simple answer cannot be given. There is a strong presumption that the biblical studies of the ancient Soferim and of the learned in the priesthood were primarily directed to the interpretation of the Scriptures, so far as they dealt with the laws, and the more precise understanding and application of what the Scripture enjoined or forbade. In this sense the Midrash form is the older.

On the other hand, a multitude of traditional laws were of immemorial antiquity and had prescriptive authority independent of Scripture, and there were besides the numerous ordinances and injunctions (Takkanot and Gezerot) of earlier authorities.

From the second century before the Christian era, if not earlier, probably in some connection with the Pharisaean movement, the Scribes annexed the whole field of traditional law, and made it their business to know and to teach its rules as a distinct branch of learning. This led to a more technical formulation, and to the endeavor to group them in some association, by numbers or otherwise, in order to facilitate memorizing them. If

---

[1] This definition is *a potiori*. There is in our Mishnah one whole book (Pirkè Abot) the contents of which are pure Haggadah in a precise formulation resembling the Halakah, and there are pieces of Haggadah elsewhere, e.g., at the end of M. 'Eduyot, on the mission of Elijah. So also there are elements derived from the juristic Midrash, which in the Tosefta are much more common.

[2] On this subject see J. Z. Lauterbach, 'Midrash and Mishnah,' Jewish Quarterly Review, N. S., V (1914–15), 503–527; VI, 23–95, 303–323.

this reconstruction of the history is sound, it may be said that, as a discipline conscious of the task of connecting the written and the unwritten law, the Tannaite Midrash assumes the existence of Halakot. The discovery of biblical texts for traditional laws was facilitated by new methods of exegesis, especially in the school of Akiba. Some weight may be laid also on the order of studies in the school, which began with the memorizing of the Halakot or Mishnayot (single sentences of the Mishnah), and went on thence to the biblical Midrash.

In the schools of the second century both branches of learning were cultivated; there were numerous Mishnah collections as there were numerous Midrash collections. Early in the third century the Mishnah of the Patriarch Judah acquired unique authority in Babylonia as well as in Palestine, but the others were not thereby extinguished. They are frequently cited in the Talmuds with the formula for Tannaite tradition, and occasionally in the name of the master from whose school they came. They contribute thus to the volume of Baraita which represents to us the teaching of second-century Judaism. It may not be superfluous to say that this matter, like the whole survival of Tannaite tradition, including the Baraita, is in "the language of the learned," the scholastic Hebrew of the Tannaim.[1]

The Mishnah — to use this name henceforth not generically, for a kind of literature, but specifically for the codification issued by the Patriarch Judah — traces its lineage through R. Meir to R. Akiba. The actual process was much more complex than this simple formula, which is in fact not concerned with history but with authority. We have no occasion, however, to involve ourselves in the origins of the Mishnah. The classification of the rules of the traditional law under certain topics for memory and discussion was probably as old as the need for it. The complete systemization is attributed to Akiba; the carrying out of the

---

[1] The often-repeated statement that Hebrew is the language of the Mishnah, while that of the Gemara is Aramaic, is true, so far as the latter is concerned, only *a potiori*.

system, to his disciples; the particular redaction which gained unique authority, to the Patriarch Judah.

In this, as in the Mishnahs of other teachers, the rules of the traditional law are brought under six heads, constituting so many grand Divisions of the work, called Sedarim,[1] viz.: 1, Zera'im; 2, Mo'ed; 3, Nashim; 4, Nezikin; 5, Kodashim; 6, Toharot. *Zera'im* ('Seeds') contains the laws on agriculture, such as the prohibition of mixed plantations, and especially the taxes for religious and charitable purposes imposed on the products of the soil. To it is prefixed the important Berakot, on the Prayers. *Mo'ed* ('Festivals') is sufficiently described by its name. It includes the laws for the Sabbath, New Moon, New Year's, and all the seasonal and occasional feasts and fasts. *Nashim* ('Women'), laws dealing with marriage and divorce, the levirate, adultery, etc.; *Nezikin* ('Injuries'), civil and criminal law;[2] *Kodashim* ('Consecrated Things'), sacrifices and offerings, ritual, etc.; *Toharot* ('Cleanness'),[3] laws of clean and unclean in things and persons, purifications, etc.

Each of these principal Divisions is made up of a number of Parts (Massektot),[4] embracing laws on particular subjects that fall under the general head, e. g., in the Division on Festivals, the Sabbath, Passover, Day of Atonement, etc. Each Part is subdivided into Chapters (Perakim), and the Chapters into Paragraphs, each of which is called a Mishnah (in the Palestinian Talmud, a Halakah).[5] The Massekta (Part) is cited by name, the Chapters and Paragraphs in the editions of the Mishnah now

[1] 'Orders,' i. e., orderly arrangement of the laws on the several subjects. Cf. Seder, or Siddur, for a book in which the prayers are arranged in order.

[2] To Nezikin is appended Pirkè Abot, the Chapters of the Fathers — aphorisms, maxims, sentences, of the teachers of successive generations from the Men of the Great Synagogue down. See below, pp. 156 f.

[3] Euphemistic for 'Uncleannesses.'

[4] Masseket, Massekta, has an etymology and an evolution of meaning similar to the Latin *textus*. The Latin translation of the Mishnah rendered it by Tractatus, whence in English the Parts are often called 'tractates' or 'tracts,' or 'treatises,' a name which gives the uninitiated reader a notion very unlike the thing.

[5] Halakah is the older name.

usually by number, e. g., M. Pesaḥim 2, 4,[1] i. e., Mishnah, Massekta Pesaḥim (Passover), Chapter 2, Paragraph 4.

The disposition of the Mishnah answers its practical purposes, though it sometimes brings in subjects in a place where in a strictly logical arrangement they would not be looked for. Thus, Vows (Nedarim) are put in the division Nashim, evidently because in Num. 30, 2–17, women's vows, and the right of the father or husband under certain conditions to annul them, are the principal subject; only verse 2 has to do with the vow of a man who is *sui juris*.[2] The only other passage which treats of the subject in any detail, Lev. 27, is concerned only with the valuation of commuted vows, which in the Mishnah is dealt with under 'Arakin ('Valuations'), in Division V (Ḳodashim). The subsumption of Vows under Women has for a further consequence that the Nazirite's vow (Nazir), the rules to be observed by him, and the ritual for the dissolution of the vow at its term (Num. 6), are also drawn into the same division. Similar observations may often be made on the contents of the several Parts (Massektot). Didactic reasons frequently prevail over strictly systematic considerations, and quite properly, inasmuch as the Mishnah was not a code but an educational instrument.

Different Parts of the Mishnah vary considerably in character, partly in consequence of the nature of the diverse subjects with which they have to do, partly because they are based upon earlier works proceeding from different individual scholars or different schools. That this was the case is recognized in traditions such as those which attribute the anonymous element in Tamid (the Daily Burnt Offerings) and Yoma (Day of Atonement) to a certain (otherwise obscure) R. Simeon of Mizpah, a contemporary of Rabban Gamaliel II;[3] in Middot (description of the Herodian temple) to R. Eliezer ben Jacob[4] (generally taken

[1] Or simply Pesaḥim ii. 4. [2] Cf. Deut. 23, 21–23.
[3] Yoma 14b (alleged for Tamid by R. Huna; for Yoma by R. Johanan). The only other notice of this Simeon is in M. Peah 2, 6.
[4] R. Huna in Yoma 16a, above. See Frankel, Darkè ha-Mishnah, p. 73 (ed. Warsaw, 1923, p. 76); Bacher, Tannaiten, I, 62 f.

for the older of the name, contemporary with Akiba); and other like testimonies.

There is strong probability for the opinion that some if not all of these remoter sources of our Mishnah were in writing, as well as the mid-century Mishnahs and Midrashes of Akiba's disciples. That the Mishnah of the Patriarch Judah was redacted and published in writing — so far as publication can be said of such a work — is affirmed by Sherira Gaon in the Response referred to above. It is demonstrable that additions and changes crept into the text of the Mishnah after the Patriarch's death; such can almost always be certainly recognized, and are relatively inconsiderable.

The Mishnah has been transmitted in manuscripts and in print as an independent work, and also in the two Talmuds as the text for the discussions of the Amoraim. Each of the Talmuds, again, has had its own channels of transmission. Some textual diversity has arisen in this way, but on the whole the constancy of the tradition is satisfactory.

A critical edition of the Mishnah, as a philologist would use that phrase, does not exist, though some individual parts have been edited unpretentiously for learners, but with a critical text and well-selected apparatus, by Hermann Strack. A more ambitious enterprise is: G. Beer and O. Holtzmann, Die Mischna. Text, Übersetzung und ausführliche Erklärung. Several parts edited by different scholars have appeared, of very variable quality. The commentary is frequently quite inadequate, while some of the authors expatiate, especially in the introductions, on things that have no relevancy to the matter in hand.

The edition that has been most useful to Christian scholars in the past is that of Surenhusius, in six folio volumes (1698–1703), with a Latin translation of the text and of the most approved Jewish commentaries (Maimonides and Obadiah of Bertinoro), together with additional comments and notes by Christian scholars, and extensive indexes. Modern Jewish editions commonly give the commentary of Bertinoro (died ca. 1500) and the notes and glosses (Tosafot) of Yom Tob (Lipmann Heller, died 1654).

[1] Beginning in 1913.

The commentary of Maimonides (d. 1204) is printed in modern editions of the Babylonian Talmud after each Part.

The Tosefta is a work of the same class with our Mishnah. The disposition in six grand Divisions, the order of the primary subdivisions,[1] and in the main the subjects treated in each are the same, and in many instances the formulation of the basic Halakah is identical. On the other hand, the Tosefta treats the subjects more at large than the Mishnah, very often giving the biblical ground of the rule or the reason for it,[2] which the Mishnah rarely does.

There is, thus, a close connection between the two, and a striking difference of method which points to a different school. R. Johanan reports that the Mishnah derives from Akiba through R. Meir, the Tosefta through another of Akiba's disciples, R. Nehemiah;[3] but this schematic filiation throws no light on the salient difference of method in two collections both of which go back to Akiba,[4] nor does it account for the frequent obvious dependency of the Tosefta on our Mishnah. The name Tosefta (probably originally plural, Tosefata), 'Supplement' (Supplements), indicates the relation which the work was thought to have to the Halakic tradition or to our Mishnah. It is, however, in many cases an amplified Mishnah giving the text of our Mishnah with additions, rather than supplementary notes to the Mishnah, while in others it has matter which is intelligible only by recourse to sentences in our Mishnah which are not reproduced.

The redaction of the Tosefta of the Babylonian schools is at-

[1] Abot, Tamid, Middot, and Ķinnim are lacking. In the subdivisions the Tosefta occasionally follows a different and perhaps an earlier arrangement of the Mishnah.

[2] It has thus an obvious affinity to the Tannaite Midrash, with which as Baraita it is coupled, and sometimes approximates a Talmudic treatment.

[3] Sanhedrin 86a.

[4] Did Akiba himself employ both methods? See Frankel, Darkè ha-Mishnah, pp. 304–307 (ed. Warsaw, 1923, pp. 322–325); Lauterbach, in Jewish Encyclopedia, XII, 207–209. This theory has not found much acceptance.

tributed by mediaeval authorities to R. Ḥiyya, an associate of the Patriarch Judah,[1] to whom the editing of Sifra is now ascribed. Whatever the relation of the work to R. Ḥiyya, the compiler probably drew on other contemporary collections, the "Large Mishnahs" of R. Hoshaʿya and others. The internal evidence goes to show that the compilation falls in the first part of the third century, but also makes it probable that various additions were early made to it.

Many hypotheses have been proposed to explain the relations of the Tosefta and the Mishnah which need not be discussed here. What is to our purpose is that, while in the Talmudic discussions of the traditional law it ranks only as a collateral authority like the Tannaite Midrash, the Tosefta is, from the historical point of view, a no less authentic, and, from its peculiar character, a more fertile, source. It has also escaped the attention of the censorship, which excised, especially from the Babylonian Talmud, whatever it found offensive to Christian sensibilities.

The Tosefta is found appended to the editions of Alfasi's Halakot (Venice, 1521, and thereafter). A separate edition, with the use of two manuscripts, was published by M. S. Zuckermandel, Pasewalk, 1881. With a supplement containing a synopsis of the contents of the Tosefta, indexes, and a glossary (Trier, 1882).

In the Mishnah there is one tractate which demands especial notice, namely the Pirḳè Abot, appended to the Division Neziḳin. These Chapters of the Fathers are wholly different in character from the rest of the Mishnah, for in an otherwise exclusively Halakic collection it contains no Halakah. Its appropriateness, and the probable reason for its inclusion, lies in the fact that it begins with the concatenated tradition of the Law from Moses down to Shammai and Hillel, with whom the school tradition starts. From the Men of the Great Synagogue on, there is attributed to each of the living links in this chain a pithy sentence, which is, so to say, his individual motto. The series was continued in the same way to Rabban Johanan ben Zakkai

---

[1] Sherira Gaon, ed. Lewin, pp. 6, 34 f.; cf. p. 39 (Ḥiyya and Hoshaʿya).

and his disciples, from whom more numerous sayings are reported. The collection grew by accretion, other memorable utterances of the older generations being introduced into it, and by extension, each new generation contributing of its wisdom.[1] Chapter 5 is made up of numerical groups, without authors' names, e. g., by ten utterances the world was created, ten generations from Adam to Noah and ten from Noah to Abraham, ten trials of Abraham, ten miracles for the forefathers in Egypt, etc. Chapter 6, called the Baraita of R. Meir from the fact that the first sayings in it are in his name,[2] is a loose appendix of obviously later date.

The first four chapters consist of moral and religious aphorisms, a kind of rabbinical Book of Proverbs with the authors' names indicated. They differ from the Proverbs of Solomon and the Wisdom of Ben Sira in being especially applicable to scholars and students. They are in a sense the ethics of a class, but of a class to which ideally all Jews should belong. It is significant that the Chapters of the Fathers were ultimately taken up into the synagogue service and are regularly read on sabbath afternoons during a certain part of the year.[3] The custom is at least as old as the age of the Geonim, being referred to in the Siddur of Rab Amram.[4] The level of these sayings is very high, and, for a knowledge of the ideals of rabbinical ethics and piety, no other easily accessible source is equal to the Abot.

There is an edition with translation and commentary by C. Taylor: Sayings of the Jewish Fathers. Cambridge, 1877 and 1897. — A Talmudic catena by Noah Kobryn (Warsaw, 1868) brings together parallels to each sentence of the Abot from the Talmuds and the Midrashim, with a running commentary, and is a most useful key to the whole body of ethical Haggadah.

[1] See Strack, l. c., p. 54: Kern der Sammlung 1, 1–15; 2, 8–14; 5, 1–5, 7–10, 13–18. Soweit reicht der Parallelismus mit Aboth deRabbi Nathan.
[2] Also called Ḳinyan Torah, "Acquisition of the Law," from the content of these initial sayings.
[3] This is the use of the German and Polish rites. See I. Abrahams, Companion to the Daily Prayer Book, pp. clxxvi ff.
[4] See below, pp.176 f.

With the Abot must be mentioned the Abot de-R. Nathan
which is sometimes called a Tosefta (supplement) to Abot.   The
R. Nathan in the title is probably meant to be Nathan the Babylonian, who filled the office of vice-president (Ab Bet Din) under
R. Simeon ben Gamaliel.   If there is anything in the attribution,
it cannot apply to any form of the work that we know, which
plainly comes from a much later time than the middle of the
second century. The relation to Abot is not the same throughout.   The first part [1] may be described as an expansive Midrash
on Abot chapters 1 and 2;   the second (cc. 19–30) is rather a parallel in form and content to Abot chapters 3 and 4 than an amplification and exposition like the preceding; cc. 31–41 are
numerical like Abot chapter 5.

In editions of the Babylonian Talmud the Abot de-R. Nathan
is printed in an appendix to the fourth Order (Neziḳin), along
with other minor tractates, chiefly from the Gaonic age, which
are no part of the Talmud itself.[2]   There are manuscripts representing a different recension, which Schechter's edition [3] puts
in parallel to the common text; the latter is also revised on manuscript authority.

A work of a different kind, the core of which at least belongs
to the Tannaite period, and which enjoyed great authority in its
field, is the Seder ʿOlam, a chronological synopsis of biblical history from Adam down to the age of Alexander (Daniel), and a
continuation in brief to the destruction of the second temple and
the war under Hadrian. The endeavor to fix the dates of Hebrew history by the data given in the Scriptures had been made
by an earlier chronologer, Demetrius, probably an Alexandrian
Jew, of whose work only scanty fragments have survived.[4]   The

---

[1] Chapters 1–18 in the common numeration.
[2] On these see H. Strack, Einleitung in Talmud und Midrasch, 5 ed., pp.
72–74, and the relevant articles in the Jewish Encyclopedia. Among them
the tracts on morals and manners (Derek Ereṣ) may be particularly noted.
[3] Aboth de-Rabbi Nathan (Vienna, 1887), with an introduction, developing a critical theory of the antecedents of the work.
[4] C. Muller, Fragmenta Historicorum Graecorum, III, 214–217.   See
Schürer, Geschichte des jüdischen Volkes, III, 349–351.

Book of Jubilees imposes its peculiar system on the history from Adam to Moses. For the post-exilic period the author of Seder 'Olam had no sufficient sources, and his schematic chronology of the Persian centuries and thereafter, as has been shown above, is widely in error. In c. 30 the destruction of the temple (70 A.D.), 490 years after the first destruction, begins a new era (from the Destruction of the Temple), while, as the author remarks, in the Diaspora the Seleucid era (312 B.C.) was commonly employed. The last chapters are evidently mutilated, and, between that and the attempts to fill up the conclusion, are often unintelligible.

The author of the Seder 'Olam displays great ingenuity both in his method and in the application of it, and, whether that was his intention or not, laid the foundation for a chronology based on the Era of Creation. A computation from the creation in even millenniums is found in 'Abodah Zarah 9a,[1] citing Tanna de-Be Eliahu.[2] Seder 'Olam is several times cited in the Talmud with the introductory formula for Tannaite tradition (Baraita).[3] The authorities cited in it are almost all prominent teachers of the early and middle second century. R. Johanan attributed the transmission of the work to R. Jose (ben Ḥalafta),[4] who had studied under Akiba and took part in the Galilean restoration after Hadrian. In several places in our Seder 'Olam, R. Jose is introduced by name (e. g., c. 28, near the end), from which it may be inferred either that these passages were inserted by a later hand (Zunz), or, if they are from his own, that for the bulk of the book he was only transmitting an older tradition.

The Seder 'Olam is in Hebrew, like the rest of the contemporary literature.

The edition cited in the present volumes is that of B. Ratner: Seder Olam Rabba, die Grosse Weltchronik. Wilna, 1897. With

---

[1] Not for historical purposes, but for the date of the beginning of the messianic age in God's original plan.

[2] See Seder Eliahu Rabba, ed. M. Friedmann, p. 6, below; and Friedmann's Introduction, p. 46.

[3] 'Abodah Zarah 8b; Megillah 11b; Shabbat 88a, etc.

[4] Yebamot 82b; Niddah 46b, below.

critical and explanatory notes (in Hebrew). — The same author published separately an introduction (Mebo leha-Seder 'Olam Rabbah). An edition of the first ten chapters, with an introduction by A. Marx, 1903, has not been completed.

In this connection mention may be made of the Megillat Ta'anit, "Fasting Scroll," a calendar of days commemorating joyous seasons or events in the history of the people on which public fasting is not permitted and on some of which mourning also is forbidden. The occasion is generally indicated, but with such brevity that, especially in our fragmentary and accidental knowledge of whole periods of the history, the reference is frequently impenetrably obscure.

The calendar, the whole of which could be printed on an octavo page, is in Aramaic, presumably because it was meant for the guidance of the unlearned as well as the educated. It is referred to as a well-known and authoritative writing in the Mishnah (Ta'anit 2, 8) and often elsewhere.[1] A Baraita in Shabbat 13b attributes the composition of the scroll to Hananiah ben Hezekiah (ben Garon) and his associates; the scholiast names his son Eleazar,[2] which would put it in the latter part of the first or beginning of the second century, but in any case would only mean the redaction, with additions to date, of a list that began much further back.[3]

On this calendar scholia in Hebrew were written in post-Talmudic times, the author of which attempts a historical commentary on the obscure allusions in the text. It is a critical error to take his learned combinations for tradition.

Of modern investigations it is sufficient here to refer to Solomon Zeitlin, Megillat Taanit as a source for Jewish Chronology and History in the Hellenistic and Roman Periods, 1922.[4]

[1] Jer. Megillah 70c; 'Erubin 62b, end.
[2] On c. 12, end. So also Halakot Gedolot, ed. Hildesheimer, p. 615.
[3] See Judith 8, 6.
[4] For the earlier literature see Zeitlin, pp. 65 f.

CHAPTER IV

HOMILETIC COMMENTARIES

THE third class of sources is the Homiletical Midrash. The works with which we have been thus far engaged are primarily Halakic. Their intention is either to define the rules of the traditional law or to connect these rules with the written law by the exegesis of the legislative parts of the Pentateuch. The classes to which we now turn are Haggadic.[1] In the dichotomous division Halakah[2] is law, and whatever is not Halakah is Haggadah;[3] but this definition gives no idea of the wealth and variety of the Haggadah. The value set on the latter is strongly expressed in Sifrè on Deut. 11, 22: "Those who interpret the implications (of Scripture)[4] say: If you would learn to know Him at whose word the world came into being, learn Haggadah, for by this means you will come to know the Holy One and cleave to his ways."[5] On Deut. 32, 14, the Sifrè has: "'With the kidney-fat of wheat'; these are Halakot, for they are the substance [lit., 'body'] of the law; 'and of the blood of the grape, thou drinkest wine,' these are Haggadot, which attract a man's heart like wine."[6] With a reminiscence of such eulogies Zunz wrote: "The Haggadah,

[1] A summary account of the most important may be found in Strack, Einleitung in Talmud und Midrasch, 5 ed., pp. 74–76. Cf. A. Marx's review of Strack, Jewish Quarterly Review, N. S., XIII, 354. For a masterly survey of this literature see J. Theodor, 'Midrash Haggadah,' Jewish Encyclopedia, VIII, 550–569, and 'Midrashim, Smaller,' ibid. 572–580.

[2] From a verb meaning 'to walk, go'; figurative like the English 'walk,' a way of living or acting; in Hebrew, specifically a rule to go by.

[3] Etymologically, 'teaching' (of Scripture); in use, specifically, non-legal teaching.

[4] דורשי רשומות. See Bacher, Tannaiten, I, 31; Terminologie, I, 183f. Bacher connects these ancient interpreters with the times of Johanan ben Zakkai.

[5] Sifrè Deut. § 49 (ed. Friedmann, f. 85a). R. Joshua ben Levi took the neglect of "the works of the Lord" in Psalm 28, 5, to be neglect of the Haggadot. Midrash Tehillim in loc.

[6] Sifrè Deut. § 317.

whose aim it is to bring heaven nearer to men and again to lift men up to heaven, appears in this mission as the glorifying of God and the comfort of Israel. Hence, religious truths, moral lessons, discourse on just reward and punishment, inculcation of the laws in which the nationality of Israel is manifested, pictures of the past and the future greatness of Israel, scenes and stories from Jewish history, parallels between the divine institutions and those of Israel, encomiums on the Holy Land, inspiring narratives, and manifold consolation — these constitute the chief content of the synagogue homilies." [1]

The high aim of the Haggadah is religious and moral instruction and edification; but its authors are aware that to catch and hold the attention it must make itself interesting, and it is not beneath its dignity to be entertaining. It is supposed to be interpretation and application of Scripture, as the name Midrash implies; but it brings freely to the illustration of the text and its lessons matter not only from all over the Bible but from far outside, and is in some ways the most characteristic product of Jewish literature and life through many centuries.

High as the estimation was in which the Haggadah was held, it did not possess authority like the Halakah. In the latter, where there was a conflict of juristic opinion, it was necessary to determine which was to be followed, and so far as it is proper to speak of Jewish orthodoxy (correctness of opinion) it is solely in this field; there was no such thing as an orthodox Haggadah. The wide agreement on the main topics of theology and morals was due to the fact that the Scripture was plain and the traditional understanding and application long established. Where this was not the case there was free diversity. There was, for example, no Jewish "doctrine of the Messiah" such as Christian scholars have often tried to construct, no "doctrine of the Last Things" (Eschatology), but many attempts to combine in an imaginable sequence the diverse representations of the Scriptures, none of which had any claim to being the sole true combination.

[1] Zunz, Gottesdienstliche Vorträge der Juden, p. 349 (2 ed., p. 362).

It has been rightly said that the completion of the Mishnah, which closes an epoch in the schools of the Law, was of no consequence in the history of the Haggadah. The following century concedes nothing to its predecessor, either in the wealth of the material that has come down to us and the number of eminent names associated with it, or in the independence and originality of its contents.[1]

The Haggadah with which we are concerned flourished chiefly in Palestine, and among the compilations presently to be described none is of Babylonian origin.[2]

"Haggadah books" are mentioned repeatedly in the third century as in the hands of several rabbis of the time, though one of the most famous Haggadists of the age, Joshua ben Levi, vehemently condemned these writings. We catch only one glimpse of what was in them when the same rabbi tells that the only time he ever looked into such a book he found in it some numerical "correspondences" between the Pentateuch and something else in the Bible; but the memory of this one experience gave him the nightmare.[3] Other rabbis had no such prejudice against Haggadah books. R. Johanan and R. Simeon ben Lakish are reported to have consulted one on a Sabbath,[4] and Johanan is said to have frequently had one about him,[5] and to have remarked that, if a man learns Haggadah out of a book, it is assured that he will not soon forget it.[6]

Among the Midrashim of this class the expository Midrash on Genesis known as Bereshit Rabbah holds first place by virtue

---

[1] W. Bacher, Agada der palästinensischen Amoräer, I, viii.

[2] The voluminous Haggadah of the Babylonian Talmud is in the man.   ⸗
a different stamp.

[3] Jer. Shabbat 15c, middle.

[4] Giṭṭin 60a; Temurah 14b. It is about the reading on the *Sabbath* that the question is raised.

[5] Berakot 23a, below.

[6] Jer. Berakot 9a, above. Along with other circumstances of learning about which there is a "ratified covenant" to the same effect, e. g., learning in an humble spirit (Prov. 11, 2).

of its age and of the extent and importance of its contents. From
its first words, "R. Osha'ya (Rabbah) opened" (sc. his discourse
on Genesis 1, 1 ff.) with the text Prov. 8, 30, the catena got the
name Bereshit de-Rabbi Osha'ya, and the like, under which it is
cited in mediaeval authors;[1] and the same explanation is probably to be given of the assumption that R. Osha'ya (or Hosha'ya),
one of the most eminent scholars of the third century, was the
author of the work. The title Bereshit Rabbah has been thought
to have originated by transferring to the book the epithet Rabbah ('the Great,' i. e., the older) which properly belonged to
R. Hosha'ya; but this explanation is dubious:[2] the name may
designate the work itself as the Large (Midrash on) Genesis.[3]
What is more certain is that from Genesis the title "Rabbah"[4]
was extended to the other Midrashim on the Pentateuch, and
later to those on the five Megillot when these were appended to
the series on the Pentateuch, and that a plural, Rabbot, was
made to cover them all.[5]

Bereshit Rabbah is an expository commentary which almost
to the end follows the text of Genesis verse by verse, and especially in the earlier chapters almost word by word, skipping only
bare genealogies and repetitions which required no fresh remark,
such as Gen. 24, 35–48 (after vss. 12–27). It is especially expansive on Gen. 1–3 (Creation, Adam and Eve in the Garden),
where a whole chapter of comment is sometimes devoted to one
or two verses of the text: chapter 1, for example, to Gen. 1, 1,
chapter 2 to Gen. 1, 2, etc. This part of the work is of peculiar
interest; it sets forth the biblical teaching on these points in

[1] See Theodor's edition, p. 1, note; Jewish Encyclopedia, III, 62.

[2] Theodor, ibid. III, 64.

[3] A mediaeval work entitled Bereshit Rabbah, by R. Moses ha-Darshan,
quoted in Raimund Martini, Pugio Fidei, is not to be confounded with our
Midrash.

[4] Note the extract from Halakot Gedolot in Zunz, Gottesdienstliche
Vorträge, u. s. w., p. 177 (2 ed., p. 187), where the adjective Rabbah is used
of Genesis only.

[5] Ekah Rabbati is a different case, being taken from Lam. 1, 1, *ha-'ir
rabbati 'am.*

Jewish interpretation in reply to cavils of objectors and in opposition to the theories of alien philosophies. It is highly probable that some of the contributors were acquainted with Philo — with his ideas, if not with his writings — which is not strange since R. Hosha'ya had his school at Caesarea and was contemporary there with Origen, whose biblical studies brought him into association with Jewish scholars.[1] Caesarea was one of the chief centres of Christianity in Palestine. It had a considerable Jewish population, and it is likely that there had been controversies between Jews and Christians there before the end of the second century, as there certainly were in the third.[2] Echoes of such discussions in Caesarea or elsewhere may be heard here and there in Bereshit Rabbah, for example, c. 8, 9 (on Gen. 1, 26).[3] The opponents are by this time catholic Christians, and the Jewish polemic is outspokenly directed against the deification of Christ, as in the utterances of Abahu.[4] The controversial element in the Midrash is, however, rare, and of minor interest.

It has been fitly said of it: "This Midrash is eminently rich in sublime thoughts and finely worded sentences, in all kinds of parables, in foreign words, especially Greek, used freely and intentionally for the sake of elegance of diction."[5]

It begins on a very large scale, nearly one fourth of the whole work being given to the section Bereshit (Gen. 1, 1–5, 8) alone. Toward the end (from about Gen. 44) it is much more cursory, and the method changes. It is suggested that it may have been left incomplete, and the deficiency supplied by other hands and from different sources.

[1] Origen (d. 253) established himself there in 231 A.D. and labored there till the Decian persecution in 250. He mentions (on Psalm 1) his acquaintance with Ἰοὔλλος πατριάρχης, probably a scribal error for Ἰούδας (Judah II).

[2] Abahu. Bacher, Pal. Amoräer, II, 96 f., 115–118; Jewish Encyclopedia, I, 36 f.

[3] R. Simlai; the same series of questions and answers, with two more, in Jer. Berakot 12d, below. Bacher, Pal. Amoräer, I, 555 f.

[4] Jer. Ta'anit 65 b, below; Exod. R. 29, 1.

[5] J. Theodor, 'Bereshit Rabbah,' Jewish Encyclopedia, III, 63.

The homiletic character is marked by the introductions prefixed to nearly all the sections, which start from a text in another part of the Bible, most frequently from the Hagiographa, and more or less ingeniously make the transition to the verse in Genesis which is to be commented on. Many of these introductions bear the names of the homilists who invented them, or whose interpretation of the text was utilized for the purpose; the greater number, however, are anonymous, and not a few are composite. Once the introduction — sometimes lengthy — is despatched, the exposition goes its way without further reference to it.

The age of such a catena is a question to which a simple answer cannot be given. It contains much material which comes from the second and third centuries, and may have been compiled from previous collections. On the other hand, the redaction, in the nature of the case, was not definitive, thus excluding later additions. The intimate relation to the Palestinian Talmud makes it probable that the redaction was made in the same environment and in the same age with that Talmud, say the early part of the fifth century. The authorities named are nearly all Palestinian, and form a succession from the second century to well on in the fourth.

A critical edition of Bereshit Rabbah was begun in 1903 by J. Theodor: Bereschit Rabba mit kritischem Apparate und Kommentare. Text, apparatus, and commentary are everything that such an edition should be. Since Theodor's death in 1923, the edition has been competently carried on by Ch. Albeck, with the use of Theodor's collations and collections. The thirteenth part (1927), pages 961–1059. Extends to Gen. 39.6 (in Section 86), where Theodor's manuscript ended.

There are many collective editions of the Midrashim on the Pentateuch and the Megillot, with a steadily increasing flow of commentaries. The most comprehensive and the most frequently used nowadays is that published by the house of Romm, in Wilna. The references in the present volumes are to this edi-

tion.[1] There is a German translation of Bereshit Rabbah and
of the other so-called "Rabbot" on the Pentateuch and the
Megillot, by August Wünsche, under the general title, Bibliotheca
Rabbinica (1880 sqq.).

The Midrash on Exodus (Shemot), down to the end of Exod.
11 (c. 14), resembles that on Genesis described above, and may
have been planned as a supplement to it, carrying on the narrative to the point where the laws and the Mekilta begin (Exod.
12). The introductions, or proems, are regularly followed by a
running exposition of the entire lection, as in Bereshit Rabbah.
From chapter 15 (Exod. 12) on, the whole economy of the
work is different. The matter is largely taken bodily from homilies in other Midrashim, especially of the Tanḥuma type.[2] The
compilation is unquestionably late; Zunz inclines to put it in
the eleventh or twelfth century.

An expository Midrash of character similar to Bereshit Rabbah and of not far from the same age is the Ekah Rabbati, on
Lamentations. Since the latter book was not divided into lections, the proems in Ekah Rabbati, thirty-six in number,[3] are
prefixed in mass to the running comments on the book verse by
verse. The proems regularly begin, "Rabbi N. N. opened (his
discourse)," with a text from somewhere else in the Bible, apt,
or applied, to the content of the Book of Lamentations taken as
an elegy on the fallen glory — an appropriate theme for the commemoration of the ninth of Ab, the destruction of the temple,
and for the eve of that day. The body of the Midrash has many
stories of the unhappy fortunes of the Jews, the disasters of the
Bar Cocheba war, the persecutions they suffered from the Romans, the mockery of which they were made the butt in comedy,
and the like, by the side of which, for variety, may be put the
match of wits between Jews and Athenians, in which the Greeks

---

[1] It is an inconvenience that the subdivisions do not correspond in all
editions, and for that reason chapter and verse of the biblical text are frequently added.

[2] See below, pp. 169 f.   [3] The older editions count 33.

come off second best. Stories make up more than one fourth of the contents (leaving out the proems).

The Midrash on Lamentations, like that on Genesis, stands close to the Palestinian Talmud, though somewhat later than those two works, and had apparently certain older collections as a source in common with Bereshit Rabbah and the Pesiḳta of Rab Kahana. Here also the first chapter is treated on a much larger scale than those that follow, as is not strange in view of the monotony of the theme. Like Bereshit Rabbah, it abounds in Greek words.

This Midrash is cited by chapter and verse of Lamentations.

Of a different type from the expository Midrash thus far described is the homiletical Midrash in the stricter sense, which is more numerously represented. One of the oldest of these, and that in which the type is most clearly seen, is the Pesiḳta (Pesiḳta de-Rab Kahana). It contains homilies on the lections for the high days of the ecclesiastical calendar, not for the continuous series of Sabbath pericopes. In the arrangement adopted by Buber in his edition there are first six homilies for the special Sabbaths;[1] then follow homilies for the Feasts (Passover to Pentecost inclusive, nos. 7–12); homilies on lections from the Prophets for the Sabbaths of retribution and consolation[2] (three Sabbaths preceding the ninth of Ab, and seven after it); homilies on lections from the Prophets (nos. 13–22); for New Year's (no. 23); Penitential homilies, between New Year's and the Day of Atonement (nos. 24–25 [26]); the Day of Atonement (no. 27); Tabernacles (nos. 28–31).

In the manuscripts there are differences in order and in some measure in contents, but the general scheme is the same. The structure of the proems is more elaborate than of those in the Midrash on Genesis or on Lamentations; the exposition, on the other hand, seldom gets far beyond the beginning of the lesson.

[1] Four of the five or six preceding the first of Nisan (M. Megillah 3, 4).

[2] From the seventeenth of the month Tammuz to the season of Tabernacles: שבעה דנחמתא, תלתא דפרענתא‎.

The Pesiḳta is one of the earlier Midrashim; that it is later than Bereshit Rabbah and Ekah Rabbati is agreed; on the question whether it is older or younger than the Midrash on Leviticus, which it strikingly resembles and with which it has some homilies in common, opinion is divided.

The only edition of the Pesiḳta is that of S. Buber: Pesiḳta, die älteste Hagada, redigirt in Palästina, u. s. w., 1868. With an extended introduction, and commentary.—A German translation by August Wünsche is included in his Bibliotheca Rabbinica.

The Pesiḳta Rabbati is a mediaeval work; if in the figures near the beginning of the first homily the author himself gives his date, it was composed in 845. It makes large use of older sources, including the Pesiḳta de-R. Kahana, from which five entire homilies are taken bodily, but in general it is of a very different character. The lucid and often elegant Hebrew is noteworthy. The latest edition is by M. Friedmann, Pesiḳta Rabbati, u. s. w., Vienna, 1880.

Whatever the relation between the Pesiḳta and the Midrash on Leviticus (Wayyiḳra Rabbah), there is no doubt that the latter is another of the older Midrashim. It is not an exposition of the Book of Leviticus, but a series of homilies on passages in Leviticus, most of them on the Sabbath lections (Sedarim) of the triennial cycle; five of them are on lessons for the Feasts, and, apart from minor variations, are identical with five homilies in the Pesiḳta.[1] An interesting feature of this Midrash is the frequent introduction of popular proverbs in Aramaic, to illustrate the turn given by the homilist to a verse of Scripture.

Another variety of the homiletic Midrash is represented by what are called the Tanḥuma homilies, by a generic extension of the title of one such collection, the Midrash Tanḥuma, named after one of the most prolific homilists of the fourth century, R. Tanḥuma bar Abba, who frequently appears in it. This collection, which exists in two recensions, covers the whole Pentateuch,

---

[1] Wayyiḳra Rabbah, Parashahs 20, 27–30; Pesiḳta 27, 9, 8, 23, 28.

though by no means evenly, following the Sabbath lections of the triennial cycle, and has homilies also on the Festival cycle which we have seen in the Pesiḳta.

A peculiarity of this species is that many of the homilies start with a morsel of halakic caviar as an appetizer. The audience — perhaps the Meturgeman for them — asks a question of this kind,[1] for example: "Let our master teach us how many kinds of clean animals there are in the world. — Thus have our rabbis pronounced; There are ten such animals" (the catalogue follows). From the standing formula of the question, *Yelammedenu rabbenu*, the Midrash (or one of its sources) is cited as Yelammedenu.[2] On this hors d'oeuvre follow several proems, and an exposition of the first verses of the lection. Many of the homilies close with a forward look to the great deliverance and the fulfilment of the hope and promise of the better time to come — what moderns sometimes loosely call "messianic" conclusions.[3]

There are, as has been said, two recensions of the Tanḥuma, one in many editions presenting the (amplified) text of Mantua, 1563, the other edited by Buber from manuscripts in 1885. They differ widely in Genesis and Exodus, and agree more nearly in the three other books. The critical problems, which are even more tangled here than in the other Midrashim, need not detain us. Buber's contention that his Tanḥuma is older than Bereshit Rabbah, and even than the Pesiḳta to which he formerly gave the seniority, has not found much acceptance.[4]

The Midrash on Deuteronomy (Debarim Rabbah) is a series of twenty-seven homilies on lessons of the triennial cycle. Each

---

[1] The question is not always on the Halakah, e. g., "How many things preceded the history of the world?" (i.e., the account of creation in Gen. 1). "The tradition of our rabbis is that seven things were created while as yet the world was not created," etc. The question and answer are usually chosen for some relevance to the subject in hand.

[2] The author of the Yalḳuṭ cites both Tanḥuma and Yelammedenu, as if he had them separately.

[3] Compare many of the homilies in Pesiḳta Rabbati.

[4] For the theory of the three Tanḥumas see Lauterbach in the Jewish Encyclopedia, XII, 45 f.

begins with a halakic exordium, introduced in a peculiar stereo-typed form and sometimes of considerable length;[1] upon this follow the proem (or proems) and the text at the beginning of the lesson. The discourse regularly concludes with promises or consolation.

Bemidbar Rabbah, on Numbers, is less homogeneous. The last third of the book (cc. 15–23, on Num. 8–35) is a series of Tanḥuma homilies, with a Halakah at the beginning. Chapters 1–5 are a large and free amplification of homilies of a similar type. The inordinately long section Naso (cc. 6–14) is a compilation which accompanies the text continuously. It draws on mediaeval sources, and is not older than the twelfth century.

In an account of the sources used in the present volumes it is unnecessary to describe particularly the Midrashim on the Megillot, Esther, Song of Songs, Ruth, Ecclesiastes. They also draw largely on their predecessors;[2] in that on Ecclesiastes there is considerable use of the Palestinian Talmud and some loans from the Babylonian Talmud; even post-Talmudic tractates are quoted.

The value of the older expository and homiletical Midrashim (Bereshit Rabbah, Ekah Rabbati, Wayyikra Rabbah, Pesikta) lies in the fact that they not only preserve much of the religious and moral teaching of the second century in the names of its authors, but are our only source (besides incidental matter of the kind in the Talmuds) for that of the third century, in which several of the rabbis flourished who most excelled in this branch of tradition and instruction, such as Joshua ben Levi, Johanan, Simeon ben Laḳish, Samuel ben Naḥman; nor was the fourth century lacking in eminent representatives of the art.

[1] The halakic exordium is simply noted, Halakah, instead of the Yelam-medenu formula. E.g., Halakah. A man of Israel, is it licit for him to write a Torah (Pentateuch) in any language? — Thus have the learned (Ḥakamim) taught: There is no difference between books (copies of the Pentateuch) and Tefillin and Mezuzot, except that books may be written in any language, etc. (M. Megillah 1, 8).

[2] These passages sometimes represent an older and better text than our editions of their sources.

The fertility and originality of the third-century Haggadah especially has been remarked above. It must be understood, however, that the originality is not in the substance of the teaching but in the ingenuity with which familiar lessons are discovered in unsuspected places in Scripture and new lessons in hackneyed texts, and in the art with which they are developed, illustrated, and applied. The doctrines of religion and the principles of morals were long since unalterably established; need, or possibility, of progress beyond them did not enter the mind of the teachers of theology and ethics. Their task, as they conceived it, could not be more aptly expressed than in the words of the Gospel about a particular topic: "Every scribe who has been instructed in the (nature of the) kingdom of Heaven is like a householder who produces out of his storeroom new things and old." [1]

To assure ourselves that in the substance of the teaching, whether the form be new or old, there is no change, it is only necessary to compare what we have in the Midrashim and in the Talmudic Haggadah from the third and fourth centuries with the older homilists and the standard authority of the Tannaite Midrash, with which again the various writings from Sirach on are in essential agreement.

But while we thus establish the continuity through four or five centuries, we do not overlook the fact that Judaism had made much history in that period. The conflict over the authority of the traditional law had ended in the complete triumph of the Pharisees; the controversy about the life after death had elevated the resurrection to the rank of a dogma and made heretics of the Sadducees. Other sectarians and schismatics had been sloughed off or reabsorbed. The Essene order had apparently long since disappeared.[2] The disciples of Jesus the Naza-

---

[1] Matt. 13, 53. See the preceding parables on the Kingdom, vss. 14–51, which may be taken as examples of the "new things" that such a scribe can bring out.

[2] There is no recognizable mention of it in the whole body of rabbinical literature.

rene, who had made some stir for a generation or two after the fall of Jerusalem, had finally put themselves outside the pale of Judaism in the Bar Cocheba war. The Christianity which the rabbis had to do with thereafter was Greek, and the controversy was with catholic doctrine. There were always skeptics to be refuted, especially on the old issue of retribution, and perhaps here and there foreign philosophical influences to be resisted. These changes of complexion can be observed in the incidence of controversy and the shifting emphasis on particular points in successive generations; but of differences in the fundamental conceptions of Judaism there is no evidence.

What is true of the Midrashim holds good equally of the contemporary Haggadah in the Talmuds, which in the Palestinian Talmud is intimately related to the Midrashim. Not only is the Baraita an important source for the second century, but so too are the utterances of the Amoraim for the third and fourth.

In the present volumes the Talmuds are cited in the customary way, the Palestinian (Jerushalmi) by the folio and column of the Krotoschin edition (1866), the Babylonian by the folios of each tractate, which are the same in all the current editions. Of the former there is a French translation by Moïse Schwab: Le Talmud de Jérusalem traduit pour la première fois. 11 volumes, 1871–1889. (Vol. I, 2d ed., 1890.)—Of the latter, a German translation by Lazarus Goldschmidt: Der Babylonische Talmud . . . möglichst sinn- und wortgetreu übersetzt. Thus far, 8 volumes, 1897–1922. The text follows the first Bomberg edition (Venice, 1520–1523).—A translation of the haggadic parts of both Talmuds by August Wünsche: Der Jerusalemische Talmud in seinen haggadischen Bestandtheilen übertragen, 1880; Der Babylonische Talmud in seinen haggadischen Bestandtheilen, wortgetreu übersetzt, u.s.w. (4 volumes, 1886–1889).[1]

It is proper to say that the Talmud is one of the books of which even the best translation is in large part to be understood only with the aid of the original and of the Hebrew commentaries.

[1] Rodkinson's so-called English translation is in every respect impossible.

CHAPTER V

VERSIONS OF SCRIPTURE. PRAYERS

The older Aramaic translations (Targums) of the Pentateuch and the Prophets, of which something has been said above, are of Palestinian origin and probably date from the second century. They show in many ways affinity to the exegesis of the Tannaim of the school of Akiba. We have the text in a Babylonian recension of perhaps the third century, which, however, does not seem to have gone much deeper than accommodation to the vocabulary of the Babylonian Jews in the use of certain words. Both were in intention as near to verbal translation as was consistent with bringing out the meaning; the midrashic element which occasionally runs loose can sometimes be proved by external evidence to be a later accretion, and in other cases the same thing may fairly be suspected. In Palestine they did not obtain the official recognition they had in Babylonia, but it may be inferred that the Babylonian schools took these Targums, along with the Mishnah, the Tosefta, and the Tannaite Midrash of the school of Akiba, because they also represented this school and were authenticated by their origin.

Besides the use that the interpreter (Meturgeman) might make of a written version in preparation for his oral rendering of the lessons in the synagogue, such translations could hardly fail to be found great aids in private study, as a supplement to oral instruction in the Scriptures. References to such a use of them are, however, rare. In Sifrè Deut. § 161, in what may be called the progress through learning to virtue and piety, the first biblical discipline, Miḳra (learning to read the Hebrew Bible), is followed by Targum (learning translation), but this need not have been from a book. A probable reference to the latter is found, however, in the precept given by R. Joshua ben Levi, head of a school at Lydda in the first half of the third century, to his sons, that they should read the lesson of the week privately twice in the course of the week, and the Targum once.[1] Later in the same century R. Ammi made this a rule for all.[2] The latter prescription supposes that copies of an Aramaic version were in the hands of the educated. This rule became general practice, and was perpetuated to times and regions where Aramaic was not spoken by the Jews; and the disuse of it evoked strong protest. The Targum of Onkelos was thus read for centuries, and it is a reasonable inference that it was this that Joshua ben Levi and Ammi meant.

The usefulness of a standard version as an authentic interpretation of the Scripture needs no words. And inasmuch as it undertook in the main only to give the "plain sense" interpretation, it did not hamper the freedom of the search for deeper meanings and new combinations which was the province of Midrash.

The Palestinian Targum on the Pentateuch ("Targum of the Land of Israel") is frequently called Targum of Jonathan (ben Uzziel, the reputed translator of the official Targum on the Prophets) or, by moderns, "Pseudo-Jonathan." The former name first appears in the fourteenth century, and probably originated in an erroneous resolution of an abbreviation. A similar origin may be conjectured for the name "Jerusalem Targum," which goes back to the twelfth century. In the form in which the Palestinian Targum is in our hands it is late, containing the names of a wife and daughter of Mohammed,[3] and, in some manuscripts, references to still later events. Such passages, however, prove only that the popular Targum was kept up to date, so to speak, as it was copied from age to age, and do not determine the age of the bulk of the work. The relation to Onkelos is capable of more than one interpretation, and both interpretations may be partially right.

The translation is sometimes close, elsewhere freely para-

[1] Berakot 8b. [2] Ibid. 8a, below. [3] On Gen. 21, 21.

phrastic; in many parts the Targum runs into Midrash. For the purposes of the present volumes, it is seldom of consequence; and the same is true of the Fragment Targum which is related to it.

The Targums on the Hagiographa are all of too late a date to serve us as sources, and need not be described here.[1]

The Targums had a time of being very much overworked by Christian scholars in consequence of the erroneous notion that they antedated the Christian era; and in particular the messianic expectations of the Jews in that age were looked for in them. Afterwards they were still more abused in the search for the Jewish idea of a God-out-of-reach who negotiated with the world only through the Memra and other intermediaries.[2]

Their true value lies in the evidence they give to the exegesis of the Tannaite period — to the real understanding of what the Bible said for itself.

In treating the subject of Piety (Part VI) much is made of Jewish prayers. It is therefore necessary to say something here about this subject. It is to be premised that prayer-books do not make their appearance for many centuries after the period with which we are here dealing. The oldest known work of the kind, the Seder Rab Amram, composed after the middle of the ninth century of our era by the head (Gaon) of the Academy at Sura in Babylonia, at the request of Spanish communities,[3] was widely disseminated, and served as a basis for subsequent compilations and as an authority on liturgical questions. In this wide use the rules for the order of prayers and the like were preserved with little change, but the text of the prayers themselves was extensively accommodated to the established custom of the

[1] See W. Bacher, 'Targum,' Jewish Encyclopedia, XII, 61 f.

[2] See Moore, 'Intermediaries in Jewish Theology,' Harvard Theological Review, XV (1922), 41–85; Strack-Billerbeck, Kommentar zum Neuen Testament aus Talmud und Midrasch, II (1924), 302–333 (on John 1, 1).

[3] Rab Amram died ca. 875. On the succession of mediaeval prayer-books see I. Elbogen, Der jüdische Gottesdienst in seiner geschichtlichen Entwicklung, pp. 358 ff.

several regions, so that the testimony of the edition or of the manuscripts (which exhibit many variations) cannot be taken as representing the Babylonian use in the ninth century. It appears, however, that prayer-books were already in use in Amram's time.

Next in order of time came the Collection of Prayers and Hymns of Praise by Saadia (d. 942), who was led to undertake the task by the variations of usage and the liberties which scholars took in the way of innovations.[1] Maimonides (d. 1204) treats the regulations concerning prayer at length in the second book of the Mishneh Torah, to which is appended an Order of Prayers for the whole year.[2] The Maḥzor Vitry, compiled by Simḥah ben Samuel (d. 1105), a pupil of Rashi, is a much more extensive work, belonging to the so-called Ashkenazic[3] branch of the liturgical tradition. The Maḥzor Vitry was edited by Simeon Hurwitz (Berlin, 1893; anastatic reprint, Nürnberg, 1923).

Of modern editions of the Prayer-Book mention is to be made, in the first place, of Seligman Baer, 'Abodat Israel (Rödelheim, 1868; anastatic reprint, 1901). — The Authorized Daily Prayer Book of the United Hebrew Congregations of the British Empire. With a new translation by the Rev. S. Singer (London, 1891, and repeatedly since); with A Companion to the Authorised Daily Prayer Book, etc., by Israel Abrahams (revised edition, London, 1922). Both of these represent the Ashkenazic rite. — A modern edition of the Sefardic rite is that of D. A. de Sola, revised by M. Gaster. London, 1901.

While the text of the prayers in our hands in these books is, at the utmost, mediaeval, there is abundant evidence that the principal prayers themselves were in use as far back as our sources go, and were, in the age of the Tannaim, believed to be of immemorial antiquity. The Men of the Great Synagogue ordained

---

[1] Probably drawn up for the use of Jews in Egypt. It is incompletely preserved, and has not been edited.

[2] Much abridged in manuscripts and editions.

[3] French (Northern) and German Jews.

the benedictions, prayers, and forms for ushering in and marking
the close of sacred time (Ḳiddush and Habdalah).[1]   Particular
benedictions or parts of the synagogue prayers are cited by
the initial words, assuming that the sequel is in everybody's
memory, and these *incipits* are prevailingly identical with those
of the prayers still in use and known by the same titles.   The
school discussions, which reach back to the generations before
the destruction of Jerusalem (Bet Shammai and Bet Hillel)
are about modalities, not matter.[2]   Substance and phraseology have biblical antecedents; extracanonical writings of the
centuries before our era afford numerous parallels.   But the
prayers of the synagogue differ from these on the one hand in
their comprehensiveness and on the other in the conciseness of
their formulation, adapted in both respects to congregational
and individual use.   The words were not prescribed, but they
tended to become fixed by repetition, and to vary chiefly by
verbal amplification.   Extensive additions appear in the festival
liturgies, not in the standard prayers.

In using these and the private prayers of individual rabbis as
witnesses to the character of Jewish piety, the date to be assigned
to them is less important, because in this respect no significant
difference is to be discovered between the religiousness of the
first centuries of our era and that of the following periods down
to the invasion of mysticism.

[1] Berakot 33a (in the name of Johanan).
[2] For a list see Elbogen, p. 247, and Notes (2 ed., pp. 554 f.).

CHAPTER VI

EXTRANEOUS SOURCES

Of Sirach and his importance as a witness to the stage at which
Judaism had arrived in the class to which he belonged, two centuries before the common era, enough has been said in an earlier
chapter. It remains here to add something about his book.

The title in the Greek Bible is Σοφία Ἰησοῦ υἱοῦ Σείραχ, or,
abridged, Σοφία Σείραχ; in Latin and the modern versions
after it, Ecclesiasticus.[1] That it was written in Hebrew is beyond
question. It was translated into Greek by a grandson of the
author who went to Egypt in the thirty-eighth year of Ptolemy
Euergetes, that is, in 132 B.C. His translation was probably
made there some years later.[2]

Among the spoils of the Genizah in Cairo were found considerable fragments of two manuscripts of the work in Hebrew,
and a scrap of a third,[3] besides some extracts. Altogether they
contain about two thirds of the book. The text of these eleventh-
or twelfth-century manuscripts differs widely, as would be expected, from the Greek and Syriac [4] versions. These variations
may be ascribed in part to transcriptional errors of the Hebrew
scribes, in part to an archetype already remote from the copy in
the hands of the first translator. The translations have had a
more intricate history, and manuscripts of the Greek version and
the secondary versions made from the Greek vary materially. The
critical problems thus presented are complicated and very difficult.[5]

[1] Cyprian; Rufinus, In symbolum, c. 38. Ἐκκλησιαστικός, Photius; title
of cod. 248 H–P. In Syriac, חכמתא דברסירא, The Wisdom of the Son of
Sirach.

[2] See the translator's Preface.

[3] Marginal notes in one of them record readings from two other codices.

[4] The Syriac was made from the Hebrew, though it did not escape the
influence of the Greek Bible.

[5] See Peters, Der . . . hebräische Text des Buches Ecclesiasticus, 1902
(Prolegomena). — For the Greek version, Cod. Vaticanus Gr. 336 (Holmes and

One question was raised shortly after the first publication of a part of the Hebrew text: is it a descendant of the original Wisdom of Ben Sira, or a translation from the Greek or the Syriac? Though the case would not be without example, scholars generally agreed in rejecting the hypothesis of translation. Several attempts have been made to reconstruct what Sirach actually wrote, on the basis of the three primary witnesses (Hebrew, Greek, Syriac),[1] but whatever success may have been achieved in particular instances, as a whole the result of such a contamination of recensions is not convincing, and the method must be pronounced fallacious.

A convenient edition of the Hebrew text, with the variants of the manuscripts, and the most important readings of the Greek and Syriac, is: H. Strack, Die Sprüche Jesus' des Sohnes Sirachs, u.s.w., 1903. — Norbert Peters, Der jüngst wiederaufgefundene hebräische Text des Buches Ecclesiasticus, 1902. Text and translation, with critical prolegomena and commentary. — R. Smend, Die Weisheit des Jesus Sirach. Hebräisch und Deutsch, 1906. — Die Weisheit des Jesus Sirach erklärt, 1906.

See also Box and Oesterley, in R. H. Charles, Apocrypha, etc. With an extensive critical apparatus to the composite translation.

A very important source from the middle of the first century before the Christian era are the so-called Psalms of Solomon, which in certain Christian lists stand with First and Second Maccabees, Wisdom of Solomon, Sirach, Judith, Tobit, etc., as "Antilegomena," [2] in a kind of appendix to the books of the Hebrew Bible. They are found in a few cursive manuscripts of

Parsons no. 248) is of peculiar importance. — An edition of this manuscript with an ample critical commentary by J. H. A. Hart, Ecclesiasticus in Greek, was published in Cambridge, 1909.

[1] See, e.g., V. Ryssel, in Kautzsch, Die Apokryphen und Pseudepigraphen des Alten Testaments.

[2] Substantially corresponding to what in Protestant versions of the Bible are entitled "Apocrypha." — Another list puts the Psalms of Solomon, along with Enoch and other apocalypses, the Testaments of the Twelve Patriarchs, etc., among the Apocrypha in the ancient and catholic use of the word, for which "Pseudepigrapha" is now commonly used.

the Greek Bible, either following the Psalms of David or in the Solomonic group, and they once stood in the Codex Alexandrinus (5th century) at the very end, after the New Testament and the Epistles of Clement.

These Psalms are preserved only in a Greek version and in a secondary Syriac translation from the Greek;[1] but there is no question that the original language was Hebrew. The age of several of them is determined by unmistakable references to the taking of Jerusalem by Pompey (63 B.C.) and to his death (48 B.C.).[2] Inasmuch as there is no reference in them to Herod, who took Jerusalem with the aid of the Romans in 37, or to the restoration of the Asmonaean Antigonus by the Parthians (40 B.C.), it is probable that the latest of the Psalms were written before these events. It is not certain that they are all the work of one author, but the internal situation so far as it is reflected in them corresponds to conditions under the last Asmonaean princes, say from the death of Queen Alexandra (67 B.C.); that the earlier rulers of the family are included in the same condemnation is no indication of date.

The author was evidently a resident of Jerusalem, and writes with personal knowledge and feeling of the calamities that befell the city and its inhabitants in those troubled times. He lays all these evils at the door of the rulers and their partisans, whom he charges with all manner of enormities. Besides all this, they were usurpers of the throne of David, which God had sworn should belong to his posterity forever. Pompey was the instrument of God's judgment upon them; but his arrogance was visited upon him in his dishonored death.

The author paints a shocking picture of the demoralization of the times. It was not, however, universal. The familiar division of men into righteous and wicked, sinners and saints,[3] runs

---

[1] In the sole known manuscript they are appended to what are called the "Odes of Solomon," Christian compositions with which they have no connection except Solomon's name.

[2] See particularly Psalms 2; 8; 17.

[3] Ὅσιοι (חסידים).

through these Psalms, as in so many of the Psalms of David.[1]
The author rails at the profane who "live in hypocrisy with
the pious" and "sit in the pious congregation, though their
heart is far remote from the Lord."[2]   The contrast between
these two kinds of men in character and destiny is a recurrent
theme.

Man is free and chooses his conduct for himself, and with it
his fate. "Our deeds are in the election and power of our soul,
to do righteousness or unrighteousness in the works of our
hands," etc. (9, 7–9). Directly opposite are the way in which the
righteous man receives the chastisement of the Lord and the be-
havior of the sinner when misfortune befalls him and he goes on
heaping sins upon sins. Diverse, too, are their ends. "The
destruction of the sinner is forever, and when God visits the
righteous no notice will be taken of him. . . . But those that fear
the Lord will arise to everlasting life, and their life in the light of
the Lord will never fail" (Psalm 3).

The Psalms that have no such salient features are not less
instructive for the piety they represent;[3] both the conception
and the sentiment are those of normal Judaism. The author of
the Psalms of Solomon (or the authors) was a religious-minded
man, full of the Scripture, reminiscences of which are pervasive.
He shared the belief of the Pharisees in the resurrection of the
righteous dead, of which he speaks without emphasis or argument as though it were accepted doctrine among those for whom
he wrote. He prays that God raise up for his people their king,
the son of David, in the time He has appointed, to be king over
Israel His servant, endued with all the qualities of which the
prophets had told. The picture of his reign is a composite of
ancient prophecies, free from apocalyptic fantasies. When we

[1] Cf. also the Wisdom of Solomon.
[2] The portrait of such a one, a man in high station, is drawn, perhaps from
life, in Psalm 4.
[3] That they were sung in the synagogues (Ryssel) is extremely improbable
in view of anything we know of the service; but so far as the contents go they
would not have been unacceptable.

come to treat of Jewish expectations of the future of the nation we shall have occasion to discuss this Psalm more particularly.[1]

The Psalms of Solomon have been repeatedly edited. Those editions whose text is based on a collation of several manuscripts are: Ryle and James, Ψαλμοι Σολομωντος. Psalms of the Pharisees, commonly called the Psalms of Solomon, etc. With introduction, English translation, notes, appendix and indexes. Cambridge, 1891. — v. Gebhart, Ψαλμοι Σολομωντος. Die Psalmen Salomo . . . herausgegeben. Leipzig, 1905 (Texte und Untersuchungen, u.s.w., XIII, 2). — Swete, The Old Testament in Greek, etc., III (1894), 765–787.
English Translation in Ryle and James, above.

Turning now to the sources to which Judaism has never accorded any authority, the so-called Synoptic Gospels (Matthew, Mark, Luke) are of the first interest, for they witness to the prevailing Jewish teaching of their time. Of the fundamental Judaism of these writings enough has been said above; their messianic and eschatological features in relation to Jewish ideas on those subjects will be discussed in that connection.[2] The severe strictures they pass on the religious leaders who opposed the movement are *ex parte* testimony, to be impartially weighed. In so doing it is to be observed that this censure is directed against persons or classes, and does not convey an implicit criticism of Judaism itself. The whole point of the scathing denunciation of the Scribes and Pharisees is that they are not true to the religion they profess and their own better knowledge. Criticism of their teaching on particular points is sometimes severe, and even goes on to the sweeping charge of nullifying the word of God by their tradition. But this is not to be taken as a rejection of tradition in principle, like that of the Sadducees, or of the authority of the Scribes as its custodians and expositors. Our concern, however, is not with a critical estimation of the testimony of the Gospels but with the sources themselves. And, it must be noted,

[1] Psalm 17; cf. also Psalm 18. See Vol. II, p. 328.
[2] Vol. II, Part vii.

as sources for contemporary Judaism, not as sources for the life and teaching of Jesus.

The Gospels in our hands in Greek are the Gospels of Gentile churches, and all of them, in different ways and measures, bear marks of this early non-Jewish Christianity. It is the prevailing opinion among critics that none of them — unless it be Mark — in its present form is earlier than the fall of Jerusalem in the year 70. Mark [1] tells more of the works of Jesus than of his words, but early brings him into conflict with the Pharisees on points of observance. Matthew has the events as in Mark, but exhibits the teaching of Jesus much more fully from another source. Luke has much of this matter, but distributed in quite a different way, and has besides a good deal to which there is no parallel in Matthew. The matter which Luke has in common with Matthew was clearly not taken from Matthew, and it is therefore inferred that in both Gospels it is derived independently from a common source (generally designated by the cipher Q), which the two authors used each in his own way.

Neither Jesus nor his immediate disciples spoke Greek.[2] The primitive tradition of his teaching was in the vernacular Aramaic dialect of Galilee, and the first written precipitate of their tradition, collected and set down for their own use, was also in Aramaic.[3] It would be nothing strange if subsequently some scholar converted to their belief should have put the Gospel (*Euangelion*) of Jeshu ha-Noṣri into the Hebrew which the learned used for such purposes.[4] It was perhaps such a work that was in the latter part of the fourth century in the hands of the Nazarenes at Beroea (Aleppo).

The Greek in which the Synoptic Gospels have come down to

[1] Matthew, Mark, Luke are used here as titles of books, not as authors' names.

[2] If they knew any Greek for market purposes, they certainly did not use a foreign language instead of their mother tongue to talk to their countrymen or with one another about religious subjects.

[3] Not, however, in dialect, but in the written language.

[4] The synagogue homilies were in the common Aramaic, but all the homiletic Midrashim are in Hebrew.

us bears in places unmistakable evidence of translation from Aramaic. The dialect which Jesus and his Galilean disciples spoke [1] is not sufficiently known to make it possible to obtain by retroversion from the Greek the actual words he used, even if we could suppose that the Greek was a verbal translation of a verbatim original. The teaching of the Synagogue, on the other hand, to which so much in the Gospels is akin in substance and phrase, is accessible to us only in the "language of the learned," the Hebrew of the Midrash. The Aramaic link between the synagogue exposition and the primitive Nazarene tradition underlying the Gospel is lost. For our purpose the loss is not serious. [2] If in most cases we do not know verbally how the rabbis expressed themselves in the language of the people, we do know how they said the same thing in their discussion with one another, and if through the Greek of the Gospels we hear this immediately, we have made the connection not only with the popular instruction of the synagogue but with the larger development in the discussions of the schools. It is to this that the interpreter of the Gospels must resort at every turn for the understanding of his text — not only its terms but its ideas, and frequently for the association of ideas.

While the Gospels are thus in large measure witnesses to the rabbinical teaching of the time, they were from the beginning apologetic documents. As with the first part of the Acts of the Apostles which is their sequel, their characteristic is the identification of their teacher, Jesus of Nazareth, with the Messiah. How far the Old Testament texts they appealed to had been interpreted messianically by the authorized expositors of Scripture, or by the greater freedom of the homilists, can, unfortunately, seldom be known. We can be sure, however, that the proof-texts the disciples of Jesus alleged as predictions of the death of the Messiah, and of the resurrection and ascension,

---

[1] See G. Dalman, Grammatik des jüdisch-palästinischen Aramäischen, u. s. w., 1894 (2 ed. 1905).

[2] Peculiarities of dialect may sometimes explain textual variations.

were used in that way for the first time by them. It seems clear also that in identifying their Messiah in the second stage with the apocalyptic "Son of Man" they were not giving an original interpretation of Daniel 7, 13 f., but either a bit of rabbinical Haggadah, or were drawing upon eschatological developments of that vision such as are found in the so-called "Parables" of Enoch.[1] The Gospel according to Matthew is, of the three, the most important source for Judaism, not only for its contents but for its attitude; it is at once the most conservatively Jewish of the Gospels and the most violently anti-Pharisaic. For the prominence of both these features it may be surmised that the history of the Nazarenes in their relations to Gentile Christianity on the one side and to the Jewish authorities on the other was decisive.

In the fourth century Jerome, then pursuing the ascetic life in the desert of Calchis, consorted with a Nazarene sect in Beroea (Aleppo), which endeavored to combine the observance of the Law with the grace of the Gospel,[2] but condemned the Scribes and Pharisees, and by name the heads of the Tannaite schools. The "houses" of Shammai and Hillel [3] were "the two houses of Israel" in Isa. 8, 12, who by their traditions and δευτερώσεις (Mishnah) dissolved and defiled the Law. They did not accept the Saviour, who became, in the words of the prophet, their downfall and stumbling-block.[4] In Isa. 8, 23 they found, first, the preaching of Christ in Galilee by which the land of Zebulun and Naphtali was freed from the errors of the Scribes and Pharisees, and shook off from their necks the exceeding heavy yoke of Jewish traditions; afterwards, by the gospel of the Apostle Paul, who was the last of the Apostles, the preaching was extended, and the gospel of Christ shone abroad to the boundaries of the nations [4] and the way of the great sea (Isa. 8, 23). They

---

[1] See below, Part VII.

[2] Comm. on Ezek. 16, 16 (Vallarsi V, 161). He applies to them Matt. 7, 16 f., the patch of new cloth on the old garment.

[3] The name Shammai is etymologized, *dissipator;* of Hillel, *profanus.*

[4] Comm. on Isa. 8, 11 f. (Vallarsi IV, 122 f.).

evidently held that it was not for them, as born Jews, to emancipate themselves from the law; [1] their hearty recognition of the missionary labors of Paul shows that they did not hold, as one wing of the believing Jews had insisted in Paul's time, that converts to the Gospel were bound to put themselves under the law.

While Matthew is a Jewish Gospel, even in its antipathies, the author of Luke pays more attention to the point of view of Gentile Christians, to which class many, in ancient as well as modern times, think that he himself belonged.

The first part of the Acts of the Apostles tells how the leading disciples of Jesus, Galileans all, shortly after his death established themselves in Jerusalem in expectation of his reappearance from heaven, and tried to convert those who would listen to them to their faith that Jesus was the Messiah of prophecy, by arguing from the Scriptures that its predictions had been fulfilled not only in his life but by his death, and that Daniel's predictions of the coming of the Son of Man to judgment also would presently be fulfilled in him. The interference of the religious authorities with this propaganda, the growth of the movement, and the internal history of the society of believers are the principal subjects of this narrative, in which the historian has used, directly or indirectly, Aramaic sources containing traditions of the church in Jerusalem in those eventful years. It was not a schismatic body; its leaders and the mass of their followers were, aside from their peculiar messianic and eschatological beliefs, observant Jews, as their teacher had been. [2] Some of their Greek-speaking converts, however, were more radical, and there were premonitory symptoms of the new direction which the movement took with Saul of Tarsus, who became Paul the Apostle.

With the Gospels may be mentioned in this connection the "Teaching of the Twelve Apostles" (Didachè). Critics are al-

---

[1] Comm. on Isa. 8, 23. (Vallarsi IV, 129 f.).

[2] See Matt. 5, 17–20. Whether this position is tolerable in Christianity is a point on which Augustine and Jerome disagreed. See Jerome, Ep. 112 ad Augustinum; Augustine to Jerome, ibid., Epp. 56 and 67.

most unanimously agreed that the first part of this little book, the Two Ways (cc. 1–6), is of Jewish origin, perhaps a compend of elementary moral instruction for Gentile converts such as are called God-fearing men (or women).[1] This little manual was early taken over by Christians for the same purpose. The Greek text of the Didachè discovered by Bryennios has an unmistakably Christian passage (1, 3–2, 1)[2] which is not found in the old Latin translation; but otherwise the Two Ways has not been Christianized. The Two Ways often appears in early Christian literature from the so-called Epistle of Barnabas on,[3] while of the rest of the book there is no such evidence, which leads to the conjecture that the Two Ways circulated by itself.[4]

Chapters 7–15 are Christian, representing a very simple type of rites, doctrine, and organization. The separation from the Jews is signalized in the appointment of Wednesday and Friday as the weekly fast days, instead of Monday and Thursday, as is the custom of "the hypocrites." Baptism is into the name of the Father and the Son and the Holy Spirit[5] — which it is an anachronism to read as a trinitarian formula. Relieved of this interpretation, the formula is one in which it is quite unnecessary to suspect the influence of Gentile Christianity. Jewish believers may well have deemed it the most appropriate for the reception of Gentile converts, who confessed their faith in the one true God, the Father, and in his Son, the Messiah, and in the Holy Spirit of inspiration in the society of believers and particularly in their prophets.[6] Baptism into the name of Jesus Christ (the Messiah), or of the Lord Jesus, was sufficient in the

[1] Σεβόμενοι (or φοβούμενοι) τὸν θεόν. Actual proselytes required much more specific instruction in the Law. See, e.g., pp. 331, 333.

[2] Part, even of this, has its closest parallels, not in the Gospels but in Jewish sources (1, 5–6).

[3] Chapters 18–20 (lacking in the single manuscript of the Latin version which ends with c. 17).

[4] It is thought by some that the eschatological close, c. 16, has a Jewish core.

[5] Matt. 28, 19. Cf. Didachè 7, 1 (ταῦτα πάντα προείποντες — namely, the Two Ways), with Matt. 28, 20.

[6] Didachè 11, 7 ff.

case of Jews or Samaritans, who had no need to profess monotheism.[1]

The Christian part of the Didachè shows the hand of an author familiar with Jewish customs and forms. The observance
of two fast days in each week, with the substitution of Wednesday and Friday for Monday and Thursday, has already been
mentioned. So the three daily hours of prayer with the recitation of the prayer "the Lord commanded in the Gospel," [2]
instead of the prayer used by "the hypocrites" (the Tefillah).
Even more conclusive is the character of the liturgical prayers
prescribed for the Eucharist (c. 9), and the Blessing after the
Meal (c. 10). The content is Christian; but they are throughout reminiscent of the Jewish forms of prayer, the place of which
they take. They begin with a substitute for the Ḳiddush,[3] then
for the blessing of the bread, and finally a Birkat ha-Mazon in
three parts, each closing with an ascription, and a conclusion to
the whole.[4]

In what region the Christian community existed which has
left us this picture of itself is a question to which no answer can
pretend to be better than a guess. There is no reason to doubt
that the original language was Greek; not, like the primitive
Gospel or the first part of Acts, Aramaic. Its age can only be
inferred from the rudimentary character of the institutions,
which would incline us to a relatively early date — say, the beginning of the second century; but primitive conditions may
have lasted much longer in outlying places than in the great
centres, and especially in Jewish-Christian communities. Nor is
the date, which is of interest in relation to the development of
Christian doctrine and discipline, of so much importance from
our point of view.

[1] Cf. Didachè 9, 5 (οἱ βαπτισθέντες εἰς ὄνομα κυρίου — condition of admission
to the Eucharist).
[2] The Lord's Prayer as in Matthew, with the doxology, from which "the
kingdom" is omitted.
[3] Therefore the blessing of the cup precedes that of the bread (cf. Luke
22, 17).
[4] See G. Klein, Der älteste Christliche Katechismus (1909), pp. 214 ff.

CHAPTER VII

TESTAMENTS. JUBILEES. SECTARIES AT DAMASCUS

MENTION may properly be made here also of one or two writings which, though exhibiting idiosyncrasies which mark them off from the main line of development, nevertheless in fundamental things are at one with it.

Such is that entitled The Testaments of the Twelve Patriarchs, in which, taking the suggestion from the Blessing of Jacob in Genesis 49, and the Blessing of Moses in Deuteronomy 33, each of the sons of Jacob, when his time comes to die, gathers his descendants about him and delivers to them his parting charge. Drawing a lesson for them from his own life, he dwells particularly on the sin (or sins) into which he had fallen, with the consequences in his case and in general, warns his children against the occasions and temptations which lead men into the like sins, and commends the contrary virtues with the disposition by which they are cultivated. In one or two cases the triumph over temptation (Joseph), or the superiority of the simple life in single-mindedness (Issachar), is the main theme; the patriarch is an illustration of virtue, rather than a warning against vice.

In the exemplification of these moralizings the biblical story is followed so far as it goes, but amplified and supplemented by legendary matter, in which the wars of Jacob and his sons with the kings of the Amorites and with Esau and his army are prominent. These prototypic conflicts, spun out of Gen. 35, 5 and 36, 6, were evidently a favorite subject; we have them in the Book of Jubilees [1] and in the late Midrash Wayissaʻu.[2]

---

[1] Jubilees 34 and 37.
[2] Found in the Yalḳuṭ on Genesis § 133; edited thence by Jellinek, Bet ha-Midrasch, III, 1–5.

The moralizing itself is throughout sound, and frequently on a high plane. Its basis is scriptural, but it shows the same kind of advance beyond its texts, by combination and by interpretation in the light of the higher principles of morality, which is characteristic of the teaching of the Scribes — for example in the repeated coupling of the commandments of love to God and love to fellow man. There is nothing of sectarian eccentricity about it. Noteworthy is the place of repentance, and the conception of it.

The affinity of the Testaments with Jubilees appears not only in the Haggadah but in the prominence of "Beliar" as the name of the chief of a realm of evil. In Beliar's train is a multitude of "deceiving spirits" which tempt and prompt men to particular sins. These spirits have no concrete reality, and are hardly more than personifications of the prompting man feels in himself of lust, covetousness, envy, jealousy, hatred, or what not.[1] It is a kind of analysis of the "evil impulse."[2] It is, however, much more elaborated than in rabbinic sources, in which moreover the name Belial occurs only in biblical contexts.

Besides the moralizing and legendary Haggadah there is another element in the Testaments of which notice must be taken. In almost every one of them there is an exhortation to be loyal to Levi and Judah, to obey them, to love them, honour them, be united to them.[3] Sometimes this is reinforced by a prediction that the tribe will fall away from them with dire consequences. The Testament of Levi narrates as a vision a tour of Levi through the scale of heavens, and in another his investiture there with the pontificals of the high priest, and how his grandfather Isaac taught him the duties of the priesthood. The exhortation he gives his sons (c. 13) to fear the Lord, and instruct their children in the law, and do righteousness, and get wisdom, is a high ideal of the office.

---

[1] See e. g. Test. Reuben 3, 3–6. To call this sort of thing "a vast demonology" (Charles) is a misnomer.

[2] Cf. the δύο διαβούλια, Test. Asher 1, 2.

[3] Levi has regularly the precedence and the emphasis. See e.g. Reuben 5, 8; Judah 21, 4.

By the side of these passages which magnify the priesthood there are, however, others, in predictive form, which match the worst things the Psalms of Solomon have to say about the priesthood in the days of the degenerate Asmonaeans.[1] These pieces seem to be thrust into their context, and are generally attributed to a later author.[2] On the other hand the eschatological closes of some of the Testaments seem to be original, though they have frequently been interpolated or glossed by Christian copyists.

The Testaments have been transmitted to us in Greek and in an Armenian translation from the Greek.[3] The Greek is less palpably a translation than the most, but there are not lacking indications that the original language was Hebrew.

The Testaments were long regarded as a Christian composition. The Christianity of many passages is indeed salient and of others is strongly probable. On the other hand the bulk of the book is *prima facie* Jewish, the morals no less than the legends. Grabe, who first edited the Greek text (1698; 2 ed. 1714), saw in it a Jewish work, interpolated by Christian hands. Evident as this solution seems, it found no favor with following critics, who disagreed only on what kind of Christian the author was; and it is only in recent times that scholars generally have reverted to Grabe's view, a confirmation of which is found in the fact that some of the Christian patches were not in the Greek manuscript from which the Armenian version was made.[4]

Before the Christian interpolators, Jewish hands had made additions to the Testaments, the most striking of which have been mentioned above.

In this state of things, and with the uncertain interpretation of references to historical situations, it is not strange that opinions

[1] See especially Levi 14, 5–16, 5.

[2] A book of Enoch is sometimes cited as the source of these predictions of degeneracy.

[3] Some fragments in Aramaic, and a Testament of Naphtali in Hebrew whose relation to our Greek is very remote, may here be ignored.

[4] On the Armenian version see F. C. Conybeare, in Jewish Quarterly Review, V (1893), 375–398; VIII (1896), 260–268, 471–485.

differ somewhat widely about the age of the original work.[1] The
Asmonaean restoration is the earliest date in this period at
which such enthusiasm for the priesthood of Levi as is manifest
in the Testaments is probable; nor is it likely to have survived
the doings of Alexander Jannaeus and his successors, who corre-
sponded only too well to the character given the degenerate
priests in an addition to the Testament of Levi, chapters 14 and
15. For our purpose greater precision is not essential.

Editions of the Greek text: Robert Sinker, Testamenta XII
Patriarcharum, etc. Cambridge, 1869. (Based on a Cambridge
manuscript, with the readings of an Oxford MS. in foot notes.)
Appendix (containing a collation of the Roman and Patmos
MSS.). Cambridge, 1879. — R. H. Charles, The Greek Versions
of the Testaments of the Twelve Patriarchs edited from nine
MSS., together with the variants of the Armenian and Slavonic
versions and some Hebrew fragments. Oxford, 1908.

Translations: R. H. Charles, The Testaments of the Twelve
Patriarchs. Translated from the Editor's Greek Text . . . with
Introduction, Notes, and Indices. 1908. — F. Schnapp, 'Die
Testamente der zwölf Patriarchen' (in E. Kautzsch, Die Apo-
kryphen und Pseudepigraphen des Alten Testaments, II (1900),
458–506).

The Book of Jubilees, to which a passing reference has been
made, has its name from the chronological scheme in which the
author dates every event from the creation to the eve of the
exodus by Jubilee periods of forty-nine years and their subdivision by sevens: thus the birth of Abram was in the thirty-
ninth Jubilee, in the second week (heptad of years), in the seventh
year of the week.[2] Frequently the exactness is carried out to
the day of the month. With this chronological system goes a
reconstruction of the calendar. Instead of a year of twelve lunar
months rudely adjusted to the solar year by the intercalation,

---

[1] It is generally believed that the Testaments, or parts of them, are related
in some way to the Book of Jubilees; but that work is itself datable only
within rather wide limits.

[2] Jubilees 11, 14 f.

when necessary, of a thirteenth month, the author would have
a solar year of fifty-two weeks (364 days), divided into four quarters of thirteen weeks each, on the first day of each of which a
memorial day was appointed, without regard to the moon, which
disorders all measures of time, getting ten days out of the way
every year.[1] In consequence of the abandonment of this divinely
appointed and revealed system, the festivals and the new moons
were not kept at the proper times; and inasmuch as the time was
of the essence of the observance,[2] this was a grave religious lapse
which was attended by many others. The angel who makes this
revelation to Moses takes pains to affirm that the system is no
innovation: he has it written in a book in his hands, and in the
"heavenly tables" the division of days is ordained, "lest they
forget the feasts of the covenant and walk according to the feasts
of the Gentiles after their error and their ignorance." [3]

The same kind of a solar year of 364 days [4] is defined in a description of the movements of the sun and the stars, and of the
moon, that has come down to us in the Ethiopic Book of Enoch
(cc. 72–75; 78), and was doubtless meant to be taken for the
astronomical observations of that explorer of the heavens.[5]

Into this eccentric calendar system it is unnecessary to enter
here. The motive for it was probably not the mere charm of
symmetry, but the desire to create a distinctively Jewish division of time fundamentally unlike those of other peoples, and
particularly that of the Greeks.[5] In the reaction against Hellenism in the second century such a motive is intelligible enough,

[1] Twelve lunations occur in 354 days; the intercalary year has 384 days.
See Jubilees 6, 29–38. In the author's scheme there would be eight months
of thirty days each, and four (presumably the first month of each season) of
thirty-one days, or — what comes to the same thing — twelve months of
thirty days, and an unnumbered day at the beginning of each season (Enoch
75, 1).

[2] See also 49, 14 f.

[3] Jubilees 6, 35.

[4] Enoch 74, 10–12; 75, 2. For the lunar year cf. 74, 13–16; 78, 9, 15 f.

[5] See Enoch 76, 14; 82, 1–8.

[6] See Jubilees 6, 35. The author of Enoch seems to be acquainted with
the eight-year cycle of intercalation (Octaeteris); see 34, 13–16.

and the end to be achieved may well have seemed of sufficient moment to outweigh the inconveniences of a year that was a day and more shorter than a mean solar year, especially as the consequences would become serious only by accumulation.[1] There is no indication that an attempt was ever made to get this calendar into use, nor that it was a party issue as the reckoning of the Feast of Weeks (Pentecost) was between the Pharisees and the Sadducees.

The Book of Jubilees may be described as a Midrash on Genesis and the first twelve chapters of Exodus, but it is peculiar in being the work of one author, composed on a preconceived plan and with a definite purpose. It presents itself as a revelation made to Moses on Mt. Sinai, where "the angel of the presence who went before the hosts of Israel," at God's command, with the heavenly chronological tables in his hands, dictated to Moses the history from the beginning (including even Moses' own biography) from the point of view of an angelic eyewitness and participant.

One of the chief ends of the author was to carry back the origins of the distinctive observances of Judaism to a remote antiquity and to connect them with epochs in the history of the patriarchs or of Noah and the antediluvians, and that not merely as ancestral customs but as laws then and there delivered by God for all future time. For this there were precedents in the Pentateuch in particular cases, such as the law against eating flesh with blood in it given to Noah and the law of circumcision given to Abraham. Later rabbis could not imagine the pious patriarchs otherwise than as knowing and keeping the whole personal and domestic law, even to its rabbinical refinements, when there was as yet no written law. But whatever anticipations of this kind there were, the Law in its completeness and

---

[1] Biblical authority for a solar year of 364 days (twelve lunar months plus ten days) may have been found in the narrative of the flood in Genesis, as was acutely conjectured by B. W. Bacon in Hebraica, VIII (1891–92), 79–88; 124–139; Charles, The Book of Jubilees (1902), p. 55.

finality was given by Moses. The festivals — Passover, Un-
leavened Bread, Tabernacles — were memorials of events in the
history of the escape from Egypt; the designation of Levi as the
priestly tribe was made after the exodus, and the whole sacrificial system and ritual was instituted only after the erection of
the tabernacle and the installation of Aaron and his sons.

According to Jubilees, on the contrary, the Feast of Weeks
was first kept on earth by Noah [1] in commemoration of the eternal covenant God made that there should not again be a flood
on the earth.[2] It fell into desuetude after Noah's death, but
was observed by Abraham [3] and his descendants down to the
generation of Moses, when it was again forgotten till it was re-
established at Sinai as is prescribed in "the first law" (Pentateuch). Tabernacles was first celebrated on earth by Abraham
for seven days.[4] Jacob kept it at Bethel, and added the eighth
day.[5] On this occasion Levi was invested with the priesthood,
and the laws of tithing were given.[6] The ritual of these festivals is described in much detail, even to the recipe for the
compound incense burnt by Abraham (16, 24), following in general the laws in the Pentateuch, but with some features of later
observance not found in Scripture, such as the procession around
the altar at Tabernacles (16, 31), and some which are not mentioned in Tannaite sources.

The occasion for the introduction of many laws is given: for
example, purification after childbirth in the days of the first
parents (3, 8–14); the laws against incest after the crime of
Reuben (33, 10–20), repeated in fuller form in connection with
Judah's sin with Tamar (41, 25 f.).[7]

---

[1] It had been celebrated in heaven from the creation till the days of Noah,
Jubilees 6, 18.
[2] Ibid. 6, 16 f.
[3] Ibid. 6, 19; 14, 20; 15, 1 f.; 22, 1–5.
[4] Jubilees 16, 20–31.
[5] Ibid. 32, 4–7, 27–29.
[6] Ibid. 32, 8–15.
[7] For an enumeration see Charles, Book of Jubilees, Introduction, pp.
lii–liii.

The author speaks of books of the forefathers (Enoch, Noah, 21, 10) handed down from father to son, as from Noah to Shem, from Jacob to Levi (10, 13 f.; 45, 16). The laws are preëstablished in the heavenly tablets, or recorded in them; these tablets contain predictions also.[1] Authority is thus occasionally given to the peculiar rules of the book (Halakah).

The Book of Jubilees sometimes follows the biblical narrative very closely, and in other places embroiders upon it freely. Much of this legendary embellishment was probably drawn from a common fund of Haggadah, but the selection from it as well as what seems to be the author's own contribution to the story is apposite to his purpose. He passes over incidents in Genesis which put the patriarchs in an unfavorable light,[2] and makes slight omissions or changes in the narrative with the same motive. Similarly he makes Mastema (his name for Satan) responsible for things that might seem to reflect on the character of God, after the example of the Chronicler in the case of David's census.[3]

Great emphasis is laid in Jubilees on the separation of Jews from Gentiles. Israel alone was chosen by God to be His people. The many nations and peoples indeed all belong to Him, "and over them He gave spirits power, that they might lead them to go astray from following Him. But over Israel He did not appoint any angel or spirit, for He alone is their ruler," etc. (15, 31 f.). Abraham in his dying charge enjoins on Jacob: "Separate thyself from the nations, and do not eat with them, and do not do as they do, and do not be their associate; for their work is uncleanness and their ways defilement," etc. (22, 16–18). Above all, intermarriage with them is stringently forbidden under pain of death (30, 7–17);[4] a man who causes his daughter to be thus defiled has given of his seed to Moloch.[5] Peculiar enmity is manifested toward the Philistines, the Edomites, and

---

[1] See Charles on Jubilees 3, 10, note.
[2] For which there was especial need in the story of Jacob.
[3] Cf. 2 Sam. 24, 1 with 1 Chron. 21, 1.
[4] See also 22, 20; 25, 9.
[5] Lev. 18, 21. See the Palestinian Targum on this verse.

the Amorites — names suitable enough to the assumed situation, but under which are to be recognized the peoples against whom the Jews in the author's time had the best grounds for hostility.

The sacramental observances of Judaism, if the word may be allowed, are circumcision and the sabbath, which are shared with the two highest orders of angels. Both belong to Israel alone.[1] The violation of these ordinances is rank apostasy and entails the supreme penalty by the hand of man and of God.

What is said about the omission or the obliteration of circumcision (15, 33 f.) evidently refers to conditions such as are described in 1 Macc. 1, 13 f.; 2 Macc. 4, 9–14.[2] The neglect of parents to circumcise their children perhaps accounts for the insistence of the author that the rite must be performed without exception on the eighth day (15, 12, 14, 25 f.),[3] as reaction from the neglect or lax observance of the sabbath may explain the unparalleled stringency of his application of that law (50, 6–13). In opposition to the opinion of the hellenizers that the law was antiquated, and the time had come to modernize it, if not to abandon it, and be like other civilized people, he unweariedly reiterates that the law is divine in origin and authority, and will continue unchangeable to the end of the present order of things.

The Judaism of the book is unimpeachable. It glorifies the Law, as the revelation in parts on earth of the Law that was inscribed on the heavenly tables before the creation of the world, and was, as we have just seen, to endure unchanged to the end. Compromise with the ways of the heathen, intermarriage with them, even commensality, are apostasy, and call down the wrath of God not only on individual offenders but on the nation. The interpretation of the biblical laws and the expansion and application of them are in cases of difference stricter than the corresponding Halakah of the Mishnah and contemporary works,

---

[1] On the exclusiveness of the Sabbath see Jubilees 2, 31.

[2] Cf. 2, 45. On the king's prohibition, 1, 48, 60; 2, 46.

[3] This is, however, the literal law in Scripture. It is unnecessary to suppose that he is controverting the opinion that in certain circumstances the rite might be postponed one or two days.

the others; but fundamental rules are given on forbidden kinds of food ("dietary laws"), uncleanness and purifications, oaths, judicial and private, judges, witnesses and testimony, vows, things lost and found, communal charities, dealings with Gentiles, etc.

Among the obligations assumed by those who entered into the new covenant in the land of Damascus, were, "to set apart the sacred dues as they are prescribed, and that a man should love his neighbor as himself, and sustain the poor and needy and the proselyte, and seek each the welfare of his brother; that no man transgress the prohibited degrees, but guard against fornication according to the rule; and that a man should reprove his brother according to the commandment, and not bear a grudge from one day to another; and to separate from all kinds of uncleanness according to their several prescriptions; and that a man should not defile his holy spirit, even as God separated for them (between clean and unclean)." The opposite vices are often held up as the cause of divine wrath and ruin. Wandering in the devices of a sinful imagination and adulterous eyes destroyed great men, caused the fall of the Watchers of heaven (Gen. 6, 4), and brought the great flood.

A minute examination of the legal rules in the book in comparison with the standard Halakah as it is in the Tannaite sources proves that, except in relation to the lawfulness of certain marriages to which we shall return below, the differences between them, taken singly, are not wider than existed between great legal lights in the first and second centuries.[1] In general the covenanters are stricter than the later rabbis; but not so liberal with the death penalty as the Book of Jubilees. Their affinities are throughout with the Pharisees, not with any other variety of Judaism.

The two points of striking diversity are, first, that the sect brands as incest the marriage of a man with his niece (daughter

---

[1] Such an investigation by a most competent authority in the Halakah is made in Professor Louis Ginzberg's Eine unbekannte jüdische Sekte, 1922.

of his brother or sister), which is not so classed in the biblical law, and by the rabbinical authorities was regarded as legitimate and even given a preference; [1] and second, that it condemns bigamy as adultery. The former of these prohibitions is derived by analogy from the biblical prohibition of such a union between aunt and nephew.[2] Bigamy was prohibited, according to their interpretation, by Lev. 18, 18.[3] They support this by Gen. 1, 27, 'a male and a female created He them,' and 7, 9, 'by pairs they went into the ark'; also by the law that the prince shall not multiply wives (have more than one wife at a time), Deut. 17, 17.

This condemnation of polygamy, like that of the marriage of uncle and niece, is not to be attributed to what are called moral considerations, but to a peculiar exegesis of the biblical laws in question. The violence of the language in which those with whom their interpretation conflicted are assailed shows that the controversy on these points was most acute.

What is more important than particular differences is that the whole method, both of the halakic interpretation of the laws and the midrashic use of the Law and the Prophets, is of the same kind with which we are familiar in Tannaite literature. And more important still is the fact that the sect had an authoritative body of Halakah, topically arranged, and formulated with a precision which reveals experience. From the nature and purpose of the writing before us, which is a warning and exhortation to the members of the sect, it may be inferred, as has been said, that only a selection of this Halakah is presented; the *Sefer he-Hago*, by which the officials, judges, and priests were to be guided, was presumably much more extensive — "a sectarian Mishnah." [4]

---

[1] Yebamot 62b–63a; Sanhedrin 76b.   See Maimonides, Issurè Bi'ah 2, 14. For cases of such marriages among the Tannaim see Ginzberg, Eine unbekannte jüdische Sekte, p. 182 n. 2.

[2] Lev. 18, 12.

[3] "Thou shalt not take one wife to another . . . in her (the first wife's) lifetime." On the reasoning in this interpretation see Ginzberg, op. cit., pp. 24 ff., and on the whole question, pp. 181 ff. The inference that they allowed no divorce is erroneous.   [4] Ibid., pp. 70 f.

A further fact of no little significance is that this organized Halakah was committed to writing not only in a book for the use of the authorities of the community, but in part at least for the people at large. Nor is there any reason to think that this was a sectarian innovation.

Professor Ginzberg has shown that the affinity of the legal element of the document to the Halakah of the Pharisees extends also to its theological position, which is in the main in accord with their teachings, with differences chiefly attributable to sectarian narrowness.[1]

The book has certain resemblances to the Book of Jubilees and the Testaments of the Twelve Patriarchs. The former is cited by its title, The Book of the Divisions of the Times according to the Jubilee Periods and their Weeks. The "three nets of Belial of which Levi the son of Jacob spoke, with which he (Belial) caught Israel" is generally thought to be a reference to the Testament of Levi, though the quotation is not found in the Testament as we have it. It is quite possible, however, that some other moralizings of Levi are cited. Whether the resemblances signify anything more than proximity in time and environment — whether, in other words, there is a literary dependence of one on another — is not certain. The citation of Jubilees is apparently to say that an exact explanation of the world-periods is to be found in that work, presumably in reference to a computation of the end; but this is apropos of nothing in the context, and is not further developed.[2] It is possible, but not self-evident, that when God "revealed to them the secrets wherein all Israel went astray, his holy sabbaths and his glorious festivals, and his righteous testimonies, and his true way, and the pleasure of his will — things which if a man do he shall live by them," the repristinated calendar of Jubilees is included; but the author at least shows no zeal about it.

---

[1] Eine unbekannte jüdische Sekte, p. 299.
[2] Ginzberg, op. cit., p. 134, suspects an unintelligent gloss to the preceding words.

The age of the migration to Damascus and the organization of the seceding community there is a point in dispute. Several of the early investigators thought of the hellenizing high priests and the vengeance inflicted by "the head of the Greek kings," which is the last event in the national history that seems to be clearly alluded to. Eduard Meyer has more recently argued strongly for a date about 170 B.C.,[1] laying some stress on the fact that there is no sign in the book of the desecration of the temple and the Maccabaean wars, nor of the Book of Daniel. Since he thinks that the author knew the Testaments and made much use of Jubilees, he accordingly puts both these writings back into the third century. Ginzberg, on the other hand, dates the origin of the movement under Alexander Jannaeus, during whose conflicts with the Pharisees its adherents sought refuge in the region of Damascus, where they developed into an intransigent sect which would have nothing to do with the moderate Pharisees in Judaea. Jubilees and the Testaments (in their original form) are now put by most critics shortly before the breach between the Asmonaeans and the Pharisees.

The stage of halakic development attested in our document is a consideration of some weight in favor of the later date of which due account must be made.

The Apocalypses — Enoch, the Syriac Baruch, Fourth Esdras, and minor works of the class — will be discussed in Part VII.

[1] 'Die Gemeinde des Neuen Bundes im Lande Damaskus, eine jüdische Schrift aus der Seleucidenzeit.' Abhandlungen der Preussischen Akademie der Wissenschaften, 1919.

CHAPTER VIII

HISTORICAL SOURCES

It remains here briefly to enumerate works on Jewish history in biblical times and later, or on the religion of the Jews.

For the history of the Maccabaean rising and the achievment of autonomy down to the death of Simon and the accession of John Hyrcanus (135 B.C.), a period of about forty years, the First Book of Maccabees is the primary source.[1] The book, which is extant only in Greek and translations from the Greek, was written in Hebrew after Old Testament models. The author was a Palestinian Jew, a partisan of the Asmonaeans who had come to the rescue of their imperilled religion and delivered their people from the dominion of the heathen, and he tells the story accordingly. It is told in a straightforward way, with frequent dates of the Seleucid era, and makes the impression of being the work of a well-informed man who stood near the events and the actors in the history he narrates. It may be probably dated in the last quarter of the second century before our era.

Loyalty to their God and the institutions of their people was the mainspring of the revolt. The author's heroes and their followers were zealous for the observance and enforcement of the laws prohibiting worship of other gods and all idolatry, and those prescribing circumcision and the sabbath and the sabbatical year; they execute ruthlessly the stern Deuteronomic law on the apostates. They manifest throughout a firm confidence in the power and purpose of God and in his will to deliver those who put their trust in him, and they fortify their faith by biblical examples from the ancient history down to the stories in the Book

[1] Many scholars since Whiston think that chapters 14–16 (or 14, 15–16, 23) are an addition to the original work, unknown to Josephus; but in view of Josephus' habits of compilation the inference is unsafe.

of Daniel; but this faith is in a God who helps those that help themselves. There is no expectation of miraculous intervention as distinguished from providential support, and no hint of anything resembling miracle. Nor is there any trace of the religious pragmatism that is so strongly impressed on Kings and Chronicles. There is no appeal to prophecies of deliverance and the future greatness and glory of the Jewish people. In contrast to 2 Maccabees, there is no suggestion of a life beyond death. For God, the author regularly says Heaven, or employs a pronoun the reference of which is self-evident.

Second Maccabees is an abridgment of a larger work in five books by an otherwise unknown Jason of Cyrene, written in a turgid rhetorical Greek. Prefixed to the book are two letters (1, 1–2, 18) from Jerusalem Jews to their brethren in Egypt, which may be left out of consideration here. The epitomator's preface occupies 2, 19–32; with 3, 1, the history begins.

The period covered is much shorter than that in 1 Maccabees, ending with the victory of Judas over Nicanor in 161, at the culminating moment of Judas's career. On the other hand the events which led up to the revolt, the intrigues and bribery by which Jason and Menelaus got themselves into the high priesthood, about which 1 Maccabees has not a word,[1] are narrated at some length, glossing nothing of the scandal.

In striking contrast to First Maccabees, the second book, not only freely employs the common Old Testament names and titles of God, but abounds in descriptive epithets and phrases, some of which come from the Old Testament, others occur only in the later Jewish literature, or seem to be original with the author. God is the Most High, whose abode is in heaven; he is the Almighty, the King of Kings, the Creator of the World, the Great Lord of the World, the Master of Life and the Spirit, the

---

[1] 1 Macc. makes the movement for Hellenization proceed from some Jewish "sons of Belial," but names no names. Perhaps regard for the honor of his people may have stayed his hand rather than particular reverence for the priesthood.

All-Seeing One, the Just Judge, the Merciful God, the Lord of
Spirits (3, 24). Angelic apparitions and miraculous interventions are frequent. The most striking instance is the physical
intervention of the splendid horseman and his two satellites who
defeat Heliodorus' purpose to seize the temple treasure; others
are the apparition of the mounted angel in white garments with
golden weapons who leads Judas and his army in the battle with
Lysias (11, 8, 10), and the five celestial horsemen who put themselves at the head of the Jews in 10, 29. The theological pragmatism of the history is well-defined in 5, 17 ff.: The Lord for a
short while was angry with the city because of the sins of its inhabitants, and for this cause permitted Antiochus to work his
will upon it; after the Mighty Ruler was reconciled, it was exalted again with glory.[1]

Moralizing reflections, grounded on this doctrine, are common, as for example, 4, 16 ff.[2] In individual cases the author is
fond of pointing out how the divine retribution overtakes sinners
in kind.[3] These edifying comments on the ways of God give occasion to exhibit a rhetorical pathos which smacks of the Greek
schools rather than of the Old Testament precedents; examples
of this pathos in different associations are also found, e. g., 4, 47;
3, 15–21, etc.

The confident belief in a restoration of life after death is the
sustaining hope of the martyrs in chap. 7, in the form of a restoration of the tortured and mutilated bodies of the victims; see
also 14, 45 f. For Antiochus and such as he there is no resurrection to life.[4] Judas offers prayers and has expiatory sacrifices
offered in the temple for some of his men who were killed in
battle and were found to be wearing heathen amulets under their
shirts; and the author adds that herein he did well, having regard to the resurrection: "For had he not expected that those
who had fallen would rise from the dead, it would have been idle

[1] See also 6, 12–17.   [2] See further 5, 6, 17 ff.; 6, 12 f.; 12, 43.
[3] See 9, 5–10; 13, 4–8, etc.
[4] 7, 17 might seem to imply a conscious existence for the tyrant after
death, but perhaps should not be pressed so hard.

and foolish to pray for dead men; and he reflected further that for those who sleep in piety the fairest reward is laid up — a holy and pious thought. Therefore he made this expiation for the dead, that they might be relieved from their sin " (12, 38–45).

Jason plainly wrote at a distance from the scene of the struggle he relates, but it cannot safely be inferred from the miraculous element in the story that it was composed long after the events. In a favorable environment the growth of legend may begin with the earliest reports of what happened. How long a time elapsed between Jason and the epitomator can only be conjectured. For our purpose it is enough that the book as we have it probably comes from the first century before our era.

It is very instructive that 2 Maccabees, and the work of Jason of Cyrene which it epitomizes, though coming from Grecian Jewry, has a closer resemblance to popular Palestinian Judaism than appears in First Maccabees, which was written in Palestine and in Hebrew. Especially noteworthy is the prominence of the life after death as a bodily life,[1] and the denial of such a hereafter to the tyrant. The difference between this and the Hellenistic conception in the Wisdom of Solomon, and especially from the use of the same martyr stories in Fourth Maccabees, on the one hand, and the complete Pharisaean doctrine on the other, is evident.

For the history of the war of 66 to 72 and its immediate antecedents Josephus writes as an eye-witness and participant in the events he narrates, or of things at least within his memory.[2] He begins, however, much farther back, with the taking of Jerusalem by Antiochus Epiphanes and the desecration of the temple in 168 B.C., and for a period of more than two centuries he was evidently dependent on preceding historians. First Maccabees is the only recognizable Jewish source,[3] and Josephus seems

---

[1] Apparently entered on by the martyrs at once, not (as in Daniel) at the great assize.

[2] Titus Flavius Josephus, Bell. Jud. ii. 13, 1 ff. Vita.

[3] Bell. Jud. i. 1, 1–i. 2, 4.

not to have used this directly but to have taken the very summary account of the struggle as he found it in the comprehensive historical work which he made his principal authority.[1]

The treatment of Herod's reign points to a Greek historian who was not only well informed about the events of the reign but had the knowledge which enabled him to correlate them with the political history of the times. The general opinion of critics identifies this historian with Nicolaus of Damascus, in whom these conditions are completely fulfilled. Nicolaus lived for many years at the court and in the confidence of Herod, and was repeatedly employed by the king in public affairs; he was the author of a universal history, in the writing of which he was encouraged by Herod. Whether Josephus, in the War, drew directly on the work of Nicolaus,[2] or through an intermediate source,[3] is not essential to our inquiry. In either case Josephus has evidently abridged his source for his own purpose.

It is a fair presumption that he used the same source for the preceding period, from the Maccabaean rising on, and this is confirmed by internal evidence of the unity of the narrative and its consistent point of view, which is that of an outsider not at all prepossessed in favor of the Jews, and particularly not of the Pharisees.[4] The famous passage in the second book of the Jewish War,[5] in which the three Jewish philosophies are classified by their attitude to the problem of fate ($\epsilon i\mu\alpha\rho\mu\epsilon\nu\eta$), is most probably ultimately from the same non-Jewish source.[6]

The problem of the sources in the corresponding part of the Antiquities is more complicated.[7] The later work not infrequently differs materially from the earlier, and it is evident that Josephus employed other sources, in particular a Jewish author

---

[1] Compare the ampler narrative in Antt. xii. 5–xiii, 7.

[2] So most recently Hölscher, in the article 'Josephus' in the Real-Encyclopädie der classischen Altertumswissenschaft, IX (1916), col. 1943 ff.

[3] W. Otto, art. 'Herodes,' ibid., Supplement, II, 1 ff. (to vol. VIII).

[4] See above, pp. 64–66.　　　[5] Bell. Jud. viii. 8, cf. Antt. xiii. 5, 9.

[6] The long description of the Essenes is a question for itself.

[7] Beginning with xii. 5. The War was written between the years 75 and 79; the Antiquities was finished in 93–94.

(or authors) strongly hostile to Herod. In the history of the Asmonaeans there is a Jewish strand which sympathizes with the nobles who supported Alexander Jannaeus, and does not like the Pharisees much better than did Nicolaus. In consequence of Josephus' easy-going way in the compilation of his work, there are many inconsistencies which he either made no attempt to harmonize or an ineffective one.

For the religion of his times Josephus is a somewhat disappointing source. As he tells us in his autobiography, he experimented with all three of the sects, and with a solitary in the desert besides, and finally addicted himself to the Pharisees. He professes also, before this perambulation, and while still very young, to have acquired an extraordinary reputation for legal learning. And he was a member of one of the great priestly families. It would not be unreasonable to expect to learn of him much about the religion of his times, especially in the Antiquities where he takes us over the Old Testament history and describes the Mosaic legislation.[1] It is true that he writes to display to Gentile readers the antiquity and excellence of the Jewish people and its institutions, and is naturally guided by this intention;[2] yet it is a striking fact that, if we were dependent on the works of Josephus alone, we should know very little about the religion of his contemporaries. In illustration it may be noted that of so important an institution as the synagogue there is no mention; the word itself occurs, if I am not in error, only of a building in Antioch in which was deposited by later Syrian kings some of the plunder of the temple carried off by Antiochus IV.[3]

It may, I think, be fairly inferred that Josephus, like most of the aristocratic priesthood to which he belonged, had little interest in religion for its own sake, and that his natural antipathy to all excess of zeal was deepened by the catastrophe which religious fanatics had brought upon his people.

[1] Whether the paraphrase of the laws is Josephus' own, or was taken with much else from some Alexandrian predecessor, does not affect the point.

[2] Cf. Contra Apionem ii, 16 ff., especially §§ 164 ff.

[3] Bell. Jud. vii. 3, 3.

With Philo the case is quite the reverse; his dominant interest is in Judaism as a religion. He was of a family of high standing in Alexandria. A brother of Philo had filled an important post in the excise; his son, Philo's nephew, Tiberius Alexander, who abandoned the religion of his fathers, rose in the Roman service to be procurator of Judaea under Claudius, and was made Governor of Egypt by Nero, where he sternly repressed a tumult of the Jews on the eve of the rebellion in Palestine. During the siege of Jerusalem he was on the staff of Titus as *praefectus castrorum*. Philo himself was the head of the delegation of Alexandrian Jews to protest to the emperor Caligula against the wrongs they suffered under the administration of Flaccus.[1] Such diversion from his philosophical pursuits into political affairs, however necessary, was regretted as a grave misfortune; he thanks God that he was not wholly submerged in them.[2]

Philo had had a broad and thorough education according to the encyclical scheme of studies followed in the Greek schools, embracing Grammar (including History and Literature), Arithmetic, Geometry, Astronomy, Music, and Rhetoric.[3] With this preparation he went on to the study of philosophy in its three branches, Physics, Ethics, and Logic,[4] and attained an extensive rather than profound acquaintance with Greek philosophical learning. Like most of his contemporaries, and probably like his teachers, he was an eclectic, taking good things where he found them, so that the result is a congeries of opinions, not a close-knit system. If we had to give his own philosophy a name, we should label it a Stoicizing Platonism with a penchant for Pythagorean number-jugglery. But we should have to add that

[1] This visit to Rome in the year 40 is the one fixed date in his life. He has given his own account of it in the Legatio ad Gaium.

[2] De spec. legibus iii. 1 (ed. Mangey II, 299 f.).

[3] On the necessity of these preparatory disciplines (propaedeutic) he peatedly insists; see De Cherubim c. 30 (Mangey I, 157 f.); De agricul. Noe cc. 3-4 (Mangey I, 302 f.); De congressu, cc. 3, 4, 14, 25, 26 (Mangey I, 520 f., 529 f., 539-541).

[4] The Stoic division. De agricultura, l. c.

adaptability to Jewish theology enters as a factor of choice into his personal eclecticism.

Of his Jewish education he tells us nothing. Yet, apart from his frequent references to the interpretations of others, it is constantly evident that he has at his command a wealth of such material accumulated by his predecessors or contemporaries. How much of this he acquired from the discourses in the synagogues of which he speaks in laudatory terms, how much he may have got from earlier writers on similar subjects, there is no means of knowing; but in either case the most natural supposition is that the discourses or the writings came out of the study of the Scriptures in Alexandrian schools of the Law, and that Philo himself had been a student, and was perhaps a teacher, in such a school.

Philo set himself to prove that between sound philosophy and revealed religion there is complete accord — they are two ways of expressing the one divine truth. With his philosophical theology and the methods by which he discovers and verifies it we are not here concerned. Neither his conception of a transcendent God, nor the secondary god, the Logos, by which he bridges the gulf he has created between pure Being and the phenomenal world, and between God so conceived and man, had any effect on the theology of Palestinian Judaism. His summary of the biblical doctrine of God as he derives it from the first chapter of Genesis in five propositions, the Existence of God, the Unity of God, the Creation of the World, the Unity of the World, the Providence of God,[1] is framed in explicit antithesis to as many false doctrines of Greek philosophical schools.[2] The articles themselves are the belief of all Jews; Palestinian Judaism had to combat some of the same errors in popular form, but never felt the need of such a formulation of the items of true doctrine.

We may therefore pass over Philo's philosophy of religion, which he no doubt valued most highly of all his work. His importance for an inquiry such as ours lies in the fact that he was

[1] De opificio mundi c. 61 (ed. Mangey I, 41).
[2] Skeptics, Peripatetics, Stoics, Epicureans.

the first to undertake a complete exposition of Judaism from the point of view of a man who had abundant observation of other religions and a wide acquaintance with the religious and ethical aspects of contemporary philosophy. That he employs the comparative method which thus imposed itself in the full conviction of the intrinsic excellence and the immeasurable superiority of Judaism, and exhibits it in its self-evidence to Jews and Greeks, does not diminish the value of his work.

This series of writings is introduced by the Life of Moses, the lawgiver; followed by the treatise on the Decalogue, subsuming under each of the Ten Commandments the positive and negative obligations expressed or implied in it in a fashion similar to Christian catechisms in later times. Then, in a corresponding distribution, he takes up in detail the specific laws in the Pentateuch in four books;[1] supplemented by a book on the Virtues in which (as in the last chapters of Book iv, *De iustitia*) he groups precepts which could not so well be brought under any one of the Ten Commandments. This book seems not to have reached us complete; a lost section on Piety (εὐσέβεια) once preceded that on Philanthropy.[2] The remaining subtitles are *De fortitudine*, *De humanitate*, *De nobilitate*.[3] To this again is appended a book on Rewards and Punishments, closing with the comminations in Lev. 26 and Deut. 28 (*De exsecrationibus*).

In the treatment of the moral precepts of the Law, and especially in the book on the Virtues, the influence of Greek, particularly Stoic, ethics is obvious. On the other hand, the allegorical interpretation so prominent in the other works of Philo plays here a relatively insignificant part.

The method is unlike either that of the Tannaite Midrash or of the organized Halakah in the Mishnah. One striking differ-

---

[1] De specialibus legibus, i–iv (ed. Mangey II, 210–374). The parts of these books have in the manuscripts and editions separate titles taken from the subjects treated in them, by which they are frequently cited.

[2] The two great commandments. See De humanitate c. 1 § 51 (ed. Mangey I, 383). See Cohn-Wendland, V, pp. xxvi f., and p. 266.

[3] περὶ ἀνδρείας, περὶ φιλανθρωπίας, περὶ εὐγενείας.

ence is that Philo does not rest the obligation of conformity to
the law on the authority of revelation, but endeavors to find a
rational and moral excellence in the individual prescriptions
which commends them to intelligence and conscience. Another
is that he makes no place for tradition beside exegesis, nor for
the enactments or the precautionary rules of the Scribes — the
oral law. The unwritten law is for him the Stoic law of nature.[1]
In particulars he is often in agreement with Tannaite Halakah,
often at variance with it.[2] No small part of these differences are
attributable to the fact that Philo operated exclusively with the
Greek translation of the Pentateuch.

In what relation the Alexandrian Jews stood to the Palestinian
schools in his day and before it, is not known. Nor would it be
safe to infer, as is sometimes done, that Philo is a representative
of Alexandrian Jewry as a whole. It is probable that there was
a more or less steady and considerable influx of Jews from Palestine, and there may have been as wide differences between the
newcomers and those whose ancestors had been in Egypt for
generations as we see under similar circumstances in modern
cities.

Philo's digest of the laws had no discoverable influence on the
rabbinical law; but it is of great interest in itself, and frequently
offers instructive parallels.

[1] Another noteworthy feature of Philo's exposition is that he so seldom
looks outside the Pentateuch, even for illustration. The abundance of
apposite citation from the Prophets and the Psalms in the Tannaite Midrash
has no counterpart in Philo, even when the quotation would seem almost to
force itself on the attention.

[2] See B. Ritter, Philo und die Halacha, and the notes to the "Einzel-
gesetze" in the German translation edited by L. Cohn, Die Werke Philos von
Alexandria, II (1910).

AIDS TO THE USE OF THE SOURCES [1]

1. *Rabbinical Sources:*

J. Winter und Aug. Wünsche, Geschichte der jüdisch-helleni-
stischen und talmudischen Litteratur. Vol. I. 1894. Pp. 696.
A description of the various sources with selected extracts from
each in translation, whence the sub-title, "Eine Anthologie für
Schule und Haus." "Litteraturnachweise," pp. 692–696.

W. Bacher, Die Agada der Tannaiten.[2] 2 vols. I, Von Hillel
bis Akiba. Von 30 vor bis 135 nach der gew. Zeitrechnung.
1884, 2 ed. 1903. II, Von Akiba's Tod bis zum Abschluss der
Mischna. (135 bis 220 nach der gew. Zeitrechnung.) 1890.
In chronological order, with brief biographical notices. The
teachings of the several masters are arranged under appropriate
topics, with notes on the text, the attribution, parallels, etc.,
making a critical and exegetical commentary of the highest value
to the student. The author reserved the anonymous Haggadah
for separate treatment; but the carrying out of the plan was
prevented by his death. Indexes of the Tannaim and of the
Amoraim quoted are given in each volume, and a subject index
to both at the end of vol. II — the latter, unfortunately, in a
very inconvenient form. The student who actually works his
way through these two volumes will acquire a knowledge of the
authentic religious and moral teaching of the period which he
could get in no other way.

W. Bacher, Die Agada der palästinensischen Amoräer. 3 vols.
1892–1899. The first volume, from the close of the Mishnah to
the death of R. Johanan (279 A.D.), includes the great homilists
of the third century.

H. Strack und P. Billerbeck, Kommentar zum Neuen Testament aus Talmud und Midrasch. I (1922), Das Evangelium
nach Matthäus. Pp. 1055; II (1924), Das Evangelium nach
Markus, Lukas und Johannes, und die Apostelgeschichte. Pp.
867; III (1926), Die Briefe des Neuen Testaments und die Offen-
barung Johannis. Pp. 857. Volume IV, containing excursuses, detached notes, and indexes, is to follow. An immense collection
of parallels and illustrations from all parts of the rabbinical literature, in trustworthy translation, with the necessary introduc-

---

[1] Those which are of use only to the advanced scholar are not included.

[2] "Agada" (Haggadah) includes all teaching that is not legal in character.

tions and explanations. The itemized index of subjects in Vol.
II, which will be followed by fuller indexes in vol. IV, makes it
possible to use the volumes not only as a commentary on New
Testament passages in their relation to Judaism but as a con-
spectus of Jewish teaching on various topics.

2. *Apocrypha and Pseudepigrapha:*

R. H. Charles, editor. The Apocrypha and Pseudepigrapha of
the Old Testament in English, with introductions and critical
and explanatory notes to the several books. In conjunction with
many scholars. 2 vols. 4° 1913. (I Apocrypha, II Pseudepigrapha.) The most comprehensive undertaking of the kind, and
the only one in English. On some of the books, as on Tobit and
Sirach, the critical notes on the text are very full. The comprehensive index at the end of the second volume is worthy of
especial notice.

E. Kautzsch, editor. Die Apokryphen und Pseudepigraphen
des Alten Testaments. With the coöperation of numerous
scholars. 2 vols. 1900. A similar enterprise in German; less inclusive, on a smaller scale, and in less luxurious form.

Translations of particular books and commentaries on them
are mentioned in connection with the books.

On the Apocrypha as a whole the commentary of Fritzsche
and Grimm has not been superseded: Kurzgefasstes exegetisches
Handbuch zu den Apokryphen des Alten Testamentes, 1851–
1860.

The only critical edition of the Greek text of the Apocrypha,
with apparatus is O. F. Fritzsche, Libri apocryphi Veteris Testamenti graece. 1871.[1]

It is not superfluous to note that Swete's Old Testament in
Greek is not such an edition, and was not intended to be. It
gives accurately the text of the Vatican codex 1209 (B), with the
variants of certain other uncial manuscripts, and this text and
apparatus is, especially in some of the Apocrypha, altogether inadequate.

[1] It includes the Psalms of Solomon, the Latin of 4 Esdras, a Latin translation of the Syriac Apocalypse of Baruch, and the Assumption of Moses
With an index of names, and of Greek words.

PART I

REVEALED RELIGION

CHAPTER I

NATIONALITY AND UNIVERSALITY

To understand what Judaism was at the beginning of the Christian era it is necessary to bear in mind the twofold character of nationality and universality which had been inseparably impressed upon it by its history.[1] It had been a national religion: Jehovah is the god of Israel; Israel is the people of Jehovah.[2] The propositions are correlatively exclusive. However wide the power of Jehovah over the nations of the world, he has no nation of his own but Israel; and whatever power may be attributed to the gods of other nations, the nation of Israel has no god but Jehovah.

This is the corner stone of the religion of Israel both in the popular apprehension and in the explicit affirmation of the religious leaders in all periods. The wars of the Israelites with the Canaanite inhabitants of Palestine or with the neighboring peoples are the wars of their god; the continually reiterated charge in the prophets and the laws is that the Israelites, leaving the worship of their own god, worship foreign gods, or other gods.[3]

[1] To express these aspects of religion the words 'particularism' and 'universalism' are often used. Inasmuch as in this contrast 'particularism' frequently implies a depreciatory judgment, while these 'ism' words of themselves suggest a conflict of theory or principle, this terminology should be eschewed by historians. On the twofold character of the religion, see Schürer, Geschichte des jüdischen Volkes im Zeitalter Jesu Christi, 3d ed. III, 114, and the literature there cited.

[2] On the history of the pronunciation 'Jehovah,' which has been established in the languages of Western Europe since the sixteenth century, see Note 1.

[3] See, e.g. Judges ch. 5; 1 Sam. 17, 45; 25, 28 (cf. Num. 21, 14); 2 Sam. 7, 24; Hos. 2, 25 (23); Jer. 7, 23; 11, 4; Amos 3, 2; Lev. 26, 12; Deut. 26, 17–19; Exod. 20, 2 f.; 34, 14. Jehovah is a 'jealous god,' Exod. 20, 5; 34, 14; Deut. 4, 24; 5, 9; 6, 15.

The common man in ancient times doubtless regarded the relation between Israel and its god as a matter of course: it was natural that every nation should have a national god, and though it was part of his religious patriotism to believe that the god of Israel was greater, that is, more powerful, and better to his people, than the gods of the neighboring peoples, the relation between Jehovah and Israel was in his mind not different in nature from that of Chemosh and Moab.[1] The religious leaders, on the contrary, at least from the eighth century, taught that the relation between Jehovah and Israel was peculiar in that it was constituted by his choice, and rested on a compact the terms of which he had prescribed and Israel had accepted.[2] The election by which Israel alone of all the nations of the earth was made the people of Jehovah is Israel's glorious prerogative; but it also imposes peculiar and heavy obligations.

As a national religion the religion of Israel has certain features which should not be overlooked. The national god was not the head of a national pantheon, like Assur in Assyria or the Egyptian Amon-Ra in the Theban empire; nor is his position similar to that of the chief city-gods of the Phoenicians and Syrians, nor those of the Greeks and Romans, like Athena in Athens or Jupiter in Rome. An organized polytheism of this kind never existed in Israel. Apart from any exclusiveness supposed to be inherent in the religion itself or in the minds of the people, the conditions which usually create such polytheisms were absent. Jehovah was the god of a group or confederacy of tribes which invaded and eventually conquered Palestine. The gods of the petty city-states into which the country was divided were not incorporated in the pantheon of the conquerors. They had apparently little individuality, they were just the *baals* (divine proprietors) of

---

[1] See Judges 11, 23 f.; 2 Kings 3, 4 ff. For the counterpart of this attitude see the inscription of Mesha, king of Moab, G. A. Cooke, Text-book of North-Semitic Inscriptions (1903), pp. 1–14; or Encyclopaedia Biblica, III, cols. 3040–3048.

[2] Amos 3, 2; Hosea; especially Deut. 7, 6–11; 9, 9 ff.; 10, 12 ff.; 14, 2; 26, 18 f.; see also 4, 37 ff.; 5, 2 ff.; 29, 9 ff.; Exod. 19, 5 f.; 24, 3–8.

this or that place. They were the protectors of the communities that worshipped them, and in that capacity they succumbed to the god of the invaders; they were also the givers of the increase of the land, and in this character, the Israelites, as they passed over to husbandry, learned from the older inhabitants with the art of agriculture the rites of the baal cultus.

With completer occupation, the god of Israel became the god of the land of Israel; the ancient 'high places' were appropriated by him with the agricultural festivals. The baals were thus absorbed by Jehovah, not given a place beside or beneath him, as the clan gods of the Israelite tribes had probably already been absorbed.[1] In the eyes of many, the Canaanite cultus, in whatever name it was celebrated, was heathenism and idolatry; Hosea stigmatizes it as like the unfaithfulness of a wife who abandons her husband to play the harlot with other lovers. The exclusiveness of the relation between the national god and his people could not find a more drastic figure; and long after the Canaanite population had been absorbed in Israel by intermarriage, as their gods had been absorbed by Jehovah, the worship of the baals remained the typical apostasy.

When the kingdom of Israel entered into political alliance with Phoenicia and the alliance was cemented by the marriage of Ahab with a Tyrian princess, the worship of the Baal of Tyre (Melkart) was introduced in the capital, with no more thought of supplanting the national god than Ethbaal would have had if in reciprocity he had built a temple of Jehovah in Tyre. But Elijah was of another mind. No foreign god should be worshipped in Israel; there can be no divided religious allegiance — Jehovah *or* Baal! The zealots for Jehovah wrought the ruin of the dynasty of Omri; the principle of exclusiveness triumphed.

In the seventh century foreign gods and cults flourished rankly in Judah. Manasseh earned for himself a particularly

---

[1] Functional deities other than agricultural do not seem to have been much developed among the Canaanites; but whatever they were, their functions also were taken over by the national god. The goddess of fertility or maternity alone seems to have kept her place in the household.

bad name by the introduction of such religions from far and wide. Under Josiah the party loyal to Jehovah had their day, and the reforms of his eighteenth year swept away the gods whom Manasseh had installed in the temple of Jehovah itself, the altars of the Queen of Heaven and the horses of the Sun, as well as the Tophet in the Valley of Hinnom just outside the city, where children were offered by fire to the divine King (Moloch). When the final catastrophe of Judah came, the prophets bade their stricken countrymen see in it the vengeance of their own god for the sins of Manasseh and his generation: Jehovah was a jealous god, who would share the worship of Israel with no other; the proof of this doctrine, enounced long ago, had overtaken them. If there were those at the moment who explained the disaster in a contrary way (Jer. 44, 15 ff.), the prophetic interpretation soon came to be uncontested.

This interpretation had momentous consequences. It was not the Babylonians in the might of their gods who had triumphed over Judah and its impotent god; it was Jehovah himself who had launched Nebuchadnezzar and his hosts against the doomed city to execute his judgment on religious treason. Henceforth for all time the principle was established that for a Jew to worship any other god is apostasy. For centuries this had been reiterated by the religious leaders in law and prophecy; the event gave their words a divine authentication.

The recognition of the exclusive right of the national god to the religious allegiance of the nation and of every member of it is sometimes described as a 'practical monotheism.'[1] The exclusive worship of one god, whether by the choice of individuals or by the law of a national religion, is not monotheism at all in the proper and usual meaning of the word, namely, the theory, doctrine, or belief, that there *is* but one God. This is the only sense in which the term has hitherto been used of Judaism,

---

[1] It has also been named 'monolatry,' in the sense of the worship of one god only. Others call it 'henotheism,' a term already appropriated to a wholly different phenomenon.

Christianity, and Mohammedanism; and since the word is needed to describe this type of religion, it is inexpedient to deflect it to another sense, even with a contradictory qualification. This is not a mere contention about words. In Israel monotheism in the proper sense was not the outcome of the exclusive principle; it was reached by a different way, and as soon as its implications were recognized they were found to collide with the exclusiveness of the reciprocal relation between God and Israel in the national religion.

Another feature of the religion of Israel which distinguishes it from those of other peoples of the time is its antipathy not only to images but to aniconic representatives of the deity, the pillars and posts at the places of worship.[1] The opposition to these things was at first because they belonged to other religions, Canaanite or foreign; but the religious leaders advanced to the higher ground that Jehovah is invisible, and therefore cannot be represented in any visible likeness, of man or beast, in earth or sky or sea, or by the host of heaven on high (Deut. 4, 12–19).[2] The narrative of Josiah's iconoclastic reforms (2 Kings 23) pictures a very different reality. But here again the fall of Judah, in the prophetic interpretation, set the stamp of Jehovah's abhorrence on idolatry in every form.

The principle that God cannot be seen in any natural object nor imaged by man's hands in any likeness is frequently called a doctrine of the 'spirituality' of God. If 'spirit' were taken in the biblical sense, there would be no other objection to the phrase than its abstractness; but in modern use spirit is the contrary of matter, and 'spiritual' equivalent to 'immaterial.' In this sense the spirituality of God is a philosophical theory derived from the Greeks, not a doctrine of Judaism in biblical times or thereafter, any more than Jewish monotheism is a doctrine of the unity of God in the metaphysical sense. Philo

[1] See Encyclopaedia Biblica, 'Idol, Idolatry,' 'High Place,' 'Massebah,' 'Asherah.'

[2] See Encyclopaedia Biblica, II, cols. 2157 f.

has both conceptions from Plato, and reads them into the Bible with the rest of his philosophy; but he did not get them from the Bible nor from Judaism at all.

The fall of the kingdom of Judah; the deportation of considerable bodies of its people, especially of the upper classes, to Babylonia, where they were settled in colonies; the flight of others during and after the wars to the neighboring countries or to Egypt, was the beginning of a dispersion which grew more extensive in the following centuries and reached great proportions under Alexander and the Macedonian kings. But however widely the Jews were scattered, they felt themselves members of the Jewish nation. Even as a subprefecture of a Persian province or in similar subordination in the empire of Ptolemies or Seleucids, Judaea, within its narrow limits, had an acknowledged political existence of a kind, and even after generations in other lands the Jews still looked to it as their native country; the national spirit survived the collapse of the national state. There were hopes, often disappointed but permanently inextinguishable, of the revival of national autonomy, and even dreams of the recovery of vanished power and glory.

The temple had been rebuilt early in the Persian period (520–516 B.C.) and the worship of the national god reëstablished in its ancient seat. But the national religion was no longer as it had been in the days of the kingdom the religion of a people occupying its own land, where men were born and brought up in the ways of their fathers without reflection or choice of their own. Now the great majority of the Jews lived in foreign countries, in daily contact with men of different races, customs, and religions. In such an environment, as the history of emigration and colonization in modern times teaches us, fidelity to the religion of their ancestors, was a matter of individual determination; and these external conditions concurred with the turn to individualism which the religion itself had received from Jeremiah and Ezekiel to give it a somewhat different character. The older ideas of national solidarity were supplemented and to some extent superseded by personal responsibility. We shall have occasion to revert to the consequences of this change at a later stage in our investigation.

The national feeling of the Jews throughout the world was greatly exalted by the achievement of Judaean independence and the reëstablishment under the Asmonaeans of a national state, with boundaries extended to the frontiers of Solomon's empire; and whatever might be thought about Herod, it could not be questioned that he made the kingdom of Judaea one of the most conspicuous powers in the Nearer East. Moreover, the friendly relations of the Asmonaeans and of Herod with Rome secured for the Jews throughout the sphere of Roman dominion or influence extraordinary privileges and exemptions, which in the main they retained through the following period.[1]

Great numbers of Jews at the beginning of our era were descendants of families which had been settled in other and often remote countries as long as the present-day descendants of the English colonists in America; they spoke another language and had appropriated more or less of alien culture. To them Judaism was in reality not so much the religion of the mother-country as the religion of the Jewish race; it was a national religion not in a political but in a genealogical sense. But notwithstanding this distinction — of which they were doubtless unconscious — the Jews were still in their own belief the only people of God, and the one God was still in a peculiar sense the god of the Jews. To them alone he had made himself known, not in nature and conscience only, but by the word of revelation; to them alone he had given in the twofold law his will for man's whole life; theirs were "the adoption (which made them alone sons of God) and the glory and the covenants and the legislation and the (divinely ordained) worship and the promises" — so Paul sums it up in Romans 9, 4. The golden age in the future, the goal toward which all history moved, was, above everything else,

[1] Juster, Les Juifs dans l'empire romain, I, 213 ff., 339 ff.

the fulfilment of Israel's destiny. Nationality was thus an essential character of Judaism.

For centuries, however, it had been the fundamental dogma of Judaism that there is but one God, creator and ruler of the world.[1] The most elementary reflection on the implications of monotheism makes it clear that a universal god's interest in mankind cannot be confined to a particular nation. The very elevation of Jehovah to the place of sole God thus seemed to threaten the foundations of the national religion, the peculiar and exclusive relation between Jehovah and Israel. The first consciousness of this antinomy is perhaps expressed in more emphatic assertions of the arbitrariness of the divine election.[2] In particular the existence of the polytheistic religions of the heathen was a new problem. According to the author of Deut. 4, 19 f., Jehovah assigned the sun, moon, and stars, the whole host of heaven, which all antiquity believed to be glorious divine beings, to the other nations, but took Israel to be a hereditary nation of his own.[3] It is obvious that this solution, which made God himself the author of polytheism, could not permanently satisfy.

In Deut. 32, 8 f. we read: 'When the Most High gave the heathen their inheritance, when he divided the children of men, he established the boundaries of the nations according to the number of the sons of Israel. For the portion of Jehovah is Israel; Jacob, his hereditary lot.' For the last words of verse 8 the Septuagint Greek has, 'according to the number of the angels of God,' rendering בני אל (literally 'sons of God') in place of בני ישראל. Many modern scholars think that the Septuagint here represents the original reading:[4] there were

---

[1] On the character of Jewish monotheism see pp. 360–362, 401, 432.

[2] Deut. 7, 6–11; 10, 14 ff.; 4, 32–39.

[3] Cf. Deut. 29, 24 f.: The Israelites 'forsook the covenant of the Lord, the God of their fathers . . . and went and served other gods and worshipped them, gods that they had not known, and he had not assigned to them.'

[4] De Goeje, Stade, Cheyne, and others; most recently, with an original interpretation of the verse, K. Budde, Das Lied Mose's, Deut. 32, pp. 17 ff. (Tübingen, 1920).

as many nations as there were inferior divine, or superhuman, beings, among whom in the author's age the heavenly bodies stood in the first rank. The passage would then correspond in meaning to 4, 19 f.: each nation has among the 'sons of God' its own national deity. Others connect the phrase, as perhaps the Greek translators understood it, with the angel champions (princes) of the nations in Dan. 10, 13, 20, 21; 12, 1; Ecclus. 17, 17 ("For each nation He appointed a prince, and the portion of the Lord is Israel"); cf. also Isa. 24, 21. The reading of our Hebrew text, and of all the versions from Aquila on, gives, however, an entirely acceptable sense: the 'number of the sons of Israel' was seventy (Exod. 1, 5), and seventy is the number of nations sprung from the three sons of Noah (Gen. 10), as the Jews early observed; the seventy nations are a standing feature of Jewish ethnography.[1] The Palestinian Targum on Deut. 32, 8 combines the seventy nations, corresponding to the seventy sons of Israel who went down to Egypt, with seventy angels, princes of the nations, who were distributed to the several nations by lot at the time of the dispersion of the peoples after the confusion of tongues at the tower of Babel.[2]

Monotheism is the fundamental dogma of the theologian among the prophets, in Isaiah 40 ff.: 'I am Jehovah, and there is none else: beside me there is no God.'[3] The negations are as emphatic and insistent as the affirmations. The author lavishes his sarcasm on the idols the heathen worship as gods, the work of men's hands in which is no help.[4] The sole God is the creator

---

[1] E. g. Pesiḳta ed. Buber f. 16a; 48a. There are correspondingly seventy languages, e.g. Sanhedrin 17a, end; Tos. Soṭah 8, 6. See below, p. 278.

[2] Christian authors (Epiphanius, Augustine, al.) generally count seventy-two. On the Jewish enumeration see further Note 2.

[3] Isa. 45, 5; see also 43, 10–15; 44, 6, 8; 45, 14, 18; 46, 9; and cf. 41, 4; 42, 8, etc. Observe the pregnant use of אֵל (without the article), 'I am God' (Isa. 43, 12; cf. 40, 18). See also Deut. 4, 35; 32, 39.

[4] Isa. 40, 18–20; 41, 6 f.; 45, 20; 46, 1 f., 5–7; at length, 44, 9–20; cf. Jer. 10, 1–16. Some of the descriptions of the image-maker's shop may be from later hands; but they are only variations on a given theme which has many echoes in Jewish literature.

of the heavens and the earth;[1] they bear witness alike to his incomparable wisdom and his almighty power. The stars which he has made come out when he musters them by number and name; not one of them fails to respond to his summons.[2] His creative activity did not cease when once the world was made; the events of the present are created in their day (48, 7). The destiny of nations is in his hands; he orders the whole course of history in accordance with his plan.[3] He alone can foretell the future, for he foreordained it and brings it to pass in his time. The heathen are challenged to produce any such evidence in behalf of their gods.[4] He is the eternal God, ever the same.[5]

In the same breath with the assertions of the unity and universality of God, his unique relation to Israel is affirmed with the utmost emphasis: "I am Jehovah, your Holy One, the Creator of Israel, your King." The author's monotheism is not a theological reflection on the nature of God, it is his religious faith: Israel's god is the only God; the almighty is the saviour of his people. The antinomy thus takes its extremest form. But in these chapters a reconciliation is also found.

If there be but one God, there can be only one religion; and the idea of unity in religion carries with it the idea of universality. Now, indeed, Israel alone knows and worships this God, but in his larger purpose it must one day be the religion of all mankind. Israel is his instrument for the accomplishment of this end; it is his prophet among the nations. It is his servant which he has chosen; he has called it to this high mission, has endowed it with his spirit and given it his message; he sustains it amid difficulties and discouragements till it shall achieve final success; it is to be a light to the nations, that God's salvation may be as wide as the world.[6] Isaiah 52, 13–53, 12 seems to be-

---

[1] Isa. 40, 12–17, 26, 28; 44, 24; 45, 12, 18; 48, 13, etc.
[2] Isa. 40, 26. Not improbably aimed at Babylonian worship of the heavenly bodies and astrological divination.
[3] Isa. 41, 26; 45, 1–6, etc.
[4] Isa. 41, 21–26; 44, 6–8.
[5] Isa. 40, 28; 41, 4; 44, 6; 48, 12, etc.
[6] Isa. 42, 1 ff.; 49, 1 ff.

long with the passages just cited. Israel is not only the prophet of the true religion but its martyr, its witness in suffering; it bears uncomplaining the penalty that others deserved, and when its day of vindication comes and God greatly exalts it, the nations which despised it in the time of its humiliation will confess in amazement that through its sufferings they were saved. It does not appear, however, that the Jews at the beginning of our era understood the passage in this way. To be more exact, they did not interpret the passage as a whole in any way, but only verses here and there in it in the way of midrash, which gives no warrant for extending the interpretation even to the next verses, much less to the whole.[1] The only continuous exposition, the Targum, refers the sufferings to Israel (deserved punishment, or trials by which God purposes to refine and purify the remnant[2] of his people and cleanse their souls from sin), while the triumph, and the deliverance of the people by intercession in their behalf and by the overthrow of the power of the heathen, are ascribed to the Messiah.[3]

The pregnant idea of the mission of Israel found little comprehension or response in the centuries that immediately followed; and it is not clear that when the Jews zealously addressed themselves to the conversion of the Gentiles in the Greek period these prophecies in Isaiah were in their mind. The belief that the true religion must in the end be the universal religion of itself made Judaism a missionary religion. God had revealed it to one nation that through them it should be proclaimed to all the nations; Israel's exclusive possession of it was not the end, but the means to a greater end. The belief in the future universality of the worship of the one true God runs like a red thread through all the later literature, a day when "the Lord

[1] See Note 3.

[2] Some manuscripts have '*the wicked* of his people.'

[3] R. Simlai (fl. early third century) applies Isa. 53, 12 to Moses (Soṭah 14a); R. Jonah (fourth century) to Akiba; others find in it the Men of the Great Assembly (Jer. Sheḳalim 48c).

shall be king over all the earth; in that day shall the Lord be one, and his name one.' [1]

The forms in which the religion of the golden age to come were imagined were naturally those of the national religion internationalized. The temple in Jerusalem should be the religious centre of the world, to which worshippers from all lands should stream bringing their sacrifices and precious gifts.[2] The Jews will not lose their prerogative in the universality of religion: they will be called the priests of the Lord, and the other peoples will minister to them in temporal things as the Jews are their ministers in sacred things.[3] The way in which the triumph is to come about is also conceived in national forms; it is by a stupendous historical catastrophe in which the heathen will be constrained to recognize the hand of the sovereign of the world vindicating his own honor in the overthrow of those who would not acknowledge him and in the deliverance and exaltation of his people.[4]

Special encouragement is given in Isaiah 56 to alien converts who felt themselves excluded by such laws as Deut. 23, 1–8, from incorporation in the people of God and participation in the promises of a glorious future made to it. Those who attach themselves to Jehovah, ministering to him, loving his name, and becoming his servants, if they keep the sabbaths and hold fast by his covenant (i.e. the law which is the condition of the promises), God will bring them to his holy mountain and make

---

[1] Zech. 14, 9. This is one of the fundamental verses for the Jewish conception of the Kingdom of Heaven. See pp. 432–434; II, 346. The providential care of God for all mankind and the future recognition of the true God by all nations are common themes in the Psalms. See Bertholet, Die Stellung der Israeliten und Juden zu den Fremden, pp. 191 f.

[2] Zech. 2, 14–17 (E. V. 10–13); Isa. 2, 2–4, etc. This is the common expectation, but not the only form. See Isa. 19, 18–25; Mal. 1, 11, 14. Cf. Sibyll. v, 492–502, where the temple of Onias is meant (Josephus, Antt. xiii. 3), but the foundation is attributed to an Egyptian priest. See Geffcken, Texte und Untersuchungen, XXIII, i (1902), p. 26.

[3] Isa. 60–61; 66, 23 f.; Zech. 14, 16 ff.

[4] See the passages cited in the preceding note; also Isa. 24–27; Dan. 2, 44 f.; 7, 9–14, etc.

them joyful in his house of prayer, accepting their sacrifices as graciously as those of Israelites by race, 'For my house shall be called a house of prayer for all peoples.' It is probable that the inferiority and uncertainty of their status had been impressed upon such converts by Jews who deemed the peculiar favor of God a matter of heredity, and that the principle of equality enounced by the prophet is meant to be taken to heart by them as much as to encourage the proselytes.[1] But the question of the religious status of converts indicates the existence of a class sufficiently numerous to raise it. The age of the passage is not certain, but it probably falls at a relatively advanced time in the Persian period. The precedence given to the keeping of the sabbath as the most distinctive external observance of Judaism is to be noted.

So long as the outlook of the religion was purely terrestrial and national, naturalization in the Jewish people was the only way by which an alien could hope to share its glorious future. The persistent denunciation of the catastrophe that was presently to overwhelm all the nations that forget God [2] in common and irremediable ruin doubtless had its effect, especially in times when the world seemed to be on the verge of the predicted disaster.

In the centuries preceding the Christian era, however, visions of a golden age when all men worship the one true God and obey his righteous and holy law amid universal and permanent peace and boundless prosperity, when nature is all beautiful and beneficent, and the very beasts of prey recover their paradisaical manners, ceased to express the sum of human desires. The thought of what is after death began to haunt men; the doctrine of resurrection and the last judgment, and the ideas of immortality and of retribution in a disembodied existence, came

---

[1] On the legal and social status of proselytes in later times see below, pp. 327, 329 ff.; 335.

[2] Psalm 9, 17.

in, and the questions they raised would not be silenced. Salvation took a new meaning and religion a new task — to show man the way and give him the assurance of a blessed hereafter according to his conception of it.

Judaism met this demand without changing its character. The way to the life of the age to come or eternal life was the old way: knowledge of the true God, faith in him, love to him, worship of him alone, obedience to his revealed will. But as the idea of salvation after death is purely individual, Judaism, in offering itself as a way of salvation in this sense, entered on a new stage of its missionary career, and prosecuted it in the dispersion with zeal and evidently with large success. In this new response to its own principle of universality the historical limitations of nationality maintained themselves. It was not enough to accept the religious doctrines of Judaism, conform to its moral standards, and even practise its peculiar observances. The significance of its initiatory rite was not entrance into a religious community, it was naturalization in the Jewish nation, that is — since the idea of nationality was racial rather than political — adoption into the Jewish race, the convert entering into all the rights and privileges of the born Jew and assuming all the corresponding obligations. For the covenant promises of God in Scripture are made inseparable from the obligations.[1] This denationalization of its converts, together with the interdiction of all those civic acts and public festivities which involved the recognition of other gods, was undoubtedly a serious obstacle to the missionary efforts of the Jews; nevertheless the number of proselytes in the two centuries before our era must have been considerable.[2]

Far larger was the number of those who in modern missionary phrase would be called 'adherents' of the synagogue, who embraced its monotheism, frequented its services and contributed to its support, kept the sabbath, abstained from swine's flesh

[1] This is the perfectly logical ground for insisting on circumcision. The opponents of Paul reasoned in the same way.
[2] See below, pp. 348 f.

and from blood, and observed other fundamental rules of the Jewish law. In the New Testament (Acts) this class is frequently mentioned under the names σεβόμενοι, or φοβούμενοι (τὸν θεόν), those who revere, or fear, God.[1]

The synagogues of the Jews were the centres of this propaganda, and gathered into them converts of both classes. Through these again Judaism penetrated more and more deeply into the circles of society from which they came. The analogy of the early Christian church and its missionary activities inevitably presents itself; but far too much is made of this resemblance when Judaism itself in that age is regarded as a church, and the transformation of a national religion into a church in the centuries between the Maccabaean struggle and the fall of Jerusalem is taken to be the most significant outcome of the history of that period. It is distinctive of a church, according to this theory, that in it religion is internationalized and in the process denationalized. In this definition the mysteries of Mithras, for example, were a church. The religion of Mithras, with rites and myths later embodied in the mysteries, was originally a national or tribal religion, most probably in Commagene and adjacent parts; but the Mithraic church (mystery) lost all connection with nationality, race, or locality. The initiate to the degree of Persa, did not become a Persian, any more than as a neophyte he was a crow, or later in his progress a lion. The Jews, on the contrary, were, both in their own mind and in the eyes of their Gentile surrounding, and before the Roman law, not adherents of a peculiar religion, but members of a nation who carried with them from the land of their origin into every quarter where they established themselves their national religion and their national customs.[2] It is upon this that their exceptional legal status and religious privileges are based; and so far as Roman law came to take cognizance of the matter, the

---

[1] See Psalm 135, 20; 115, 11, 13; 118, 4. See further below, pp. 325 f.

[2] In the Roman codes and legal text books they are called *natio, gens, populus,* in Greek ἔθνος. See Juster, Les Juifs dans l'empire romain, II, 20; cf. I, 416. For the testimony of Cassius Dio see Note 4.

hereditary *privilegia* of born Jews were not conceded to other subjects who became proselytes to Judaism.[1] Juster therefore rightly says: "Il faut avoir présent à l'esprit le caractère *ethnico-religieux* des Juifs et ne pas essayer de diviser des choses indivisibles." [2]

It was in fact this indivisibility that determined the altogether anomalous treatment of the Jews by the emperors and in Roman law. The Patriarch[3] in hereditary succession from Hillel, for whom a Davidic genealogy was found,[4] was, for the purpose of the Roman administration, treated as the head, not of a religious body, but of the Jewish people. According to Origen, the patriarchs exercised in his time an authority in no way different from that of a king of the nation, even condemning men to death, with the sufferance of the Roman authorities.[5]

Inasmuch as the law of the Jews was not only a religious law, but by inheritance from the days of their political autonomy included as an integral part and under the same sanctions a civil law, the Romans left them their own jurisdiction in cases in which both parties were Jews; and since offenses against the religious law were visited with corporal punishment, such measure at least of penal jurisdiction was vested in their tribunals.[6] Even the transformation after the destruction of the temple in 70 A.D. of the didrachm poll-tax for the maintenance of worship in the national temple in Jerusalem into the *fiscus judaicus*[7] applied to the Jews throughout the empire as members of a people.

---

[1] Juster, op. cit. II, 19 f.   [2] Ibid., I, 233 n. 2.

[3] Hebrew *Nasi*. In Ezek. 40–48 this title is constantly given to the political head of the Jewish commonwealth in the future restoration.

[4] Gen. R. 98, 8 (on Gen. 49, 10): R. Levi said, a genealogical scroll was found in Jerusalem, in which it was written, 'Hillel from David.' Christian writers controverted the claims of the Jewish patriarchs to Davidic lineage in the interest of their own application of Gen. 49, 10 to Christ. See Pamphilus, Apologia pro Origene, in Routh, Reliquiae Sacrae, ed. 2, IV, 310. The title of the patriarch in Greek is ἐθνάρχης, in Rufinus's Latin, *patriarcha*. See Note 5.

[5] Origen, Epist. ad Africanum c. 14. See Note 6.

[6] On the subject of jurisdiction see Juster, Les Juifs dans l'empire romain, II, 94 ff.

[7] Juster, op. cit. II, 282 ff.

CHAPTER II

THE SCRIPTURES

THE characteristic thing in Judaism at the beginning of our era is not its resemblance to a church, but that it conceived itself as revealed religion, and drew all the consequences of this conception. God had not only made himself known to men, but had given them in his twofold law a revelation of his will for man's whole life, and of the way of salvation through the fulfilment of his righteous and holy will. This attitude resulted no less from the teaching of the prophets than from the possession of the Law.

In this aspect Judaism falls into the same class with Zoroastrianism, the prophetic reform religion of the Iranians, and with the religions of India, Brahmanic, heretical, and sectarian. Wherever, indeed, men have taken the idea of revealed religion seriously and logically, a divine law embracing not only what we call the principles of religion but their manifold application to all man's relations to God and to his fellow men, a law not only of rites and observances but for the civil and social side of human life, forms a large and fundamental part of the revelation; and partly under the necessity of new situations, partly by scholastic interpretation and casuistic development, it becomes progressively more comprehensive and more minute. As revelation, explicit or by clear implication, all this law has the same divine origin and authority; the infraction of even the seemingly most trivial prescription may be followed by incommensurable consequences, for it is not the trivial rule that is transgressed or neglected, but the unitary law of God which is broken.

Such religions are often called 'nomistic,' that is to say, religions founded on and concluded in a law (*nomos*) given by God.

The important thing is not what we call them, but the recognition that this development is a logical consequence of the idea of revealed religion; for in the ancient world religion was not a sphere apart from, or above, everyday life, but a system of observances which embraced every side of life. Even Christianity, in spite of its Pauline antinomianism and its actual emancipation from the Old Testament law, had hardly got fairly started in the Greek and Roman world when it began to think of itself and talk of itself as a 'new law,' and to develop this idea not only in the sphere of ritual, where it made large borrowings from the laws of the Levitical priesthood, but with much more serious consequences in the realm of doctrine. Eventually, recondite dogmas derived from alien philosophies were defined not only as revealed truth to guide man in his search for God, but as a divinely prescribed norm of opinion and belief upon intellectual conformity to which the issues of eternal life depended. This tendency has appeared also in other nomistic religions. It was only in its beginnings in Judaism in the age with which we are here engaged,[1] but in some later theologians it is strongly asserted. Maimonides, after defining the faith of Judaism in his famous Thirteen Articles, adds that the Jew is bound sincerely to accept every one of these articles, and is not to be regarded or treated as a Jew if he does not.[2] In Mohammedanism, which is a thoroughly nomistic religion, the theologians got so far as to assert that a man is not only bound to accept the creed and understand it, but even to understand and accept the arguments by which the theologians professed to establish or demonstrate it.

For the Jews at the beginning of our era the revelation of God was in part embodied in writings which had come down

[1] See M. Sanhedrin 10, 1: An Israelite who denies that the resurrection of the dead is proved from the Law, or that the Law is from Heaven (God), and the Epicurean (here perhaps a man who denies divine retribution), have no part in the world to come.

[2] Maimonides, Comm. on M. Sanhedrin 10, 1; Article 13 of the "Fundamentals." M. was doubtless influenced by Moslem and Christian examples.

from earlier times — the Law of Moses, the Prophets, the histories attributed to prophetic authorship and conveying religious and moral lessons, the poetry of religious devotion in the Psalms, prudent counsels for the guidance of life in the Proverbs, and story books like Ruth and Esther, to all of which the quality of inspiration, the character of sacred Scripture belong.

Various modes of revelation are described in the Old Testament: actual appearances of God, or of a messenger of God ('angel') in human form, visions, dreams, communications by speech in murmured or distinctly uttered words. In all except the first two forms, the experience is often associated with, or mediated by, the spirit of God or of Jehovah. This is especially the case in the prophets. God's promise (Deut. 18, 15 ff.) to raise up prophets in Israel and put his words in their mouth to deliver to the people is fulfilled by putting the holy spirit in the mouth of the prophets after Moses.[1] The holy spirit is the spirit of prophecy; all the prophets spoke by the holy spirit. The holy spirit is so specifically prophetic inspiration that when Haggai, Zechariah, and Malachi, the last prophets, died, the holy spirit departed from Israel.[2] Consequently all inspired men were reckoned prophets — Abraham, Isaac, and Jacob; David and Solomon; Ezra and Mordecai, besides all those to whom the name prophet is given in the Old Testament. According to a Baraita, forty-eight prophets and seven prophetesses prophesied to Israel.[3]

---

[1] Zech. 7, 12. Sifrè on Deut. 18, 18 (§ 176); cf. also Targum Isa. 40, 13, "Who put the holy spirit in the mouth of all the prophets." The phrase 'the holy spirit' is very rare in the Old Testament (Isa. 63, 10 f.; Psalm 51, 11), and never in connection with prophecy. It is common in rabbinical literature of prophetic inspiration and the inspiration of Scripture. On the various uses of the phrase see the classified collection of instances in Bacher, Terminologie, II, 202–206; on its meaning, ibid. I, 169 f.

[2] Tos. Soṭah 13, 2; Sanhedrin 11a. Subsequent revelations were given by a *bat ḳol*; see below, pp. 421 f.

[3] Megillah 14a. Seder 'Olam R. cc. 20–21 enumerates them, with the same total. A bare catalogue in R. Hananel on Megillah *l. c.* Besides these, who have a place in Scripture, there were innumerable prophets none of whose utterances were written (Seder 'Olam c. 21).

From the books of the prophet Moses and the books containing the oracles of prophets and bearing their names it was an
easy and perhaps unconscious step to the position that all the
books of the Bible were written by prophets, that is, by men who
had the holy spirit. This is the assumption of the oldest catalogue of the authors of the canonical books.[1] Josephus held a
similar theory, and his singular classification of the books is
apparently due to his desire to include as many as possible in
the number of prophetic histories, the motive being to vindicate
the superior trustworthiness of biblical history. What has been
written since the time of Artaxerxes (I) is not deemed equally
trustworthy, because the exact succession of prophets no longer
existed.[2] The production of the books of the Bible was thus
connected through their prophetic character with the holy spirit.
It was perhaps the question about the canonicity of the writings attributed to Solomon that led to reiterated and emphatic
assertions of the inspiration of his writings: "The holy spirit
rested upon him, and he spoke three books, Proverbs, Ecclesiastes, and the Song of Songs."[3] A somewhat similar controversy
about Esther leads to a singular distinction in the Talmud,
evoked by the reported opinion of a Rabbi of the third century
that the roll of Esther is not sacred: Did he think that it
was not spoken through the holy spirit? He did not deny that
it was spoken through the holy spirit, but only to be recited,
not to be written.[4]

The notion of inspired scripture thus grew naturally out of
the nature of prophecy, and it was held that everything in the
Scriptures is inspired, though not everything that had through
the centuries been given by the holy spirit was contained in the
books of Scripture, or had ever been written at all. There had
been many prophets who produced no books.

[1] Baba Batra 14b–15a.
[2] Josephus, Contra Apionem i. 8 § 41. Josephus puts Esther in the reign
of Artaxerxes (I) son of Xerxes, and assumes the same age for the book;
Antt. xi. 6, 1.
[3] Cant. R. on Cant. 1, 1 (ed. Wilna f. 2a).   [4] Megillah 7a.

The rabbinical schools had no theory of the mode of prophetic inspiration such as Philo appropriates from Plato,[1] a state of ecstasy or enthusiasm; but it was with them an uncontested axiom that every syllable of Scripture had the verity and authority of the word of God. It followed that the contents of the sacred books were throughout consentaneous, homogeneous. There were not only no contradictions in them but no real differences. The notion of progressive revelation was impossible: the revelation to Moses was complete and final; no other prophet should ever make any innovation in the law.[2] The forty-eight prophets and seven prophetesses who came after him neither took away anything that was written in the Law, nor added anything to it except the reading of the roll of Esther.[3] Moses is the fountain head of prophecy in so literal a sense that it is said that he uttered all the words of the prophets besides his own.[4] The prophetic books are comprehended with the hagiographa under the name 'tradition' (kabbalah);[5] the prophets are transmitters of a continuous tradition beginning with Moses; the Prophets and the Hagiographa explain the Pentateuch.[6] Thus all the rest of the sacred books, with no detraction from their divine inspiration and authority, are an authority of the second rank: they repeat, reinforce, amplify, and explain the Law, but are never independent of it. Proof-texts are often quoted in threes, a verse from the Pentateuch, another from the Prophets, and a third from the Hagiographa, not as though

[1] Philo, De spec. legg. i. 9 § 65 (ed. Mangey, II, 222); esp. iv. 8 § 49 (II, 343); cf. Quis rerum divin. heres c. 53 § 265 (I, 511). Plato, Timaeus 71 E; Ion 534 B.

[2] Deut. 4, 2; 13, 1 (E. V. 12, 32); Lev. 27, 34. Shabbat 104a; Megillah 2b. Maimonides, Yesodè ha-Torah 9, 1.

[3] Megillah 14a. See below, p. 245.

[4] Joshua ben Levi and Samuel ben Naḥman (third century), Exod. R. 42, 8. Bacher, Pal. Amoräer, I, 164, cf. 500.

[5] Throughout the age of the Tannaim and Amoraim, down to the close of the Talmuds, Ḳabbalah is used only of the tradition in Scripture, not of the unwritten law, nor of the theosophic tradition to which the name was subsequently attached. Bacher, Terminologie, I, 165 f.

See Bacher, Terminologie, I, 155.

the word of the Law needed confirmation, but to show how the Scripture emphasizes the lesson by iteration.[1]

In consequence of their origin the books of the Bible as a whole are 'The Scripture' or 'The Holy Scriptures,'[2] and by this character separated from all other writings. With this the usage of the New Testament agrees.[3] A sense of the unity of Scripture endows it with a kind of personality in such phrases as 'the Scripture says,' 'the Scripture speaks,' 'the Scripture teaches,' and many other more technical terms.[4] Quotations are also often introduced by, "it is written," sc. in the Scripture, as in the New Testament.

The author of Zechariah 13, 1–6 speaks very ill of the prophetic profession in his day: when God purifies his people he will make the very names of their idols to be forgotten, and exterminate from the land the prophets and the unclean spirit together; public opinion will be so strongly against them that their lives are not safe even in their parents' houses.[5] A century or two later the Maccabaeans have no prophet at hand to tell them what to do with the stones of the polluted altar, and put them in safe keeping till one shall come. So also Simon is created ruler and high priest permanently, "until a trustworthy prophet shall arise." From another passage in the same book we learn that it had already been long since a prophet was seen. Probably the author meant, since the time of Haggai, Zechariah, and Malachi, with whom, according to Josephus as well as the rabbis, prophecy ceased.[6]

Inspiration being thenceforth a thing of the past, men had the ancient word of God in the Scriptures that had come down from

---

[1] E.g. Megillah 31a (Joḥanan). Bacher, Terminologie, I, 193, cf. p. 65; many examples in Blau, Zur Einleitung, pp. 22 f.

[2] See Note 7.

[3] Thus, ἡ γραφή, of Scripture generally or of a particular passage; αἱ γραφαί, γραφαὶ ἅγιαι. τὰ ἱερὰ γράμματα in New Test. only 2 Tim. 3, 15 (Philo, Josephus).

[4] See Bacher, Terminologie, I, 90–92.

[5] Cf. Deut. 13, 1–5; Ezek. 14, 6–11.

[6] 1 Macc. 4, 46; 14, 41; 9, 27; cf. Psalm 74, 9.

former times, a closed body of books differing from all others in possessing the quality of inspiration. Since such books alone were normative, it was of fundamental religious importance to determine what they were. When this need first made itself felt, prescription left no room for question about the Pentateuch or the Prophets; [1] for generations lessons had been regularly read from these books in the synagogues. Besides these there were other books of more miscellaneous character for which no more descriptive and distinctive name was found than 'The Writings.' [2]

The last named books were not read in the synagogue, and consequently had not the same prescription of liturgical use as the Law and the Prophets. [3] Some of them were probably rarely found in private possession. There were, moreover, other books of similar kinds, some of which enjoyed much popularity, as their adoption by Christians in Greek translations proves — story books like Judith and Tobit, the Proverbs of Jesus son of Sirach, apocalypses such as have been preserved to us in the Book of Enoch, and many more. It was here, therefore, that discrimination was necessary and dispute possible. About the Psalms there was no question; though they furnished no lessons for the synagogue, some of them had a place in the temple liturgy which was believed to have been instituted by David himself; [4] many of them were ascribed in their titles to him,

[1] The Prophets are Joshua, Judges, Samuel, Kings; Isaiah, Jeremiah. Ezekiel, and The Twelve (Minor Prophets), eight books in all. Baba Batra 14b. (The order is: Jeremiah, Ezekiel, Isaiah, The Twelve.)

[2] *Ketubim*, properly the name for all Scriptures, and often so used. Since the Law and the Prophets had names of their own, *Ketubim* came to be used specially for the rest of the Scriptures which had no such proper name. See Note 8.

[3] The custom of reading five of these books (the Five Rolls, Megillot), Song of Songs, Ruth, Lamentations, Ecclesiastes, Esther, at Passover, Pentecost, the Ninth of Ab, Tabernacles, and Purim respectively, was not established till long after our period. Esther alone was from the beginning inseparably connected with Purim. The reading of the others came in gradually in post-Talmudic times. See Elbogen, Der jüdische Gottesdienst, pp. 184 ff.; Blau, in the Jewish Encyclopedia, VIII, 429 f.

[4] 1 Chron. 15, 16–16, 36; Ecclus. 47, 8–10.

and he was universally regarded as the author of the whole collection.[1] Undoubtedly most of the other Writings which now constitute the third part of the Jewish Bible were at the beginning of our era by long established consent included in the class of inspired and sacred scriptures. But this was not true of all of them, while there were other books for which this character was claimed.[2] The Jewish authorities thus found it necessary to define the canon of Scripture, as the Christian church subsequently did under a similar necessity.

The most serious controversy was over Ecclesiastes and the Song of Songs, the dissensus about which seems to have lasted through most of the first century after Christ. The Mishnah affirms specifically that both these books are sacred, i.e. canonical,[3] and records a tradition in the name of Simeon ben 'Azzai, who had it on the authority of the members of the council itself, that it was so decided on the memorable day on which the council at Jamnia deposed the patriarch Gamaliel II and installed R. Eleazar ben Azariah in his room, and this tradition is declared in the Mishnah to be authentic. It preserves, however, diverse reports of the differences. Ecclesiastes was one of the old disputes between the rival schools of Shammai and Hillel, the former rejecting, the latter accepting the book as sacred,[4] and the decision at Jamnia did not secure unanimity of opinion. Not only does a contemporary of the Patriarch Judah assert that while the Song of Songs is canonical because it was spoken by the holy spirit, Ecclesiastes is not, because it is Solomon's own wisdom,[5] but Jerome, at the end of the fourth century, heard from his Jewish teachers that it had been proposed to commit the book to oblivion on internal grounds, but

---

[1] David included Psalms by ten other poets. Baba Batra 14b-15a.

[2] It may not be superfluous to say that books written on rolls were not physically united as they were later in manuscript codices and in printed editions.

[3] M. Yadaim 3, 5. See Note 9.

[4] M. 'Eduyot 5, 3; M. Yadaim 3, 5; Megillah 7a (Simeon ben Yoḥai).

[5] Simeon ben Menasya, Tos. Yadaim 2, 14; cf. Megillah 7a.

the rabbis had been withheld from doing so by the closing words (Eccles. 12, 13 f.), which of themselves warranted putting it among the divine books.[1]

That the right of the Song of Songs to a place among the sacred Scriptures was also contested would be evident from the necessity of a formal affirmation of it in the Mishnah even if we had not direct testimony to the fact; and if any further evidence were needed, the vehemence of Akiba's protest would supply it: "God forbid! No man in Israel ever dissented about the Song of Songs, holding it not to be sacred. The whole age altogether is not worth as much as the day on which the Song of Songs was given to Israel; for all the Scriptures are holy, but the Song of Songs is the holiest of all. If there was a division, it was only over Ecclesiastes." [2]

About the same time with the deliverance concerning Ecclesiastes and the Song of Songs, though the occasion is unknown, a decision was given that certain other books are not canonical: "The gospel and the books of the heretics are not sacred Scripture. The books of Ben Sira, and whatever books have been written since his time, are not sacred Scripture." [3] For the exclusion of Sirach, a book highly esteemed by the Jewish masters, more than one reason may be conjectured; but one is sufficient: the author was known to have lived in comparatively recent times, in an age when, with the death of the last prophets, the holy spirit had departed from Israel. The same principle applied *a fortiori* to later writings, including the Gospels and other Christian books. The specification of the latter, however, is one of several indications that in the generation following the disastrous end of the Jewish war the 'disciples of Jesus the Nazarene,' finding an effective argument in the calamity of the people and the destruction of the temple, which they interpreted as a judgment on the nation for its rejection of the Messiah

---

[1] Comm. in Eccles. 12, 13 f. See Note 10.
[2] M. Yadaim 3, 5. See Note 9.
[3] Tos. Yadaim 2, 13; cf. Tos. Shabbat 13 (14) 5. See Note 11.

and the precursor of the direr judgments to follow, had had such success as to rouse the apprehension of the rabbis and prompt them to take measures to check the growth of the sect.

The chief book of the Nazarenes was their 'gospel,' [1] for which they evidently claimed the character of sacred Scripture. The holy spirit might have departed from Israel centuries ago, but it had come back again and rested upon their apostles and prophets; [2] inspiration was no longer a thing of the past, and inspired books were again possible. The vehemence with which the leading rabbis of the first generation of the second century express their hostility to the gospel and other books of the heretics, and to their conventicles, is the best evidence that they were growing in numbers and influence; some even among the teachers of the Law were suspected of leanings toward the new doctrine. [3] The war under Hadrian brought about a complete separation of the Nazarenes from the body of Judaism, and after the war the animosity diminished with the danger of the spread of infection within the synagogue.

Besides Ecclesiastes and the Song of Songs, there was debate about some other books of the Hagiographa. In the account of these differences in Megillah 7a, R. Simeon ben Yoḥai, after remarking that Ecclesiastes was in controversy between the schools of Hillel and Shammai, continues, "but Ruth, and the Song of Songs, and Esther are sacred Scriptures," that is, three other of the smaller Writings. [4] Esther was, however, not uncontested. From as late a time as the third century we have the opinion of Samuel that the volume was not sacred, a position which caused embarrassment to later teachers and led to the apologetic distinction noted above. [5]

---

[1] They called it *euangelion*, and by this name, or punning distortions of it, it is referred to in rabbinical literature.

[2] Mark 1, 10; Acts 2, 1 ff.; 4, 31; 1 Cor. 14, etc.   [3] See Note 11.

[4] A Baraita in Berakot 57b names three larger *Ketubim*, Psalms, Proverbs, and Job, and three smaller, Song of Songs, Ecclesiastes, and Lamentations, and mentions Esther in the immediate context. Ruth is not named, but no significance is to be ascribed to the omission.

[5] Page 238. See Note 12.

The nature of the objection that the Book of Esther at once raises is plainly stated in Jer. Megillah 70d. The keeping of the new Days of Purim conflicted with the fundamental principle that the law of Moses was complete (Lev. 27, 34), and that no other prophet should ever arise after him to introduce any new institution; yet here were Mordecai and Esther trying to do that very thing. According to tradition this difficulty was felt when the letters of Mordecai and Esther enjoining the observance (Esther 9, 20 ff.; 29 ff.) first reached Palestine, and was resolved at that time by an assembly of eighty-five elders among whom were thirty prophets and more, who succeeded in finding the necessary warrant in all three parts of the canon. We know that the Mordecai Day, Adar 14, was a calendar date at the time when 2 Maccabees was written (2 Macc. 15, 36).[1]

The Book of Esther was read at Purim; but as that festival had a markedly popular and even secular character, it does not necessarily follow that Esther was at once accepted as sacred Scripture. That inevitably followed however; and when in the third century Johanan said that (in the days of the Messiah) the books of the Prophets and the Hagiographa were destined to be abrogated,[2] but the five books of the Law will not be abrogated, Simeon ben Lakish amended him, saying that the roll of Esther also and the rules of the traditional law (Halakah) will not pass away; while an array of rabbis, including Bar Kappara and Joshua ben Levi, declared, as has been noted above, that the roll of Esther was spoken to Moses from Sinai.[3]

[1] See Note 13.

[2] Jer. Megillah 70d, below, alleging Deut. 5, 22. The burden of the later revelations is reproof and correction for Israel's sins; if Israel had not sinned, a later rabbi said, they would not have been given (Aha bar Hanina, Nedarim 22b; Bacher, Pal. Amoräer, III, 543). Esther on the contrary is necessary to the observance of Purim. On the perpetuity of the rules of the unwritten law see below, p. 271.

[3] Jer. Megillah l. c., on the principle, "there is no earlier and later (chronological order) in the Bible." On this rule of the exegetical school of Ishmael see Bacher, Terminologie, I, 167 f. The Book of Esther was not supposed to have been written until the days of Mordecai and Esther, but as it had been revealed to Moses it is no illegitimate addition to Mosaic institutions.

Much weight has been attached to the fact that in the list of the books of the Old Testament obtained in Palestine by Melito, Bishop of Sardis in the reign of Marcus Aurelius, the Book of Esther is not named,[1] from which it is inferred that Melito's informants did not acknowledge Esther as inspired Scripture. In view of the whole character of the list the inference is by no means certain; but, granting its correctness, if Melito got his information from Christian Jews, as is most probable, it would prove nothing about the estimation in which the book was held by others. Christian Jews, after the complete breach with their countrymen made by the Bar Cocheba war, can hardly be supposed to have kept up by themselves so emphatically national a festival as Purim, and with the observance the book would fall into desuetude. The Mishnah and Tosefta are proof that in Melito's time the Jewish authorities in Palestine, so far as we know without dissent, treated Esther as sacred Scripture.

The objection to Ecclesiastes, that it contradicted itself, could be raised against Proverbs also. Proverbs 26, 4 bids, 'Answer not a fool according to his folly;' verse 5, 'Answer a fool according to his folly.' There is no difficulty, it was replied; the former verse refers to discussions of words of the Law, the latter to secular matters.[2] The account does not make the impression that there was a serious move to put away the Book of Proverbs; it sounds more like an incident in the argument about Ecclesiastes.

About Ezekiel we have a more picturesque story: The learned considered putting away the Book of Ezekiel because it contained things in conflict with the Pentateuch, and they would have done so but for the labors of Hananiah ben Hezekiah, who, supplied with three hundred jars of oil, sat in his study on the roof of the house until by a profounder exegesis he harmonized

---

[1] Melito's catalogue is preserved in Eusebius, Historia Ecclesiastica iv. 26. Uncertainty about Esther appears in several later Christian lists; these are, however, without significance for the canon of the Jews.

[2] Shabbat 30b; cf. Megillah 7a.

them.[1] The programme for the age of restoration in Ezek. 40 ff. differs in many and not unimportant points from the Law of Moses, and much midnight oil might well be consumed in converting difference into sameness. The case of Ezekiel was, however, wholly different from that of Ecclesiastes and the Song of Songs in the Mishnah, or of Sirach. The question was not, Is this book sacred, or inspired, Scripture?[2] but, assuming its prophetic authorship and inspiration, is it expedient to withdraw the book from public use lest the unlearned or the half-learned be stumbled by the apparent discrepancies between it and the Law? The word I have rendered 'put away' (ganaz) means 'store away in safe-keeping,' and is used only of things of intrinsic value or things of sacred character.[3] The translation, 'pronounce apocryphal,' is erroneous. According to Talmudic authority, a copy of the Pentateuch in which there are as many as three (or four) errors to a column must be 'put away'[4] in a place where it cannot be used but is safe from profanation; it is assuredly not declared apocryphal! The Torah which God had kept by him in heaven for nine hundred and seventy-four generations[5] was a 'hidden treasure' (ḥamudah genuzah)[6] — certainly not an apocryphon!

The principles and method of interpretation were determined by the idea of revealed religion embodied in sacred Scripture. In all its parts and in every word the Scripture was of divine origin and authority, being either an immediate revelation, such

---

[1] Hananiah ben Hezekiah ben Garon was of the school of Shammai, and prominent in the generation before the fall of Jerusalem. See Bacher, Tannaiten, I, 18 f. For the story see Shabbat 13b; Ḥagigah 13a; Menaḥot 45a.

[2] I.e., "Does it make the hands unclean?" (see Note 9), or "Was it spoken by the holy spirit?"

[3] The verb ganaz is a denominative from a Persian noun meaning 'treasure,' which was borrowed by the Jews in the form genazim, Ezek. 27, 24; Esther 3, 9; 4, 7. See W. Bacher, 'Genizah,' in Encyclopaedia of Religion and Ethics, VI, 187–189; and Note 13.

[4] Menaḥot 29b, below.

[5] Shabbat 88b, below; Bacher, Pal. Amoräer, I, 160 f.

[6] Or ḥemdah genuzah. See Diḳduḳe Soferim in loc.

as was made to Moses by God *propria persona,*[1] or through visions
and dreams, or given to the prophets and the authors of the
various sacred books through the inspiration of the holy spirit.
What is of no less importance, though it is less frequently remarked, is that the Scriptures are throughout a *revelation of
religion,*[2] in the widest meaning of that word. They are all
Torah, not by an extension *a potiori* of the name of the Pentateuch to all the Scriptures, but because in them all, πολυμερῶς
καὶ πολυτρόπως (Heb. 1, 1), God has revealed what he has chosen
to make known of his character and his ways, and what he requires of men in their relations to him and to their fellows. This
is the content and meaning of every word of Scripture; sometimes in the plain letter intelligible even to the superficial reader,
sometimes to be discerned only by those who know how to
penetrate to the deeper sense that lies beneath the letter. The
conviction that everywhere in his revelation God is teaching
religion and that the whole of religion is contained in this revelation is the first principle of Jewish hermeneutics. To discover,
elucidate, and apply what God thus teaches and enjoins is the
task of the scholar as interpreter of Scripture. Together with
the principle that in God's revelation no word is without significance, this conception of Scripture leads to an atomistic exegesis,
which interprets sentences, clauses, phrases, and even single
words, independently of the context or the historical occasion,
as divine oracles; combines them with other similarly detached
utterances; and makes large use of analogy of expressions, often
by purely verbal association.

So important a work was not left to the competitive ingenuity
of individuals. Besides the training and tradition of the schools,
certain hermeneutic rules were evolved as norms of method and
criteria of the validity of a particular procedure. The formulation of seven such rules was attributed to Hillel, about the beginning of the Christian era; a century or more after him R.

---

[1] "Mouth to mouth," Num. 12, 6–8; "face to face," Deut. 34, 10.
[2] This is the nearest equivalent to the Jewish conception of Torah.

Ishmael expanded them to thirteen without material change in their substance, and in this form the rules became the standard of rabbinical exegesis, particularly in juristic deductions and inferences — homiletic interpretation for ends of edification was less strictly regulated.[1] The methods and results of this exegesis must be viewed in the light of its own presuppositions as they have been exhibited above, not of ours. We need to remind ourselves that the conception of development as applied to re-vealed religion, or in theological phrase an economy of revela-tion, is eminently modern. To the rabbis, if it could have been explained to them, it would have seemed a contradiction of the very idea of religion: the true religion was always the same — how otherwise could it be true? The revelation of God's char-acter and will was unchanging as God himself was unchanging.

With the consequences of this apprehension of the nature of revelation in the development of the unwritten law by juristic exegesis we are not at this point concerned. In the sphere of what we should call religion and morals the result was that by their methods of interpretation, however faulty they may seem to those who are accustomed to regard modern philological and historical methods as the only legitimate art of interpretation, the Jewish teachers found in all parts of the Scriptures their own worthiest conceptions of God's character and man's duty, con-ceptions which, as we shall see hereafter, were derived from the highest teachings of the Scriptures and are in some important respects an advance beyond them. Hellenistic Jews accom-plished the same thing by means of the more elaborate and self-conscious methods of sustained allegory, and in literary forms. In this way Philo discovers in the Scriptures not only the loftiest teachings of his religion, but the most recondite doctrines of his philosophy, which he holds to be equally of divine origin, and in essence identical with the truth revealed in Scripture.[2]

The interpretation of the Scriptures in the New Testament is of precisely the same kind. Familiar illustrations of an exegesis

[1] See Note 14.   [2] See Note 15.

comparable to that of the Palestinian rabbis are Jesus' proof of the resurrection of the dead from the Pentateuch in Matt. 22, 31 f.,[1] and Paul's allegory of Hagar in Gal. 4, 24 f., or his allegorizing upon Jewish midrash in 1 Cor. 10, 1–4, while the Epistle to the Hebrews exemplifies throughout the Hellenistic art.

It was on the same assumption of the consistency of revelation, and with methods from our point of view as uncritical, that Christians from the beginning found the distinctive doctrines of Christianity expressed or implied in all parts of the Old Testament, and that in more recent times Protestant dogmatists found the mystery of the Trinity revealed in the first chapters of Genesis, or proved the deity of the Son from Psalm 2, 7 and Prov. 30, 4. In fact the application of modern historical and critical methods to the Scriptures, and above all the introduction of the idea of development, involves, consciously or unconsciously, a complete change in the idea of revelation, a change which orthodoxy, whether Jewish or Christian, has resisted with the instinct of self-preservation.

[1] Rabbinical deductions of the resurrection from passages of Scripture: Sifrè Deut. § 329 (on Deut. 32, 29); Sanhedrin 90 b. For others see Strack, Kommentar zum Neuen Testament aus Talmud und Midrasch, on Matt. 22, 32.

CHAPTER III

THE UNWRITTEN LAW

The whole revelation of God was not comprised in the sacred books. By the side of Scripture there had always gone an unwritten tradition, in part interpreting and applying the written Torah, in part supplementing it.[1] The existence of such a tradition in all ages is indubitable. The priests' traditional knowledge of details of the ritual, for instance, is constantly assumed in the laws in the Pentateuch on the subject of sacrifice. The rules for the private burnt offering and peace offering in Lev. 1 and 3 are formulated with expert precision, but in the actual offering of even such simple sacrifices they require at every step to be supplemented by a customary practice. The law requires a lamb as a burnt offering every morning and evening, with the accompanying quantum of flour, oil, and wine (Exod. 29, 38–42), but gives no further particulars. As these perpetual daily sacrifices for the whole people were the constant element in the *sacra publica* and so to speak the basic rite of the cultus, they were doubtless always celebrated with a solemnity accordant to their importance. But the whole elaborate and splendid ritual as it was developed in the use of the temple was preserved and transmitted only in tradition until after the worship ceased with the destruction of the temple in the year 70.[2] For the performance of the solemn piacula of the Day of Atonement the directions in Lev. 16 are altogether inadequate; the actual conduct of the complicated rites must always have been directed by priestly

[1] The tradition of the Elders, Mark 7, 3–13; see Josephus, Antt. xiii. 10, 6. Note 16.

[2] For the ritual as it was in the generation before the destruction of the temple see M. Tamid—perhaps the oldest tractate of the Mishnah; see above, p. 153.

tradition.[1] Doubtless in the course of time the ritual developed in practice by that tendency to enrichment which is strong in all liturgies, or was revised by recurrence to the prescriptions of the Law; but whatever it was, it rested on tradition and was embodied in tradition. These instances may suffice to illustrate what was true of the whole ritual and ceremonial law.

Nor was the Scripture by itself more sufficient in the field of civil and criminal law. What is found in the Pentateuch appears to modern critics to be the fragmentary remains of codes or collections of laws from the times of the kingdoms. One such code, of which a single title intact and several others more or less incomplete are preserved in Exod. 21–23, was formulated with juristic precision and evidently laid out on a large scale. Much the greater part of it, and of other collections of the same age, probably perished with the fall of the national state; and in the following ages under foreign rule the lost parts were never methodically replaced, though patched in many places with material that is distinguished by an entirely different formulation. Nor was any considerable attempt made to adapt or extend the civil law to the changed conditions of the Jews in this period by additions to the Pentateuch. The major part of the native law under which the Jews lived during the centuries of Persian and Greek dominion must have been an unwritten common law, the custom of the community, preserved particularly by the elders or judges before whom cases came. Their jurisdiction itself rested on the same ground. The Pentateuch directs the appointment of judges in cities and towns (Deut. 16, 18), but says little or nothing about the constitution or procedure of the tribunals.

The law in Deut. 24, 1–4, on the remarriage of a divorced woman, presumes that a legal divorce demands a certificate of repudiation (*sefer keritut*) given to the woman by the man as evidence that she was free to marry again. There is however no law prescribing such a writing nor any direction concerning its

[1] M. Yoma, Tos. Yom ha-Kippurim, Sifra on Lev. 16.

form, though as a legal instrument it must be supposed that a certain form, and probably also the proper witnessing of the instrument, were necessary to its regularity if not to its validity, since in such matters ancient law was as insistent as modern on formal correctness. In many other things enjoined in the religious law, e.g. the payment of the taxes for the support of the priesthood and other ministers of worship, the obligatory offerings, the observance of holy days, the mode of fulfilment must have followed custom which had the force of law, and when defined became tradition.

The prohibitions of labor on the Sabbath in the Pentateuch are as general and indefinite as they are emphatic. The prophets are more explicit. Amos condemns trading on that day (8, 5), Jeremiah the bearing burdens on the Sabbath day and carrying them into the city or out of houses (17, 21–24; cf. Neh. 10, 32), thus giving testimony to the antiquity of some of the most important principles of Jewish sabbath observance. But nowhere in the Old Testament is there such a definition of the works which are forbidden on the Sabbath that a man could know in all cases whether the thing he was doing was permissible or prohibited. The necessity of definition in this case was peculiarly great because of the severity of the penalties denounced in the Pentateuch against the profanation of the day. The regulations which we find in the Mishnah are in part the formulation of custom, in part of exegetical study of the Scriptures, in part of juristic casuistry; but upon the premises of revealed religion such things cannot be too exact or too minute.

Thus in every sphere there always existed beside the written law a much more extensive and comprehensive body of unwritten law more or less exactly and permanently formulated. From our point of view the authority of this consuetudinary law was common consent or the prescription of long established usage. To the Jews, on the contrary, inasmuch as the written law took into its province all spheres of life, the unwritten law, dealing with the same subjects and often defining how the former should be carried out or enforced, was equally of religious obligation. And since religion with all its duties and observances was revealed by God, the revelation necessarily included the unwritten as well as the written law. The written law, again, was all revealed to Moses, and it was a very natural inference that its inseparable complement the unwritten law, which shared the immutability of all revelation, was revealed to him at the same time.[1] Sweeping statements to this effect are, however, homiletic hyperbole rather than juristic theory; this character is particularly alleged only of a few laws.

Between the written and the unwritten law there could be no conflict. It was one of the principal works of the schools to exhibit and establish the complete accord between Scripture and tradition; not as though the authority of the unwritten law as such depended on the written, but because the agreement was a criterion of the soundness of a particular tradition or interpretation. For not every thing that was customary at any time had by that fact the force of divine law; nor, where revelation was the only norm, could usage at variance with it acquire authority by prescription.

In the methodical study of the written law as it was prosecuted in the schools many questions of interpretation and application arose and were discussed, the implications of the law were followed out and compared with other rules, and the results of all this investigation were concisely and clearly formulated. This process led to the discovery of many things which formed no part of existing custom or tradition; but when they were ascertained, the effort was made to secure conformity to them, not as innovations, but as a revival of ancient commandments of God which had fallen into desuetude and oblivion. When God said to Moses: "If ye shall diligently keep all this commandment which I command you," etc. (Deut. 11, 22), the words, 'all this commandment' include the juristic exegesis, the formu-

[1] See Note 17.

lated rules, and the edifying applications.[1] The Pharisees were especially zealous in this endeavor, which brought them into conflict with more than one of the Asmonaean rulers,[2] and into many controversies with the Sadducees.

An expansion of the unwritten law came about also by the search in the Scriptures for a principle, an implied provision, or a precedent, by which a new question could be answered or new actual conditions or emergencies met. In such cases also the result, if approved by the authorities as deduced by valid exegetical procedure from the Scripture in which it was implicitly contained, was itself revealed, and became part of the Mosaic tradition.

The authenticity of the unwritten law delivered by Moses could be assured only by an uninterrupted and trustworthy transmission from generation to generation down to the schools of the first century of our era. Such a chain of tradition is given at the beginning of M. Abot: "Moses received the Law (written and unwritten) from Sinai (from God) and transmitted it to Joshua, and Joshua to the elders, and the elders to the prophets, and the prophets transmitted it to the men of the Great Assembly.[3] . . . Simeon the Righteous was one of the last survivors of the Great Assembly. . . . Antigonus of Socho received the tradition from Simeon the Righteous," . . . He was succeeded by the so-called Pairs:[4] Jose ben Joezer and Jose ben Johanan (in the time of the Maccabaean struggle); Joshua ben Peraḥiah and Nittai of Arbela; Judah ben Ṭabai and Simeon ben Shaṭaḥ (under Alexander Jannaeus and in Queen Alexandra's time); Shemaiah and Abṭalion (in the days of Herod); the last

---

[1] See below, p. 256 f.

[2] Josephus, Antt. xiii. 10, 6; 15, 5; 16, 1.

[3] See Note 18.

[4] M. Ḥagigah 2, 2. According to this Mishnah the first named in each pair was president of the Sanhedrin (*nasi*), the second, vice-president (*ab bet din*), the old political Sanhedrin presided over by the high priest being organized after the model of a rabbinical council. See H. Strack, Einleitung in Talmud und Midrasch, 5 ed. p. 117 f., and Note 18a.

pair being Shammai and Hillel at the beginning of the Christian era, with whom the school tradition proper begins.

Certain rules of the unwritten law are specifically called 'Mosaic rule of law from Sinai,' that is, a rule that was given to Moses by God. These rules come in part from the time of Rabban Gamaliel or from the school at Jamnia, and are thus designated to give the authentication of immemorial prescription and divine origin to traditional laws for which no biblical support could be adduced.[1]

Many rules of the unwritten law were found, by more penetrating exegesis or by combination with other passages in the Pentateuch or elsewhere in the Scriptures, to be implicit in the written law. It was assumed that these were made known to Moses, to whom the whole twofold law was revealed; but it was not necessary to suppose that they had been handed down in continuous tradition like the Mosaic rules from Sinai. Many which were delivered by Moses to his contemporaries were forgotten even in the first generation. In the days of mourning for Moses, it is said, grief caused no less than three thousand thus to fall into oblivion; Joshua himself forgot three hundred as a punishment for his self-sufficiency, and neither was he nor were the priests and prophets who came after him able to restore them. Many hundreds of exegetical proofs were also forgotten, but these the acumen of Othniel rediscovered.[2] Evidently, scholars in later times could do the same thing, if they were acute enough. Akiba, in particular, by a more subtle hermeneutic and a fabulous ingenuity in the exercise of it, found in the written law many rules for which before him there had been only the traditional authority of Moses from Sinai.[3] We have seen that in Sifrè on Deut. 11, 22 the words, 'all this commandment,' are understood to include juristic exegesis (*midrash*),

---

[1] הלכה למשה מסיני. See Note 19.

[2] Temurah 16a. These legends come from rabbis of the third and fourth centuries. They are adduced only as illustrations of the general attitude toward the Mosaic revelation.

Menaḥot 29b. Bacher, Tannaiten, I, 263 ff. See Note 20.

formulated rules (*halakot*), and practical religious and moral application (*haggadot*), as well as the text of Scripture itself.[1]

In all religions which profess to be wholly and solely based on a revelation, fixed and final, embodied in certain books, tradition is necessarily called in to interpret and supplement the scriptures; the origin of this tradition must lie in the age of revelation itself; and to be authoritative it must ultimately derive from the fountain-head of revelation. In Mohammedanism an oral tradition is therefore traced back through an unbroken line to the companions of the Prophet, witnesses of his words and example. In Christianity the record of the words and deeds of Jesus in the Gospels was ascribed to the Apostles immediately or through disciples under their direction; the Apostles were the inspired authors of the other books which, with the Gospels, constitute the Scriptures of the new dispensation. Apostolic tradition was the formative and normative principle of the ancient catholic church in organization, worship, doctrine, and discipline. A long series of writings, from the Teaching of the Twelve Apostles early in the second century to the eight books of the Apostolic Constitutions with the appended Canons in the fourth, bear witness to the strength of the feeling that whatever is Christian ought to be apostolic. The symbol called the Apostles' Creed was early imagined to have been framed by the Apostles in a kind of symposium, each of them contributing an article. The theory of apostolic tradition is still held unchanged by the great body of Christian churches, East and West. It was uncompromisingly affirmed by the Council of Trent against the contention of the Reformers that the Scriptures alone had divine authority; and the dogma of papal infallibility defined at the Vatican Council in 1870 is declared to be in accord with a tradition which has been received from the beginning of the Christian faith.

The rabbinical doctrine, therefore, so far from being singular, is essentially the same as that of other 'book religions.' Over

---

[1] See further Note 21.

it Karaites and Rabbanites divided in the eighth century, and it is the primary line of cleavage between Reform Judaism and the Orthodox, as it is between Protestants and Catholic Christians. The Christian church, however, very early developed a strong and gradually unified organization, whose bishops in regular succession from the Apostles, custodians of the apostolic tradition, and themselves under the guidance of the Holy Spirit, exercised an authority in the definition of doctrine and the regulation of life for which neither of the other religions possessed a comparable organ; and because it had this living tradition, Christianity had no need to create a great corpus of traditions, like the Talmud or the Moslem Ḥadith collections, to be the norm and final authority for codes of law and the conduct of life.

Whatever the critic may think about the historical character of the actual traditions of any of these religions or of the doctrine of tradition itself, he cannot deny that upon their premises, namely, that everything that is of religious obligation is revealed and that revelation is long since closed, nothing but a belief in such an interpretative and complementary tradition could maintain unity and continuity, conserve the acquisitions of the past, and adapt the religious law to the changing conditions of the present.

The actual content of Jewish tradition was of diverse origin. Part of it was long established custom for which the schoolmen might seek an explicit or implicit scriptural warrant, or, failing that, fall back on the half-conscious fiction of a Mosaic rule from Sinai. But an important part consisted, as they were well aware, of regulations or prohibitions issued and imposed by those in whom at different times such virtually legislative authority was vested. Enactments of this kind, whether proceeding from an individual or a corporate body, are called 'decrees' (*gezerot*) or 'enactments' (*takkanot*), using the former term for prohibitions, the latter for ordinances of a positive character.[1] One of the

[1] See Jewish Encyclopedia s. vv. 'Gezerah,' 'Takkanah.'

maxims ascribed to the men of the Great Assembly (Abot 1, 1) is, "Make a fence for the Law," that is, protect it by surrounding it with cautionary rules to halt a man like a danger signal before he gets within breaking distance of the divine statute itself.[1] A warrant for this was found in Lev. 18, 30, interpreted, "Make an injunction additional to my injunction." [2] The explicit prohibition in Deut. 4, 2, 'Ye shall not add unto the word which I command you, nor shall ye take aught from it,' was easily got over by the exegesis of the schools: in Deut. 17, 11 they found implicit confidence in the courts of each generation and obedience to them prescribed, and they extended the same authority to the decisions and decrees of the rabbinical *bet din*.[3]

Nor were these deliverances confined to laying down the proper way of fulfilling the requirements of the law under changing conditions, or to protecting the law from infringement by a thickset hedge of prohibitions more stringent than the letter. When the exigencies of the time seemed to them to demand it, the rabbis in council or individually did not hesitate to suspend or set aside laws in the Pentateuch on their own authority, without exegetical subterfuges or pretense of Mosaic tradition. Where justification is offered for extraordinary liberties of this kind, Psalm 119, 126 is frequently quoted, with a peculiar interpretation. Instead of, "It is time for the Lord to do something, they have made void thy law," the verse is taken, "It is time to do something for the Lord."[4]

There are in fact numerous rabbinical enactments from all periods which are more or less directly at variance with the plain letter and intent of the law.[5] Among the most noteworthy was the legal fiction called *prozbul* (or *prosbul*) devised by Hillel.

[1] See Note 22.
[2] Moʻed Ḳaton 5a; cf. Sifra, Aḥarè, end (f. 86d, ed. Weiss); Weiss, Dor Dor we-Doreshau, II, 47.
[3] Sifrè Deut. § 154; Midrash Tannaim on Deut. 17, 11 (p. 103). See Note 23.
[4] M. Berakot 9, 5, end. See Note 24.
[5] Weiss, Dor, II, 50-52.

The law of Deut. 15, 1–3 by which all loans were cancelled at
the beginning of every seventh year worked as, in human nature,
such a utopian economic experiment might be expected to work.
Notwithstanding the pathos of the exhortation in verses 7–11,
and no matter what the distress of the borrower might be, money-
lenders could not be induced to make a loan in the fifth or sixth
year which would automatically become a donation in the
seventh.   Like much equally well-meant legislation in later
times, the effect of the law was the diametrical opposite of its
intent.   Hillel's remedy was the execution in court of an instrument, attested by the seals of the judges or witnesses, by which the
lender retained the right to reclaim the loan at any time he saw
fit.[1] Shortly before the outbreak of the Jewish War in 66 A.D.,
in consequence of the multitude of adulterers, R. Johanan ben
Zakkai did away with the ordeal of jealousy (Num. 5, 11–31),
alleging as a warrant for the abrogation of the law Hos. 4, 14:
'I will not punish your daughters when they commit harlotry,
nor your daughters-in-law when they commit adultery; for they
themselves go apart with harlots and sacrifice with the pros-
titutes of the sanctuary.'[2] In a similar way the frequency and
boldness of murders led, we are told, to the abolition of the
antique rite prescribed in Deut. 21, 1–9, when the victim of a
murder by an unknown hand was found lying in the open field.[3]

There was thus a large body of law that grew out of the needs
of the times and changed with them.   Such laws and regulations were probably made in the Persian and earlier Greek
periods by the priests and the council of the elders in their respective spheres or concurrently; many are attributed to the
Men of the Great Assembly.   The Asmonaean princes and kings
doubtless made law by their own edicts, encroaching especially
on the powers of the elders.   It is not without significance that

[1] M. Shebi'it 10, 3 f.; M. Giṭṭin 4, 3, etc.   Jewish Encyclopedia s. v.
'Prosbul'; Schürer, Geschichte des jüdischen Volkes, II, 363. See Note 25.
[2] M. Soṭah 9, 9. The words of the prophet are taken as a warrant for
abandoning the ordeal in a time of general corruption of morals.
[3] M. Soṭah 9, 9.

the older name γερουσία (*senatus*) is replaced by συνέδριον (Sanhedrin), which in the language of the time had come to mean 'court' rather than 'council.'[1] It is to be remembered, however, that a sharp distinction between legislative and judicial powers is very modern; and, further, that law is made by the decisions of a court as much as by the enactment of statutes, especially if the court decides cases submitted *in thesi*, as seems to have been the Jewish practice. That under the later Asmonaeans, their supporters, the party of the Sadducees which embraced the priestly aristocracy, constituted the majority in the Sanhedrin was but natural, and as natural that they made laws and ordinances in accordance with their own traditions or their own notions. Meanwhile the scholars of the rival party of the Pharisees were busy with their juristic studies of the law of Moses and the traditions of the elders, and arrived at results often widely at variance with those of the Sadducees. Under John Hyrcanus they came into open conflict with the rulers, which in the reign of Alexander Jannaeus grew into a civil war. From Queen Alexandra they demanded and obtained the abrogation of the Asmonaean-Sadducean code of civil and criminal law and the substitution of their own ordinances (νόμιμα) which had been annulled by John Hyrcanus. They even constrained the priesthood to make modifications in the ritual of the temple and matters connected with it to conform to their interpretation of the law.[2] The representation and influence of the Pharisees in the Sanhedrin was doubtless much increased in Alexandra's time, and probably maintained after her.

With the fall of Jerusalem the Sanhedrin as a council or court recognized by the government came to an end. What succeeded it, taking its name 'high court' and claiming succession to its functions, was in fact only a self-constituted body of scholars, at first under the presidency of Johanan ben Zakkai at

---

[1] See Schürer, Geschichte des jüdischen Volkes, II, 194. The Jewish name for it is *Bet din ha-gadol*, which we might render the Supreme Court.

[2] Josephus, Antt. xiii. 16, 2, cf. 10, 6. See Note 26.

Jamnia, later under the Patriarchs, beginning with Gamaliel II. So completely did this character predominate that the Jews of later times imagined the old political Sanhedrin as in all respects similar to their rabbinical assemblies.[1]

The unwritten law, as we have seen, was in no wise inferior in authority to the law written in the Pentateuch, both being God's revealed will. The covenant at Sinai, the Magna Charta of Judaism, was made upon both. As in other religions where it is thus raised to an equal rank with Scripture, tradition, as the living word, interpreting, supplementing, adapting, applying, the written word, asserts its superior authority, and its claims are wont to be more strongly expressed if its authority is questioned either in general or on a particular point. So it was in Judaism. Thus it is declared: "A more serious matter is made of the words of the scribes than of the words of the (written) Law." A later teacher sets himself formally to prove that the words of the elders are of more weight than those of the prophets: the prophet has to authenticate himself and his message by a sign (Deut. 13, 2), while for the teachings and decisions of the elders (i.e., the members of the high court in Jerusalem) unquestioning obedience is commanded (Deut. 17, 11).[2] This is the παράδοσις τῶν πρεσβυτέρων, against which Jesus directs his criticism.[3] It is to be observed, however, that notwithstanding all the fault he finds with the Scribes and Pharisees, Jesus recognizes them as the legitimate interpreters of the law, and bids his disciples obey their injunctions, but not follow their example in shirking the heavy burdens they load on other men's backs.[4]

---

[1] On the Sanhedrin see Schürer, *op. cit.*, II, 188–213; Juster, Les Juifs dans l'empire romain, I, 400–402; Jewish Encyclopedia s. v. 'Bet Din,' III, 114 f. (L. Ginzberg), and s. v. 'Sanhedrin,' XI, 41–46 (Lauterbach).

[2] See Note 27.

[3] Mark 7, 1–13; Matt. 15, 1–19.

[4] Matt. 23, 1 ff. It is indeed laid down by rabbinical authority that a decree is not to be imposed on the public unless the majority are able to abide by it (Horaiyot 3b, and elsewhere); but that the restrictions and prescriptions were often onerous is indubitable. See Weiss, Dor, II, 50.

CHAPTER IV

THE PERPETUITY OF THE LAW

THE comprehensive name for the divine revelation, written and oral, in which the Jews possessed the sole standard and norm of their religion is *Torah*. It is a source of manifold misconceptions that the word is customarily translated 'Law,' [1] though it is not easy to suggest any one English word by which it would be better rendered. [2] 'Law' must, however, not be understood in the restricted sense of legislation, but must be taken to include the whole of revelation — all that God has made known of his nature, character, and purpose, and of what he would have man be and do. The prophets call their own utterances 'Torah'; and the Psalms deserved the name as well. To the unwritten law the religious and moral teachings of the Haggadah belong no less than the juristically formulated rules of the Halakah. In a word, Torah in one aspect is the vehicle, in another and deeper view it is the whole content of revelation. [3]

For the Jewish conception of law in this broad sense it is fundamentally significant that it was early identified with wisdom. In Deut. 4, 6, it is urged upon the Israelites as a motive for keeping the statutes and ordinances which Jehovah has enjoined upon them: 'For this is your wisdom and understanding in the sight of the nations, who, when they hear all these statutes, will say, Surely this great nation is a wise and understanding people.' [4] Since this law, the distinctive wisdom of Israel, was revealed by God, it, like all true human wisdom, was God's

---

[1] In the Greek Pentateuch νόμος, and correspondingly in all subsequent versions.

[2] On the word Torah see Note 28.

[3] See Schechter, Some Aspects of Rabbinic Theology, pp. 116 ff.

[4] Note the whole context, Deut. 4, 1-20.

wisdom, of which so much is said in the Proverbs and other works of the Jewish sages. Prov. 8, 22 ff. is the most fruitful of the passages in which this identification of divine revelation (*Torah*) with the divine wisdom (*Ḥokmah*) is made, but many others contributed to the doctrine.

In the eulogy of wisdom in Ecclus. 24, which like Prov. 8 is put into the mouth of Wisdom itself, verse 23 (32) continues: "All this is the book of the covenant of the Most High God, the law which Moses commanded, an inheritance to the congregation of Jacob," [1] and goes on to compare the way the Law pours out wisdom in a flood with the inundations of great rivers (verses 25–29). It is inexhaustible; all the generations that have studied it have not discovered its whole meaning (vs. 28).[2] In the first of the poems in the Book of Baruch, reminiscent of the praises of Wisdom in Proverbs 8 and Job 28, God, the omniscient creator, who alone knows wisdom (3, 32), "Found out every way of knowledge, and gave it to Jacob his servant and to Israel his beloved. After that it was seen upon earth and conversed among men.[3] This is the book of the commandments of God, and the law which abideth forever; all who hold it fast are (destined) to life, but those who abandon it shall die" (3, 37–4, 1).[4] The author of 4 Maccabees, after the definition: "Wisdom (σοφία) is a knowledge of things divine and human, and of their causes" (1, 16),[5] continues: "This (wisdom) is the education

[1] Ταῦτα πάντα is the logical predicate: the Law is all that is said in the foregoing verses. The Greek translator of Ecclesiasticus has κληρονομίαν συναγωγαῖς Ἰακώβ, as in Deut. 33, 4 (Hebrew, singular), having in mind the reading of the Law in the religious assemblies of his time.

[2] Cf. Ecclus. 21, 1: "All wisdom is from the Lord, and with him it is eternally"; 19, 20: "In all wisdom is a doing of the law."

[3] Cf. Ecclus. 24, 10 ff. This verse was often quoted by Greek and Latin Fathers as a proof-text for the incarnation of the Logos (Wisdom). Some modern scholars, similarly misunderstanding the words, reject them as a Christian interpolation. It is as revealed in the Law that Wisdom abides among men unto life.

[4] The author has in mind Deut. 30, 11–18. Note also Baruch 4, 4, "Blessed are we, Israel, for what is well-pleasing to God is known to us."

[5] The current Stoic definition. See Note 29.

given by the law, through which we learn divine things in a manner befitting them, and human things in a way profitable to us" (1, 17).[1] In the apostrophe to the martyr Eleazar he exclaims, ὦ σύμφωνε νόμου καὶ φιλόσοφε θείου βίου (7, 7; cf. also 7, 21–23). Philosophy is for him equivalent to revealed religion; piety and wisdom are interchangeable terms.

The identification of revelation, and more specifically of the Mosaic Law, with divine Wisdom, was thus established in Jewish teaching at least as far back as Sirach (ca. 200 B.C.), and his way of introducing it makes the impression that it was a commonplace in his time, when the study of the law and the cultivation of wisdom went hand in hand, and as in his case were united in the same person.[2]

The identity of the Law and Wisdom is of frequent occurrence in the rabbinical books also, and even in the oldest passages is assumed as something universally acknowledged, from which further inferences are drawn.[3] Besides Prov. 8, 22 ff., several other passages are quoted in which 'Wisdom' is made equivalent to 'Law.' Bar Ḳappara so interprets Prov. 9, 1–3 (combined with 2, 6; 8, 22); and, by reckoning Num. 10, 35 f. as a book by itself, finds seven books of the Law, corresponding to the seven pillars with which Wisdom built her house (Prov. 9, 1).[4] Once this equivalence was established, all that was said in the Scriptures about the nature of wisdom, its source, its fruits, and its inestimable worth, was applied to the Law, either in the larger sense of revelation, or with special reference to the law of Moses; and in the same way Law acquires the vivid poetical personification that is given to Wisdom in the higher flights of the sapiential books.[5]

---

[1] Αὕτη δὴ τοίνυν ἐστὶν ἡ τοῦ νόμου παιδεία, δι' ἧς τὰ θεῖα σεμνῶς καὶ τὰ ἀνθρώπινα συμφερόντως μανθάνομεν.

[2] See Note 30. [3] Sifrè Deut. § 37 and elsewhere. See Note 31.

[4] Lev. R. 11, 3. Bar Ḳappara, a pupil of the Patriarch Judah, taught at Caesarea in the early third century. In Shabbat 116a this combination is attributed to Jonathan. See Bacher, Tannaiten, II, 509 n. Probably the Amora of that name, teacher of Samuel bar Naḥman, is meant.

[5] See Note 32.

The most important consequence of this appropriation to the Law of the attributes of the divine Wisdom is that the Law is older than the world. In Prov. 8, 22 ff., Wisdom (the Law) says of itself: 'The Lord created me as the beginning of his way, first of his works of old. I was installed ages ago, from the beginning, before the earth was,' etc. Thus, in Sifrè on Deut. 11, 10, to prove that, in God's way of doing, what is most highly prized by him precedes what is less prized: "The Law, because it is more highly prized (literally, 'dearer') than everything, was created before everything, as it is said, The Lord created me as the beginning of his way" (Prov. 8, 22).[1] The Law stands first among the seven things which were created before the creation of the world, with Prov. 8, 22 again for the proof-text; and repentance is next to it.[2] This collocation is not accidental. That God did not make the Law, with all its commandments and prohibitions and its severe penalties, without knowing that no man could keep it, nor without creating a way by which his fault might be condoned, is as firm a conviction as there is in all the Jewish thought of God. Repentance must therefore be coeval with Law. And so they found it revealed by God himself in the ninetieth Psalm: 'Before the mountains were brought forth, or ever thou hadst formed the earth and the world, even from everlasting to everlasting, thou art God. Thou turnest man to contrition, and sayest, Repent, ye children of men.'[3]

Wisdom was present at the creation of the world, not as a passive onlooker, but a sharer in the work of making it and the joy of the maker (Prov. 8, 30 f.); she was at God's side, a skilled craftsman, or artist. The identification of Wisdom with the Law led in this way not only to the antemundane existence of the Law but to a connection of the Law with creation. Akiba called it the instrument of God in creation: "Beloved (of God) are

---

[1] Sifrè Deut. § 37 (f. 76a–b).   [2] See Note 33.

[3] This is the Jewish interpretation of the words rendered in the English versions, 'Thou turnest man to destruction.' See Note 34.

Israel, for to them was given the instrument with which the world was created;[1] still greater love is shown in that it was made known to them that there was given to them the instrument with which this world was created, as it is said, 'For good instruction have I given you, my Law forsake not'" (Prov. 4, 2).[2] An interesting development of this idea is given in Genesis Rabbah: "*Amon* (Prov. 8, 30) is equivalent to *Omen* ('artificer, architect'). The Law says, I was an architect's apparatus for God. As a rule an earthly king who is building a palace does not build it according to his own ideas, but to those of an architect; and the architect does not build it out of his head, but has parchments or tablets to know how he shall make the rooms and openings; so God looked into the Law and created the world." [3]

The resemblance of this interpretation to a passage in Philo's De Opificio Mundi is obvious. When God proposed to create this visible world, he first made the intelligible world (κόσμον νοητόν, the universe of ideas) as a model, in order that employing an immaterial and most godlike pattern he might produce the material world, a younger copy of the elder.[4] The parallel is made the more striking by the fact that in the sequel Philo illustrates this Platonic philosophy of creation by a comparison of God's procedure to that of a king who proposes to found a new city: he calls to his aid an expert engineer, who, having surveyed the ground, lays off the whole city in his mind, and then, looking into the plan, proceeds to reproduce it in stone and wood.[5] Just so God, being minded to create this megalopolis (the world), first conceived its types, by combining which in a system he produced the intelligible world, and, using it as a pattern, the sensible world.

[1] The word אמון in Prov. 8, 30 being taken as the 'instrument' of an art or craft. Gen. R. 1, 1. See Note 35.
[2] Abot 3, 14. לקח טוב is God's Torah. Berakot 5a.
[3] Gen. R. 1, 1.
[4] De opificio mundi c. 4 § 16 f. (ed. Mangey, I, 4); cf. Plato, Timaeus 28 ff.
[5] Philo may well have had in mind the laying out of the city of Alexandria by the engineers of Alexander the Great.

R. Hosha'ya, to whom the midrash in Genesis Rabbah is attributed, taught in Caesarea, and was a contemporary there of Origen, whose Old Testament studies, as we know, brought him into intercourse with Jewish scholars. It is not impossible, therefore, that Hosha'ya may have been acquainted with Philo's ideas, if not with his writings; but the coincidence is not of a kind to demonstrate dependence.[1] Another teacher of the third century, R. Simon, arrives by an entirely different route at a similar goal: God studied Genesis, the first chapters of which are, so to speak, a programme of creation, and created the world to correspond.[2]

Another idea which finds frequent expression is that the world was created *for* the Law. So R. Benaiah: "The world and everything in it was created solely for the sake of the Law, as it is said The Lord founded the earth for the sake of Wisdom" (Prov. 3, 19).[3] Much older is the aphorism of Simeon the Righteous: "The stability of the world rests on three things, on the Law, on worship, and on deeds of personal kindness."[4]

In such utterances, under forms that strike us as fantastic, and supported by an exegesis more subtle than convincing, ideas are expressed which lack neither insight nor significance. Religion was not an afterthought of God; it was impossible to conceive a world like this without religion. Since the two are thus indissolubly connected, the world must be made, we might say, on a religious plan. And since religion was in Jewish apprehension a complete system of divinely revealed beliefs and duties, obligatory, not discretionary — a law — this system in its integrity must have existed before the world, and the world must have been made to correspond to it.[5] It is a finer conception still that the world was made *for* the Law — for religion,

---

[1] See Bacher, Pal. Amoräer, I, 107 (cf. p. 92); J. Freudenthal, Hellenistische Studien, I, 73; Jewish Quarterly Review, III, 357–360.

[2] Gen. R. 3, 5. Cf. Philo, Legg. allegor. i. 8 § 19.

[3] See Note 36.

[4] Abot 1, 2. See Note 37.

[5] See Philo, De opificio mundi c. 1 § 3, quoted in Note 38.

we should say — that is, as a sphere for the realization in thought and life of the true relation between God and man through man's conformity to God's holy will.

This law, being perfect, is unchangeable. The Law that was in time revealed in writing and by word of mouth to Moses is the same that was with God before the world was created; and it shall endure in its entirety unchanged as long as the world exists. [1] Philo, contrasting it with the ever changing legislation of other nations, writes: "The provisions of this law alone, stable, unmoved, unshaken, as it were stamped with the seal of nature itself, remain in fixity from the day they were written until now, and for the future we expect them to abide through all time as immortal, so long as the sun and moon and the whole heaven and the world exist." [2]

The association of the Law with the divine Wisdom was another ground for asserting the perpetuity of the Law. We have already seen this result in Baruch 4, 1, where the wisdom God has searched out and given to Israel is "the book of the commandments of God and the Law that exists to eternity," and in Sirach where the wisdom that says of itself: "Before time, from the beginning He created me, and unto the end of time I shall not cease" is "the law which God commanded Moses." [3] It is the "eternal law" in Enoch 99, 2, cf. 14; its prescriptions are an "eternal commandment" in Tobit 1, 6. It could serve no purpose to multiply quotations.

The rabbinical doctrine could not be better expressed than in Matt. 5, 18: "Until heaven and earth pass away,[4] not the smallest letter, not an apex of a letter, shall pass away from the Law till it all be done." Note also the sequel: "Whoever shall

[1] No other Moses will come and bring another Law, for there is no Law left in heaven. Deut. R. 8, 6. Perhaps against the Christians and their "new law."
[2] Philo, Vita Mosis, ii. 3 §§ 14–16 (ed. Mangey, II, 136 f.); Josephus, Contra Apionem ii. 38 §§ 277 f., cf. i. 8 § 42; Antt. iii. 8, 10 § 223.
[3] Ecclus. 24, 9 with vs. 23; see above, p. 264.
[4] That is, never; Job 14, 12

relax one of these very least commandments and teach men so
shall be called the least in the kingdom of Heaven." So also
Luke 16, 17: "It is easier for heaven and earth to pass away
than for one apex of the Law to fall." [1] A parallel is found in
Genesis Rabbah (10, 1) on Gen. 2, 1, whence, by combination
with Psalm 119, 96 and Job 11, 9, it is elicited that heaven and
earth have measures (limit),[2] but the Law has none; a statement
which the commentators understand of time as well as space:
heaven and earth will have an end (Isa. 51, 6), but the Law
will not.

Such utterances are not to be pressed into the strict sense of
eternity: the authors may not push their vision at the farthest
beyond the present order of things, the world as it now is. But
the Jews, through all the vicissitudes of their fortunes, held
fast to the faith that there was a better time coming, as the
Scriptures foretold. The visions of this time in the prophets are
numerous and diverse. Many of them are the promise of a kind
of national millenium, deliverance from subjection to the Gentiles, the restoration of an independent Jewish state expanded
to its ancient boundaries and exercising dominion over the
countries around it far and wide. Some of these prophecies
predict a revival of the Davidic monarchy, while others say
nothing about the political constitution of the state. All agree in
picturing, often in idyllic imagery, a time of lasting peace and
prosperity under the favor of God. The seventeenth of the
Psalms of Solomon best represents to us, in a composite of Old
Testament prophecies, how the messianic times were imagined
by an orthodox Jew a half century before our era. Philo shows
us how the golden age could be conceived without reference to
a restoration of the monarchy.

But there were also in the Prophets predictions of a greater
change, of a catastrophe in which all nature is involved, of new
heavens and a new earth, and of a new order of things, a new
age of the world, beyond this crisis.[3] For this new order of

[1] See Note 39.   [2] See Note 40.   [3] E.g. Isa. 24–27; 65, 13 ff.

things the Jewish name is "the age to come" ('*olam ha-ba*) in contrast to "this age" ('*olam ha-zeh*), the world we live in. The vaguer phrase, "the future" ('*atid la-bo*), refers sometimes to the messianic times, sometimes to the age to come, sometimes includes them both without distinction. Even between the two more descriptive terms the distinction is not strictly maintained; the biblical imagery of the national golden age in the present order being carried over into the age to come, while the convulsions of the final crisis are made to usher in the days of the Messiah. Added to all this, the difficulty of distinguishing earlier from later ideas is at its greatest just here where it is most important. The temptation to be clearer than our sources or their authors is here peculiarly strong, and must be guarded against at every step. So much, in anticipation of a fuller discussion in a later chapter, it seems necessary to premise here.[1]

Inasmuch as the days of the Messiah are the religious as well as the political consummation of the national history, and, however idealized, belong to the world we live in, it is natural that the law should not only be in force in the messianic age, but should be better studied and better observed than ever before; and this was indubitably the common belief. The priesthood and the sacrificial worship in the new temple are constantly assumed. The harps of the temple musicians will have more strings than now.[2] A high priest in the messianic times is frequently mentioned; religion without sacrifice was in fact unimaginable. Nor are the expiatory institutions of the law unnecessary, for even in the messianic times men will not be without sin; their superabundant prosperity may even be the cause of such rebelliousness as their fathers so often fell into when they were too well off.[3] The rules of the unwritten law will remain beside the written, and there must of course be schools for the study of both. A Palestinian rabbi in the circle of the Patriarch Judah

---

[1] See Part VII, chap. ii (Vol. II, pp. 377 ff.).

[2] Tos. 'Arakin 2, 7 (R. Judah), and elsewhere; see Friedmann's note on Pesiḳta Rabbati 99a. Bacher, Tannaiten, II, 223.

[3] Deut. 32, 15; Sifrè Deut. § 318.

even discovered in the Scripture that the synagogues and schools
of Babylonia would then be transplanted to Palestine.[1]

With the Law in the Age to Come the case was different. The
scene of that age was indeed the earth, but a transformed and
glorified earth, where all the conditions of existence were so unlike those of human experience as to be imaginable only by contrast. Between this and that lay the judgment that was the end
of history and of the very stage on which the tragedy of mankind
had been played. The new age began, so the Pharisees taught
and the mass of the people believed, with the resurrection of the
dead, who entered thus on a new and different life. To the cavilling question of the Sadducees, to which of her seven husbands
the woman should belong who had six times been passed on from
brother to brother in levirate marriage, Jesus answered, "When
men rise from the dead, they neither marry nor are given in
marriage, but are as angels in heaven." [2] It is sound Pharisean
doctrine: "The age to come is not like this age. In the age to
come there is no eating and drinking, no begetting of children,
and no trading, no jealousy, no hatred, and no strife," etc.[3] In
the Mishnah itself it is taught that there is no death there, no
sorrow, and no tears (Isa. 25, 8).[4] The following quotation also
is apposite: "In this age Israelites contract uncleanness and
get themselves purified according to the directions of a priest;
but in the future it will not be so, but God himself is going to
purify them, as it is written, I will dash pure water upon you
and you shall be pure; from all your uncleannesses and from
all your idols I will purify you" (Ezek. 36, 25).[5]

It is evident that in such a world the greater part of the laws
in the Pentateuch would have no application or relation to any-

---

[1] Megillah 29a. On the law in the messianic age see Klausner, Die
messianischen Vorstellungen des jüdischen Volkes im Zeitalter der Tannaiten,
pp. 115 ff. See Note 41.

[2] Mark 12, 25.

[3] Berakot 17a, and often. A favorite saying of Rab (first half of the third
century).   [4] M. Moʻed Ḳaton 3, 9.

[5] Pesiḳta ed. Buber f. 41b; Tanḥuma ed. Buber, Ḥuḳḳat § 28 (f. 60b).

thing actual. This was true, however, of many of the laws in the rabbis' real world. Not only the laws for the king, but much of the civil and criminal law, necessarily fell into desuetude under foreign rule; many of the laws, especially those concerning agriculture and the taxation of agricultural produce for the support of the ministry and public worship, applied only to the land of Israel; [1] after the destruction of the temple not alone the laws regulating the cultus and the functions of the priesthood, but many laws treating of uncleanness requiring offerings for purification were no longer practicable. Yet the Law was studied with more diligence than ever, not only that a knowledge of it might be preserved for the restoration they believed to be near, but because the occupation of the mind and heart with laws which were for the present in abeyance, like those of sacrifice, was a surrogate for the fulfilment in act that had for the time been rendered impossible. [2]

Nor is this all. No one can read the works in which the results of the scholastic occupation with Scripture are embodied without feeling that teachers and learners not only took keen intellectual pleasure in their labors, but that many approached the subject in a truly religious spirit, and sought edification as well as enlightenment in the profound study of God's character, will, and purpose, as revealed in his word. It is not strange, therefore, that they should have imagined this study, the occupation of mind and heart with religion, as continuing in the Age to Come, and that then God himself would be their teacher. [3] They knew that it would not content them forever to sit "with their crowns on their heads enjoying the effulgence of the divine presence." [4] They could not imagine themselves in another life without the intellectual interests of the present life; and, like the rest of us, they found many things in nature and revelation

---

[1] For the discrimination between laws everywhere binding and those obligatory only 'in the land,' see Sifrè Deut. § 59, cf. § 44. See Note 42.

[2] Menaḥot 110a; Pesiḳta ed. Buber f. 60b; Tanḥuma ed. Buber, Aḥarè § 16 (f. 35a), etc. It is accepted as an atonement in lieu of all sacrifices.

[3] See Note 43.   [4] Berakot 17a.

that they would like to have God explain, especially those commandments and prohibitions of the law for which they could discover no rational or moral ground. As religious men they obeyed the divine statutes without question; as reasonable men they could not help wanting to know the reason of them. Such explanations, they thought, must have been given to Moses, but they had not been handed down in the unwritten tradition. God doubtless meant to put men in this world to the test of implicit obedience; but in the Age to Come this motive would no longer exist.[1]

The Jews could no more conceive a world in the past without a revelation of God's will for man's life than in the present or the future. Accordingly they believed that certain laws for all mankind were given to Adam. Six such commandments are enumerated with slight variations in order and exegetical derivation. The following is the list given by Levi: 1. Prohibition of the worship of other gods;[2] 2. Blaspheming the name of God; 3. Cursing judges; 4. Murder; 5. Incest and adultery; 6. Robbery.[3] Levi's teacher Johanan, gives them thus: Command to establish courts of justice;[4] prohibition of blaspheming the name of God; of the worship of other gods; murder; incest and adultery; theft.[5]

These commandments were given again to Noah after the flood for all his descendants, with the addition of a seventh, consequent upon the permission then given to eat the flesh of animals (Gen. 9, 3); namely, the prohibition of flesh with the blood of life in it (Gen. 9, 4).[6] Other laws were held by some authorities

---

[1] See Note 44.
[2] That there was a primaeval revelation of the unity of God and the sin of idolatry was commonly assumed. More philosophically minded men like the author of the Wisdom of Solomon saw in nature evidence to which men shut their eyes (Wisdom 13, 1 ff.); Philo, e.g. De decalogo cc. 13 f. (ed. Mangey II, 190, 191). Cf. Paul, Romans 1, 18 ff.; see also Acts 14, 17; 17, 24 ff.
[3] Gen. R. 16, 6. Bacher, Pal. Amoräer, II, 316 and n. 3.
[4] On this commandment see Tos. 'Abodah Zarah 8, 4; Sanhedrin 56b, end.
[5] Sanhedrin 56b. See Note 45.
[6] Tos. 'Abodah Zarah 8, 4; Sanhedrin 56a, end. See Note 45.

to be binding on the descendants of Noah (Gentiles); but the prevailing opinion limited them to these seven. The Gentiles, it was taught, had undertaken to keep these laws, but did not do so, or they proved unable to live up to them. Other commandments were given to the patriarchs; circumcision to Abraham, the prohibition of 'the sinew that shrank' to Jacob.[1]

Whereas in the Pentateuch the whole system of festivals, the ritual of sacrifice with the functions and prerogatives of the priesthood, are revealed first at Sinai, the Book of Jubilees narrates how they were introduced upon some specific occasion centuries before. Thus Pentecost was instituted by Noah after the flood, and was kept by Abraham, Isaac and Jacob, and by their descendants down to the generation of Moses (6, 17 ff.); Tabernacles was celebrated by Abraham in booths (16, 20 ff.), and later by Jacob, who added to it the eighth day (32, 4 ff., 27); the fast of the Day of Atonement is given a historical motive in the life of Jacob (34, 17–19); the priesthood has its beginning in the solemn consecration of Levi himself (32, 1–15); the elaborate sacrificial ritual of the priests' law in the Pentateuch is practiced on the proper occasions from Noah down (see, e.g., c. 7); the injunctions given by Abraham to his children (20, 1–10), especially to Isaac (c. 21), anticipate not only the legislation of Moses but in part the temple regulations of the Greek period (21, 12 f.). There are also in Jubilees many legal regulations differing from those of the Mishnah and kindred works, generally in the direction of greater strictness, which are attributed to the ages before Moses.

In rabbinical circles the question was raised whether the laws given to Israel by Moses had not been known to the Patriarchs — does it not say that the law which Moses gave was an "inheritance of the congregation of Jacob," coming to them, that is, from the Fathers?[2] Abraham, in particular, it was said, was

---

[1] Gen. 17, 10 ff.; 32, 33. There is no prohibition in the Law of eating the 'sinew that shrank.' According to M. Hullin 7, 6 such a law was given at Sinai, "but it was written only in its place," *sc.* in the narrative.

[2] Deut. 33, 4; Sifrè Deut. § 345.

thoroughly versed in both the written and the unwritten law, and kept them both. He followed all the commandments most scrupulously; even the *'erub tabshilin* was observed in his household.[1]

Whatever previous revelations there had been, they were all included in the complete and final revelation, the twofold Law given to Israel at Sinai. The religion thus revealed was the religion of Israel and of no other nation — that was the history of the past and the present fact. But the Jews had long since come to believe that as the one true religion it was destined to be the religion of all mankind; and the question which emerged with the beginning of reflection on the implications of the idea of universal revealed religion still pressed for an answer: How can the revelation have been made to one nation only? The author of Isa. 40 ff., who found his solution in the prophetic mission of Israel, confronting the idolatrous polytheism of his surroundings, concentrated the idea of true religion into a pure monotheism and a moral life; of Jewish observances he emphasizes only the sabbath, which in the exile became the symbol of Judaism. A similar situation produced a similar simplification in much of the literature of Jewish apologetic and propaganda in the Hellenistic dispersion.

In Jewish Palestine, however, monotheism was not a question; there was no active propaganda, and the condemnation of idolatry was not addressed to Gentiles. Naturally, therefore, when men thought of revealed religion, it was religion as a rule of life rather than as the recognition of the one true God; and this the more because it was the interpretation and application of the rule of life, not the knowledge of God, on which there was discussion in the schools and controversy between sects. With the emphasis thus given the divine law as the content of revelation — a law to which the intrinsic universality of true religion itself was neces-

---

[1] Tanḥuma ed. Buber, Lek leka § 1 (see Buber's note), and cf. § 23; Yoma 28b. In other parallels the *'erub ḥaṣerot* is specified, e.g. Gen. R. 64, 4. See Note 46.

sarily ascribed — the exclusiveness of the revelation to Israel was a more difficult problem. The difficulty was enhanced by the fact that, as it was now conceived, not only the fortunes of nations were determined by their attitude toward the true religion, but the fate of individuals after death. Did it consist with the justice of God that the heathen of all generations should be doomed for not keeping a law which neither they nor their fathers had ever known?

Some such reflections, I conceive, gave rise to the persuasion that the law must have been revealed to the Gentiles also; not alone the rudimentary law given to Adam and repeated to Noah, but the Law in its Sinaitic completeness. From the conviction *a priori* that God must have done something to the assertion that actually he did, and then to the discovery in Scripture of proofs of the fact, is a process too familiar in the history of religious thought to require explanation or extenuation in the particular case.

That the whole law was revealed at Sinai to all nations and offered to them for their acceptance, but refused by all except Israel, is not, like many of the things we have had occasion to note — like Abraham's expertness in the study and practice of the twofold law, for example — a scholastic conceit or a play of homiletical subtlety; it was the teaching of both the great schools of the second century, the schools of Ishmael and Akiba, and is therefore presumably part of the earlier common tradition from which they drew; and it is repeated in many places with varying circumstantial details. The law was given in the desert (Exod. 19, 1), given with all publicity in a place which no one had any claim to, lest, if it were given in the land of Israel, the Jews might deny to the Gentiles any part in it;[1] or lest any nation in whose territory it was given might claim an exclusive right in it. It was given in the desert, in fire and in water, things which are free to all who are born into the world. It was

---

[1] Mekilta, Baḥodesh 2 (ed. Friedmann f. 62a; ed. Weiss f. 70a), on Exod. 19, 2. See Note 47.

revealed at Sinai, not in one language but in four — Hebrew, Roman, Arabic, and Aramaic.[1] The foreign languages here named — "Roman" being the language of Seir (Esau) — are those of peoples living, one might say, within hearing distance of the thunder tones of revelation at Sinai, and it is these three neighboring peoples which in the often repeated story refused the law because it forbade the sins to which they were by heredity addicted, murder, adultery, and robbery.[2]

In Jewish computation, however, based on Gen. 10, the nations of the world were seventy, and the notion that the law was given to all nations takes the form of a revelation in seventy languages. Sometimes it is God's voice at Sinai that is heard in all seventy at once;[3] or Moses in the plains of Moab interpreted the law in seventy languages;[4] or, again, the law was inscribed on the stones of the altar on Mount Ebal (Josh. 8, 31 f.), and the nations sent their scribes who copied it in seventy different languages.[5] Everywhere the nations refused to receive the law thus offered to them; Israel alone accepted it and pledged obedience to it. God foreknew that the Gentiles would not receive it, but he offered it to them that they might have no ground to impugn his justice; it is not his way to punish without such justification, he does not deal tyrannously with his creatures.[6]

That Israel alone among the nations has the true religion argues, therefore, no partiality or injustice in God; it is because, while all the rest refused the revelation he made of his character and will, Israel joyfully received it and solemnly bound itself to live in conformity to it.[7] In content and intention the Law is

---

[1] Sifrè Deut. § 343 (ed. Friedmann f. 142b, near the top).

[2] Ibid. See Note 48.

[3] Shabbat 88b. See Note 49.

[4] Gen. R. 49, 2; Tanḥuma ed. Buber, Lek leka § 23 (f. 40a); Agadat Bereshit c. 16, 2.

[5] Tos. Soṭah 8, 6 (Judah ben Ilaʿi); cf. Soṭah 35b.

[6] Pesiḳta ed. Buber f. 200a; Tanḥuma ed. Buber, Berakah § 3 (f. 28a). See Note 50.

[7] In that moment and by that act the Reign of God (*malkut Shamaim*, 'Kingdom of Heaven'), which till then had been acknowledged only by individuals, became national.

universal; and, notwithstanding the collective rejection by the
Gentiles, individual Gentiles who obey its commandments share
in its promises. Thus, in Lev. 18, 5, 'Ye shall therefore keep my
statutes and my ordinances, which if a man do, he shall live by
them,' R. Meir is reported to have found proof for the assertion
that even a foreigner (or Gentile) who occupies himself with
the Law is like the high priest; for in that verse it is not said
that priests, levites, and (lay) Israelites shall live by them, but
"a *man*," therefore even a Gentile.[1] This view is set forth more
fully in Sifra on Lev. 18, 5 in the name of R. Jeremiah: "If you
ask whence we learn that even a Gentile who obeys the law is
like the high priest, the answer is found in the words, 'Which if
a *man* (any human being) do, he shall live by them.' So again
it is said, 'This is the law of mankind, Lord God' (2 Sam. 7,
19); not this is the law of priests and levites and Israelites,[2] but
of *mankind*. And again, 'Open the gates that a righteous Gentile
keeping faithfulness may enter by it' (Isa. 26, 2); not open the
gates that there may enter priests, levites, and Israelites, 'This is
the gate of the Lord; the righteous shall enter by it' (Psalm
118, 20); not priests, levites, Israelites. It does not say, Rejoice,
priests and levites and Israelites, but, 'Rejoice, ye righteous, in
the Lord' (Psalm 33, 1). Not, Do good, O Lord, to the priests,
levites, Israelites, but 'Do good, O Lord, to the good' (Psalm
125, 4). Hence it follows that even a Gentile who obeys the
law is like the high priest." [3]

The Sadducees denied the authority of the unwritten law;
they acknowledged no revelation but that in Scripture.[4] They
had traditions of their own, ritual and jural, but their authority
rested on prescription or the legislative powers of rulers or

[1] Sanhedrin 59a; Baba Ḳamma 38a; 'Abodah Zarah 3a.

[2] Priests, levites, lay Israelites, are not social classes, but the three worshipping congregations. The high priest is not counted among them, and
therein lies the resemblance between the Gentile student of the Law and the
high priest specifically.

[3] Sifra, Aḥarè Pereḳ 13 (ed. Weiss f. 86b). See Note 51.

[4] Josephus, Antt. xiii. 10, 6; see above, pp. 57 f.; 68.

of the Sanhedrin, not on supplementary instructions given to Moses at Sinai. In their interpretation of the written law for practical purposes — they had no scholastic interest in the subject — the Sadducees were common-sense literalists, and consequently often more rigorous than the Pharisees, not only in the field of criminal law,[1] but in various other matters in regard to which the 'tradition' of the Pharisees was more accommodating. On the other hand, they ridiculed the absurdity of the Pharisaic dictum that manuscripts of sacred Scriptures render unclean the hands of one who touches them, while profane books do not.[2]

The points in dispute between Pharisees and Sadducees in the days when the latter were a powerful or even a dominant party were undoubtedly much more serious than the trivialities that are incidentally reported in our sources. Even in the first generations after the fall of Jerusalem the real issues had fallen into oblivion. The destruction of the temple and the abolition of the Sanhedrin left the surviving Sadducees a mere sect, small in numbers, without influence among the people, and standing for nothing in particular except their hereditary antipathy to the Pharisees, an antipathy which found expression in cavilling questions and paltry annoyances rather than in serious controversy. Thenceforth the authority of the unwritten law and of the Pharisaean interpretation of the Scriptures was uncontested; the teaching of the schools and the decisions of rabbinical assemblies more and more completely dominated Judaism not only in Palestine but in the Dispersion.

[1] Josephus, Antt. xiii. 10, 6.
[2] M. Yadaim 4, 6.

CHAPTER V

THE SYNAGOGUE

A consequence of the idea of revealed religion which was of the utmost moment in all the subsequent history of Judaism was the endeavor to educate the whole people in its religion. Such an undertaking has no parallel in the ancient Mediterranean world. The religion of the household in Egypt or Greece or Rome was a matter of domestic tradition, perpetuated by example rather than by instruction, and no attempt was ever made to systematize it and make it uniform, or even to fix it; the religion of the city or the state was a tradition of the priesthoods, in whose charge the public cultus was, and who gave directions and assistance *pro re nata* to individuals in private sacrifices and expiations. If the usage of the sanctuary was reduced to writing, it was done privately for the convenience of the priests themselves. The possession of a body of sacred Scriptures, including the principles of their religion as well as its ritual and the observances of the household and the individual, of itself put the Jews in a different case.

What gave the motive to the unique endeavor of which we have spoken was not the mere possession of such sacred Scriptures, but the conviction that in these Scriptures God had revealed to his people his will for their whole life, and that the welfare of the nation and the fulfilment of its hopes for the future depended upon its conformity to his revealed will. The recovery of independence, with all the political and material prosperity the prophets depicted in such splendid imagery, would not come until they proved themselves fit for it by doing their best to fulfil the obligation they had undertaken when at Sinai their fathers professed, "All that the Lord hath spoken will we do and obey." [1] This was the religious motive in the zeal with which the Pharisaic party in New Testament times not only took pains to instruct the masses in the proper observance of the law but strove to impose on them the "traditions of the elders," and to induce individuals voluntarily to pledge themselves to be scrupulous in certain matters about which there was general laxity. It was for this that they made an ever thicker and thornier hedge about the letter of the law "to keep men at a distance from transgression."

The Pharisees made of the resurrection of the dead an article of faith, and taught that between death and the resurrection the souls of the righteous awaited the last judgment in blessedness and those of the wicked in misery. Inasmuch as righteousness and wickedness are defined by man's conformity to the divinely revealed norms of character and conduct or disregard of them, the well-being of the individual after death as well as the realization of the national hope demanded education in religion. For with the Jewish conception of religion it was not to be imagined that a man or a people could be righteous without knowing God's holy character, and what was right in his eyes and what wrong. And if God had revealed these things, plainly revelation was the only place to go to learn them.

To those who are accustomed to regard religion as primarily a way by which a man may be assured of salvation for his own particular soul, this personal motive for study and observance might seem more compelling than the desire to bring near the national salvation, and this impression is strengthened by Paul's argument, which implies that the salvation of the individual by the works of the law was the chief end of Jewish religiousness. The inference would, however, be erroneous, at least for Palestinian Judaism in the period under our consideration, as will be made clear in a subsequent chapter.

[1] The Asmonaean failure, charged to the religious shortcomings of princes and people (Psalms of Solomon 2, 15–18, and passim), doubtless contributed to this conviction, and the memory of this failure made the Pharisees averse to messianic enthusiasm and agitations for independence.

For the education of the whole people in the principles and practice of its religion Judaism had two institutions, outgrowths of the religion itself, which were in their respective spheres admirably adapted to this end, the synagogue and the school; and these two, though of independent origin and never organically connected, worked together in a harmony which resulted in substantial unity of instruction.

It is not probable that the synagogue began with so definite a purpose.[1] Its origin is unknown, but it may be reasonably surmised that it had its antecedents in spontaneous gatherings of Jews in Babylonia and other lands of their exile on the sabbaths and at the times of the old seasonal feasts or on fast days,[2] to confirm one another in fidelity to their religion in the midst of heathenism, and encourage themselves in the hope of restoration. In such gatherings we may imagine them listening to the words of a living prophet like Ezekiel[3] or the author of Isa. 40 ff., or reading the words of older prophets; confessing the sins which had brought this judgment upon the nation and beseeching the return of God's favor in such penitential prayers as ere long became an established type in Hebrew literature, or in poetical compositions of similar content such as are found in the Book of Lamentations and in the Psalter.

The proved religious value of such gatherings would lead to custom and to the spread of the institution to other communities; the things which it would be most natural to do and say under such circumstances at least contain the elements of the later synagogue service.[4] Wherever and however it arose, the

---

[1] See Note 52.   [2] Zech. 7, 5; Isa. 58.

[3] Ezek. 8, 1; 14, 1; 20, 1. Many of the prophecies of Ezekiel may nave been delivered on such occasions. Perhaps such chapters as Deut. 4; 29 f., may have been composed to be read in such assemblies; cf. also Lev. 26.

[4] Possible mention of such associations in the Old Testament: קהל חסידים, ἐκκλησία ὁσίων, Psalm 149, 1; עדת צדיקים, Psalm 1, 5; cf. οἱ ἀγαπῶντες συναγωγὰς ὁσίων, Psalms of Solomon 17, 18. See also Enoch (Parables) 38, 1; 53, 6; 62, 8. In 53, 6 we read that "the righteous and elect one shall cause the house of his congregation to appear," which Charles and Beer understand of synagogues (restored by the Messiah—Beer). Is it rather the temple of the new age?

synagogue was at the beginning of our era already an institution of long standing, which like all the religious institutions of Judaism was believed to have been established by Moses,[1] while the liturgical prayers were said to have been appointed by the Men of the Great Assembly.[2] It was to be found in the Dispersion wherever there were Jews enough to maintain one. In Palestine there were synagogues in all the cities and towns; there were many in Jerusalem itself, under the very shadow of the temple, and even one within its precincts.[3]

If the synagogue as we know it in New Testament times or from the Mishnah is compared with the voluntary private assemblies which we have supposed to be its forerunners, two important differences appear: *First*, before the beginning of the Christian era it had become a public institution, commonly possessing an edifice for religious gatherings erected by the community or given to it by individuals — sometimes by pious Gentiles (Luke, 7, 5). It was no longer a surrogate for the worship in the temple among Jews who were deprived of participation in the cultus by the cessation of sacrifice or by their remoteness from Jerusalem,[4] but had attained an independent position as the seat of a worship of different character, a rational worship without sacrifice or offering. And, *Second*, regular instruction in religion had taken its place as an organic part of worship, and even as its most prominent feature.

In this double character the synagogue was a wholly unique institution. To the observation of the Greeks it suggested a school of philosophy. The preliminary purifications and the prayers which preceded the reading and exposition of its books were not without analogies in certain Greek religious and philosophical circles such as the Pythagoreans. The teaching of the

---

[1] Philo Vita Mosis iii. 27 (ed. Mangey II, 167 f.); Josephus, Contra Apionem ii. 17.

[2] Berakot 33a. See Note 53.

[3] M. Yoma 7, 1; M. Soṭah 7, 7 f.; Tos. Sukkah 4, 11. See Note 54.

[4] Ezek. 11, 16; see Note 55.

synagogue also, particularly its fundamental monotheism and its emphasis on morals, was to Greek apprehension purely philosophical doctrine. Hellenistic Jews like Philo described the Sabbath services of the synagogue for Greek readers in the same way: the Jews laid aside all their ordinary occupations, not to take the time for sports and shows, but to devote themselves wholly to philosophy — real philosophy, their national philosophy.[1]

To the Jews, however, as appears clearly enough in Philo himself, the synagogue was a place for instruction in the truths and duties of revealed religion; and in imparting and receiving this divine instruction no less than in praise or prayer they were doing honor to God — it was an act of worship. The consequence of the establishment of such a rational worship for the whole subsequent history of Judaism was immeasurable. Its persistent character, and, it is not too much to say, the very preservation of its existence through all the vicissitudes of its fortunes, it owes more than anything else to the synagogue. Nor is it for Judaism alone that it had this importance. It determined the type of Christian worship, which in the Greek and Roman world of the day might otherwise easily have taken the form of a mere mystery; and, in part directly, in part through the church, it furnished the model to Mohammed. Thus Judaism gave to the world not only the fundamental ideas of these great monotheistic religions but the institutional forms in which they have perpetuated and propagated themselves.

How the synagogue became a universal public institution of Judaism, and when the regular reading and exposition of the Law came to have a central place in the worship, history gives no hint. There is indeed no mention of synagogues at all in Jewish writings surviving from the centuries preceding the Christian era, unless, as is commonly thought, Psalm 74,8,

---

[1] Vita Mosis iii. 27 § 211 (ed. Mangey II, 167); cf. De septenario c. 6 §§ 61 f. (II, 282); De somniis ii. 18 (I, 675). Similarly of the Therapeutae, De vita contemplativa c. 3 §§ 30 ff. (II, 476). Cf. Josephus, Antt. xviii. 1, 2. See Note 56.

"They have burned all the meeting places of God in the land,"
be such a reference.[1]

It is hardly likely that this double development of the synagogue came about of itself by a kind of natural evolution unconscious of its ends. In its singular adaptation to the religious
education of the whole people it seems rather to give evidence
of intelligent purpose; and all that we know about the times, as
well as the subsequent history of the synagogue, would incline
us to conjecture that the leading part in this development was
taken by the Pharisees from the second century before our era.
The Pharisees were an outgrowth of the Ḥasidim, representing the active and progressive element in that party—those who
thought that when men had nullified God's law, it was "time
to do something for the Lord." The Maccabaean struggle was
eminently such a time, and men of insight must have learned
from the apostasy of many in high places and the indifference
of the most that there was nothing more urgent to do than to
inculcate and confirm religious loyalty by worship, knowledge,
and habit, through some such means as the synagogue. The
permanent security of the religion, to say nothing of the greater
things it held in prospect, could only be attained by bringing all
classes to an understanding of the distinctive nature of Judaism,
an appreciation of its incomparable worth, and a devotion to
its peculiar observances like that which the Pharisees themselves cultivated in their pledge-bound societies. Education in
revealed religion which has its revelation in sacred scriptures is
of necessity education in the Scripture: methodical instruction
in the Law, was, under these conditions, the foundation of everything. Hence the regular readings from the Pentateuch, accompanied by an interpretative translation into the vernacular,
and followed by an expository or edifying discourse, usually
taking something in the lesson as a point of departure, became
constant elements of the synagogue service.

Among the Pharisees were many of the Scribes (biblical

[1] See Note 57.

scholars), who seem hitherto, as we gather from the references to them in Sirach, to have stood as a class somewhat aloof from the populace, conscious of a learning and intelligence beyond the comprehension of the vulgar.[1] Once drawn into the movement, however, they naturally took an important part in instruction of the people, and the interpretation of the Scripture in the synagogue was thus directly connected with the traditional learning of the Scribes as it was in later times with that of the schools. Whether or not the Pharisees adapted the synagogue more completely to the ends of religious education in some such way as has been suggested, it is certain that they took possession of it and made most effective use of it. Through it, more perhaps than by any other means, they gained the hold upon the mass of the people which enabled them to come out victorious from their conflicts with John Hyrcanus and Alexander Jannaeus and to establish such power as Josephus ascribes to them.[2]

The synagogue in the hands of the Pharisees was doubtless the chief instrument in the Judaizing of Galilee. In the days of Judas Maccabaeus, the Jews, or at least those who were faithful to their religion, were a very small part of the mixed population of Galilee — so few that Simon, after defeating the heathen who threatened to exterminate them, carried the Galilean Jews and all their belongings off to Jerusalem for safety.[3] Within not much more than a century, Galilee had become as Jewish as Judaea, and more inclined to excesses of national and religious zeal which brought them repeatedly into conflict with the Roman government.

The necessity of such an institution as the synagogue was even greater outside of Palestine than in it; for while at home the Jews had a religious centre in the temple and a bond of union in its worship, especially at the festivals, in foreign lands there was nothing of the kind. It is probable that the Jews in the Disper-

---

[1] Ecclus. 6, 32 ff.; 9, 14 ff.; 14, 20 ff.; especially 38, 24 ff.

[2] Josephus, Antt. xiii. 10, 5 f.; 15, 5; 16, 1 f.; Bell. Jud. i. 5, 1-3.

[3] 1 Macc. 5, 21-23. Making all allowance for exaggeration, it remains that Galilee in those days was mainly heathen.

sion were from the beginning accustomed to gather on the sabbath as a day of leisure, if only to meet their countrymen, and
their gatherings would naturally assume in some degree a religious character. Without some such association, indeed, it is
hardly imaginable that the Jewish communities, deprived of every
form of public cult, should have maintained the religion of their
fathers. It is now the general opinion of scholars that the Greek
translation of the Pentateuch early in the third century B.C. was
undertaken, not to enrich Ptolemy's Library as the fictitious
letter of Aristeas narrates, but for the use of Jews among whom
knowledge of Hebrew was becoming rare; though it does not
follow that it was made especially for public reading in the
Alexandrian synagogues.

   Much in the history of the synagogue is thus obscure, but
what is certain is that for several generations, at least, before our
era the synagogue had been what it was in subsequent centuries,
an institute of religious education, universal, unique in aim and
method, and in a high degree effective. A good measure of this
effectiveness is given by the earliest Gospels. Jesus and his
disciples were Galilaeans, from a region in which the expansion
of Judaism was comparatively recent, and where the great
rabbinical schools were still of the future. Jesus himself grew
up in an obscure little town even the name of which is not found
outside of the New Testament. All were men of the people;
there was no scholar among them. What they knew of the words
of Scripture and its meaning they had learned in the synagogue
from the readings and the homilies; no other sources of knowledge were accessible to them.[1] Many apposite references to the
Scriptures, or quotations from them, were probably introduced
into the Gospels in the course of transmission, but when all
deductions are made, and within the limits of what has the presumption of being authentic tradition of the words of Jesus, the
range of quotation and allusion is remarkably wide, embracing
the Pentateuch, the Prophets, the Psalms, and occasionally some

   [1] See Note 58.

others of the Hagiographa; the number of references is large, and the aptness with which they are adduced evinces notable intimacy with Scripture. That the synagogue gave opportunity to acquire such familiarity is sufficient testimony to the quality of its instruction. For the Hellenistic synagogues, the knowledge of Scripture which Paul assumes that his hearers possess gives similar witness.

Each synagogue was presided over by a Head of the Synagogue,[1] probably chosen from among the 'elders' by coöptation, who had general oversight of the exercises in the synagogue, maintaining order (Luke 13, 14), inviting strangers to address the assembly (Acts 13, 15), and the like. A salaried officer was the synagogue attendant, the 'minister' (Luke 4, 20).[2] In his charge were the synagogue building and its furniture, especially the rolls of the Scriptures; sometimes he had his dwelling under the same roof. From the roof of the synagogue he gave the signal to people to stop work on the approach of the sabbath by a thrice repeated blast on a trumpet,[3] and similarly gave notice of the close of the holy day. In the service of the synagogue the attendant brought the roll of Scripture from the press and delivered it to the reader; when the reading was concluded he received it back (Luke 4, 20), rolled it up, and after holding it up to the view of the congregation returned it to the press.[4] He also indicated to the priest the point at which the benediction should be pronounced,[5] and at the fasts he told the priests when to blow the trumpets.[6]

In smaller communities the Ḥazzan often had to fill a variety of other offices. When there were not readers enough at the

---

[1] *Rosh ha-keneset*, M. Soṭah 7, 7 f., and elsewhere; ἀρχισυνάγωγος, Mark 5, 22, etc. See Note 59.

[2] *Ḥazzan ha-keneset*. M. Soṭah 7, 7 f. and often. See Note 60.

[3] Tos. Sukkah 4, 11 f.; Shabbat 35b.

[4] Compare the more elaborate ceremony described in M. Soṭah 7, 7–8.

[5] Sifrè Num. § 39, end; Soṭah 38a.

[6] Ta'anit 16b. See in general W. Bacher, 'Synagogue,' in Hastings' Dictionary of the Bible, IV, 640 ff.

service he had to fill out the number, or even to read the whole
lesson himself;[1] he might also have to lead in prayer.[2] The
inhabitants of Simonias asked the Patriarch Judah to give them
a man who could serve them as preacher, judge, sexton (*haz-
zan*), school master, teacher of the traditional law, and whatever else they needed, and he sent them such a universal func-
tionary in the person of Levi ben Sisi.[3] Especially frequent
was the combination of sexton and schoolmaster.[4]

The synagogues in prosperous communities were often fine
edifices according to the taste of the time and place; the community did not spare money on the decoration and furnishing.
The essential parts of the synagogue furniture were a chest,
or press, in which the rolls of the Scriptures were kept, usually
standing in an alcove or recess shut off by a curtain from the
body of the synagogue; and a *bema*, or platform, with a reading
desk on which the roll of the Pentateuch or the Prophets was
laid for the reading of the lessons. Lamps and candelabra also
belonged to the furnishings of the synagogue. The notices we
possess about the internal arrangement and furniture of the
Palestinian synagogues are from the second century, and it is not
improbable that after the destruction of the temple there was a
tendency to assimilate the synagogue in such externals to the
temple, as certain features of the temple worship were taken over
into the service of the synagogue and terms of the sacrificial
cultus were appropriated to prayers of the synagogue; but we
have no reason to question that the synagogue and its services
had essentially the same character before the destruction of
Jerusalem as after. This is confirmed by the descriptions Philo
gives of the worship in Alexandrian synagogues.[5]

---

[1] For an example see Megillah 25b. When the Ḥazzan read, another had
to take upon him the Ḥazzan's ordinary offices, Tos. Megillah 4, 21.

[2] An instance, Jer. Berakot 12d, middle.

[3] Jer. Yebamot 13a. Levi did not acquit himself of the task to their satisfaction. Cf. Jer. Shebi'it 36d, top, the story of R. Simeon ben Laḳish at
Bosra.

[4] See Note 61.

[5] On the architecture and furnishings of the synagogues see Note 62.

The constant parts of the synagogue service were prayer, the reading of the lessons from the Scripture, followed, if a competent person was present, by a homily. The prayer was preceded by the recitation of what may be called the Jewish confession of faith, usually named from its first word, the Shema': 'Hear, O Israel, the Lord our God, the Lord is One,[1] and thou shalt love the Lord thy God with all thy heart, and with all thy soul, and with all thy might' (Deut. 6, 4 f.),[2] introduced and followed by sentences of ascription, called Berakot because they regularly begin, after the pattern of similar ascriptions in the Psalms, with the word, 'Blessed.' Thus in the first of the ascriptions which constitute the regular preface to the Shema', whether said privately morning and evening or in public worship, runs: "Blessed art thou, O Lord our God, King of the world, former of light and creator of darkness, author of welfare (peace), and creator of all things." [3]

The recitation of the Shema' is followed by the prayer, Tefillah.[4] In the oldest form in which it is known to us, it consists of a series of 'Benedictions,' so called from the responses at the close of each ascription or petition: "Blessed art thou, O Lord," etc. In an arrangement made toward the end of the first century there were eighteen such prayers, whence the common name, 'The Eighteen' (sc. Benedictions), Shemoneh 'Esreh,[5] and this name was perpetuated unchanged when subsequently a nineteenth was added; it is popularly used also of the prayers on sabbaths and festivals, when only six of the eighteen (nineteen)

---

[1] That is, 'sole God.' This is doubtless the way in which the words were construed and understood. Cf. Deut. 4, 35, 39; 7, 9.

[2] Mark 12, 29 f. and parallels. On the Shema' of the liturgy and the Berakot see Note 63.

[3] The Decalogue once had a place in the synagogue liturgy, but was dropped to give no occasion to "the cavils of heretics." See Note 64.

[4] Tefillah is the Biblical word for prayer as petition (Isa. 1, 15; 1 Kings 8, 38) or intercession (2 Kings 19, 4; Jer. 7, 16; 11, 14, etc.). For the Jewish use see Note 65.

[5] E.g. M. Berakot 4, 3: Rabban Gamaliel said, "A man should pray the Eighteen every day."

are said.[1] The prayer opens with the praise of God (Nos. 1–3); and closes with thanksgiving to God (Nos. 17–19); the petitions (Nos. 4–16) are thus enclosed in ascriptions.[2]

The ordaining of the ascriptions and of the prayers in general was attributed to the Men of the Great Assembly, with whom so many others of the institutions of Judaism were reputed to have originated.[3] The same body is probably meant when it is said elsewhere that "a hundred and twenty elders, among whom were a number of prophets," prescribed the Eighteen Benedictions in their order.[4] But by the side of this stands a historical statement that a certain otherwise unknown Simeon ha-Pakuli, in the presence and presumably under the direction of R. Gamaliel (II) at Jamnia, arranged the Eighteen Benedictions in the order in which they were to be said.[5] Inasmuch as Gamaliel made the daily repetition of the Eighteen obligatory on every man — a rule which was disapproved by some of his influential contemporaries [6] — fixing of the order of the prayers was a natural corollary, and perhaps the exact number of prayers that should constitute a complete Tefillah (eighteen) was fixed at the same time.[7] The prayer for the extirpation of heretics, formulated by another of his disciples, Simeon the Little, was introduced into the prayers by order of Gamaliel.[8]

All forms of the Tefillah that are known to us in the past or the present go back to this redaction by the authority of Gamaliel II about the end of the first century of our era, and, with many verbal variations and much amplification, they exhibit a constant order and an essential unity of content. There is no doubt, however, that the work of the redactor was principally, as the tradition describes it, to arrange in appropriate order

[1] See below, p. 295.

[2] Sifrè Deut. § 343. See Note 66.

[3] Berakot 33a.

[4] Megillah 17b; Jer. Berakot 4d.

[5] Megillah 17b; Berakot 28b, end.

[6] M. Berakot 4, 3.

[7] See Note 67.

[8] The oldest Palestinian form of this petition is: "For apostates may there be no hope, and may the Nazarenes and the heretics suddenly perish." See Note 68.

existing topics of prayer, probably with the exercise of a certain selection among nearly equivalent petitions and the adoption of a normal, though not obligatory, phraseology. The petitions themselves, upon internal evidence, had their origin at various times and under different circumstances, and they have often been recast or modified to adapt them to changed situations.[1] In their religious spirit they resemble the Psalms, from which their diction also is chiefly drawn. Some of them were brought over into the service of the synagogue from the temple liturgy; others were perhaps originally framed for the private use of individuals; while others still, expressing feelings and desires of the community or the people, seem to have their origin in the synagogue itself.

Certain evidences of the age of individual petitions are rare. The resurrection of the dead in the second benediction is an indication not only of age but of the circles in which the prayer was framed; it is specific Pharisaic doctrine, and cannot well have got into the synagogue prayers till the Pharisees obtained control of the synagogue. There are, as we should expect, expressions which imply the destruction of Jerusalem and the cessation of the sacrificial cultus, but these seem to be engrafted on older petitions or to be modifications of them, rather than the substance of new ones. On the other hand the nucleus of the prayers is doubtless of greater antiquity.[2] In second century sources and thereafter there is abundant evidence of familiarity with the prayers, which are cited by their opening phrase or by characteristic words.[3]

The three prefatory benedictions bless the God of the Fathers, Abraham, Isaac, and Jacob; the Mighty God, who nourishes the living and revives the dead; the Holy God. Petitions follow for knowledge, repentance, forgiveness, deliverance from affliction, healing, for a bountiful year, the gathering of the dispersed

[1] See Note 69.

[2] See Elbogen, Der jüdische Gottesdienst, p. 30.

[3] The names of the first three and the last two are given in M. Rosh ha-Shanah 4, 5. See Note 70.

of Israel, the restoration of good government, the destruction of heretics and apostates, for the elders of the people and upright converts, for the rebuilding of the temple and the reign of the Davidic dynasty, for the hearing of prayer, the restoration of sacrificial worship; closing with thanksgiving for God's goodness and loving-kindness, and a final prayer for peace and the welfare of all God's people.

It will be observed that the first group of petitions are of a personal nature, though they are the needs of all men, and that religious needs — knowledge and intelligence, repentance, forgiveness of sins — take precedence of natural needs. These are succeeded by a less coherent and well-ordered group of petitions chiefly for public or national goods, which, as might be expected, have suffered more extensive changes than the preceding individual petitions. Repeated changes have been made also in the names of the adversaries in the *Birkat ha-Minim*, in consequence of the change of times or environment.[1] An increasingly eschatological direction of the individual hope led also to the more frequent mention of the resurrection of the dead.

The last three prayers are, as we have seen, called 'Thanksgivings'; in fact, however, this character belongs only to the penultimate, the other two being petitions. After the prayer of thanksgiving came the priestly benediction when it was pronounced; and this was followed by a prayer for peace which was a kind of congregational response to the priest's benediction, whose words, "The Lord lift up his countenance upon thee and give thee peace," are taken up: "Bestow peace . . . upon us," etc., with the corresponding benediction, "Maker of peace." From this relation, the last prayer is itself called 'the priests' benediction' (*Birkat Kohanim*).[2]

The priestly benediction was taken over into the synagogue from the temple,[3] where, in conformity with Num. 6, 22–28, the

---

[1] In Jer. Berakot 4d the petition is summarized, "Bring low our adversaries." See Note **68**.

[2] M. Rosh ha-Shanah 4, 5; M. Tamid 5, 1.

[3] See Note **71**.

priests blessed the worshipping congregation in the words: "The Lord bless thee and keep thee. The Lord make his face to shine upon thee and be gracious unto thee. The Lord lift up his countenance upon thee and give thee peace." [1] In the temple the blessing was pronounced in the course of the regular daily burnt-offering, where, as soon as the parts of the victim had been laid on the altar, the priests took their place on the steps leading up to the portico. [2] In the synagogue it occupied a corresponding position, following the prayer for the acceptance of sacrifices, or (after 70 A.D.) for the restoration of sacrifice. The blessing was not pronounced at every service of the synagogue: in the first centuries of our era it was given at daily morning prayer when a legal congregation (ten men) was assembled and a priest was present, and at additional services on the sabbaths and festivals.

Of the regular daily morning prayer (*Tefillah, Shemoneh 'Esreh*) described above only the first three and the last three prayers are recited on sabbaths and festivals, and the concurrence of all the rites in this gives good ground for inferring that it was the oldest custom. The place of the thirteen intervening petitions is filled by a single prayer having for its subject the day and its proper observance, so that the prayer consists of seven parts; New Year's, however, has in this place three special prayers instead of one.

The ascriptions and petitions in the prayer in their earliest form were all short, several of them consisting of but two clauses with a correspondingly brief benediction; and even in the expanded form of later times they are of moderate dimensions compared with other parts of the liturgy. The Shema' and the Tefillah may be said in any language; the priestly benediction must be in Hebrew. [3] After the end of the public prayer, place

---

[1] For references to benediction by priests see Lev. 9, 22; Deut. 10, 8; 21, 5; Josh. 8, 33; 2 Chron. 30, 27.

[2] M. Tamid 7, 2, where the differences between the use in the temple and in the synagogue are enumerated; cf. M. Soṭah 7, 6; Tos. Soṭah 7, 8.

[3] M. Soṭah 7, 1-2; Tos. Soṭah 7, 7.

was made for the private silent petitions of individuals out of
their own hearts. Such prayers might be prolonged even to
the extent of the longest prayer in the liturgy, the confession of
sins on the Day of Atonement.[1]

Whether the use of select Psalms had established itself in the
service of the synagogue at as early a time as that with which we
are here occupied is not entirely certain, though it would seem
natural that with other features of the temple worship the songs
of the levites at the morning and evening sacrifices should be
imitated in the synagogue. The first group of Psalms to be so
employed was Psalms 145–150; but it appears that in the middle
of the second century the daily repetition of these Psalms was
a pious practice of individuals rather than a regular observance
of the congregation.[2]

The reading of the Scriptures was, as has been said above, a
characteristic feature of the synagogue service, and probably
goes back in some form or other to the beginnings of the institution. Moses is said to have ordained that portions of the
Law should be read on sabbaths, holy days, new moons, and
the intermediate days of the festivals; while Ezra is said to have
prescribed the reading on market days (Monday and Thursday)
and at the afternoon service (*minḥah*) on the Sabbath[3] —
another way of saying that at the beginning of our era the
custom was of immemorial antiquity.

In the Bible itself the only prescription for the public reading
of the Scriptures is in Deut. 31, 10, where Moses directs that
"this law" (that is, in the writer's intention, the Book of Deuteronomy or some part of it) be read in the hearing of the as-

---

[1] Tos. Berakot 3, 10; cf. Berakot 31a. At a much later time a text for such
taḥnunim was provided in the prayer-books, but the use of them was optional.

[2] Shabbat 118b (Jose ben Ḥalafta); cf. Soferim 17, 11.

[3] Jer. Megillah 75a. Elsewhere the reading on Sabbaths and market days
is an ordinance of the prophets and elders (of the Great Assembly); Mekilta
on Exod. 15, 22 (ed. Friedmann 45a, ed. Weiss 52b, end). Cf. also M. Megillah 3, 6, end; Sifra on Lev. 23, 44 (ed. Weiss f. 103b); Sifrè Deut. § 127. See
Elbogen, Der jüdische Gottesdienst, pp. 156 f., 538.

sembled people once in seven years at the Feast of Tabernacles.[1]
In Nehemiah 8 a description is given of the public reading, at
the request of the people of Judah, of the book of the Law of
Moses which Ezra the scribe had in his possession. Some of
the features of this narrative, as will be shown further on, have
a striking resemblance to the reading of the Scriptures in the
synagogue.[2]

It would be most natural that at the festal seasons passages
from the Pentateuch in which the feast is appointed and its
rites prescribed should be studied in the schools and read and
expounded in the synagogues,[3] and that among several possible
selections of this kind one should become customary. This is
the case in the oldest list of appointed lessons, M. Megillah 3,
4–6, which includes not only readings for the great festivals, and
for New Years and the Day of Atonement, but for all the eight
days of Tabernacles, the Feast of Dedication (Ḥanukkah),
Purim, New Moons, Fast Days, and for four sabbaths out of five
or six preceding the first day of Nisan. The lessons are designated by the first words of the pericope, or by a general description of the passage, without indication where the reading
ended.[4] The natural limits of most of the lessons are not large;
that for the Passover, for example, contains only five verses,
New Years only three. The longest, that for the Day of Atonement, has but thirty-four verses if the whole was read.[5] Evidently, the principal thing must have been the exposition of the
ritual and proper observance of the day, based on these short

[1] See Note 72.

[2] The Chronicler, from whose hand we have this narrative, wrote about
300 B.C. and apparently had Deut. 33, 10–13 in mind. Had he also the example of the synagogue? The contrary — that his narrative served as model
for the synagogue — is commonly assumed.

[3] See Megillah 32a, end: Moses ordained that the traditional law (*halakah*)
should be studied in connection with the season; the laws of the Passover
at Passover, etc. Sifrè Deut. § 127; Tos. Megillah 4, 5.

[4] See Note 73.

[5] The blessings and curses on public fasts (Lev. 26; Deut. 28) are longer;
but this was an exceptional all-day service.

pericopes and introducing the substance of other laws in the
Pentateuch on the same subject with the definitions of the oral
law, rather than the mere reading of the paragraph which
served as the starting point.

The four special sabbaths mentioned above had fixed lessons,
from the catch-words of which they got their names (Shekalim,
Zakor, Parah, ha-Ḥodesh).[1] The motives for the selection of
these passages for the particular sabbaths to which they are
assigned are easily discovered; Shekalim reminds the people of
the approaching collection of the annual half-shekel poll-tax;
Zakor, with its command to exterminate Amalek, is associated
with Purim through Haman the Agagite;[2] Parah suggests the
purifications necessary in preparation for the Passover; ha-
Ḥodesh (on the sabbath preceding the first of Nisan or falling
on that day) is the law of the Passover itself, the celebration of
which comes in the middle of the month.

The provision in this Mishnah for all kinds of holy days has
a systematic look, and may be later than the fall of Jerusalem;
but the lessons for the high festivals and the Day of Atonement
are probably much older, and this may be the case also with
the special sabbaths, or the most of them.[3] About the lessons
from the Pentateuch on other sabbaths nothing is certainly
known, nor is it known when the custom of reading it through
in order and within a certain number of sabbaths established
itself. It is intrinsically probable that when readings on ordinary sabbaths first came to be customary, a passage from the
Pentateuch was freely selected by the head of the synagogue or
by the reader, as long continued to be the case with the Prophets;
and even that successive readers might take passages from different parts of the volume; the prohibition in M. Megillah 4, 4,[4]

---

[1] Exod. 30, 11–16; Deut. 25, 17–19; Num. 19, 1–22; Exod. 12, 1–20.

[2] Descendant of Agag, king of the Amalekites, 1 Sam. 15.

[3] The introduction of Purim into the calendar is the extreme upper limit
for Zakor, which is, indeed, something of an intruder in a natural series preparatory to the Passover. It may be noted that in the lists of lessons the
special sabbaths precede the feasts.

[4] See Note 74.

"Readers may not skip from place to place in the Pentateuch" (as they may in the Prophets), would otherwise be meaningless. Of the reasons given for this rule in later discussion the most probable is, "that Israel may hear the Law consecutively."[1] It may not be inferred from this rule, which has reference only to the reading at a single service, that the reading was continuous from one service to another. This was a natural next step, and is represented in the middle of the second century by R. Meir: "At the place where they leave off at the Sabbath morning service, they begin at the afternoon service; where they leave off at that service, they begin on Monday; where they leave off on Monday, they begin on Thursday; and where they leave off on Thursday, they begin on the following Sabbath." Meir's contemporary, R. Judah (ben Ila'i), holds that the proper order is to begin at each Sabbath morning service where the reading ended at the morning service of the preceding Sabbath.[2] It is clear from this that authorities recognized no division of the Pentateuch into lessons of fixed length, or of a cycle of lessons to be finished within a fixed time. Assuming the normal number of readers prescribed in the Mishnah and the minimum number of verses for each reader, it has been reckoned that on R. Meir's plan it would take about two years and a third to go through the Pentateuch, and on R. Judah's not less than five and a half.[3]

Ultimately the Pentateuch was divided into sections (*sedarim*) of such length as to complete the cycle at the completion of a definite time. In the Babylonian Talmud it is noted that the Jews in the West (Palestine) read the Pentateuch through once in three years, at variance with the Babylonian Jews, who at that time were accustomed to finish it in one year. Inasmuch as there is no suggestion of such a division or practice in the

---

[1] Jer. Megillah 75b. The practical reason that rolling and unrolling the volume to find a new place was tedious for the congregation is also considered.

[2] Tos. Megillah 4, 10; Megillah 31b. See Note 75.

[3] Elbogen, Der jüdische Gottesdienst, p. 160; cf. 539.

Mishnah or Tosefta, which minutely regulate so many things about the reading of the Law, it may be inferred that it was not authoritatively established before the third century, though it may have earlier become customary.[1] The Babylonian custom, which eventually prevailed everywhere, is presumably later than the triennial system; its lessons (*parashiyot*) are in the average three times as long.[2]

The sequence of regular readings in the Pentateuch was probably at first suspended on the four special sabbaths and on sabbaths which fell in a festival; later the proper lessons for these sabbaths were made a second lesson, following the section for the day in the order of continuous reading.

The reading at certain services in the synagogue of a selection from the Prophets as a close to the lesson from the Pentateuch is mentioned in the Mishnah as a familiar custom,[3] but without any regulations concerning it further than that a legal congregation (ten men) must be present, and that Ezek. 1 is not to be read.[4] The Tosefta gives the proper selections for the four special sabbaths, chosen for their relevancy to the occasion and to the preceding lesson from the Pentateuch.[5] Evidence of the reading from the Prophets is given by Luke 4, 16 ff., which tells how Jesus, going into the synagogue in Nazareth on a sabbath, stood up to read; the volume that was handed to him was the Book of Isaiah; he opened it and found the place where it is

[1] Indications of such a custom may perhaps be found in the direction of R. Simeon ben Eleazar that the curses in Lev. 26 be read before Pentecost and those in Deut. 28 before New Years (Megillah 31b). This was, according to Simeon ben Eleazar, an ordinance of Ezra. Note also the examples in Tos. Megillah 4 (3), 31 ff. (authorities of the early second century).

[2] See Note 76.

[3] M. Megillah 4, 3; cf. 4, 9, end. See Note 77.

[4] The *merkabah*, forbidden because of the use made of it in theosophical speculations. Ezek. 16, 1 ff. also was forbidden by some (cf. Tos. Megillah 4, 34). Ultimately both were permitted.

[5] Thus the Hafṭarah to Sheḳalim (Exod. 30, 11–16) is 2 Kings 12, 3 ff (English Bible 12, 9 ff.); to Zakor (Deut. 25, 17–19), 1 Sam. 15, 2–9; to Parah (Num. 19, 1–22), Ezek. 36, 25 ff.; to ha-Ḥodesh (Exod. 12, 1–20), Ezek. 45, 18 ff.

written, "The Spirit of the Lord is upon me," etc. (Isa. 61, 1 f.); having read the verses, he rolled up the book and handed it back to the attendant, and sat down to expound the passage.[1] The language leaves it uncertain whether Jesus selected the passage himself, or whether the roll had been so prepared beforehand that when it was opened the column containing it was exposed. Inasmuch, however, as there was never any thought of continuous reading in the prophetic books, it is likely that on ordinary sabbaths the selection was left to the head of the synagogue, or to the reader — for this lesson there was only one reader.

In the choice of the selection from the Prophets appropriateness to the preceding reading from the Pentateuch, such as has been observed above in the case of the special sabbaths, is elsewhere noted.[2] In a Baraita in Megillah 31a–b we find lessons selected on this principle not only for the three great festivals but for the sabbaths in the festival weeks, sabbaths on which a new moon falls, the Feast of Dedication, and the Ninth of Ab. For other sabbaths the choice was apparently still free. The assigning of a particular lesson from the Prophets as a pendant to every lesson from the Pentateuch must be later than the division of the Pentateuch into sections of definite length and the establishment of the custom of reading not only in course but in cycle.

The lessons from the prophetical books (*haftarah*) designated in the older lists to which reference has been made above are, like the readings from the Pentateuch in the same lists, generally short; and this is true of many of the Haftarahs in the Palestinian triennial cycle. Even more evidently than in the oldest Pentateuch pericopes the prophetic selections were texts rather than lessons.

In the Mishnah the number of readers for the lesson from the Pentateuch at the various services is exactly prescribed: on

---

[1] The description corresponds accurately to the usage of the synagogue as we find it in the Mishnah and later texts.

[2] Megillah 29b.

Monday and Thursday and at the Sabbath afternoon service, three; on New Moons and the days in the festivals which are not sabbatical, four; and so on. At the Sabbath morning service seven are called up for the reading of the Law;[1] and since each reader must read at least three verses, the shortest possible Pentateuch lesson had twenty-one verses. At a later time the text of each sabbath lesson (*parashah*) of the annual cycle was divided for the guidance of readers into seven sections or paragraphs, which are indicated in manuscripts and editions. This subdivision is evidently comparatively late, and has only the authority of usage.[2] The first reader pronounced a benediction before beginning his portion of the Law, and the last said one after his portion.[3] In calling up the readers precedence was given to a priest, if one was present, and after him to a levite.[4]

The necessity of a translation of the lessons from the Scriptures must have been early felt, perhaps as early as the institution of the reading itself.[5] The language of the Bible had long since ceased to be the vernacular of the Jews anywhere. In Palestine and Babylonia and interior Syria they spoke distinct dialects of Aramaic; in Egypt Aramaic had given way in our age to Greek, which was the speech of almost all the Jews in the western Dispersion; in the remoter provinces of the Parthian empire they spoke the languages of their surroundings, perhaps in addition to Aramaic. However great the reverence of the Jews for the 'sacred tongue,' they had no superstition about it, and put understanding above sentiment. The traditional interpretation

[1] See M. Megillah 4, 1-4. The provision for a large number of readers points to a time when, as in the latter part of the second century, there were schools in almost every city, and multitudes of scholars.

[2] The divisions vary greatly in different manuscripts. Maimonides (d. 1204) gives a list copied from an ancient standard codex of the Bible attributed to the famous Massorete, Ben Asher (first half of the ninth century). See Mishneh Torah, Sefer Torah c. 8.

[3] M. Megillah 4, 1.

[4] M. Giṭṭin 5, 8. Not as an acknowledged right, but "for the sake of peace." On the precedence of scholars see M. Horaiot 3, 8.

[5] On the following see Elbogen, Der jüdische Gottesdienst, pp. 186 ff.

of Neh. 8, 8 is that the reading of the Law by Ezra was accompanied by a translation into Aramaic.[1]

In the Palestinian synagogues the lessons were read in Hebrew,
and an interpreter standing beside the reader translated them
into Aramaic. The rules for the readers and the interpreter are
laid down in the Mishnah with considerable detail.[2] In earlier
times the practice was probably simpler and more elastic. With
such short pericopes as seem at first to have been customary
there can hardly have been more than one reader, who may
even, upon occasion, have been his own interpreter.[3] It must
be borne in mind that for the order of worship in the synagogue
the Mishnah is a late source, representing things as they were
after the destruction of Jerusalem and especially after the war
under Hadrian, a period in which the new importance of the
synagogue would naturally lead to amplification and regulation
of the service. The older custom can be read in it only as in a
kind of palimpsest.[4]

So far as the rule went, any competent person, even a minor,
might act as interpreter, subject of course to the control of the
head of the synagogue. The number of qualified interpreters in
an ordinary synagogue must usually have been small, and it is
probable that the synagogue attendant, who was frequently
also the school teacher, often served in this capacity.[5]

The translation was supposed to be extempore; the interpreter
listened to the reading of a verse (in the Prophets it might be
three, if the subject was the same) and gave the meaning of it
to the congregation in their own language. Nothing hindered

---

[1] Megillah 3a and parallels. See Note 78.

[2] See Note 79.

[3] In Luke 4, 16 ff. there is no mention of translation; but the author of
the Gospel was doubtless better acquainted with the Hellenistic synagogues,
in which there was no need of one, the reading being in Greek.

[4] The regulations in the Mishnah sometimes seem to be ideals or desiderata rather than realities. They would do very well in the cities where there
were great rabbinical schools, and such may have been chiefly in mind.

[5] An instance, Jer. Megillah 74d. The story is told of Samuel ben Isaac,
early in the fourth century.

his preparing himself beforehand; but in the synagogue he must have nothing written before him.[1] The object of the translation was not to turn the scripture word for word into another language, but to give the hearers an understanding of the sense; it was in intention, therefore, a free interpretation rather than a literal reproduction.[2]

The vagaries to which such freedom is exposed did not fail to arise. In an example adduced in the Mishnah the congregation is bidden to silence the interpreter who takes liberties with his text and give him a smart admonition besides.[3] R. Judah (ben Ila'i) sets a difficult standard for the translator: "He who translates a verse with strict literalness is a falsifier, and he who makes additions to it is a blasphemer."[4]

The synagogues were, however, not under rabbinical control, and it is hardly to be questioned that the early interpreters in some cases exercised considerable freedom in paraphrase. The Palestinian Targums, as we have them, come from a much later time, but in the freedom with which translation runs into midrash they may be taken to illustrate the fashion of the older interpreters, though in their actual form the midrashic element may be largely literary contamination. It is even possible that in the first age of the institution translation and homily were not yet differentiated, and the interpreter was also the expository preacher. In the second century the attempt was made to provide a standard Aramaic translation of the whole Pentateuch, and the result is in our hands in the Targum of Onkelos. In

---

[1] See Jer. Megillah 74d. The reason was that the Targum might not seem to be a kind of second Scripture. Oral tradition and Scripture must be sharply distinguished. To avoid any possible confusion the reader was forbidden to prompt the translator, lest some might think that the translation was in the roll before him.

[2] Literal translation is, however, ordinarily the easiest, and the synagogue interpreters often stick close to their text.

[3] M. Megillah 4, 9. With the rendering of Lev. 18, 21 here condemned compare the Palestinian Targum. See Note 80.

[4] Tos. Megillah 4, 41; Ḳiddushin 49a. See Berliner, Targum Onkelos, II, 173 f.

Babylonia it soon came to authority, but whatever esteem it enjoyed in Palestine, it did not supersede the freer kind.[1]

How early the homily became an independent part of the synagogue service is not known.[2] It was so in the times of Jesus; it was so in the Hellenistic synagogues of which Philo writes, Paul in his missionary expeditions habitually used the opportunity the discourse gave to introduce his gospel to Jews and proselytes and Gentiles frequenting the synagogue. Preaching in the synagogue was not the prerogative of any class, nor was any individual regularly appointed to conduct this part of the service; but it was only natural that those whose life study had been the Scriptures and the religion of their people should be found more profitable for instruction than unschooled men, and that such as had the gifts of interesting and edifying discourse (Haggadah) were more popular than those who excelled only in juristic refinements.

The homily was in the nature of the case the freest and most variable part of the service, and its fashion changed greatly with changing times and circumstances. We find in the Mishnah and kindred authorities no attempt to regulate either its matter or its method. The homiletical and expository Midrashim which have come down to us from the fifth century and later give a good notion of the nature of the Haggadah in all its varieties; the sermonic form is perhaps most nearly represented in the Pesikta.[3] The important thing for our present purpose is that the homilists in all ages worked into their discourses a great deal of quotation, not only from the Law and the Prophets but from the Hagiographa, thus familiarizing their hearers with books that were not regularly read in the synagogue, and with which, consequently, the mass of the people could hardly otherwise have been extensively acquainted. The sermon in the synagogue was in the mother tongue; the discourses in the school (*Bet ha-*

[1] See Note 81. [2] See Note 82.
[3] On these Midrashim see above, pp. 161 ff.

midrash), being addressed to scholars and students, were probably, at least in Palestine, in 'the language of the learned,' the Hebrew of the schools.[1]

The preacher closed his homily with a brief prayer in the language of the discourse itself (Aramaic), upon which followed the ascription, "May his great name be blessed forever and for ever and ever." [2] The precise language of this closing prayer, as in other cases, was not at first fixed. In the course of time it was much expanded, and was introduced, with variations for which there are distinctive names, in other places in the liturgy, retaining by exception the Aramaic language, and being known by an Aramaic name, the Ḳaddish.[3]

Philo briefly describes the service of the Hellenistic synagogue, particularly as an institute of instruction in the Scriptures. Moses commanded that the Jews should assemble on the seventh day, and being seated should reverently and decorously listen to the Law, in order that no one might be ignorant of it; and such is the present custom. One of the priests who is present, or one of the elders, reads to them the divine laws and expounds them in detail, continuing till some time in the late afternoon; then the congregation disperses, having acquired knowledge of the divine laws and making much progress in religion.[4] In another work Philo writes: "Innumerable schools (διδασκαλεῖα) of practical wisdom and self-control and manliness and uprightness and the other virtues are opened every seventh day in all cities. In these schools the people sit decorously, keeping silence and listening with the utmost attention out of a thirst for refreshing discourse, while one of the best qualified stands up and instructs them in what is best and most conducive to welfare, things by which their whole life may be made better." The two comprehensive

---

[1] The Midrashim in our hands are with small exceptions in Hebrew.
[2] See Note 83.
[3] See Note 84.
[4] Fragment (from the first book of the Hypothetica) in Eusebius, Praeparatio Evangelica viii. Philo, ed. Mangey, II, 630 f.

topics of this manifold discourse are piety and holiness toward
God, and benevolence and uprightness toward men.[1]

It does not lie in Philo's purpose in these places to speak of the
worship of the synagogue, but the name 'places of prayer'[2] is of
itself testimony to the fact that instruction was not their sole
function.

---

[1] De special. legg. ii. De septenario c. 6 §§ 62 f. (ed. Mangey II, 282).
See Note 85.

[2] Προσευχαί. See Note 59. On the Day of Atonement the Jews spend
this whole day in prayers and suplications; Philo, De septenario, c. 23 § 196
(ed. Mangey II, 296).

CHAPTER VI

THE SCHOOLS

THE second of the great institutions of religious education in Judaism was the school. In some form or other the school is as old as the synagogue if not older, and the synagogue was always dependent upon it. The reading of the Scriptures in the ancient language; the vernacular interpretation; the homiletical exposition drawing out of the Scripture its religious and moral lessons; the instruction in the peculiar observances of Judaism and their significance, all required a considerable measure of education, while to fulfil its possibilities as a school of revealed religion the synagogue needed to have behind it a higher learning upon which it could draw directly or indirectly.

When in the Bible the instruction of the people in the Torah is spoken of as an office of the priesthood,[1] it is doubtless the Torah of the priests that is primarily meant, their answers and instructions about clean and unclean, purifications and expiations, obligatory offerings, and the like.[2] In the narrative of Ezra's reading of the Law, however, the levites expounded its provisions more generally; the Chronicler has such more general instruction in mind also in describing the mixed commission which Jehoshaphat sent around to teach in the cities of Judah, 'having the book of the law of the Lord with them.'[3] It is certain, however, that the study of the Scriptures and the teaching of religion from them was not a prerogative of the priesthood.

The men who took the lead in this work in the last century of Persian rule and the Greek period that followed are called

---

[1] Deut. 33, 10; Jer. 2, 8; 18, 18; Mal. 2, 4–9.
[2] E.g., Haggai 2, 11–13.
[3] 2 Chron. 17, 7–9; cf. 15, 3. Compare the institution of a mixed court of last resort in Jerusalem, 2 Chron. 19, 8–11.

soferim, commonly translated 'scribes,' more exactly, 'biblical scholars.'[1]   The ideal of such a scholar is well expressed in Ezra 7, 10: 'Ezra (the priest, the *sofer*, ibid. vss. 11 f.) had set his mind intently to study the law of the Lord, and to do it, and to teach in Israel statute and ordinance.'[2]   A century later Jesus son of Sirach describes in eulogistic terms the station and occupation of the scribe, contrasting him with the classes who have to give all their time and thought to making a living.   The learning of the scholar (*sofer*) can be acquired only by such as are free from these necessities and have the opportunity of leisure to consider and discuss matters of higher interest.[3]

The ideal scholar of Sirach is a cultivated man, who has broadened his mind by travel in foreign countries and had experience of the good and the bad in men, and was a presentable person in the highest company.[4]   His studies have a wide range.   He devotes his mind to the understanding of the law of the Most High, and is thus qualified to take a leading part in the assembly of the people or to sit on the judge's bench and give out right and just sentence.   He occupies himself with prophecies, and seeks out the wisdom of all the ancients, and preserves the utterances of famous men; he is well versed in the elusive turns of parables and in making out enigmatical utterances.   He sends up his petition at the beginning of the day to the Lord who made him, opening his mouth in prayer and in supplication for his sins.   "If the great Lord will, he shall be filled with an understanding spirit and will pour out words of wisdom, and celebrate the praises of God in prayer."[5]

It is worthy of particular notice in this description of the scholar's pursuits that the study of the Scriptures and skill in

---

[1] See Note 86.

[2] The obligation of the learned to teach is strongly expressed by R. Jose ben Ḥalafta (second century A.D.): "To learn and not to teach — there is nothing more futile than that!"

[3] Ecclus. 38, 24–39, 11. See Note 87.

[4] Ecclus. 39, 4 ff.

[5] Ecclus. 39, 6.   This verse and the following seem to refer to a public occasion, such as a homily in the synagogue or a discourse in the school.

parables and proverbs go hand in hand. Of the author's proficiency in the latter art the book is proof; his familiarity with the
Scriptures is manifest throughout, and is brilliantly exhibited in
the Hymn in Honor of the Fathers,[1] which is an epitome of the
famous men and memorable events of the Bible from Genesis
down to his contemporary, Simon son of Onias, whose ministry
as high priest in all the splendor of the temple liturgy he extols
in his loftiest style.[2]

It is common to think of the sages, such as the authors of
Proverbs and Jesus son of Sirach, as a new kind of teachers in the
later Persian and Greek centuries, whose calling it was to impart
to youths, especially of the higher classes, principles or maxims
of moral and social conduct — a kind of Hebrew sophists, distinct from priests on the one hand and scribes on the other.
In Sirach's case, at least, the latter distinction does not hold; a
scribe (*sofer*) is precisely what he was, a man expert in the Scriptures and in the religious learning of his people, such as he describes in the passage summarized above. His grandson and
translator writes of him: "Having given himself especially to the
reading of the Law and the Prophets and the other ancient books
of his people, and having acquired much proficiency in them, he
was moved himself to write something on subjects profitable for
education and wisdom."[3] It should be noted that the schoolmen
of later times also cultivated the parable and the apophthegm as
an art,[4] and some of them achieved a notable mastery in it. The
Chapters of the Fathers (Pirkè Abot), appended to the fourth
series (Nezikin) of treatises in the Mishnah and the Babylonian
Talmud, contains favorite maxims or memorable aphorisms of
eminent teachers from the Men of the Great Assembly down to
the first half of the third century of our era (chapters 1–4); and
a great many maxims of similar form and content from every

---

[1] Ecclus. 44–49.

[2] Ecclus. 50. This Simeon was himself, according to Jewish tradition
(Abot 1, 2), one of the last survivors of the Great Assembly, that is of the
early Soferim, whose institutions and decrees are so often referred to.

[3] Translator's Preface.   [4] Cf. Eccles. 12, 9–12. See Note 88.

period are scattered through the Talmud and Midrashim. Such epigrammatic sayings were evidently one of the most highly appreciated features of homiletic discourse in the synagogue and the school house. The teaching of Jesus in the Synoptic Gospels exhibits the same popular forms.

The sayings attributed to the oldest authorities in the Pirkè Abot revert frequently to study and teaching as one of the fundamental institutions of Judaism. The Men of the Great Assembly themselves are said to have given three injunctions: "Be deliberate in giving judgment, and raise up many disciples, and make a fence about the Law." The favorite maxim of Simeon the Righteous is: "The world rests on three supports: the Law (i.e. the study of God's revelation, the sacrificial worship, and deeds of personal kindness." Jose ben Jo'ezer, in the beginning of the Seleucid dominion, said: "Let thy house be a regular meeting place [1] for learned men, and sit in the dust at their feet, and thirstily drink in their words." In the next generation, Joshua ben Perahiah's word was: "Get thyself a master (teacher, *rab*), and take to thyself a fellow student,[2] and judge every man on the good side."

It is probable that organized schools such as emerge in our sources shortly before the beginning of the Christian era were preceded at an earlier time by stated or occasional meetings of the Soferim for study and discussion, the results of which were sometimes embodied in decisions or in rules promulgated by their authority.[3] Younger scholars, who pursued their studies, we may conjecture, under the guidance of individual masters, frequented these conventions as auditors, and profited by listening to the discussions of their elders. To such gatherings, held in private houses, Jose ben Jo'ezer seems to refer in the words quoted above from the Pirkè Abot. The phrase *bet wa'ad*, 'stated place of meeting,' there employed occurs frequently,

---

[1] בית ועד.
[2] That is, Do not try to learn of yourself or by yourself.
[3] *Gezerot* and *takkanot*; see above, p. 33 and p. 258.

especially in the Palestinian Talmud, apparently always of a meeting-place of scholars, or school, not of the gathering of the congregation in the place of prayer, or synagogue.

As early as Sirach another term is found which eventually prevailed, *bet ha-midrash*, 'place of study,' [1] a name often coupled with that of the synagogue in combinations which show that the two were distinct, though closely associated. It is fairly to be inferred that as early as the generation before the attempt of Antiochus IV on the Jewish religion the school was an established institution. A generation later, a considerable company of scholars (συναγωγὴ γραμματέων),[2] went to meet Alcimus, the new high-priest sent by Demetrius. As has been already remarked, in the eulogy of wisdom (c. 24), Jesus son of Sirach identifies Wisdom with the Law which Moses gave, applying to it Deut. 33, 4: "All this is the book of the covenant of the Most High God, the law which Moses commanded, an inheritance to the assemblies of Jacob." Wisdom is not only the Jewish religion but specifically the revelation of it in the Pentateuch. Subjectively wisdom is "the fear of the Lord" (Ecclus. 1, 1–15); objectively it is the law of Moses.[3]

Of this law Sirach was a teacher. In his school he doubtless imparted to his hearers such religious and moral aphorisms as are collected in his book, as the rabbis did in later times; but that he also interpreted to them the Scriptures and inculcated the rules which earlier authorities had made to define the law and to keep men far from transgression by putting a fence about it is as certain as any inference can be. It may also be surmised with much probability that what he has to say about public discourse reflects his own experience as a preacher in the synagogue or school.[4]

[1] See Note 89.

[2] Equivalent to a Hebrew כנסת סופרים. Whether the sixty whom Alcimus put to death on one day were all scribes is not quite clear. See 1 Macc. 7, 12–18. On Jose ben Jo'ezer see pp. 45 f.

[3] Smend, Die Weisheit des Jesus Sirach, p. xxiii.

[4] Ecclus. 39, 6 ff. Above p. 309.

It is difficult to form a definite notion of the schools before the fall of Jerusalem, because in later references to them it was naturally assumed that they were altogether like those of the authors' own time.[1] For our present purpose, however, this question is not of prime importance. The existence of many biblical scholars (Soferim) from the third century B.C. down shows that there was regular provision for transmitting the learning of former generations and adding to it.

An anecdote narrated to illustrate Hillel's eagerness for learning tells how he supported himself and his family by day labor, and out of his wages of a victoriatus[2] a day paid one half to the janitor of the school. One day he had not earned anything, and as the janitor would not let him in without the entrance fee, he climbed up, fastened himself, and sat on a window-sill, "that he might hear the words of the living God from the lips of Shemaiah and Abtalion,"[3] the greatest scholars and the greatest expositors of the generation.[4] In this situation he was found next morning buried in snow and nearly frozen to death.

Hillel had come to Palestine from Babylonia when already a mature man to study under these masters.[5] He had, however, already been a student of the Law, and we are told that he brought with him from Babylonia certain definitions or interpretations which he desired to compare with those accepted in Palestine,[6] and perhaps to get the judgment of the authorities there on his method of interpretation.[7] It is to be inferred from this instance that schools of the Law were already established in

[1] See Note 90.

[2] A small coin worth about half a denarius.

[3] Yoma 35b.

[4] Pesaḥim 70b. Abṭalion is commonly identified with the 'Pollion' of Josephus, Antt. xv. 1, 1 (cf. 10, 4 § 370), a leader of the Pharisees in the reign of Herod. 'Samaios' his disciple (in xv. 1, 1) would seem to be Shammai rather than Abṭalion's colleague Shemaiah. See Note 89a.

[5] Jer. Pesaḥim 33a.

[6] Jer. Pesaḥim l.c.; Tos. Negaʿim 1, 16; Sifra, Tazriʿa Pereḳ 9, end (ed. Weiss f. 66d–67a). See Bacher, Tannaiten, I, 2.

[7] On Hillel's hermeneutic rules (Tos. Sanhedrin 7, 11) see H. Strack, Einleitung in Talmud und Midrasch, 5 ed. pp. 96 ff.

Babylonia, where a method of juristic deduction was developed
in advance of the Palestinian schools, which rested more exclusively on the authority of tradition.[1]   In the following century,
before the fall of Jerusalem, there was a famous school at Nisibis, presided over by Judah ben Bathyra,[2] and doubtless there
were others in many of the Jewish centres.

In Palestine, and probably elsewhere, the school (*bet ha-
midrash*) was frequently adjacent to the synagogue, and in later
accounts it is assumed that each synagogue had its own,[3] which
implies, of course, that they were not exclusively what we should
call professional schools, but ministered to the instruction of the
whole educated part of the community as in more recent times.
The building occupied by a synagogue may be transformed into
a school, but not contrariwise; it would be a descent in rank,
such as is forbidden in M. Megillah 3, 1.[4]

The hall of the school was used on Sabbath afternoons for
popular instruction both in the Scripture and in the rules of the
unwritten law.[5]   It was forbidden to read the Hagiographa privately on the Sabbath (at least till after Minḥah),[6] because the
readers were in danger of becoming so much interested in them
as to neglect this opportunity of instruction and edification.[7]   An
anecdote about R. Eleazer ben Azariah, in the first generation

[1] This is the point of the discussion with the Bene Bathyra in Jer. Pesaḥim
l.c.

[2] Sanhedrin 32b.   [3] See above, p. 104.

[4] Megillah 27a, top (R. Joshua ben Levi, first half of the third century of
our era).   Note the distinction there between the *bet ha-midrash* as a place
where men magnify the law and the synagogue as a place where they magnify
prayer (R. Joḥanan and R. Joshua ben Levi).

[5] The earliest mention of this custom comes from the second century (R.
Nehemiah, Shabbat 116b); but there is no reason to infer that it was of
recent origin.

[6] The hour of prayer, corresponding to the time of the afternoon sacrifice
in the temple.

[7] M. Shabbat 16, 1; Shabbat 116b; Jer. Shabbat 15c, top.   These writings might however be taught and expounded in the school.   At a later time
lessons from the Hagiographa were read in Babylonia (Nehardea) at the
Sabbath afternoon service (Shabbat 116b).   See Elbogen, Der jüdische
Gottesdienst, p. 118. — Frequent blessings are pronounced on such as hasten
from the synagogue to the school.

of the second century, illustrates the character of the discourse in the school house. Two rabbis, Johanan ben Beroka and Eleazar Ḥisma, on their way to Lydda from Jabneh, then the seat of the great rabbinical academy, where they had spent the Sabbath, passed on the way through a village where the aged R. Joshua (ben Hananiah) was living and called on him. He asked them, What did you have new in the school today? They made an evasive reply, politely implying that they could bring nothing new to so eminent a scholar, but he understood their reticence and pressed his question. Impossible that there should be a meeting in the school without something new! Whose sabbath was it? It was the sabbath of R. Eleazar ben Azariah,[1] they answered. And what did he preach about? Thereupon they told him how Eleazar applied Deut. 31, 12 ('Assemble the people, men, women, and children') to the congregation: the men come to learn, the women to hear, but what are the children there for? To acquire a reward for those who bring them. He had also expounded two other texts, Deut. 26, 17 f., and Eccles. 12, 11 ('The words of the learned are like goads,' etc.), giving on the latter a characteristic piece of midrash, with an application for the benefit of students who were distracted by the conflict of authorities to the point of abandoning the attempt to become scholars.[2]

The combination of instruction in the rules of the unwritten law with the exposition of Scripture in these discourses in the school has perhaps left a memorial in certain Midrash collections where the homilies are introduced by a juristic question: "Let our rabbi teach us," etc. (*Yelammedenu*),[3] with its answer; and others which begin, without the formal fiction of a question, with a sentence or two of the same kind, designated 'Halakah,' though the extant collections of this type are more recent than the period under our present consideration.

[1] See Vol. II, p. 220.
[2] Tos. Soṭah 7, 9 ff.; Ḥagigah 3a–b; Jer. Ḥagigah 75d. Bacher, Tannaiten, I, 213 f.
[3] ילמדנו רבינו. See above, pp. 170, 171 n.

Elementary instruction was doubtless for a long time left to parents, and was given by them or by tutors employed by them, or in private schools. This restricted education in general to the children of parents who were able to teach them or to pay for having them taught, and had the interest to do it. Such a limitation could not be to the mind of the leaders, whose ideal was the education of the whole people in revealed religion. The studies of the high school, as we might call it, the Bet ha-Midrash, required a knowledge of the ancient Hebrew language in which the Scriptures were written and of the Hebrew of the schools, the 'language of the learned,' in which the unwritten law was always taught, and in which throughout our period the discussions of the school were conducted. The latter might be learned in the high school itself; but reading and writing and a grounding in the language of the Bible must be acquired previously.

To meet this need elementary schools were established, called, in distinction from the Bet ha-Midrash, or advanced school, Bet ha-Sefer, or Bet ha-Sofer — we might paraphrase, reading and writing schools.[1] Private schools of this kind had doubtless long existed before any attempt was made to establish public schools in every community, and they continued to exist beside the public schools. About the institution of the latter we have no certain information.[2] It is evident, however, that whatever may have been done before the fall of Jerusalem had to be begun anew after the war, and again after the war under Hadrian. In the latter period, at least, it was regarded as the normal thing for each community to maintain, besides the synagogue, an elementary school and an advanced school (Bet Sefer and Bet Midrash). R. Simeon ben Yoḥai [3] said: If you see cities in the land of Israel that are destroyed to their very foundations, know that it is because they did not provide pay for teachers of the Bible and of tradition, according to Jer. 9, 11 f., 'because they

---

[1] See Note 91.   [2] See Note 92.
[3] Disciple of Akiba, after the war under Hadrian.

abandoned my Law.'¹ In the same context it is related that the
Patriarch Judah sent out a commission headed by R. Ḥiyya to
make a tour of the cities in the land of Israel and establish in each
a teacher of the Bible and one of the tradition. They found
one small place where there was a village watchman, but no
teacher at all, and proceeded to impress on the townsmen that
the true keepers of a city were the teachers of the Bible and tradition, for which they found authority in Psalm 127.²

The obligation to maintain schools is repeatedly emphasized.
A scholar should not take up his abode in a town in which there
is not, among other requisites of civilization, an elementary
teacher.³ A town in which there are no children attending school
is to be destroyed, or, as another reporter has it, put under the
ban.⁴ The salary of the school teachers of both grades was paid
by the community, who taxed themselves for this purpose; and
the collector was authorized to distrain for this tax, which he
might not ordinarily do for the poor-rates.⁵ The school teacher is
given a rank in the hierarchy of education beneath the learned
(ḥakamim) but above the synagogue attendant (ḥazzan);⁶ though
in eligibility as a husband he is put at the bottom of the list,
perhaps because the class, though respectable, was poorly paid.⁷
As has been noted above, in small communities the same man
often served as school teacher (sofer) and as synagogue attendant (ḥazzan), and sometimes one scholar presided over both the
advanced and the elementary schools, as in the case of Levi

¹ Jer. Ḥagigah 76c; Pesiḳta ed. Buber f. 120b.
² Compare R. Ḥiyya's account of what he did in a town where there was
no teacher of the Bible, Ketubot 103b; Baba Meṣi'a 85b.
³ מלמד תינוקות, Sanhedrin 17b, end.
⁴ Shabbat 119b. Bacher, Pal. Amoräer, I, 347, n. 2.
⁵ Pesiḳta ed. Buber f. 178a–b; cf. Baba Batra 8b. Apparently only men
who had children were assessed for the support of the teacher. Particular
praise is given by a fourth century preacher to a bachelor who voluntarily
contributes to the salary of the teachers of the Bible and of tradition: God
will reward him by giving him a boy of his own (Lev. R. 27, 2). For other
passages on teachers and school children see Note 93.
⁶ Soṭah 49a, end.
⁷ Pesaḥim 49b, top. See Note 93a.

ben Sisi cited above; still oftener, probably, the school teacher was the interpreter (*meturgeman*) in the synagogue.

The boys' school maintained by the community was held in the synagogue, as the mosque is used today in Mohammedan countries. There were also private schools in the teachers' houses, and the children often made so much noise coming and going and shouting their lessons in concert, that the neighbors seem at one time to have had a right to prevent the setting up of a school in the block, as they might the introduction of a trade that created a nuisance.[1]

Boys learned to read in the Hebrew Bible as Moslem boys today learn to read in the Koran. School copies of parts of the Pentateuch were given them for this purpose, and by long established custom the beginning was made with the Book of Leviticus in the elementary school,[2] as well as subsequently in the advanced school in which tradition was studied. The reading was necessarily accompanied by an explanation in the mother-tongue, and the pupils thus learned the meaning of Scripture along with the words. In an age when dictionaries and grammars were unheard of, it was the only way, and a very effective way as far as it went. From the Pentateuch the reading progressed to the Prophets and the Hagiographa. It is probable that many pupils did not follow this course to the end; but what we might call a graduate in Scripture was expected to be able to read all three groups of books.[3]

The religious leaders regarded the study of the Scripture as the foundation of all learning, but, if it stopped there, as an incomplete education, since it dealt only with the letter and the literal sense, to the exclusion of that comparison of scripture with scripture by which its more recondite teachings were discovered,

---

[1] Baraitas quoted in Baba Batra 21a. See Bacher in Jahrbücher für jüdische Geschichte und Literatur, 1903, p. 67. The rule in M. Baba Batra 2, 3; Tos. Baba Batra 1, 4 is to the contrary. Compare the attempted reconciliation in Baba Batra 21a.

[2] Pesiḳta ed. Buber f. 60b, end; Lev. R. 7, 3. Reasons are given for not beginning with Genesis.   [3] Ḳiddushin 49a. See Note 94.

and of the unwritten tradition, religious as well as juristic, which
supplemented the written word and interpreted it. They felt
much as a trained Old Testament scholar today feels about a
man who, ignoring all the learning of the past embodied in an
exegetical, historical, and theological tradition that fills hundreds
of volumes, and ignorant of the methods of what is called biblical
science, or ignoring its worth and rejecting its authority, under-
takes to interpret the Scriptures out of his own head. To occupy
one's self exclusively with the study of Scripture "is a way, but
not the real way." [1]

The higher religious education had for its principal subject
matter tradition in a wide extension of the term. The name for
this tradition in its whole extent is *Mishnah*,[2] in distinction from
Mikra, Bible study. In this wider sense, Mishnah, or the teaching and learning of tradition, included, in our period, three
branches, *Midrash* (also called *Talmud*),[3] *Halakah*, and *Haggadah*. 'Midrash' was the higher exegesis of Scripture, especially
the derivation from it, or confirmation by it, of the rules of the
unwritten law; 'Halakah,' the precisely formulated rule itself;
'Haggadah,' the non-juristic teachings of Scripture as brought
out in the profounder study of its religious, moral, and historical
teachings.[4] All this belonged to the Jewish science of tradition.
Even a moderate proficiency in it was not to be attained without
long and patient years of learning; mastery demanded unusual

[1] R. Simeon ben Yoḥai, Jer. Shabbat 15c. See Bacher, Tannaiten, II,
91 f.
[2] This use of the term is not to be confounded with the specific use in
which 'Mishnah' is applied to rules of the unwritten law (*halakot*) as the
crowning branch of the study of tradition, and still more narrowly to the
collection of the Patriarch Judah which we call 'the Mishnah.' Jerome uses
the word δευτερώσεις as equivalent to Mishnah in the wider sense.
[3] Again not to be confounded with the great body of organized tradition
and discussion which we call 'the Talmud.'
[4] On the value set on the Haggadah see Sifrè Deut. § 49, end (on 11, 22):
"Those who search out the intimations of Scripture say, if you wish to
know the Creator of the world, learn Haggadah; from it you will come to
know God and cleave to his ways." Cf. above, pp. 161 f.

capacity. The method of the schools developed not only exact and retentive memory and great mental acuteness, but an exhaustive and ever-ready knowledge of every phrase and word of Scripture.

A late appendix to the Pirkè Abot (5, 21) would have a boy begin in the Bible school at five years, go on to the study of tradition (Mishnah) at ten, advance to Talmud at fifteen,[1] marry at eighteen, and so on. It is needless to say that reality did not exhibit so neat a scheme; but it is probable that boys ordinarily passed from the elementary school to the more advanced studies of the Bet ha-Midrash between the years of twelve and fifteen, an age in which they came to personal responsibility for compliance with all the rules of the law. Before this age, boys who knew how were competent to take part in the reading of the lessons from the Pentateuch or Prophets in the synagogue, and to serve as translator.[2] This of itself does not prove very much, for they could be coached on the particular paragraph, as has often been done since.

Only a small proportion of those who went through the elementary school, or even of those who began the study of tradition, had either the opportunity or the ability to go on to the higher stages by which men advanced to the rank of what we might call professor, with the *venia docendi* (*et decernendi*). A later Midrash gives this turn to the words, 'I have found one man out of a thousand' (Eccles. 7, 28):[3] "Such is the usual way of the world; a thousand enter the Bible school, and a hundred pass from it to the study of Mishnah; ten of them go on to Talmud study, and only one of them arrives at the doctor's degree (rabbinical ordination)." But the measure of education attained by many men enabled them to profit by the expositions in the Bet ha-Midrash on Sabbath afternoons and at other

---

[1] 'Mishnah' is here used in the narrower sense, formulated and memorized rules (*halakot*); 'Talmud,' in the later meaning, explanation and discussion of the rules. This classification makes four disciplines: Bible, Mishnah (i.e. Halakah), Talmud, Haggadah. So Jer. Peah 17a, below, and parallels.

[2] M. Megillah 4, 5 f.   [3] Eccles. R. *in loc.*

times, and to listen with interest to the lively discussions of the teachers and more advanced students.[1]

When such opportunities of acquiring a knowledge of religion were open to all, it is not strange that those who neglected them and consequently remained in ignorance of the revealed will of God, unconcerned about the distinctions of clean and unclean further than they had become matters of habit among their kind — that such 'amme ha-areṣ should be regarded by the Pharisees as little better than the indigenous heathen who were properly designated by that opprobrious name.[2]

As has been already remarked, our definite information about the schools comes from the second century, and chiefly from a time after the war under Hadrian, and it may well be that the leaders who reorganized Jewish institutions after that catastrophe made the school system more universal and regular than it had been previously; but it is certain that they introduced nothing novel into its character.

Schools of a similar kind existed in Babylonia before the Christian era, as is shown by the case of Hillel; and that the Greek speaking Jews had schools for the study of the Scriptures and of their religious law, we have the testimony of Philo: The Jews, "from their very swaddling clothes are taught by parents and teachers and masters, and above all by their sacred laws and unwritten customs, to acknowledge one God, the father and creator of the world." [3] Philo's own acquaintance with parts of the traditional law and the current homiletical exegesis is well established.[4]

[1] The very assumption that in an ordinary Sabbath morning synagogue service seven readers, besides at least one interpreter, and one (or more) leaders in prayer, took part, indicates that the Bible schools of the later second century were well attended and effective.
[2] "Peoples of the land."
[3] Legatio ad Gaium c. 16 § 115 (ed. Mangey, II, 562); cf. ibid. c. 31 § 210 f. (II, 577). The similar expressions in Josephus refer to Jews in general, not particularly to Palestinian Jews; see C. Apionem, i. 12 § 60; ii. 18.
[4] B. Ritter, Philo und die Halacha, 1879; Z. Frankel, Ueber den Einfluss der palästinensischen Exegese auf die alexandrinische Hermeneutik, 1851, pp. 190–200.

The Hellenistic Jews, having provided themselves with Greek translations of the Scriptures, used this version in their synagogues and schools, and emancipated themselves from the task of learning to read the original Hebrew. Learned men might study the ancient language, but it had no such place in general education as in Palestine or in Babylonia. If Philo knew Hebrew, the chief use he makes of it is to perpetrate etymologies which have sometimes led to the inference that he had only that little knowledge which in this field, if anywhere, is a dangerous thing.[1] It should not be forgotten that these interpretations of names were not put forth for the satisfaction of modern philologists but for the edification of his contemporaries; and they are not, after all, so much worse than similar adventures of Palestinian scholars whose knowledge of Hebrew is beyond question. It is likely, however, that in Philo's time knowledge of Greek was more common among the upper classes in Jerusalem than of Hebrew in Alexandria.[2]

In conclusion it may be repeated that the endeavor to educate the whole people in its religion created a unique system of universal education, whose very elements comprised not only reading and writing, but an ancient language and its classic literature. The high intellectual and religious value thus set on education was indelibly impressed on the mind, and one may say on the character of the Jew, and the institutions created for it have perpetuated themselves to the present day.

[1] See Note 95.
[2] This seems to be assumed in the account of the translation of the Pentateuch given in the Letter of Aristeas. Not only the authentic copy of the Law but the qualified translators are brought from Jerusalem. — Since we are here concerned only with religious education and the schools in which it was given, it is unnecessary to discuss the extent to which secular subjects, especially the Greek language and Greek science, were cultivated in Palestine in the centuries under investigation, or the attitude of the religious authorities toward such studies. The only branch of science that could be brought immediately into the service of religion was mathematics and astronomy for calendar purposes, particularly the determination of the exact time of the lunar conjunction, the solstices and equinoxes, etc.

CHAPTER VII

CONVERSION OF GENTILES

THE conviction that Judaism as the one true religion was destined to become the universal religion was a singularity of the Jews. No other religion in their world and time made any such pretensions or cherished such aspirations. It was an exclusiveness the rest of mankind did not understand and therefore doubly resented. And it must be admitted that the manner in which the Jews asserted their claim and descanted on the sin and folly of polytheism and idolatry and the vices of heathen society was not adapted to make them liked in an age that knew nothing of jealous gods, and when all manner of national and personal religions, native and foreign, lived amicably and respectfully side by side.[1] If the Jews alone were excepted from this universal toleration, as Philo complains,[2] it was chiefly because they alone were intolerant.[3] The Christians, who inherited their exclusive and aggressive monotheism, provoked the same exceptional intolerance in the habitual *laissez faire* of pagan religion.

But if some of the methods of Jewish apologetic and polemic provoked prejudice rather than produced conviction, the belief in the future universality of the true religion, the coming of an age when "the Lord shall be king over all the earth," when "the Lord shall be one and his name One," [4] led to efforts to convert the Gentiles to the worship of the one true God and to faith and obedience according to the revelation he had given, and made

---

[1] The religion of the Egyptians, with its beast-gods and its strange taboos, was indeed a common object of ridicule for Gentiles as well as Jews; see e.g. Juvenal, Sat. 15.

[2] Legatio ad Gaium c. 16 § 117 (ed. Mangey II, 562).

[3] The antipathy to the Jews as a people had many other causes. See Schürer, Geschichte des jüdischen Volkes, III, 105 f.

[4] See above, p. 229 f.; and Vol. II, p. 346.

Judaism the first great missionary religion of the Mediterranean world. When it is called a missionary religion, the phrase must, however, be understood with a difference. The Jews did not send out missionaries into the *partes infidelium* expressly to proselyte among the heathen. They were themselves settled by thousands in all the great centres and in innumerable smaller cities; they had appropriated the language and much of the civilization of their surroundings; they were engaged in the ordinary occupations, and entered into the industrial and commercial life of the community and frequently into its political life. Their religious influence was exerted chiefly through the synagogues, which they set up for themselves, but which were open to all whom interest or curiosity drew to their services. To Gentiles, in whose mind these services, consisting essentially of reading from the Scriptures and a discourse more or less loosely connected with it, lacked all the distinctive features of cultus, the synagogue, as has been observed above, resembled a school of some foreign philosophy. That it claimed the authority of inspiration for its sacred text and of immemorial tradition for the interpretation, and that the reading was prefaced by invocations of the deity and hymns in his praise, was in that age quite consistent with this character. That the followers of this philosophy had many peculiar rules about food and dress and multiplied purifications was also natural enough in that time.

The philosophy itself, whose fundamental doctrines seemed to be monotheism, divine providence guided by justice and benevolence, and reasonable morality, had little about it that was unfamiliar. Even what they sometimes heard about retribution after death, or a coming conflagration which should end the present order of things, was not novel. But at the bottom Judaism was something wholly different from a philosophy which a man was free to accept in whole or in part as far as it carried the assent of his intelligence. It might be a reasonable religion, but it was in an eminent degree a religion of authority; a revealed religion, which did not ask man's approval but demanded obedience to the whole and every part, reason and inclination to the contrary notwithstanding; an exclusive religion which tolerated no divided allegiance; a religion which made a man's eternal destiny depend on his submission of his whole life to its law, or his rejection of God who gave the law. Such, at least, was the rigor of the doctrine when it was completely and logically presented.

It is certain that it was not always preached so uncompromisingly. Especially in the Hellenistic world, polytheism and idolatry was so decisively the characterististic difference between Gentile and Jew that the rejection of these might almost seem to be the renunciation of heathenism and the adoption of Judaism; and if accompanied by the observance of the sabbath and conformity to the rudimentary rules of clean and unclean which were necessary conditions of social intercourse, it might seem to be a respectable degree of conversion. Nor are utterances of this tenor lacking in Palestinian sources; e.g., The rejection of idolatry is the acknowledgment of the whole law.[1]

Such converts were called religious persons ('those who worship, or revere, God'),[2] and although in a strict sense outside the pale of Judaism, undoubtedly expected to share with Jews by birth the favor of the God they had adopted, and were encouraged in this hope by their Jewish teachers. It was not uncommon for the next generation to seek incorporation into the Jewish people by circumcision.[3]

In those days it was nobody's business what gods a man believed in, or how many, or whether he believed in any; and the observance of the sabbath or the regulation of diet might expose him to social disapproval and to ridicule, but had no more tangible consequences. It was a different matter to refuse to take part in the ceremonies of the established religion of the city or

[1] Sifrè Num. § 111; Deut. § 54; Ḥullin 5a, and parallels. One who renounces idolatry is called in Scripture a Jew. Megillah 13a, top.

[2] Φοβούμενοι τὸν θεόν, σεβόμενοι τὸν θεόν, or abbreviated, σεβόμενοι. In Hebrew, יראי שמים. See Note 96.

[3] Juvenal, Sat. 14, 96 ff.

in the cult of the emperors; but so far as the former was concerned only those who had the rights and the corresponding obligations of citizens were affected by it; and as to the latter,
unless a common man made ostentation of his disrespect, his
neglect provoked no remark. Women in general had only their
fathers or husbands to reckon with; and partly from excess of
religiousness, partly because they had no public religious duties,
women were in the large majority among these adherents of
Judaism, and a still larger proportion, doubtless, of the proselytes.
Men who occupied a place of prominence in the community, or
held office in the city or state, must have made a compromise like
Naaman between their belief and the duties of their station,
and performed their part in the festivals and other ceremonies of
the public religions — if you did not *believe* in the gods, it was an
empty form.

However numerous such 'religious persons' were, and with
whatever complaisance the Hellenistic synagogue, especially,
regarded these results of its propaganda, whatever hopes they
may have held out to such as thus confided in the uncovenanted
mercies of God, they were only clinging to the skirt of the Jew
(Zech. 8, 23); they were like those Gentile converts to Christianity who are reminded in the Epistle to the Ephesians that in
their former state, when they were called uncircumcised by the
so-called circumcision, they were aliens to the Israelite commonwealth, foreigners without right in the covenanted promises.[1]

Much confusion has arisen from the habit of describing such
adherents of the synagogue as a class of proselytes, or, as it is
sometimes said, semi-proselytes, and trying to find a category
for them in the rabbinical deliverances concerning proselytes.
It may, therefore, be said at the outset that Jewish law knows
no semi-proselytes, nor any other kind of proselytes than such

[1] Ἀπηλλοτριωμένοι τῆς πολιτείας τοῦ Ἰσραὴλ καὶ ξένοι τῶν διαθηκῶν τῆς
ἐπαγγελίας, Ephes. 2, 12. Proselytes, on the contrary, have come over to
καινῇ καὶ φιλοθέῳ πολιτείᾳ, Philo, De Monarchia c. 7 § 51 (ed. Mangey II,
219).

as have, by circumcision and baptism, not only become members of the Jewish church but been naturalized in the Jewish nation — to make a distinction where none existed.[1]

Proselyte, the Greek προσήλυτος, is thus explained by Philo:[2] They are such as have resolved to change over to (true) religion, and are called proselytes because they have become naturalized in a new and godly commonwealth,[3] renouncing the mythical fictions and adhering to the unadulterated truth. . . . Under the law of Moses the proselytes enjoy equal rights in all respects with the native born,[4] as is only just, inasmuch as they have left country, friends, and kinsfolk for the sake of virtue and holiness. There can be no question that Philo means by 'proselyte' one who has deserted[5] his gods and his people to cast in his lot with the Jews. Tacitus speaks of proselytes as *transgressi in morem eorum*. Such practice circumcision like the Jews: "nec quidquam prius imbuuntur, quam contemnere deos, exuere patriam, parentes liberos fratres vilia habere."[6]

An examination of all the passages in Philo shows conclusively

---

[1] It is not a question in what loose senses *we* may use the word 'proselyte,' nor even whether the Greek προσήλυτος is ever used loosely; but whether Judaism — rabbinical and Hellenistic — recognized more than one kind of proselyte in *its* sense of the word. Precisely the same conditions exist in modern Christian missions: there are the baptized members of the church, and a fringe of adherents, who may have given up some heathen practices and adopted some Christian ones, but are nevertheless outside the pale of the church.

[2] De monarchia c. 7 §§ 51–53 (ed. Mangey II, 219). See also De sacrificantibus c. 10 § 308 f. (II, 258); De iustitia c. 6 § 176 ff. (II, 365); De humanitate c. 12 § 102 ff. (II, 392); De poenitentia c. 1 § 175 ff. (II, 405). Philo, whose fondness for exhibiting the resources of his vocabulary is well known, employs more frequently ἐπήλυτος, ἐπηλύτης, ἔπηλυς — classical Greek words in a political sense.

[3] Τούτους δὲ καλεῖ προσηλύτους ἀπὸ τοῦ προσεληλυθέναι καινῇ καὶ φιλοθέῳ πολιτείᾳ. Josephus (Antt. xviii. 3, 5 § 82) describes Fulvia as τῶν ἐν ἀξιώματι γυναικῶν καὶ νομίμοις προσεληλυθυῖαν τοῖς Ἰουδαικοῖς, evidently with the same etymology in mind.

[4] Ἰσοτιμία, ἰσονομία, ἰσοτέλεια.

[5] This is Philo's word: they are αὐτομολοῦντες. Similarly in the fragment, ed. Mangey II, 677, foreigners who join Israel are ἐπήλυδες . . . νομίμων καὶ ἔθων.

[6] Tacitus, Hist. v. 5.

that προσήλυτος and its synonyms designate a man who has not
merely embraced the monotheistic theology of Judaism, but has
addicted himself to the Jewish ordinances and customs, and
in so doing severed himself from his people, friends, and kins-
men; for which reason he is to be treated with peculiar benevolence. He has become a naturalized citizen of a new religious
commonwealth in which he is on a full equality of rights and
duties with born Jews.[1]

In the Greek Bible προσήλυτος is the usual, though not the constant, translation of the Hebrew *ger*.[2] The older associations of
this word were civil and social. The *ger* was an alien immigrant,
or the descendant of such an immigrant, resident in Israelite
territory by sufferance, without any civil rights, like the μέτοικος
in a Greek city. This is the position of the *ger* in the older Hebrew
legislation and in Deuteronomy. They are distinguished from
foreigners (*nokrim*), who may be casually and temporarily in
the country, and from the descendants of the ancient Canaanites.
Israelites are enjoined not to oppress these aliens, who had no
legal remedy;[3] and they are frequently presented as objects of
charity.

In the Persian period the word comes to be applied to foreigners (men of other than Jewish descent) who join themselves to
Jehovah, or to Israel as the worshippers of Jehovah. Thus in
Isaiah 14, 1, in the restoration, when God reëstablishes Israel
in its own land, "the *ger* (the converts they have made in the
exile) will join themselves to them and attach themselves to the
house of Jacob."[4] Such converts are described in Isa. 56, 6 ff.:

[1] When he says that what makes a proselyte is not circumcision of the
flesh but the circumcision of pleasures and appetites and the other affections
of the soul (Fragment, ed. Mangey II, 677; cf. Paul, Rom. 2, 28 f., and with
both, Jer. 4, 4), he is not talking about uncircumcised proselytes; he is only
saying of proselytes what the prophet and the apostle Paul say about Israelites. Cf. De sacrificantibus c. 9 §§ 304 f. (ed. Mangey, II, 258).

[2] See Note 97.

[3] They may often have attached themselves to a citizen as clients for
protection.

[4] The LXX here takes over the word in Aramaic form, γειώρας. See also
Ezek. 14, 7, converts (*ger*) who relapse to the worship of idols.

'The aliens [1] who join themselves to Jehovah to minister unto him, and to love the name of Jehovah, to be his servants, every one that keeps the sabbath from profaning it, and holds firmly to my covenant (law), I will bring them to my holy mountain and make them rejoice in my house of prayer; their burnt offerings and their sacrifices shall be acceptable upon my altar, for my house shall be called a house of prayer for all peoples. Thus saith the Lord Jehovah who gathers the dispersed of Israel, yet will I gather others unto him (Israel), besides those that are gathered of (Israel) himself.' [2]

The laws for the *gerim* in Lev. 17–25 put them, so far as religious duties and privileges go, in all respects on the same footing with Israelites by birth; they are subject to all the obligations of the law, precisely as the *gerim* (proselytes) in the rabbinical law are.[3] This is true, not only of religious commandments and prohibitions (Lev. 17, 8 f., 10–12, 13, 15; 22, 18; 18, 26 ff.), but before the civil law (24, 15–22): "You shall have one civil law; the proselyte (*ger*) shall be treated like the native born, for I am the Lord your God." This change in the meaning of *ger* from an *advena* in Jewish territory to an *advena* in the Jewish religion is significant at once of the change in the situation of the Jews in the world after the fall of the kingdom and of the changed conception of the character and mission of their religion — the metic has given place to the proselyte. This change is reflected in the language. For living as a resident alien (*ger*, in the original civil sense) in the land of Israel the verb is *gur*, 'sojourn'; for conversion to Judaism and adoption into the people as well as the religion a new form was needed and created, the

---

[1] בן הנכר.

[2] That is, many other Gentile converts will be added to the Israelites who are gathered from the dispersion, besides the converts they have made there.

[3] See also Lev. 16, 29 (Day of Atonement); Num. 19, 10 f.; cf. 15, 14–16, 26, 29. Especially important, as is recognized in the rabbinical law, are the prescriptions concerning the Passover, Exod. 12, 19; Num. 9, 14: "When a *ger* (interpreted 'proselyte') dwells with you and keeps the Passover to the Lord, he shall keep the Passover according to its statute and ordinance; you shall have one statute for the proselyte and for him who is native to the land."

denominative *nitgayyer*, 'become a proselyte' (*ger* in the religious sense), with a corresponding active denominative, *gayyer*, convert some one to Judaism, make a proselyte of him. Another word used with the same meaning is *hityahad* (denominative from *yehud*), 'turn Jew,' adopt the religion and customs of the Jews.[1]

A favorite figure in the Psalms for the confident security of the religious man is having a refuge, or shelter, beneath the wings of God, or beneath the shade of his wings, as the young of birds do under their mother's wings for safety from danger.[2] The same figure is frequently employed of conversion. The proselyte comes beneath the wings of the Shekinah; one who converts a Gentile brings him under the wings of the Shekinah. The origin of this use is doubtless Ruth 2, 12, where Boaz bespeaks for the Moabitish convert (1, 16) the reward for her goodness to Naomi from "the God of Israel, beneath whose wings thou art come to take refuge."[3]

The legislation in the middle books of the Pentateuch thus puts the *gerim* on the same footing with native Israelites, not only before the civil law, but in religious duties and privileges, and Philo repeatedly emphasizes this parity of the naturalized and the native Jew as one of the notable features of the Mosaic polity. The same principle runs through the traditional law. The Passover, in its memorial features, was the most distinctively national of all the festivals, but the law admits the proselyte to it, though no foreigner, no settler, no hired servant (not Israelite) may eat of it.[4] For such participation it is necessary

---

[1] See Note **98**.

[2] See Psalm 17, 8; 36, 8; 57, 2; 61, 5; 91, 4. Hos. 14, 7 is interpreted in this sense and applied to proselytes; see Num. R. 8, 7 (beginning). See also Isa. 54, 15 LXX: ἰδοὺ προσήλυτοι προσελεύσονταί σοι δι᾽ ἐμοῦ καὶ παροικήσουσί σοι καὶ ἐπὶ σὲ καταφεύξονται.

[3] Ruth R. *in loc.*, quoting Psalm 36, 8.

[4] שכיר, תושב, בן נכר. The criterion, which decides whether a man is a proselyte or not is whether he may participate in the passover meal, as among converts to Christianity it was whether he might participate in the sacrament of the Eucharist. Cf. Sifrè Num. § 71; Tos. Pesaḥim 8, 4; cf. Jer. Pesaḥim 36b. In Ḳiddushin 70a, top, a definition of *ger* is deduced from the Passover of Ezra 6 (כל הנבדל וגו', Ezra 6, 21).

that he should be circumcised, "for no uncircumcised man shall eat of it" (Exod. 12, 48). In Num. 9, 14, it is assumed that the proselyte is circumcised, and the only prescription is that he shall conform strictly to the ritual of the Passover: "Whether proselyte or native, you shall have the same ordinance." From the generality of the last clause, which contains no specific reference to the Passover, it is deduced that this scripture puts the proselyte on the same footing with the native in all the commandments contained in the Law.[1] "As the native born Jew takes upon him (to obey) all the words of the Law,[2] so the proselyte takes upon him all the words of the Law. The authorities say, if a proselyte takes upon himself to obey all the words of the Law except one single commandment, he is not to be received."[3] So Paul to the Galatians: "I solemnly warn every man that gets himself circumcised that he is under obligation to fulfil the whole law" (Gal. 5, 2). Paul had been brought up a Pharisee, and doubtless meant the unwritten as well as the written law. The Law was not solely the law written in the Pentateuch, but its complement and interpretation in tradition, the unwritten law; and with strenuous logic a contemporary of the Patriarch Judah held that the proselyte's acceptance of Judaism was incomplete and his admission not to be allowed so long as he made reservation of a single point in the rules established by the scribes without obvious support in the Scripture.[4]

The initiatory rite by which a man was made a proselyte comprised three parts: circumcision, immersion in water (baptism), and the presentation of an offering in the temple.[5] In the case of

---

[1] Sifrè Num. § 71; Mekilta on Exod. 12, 49 (Bo, 15, end; ed. Friedmann, f. 18a; ed. Weiss, f. 22a).

[2] An obligation which he acknowledges and renews every time he recites the Shema'. See below, p. 465.

[3] Sifra, Ḳedoshim Pereḳ 8 (ed. Weiss f. 91a); Mekilta de-R. Simeon ben Yoḥai on Exod. 12, 49; cf. also Bekorot 30b, top.

[4] See the passages cited in the preceding note, and Note 99.

[5] Sifrè Num. § 108 (on Num. 15, 14); Mekilta de-R. Simeon ben Yoḥai on Exod. 12, 48; Keritot 9a. See Maimonides, Isurè Biah, c. 13, 4.

a woman there was no circumcision, and after the destruction of
the temple no offering. Circumcision alone is prescribed in the
written law. The sacrifice of the proselyte is assimilated to four
cases in which a sacrifice is required of Israelites who have otherwise completed their purification but not offered the piacular
victim.[1] The practical effect of the rule was that if the proselyte
went to Jerusalem, he, like Jews of the classes enumerated who
were "lacking an expiatory offering," might not participate in a
sacrificial meal and eat consecrated food (*kodashim*) until he had
brought his piaculum.[2] The sacrifice to be made by a proselyte
was a burnt-offering for which doves or pigeons sufficed.

The offering of a sacrifice is, thus, not one of the conditions of
becoming a proselyte, but only a condition precedent to the
exercise of one of the rights which belong to him as a proselyte,
namely, participation in a sacrificial meal.[3] As soon as he was
circumcised and baptized, he was in full standing in the religious
community, having all the legal rights and powers and being
subject to all the obligations of the Jew by birth.[4] He had
"entered into the covenant."[5]

The origin of the requirement of baptism is not known. The
rite has a superficial analogy to the many baths prescribed in
the law for purification after one kind or another of religious
uncleanness, and modern writers have frequently satisfied themselves with the explanation that proselytes were required to
bathe in order to purify themselves, really or symbolically, from
the uncleanness in which the whole life of the heathen was passed.
This explanation seems to be nowhere explicitly propounded by

---

[1] M. Keritot 2, 1. They must make an offering before they can eat
kodashim; Lev. 15, 13–15, 28–30; 12, 6–8; 14, 10 ff.

[2] So R. Eleazar ben Jacob. For a different explanation see Note 100.

[3] Any Gentile could have a *burnt* offering made for him at his expense,
Sifrè Num. § 107, end, etc.

[4] Yebamot 47b: "When he is immersed and comes up (from the water)
he is in all respects like an Israelite."

[5] נכנס לברית. Hence he is called גר בן ברית, 'a covenant-proselyte,' in
contrast to the (heathen) גר תושב, 'resident alien'; e.g. Sifra, Aharè Pereḳ
12 (ed. Weiss, f. 84d, end). See below, p. 339.

Jewish teachers in the early centuries.[1] The rite itself differs fundamentally from such baths of purification in that the presence of official witnesses is required.[2]

The ritual for the admission of proselytes in Palestine in the second century, after the war under Hadrian, is described in detail in the following Baraita:[3]

When a man comes in these times seeking to become a proselyte, he is asked, What is your motive in presenting yourself to become a proselyte? Do you not know that in these times the Israelites are afflicted, distressed, downtrodden, torn to pieces, and that suffering is their lot? If he answer, I know; and I am unworthy (to share their sufferings), they accept him at once, and acquaint him with some of the lighter and some of the weightier commandments; they instruct him about the sin he may commit in such matters as gleaning close, picking up the forgotten sheaf, reaping the corner of the field, and the poor-tithe.[4] They acquaint him also with the penalties attached to the commandments, saying to him, Know that until you came to this status you ate fat without being liable to extirpation, you profaned the sabbath without being liable to death by stoning, but now if you eat fat you are liable to extirpation, and if you profane the sabbath you are liable to stoning. As they show him the penalty of breaking commandments, so they show him the reward of keeping them, saying to him, Know that the World to Come is made only for the righteous, and Israelites in the present time are not able to receive exceeding good or exceeding punishments. This discourse should not, however, be too much prolonged nor go too much into particulars. If he accepts, they circumcise him forthwith.[5] . . . When he is healed they at once baptize him, two scholars standing by him and rehearsing to him some of the lighter and some of the weightier command-

---

[1] See Note 101.
[2] Yebamot 46b; Ḳiddushin 62b, top; Maimonides, Isurè Biah, 13, 6.
[3] Yebamot 47a–b. On the antiquity of the rite, etc., see Note 102.
[4] Lev. 19, 9 (23, 22); Deut. 24, 19; Deut. 14, 28 f.
[5] Certain details of the operation are here omitted.

ments. When he has been immersed and has come up (from the water), he is like an Israelite in all that he does.[1]

In the case of a woman (proselyte), women make her sit in the water up to her neck, while two scholars standing outside rehearse to her some of the lighter and some of the weightier commandments.[2]

In the whole ritual there is no suggestion that baptism was a real or symbolical purification; the assistants rehearse select commandments of both kinds as an appropriate accompaniment to the proselyte's assumption of all and sundry the obligations of the law, "the yoke of the commandment." It is essentially an initiatory rite, with a forward and not a backward look.[3]

Rabbi (Judah, the Patriarch) remarked the correspondence between the admission of a proselyte and the experience of Israel. As the Israelites came into the covenant only by three things, circumcision, baptism, and sacrifice, precisely so the proselyte comes into the covenant by the same three things.[4] For the proselyte is equally a 'son of the covenant' with the born Jew.[5] In discussions from the first half of the second century on, it is frequently adduced as a principle that the legal status of a proselyte who embraces Judaism is (at the moment of his

---

[1] So completely so that if he subsequently relapses, he is legally treated (e.g. in questions of marriage) as an apostate Israelite (ישראל מומר); Yebamot 47b, near end. In religious matters — sacrificial meals, the Passover, etc. — the apostate Israelite, and of course the apostate proselyte, was treated as a heathen; Mekilta, Bo 15 (ed. Friedmann f. 17a; ed. Weiss f. 20b, top).

[2] Baptism requires the same minimum quantity of water as a woman's bath of purification, namely forty *seahs* — one or two hogsheads, according to varying estimates of the contents of a seah; Yebamot 47b. As in ritual ablutions, the water must touch every part of the flesh.

[3] On the question whether a man who had been circumcised but not baptized, or baptized but not circumcised, might be admitted to the Passover, see Note 103.

[4] They were circumcised before leaving Egypt (inferred from Josh. 5, 2 f., "the second time"); they were baptized in the desert (Exod. 19, 10, "Sanctify yourselves"); after they pledged themselves to keep all God's commandments they were sprinkled with the blood of the covenant sacrifice (Exod. 24, 3–8).

[5] Sifra, Aḥarè Pereḳ 12: מה אזרח בן ברית אף גר בן ברית.

reception) like that of a new born child; the casuistic question
is raised whether a son born after his conversion is his firstborn son and legal heir.[1] This principle is cited in a discussion
between scholars of the first half of the second century with
a different application. The question there is, why in those
days proselytes suffered so severely, and in reply to an opinion
that it was because before their conversion they had not strictly
observed the seven commandments given to the descendants
of Noah (i.e. to all the heathen), R. Jose quotes, "A proselyte
who embraces Judaism is like a new-born child." [2] God cannot
therefore now chastise him for deeds done or duties neglected
before his new birth. In other words, all former sins are done
away by conversion and reception into the Jewish religious community through circumcision and baptism.

Equality in law and religion does not necessarily carry with
it complete social equality, and the Jews would have been singularly unlike the rest of mankind if they had felt no superiority
to their heathen converts. To the old classification, Priests,
Levites, (lay) Israelites, a fourth category was added, Proselytes; [3] and sometimes a subdivision puts them far down in the
table of precedence, after (Israelite) bastards and Nethinim
(descendants of old temple-slaves), and only above (heathen)
slaves who had been circumcised and emancipated by their
masters.[4]

The autonomy of Judaea was achieved and successfully maintained by the Maccabaean brothers, Jonathan and Simon.
Their successors entertained larger ambitions, and by a series of
aggressive wars extended their dominion in all directions, to the

---

[1] Yebamot 62a; Bekorot 47a, top. The laws of prohibited degrees also
offer problems for casuistry; Yebamot 22a; 62a, near the end; 97b–98a; 98b.

[2] Yebamot 48b. That the proselytes suffer for their neglect of the laws
which as heathen they were bound to obey is the view of R. Ḥanina, son of
R. Gamaliel; the reply is made by R. Jose ben Ḥalafta. Other explanations
follow.

[3] Tos. Ḳiddushin 5, 1.

[4] M. Horaiyot 3, 8; Horaiyot 13a.

south over Idumaea, to the north over Galilee, east of the Jordan and the Dead Sea to the edge of the desert, and on the Mediterranean seaboard from the desert in the south to Mt. Carmel in the north. In the break up of the Seleucid kingdom, no neighboring state arose permanently to contest their power; and this superiority the Asmonaean dynasty held for eighty years. John Hyrcanus imposed the Jewish religion on the Idumaeans by compulsory circumcision; his successor Aristobulus did the same for the mixed population of northern Galilee and the Ituraeans of the southern Lebanon; and it would be quite in character if Alexander Jannaeus multiplied Jews in a similar impromptu manner in the fields of his conquests. Besides such forcible and skin-deep conversions, many doubtless of their own accord sought to be enrolled in the governing people from motives in which religious conviction had small place. The Jews, thanks in part to their independence at home, in part to their dispersion abroad which gave them ready-made commercial connections everywhere, were under the Asmonaeans and under Herod, a highly prosperous people; and in the Hellenistic cities and by Roman favor enjoyed exceptional privileges and exemptions. Under such circumstances it is not strange that conversions were numerous; all the more because the religions in which men had been born had little real hold upon them when civic duties and local associations were dissolved by distance and they mingled in the heterogeneous population of foreign lands.[1]

That many did in fact embrace Judaism from purely worldly motives the religious leaders were painfully aware. Several kinds of what we might call counterfeit converts are enumerated.[2] There is the 'love proselyte,' a man who becomes a proselyte for the sake of marrying a Jewish woman, or a woman for the

---

[1] In an interesting passage in Sifrè on Deut. 33, 19 (§ 354), the spectacle of the Jews, all worshipping one God, all eating the same kinds of food, makes so great an impression on heathen visitors to Jerusalem, who have many different gods and different rules about food, that they make haste to become proselytes to such a unifying religion.

[2] Jer. Ḳiddushin 65b; cf. Yebamot 24b.

sake of taking a Jewish husband; another professes conversion for a place at the king's table (advancement at court), or like Solomon's servants (probably with a similar motive).[1] Such are declared by R. Nehemiah to be no proselytes;[2] and he passes the same judgement on 'lion proselytes' (like the Cuthaeans in Samaria, who took to the worship of the Lord out of fear of lions, but at the same time kept on with their heathen worship and ways; 2 Kings 17, 24–33); men who become proselytes in consequence of a dream (interpreted as commanding them to become Jews); the proselytes of the days of Mordecai and Esther ("for the fear of the Jews was fallen upon them," Esther 8, 17)— "these are no proselytes!" Only those, he continues, who are converted in a time like this — the dire days after the war under Hadrian, when there was nothing to gain and nothing to fear from the Jews, no worldly advantage, therefore, to be got by casting in a man's lot with them — only such are genuine proselytes.[3] Ultimately, however, the view prevailed that they are to be regarded and treated as proselytes so long as they have been properly received and do not openly apostatize; motives for conversion lie beyond legal cognizance.[4]

One class of converts who were brought into the body of Israel by improper motives are those who are called *gerim gerurim*, of which the Gibeonites (Josh. 9) are the typical example. The participle signifies 'dragged in,' and is applied to heathen who Judaize in mass, as whole peoples, under the impulsion of fear, like the Gibeonites. Instances of such mass conversions in more recent times were the Idumaeans, who were forced by John Hyrcanus to submit to circumcision, and the Ituraeans, who were similarly Judaized by Aristobulus. They doubtless proved for a good while to be very unsatisfactory Jews, and while

[1] Proselytes of this variety may have been numerous in the days of the later Asmonaeans.

[2] Disciple of R. Akiba.

[3] Yebamot 24b. According to Jer. Ḳiddushin 65b proselytes of the classes enumerated above "are not received."

[4] So Rab, in the places cited.

there is, so far as I know, no specific mention of their case, it is very likely that they were thought of when the *gerim gerurim* were discussed. The rule finally established was that, although they did not accept Judaism for God's sake, they are legally proselytes, and to be protected in their rights as such.[1]

In contrast to all these spurious or dubious proselytes, the sincere and genuine proselyte is called *ger ṣedeḳ*, 'righteous proselyte.'[2] They are such as embrace the religion from religious motives, 'for the sake of God,' (*le-shem Shamaim*),[3] and thenceforth live in conformity to his will revealed in the twofold law as they pledged themselves to do at their reception. Another name applied to such converts is *gere emet*, 'true, or genuine, proselytes.'[4] To the righteous proselytes are sometimes applied texts in the Old Testament which speak of the righteous, or of such as fear God, i.e. are truly religious.[5] In the daily prayers, as we have seen, the petition for God's blessing upon the righteous proselytes stands in significant juxtaposition to an imprecation of his wrath upon Jewish apostates.

The word *ger* by itself having come to mean proselyte, that is, a convert to Judaism who had been received by circumcision and baptism not only into the religion but into the Jewish people, it was necessary to find a distinctive term for the resident alien.

---

[1] The proof is the famine that God sent on Israel for Saul's treatment of the Gibeonites and the expiation demanded for his sin (2 Sam. 21, 1–9). Jer. Ḳiddushin 65b–c; Midrash Shemuel 28, 5; Num. R. 8, 4.

[2] גר צדק. See Shemoneh 'Esreh 13; על גרי הצדק יחמו רחמיך (Palestinian recension); ועל גרי הצדק יהמו רחמיד . . . על הצדיקים (Babylonian recension; cf. Megillah 17b, end); Sifra, Aḥarè Pereḳ 13 (ed. Weiss, f. 86b), citing Psalm 118, 20. Other references below, p. 340. The common translation, 'proselyte of righteousness,' in verbal imitation of the Hebrew idiom, instead of the idiomatic English 'righteous proselyte,' has doubtless contributed to the erroneous notion that the phrase was originally intended to distinguish the 'full' proselyte from the 'half' proselyte ('proselyte of the gate,' see below, p. 340 f.).

[3] On this motive as a principle of conduct, see Vol. II, p. 98.

[4] גירי אמת e.g. Niddah 56b; Sanhedrin 85b; גרים של אמת, Tanḥuma ed. Buber, Bemidbar § 31. The opposite is גר שקר, Jer. Baba Meṣi'a 10c.

[5] So e.g. Midrash Tehillim on Psalm 22, 24 (ed. Buber f. 98a). R. Samuel bar Naḥman. See Note 96.

This term in rabbinical law is *ger toshab*. The doctrine of the lawyers about the *ger toshab* may be briefly summarized as follows: He is an alien, resident in Jewish territory by sufferance, but on condition that while thus resident he do not engage in the worship of other gods or in idolatrous practices, and do not blaspheme the name of God; that he hold himself subject to the jurisdiction of established courts; that he keep himself free of flagrant crimes, homicide, robbery and theft, incest and adultery; and finally, that he abstain from eating flesh with the life blood in it — the seven commandments which, as we have seen above, were said to have been given by God to Adam and Noah, and to be consequently binding upon all mankind.[1] He was not required to join in the worship of the God of Israel, nor to take upon him any further obligation to observe the commandments of God to Israel, though he enjoyed with all others the exemption from labor on the Sabbath which gives rest on that day to slaves and hirelings of every race and estate, as well as to oxen and asses which precede him in the enumeration.

Nothing but misunderstanding can come from calling the *ger toshab* a 'proselyte' or 'semi-proselyte'; he was not a convert to Judaism at all. The *ger toshab*, as uncircumcised (*ger 'arel*), is expressly distinguished from the circumcised proselyte (*ger ben berit*) who has come into the covenant of God with Israel, or the *ger mahūl*, which is the same thing. Conclusive proof that the *ger toshab* is a heathen may be taken from two items of the law: he may eat 'carrion' (*nebelah*),[2] which no Israelite or proselyte may touch; and, in the sphere of civil law, it is permissible to take usury from a *ger toshab* equally with any other heathen, while it is strictly forbidden to take usury, either in the biblical or the rabbinical definition, from an Israelite, native or adventitious.

---

[1] 'Abodah Zarah 64b. On the commandments for the descendants of Noah, see above, pp. 274 f. A simpler definition of the *ger toshab* is "one who pledges himself in the presence of three scrupulously observant persons (חברים) to abstain from idolatry'; 'Abodah Zarah 64b; cf. 65a.

[2] *Nebelah* is the flesh of animals not correctly slaughtered (M. Ḥullin 2, 4). The *ger* to whom an Israelite may give it (Deut. 14, 21) is the *ger toshab*; Sifrè

Much of what is said in our rábbinical sources about the *ger toshab* was only of exegetical or casuistical interest in the age from which those sources come. Whatever definitions and rules the rabbis made applied only to the land of Israel and to times when it lay in the power of the Jews to determine upon what conditions aliens should be allowed to establish residence among them.[1]

Since the eighteenth century another category of proselytes has figured largely in the Christian books, the so-called 'proselytes of the gate,' with whom, in contrast to the 'proselytes of righteousness,' or 'full proselytes,' the God-fearing Gentiles [2] discussed above are identified. The name, which to the uninformed might suggest converts who lingered at the door of the synagogue, is derived indirectly from passages in the Bible which speak of the '*ger* (alien) who is in thy gates' (resident in Israelite cities or towns).[3] In the second century the question was raised whether in the Fourth Commandment of the Decalogue (Exod. 20, 10) this *ger* was a *ger ṣedek*, i.e. a proselyte, who was under a personal obligation to keep the sabbath like a born Jew, or a *ger toshab*, who was subject to no such obligation. The former opinion prevailed.[4]

---

in loc., § 104. The *ger* of Lev. 17, 15, for whom the law of *nebelah* is the same as for the Israelite, is therefore the *ger ben berit*, not the *ger toshab*; Sifra, Aharè Perek 12 (ed. Weiss, f. 84d, end). See Note 104. On usury (*neshek, tarbit*, Deut. 23, 20 f.; Lev. 25, 36 f.) on loans between Israelites and the *ger toshab* see M. Baba Meṣi'a 5, 6. What is to be done if a Gentile becomes a proselyte (*nitgayyer*) while a loan on interest between him and an Israelite is outstanding, see Tos. Baba Meṣi'a 5, 21; Jer. Baba Meṣi'a f. 10c; Baba Meṣi'a 72a. On the *ger toshab*, see further Note 104.

[1] In an enumeration of laws and institutions that fell into desuetude from the time when the year of Jubilee ceased to be kept (i.e. since the exile), R. Simeon ben Eleazar (latter part of the second century) includes the *ger toshab* (see Lev. 25, 47–54); 'Arakin 29a. This may however refer only to the particular case contemplated.

[2] Σεβόμενοι (φοβούμενοι) τὸν θεόν; see above pp. 325 f.

[3] Exod. 20, 10; Deut. 5, 14; 31, 12, etc. Often named in Deuteronomy, with widows, orphans, and the landless levites, as objects of charitable provision; e.g. Deut. 16, 11, 14; 14, 29; 26, 12. See also Sifrè Deut. on 14, 29 (§ 110).

[4] Mekilta on Exod. 20, 10 (ed. Friedmann f. 69b; ed. Weiss f. 77a); cf. on 23, 12 (Friedmann, f. 101a; Weiss f. 107b); Yebamot 48b.

From much that has been written about the 'proselyte of the gate' it would be inferred that the name was in common use among the rabbis to designate a class of 'semi-proselytes.' This is an error. The phrase *ger sha'ar*, 'gate proselyte,' is not found in any Talmudic source. I know no occurrence earlier than R. Moses ben Naḥman (d. 1270), who uses it in his commentary on Exod. 20, 10 merely as an abbreviated expression for the *ger* "who is in thy gates," and is so far from knowing it as an established designation for a special class of 'proselytes' that he reverts to the old discussion whether the *ger sha'ar* was a *ger ṣedeḳ* (proselyte) or a *ger toshab*, that is, an alien who eats the flesh of animals not properly slaughtered.

The attitude of the religious leaders of Judaism toward proselytes differed in different circumstances, and individual teachers had their own sympathies or antipathies. Shammai would have nothing to do with one who was not prepared to give implicit assent, before knowing its contents, to the unwritten law as well as the written. In the generation that came after the fall of Jerusalem, R. Eliezer ben Hyrcanus, in this also a true heir of Shammai's spirit, had a bad opinion of all proselytes: They are prone to fall back into their old ways, because they are naturally bad; it is for this reason that the Scripture had so often to admonish Israelites not to give them offense by word or deed;[1] such a relapsed proselyte is meant in Exod. 23, 4 by the word 'enemy.'[2] Their misfortunes come from obeying the law not out of love to God, but out of fear of his punishments.[3] It may be assumed that a foreigner's mind is always set on idolatry.[4]

[1] Mekilta, Mishpaṭim 18, on Exod. 22, 20 (ed. Friedmann f. 95a; ed. Weiss f. 101a). According to Mekilta de R. Simeon ben Yoḥai on Exod. 23, 9, R. Eliezer counted thirty-six such admonitions; another found forty-eight (Tanḥuma ed. Buber, Wayyiḳra § 3). See also Baba Meṣi'a 59b, end.

[2] Mekilta, Mishpaṭim 20 (on Exod. l.c.), ed. Friedmann f. 99a; ed. Weiss f. 104b.

[3] Yebamot 48b. See also Baba Batra 10b, middle.

[4] Jer. Beṣah 60a; Giṭṭin, 45b. On Eliezer's attitude toward proselytes and heathen see Bacher, Tannaiten, I, 106 f.

The school of Hillel, on the contrary, like their master, wel-
comed converts, and admitted them even though their knowledge
was imperfect and their observance faulty. Hillel's motto was:
"Be one of the disciples of Aaron, a lover of peace, following after
peace, loving mankind, and drawing them to the Law (religion)."[1]
In another anecdote illustrating the different temper of the two
masters, a foreigner comes to Shammai saying, "Make a proselyte of me, on condition that you teach me the whole of the Law
while I stand on one foot." Shammai drove him off with a
measuring-stick he had in his hand. Thereupon he repaired to
Hillel with the same proposition; Hillel received him as a proselyte and taught him: "What you do not like to have done to you
do not do to your fellow. This is the whole of the Law; the
rest is the explanation of it. Go, learn it."[2]

Speaking generally the tone of the utterances about proselytes
is friendly, though not unduly enthusiastic. This is the more to
be noted because the Jews' experience with proselytes must at
times have been decidedly discouraging. It can hardly be
doubted that in perilous times many apostatized. In the outside lands, at least, many went over to Christianity. In the
persecution under Hadrian they were under strong temptation
to clear their own skirts by turning informers.[3] It would be
nothing surprising if under such circumstances the rabbis should
have looked askance at all proselytes. There is, however, little
evidence of such a temper. The following extracts may serve
to illustrate the biblical method of the schools as well as the substance of their teaching about the treatment of proselytes. The
first is from the Mekilta on Exodus 22, 20, "An alien (*ger*) thou
shalt not injure nor oppress, for ye were aliens in the land of
Egypt." Taking *ger* of an alien who has come over to the religion
of Israel, a proselyte, it comments thus:[4]

---

[1] Abot 1, 12.
[2] Shabbat 31a.   See Vol. II, pp. 86 f.
[3] See Note 106.
[4] Mekilta, Mishpaṭim 18 (ed. Friedmann f. 95a–b; ed. Weiss f. 101a–b);
cf. also Baba Meṣi'a 58b, 59b.

Do not injure him with words and do not oppress him in money matters. One must not say to him, Yesterday you were worshipping Bel, Ḳores, Nebo, and with swine's flesh still between your teeth you answer back to me! And whence do we see that if you insult him, he can retort the insult? Because the Scripture says, 'for ye were aliens.' Hence R. Nathan used to say, Do not throw up to your fellow a blemish you have yourself. Proselytes are dear to God, for he is everywhere admonishing about them, 'Do not wrong a proselyte,' and 'you shall love the proselyte,' and 'you know the feelings of the proselyte.'[1] R. Eliezer said: It is on account of the proselyte's natural depravity that the Scripture admonishes about him in many places.[2] R. Simeon ben Yoḥai said: It says, 'And those that love him are like the sun when it rises in its power.'[3] Which is greater, he who loves the king or he whom the king loves? You must say, he whom the king loves, as it is said (of God), 'And he loveth a proselyte.'[4] Proselytes are dear to God, for you will find that the same things are said about them as about Israel:[5] the Israelites are called servants,[6] as it is said, 'For to me the Israelites are servants' (Lev. 25, 53), and proselytes are called servants, as it is said, 'To love the name of the Lord and to be servants to him' (Isa. 56, 6); the Israelites are called ministers,[7] as it is said, 'And ye shall be called the priests of the Lord, ministers of our God shall be said of you' (Isa. 61, 6), and the proselytes are called ministers, as it is said, 'The foreigners who attach themselves to the Lord to minister to him' (Isa. 56, 6); the Israelites are called friends, as it is said, 'The offspring of Abraham, my friend' (Isa. 41, 8); the proselytes are called friends,[8] as it is said (of God), 'Friend of the proselyte' (Deut. 10, 18); the word 'covenant' is used of the Israelites, as it is said, 'And my covenant shall be in your flesh' (Gen. 17, 13); and so it is used of proselytes, as it is said,

---

[1] Exod. 22, 20; Deut. 10, 19; Exod. 23, 9, etc.
[2] See above, p. 341, n. 1.
[3] Judges 5, 31.
[4] Deut. 10, 18.
[5] With these parallels cf. also Num. R. 8, 2.
[6] עבדים, 'bond servants.'
[7] משרתים, free servants, or attendants.
[8] אוהבים, literally, 'lovers.'

'Who hold fast my covenant' (Isa. 56, 6); 'acceptance' is
used of the Israelites as it is said, 'With acceptance before
the Lord' (Exod. 28, 38); and of proselytes, as it is said,
'Their burnt offerings and sacrifices with acceptance on my
altar' (Isa. 56, 7); 'keeping' is spoken of the Israelites, as
it is said, 'He that keepeth Israel will neither slumber nor
sleep' (Psalm 121, 4), and of proselytes, as it is said, 'The
Lord who keeps the proselytes' (Psalm 146, 9). Abraham
calls himself a proselyte, as it is said, 'A stranger (*ger*) and
a sojourner am I with you' (Gen. 23, 4);[1] David calls himself a proselyte, as it is said, 'A stranger (*ger*) am I in the
land' (Psalm 119, 19); and it says, 'For we are strangers
and sojourners before thee like all our fathers, for our days
are a shadow on the earth and there is no abiding' (1 Chron.
29, 15); and again, 'I am a stranger with thee, a sojourner
like all my fathers' (Psalm 39, 13). Dear (to God) are the
proselytes,[2] for our father Abraham was not circumcised till
he was ninety-nine years old. If he had been circumcised
at twenty or at thirty a man could have become a proselyte only at a lower age than twenty or thirty; therefore
God postponed it in his case till he arrived at the age of
ninety-nine, in order not to bolt the door in the face of
proselytes who come,[3] and to give a reward for days and
years, and to increase the reward of one who does his will,
as it is said, 'The Lord was pleased for his righteousness'
sake to magnify the law and glorify it' (Isa. 42, 21). And
so you will find it of the four classes who answer and say before him who spake and the world came into being, 'I am the
Lord's'; for it says (Isa. 44, 5), 'One says, I am the Lord's,

[1] Abraham was not only a proselyte who came over from heathenism to
the true religion, but a great maker of proselytes. Gen. 12, 5, 'the souls they
had gotten (literally, 'made') in Haran,' are the proselytes they had made
there; see e.g. Gen. R. *in loc.* (39, near end): "The verb 'made' is used to
teach that one who brings a foreigner (*nokri*) near and makes a proselyte of
him is as if he created him." Cf. Gen. R. 84, 2 (on Gen. 37, 1). To 'bring
near' (sc. to God) is frequent for 'make a proselyte,' e.g. Jer. Ḳiddushin 65b,
end. See also below, p. 348, n. 4.

[2] To illustrate God's singular love for proselytes Num. R. has a pretty
parable of a king's affection for a stray gazelle of the desert that had joined
itself to his flocks and went in and out with them. In the parable of the lost
sheep (Matt. 18, 12 f.) the point is the shepherd's anxiety over one of his own
flock that has wandered away. See also Note 107.

[3] Cf. Gen. R. 46, init. (cf. Gen. 17, 1).

and one calls on the name of Jacob, and one inscribes with his hand, Unto the Lord, and (another) takes Israel for a surname.' 'I am the Lord's'—and may there be no admixture of sin in me! 'One calls on the name of Jacob'—these are the righteous proselytes. 'One inscribes with his hand, Unto the Lord'—these are the penitents; 'And takes Israel for a surname'—these are they that fear Heaven."

From the other great school of the period, that of Akiba, a corresponding deliverance is found in the Sifra on Lev. 19, 34:[1]

"'Thou shalt not wrong him.' That is you shall not say to him, Yesterday you were an idolater and now you have come beneath the wings of the Shekinah. 'Like the native born.' As the native born is one who takes upon him all the commandments of the law, so the proselyte is one who takes upon him all the commandments of the law. Hence the rule: A proselyte who takes upon him all the commandments of the law with a single exception is not to be admitted. R. Jose son of R. Judah says, Even one of the minutiae of the scribal regulations. 'Shall the proselyte be who sojourns with you, and thou shalt love him as thyself.' Just as it is said in relation to Israelites, 'Thou shalt love thy neighbor as thyself,' so in relation to proselytes (gerim) it is said, 'Thou shalt love him as thyself, for ye were strangers (gerim) in the land of Egypt.' Understand how proselytes feel; for ye were strangers in the land of Egypt.

These passages from the juristic Midrash express with authority the teaching of the schools in the second century. There is no reason to doubt that it is what they taught before the war under Hadrian; it was preserved and transmitted by the disciples who restored the schools after the war, and is repeated in Baraitas in the Talmud as the accepted doctrine and rule.[2]

---

[1] Sifra, Ḳedoshim Pereḳ 8 (ed. Weiss f. 91a). The chapter begins with the reasonable requirement that a man who comes to a Jewish community professing to be a proselyte must present evidence of the fact. Cf. Mekilta de-R. Simeon ben Yoḥai on Exod. 22, 20; Baba Meṣi'a 58b; 59b.

[2] In a much later homiletical Midrash, Num. R. 8, is a large compilation of matter about proselytes from various sources and ages, but throughout in the same spirit. The post-Talmudic Masseket Gerim brings together chiefly juristic material from the Talmuds.

It is not at variance with this attitude when it is taught that in the Days of the Messiah proselytes will not be received, as they were not received, it is said, in the times of David and Solomon.[1] The presumption is that those who sought to be naturalized when Israel was enjoying extraordinary power and prosperity did so only from motives of self-interest, not from religious motives; how much more in the messianic age![2] Heathen who in that age profess Judaism in mass (*gerim gerurim*)[3] and put on phylacteries and fringes, and fasten *mezuzot* on their door posts in imitation of Jewish custom, when the war of Gog and Magog breaks out will abjure their profession and desert the Jewish cause.[4]

This was not, however, a unanimous opinion. R. Jose (ben Ḥalafta) taught, on the contrary, that in the time to come (the messianic age) the heathen would come and become proselytes.[5] In the same spirit we read in a later Palestinian Midrash: "God says, In this age, through the efforts of the righteous, individuals become proselytes, but in the Age to Come, I will draw the righteous (Gentiles) near, and bring them beneath the wings of the Shekinah, as it is written, 'For then will I give the peoples, in exchange for their own, a pure language, that they may all of them call on the name of the Lord and serve him with one consent," (Zeph. 3, 9).[6]

Strong antipathy to proselytes is rarely expressed. R. Ḥelbo, a Palestinian teacher of the latter part of the third century, declares that proselytes are as troublesome to Israel as the itch.[7] This peculiar form of trouble is discovered by an ingenious combination of the word *sappaḥat* (a cutaneous eruption, Lev. 13, 2)

---

[1] Yebamot 24b; 'Abodah Zarah 3b.
[2] See above, p. 337.
[3] Ibid.
[4] 'Abodah Zarah 3b.
[5] Ibid.
[6] Tanḥuma ed. Buber, Wayyera § 38. See Vol. II, pp. 371 ff.
[7] Yebamot 47b, cf. 109b; Ḳiddushin 70b; Niddah 13b. In the passage cited last it is said on Tannaite authority (תנו רבנן) that proselytes and משחקים בתינוקות hinder the coming of the Messiah. On the meaning of the latter phrase see Klausner, Die messianischen Vorstellungen des jüdischen Volkes, u. s. w., p. 37.

with *nispaḥu* (the proselytes 'will cleave' to the house of Jacob, Isa. 14, 1). Whether R. Ḥelbo was seriously ill-affected to proselytes or only proud of his pun, and if the former, what his grievance was, is not revealed. The contexts in which his words are quoted are not more enlightening, and in any case, come from a time that lies beyond our present concern.

It gratified Jewish pride in the demonstrated superiority of the true God and the true religion to play with the imagination that bitter enemies of Israel had been constrained to acknowledge this superiority and become converts to Judaism, like Nebuzaradan, who was a righteous proselyte; or that their descendants were converted and became teachers of the Law in Palestine, like those of Sisera and Sennacherib. God would have brought the grandsons of Nebuchadnezzar beneath the wings of the Shekinah, had not the ministering angels made too strong a protest. Shemaiah and Abṭalion were descendants of Sennacherib; descendants of Haman were also among the teachers of the Law.[1] It must be observed, however, that in the latter cases there is another idea: The sins of heathen fathers are not an attainder which excludes their posterity from the Jewish people or from the highest honor the rabbis could conceive, that of being Doctors of the Law.[2]

Some of the most eminent schoolmen of the second century were, or are reputed to have been, of proselyte ancestry. This is said of both Akiba and his great disciple R. Meir. The name of the proselyte Aquila, is, thanks to his translation of the Bible, the best known of all to Christian scholars.

The emphasis laid by the rabbis on sincerity in conversion led them, as appears in the rite of admission quoted above, to an inquiry into the candidate's motives, and to a setting forth of the difficulties and dangers to which a proselyte exposed himself which might well dissuade him from his purpose if it was not

---

[1] Sanhedrin 96b; Giṭṭin 57b.
[2] On the legends of the imperial proselyte 'Antoninus' (Jer. Megillah 72b, 74a) and his relations to the Patriarch Judah, see Bacher, Tannaiten, II, 457 f.; Ginzberg, Jewish Encyclopedia, I, 656 f.

honest and strong.   Caution is enjoined against carrying this
dissuasive so far as to turn away even the sincere.[1]   The same
caution is given elsewhere.   R. Johanan quotes Job 31, 32:
"The proselyte shall not lodge without; I will open my doors to
the wayfarer," as a proof text for the rule that proselytes should
be held back with the left (the weaker) hand and drawn near with
the right; men should not do like Elisha, who thrust Gehazi away
with both hands.[2] So in a Baraita: "Always the left hand should
repel and the right hand draw near; not like Elisha, who thrust
Gehazi away with both hands; nor like Joshua ben Peraḥiah,
who thrust away Jesus the Nazarene with both hands."[3]

A contemporary of R. Johanan, R. Abba Arika (Rab), the
first great name in the history of the Babylonian schools, remarks on the dictum quoted in a previous connection that those
who seek to become proselytes from motives of self-interest are
not to be received: "The rule is, They are proselytes; and they
are not to be repelled as proselytes are repelled at the outset, but
received; and they must have friendly treatment, for perhaps
after all they have become proselytes for religious motives (for
God's sake)." [4]

There is no way of estimating statistically the results of Jewish
propaganda in the centuries that fall within the limits of our
inquiry, but they were indisputably very large, even if only
proselytes in the proper sense be taken into account.[5]   The con-

[1] See above, p. 333.

[2] Jer. Sanhedrin 29b.   On the legend of Gehazi and Elisha's fruitless
journey to Damascus to try to reclaim him, see Jewish Encyclopedia, V,
580 f.

[3] Sanhedrin 107b; Soṭah 47a. On the latter example of such excess of
zeal and its consequences (which is suppressed in the censored editions of the
Talmud), see H. Strack, Die Häretiker und die Christen nach den ältesten
jüdischen Angaben, 1910, pp. 10 f., 32* f.

[4] Jer. Ḳiddushin 65b (see above, p. 337).   Cf. Mekilta, Yitro 1 (ed. Friedmann f. 58a–b; ed. Weiss f. 66a, end).   As God brought Jethro near and did
not repel him, so, "When a man comes to thee to become a proselyte, he
does not come except for God's sake (from religious motives); do thou
therefore bring him near and do not repel him."   See Note 107.

[5] On this point see Harnack, Ausbreitung des Christentums, 4 ed., pp. 13 ff.

verts were of many races, and of all ranks in society. According to Dio Cassius, Flavius Clemens, an uncle of the emperor, consul in 95 A.D., who was put to death by Domitian in the same year on a charge of ἀθεότης, and his wife Flavia Domitilla, who was exiled on the same charge, were probably proselytes to Judaism.[1] Josephus narrates at length and with evident satisfaction the conversion to Judaism of the royal family of Adiabene,[2] which in the first century of our era was ruled by native kings in some kind of dependence on Parthia. In the first half of the century the queen, Helena, embraced Judaism, and her son, Izates, who was at the time living abroad, was independently converted to the same religion. After Izates succeeded to the throne, he was circumcised, and many of his kindred were moved to follow his example. Queen Helena spent many years in Jerusalem, and her body was conveyed thither to be buried in a tomb that is still standing. Izates died about 55 A.D., and was also buried in Jerusalem, leaving the kingdom to his brother Monobazus II. His successors also adhered to Judaism. The dynasty came to an end in 116 A.D., when Trajan conquered Adiabene and made it the province of Assyria. It may safely be assumed, as in like conditions in the expansion of Christianity, that a large part of the people of Adiabene adopted the religion of their rulers, and the Judaizing of the population may have been furthered by the strong Jewish settlements and flourishing schools at Nisibis.[3]

[1] Dio Cassius, lxvii. 14. See Juster, Les Juifs dans l'empire romain, I, 257, and the literature there listed. It is thought by a majority of scholars that Dio Cassius did not discriminate Christians from Jews, and that the victims were in fact Christians. If it were certain that the Flavia Domitilla whose name appears in a Christian inscription was the wife of Clement, the evidence would be decisive.

[2] Adiabene embraced at this time most of the territory of ancient Assyria east of the Tigris. In Izates' reign the Parthian king Artabanus added to it the district of Nisibis.

[3] Josephus, Antt. xx. 2–4; Bell. Jud. ii. 19, 2; iv. 9, 11; v. 2, 2; 3, 3; 4, 2; 6, 1; vi. 6, 3 f. See Schürer, Geschichte des jüdischen Volkes, III, 118 ff. (with literature). For the Talmudic legends about this dynasty see Brüll, Jahrbücher, u. s. w., I, 72–80.

The Jews in the Roman empire, as has been already said, enjoyed certain extraordinary privileges and exemptions, the most important of which was that they were not required to do anything which implied a recognition of another god.[1] Thus, after Augustus, when the worship of the Roman emperors became an imperial religion and was cultivated with obsequious zeal in the provinces, the Jews, and they alone, were not required to manifest their loyalty in any of the usual forms of adoration such as burning incense before the image of the emperor, or to take oath by the emperors. In strictness this exemption would have extended only to peregrine Jews, not to such as acquired the status of Roman citizens, and particularly not to freedmen, who in law were bound to worship the *sacra* of their former masters. But here also an exception was made in their favor, and various other privileges were accorded to them.

These rights and privileges belonged, however, only to those who were by birth members of the Jewish nation. If a proselyte did not worship the gods, he made himself liable to prosecution for 'atheism.'[2] The abstention was not likely to attract remark except in the case of officials whose duty it was to conduct pagan rites or assist in them. Converts of this class were, however, not numerous, and probably few of those who would otherwise have embraced Judaism were deterred by apprehension that this law might be invoked against them. Domitian's energetic collection of the special poll-tax on Jews, the *fiscus Judaicus*, which was exacted from those who without openly professing their adhesion to Judaism lived like Jews, as well as from born Jews who concealed their race,[3] gave occupation to the informers whom he

[1] Hellenistic monarchs had long before followed the same policy, granting to Jews the rights of citizens, but exempting them from participation in heathen cults which otherwise were incumbent on all citizens. See on the whole subject, Juster, Les Juifs dans l'empire romain, I, 245 f.

[2] 'Atheism,' in law, was not the theoretical denial of the existence of gods, but the failure to worship the gods that the state recognized.

[3] The half-shekel tax raised by the Jews everywhere for the maintenance of the public sacrifices in the temple in Jerusalem was converted by Vespasian after the destruction of the temple into a special tax of two drachmae per

encouraged; and their denunciations probably included some more highly placed in society than the mass of Roman Jewry. This seems to be implied in the measures of his successor, Nerva, who discharged those who were under accusation of ἀσέβεια, recalled those who had been banished, and prohibited delations either for ἀσέβεια and adopting the Jewish way of living, or about the poll-tax.[1] The laws, however, were not changed.

A much more serious check must have been given to the accession of proselytes when Hadrian made circumcision itself a crime, a measure which is said to have provoked the revolt of the Jews in 132 A.D.[2] The law, which was not directed particularly against the Jews, apparently put circumcision in the same category with castration, a capital crime.[3] In the more general proscription of the Jewish religion after the war we read of fathers who were put to death for circumcising their sons.[4] Antoninus Pius made an exception from this general law in favor of the Jews only, who could therefore legally circumcise their own sons. For all others the law remained in full force.[5] The penalties underwent some changes in the history of legislation, but were always most severe. Notwithstanding the severity of the laws, proselytes continued to join themselves to the Jews, as the renewal of the laws itself proves; but probably in diminished numbers. The laws expressly forbid masters to circumcise their slaves.

The preaching of Christianity made converts among the

capita to be paid into the public treasury of Rome (Josephus, Bell. Jud. vii. 6, 6). On Domitian's enforcement of this law, see Suetonius, Domitian, c. 12; and on the whole subject, Juster, Les Juifs dans l'empire romain, II, 282 ff.

[1] Dio Cassius, lxviii. 1, 2. Medals with the inscription, Fisci judaici calumnia sublata. Juster, op. cit. I, 258; II, 385.

[2] Historia Augusta, Hadrian, 14, 2. Down to his time circumcision seems not to have been against the law.

[3] Juster, op. cit., I, 264 ff.; cf. II, 191.

[4] Mekilta, Yitro 6, end; Lev. R. 32, 1.

[5] Circumcidere Judaeis filios suos tantum rescripto divi Pii permittitur: in non eiusdem religionis qui hoc fecerit castrantis poena irrogatur. Digest xlviii. 8, 11 (Modestinus). See Juster, Les Juifs dans l'empire romain, I, 266 ff., where the later legislation is also cited.

proselytes to Judaism as well as among the looser adherents of
the synagogue. There were such, according to Acts 2, 10, among
the converts of the Day of Pentecost. One of the seven admin-
istrators of charity to the Hellenistic community in Jerusalem
('deacons') was Nicholas, an Antiochene proselyte (Acts 6, 5).
There were, on the other hand, proselytes to Judaism who came
over from the Gentile church. Epiphanius narrates how Aquila,
the translator of the Bible, embraced Christianity and was
baptized, but subsequently, in resentment of church discipline,
turned to the Jews.[1] In the absence of any other support for
the story, it receives, and probably deserves, little credit, though
there is nothing intrinsically improbable in such a change of
faith. In times of persecution Christians sometimes joined the
Jews, presumably to evade the test applied by the officials, adoration of the emperor, to which Jews were not subject.[2]

The edicts of Christian emperors against circumcision are not
confined exclusively to Jewish proselytism; they strike also
various Christian sects which practiced circumcision.[3] The
renewal of particular legislation about circumcision, was however, of less consequence, for the Christian emperors made conversion of Christians to Judaism a crime in itself, with increasingly severe penalties both for the Christian convert and the
Jew who converted him. The net of the law is spread wide; it
takes in adherence to Judaism and its teachings, frequenting the
synagogue, and calling oneself a Jew; thus including not only
male proselytes, who were also liable to the laws prohibiting
circumcision, but to women proselytes in the strict sense, and to
the looser adherents of Judaism. The penalty was at first arbitrary with the magistrates; then the law added confiscation
of property and the inability to make a will. For the proselyte-

---

[1] Epiphanius, De mensuris et ponderibus, cc. 14 f.

[2] To one such, probably a man of some standing, who sought thus to save
himself from prosecution under Septimius Severus, Serapion, bishop of
Antioch at the end of the second century, addressed a letter. Eusebius, Historia ecclesiastica vi. 12.

[3] On these sects see Juster, Les Juifs dans l'empire romain, I, 270 n.

maker the legislation went on to equate the crime to *laesa maiestas*, and finally made it simply capital, whether the convert was freeman or slave.[1] Against all such attempts of pagan or Christian rulers to shut up Judaism in itself and prevent its spread, the Jews persisted in their missionary efforts to make the religion God had revealed to their fathers the religion of all mankind.

[1] Quicumque servum seu ingenuum, invitum vel suasione plectenda, ex cultu Christianae religionis in nefandam sectam ritumve transduxerit, cum dispendio fortunarum capite puniendum. Nov. Theodos. iii. § 4. See further Juster *op. cit.* I, 260–262.

PART II

THE IDEA OF GOD

CHAPTER I

GOD AND THE WORLD

JUDAISM, in the centuries with which we are concerned, had no body of articulated and systematized doctrine such as we understand by the name theology. Philo, indeed, endeavored to harmonize his hereditary religion with a Hellenistic philosophy, but the resulting theology exerted no discoverable influence on the main current of Jewish thought. As in the case of the Bible itself, any exposition of Jewish teaching on these subjects, by the very necessity of orderly disposition, unavoidably gives an appearance of system and coherence which the teachings themselves do not exhibit, and which were not in the mind of the teachers. This fact the reader must bear constantly in mind. It must further be remarked that the utterances of the rabbis on this subject are not dogmatic, carrying an authority comparable to the juristic definitions and decisions of the Halakah; they are in great part homiletic, often drawing instruction or edification from the words of Scripture by ingenious turns of interpretation, association, and application, which seized upon the attention and fixed themselves in the memory of the hearers by the novelty, not of the lesson, but of the way the homilist got it into the text and out again. Large liberty in such invention has always been accorded to preachers, and every one knows that scholastic precision is not to be looked for in what is said for impression. Even in the more regulated Midrash of the schools there was much freedom, especially in combining scripture with scripture according to the hermeneutic rules.

But with this fertility in derivation, and notwithstanding a liberty that was only at two or three points restrained by anything resembling a definition of orthodoxy, there is on most topics a real consensus in substance which is only made the more emphatic by the great variety of form.[1] This essential unity of conception exists not only in the rabbinical literature but may be traced back through the writings of the preceding centuries, thus showing, as should be expected, a continuity in the tradition of the schools and its reflection in popular instruction. The ultimate source is the Bible itself, interpreted in the same sense and spirit.

From the historical point of view the Bible of the Jews is the collective name for twenty-four — or as we count them, thirty-nine — books, many of which are themselves collections of writings by different authors, or compilations from earlier sources; a national religious literature of widely varying character, covering many centuries, by many hands, and reflecting not merely different situations and circumstances in the life of the nation and the mind and temperament of individual authors, but successive stages in the development of the religion itself. To the religious apprehension, on the other hand, the whole is one divine revelation, completely consentient in all its parts, and in the minutest particulars.[2] However many human authors may have been concerned in recording it, the Scriptures have, in the language of Protestant theologians, but one *auctor primarius*, even God. Upon these premises, what the modern historian calls the 'development of religion' is properly only a divine paedagogic, an 'economy of revelation.' The Jews, whose minds were untroubled by any notions of development, had not even this concession to make: the twofold revelation to Moses was complete — nothing was held back in heaven. The Prophets and the Hagiographa reiterated, emphasized, and applied the Torah for their own and following generations; they added nothing.[3]

With a conception of revelation which made an axiom not merely of its unity but of its identity throughout, it might seem

[1] The substantial diversity is greatest, as would be expected, in the eschatological sphere — the destiny of the nation and the rest of the world, and the hereafter of individuals.

[2] See above, pp. 239 ff., 269 f.

[3] See above, p. 239.

logically to follow that Jewish doctrine on any subject — say, on the character of God — would be drawn comprehensively or indiscriminately from the manifold utterances and exhibitions in the Scriptures, from the naïve anthropomorphisms of Gen. 18 and Exod. 4, 24 ff., or such vindication and expiation as is narrated in 2 Sam. 21, to passages of incomparable elevation. In fact, however, Jewish conceptions are not drawn thus collectively from everything in the Bible, nor are they an attempted harmony of discrepant representations; they are the result of a selective process. The unconscious principle in this selection was affinity with their own highest conceptions, and it fastened first of all on the passages in Scripture which most fully expressed these conceptions, and from which the latter were in fact historically derived. The rabbis then deduced them exegetically from these texts, moving thus in a circle which is the real logic of doctrine in all similar matter. Christian theology has operated from age to age in just the same way with revelation in the Old Testament and the New.

It is not the whole truth to say that Jewish teaching at the beginning of our era appropriated the best that there is in the Bible, virtually ignoring or ingeniously adapting much that did not tally with it. In the generations that intervened Judaism had advanced farther in the direction it had taken, if not in new ideas at least in new proportion and emphasis, as, for example, in the development of teaching concerning the 'reign of God' (kingdom of Heaven), and the prominence of the conception of God as 'our Father who is in heaven.' [1]

Nowhere is the selection by affinity more conspicuous than in Jewish teaching about God, to which we now turn.

In accordance with the principle of revelation, the existence of God is not a subject for question or argument; he has revealed himself in Scripture, and Scripture teaches men to recognize the manifestations of his power, his wisdom, his goodness, in nature

[1] See pp. 229 f., 401, 432 ff. Vol. II, pp. 346 f.; 201 ff.

and history and providence. Dogmatic atheism and theoretical
skepticism are the outcome of philosophical thinking, to which
the Jews had no inclination. They knew the man who thought
there was no God and conducted himself accordingly; but what
such men really meant was that no higher power concerned itself about men's doings — there was no providence and no
retribution.[1] Even the radical disbelief of the man who "denies
the root" (namely, God), comes to this end by the practical,
not the theoretical road; it begins with not hearkening to the
word of the Lord as defined and expounded by scholars, and not
doing all His commandments (Lev. 26, 14).[2] Philo, living in a
centre where all the conflicting currents of Hellenistic philosophy met and strove together, had to debate this question from
philosophical premises and with philosophical arguments, and
to confute both skepticism and materialistic atheism.[3]

The first great question of religious philosophy, as Philo puts
it, is Whether the Deity exists?; the second, What is it in its
essential nature?[4] The former he thinks it easy to prove; the
latter question is not only difficult but perhaps unanswerable.
In the ontological sense in which Philo means it, Palestinian
Judaism, to which all metaphysic was alien, never speculated
on the nature of God at all.[5]

Monotheism also, the corner-stone of Judaism, remains, as
in the Bible, the religious doctrine that there is one God and no

[1] The denial of these was frequent. See Eccles. 7, 15; 8, 14; 9, 2, et
passim. So the ungodly (ἀσεβεῖς) in Wisdom of Solomon, 1, 16–2, 20. The
wicked man contemns God, saying to himself, 'Thou wilt not require'
(Psalm 10, 13): לית דין ולית דיין, that is, "there is no judgement and no
judge," Gen. R. 26, 6.

[2] כופר בעיקר, e.g. Sifra, Beḥuḳḳotai Pereḳ 3, end (ed. Weiss f. 111c), the
nearest Hebrew equivalent of 'atheist.' The downward progress of such a
one is there analysed. See further below, p. 467.

[3] De opificio mundi c. 61 § 170 (ed. Mangey I, 41). For a synopsis of
Philo's arguments see Drummond, Philo Judaeus, II, 1 ff.

[4] De monarchia c. 4 § 32 (ed. Mangey II, 216). The two questions:
ἐν μὲν εἰ ἔστι τὸ θεῖον . . . ἕτερον δὲ τὸ τί ἐστι κατὰ τὴν οὐσίαν.

[5] There is no reason to think that the theosophy which counted among its
adepts some of the leading schoolmen at the beginning of the second century
had any philosophy in its composition. See below, pp. 411 ff.

other, or, if it must be expressed abstractly, the doctrine of the *soleness* of God, in contradiction to polytheism, the multiplicity of gods.[1] There is no assertion or implication of the unity of God in the metaphysical sense such as Philo means when he says, "God is sole, and one (ἕν), not composite, a simple nature,[2] while everyone of us, and of all other created things, is many" (πολλά), etc. Wholly remote from Jewish thought is the idea of God as pure and simple *being* (τὸ ὄν), in his proper nature an unknowable and unnamable Absolute, as Philo conceives it when he develops his fundamental philosophy.[3] Jewish monotheism was reached through the belief that the will of God for righteousness is supreme in the history of the world; *one* will rules it all to *one* end — the world as it ought to be. In this way a national god became the universal God.[4] Its origin was thus, to put it in a word, moral, rather than physical or metaphysical; and it was therefore essentially *personal*.

Monotheisms of diverse characters and tendencies have arisen in other ways. The sovereign god in a monarchically organized pantheon may be exalted so far above all others that they become only the ministers of his sole supreme will. Not infrequently their godhead is saved by the discovery that they are names, forms, manifestations, of the god who is the whole pantheon in one (*pantheus*). A physical philosophy may call the whole of nature god, and more particularly the all-pervading energetic mind; while religious feeling, aided by the mere necessities of language, may give a measure of personality to this immanent reason of the universe in nature and in man. Or, again, the one

---

[1] See above, pp. 222 ff., and Note 108.

[2] Philo's philosophy concurs with his religion in the proposition that there is but *one* God. See e.g. De opificio mundi c. 61 § 171 (ed. Mangey I, 41). In De confusione linguarum c. 33 § 170 (ed. Mangey I, 431) he quotes to this effect, Homer, Iliad ii, 204 f., just as Aristotle does at the end of Metaphysics xi. On the unity and simplicity of the divine nature, see Legg. allegor. ii. 1 § 1 f. (ed. Mangey I, 66): ὁ θεὸς μόνος ἐστὶ καὶ ἕν, οὐ σύγκριμα, φύσις ἁπλῆ κ.τ.λ.

[3] See Drummond, Philo Judaeus, II, 16 ff.

[4] See above, Part I, chap. i.

reality of an idealistic monism, the Absolute, may be similarly
personified, and become a god to worship. In none of these is
the moral character of God predominant; and therefore in none
of them was personality essential to the very idea of God, as it is
in Judaism. Jewish monotheism had no tendency toward monism, whether ontological or cosmic, or to the religious counterpart of monism, pantheism.

The assertion of the soleness of God and argument against the
many gods have naturally a larger room in the apologetic of
Hellenistic Jews than in the Palestinian schools and synagogues.
The authors of the former lived in the midst of polytheism; they
wrote to exhibit the superiority of Judaism, whether it be considered philosophically, religiously, or morally, and in the endeavor to convert Gentile readers from their vain idols to serve
the living God. They were conscious of having, so far as the
unity of the godhead is concerned, the best Greek thought on
their side. They made florilegia of the monotheistic, or mono-
theistic-sounding, utterances of Greek poets, and to make the
volume of testimony more impressive fabricated many more.
The venerable Sibyl became a prophetess of the one God:

$$αὐτὸς\ γὰρ\ μόνος\ ἐστὶ\ θεὸς\ κοὐκ\ ἔστιν\ ἔτ'\ ἄλλος\ [1]$$

or, with more doctrine:

$$εἷς\ θεός\ ἐστι\ μόναρχος\ ἀθέσφατος\ αἰθέρι\ ναίων$$
$$αὐτοφυὴς\ ἀόρατος\ ὁρώμενος\ αὐτὸς\ ἄπαντα.\ [2]$$

Polytheism did not confront them, however, as a theoretical
pluralism of gods — in *theory*, most educated Greeks in that age
were not pluralists — but practically as the worship of a multiplicity of gods represented by images or, as among the Egyptians,
by living animals. Idolatry was the universal concomitant of
polytheism, and the Jews made no difference between them.
The satire on idolatry which begins in the prophets [3] is a common-

[1] Oracula Sibyllina, iii, 629.
[2] Ibid. iii, 11 f.; cf. Frag. 1, 7 ff. (ed. Geffcken, p. 227 f.).
[3] See above, p. 227.

place of Hellenistic polemic; by its side are denunciations of it
as the most heinous of sins, giving to the work of men's hands the
honor that belongs to the God that made heaven and earth.[1] So
monstrous is this aberration that the author of the Wisdom of
Solomon endeavors to explain it as a progressive declension from
natural and comparatively harmless beginnings till the depth of
degradation is reached in Egyptian theriolatry.[2]

In Judaea the hostility of the Jews to everything resembling
idols or idolatry forced regard upon contemptuous governors,
little wont to respect the prejudices of their subjects. They
would not even suffer Roman ensigns to be brought into the city
of Jerusalem because they had images on them, and when Pilate
introduced them nevertheless, constrained him to withdraw
them.[3] It was not necessary to go far from Jerusalem, however,
to find the obnoxious cults flourishing. Herod, who rebuilt the
Jewish temple with such magnificence, erected in Samaria —
renamed Sebaste — a great temple to the emperor Augustus.
Caesarea, Herod's new seaport, and later the usual residence of
the procurators, was predominantly a heathen city, as were the
cities of the Decapolis.

But however familiar the spectacle of heathenism may have
been, the teachers of Palestine, addressing themselves to men of
their own religion, did not feel it necessary to polemize against
polytheism and idolatry as the Hellenistic literature does.[4]

---

[1] Wisdom of Solomon, 13–15; Ep. of Aristeas § 134 ff.(ed. Wendland);
Orac. Sibyll. iii, 29–31; 586–590; v, 75 ff.; Frag. 3, 21–31, and in many other
places; Philo, De decalogo c. 2 § 6–9 (ed. Mangey II, 181); De monarchia
c. 2 § 21 (II, 214), and elsewhere.

[2] Wisdom of Solomon, 15, 18 f.; cf. 11, 15; 12, 24; Ep. of Aristeas § 138;
Philo, De decalogo c. 16 § 76–80 (II, 193 f.); Josephus, Contra Apionem, i.
28 init. etc.; Sibyllines, see the preceding note.

[3] Josephus, Antt. xviii. 3, 1. Cf. also the tearing down of the golden eagle
which Herod had set over the main entrance to the temple, ibid. xvii. 6, 2–4.

[4] As Schechter says, the laws against idolatry were not a practical issue.
(Some Aspects of Rabbinic Theology, p. 141.) Such passages as Enoch 99,
7–9; Jubilees 11, 4–7; 12, 2–8; 22, 18–22; Test. of the Twelve Patriarchs,
Naphtali, 3, 3 f., have a historical appropriateness in the mouth of the supposed speakers rather than an actual interest.

Under the head of 'heathenism' ('*abodah zarah*) in the Mishnah and elsewhere they are concerned to ordain precautions, first, against acts which might seem by inference to recognize the objects and places the Gentiles regard as divine or sacred, as well as against becoming in even the most remote way accessory to idolatrous worship; and, in the second place, to warn Jews against the vices which they regarded as the offspring of heathenism, and to avoid situations and associations which might invite suspicion that they were contaminated by such vices.[1]

If the leaders of Palestinian Jewry had little fear of actual lapse into polytheism and idolatry, they had greater concern about a defection from the strict monotheistic principle of a different kind, the currency of the belief that there are 'two authorities.'[2] The references to this error do not define it. A theory of 'two authorities' might be entertained by thinkers who held that God is the author of good only, and that for the evil in the world another cause must be assumed;[3] or by such as in their thinking so exalted God above the finite as to find it necessary to interpose between God and the world an inferior intermediate power as demiurge;[4] or — as frequently happened — both these motives might concur. It is evident also that Gentile Christianity, with its Supreme God, the Father, and its Son of God, creator and saviour, was founded on a doctrine of two powers. Judged by the standard of the numerically exclusive and uncompromisingly personal monotheism of Jewish ortho-

---

[1] See Note 109.

[2] Or "two powers" (שתי רשויות). See Note 110.

[3] Philo attributes this doctrine to the Essenes. It is with them one of the evidences of godliness (τοῦ φιλοθέου) τὸ πάντων μὲν ἀγαθῶν αἴτιον, κακοῦ δὲ μηδενὸς νομίζειν εἶναι τὸ θεῖον. Quod omnis probus liber c. 12 § 84 (ed. Mangey II, 458). The doctrine is Platonic, De republica ii. 379c: God is good, and therefore cannot be the cause of any kind of evils; cf. ibid. 380c. Philo himself often affirms it: e.g. De confusione lingg. c. 36 § 180 (ed. Mangey I, 432).

[4] Philo's own transcendent conception of the Deity requires such mediation, which he finds in the Logos, δι᾽ οὗ σύμπας ὁ κόσμος ἐδημιουργεῖτο (De sacerdotibus c. 5, § 81 ed. Mangey II, 225).

doxy, all these were dualistic heresies, and in the condemnation of them the orthodox probably made no superfluous discriminations. This is no reason, however, why we should be equally indiscriminate and introduce a new confusion into a perplexed matter by labelling the Jews who held such theories 'Jewish Gnostics.' [1]

The controversy with catholic Christians over the unity of the godhead, considerable as it is both in volume and interest, lies outside our purpose.[2] It is sufficient to remark that the arguments employed on both sides are in large part the same as are found earlier in discussions of the 'two powers' in which both parties were Jews; they quote the texts of the Bible which most strongly affirm the soleness of God; and refute the inferences from the plural *elohim* ('God,' not 'gods') by scriptures equally relevant against heathen polytheists, Jewish dualists, and Christian apologists.

How easily the pious desire to associate God with good only might glide into constructive heresy is illustrated by the interdiction of certain turns of phrase in prayer. Thus, to say "Good men shall bless Thee" is a 'heretical form of expression.' [3] If the leader in prayer says, "Thy mercy extends even to the sparrow's nest, and because of good (i.e. benefits bestowed) be Thy name remembered," he is to be silenced.[4] Even a bare liturgical repetition such as "(We) thank, thank," is, with some excess of scruple, suspected of acknowledging 'two powers.' [5]

One of the earliest mentions of two powers is in Sifrè on Deut.

---

[1] On Jewish "Gnosticism" see L. Blau, Jewish Encyclopedia, V, 681–686, with the literature cited there (p. 686).

[2] Most of the rabbis of whom such discussions are reported taught or resided in Caesarea in the third century, when Caesarea was an important episcopal see and a noted centre of Christian learning in Palestine. See Note III.

[3] M. Megillah 4, 9. The nature of the heresy is not defined. Jer. Megillah 75c finds it in an implication of "two powers"; see also Tosafot on Megillah 25a, top. A different explanation is given by Rashi.

[4] See the passages cited in the preceding note; also M. Berakot 5, 3; Berakot 33b. See Note 112.

[5] M. Megillah, M. Berakot ll. cc.

32, 29, which verse is shown to be an arsenal of weapons against divers heretics — those who say that there is *no* ruling power in heaven, and those who say that there are *two* — 'there is no God beside me'; or such as hold that whatever power there is cannot bring to life nor cause death, cannot inflict injury or confer benefits.[1] On what grounds the assertion of two powers rested is not indicated.   Nothing much more definite is to be got out of another relatively old passage in the Mekilta on Exod. 20, 2 ('I am the Lord thy God').   These words guard against the inference of a plurality of gods from different ways in which God is described in Scripture — at the Red Sea as a man of war (Exod. 15, 3), or when the elders of Israel saw him, as a venerable man, full of compassion (Exod. 24, 10; Dan. 7, 9).   Here the dualists are supposed to be Gentiles (אומות העולם).   R. Nathan, however, finds in the words (and in such parallels as Isa. 44, 6; 41, 4[b], etc.) an answer for the heretics (*minim*) who assert that there are two powers; but gives no intimation who the heretics were or why they made the assertion.[2]

That two powers gave the Law and two powers created the world was argued by some from the *elohim* in Exod. 20, 1 and Gen. 1, 1, taken as a numerical plural; to which the answer is given that in both cases the *verbs* of which *elohim* is the subject are in the singular number.[3]   The first chapter of Genesis offered other opportunities for heretical argument, especially, "Let *us* make man in *our* image, after *our* likeness" (Gen. 1, 26; cf. 3, 22).[4]

The difficulty of reconciling the evils in the world with the goodness of God was so strongly felt in the early centuries of our era in the East and the West, and a dualistic solution of one kind or another was so widely accepted in philosophy and religion,

[1] Sifrè Deut. § 329.
[2] Mekilta, Baḥodesh 5 (ed. Friedmann f. 66b; ed. Weiss f. 74a).
[3] Gen. R. 8, 9.
[4] See e.g. Gen. R. 8, 8.   The heretics here were probably Christians; cf. Justin Martyr, Trypho, 62, 1 ff.   See Sanhedrin 38a, where a number of such contentious plurals are adduced, including Dan. 7, 9 (cf. Justin, l.c. 31).

that it is idle to attempt to identify the Jewish circles which adopted this solution. It must suffice us to know that there were such circles; that they tried to fortify their position with texts of Scripture; and that the rabbis refuted them with their own weapons. It is certain also that, whatever leanings there may have been in this direction, Judaism, with its inveterate monotheism, was not rent by dualistic heresies as Christianity was for centuries.

As in the Bible, heaven — the celestial spaces above the sky — is the place of God's abode.[1] In later books and in the uncanonical literature the name "God of heaven" is frequently both in the mouth of foreigners [2] and of Jews.[3] In the next stage Heaven became a common metonymy for God, as in 1 Maccabees,[4] and in the language of the Palestinian schools and synagogues,[5] e.g. "the kingdom of Heaven." That the heavens were the seat of the highest god was the universal belief of the age, and various Syrian gods of heaven were seeking their fortunes in the Roman world under the name of the sky-god Jupiter — Jupiter Heliopolitanus of Baalbek, Jupiter Dolichenus of Commagene, and the rest; while conversely the Zeus whom Antiochus IV installed in the temple in Jerusalem was in Syrian speech a "Lord of heaven."[6]

---

[1] 1 Kings 8, 30–49, and parallel in 2 Chron. 6; Psalm 2, 4; 11, 4, etc. Cf. also Isa. 57, 15; Psalm 103, 19; 2 Macc. 3, 39.

[2] Ezra 1, 2 (Jehovah, God of heaven); 6, 9, 10; 7, 12, 21, 23.

[3] Ezra 5, 11, 12; Neh. 1, 4, 5; 2, 4; Dan. 2, 18, 19, 37, 44; Psalm 136, 26; 1 Macc. 3, 18; Judith 5, 8; 6, 19; Tobit 10, 11, 12. Enoch 13, 4; 106, 11; Jubilees 12, 4; 20, 7; 22, 19; Testaments, Reuben, 1, 6, etc. In the Sibyllines, θεὸς ἐπουράνιος, οὐράνιος.

[4] 1 Macc. 3, 50; 4, 10, 24, 40; 12, 15; 16, 3; cf. Dan. 4, 23. Not, however, it should be observed, in the nominative as subject.

[5] See Vol. II, 98.

[6] 2 Macc. 6, 2 bis, Ζεύς is rendered in the Syriac version בעלשמין. In Dan. 12, 11 שקוץ שמם (βδέλυγμα ἐρημώσεως) is probably a substitute for an original בעל שמים, the altar of Zeus which Antiochus set up on the great altar of burnt offering when he dedicated the temple to Zeus. See Nestle, Zeitschrift für die alttestamentliche Wissenschaft, IV (1884), 248; and on other such opprobrious substitutions, Encyclopaedia Biblica, II, cols. 2148–2150.

From such expressions as "the heaven and the heaven of heavens," [1] a plurality of heavens was inferred.[2] Under the influence of astronomical doctrine, a scheme of seven heavens was evolved, and Biblical names and proof-texts discovered for them. In the highest ('arabot, Psalm 68, 5) are righteousness and judgment;[3] the treasuries of life and peace and blessing; the souls of the righteous dead; the souls and spirits that are yet to be created; the dew with which God will revive the dead; there are the ofannim and seraphim, the holy beasts ('living creatures') and the ministering angels; while above them is the glorious throne of the King, the living, lofty, and exalted God.[4] From the earth to the firmament above us was said to be a journey of five hundred years, the thickness of the firmament was the same, and the same interval separated one heaven from another.[5]

But although God is thus supramundane, throned high above the world, he is not extramundane, aloof and inaccessible in his remote exaltation. The subject of the passage in the Talmud in which R. Levi's astronomical wisdom about celestial distances is introduced without dissent is the nearness of God, taking as its text Deut. 4, 7: 'What great nation is there that has a god as near to it as the Lord our God is whenever we call to him?' Near, with every kind of nearness, as is intimated by the plural of the predicate.[6] A false god (idol) seems to be near, but is really remote (Isa. 46, 7); a man has such a god with him in his house, but if the man cry to it for help until he dies, it will not hear him nor save him from his straits. The Holy One (the true God) seems to be far off, but there is nothing nearer than He. For

---

[1] Deut. 10, 14; 1 Kings 8, 27; Psalm 68, 34.

[2] From Deut. 10, 14, R. Judah (ben Ezekiel (?)) deduced that there were two firmaments (רקיעים), Ḥagigah 12b; others counted three, Midrash Tehillim on Psalm 114, 1, with Buber's note, f. 236a. Cf. Paul's rapture 2 Cor. 12, 2–4.

[3] The support of God's throne, Psalm 89, 15.

[4] Ḥagigah 12b, and elsewhere. See Note 112.

[5] Ḥagigah 13a; Jer. Berakot 13a, cf. ibid. 2c, below; Gen. R. 6, 6; Tanḥuma ed. Buber, Terumah § 8.

[6] אלהים קרובים, in which the cavillers found a plurality of gods; cf. Vulgate "deos appropinquantes sibi."

the seeming distance R. Levi is here cited, and a further calculation of the room occupied by the holy beasts,[1] all showing how
high the abode of God is above the world. "But let a man go into
the synagogue and take his place behind the pulpit and pray in
an undertone, and God will give ear to his prayer, as it is said:
'Hannah was speaking within herself, only her lips moved, but her
voice was not audible,'[2] and God gave ear to her prayer; and so
he does to all his creatures, as it is said, 'A prayer of the afflicted
when he covers his face and pours out his thought before the
Lord.'[3] It is as when a man utters his thought in the ear of his
fellow, and he hears him. Can you have a God nearer than this
who is as near to his creatures as mouth to ear?"[4]

God's earthly dwelling place was the tabernacle and afterwards the temple. His great love to Israel is manifest in that,
from his throne above the seven heavens, so far away, leaving
them all, he came to dwell near his people in the goat-skin tent
he bade them set up for him.[5] At the dedication of Solomon's
temple, the cloud that hid God's glory filled the sanctuary (1
Kings 8, 10 f.). Even after the destruction of the temple, it was
maintained by Eleazar ben Pedat that God's Presence (*shekinah*)
still abode on the ruined site in accordance with his promise,
'My eyes and my mind will be there perpetually' (1 Kings 9,
3).[6] In Solomon's dedication prayer, however, there is clear distinction made between God's abode in heaven and his manifes-

---

[1] Ezek. 1, 5 ff.
[2] 1 Sam. 1, 13.
[3] Psalm 102 (title).
[4] Jer. Berakot 13a. The passage is not older than the fourth century, but
the doctrine was good in any century. The lesson from the Prophets at the
principal service on the Day of Atonement begins with Isa. 57, 15: 'Thus
saith the lofty and exalted One, abiding for ever, Holy is his name; I dwell
in the high and holy place (heaven), and with the contrite and lowly in spirit.'
Megillah 31a.
[5] Tanḥuma ed. Buber, Terumah § 8; cf. ibid. Bemidbar § 14; Naso § 19.
[6] Ibid. Shemot § 10. Contrary to the opinion that at the destruction of
the temple the Shekinah ascended to heaven (Samuel ben Naḥman, ibid.),
Eleazar ben Pedat quotes also Psalm 3, 5; Ezra 1, 3.

tation in the temple: 'The heaven and the heaven of heavens cannot contain thee, much less this house which I have built' (1 Kings 8, 27). Solomon prays that when men present their offerings or their petitions in the temple, or turn toward it in prayer even though in exile, God in heaven, his dwelling place, will hear their prayer, and grant their supplication. If God has a tabernacle or temple on earth, it is not that he needs a place to dwell in, for his holy house on high was there before the world was created,[1] but, we might put it, because men need some visible thing by which to realize his loving presence.

In reality God is everywhere present. The whole vast universe is his house, as the author of the Book of Baruch, in an eloquent passage, sets forth.[2] Because he is in one place he is no less elsewhere. In R. Levi's comparison: "The tabernacle was like a cave that adjoined the sea. The sea came rushing in and flooded the cave; the cave was filled, but the sea was not in the least diminished. So the tabernacle was filled with the radiance of the divine presence, but the world lost nothing of that presence." [3] Another comparison for this all-pervading presence of God in the world is the soul of man. As the soul fills the body, so God fills his world, as it is written, 'Do not I fill heaven and earth? saith the Lord.' The likeness of the soul to God is carried out in particulars: The soul sustains the body — God sustains the world (Isa. 46, 4); the soul outlasts the decrepit body — God outlasts the world (Psalm 102, 26); the soul is one only in the body — God is one only in the world (Deut. 6, 4); like God, the soul sees but is not seen; it is pure; it never sleeps, etc.[4]

This comparison must not be taken to imply that God was conceived as a kind of *anima mundi*, or as the all-permeating

---

[1] Tanḥuma ed. Buber, Naso § 19.

[2] Baruch 3, 24 ff.

[3] Cant. R. on Cant. 3, 10, and with slight verbal variations Pesiḳta ed. Buber f. 2b; Num. R. 12, 4. Cf. Augustine's figure of the boundless sea and the sponge (Confessions vii. 5, 1). God, who fills heaven and earth (Jer. 23, 24), spoke with Moses between the staves of the ark. R. Meir, Gen. R. 4, 4.

[4] Lev. R. 4, 8; Berakot 10a.

directing mind in the universe like the Stoic Logos.[1] Its meaning is that God is everywhere present. He appeared to Moses in a despised thorn-bush, not in a carob tree or a fig (trees that men value), it is explained, to teach that there is no place on earth void of the divine presence (*shekinah*).[2] The ubiquity of God is affirmed in many other places, with diverse proofs. Thus from Job. 38, 35, 'Canst thou despatch lightnings, and they go, and say unto thee, Here we are?' it is deduced: "God's messengers are not like men's. Men's messengers have to return to him that sent them; but with Thee it is not so. Thou sendest lightnings and they go. It does not say 'and they return,' but 'they go, and they say' etc. Wherever they go, they are constantly in Thy presence, and say, We have accomplished Thy commission, confirming what is written, 'Do not I fill heaven and earth?'" (Jer. 23, 24).[3] On Exod. 17, 6, 'Behold I stand before thee there,' the Mekilta has: "In every place where thou findest the prints of a man's foot, there am I before thee." [4]

The interest of the Jews in affirming that God is in every place was not philosophical nor primarily theological, but immediately religious. The great text was Jer. 23, 23 f.: 'Am I a god at hand, saith the Lord, and not a god afar off? Can any hide himself in secret places that I shall not see him? Do not I fill earth and heaven, saith the Lord?' No sin, however done in secrecy and in darkness, can escape the eye of him who fills heaven and earth.[5] On the other hand, that wherever we are, and in whatever estate, God is present with us, gives a realizing sense of his providence.[6]

Hellenistic Jewish literature exhibits similar conceptions. "The spirit of the Lord fills the world, and the spirit that em-

---

[1] Heinze, Die Lehre vom Logos in der griechischen Philosophie, 1872.

[2] Exod. R. on Exod. 3, 3 (c. 2, 5).

[3] Mekilta, Bo 1 (ed. Friedmann f. 2a; ed. Weiss f. 2a, below); Baba Batra 25a. See Note 113.

[4] Mekilta, Beshallaḥ 6 (ed. Friedmann f. 52b; ed. Weiss f. 60b); cf. Mekilta de R. Simeon ben Yoḥai ed. Hoffmann, p. 81.

[5] Tanḥuma ed. Buber, Naso § 6 (f. 14b–15a).

[6] See further below, pp. 373 f.

braces the universe takes knowledge of every word; wherefore no one who gives utterance to unjust speech can escape notice, nor will reproving justice pass him by." [1] So also the Letter of Aristeas: "Our lawgiver (Moses) . . . showed first of all that there is only one God, and his power is manifest throughout all things, every place being full of his dominion; and that nothing of all that men do secretly on earth escapes him, but whatever any one does stands open to his sight, and even what is not yet done. . . .   Even if a man purposes in his mind to do an evil, he does not escape God's knowledge, to say nothing of the evil he has already done." [2]

Philo's religious doctrine is the same.[3] God does not go anywhither, since he fills all things.[4] On Gen. 3, 8, he comments: It is impossible to hide from God, "for God fills all things and pervades all things, and has left nothing, no matter how solitary, void of himself. What kind of place can a man occupy in which God is not? As the Scripture testifies elsewhere: 'God is in the heaven above and on the earth beneath, and there is no other but He.' (Deut. 4, 39). And again: 'Here I stand, before thou dost' (Exod. 17, 6).[5] For God exists prior to every creature and is found everywhere; wherefore no one can hide from him." [6] Similarly, on Cain's words, 'If thou dost drive me out today from the face of the earth, and from thy face I shall be hidden' (Gen. 4, 14): "What do you say, my dear sir? If you were cast out from the whole earth, would you then be hidden? How? . . .   Would it be possible for a man, or any creature, to be hidden from God, who is before him everywhere, whose

---

[1] Wisdom of Solomon 1, 7 f.; see also what follows.

[2] Aristeas, ed. Wendland § 132 f. With the inclination of these writers to avoid the semblance of anthropomorphism by speaking of the ubiquity of the spirit or the power of God, cf. pp. 434 ff.

[3] With his metaphysical doctrine we are not here concerned.

[4] Quod deus sit immutabilis c. 12 § 57 (ed. Mangey I, 281); see also De confusione linguarum c. 27 (I, 425).

[5] ὧδε στὰς ἐγὼ πρὸ τοῦ σέ. Compare the turn given to these words in the Midrash, above p. 371.

[6] Legg. allegor. iii. 2 § 4 (ed. Mangey I, 88).

sight reaches to the ends of the earth, who fills the whole, of whom not the smallest of existing things is devoid?"[1]

The interest in the universal presence of God is in the universality and immediacy of his knowledge and of his providential activity. That God knows everything that is, and all that goes on in the world, is so often reiterated in the Bible and is illustrated and emphasized in so many ways, it is of such fundamental importance in a religion which sees the history of the nations and the life of individuals ordered by the moral will of a personal God, that the all-embracing and immediate knowledge of God is necessarily one of the pillars of Jewish faith. God knows all the secrets of nature as only the author of nature can know them, from the movements of the stars in the heavens to the habits of the shyest creatures of the desert (Job. 38 f.). To the ends of the earth he sees everything under the whole heaven (Job 28, 24); the abyss beneath, the abode of the shades, lies uncovered before him (Job. 26, 6). He knows the past from the beginning of the world, and the future to its end, for he has ordained, and he brings to pass; what he reveals of his plan by his prophets infallibly comes true.[2]

For personal religion it is of even greater moment that he knows *men* with an all-embracing, an inescapable, knowledge — their fortunes and their character, their most secret deeds, their unarticulated words, their thoughts before they have taken shape in their own minds; no concealment and no deception avails aught with him.[3] The theme is a favorite one with the moralists. Sirach frequently reverts to it: "He explores the great abyss and the mind of man, and sees through all their subtleties; he reveals bygone things and things yet to be, and

---

[1] Quod deterius potiori insidiatur c. 41 § 150 f. (ed. Mangey I, 220). On God as τόπος, encompassing all and encompassed by nothing (De somniis, i. 11) see Note 113a.

[2] See e.g. Isa. 41, 22–24; 43, 10–13; 44, 6–8, etc.

[3] See e.g. Amos 9, 2–4; Jer. 23, 23 f.; Prov. 5, 21; 15, 3; Job 34, 21; Psalm 139, etc.

uncovers the trace of secrets. He lacks no kind of intelligence, and nothing escapes him." [1]

That God knows the thoughts of all the multitude and variety of mankind is especially dwelt on in the Palestinian literature. "If a man sees crowds of men, he should repeat the eulogy: 'Blessed is He who is wise in mysterious things,' for as the features of no two are alike so the thoughts of no two are alike." [2] From 1 Chron. 28, 9, 'For the Lord searches all hearts (minds), and understands all the formation of thoughts,' R. Isaac teaches: "Before a thought is formed in a man's mind, it is already manifest to Thee," or, according to another reporter, "Before an embryo is formed, its thoughts are already manifest to Thee." [3]

The almighty power of God, also, is written large in the Bible. The creator of the heavens and the earth and all that in them is does in his world whatever he wills. Among the Jews in the age with which we are dealing, as among Christians in all ages, 'the Almighty' was frequently used by metonymy for 'God' (*ha-geburah*, literally, 'the Might'). [4] In the Greek Bible παντοκράτωρ, 'all-powerful ruler,' is common as a translation of *ṣebaot* especially in the phrase Ihvh *ṣebaot*, κύριος παντοκράτωρ; also for *shaddai*. It is frequent also in later writings, both in translations from Hebrew and in works of Hellenistic origin. [5] To the power of God, creation, the order of the universe, and the course of history bear witness.

[1] Ecclus. 42, 18–20; cf. 16, 17–23; 17, 15–20; Wisdom of Solomon 1, 6 ff.; Baruch 3, 32; Psalms of Solomon 14, 8, etc.

[2] Jer. Berakot 13c; Tos. Berakot 7, 2; cf. Tanḥuma ed. Buber, Phineas § 1.

[3] Gen. R. 9, 3. The idea is developed at length in Agadat Bereshit 2 (ed. Buber, p. 4). See Note 114.

[4] E.g. Sifrè Deut. § 9 (on Deut. 1, 9). Moses said to them: Not of myself do I say to you these things; I speak from the mouth of the Almighty (מפי הגבורה). See Note 115.

[5] Ecclus. 42, 17; 50, 14; Judith 4, 13; 8, 13; Wisdom of Solomon 7, 25; 2 Macc. 1, 25; 5, 20; 6, 26; 3 Macc. 2, 2, 8; 5, 7. In the New Testament Rev. 4, 8; 11, 17; 15, 3, etc.

The almighty power of God was not in Judaism a theological attribute of omnipotence which belongs in idea to the perfection of God; it was, as in the prophets, the assurance that nothing can withstand his judgment or thwart his purpose.[1] The omnipotence of God is thus interlocked with the teleology of history. The creator and ruler of the world comprehends all things in one great plan, glimpses of which he has given to his prophets. This plan includes a golden age for his people, the visions of which merge into a golden age for all mankind, when in the universality of the true religion, and of conformity to his righteous and gracious will, peace and prosperity shall also be universal, while nature itself shall be transformed to make the earth a fit dwelling place for such transfigured inhabitants.

The obstacles to the realization of this plan were to human view insuperable; but to God insuperable obstacles were nothing. When His time came, the proud empire that bestrode the world like the colossus in Nebuchadnezzar's dream should collapse at a stroke and utterly vanish away.[2] In that *dies irae* the superhuman powers of evil share the doom of the human: 'The Lord will punish the host of high heaven on high and the kings of the earth upon the earth.'[3]

Faith in the fulfilment of God's promised purpose dwelt upon the mighty deeds of God in olden times, in Egypt and at the Red Sea, in the conquest of Canaan. The so-called historical Psalms which recite — sometimes in prosaic enumeration — such *magnalia dei* frequently have this for one of their motives.[4] Omnipotence, which, like finite force, has in itself no religious character, acquires profound religious significance through its relation to God's end in the world; it is a cornerstone of faith.

God's power has no limit but his own will; he can do anything that he wills to do. In general, the power of God in nature is conceived as exercised directly; forces of nature acting as 'second causes,' and laws of nature according to which these forces

[1] See especially Isa. 40 ff.
[2] Dan. 2, 31 ff.
[3] Isa. 24, 21–23.
[4] E.g. Psalm 106.

operate, have no place in the native religious thought of the Jews.[1] The regularity of nature, so far as it is an observed fact, if it be reflected on at all, is merely the ordinary way of God's working. Of the uniformity of nature, the postulate of modern science — "a question begged at the outset" — no anticipation entered their minds. God was as free to act in an extraordinary way, if he saw occasion for it, as in his ordinary way; with this view of nature the one was as natural as the other. The contrast we make between natural and supernatural events did not exist; all events were equally the immediate work of God.

To understand the Jewish conception of miracle, we must enter into their way of thinking about God and nature. A miracle, from this point of view, is an extraordinary phenomenon or occurrence wrought by God, presumably for some special purpose. It cannot be described as something at variance with the laws of nature, transcending or suspending them, for, as has been said, there was no idea of laws of nature in the modern sense. Nor is it the mere wonder of it that makes such an event a miracle; it is the religious interpretation of the occurrence, the belief that in this phenomenon or event God in a peculiar way manifests his presence, reveals his will, or intervenes for the deliverance of his worshippers and the discomfiture of their enemies, to provide for their needs in distressful times, to avert calamities, to heal mortal diseases, and to save from a thousand evils where human help is vain. The greatness, the power, of God is abundantly manifest in the ordinary course of nature; it is his goodness that is peculiarly revealed in the miracle as faith interprets and appropriates it.

It could not be conceived, therefore, that the age of miracle was past. Signal interventions in history such as stood out on the pages of the ancient Scriptures there were not; but greater

---

[1] God has imposed on the elements bounds and measures; for the movements of the stars, and in the instincts of animals, he has established norms which they may not transgress and bring disorder into the cosmos. These ordinances are laws which God has imposed upon his creatures, as he has imposed laws upon men.

even than the deliverance from Egypt would be the wonders God would work in the greater deliverance that was to come. Meanwhile miracles on the individual scale continued; and if the question sometimes arose why they had become less frequent than formerly, it was a sufficient answer that their contemporaries were less worthy that God should work a miracle for them or by their hands.[1] The coming of rain in a season of drought in answer to the prayers of individuals is a kind of miracle about which there are many stories, and some such rain-making saints are the subject of what may aptly be called a professional legend.[2] Others wrought a greater variety of miracles. Among these Ḥanina ben Dosa, a disciple of Johanan ben Zakkai at the end of the first century of our era, is particularly remembered. By his prayers a son of his master Johanan ben Zakkai was healed of a grave illness.[3] Again when a son of Gamaliel II was very ill, the father sent two of his disciples to Ḥanina ben Dosa that he might beseech God's mercy upon the son. Ḥanina at once went up to the chamber on the roof and prayed for him; when he came down he said to the messengers, Go, for the fever has left him. They asked, Are you a prophet? He replied, I am neither a prophet nor the son of a prophet, but I have learned that if I have freedom in prayer, I know that it is accepted; if not, I know that it is rejected.[4] They noted down in writing the hour at which he said this, and when they arrived at Gamaliel's house and reported the matter, he said: By the divine service![5] At that exact hour, no more and no less, the fever left him and he asked for a drink of water.[6] Ḥanina's prayers once caused a shower of rain to hold

[1] Berakot 20a. See Note 116.

[2] The Talmuds on Taʿanit iii. have various legends of this kind. The most famous name is Ḥoni ha-Meʿaggel in the first century B.C. See Jewish Encyclopedia, IX, 404 f., and Note 117.

[3] Berakot 34b.

[4] Berakot l. c.; Jer. Berakot 9d; cf. M. Berakot 5, 5. This sign is attributed in Tos. Berakot 3, 4 to Akiba.

[5] העבודה. A common oath, especially after the destruction of the temple; e.g. Yebamot 32b.

[6] Berakot 34b. Compare the similar story of Jesus at Cana and the courtier's son at Capernaum, John 4, 46–53.

up for his own convenience, and then to fall again. His prayer
on that occasion seemed to countervail that of the high priest.[1]
So great was his reputation that it is said, in an apocryphal
Mishnah, "When Ḥanina ben Dosa died there were no workers
of miracles left." [2] Besides such saints in answer to whose prayers God wrought wonders, there were healers and exorcists who
effected their cures by the use of charms and the power of names,
as the disciples of Jesus are said to have done by his name.[3]

That what we should call the ordinary operations of God's
providence are no less wonderful than miracles is observed by
more than one teacher. Mention of rain is made in connection
with the resurrection of the dead in the second of the Eighteen
Prayers (M. Berakot 5, 2), because in the Scripture the miracle
of rain is made equal to the miracle of resurrection. Both are
wrought by the hand of God; of both it is said 'God opens'
(Deut. 28, 12; Ezek. 37, 12). . . . Nay, greater than the
resurrection of the dead, for resurrection is only for men, rain
for animals too; resurrection only for Israelites, rain for the other
nations as well; or resurrection is for the righteous alone, while
rain comes upon the righteous and the wicked.[4]

R. Eleazar (ben Pedat) said, The Scripture puts provision for
man's needs in the same category with deliverance; as this provision is of every day, so deliverance is of every day. R. Samuel
ben Naḥman said, It is greater than deliverance, for deliverance
comes by the hand of an angel — 'the angel who delivers me
from every evil ' (Gen. 48, 16) — but provision for man's need's
by the hand of God himself, who 'opens his hand and satisfies
the desire of every living being' (Psalm 145, 16). R. Joshua ben

[1] Ta'anit 24b.

[2] M. Soṭah 9, 15 (a late appendix). On the meaning of the phrase 'men
of deed' see Büchler, Types of Jewish-Palestinian Piety, pp. 79 ff. See also
Vol. II, p. 206 n. For other stories of his miracles, see Jewish Encyclopedia,
VI, 214–216.

[3] Particularly one Jacob of Kefar Sekanya (or Samma) in Galilee. 'Abodah
Zarah 27b; Tos. Ḥullin 2, 22 f. Cf. Acts 3, 6; 4, 10, etc.

[4] Gen. R. 13, 6; Berakot 33a; Jer. Berakot 9a, below; Ta'anit 7a, top;
cf. Matt. 5, 45.

Levi declared that this constant provision was no less a wonder than the cleaving of the Red Sea (Psalm 136, 13 and 25).[1] God is continually working miracles without men's knowing it, in protecting them from unknown evils (Job 37, 5).[2] But a man should not needlessly expose himself to peril in the expectation that God will miraculously deliver him; God may not do so; and even if a miracle is wrought for him, the man earns demerit by his presumption.[3]

God has the power to do in his world whatever he wills,[4] and he has the right of the creator to deal as he wills with his creatures.[5] But nothing is more firmly established in the Jewish thought of God than that he does not use this power wilfully like some almighty tyrant, but with wisdom and justice and for a supremely good end. A certain Pappos, paraphrased Job 23, 13 ('He is one,[6] and who shall gainsay him; he wishes a thing and does it'): God is sole judge over all the inhabitants of the world, who can contradict his sentence? Against this implication of an arbitrary and irresponsible God Akiba protested energetically. There is indeed no gainsaying him who created the world by a word, but his judgment is always according to truth and justice.[7] The words of God in Isa. 27, 4 ('I would stride upon it') are interpreted as a reflection: If by one step I overstepped and transgressed justice, 'I should set it all on fire' — at once the world would be consumed.[8]

That God is almighty makes it possible for him to be lenient.

[1] Gen. R. 20, 9; cf. Pesaḥim 118a; Pesiḳta R. ed. Friedmann f. 152a. (This bit of bread that a man puts into his mouth is a more difficult thing than the deliverance of Israel). See Bacher, Pal. Amoräer, I, 178, 487; II, 21.

[2] Midrash Shemuel 9, 2; Midrash Tehillim on Psalm 106, init. Bacher l. c. II, 85.

[3] Shabbat 32a; Taʿanit 20b. See Note 118.

[4] Jer. 32, 17 ff.

[5] Jer. 18, 2–6; Isa. 45, 9; cf. Paul, Rom. 9, 14 ff.

[6] So the text was understood.

[7] Mekilta, Beshallaḥ 6 (ed. Friedmann f. 33a: ed. Weiss f. 40a, top). Somewhat expanded, Tanḥuma ed. Buber, Shemot § 14; ibid. Wayyera § 21; cf. Akiba, Abot, 3, 15.

[8] Tanḥuma ed. Buber, Mishpaṭim § 4. (Cf. Heraclitus, Frag. 29, Bywater.)

"Thou hast compassion upon all men because thou canst do all things, and dost overlook the sins of men unto repentance." "Thy might is the basis of justice, and that thou art sovereign over all makes thee spare all." [1] The author implies that only conscious weakness in a government makes unsparing and indiscriminate severity necessary even in the administration of justice, lest evil doing or rebellion get beyond control. A similar thought is expressed by R. Joshua ben Levi: Moses called God 'the great and mighty and terrible.' [2] But when foreigners danced in his temple he seemed no longer terrible; when foreigners reduced his people to servitude he seemed no longer almighty. Then came the men of the Great Assembly and restored the crown (of the divine attributes) to its ancient completeness, by teaching that the very culmination of his almightiness is that he represses his wrath and is longsuffering with the wicked. [3]

God is the creator of the heavens and the earth and all things in them. So it was written in the first columns of the Pentateuch by revelation of the Creator himself. The theme inspired some of the finest passages in Hebrew poetry: [4] through the prophets it became a fundamental doctrine of religion. [5] The growing self-consciousness of Jewish monotheism and the proclamation and defence of it in the Gentile world gave the doctrine an enhanced importance; it figures largely in the uncanonical literature, both Palestinian and Hellenistic. [6]

In the Palestinian schools the study of the narrative of creation in Gen. 1–3 by the hermeneutic methods of the Midrash gave opportunity for much ingenuity and a great variety of

---

[1] Wisdom of Solomon 11, 23; 12, 16–18. See the whole fine passage.

[2] Deut. 10, 17.

[3] Yoma 69b. Cf. Jer. Berakot 11c; Jer. Megillah 74c. Bacher, Pal Amoräer, I, 182 f. See Note 119.

[4] E.g. Job 26, 7–14; 38 f.; Psalm 19, 1–7; 104; Prov. 8, 22–31.

[5] See especially Isaiah 40 ff.

[6] Baruch 3, 32 ff.; Ecclus. 16, 26–17, 9; cf. 42, 15–43, 33; Enoch 69, 16–24; Jubilees 2, 1–33; 4 Esdras 6, 38–54; Orac. Sibyllina, iii, 20–28; Fragment 3, 3–14, etc.

fragmentary interpretations in a field in which there was no authoritative orthodoxy.[1] It was asked, for example, on what day the angels were created, of whom there is no express mention in the text. One put them on the second day, basing his opinion on the sequence in Psalm 104, 3 f.;[2] another connected them, as flying creatures (Isa. 6, 2), with the creation of other flying things on the fifth day (Gen. 1, 20). Either way, another adds, all agree that they were certainly not created on the first day, in order that no one might say that Michael and Gabriel helped God stretch out the canopy of heaven, which was the work of God alone (Isa. 44, 24); he had no partner in the creation of the world.[3] The jealousy with which the heresy that two powers created the world is rejected[4] extends even to the suspicion that he employed the assistance of created beings such as angels. Even man was created only last of all God's works, at the end of the sixth day, for the same reason.[5]

The question whether the world the creation of which is described in Genesis was brought into existence *de nihilo*, or whether the cosmos was formed from a chaos of previously existing formless matter, and in the latter case, whether this matter was created or eternal, did not excite discussion in the Palestinian schools, and there are few utterances that bear on it in any way. A 'philosopher' (i.e. a skeptic) said to Rabban Gamaliel: Your God was a great artist, but he found excellent colors at his disposal. What were they? asked the rabbi. Chaos (*tohu wa-bohu*) and darkness and water and wind and abysses. Gamaliel, with an imprecation, proceeded to quote texts to show

[1] The discussion of some of these questions, e.g. whether the heavens or the earth was created first, engaged the schools of Shammai and Hillel in the first century of our era. Ḥagigah 12a; Gen. R. 1, 15, and elsewhere. The harmonistic view is that they were both created at once, Gen. R. 12, 12.

[2] God "erects the framework of his upper chambers (the firmament) upon the waters (Gen. 1, 6 f.) . . . he makes his angels spirits."

[3] Gen. R. 1, 3; cf. Tanḥuma ed. Buber, Bereshit § 12. Jubilees 2, 2, on the contrary, puts the creation of all kinds of angels on the first day.

[4] Above, pp. 364 ff.

[5] Tos. Sanhedrin 8, 7; Sanhedrin 38a.

that each of these is expressly said to have been created.[1] From
Eccles. 3, 11 ('He made the whole (the universe) beautiful in its
time') and Gen. 1, 31 ('God saw everything that he had made
and behold it was very good'), a teacher of the end of the third
century discovers that God had created and destroyed many
worlds before he made this one, but did not get one till this to
satisfy him.[2] Abahu, to whom this is attributed, had a reputation for his knowledge of Greek, and it can hardly be doubted
that his worlds before this one are a surreptitious piece of Greek
wisdom.[3] Such inspiration is by no means infrequent in the
Midrash, especially in the cosmological parts, and the example
may serve not only as a specimen of the kind but as a warning
against the indiscriminate use that is often made of these relatively late and heterogeneous sources.

Whatever individuals may thus have picked up, Judaism
firmly maintained the biblical doctrine that God, and God alone,
made the world. That he made it in accordance with a preconceived plan has already been noted. Unlike man, he made no
changes in this plan when he came to carry it out.[4] He created
the world by a word, instantaneously, without toil and pains.[5]
Everything that he fashioned was perfect, as all his dealing with
men is just and right (Deut. 32, 4). It is not for men to imagine
improvements in his creation or question his providential rule in
the world.[6] And, finally, everything that God made belongs to
the completeness of the created world, however superfluous flies
and fleas and mosquitos may seem to men.[7]

[1] Gen. R. 1, 9. Bacher, Tannaiten, I, 81 f. See Note 120.
[2] Gen. R. 3, 7; 9, 2. Bacher, Pal. Amoräer, II, 138.
[3] Freudenthal, Hellenistische Studien, pp. 71 f.
[4] Gen. R. 1, 13.
[5] Gen. R. 3, 2; 10, 9; cf. Tanḥuma ed. Buber, Bereshit § 11. Cf. Josephus, Contra Apionem ii. 22 § 192. On creation by a word (fiat) see below,
p. 415.
[6] This theme is developed at some length in Sifrè Deut. § 307; cf. Gen. R.
12, 1.
[7] Eccles. R. on 5, 8. God made nothing in vain; he employs frogs and
mosquitos and hornets and scorpions on his errands. Tanḥuma ed. Buber,
Ḥuḳḳat § 1; Shabbat 77 b.

To the question why the world was created different answers are given: it was made for man (not man for the world);[1] or for the sake of the righteous, such as Abraham and the patriarchs;[2] or for the sake of Israel;[3] or for the sake of the Torah (religion).[4]

Besides the public teaching of the school and synagogue, the first chapter of Genesis became the subject, or at least the starting point, of cosmogonic or cosmological speculations which were carefully guarded from publicity. The name for this esoteric doctrine was Ma'aseh Bereshit, 'The Work of Creation,' and in the Mishnah it is forbidden to expound it except privately to a single auditor.[5] The restriction, which is made on the authority of Deut. 4, 32, does not apply to the exposition of what took place on the six days of creation,[6] nor to what is within the expanse of heaven. But what was before the first creative day, or what is above, beneath, before, behind, it is forbidden to teach in public. There is no reserve about the seven heavens and what is in each;[7] but of what is above the firmament that is over the heads of the beasts (ḥayyot, Ezek. 1, 22), one must not speak.[8] Against such speculations Sirach had given a warning which is quoted in the Talmud in this connection thus: "Do not inquire into what is beyond thine understanding, and do not investigate what is hidden from thee. Reflect on things that are permitted to thee; thou hast nothing to do with the study of mysteries."[9]

[1] Syriac Baruch 14, 18; 4 Esdras 8, 44.   [2] Ibid. 15, 7; 21, 24.
[3] Sifrè Deut. § 47 (on Deut. 11, 21); Tanḥuma ed. Buber, Bereshit § 3; § 10; 4 Esdras 6, 55, 59; 7, 11; Assumption of Moses 1, 12. Similarly, Hermas Vis. I. 1, 6: "God created that which is, out of that which is not . . . for the sake of his holy church"; cf Vis. ii. 4, 1.
[4] Gen. R. 12, 2. See above, pp. 268 f. On the subject of creation see further Note 121.
[5] M. Ḥagigah 2, 1; Tos. Ḥagigah 2, 1.
[6] But there is presumption in professing to know the order of creation in detail. Gen. R. 12, 1.
[7] Ḥagigah 12b–13a; Jer. Ḥagigah 77c; Gen. R. 1, 10; 8, 2. See above, p. 368.
[8] Ḥagigah 13a.
[9] Ecclus. 3, 21 f. (Hebrew). Quoted Ḥagigah 13a; Jer. Ḥagigah 77c; Gen. R. 8, 12.

The following verses of Sirach are in the same vein: "With what is too much for thee do not concern thyself; for thou hast been shown more than thou art capable of. For men have many strange notions, and false conceits lead into error."

Of the content of this esoteric cosmology we are left to make our conjectures, partly from the prohibitions themselves, partly from such apparent leakages as have been remarked elsewhere.[1] Considerable parts of some of the apocalypses, especially of the Book of Enoch,[2] purport to be exhibitions of the mysteries of the universe beyond the bounds of human ken, extending even to heaven and hell; but it would be rash to assume a relation, or even any special resemblance, between such revelations and the speculations which the rabbis communicated to initiates as a secret tradition. In leaving this subject it may be observed that the esoteric cosmology of the Maʻaseh Bereshit, like its counterpart, the theosophic Maʻaseh Merkabah,[3] was in high estimation among the most correct of the schoolmen. Its vulgarization was prohibited, not for any suspicion of the doctrine itself, but that it might not be exposed to vulgar misunderstanding, and misunderstanding lead to skepticism or heresy.

God is not only the sole creator of the world, he alone upholds it, and maintains in existence by his immediate will and power everything that is.[4] This universal teaching of the Bible is equally the doctrine of Judaism: "God created and he provides; he made and he sustains." [5] The maintenance of the world is a kind of continuous creation: God in his goodness makes new every day continually the work of creation.[6] The history of the world is his great plan, in which everything moves to the fulfilment of his purpose, the end that is in his mind. Not only the great whole, but every moment, every event, every individual,

---

1 Cf. pp. 412 f.
2 Particularly Enoch 17–36; 39–44; 72–82.
3 See below, pp. 411 ff.
4 E.g. Psalm 104, 10–30.
5 Tanḥuma ed. Buber, Wayyera § 24.
6 So the old prayer, Yoṣer Or.

every creature is embraced in this plan, and is an object of his particular providence.[1] All man's ways are directed by God (Psalm 37, 23; Prov. 20, 24). A man does not even hurt his finger without its having been proclaimed above that he should do so.[2] It is unnecessary to dwell further on this point here. The difficulties into which the belief in such providential ordering of men's lives and fortunes gets when it is confronted with the doctrine of retribution on the one hand, and on the other by the problem of human freedom and divine determination, remain for discussion in another connection;[3] while the religious response of faith in this all-comprehensive providence will engage our attention when we come to treat of Jewish piety.

[1] See Note 122.
[2] Ḥullin 7b, below; Matt. 10, 29 f.
[3] See below, pp. 453 ff.

CHAPTER II

THE CHARACTER OF GOD

So far we have presented the theistic postulates of Judaism as it received them in the Scriptures and appropriated them in its own way. More distinctive is the Jewish conception of the character of God, to which we now proceed. This also is derived from the Bible, but here the selective process indicated above has larger room, and the advance beyond the highest attainments of the former centuries is most marked.

Thus, the holiness of God, which in old times conveyed before all else the idea of inviolability, of exalted majesty and consuming purity,[1] or was his godhead in itself, all wherein he is unlike man, came more and more to signify his godhead morally conceived, the sum of those moral perfections in which it is man's chief end to be in human measure like God, thus arriving at the sense which is now ordinarily attached to the word.

In one of the most pregnant narratives in the Bible, Moses, on the point of departing from the Mount of God to lead the people to the land of promise, asks, as if the seal of his commission, to see the glory of God. That vision is denied to eyes of flesh and blood, but God promises: 'I will make all my *goodness* pass before thee, and will proclaim the name of the Lord before thee.' 'And the Lord passed by before him, and proclaimed: The Lord, the Lord God, merciful and gracious, slow to anger and abundant in loving-kindness and faithfulness; keeping loving-kindness to the thousandth generation, forgiving iniquity and transgression and sin; one who will by no means clear the guilty, visiting the iniquity of the fathers upon the children and upon the children's children to the third and to the fourth generation.'[2] The two aspects of God's character which are here dis-

---

[1] Isa. 6; 57, 15; Psalm 99, etc.
[2] Exod. 33, 19; 34, 6 f.; cf. Deut. 5, 9 f.; Jer. 32, 17–19. See below, pp. 395 f.

played, his mercy and his justice, are the essential moral attributes on which religion in Jewish conception is founded. Amos's message is the inflexible righteousness of God, Hosea's, his inextinguishable love. These attributes, or their active manifestations in justice and mercy, run through the Bible like a cord of two colors intertwined. In the warnings and pleadings of the prophets,[1] in the prayers of the servants of God,[2] in the hymns of praise,[3] the righteousness and the love of God, his justice and his gracious mercy, are ever-recurrent motives.

In the Palestinian schools justice and mercy are frequently coupled as the two primary 'norms'[4] of God's dealing with men individually and collectively. Jewish exegesis found in these two norms an explanation of the alternation in the Bible of the divine names the "Lord" and "God" (Ihvh and *Elohim*) which has played such a part in modern analysis of the Pentateuch. The interchange is significant: Jehovah denotes God in his merciful and gracious character and attitude; Elohim in the character of strict judge. Thus R. Meir interpreted Hos. 14, 2 ('Return, Israel to (עד) the Lord, thy God:' "Repent while he is standing in the attitude (lit., 'attribute') of mercy (indicated by the name Ihvh, the Lord); if you do not, he will be 'your God' (*Elohim*, the austere judge); repent, that is, before the advocate becomes the accuser."[5] The conjunction of the two attributes of justice and mercy is so common that it is superfluous to adduce particular instances.

God's justice is first of all man's assurance that God will not

---

[1] E. g. Hos. 2, 21 f.

[2] E. g. Dan. 9, 7 and 9.

[3] E. g. Psalm 25, 8–10.

[4] מדות; respectively מדת הדין, מדת חרחמים, מדת הרחמים. Jer. Ta'anit 65b, below; Gen. R. 12, 15, and often. The juxtaposition of these attributes follows Biblical precedent; see Jer. 9, 23; 32, 17–20; Psalm 101, 1; 103, 6–18; etc. 2 Macc. 1, 24. See further Note 123.

[5] Pesiḳta ed. Buber f. 164a. The interpretation turns on the unusual preposition עד, taken to mean 'while.' In the attitude of mercy he is advocate (συνήγορος); in that of justice he is accuser (κατήγορος). Cf. also Gen. R. 33, 3; 73, 3 (Samuel ben Naḥman).

use his almighty power over his creatures without regard to right. The remonstrance of Abraham at the very thought that in the doom of the cities of the plain God would destroy the righteous with the wicked, 'Far be it from Thee! shall not the judge of all the earth do justly!'[1] is often recalled, and the homilists love to embellish the scene.[2] From more than one example in the sacred history the lesson is drawn that God does not deal with men as a king does in putting down a rebellion, slaying the innocent and the guilty indiscriminately because he does not know the one from the other. God, who knows men's thoughts and the counsel of their hearts and reins, knows who has sinned and who not, knows the spirit of each individual, and will distinguish the guilty from the guiltless.[3]

In relation to individuals, God's distributive justice is often represented as a strict *suum cuique* which gives its full meed to the good deeds of bad men, and inflicts on none more punishment than he has deserved.[4] This aspect of justice, however, will be more conveniently reserved for a later chapter.

God's rectoral justice does not mean that, having given laws and attached general or specific penalties to the violation of them, he inflexibly exacts the whole penalty of every infraction by transgression or neglect. It is not the justice of inexorable law, nor of an impersonal divine attribute, but of an all-wise and almighty sovereign whose end is not the vindication of the law or of his own majesty, not the demonstration or satisfaction of a realistically conceived attribute, but the best interest of the individual, the people, the race, and the fulfilment of his great purpose in the universal reign of God. Even when sentence has been pronounced, he can revoke it and freely pardon.[5]

[1] Gen. 18, 25.
[2] E. g. Gen. R. 39, 6; 49, 20; Lev. R. 10, 1. See also the references below, pp. 528 f.
[3] Tanḥuma ed. Buber, Korah § 19; cf. ibid. Noah § 10, and Bemidbar § 32.
[4] R. Akiba is frequently cited for this view of the divine justice; e. g. Gen. R. 33, 1.
[5] See Note 124.

A theme with many repetitions and variations is that the world would never have been created and could not endure if justice were to rule in it untempered by mercy. On Gen. 2, 4, 'The Lord God (Iнvн-*Elohim*) [1] made earth and heaven,' a Midrash represents God as deliberating: If I create the world in my merciful character (alone),[2] sins will abound; if in my just character (alone),[3] how can the world endure? I will create it in both the just and the merciful character, and may it endure! [4] So when God is about to inflict just judgment on Sodom, Abraham argues with him: "If thou seekest justice, there will be no world here; if thou seekest a world, there will be no justice here." God it is said, would take the string by both ends (have both alternatives); he wants to have a world, he wants also to have exact justice; but unless he relaxes its demands somewhat, the world cannot endure.[5]

The same idea which is here expressed in what we may call homiletic form is put into theology by Philo in a passage where he is commenting on God's dealing with the generation of the Flood (Gen. 6, 7 f.). In the deliverance of Noah while the rest of mankind was destroyed, God's saving mercy was mingled with the judgment of the sinners, as the Psalmist says, 'I will sing of mercy and judgment' (Psalm 101, 1). For if God should will to judge the mortal race without mercy, he would render a condemnatory verdict, since no man goes through his whole life without a fall, some by voluntary slips, some by involuntary. "In order, therefore, that the race may continue to exist, even though many individuals go to the bottom, he mingles with justice, mercy, which in his benevolence he employs even to the unworthy; and not only has he mercy where he has inflicted judgment, but inflicts judgment where he has had mercy.[6] For

---

[1] The former standing for God in his merciful character (Psalm 145, 9; Gen. R. 33, 1), the latter in his justice. See above, p. 387.
[2] במדת הרחמים.   [3] במדת הדין.
[4] Gen. R. 12, 15; cf. 8, 4 f.
[5] Gen. R. 39, 6; Lev. R. 10, 1; Pesiḳta ed. Buber f. 139a.
[6] Καὶ οὐ μόνον δικάσας ἐλεεῖ ἀλλὰ καὶ ἐλεήσας δικάζει.

with him mercy is antecedent to judgment, inasmuch as he knows
that a man is deserving of punishment, not after judgment rendered, but before judgment." [1] The manifoldness of God's mercy
is brought out by an enumeration of the words and phrases in
Exod. 34, 6 f., in which way thirteen 'norms of mercy' — specific
forms or manifestations of the attribute of mercy — are discovered.[2] God has no pleasure in the death of the wicked, but
that the wicked turn from his way and live (Ezek. 33, 12).

The merciful qualities of God enumerated in the rabbinical
sources after Exod. 34, 6 f. as the 'thirteen norms' are appealed
to in 4 Esdras in a moving plea for mankind, which has no other
escape from its doom.

> "I know, Sir, that the Most High is called merciful (רחום)
> because he has mercy on those who have not yet come into
> the world; and gracious (חנון), because he is gracious to
> those who turn in repentance to his law; and longsuffering
> (ארך אפים) because he shows longsuffering toward those
> who have sinned, as to his own works; and liberal (רב חסד)
> because he had rather give than exact; and of abundant
> compassion (נוצר חסד ?) because he makes his compassions
> abound to those now living and to those who are gone
> and to those yet to come, for if he did not make them
> abound, the world and those who inhabit it could not live;
> and the giver (נשה עון ?), because if he did not give out of
> his goodness, that those who have done iniquities should be
> relieved of their iniquities, not the ten-thousandth part of
> men could survive; and the judge (ונקה), because if he
> did not pardon those who were created by his word, and
> blot out the multitude of their sins, very few would be left
> of all the innumerable multitude."

A reconstruction of the orginal Hebrew text from a translation
of a translation is impossible, and the somewhat eclectic render-

---

[1] Quod deus sit immutabilis c. 16 (ed. Mangey I, 284). The whole passage is relevant.

[2] Sifrè Deut. § 49; Pesiḳta ed. Buber f. 57a, and in other places. The list
is taken up into the liturgy; see Note 125. In these qualities God is an example for men to imitate, Sifrè Deut. l. c. See below, p. 396.

ing essayed above is in more than one place doubtful.[1] The main
thing, however, is not doubtful, namely that the passage is a
kind of midrash on the *middot*, of which seven seem to be accounted for; and that they are pleaded in Ezra's remonstrance
quite as they might be in Jewish prayers for forgiveness (*selihot*).
In the sequel Ezra concentrates it upon the fate of Israel (8,
15 ff.).

R. Phineas bar Ḥama, a much quoted homilist of the fourth
century, brings together texts to prove that God does not desire
to convict any human being (Ezek. 18, 32; Psalm 5, 5); but to
acquit (justify) all his creatures (Isa. 42, 21; 46, 10). He even
appoints an advocate for sinners to bring out their good points,
and gives him full opportunity to do so, for which biblical instances are cited, such as Jer. 5, 7; Gen. 18 (Abraham's intercession for Sodom); 1 Kings 18 (Elijah),[2] etc.

In his providential dealings with men, God is longsuffering;
he seeks by warnings and chastisements to bring men to recognize and acknowledge their sins, and to turn from them unto him
in repentance, that he may forgive.[3]

God's inclination in judgment is always in man's favor. In a
picturesque application of Job 33, 23 by a Rabbi of the second
century, if nine hundred and ninety-nine angels give a bad account of man and only one a favorable account, God inclines the
balance to the meritorious side; and even if nine hundred and
ninety-nine parts of the one angel's report are bad and only one
thousandth good, God will still do the same.[4]

It would be easy to multiply indefinitely such examples from
the Haggadah. The proof-texts may seem to the uninitiated to
be irrelevant and the exegesis ingeniously misdirected; the thing
we are concerned to note is that God's justice and his mercy are
thus constantly associated in Jewish thought, which here again

[1] For a different distribution see Simonsen in Festschrift zu Israel Lewys
siebzigsten Geburtstag (1911), pp. 270–278.

[2] Tanḥuma ed. Buber, Wa'era § 11, see Note 126.

[3] See below, pp. 527 ff.

[4] Eliezer ben Jose ha-Gelili.   Jer. Ḳiddushin 61d; cf. Shabbat 32a.

is in the track of the Law and the Prophets. We shall see when we come to the article of retribution that much stricter views of divine justice prevailed than that which hyperbolically imagines God rendering a verdict in accordance with a millionth part of the evidence; and that God's mercy is so related to repentance as to give it a wholly moral character and value.[1]

Justice and mercy, or benevolence, in the abstract, may be regarded as conflicting principles — they were so regarded by the Stoics — and it is evident that in the sphere of law, if justice is defined as the rigid exaction of the penalty, and mercy be understood as unwillingness to inflict suffering, they do conflict. Moses' maxim was, "Let justice pierce the mountain" — *fiat justitia ruat caelum!* Aaron sought to make peace between men, and to recall men from their evil ways by mildness and persuasion.[2] In striving for sermonic vividness, the justice of God is sometimes dramatically personified. If God had shown to the ministering angels with whom he consulted about the making of man [3] the wicked who would spring from Adam, "the attribute of justice would not have permitted him to be created."[4] When God proposed to make Hezekiah the Messiah, the attribute of justice (*suum cuique*) objects that Hezekiah, who has not made a single hymn praising God for all the miracles wrought in his behalf, should not be thus preferred to David.[5] No one at all acquainted with the ways of preachers will suspect in these personifications a philosophy of hypostatic attributes, or discover dogma in the precedence which is often ascribed to mercy over justice.[6]

[1] See below, pp. 393, 527 f.; II, 252.

[2] Tos. Sanhedrin 1, 2; Jer. Sanhedrin 18b; Sanhedrin 6b; homiletically amplified, Tanḥuma ed. Buber, Ḥuḳḳat (Addit.) f. 66a–b.

[3] Gen. 1, 26, "Let *us* make man."

[4] Gen. R. 8, 4. In the preceding context the attribute of mercy is similarly personified; God made it his associate in creating the world.

[5] Sanhedrin 94a; Bacher, Tannaiten, II, 519. In the end it remains God's secret whom he has designated to this office.

[6] Tanḥuma ed. Buber, Tazri'a § 11: In dealing with Adam, He gave the attribute of mercy precedence over the attribute of justice.

For Jewish apprehension justice and mercy are not jealous attributes between which God is somehow distracted, but complementary aspects of his character which are harmoniously exhibited in his moral government of the world and his particular providence. 'Good and upright [1] is the Lord; therefore doth he instruct sinners in the way' (Psalm 25, 8). "Why is he good? Because he is upright. And why upright? Because he is good. 'Therefore doth he instruct sinners in the way'; because he teaches the way of repentance." [2]   Christian theologians have sometimes laid it down as an axiom that God *must* be just, he *may* be merciful. The rabbis, as we have seen, had confidence that upon such conditions God would never have made a world of peccable men; and in the theory that Justice could deter God from ruling his world in his own way, they would have scented the heresy of 'two powers' in its most obnoxious form. To them, justice and mercy were not attributes of a Divine Being, but the character of a personal God, whom they could not imagine as either unjust or unmerciful; hence they did not even see the difficulty the theologian finds in reconciling the attributes.

Mercy is not only a principle of the divine government of the world; it is the expression of a divine compassion which embraces all his creatures, men and women, the righteous and the wicked (Psalm 145, 9); [3] it extends to the brute creation. [4] The Midrash abounds upon this subject. God lamented the severe sentence he had to pass on Adam; he mourned for six days before the flood; the death of Nadab and Abihu was twice as hard for him as even for their father Aaron. [5]   God himself suffers in the sufferings of men: 'In all their affliction he was afflicted,' etc. (Isa. 63, 9). He was with Israel in Egypt; he went into exile with them to Babylon, and was delivered with them. [6]   'The

---

[1] טוב וישר.   The second word might be translated 'equitable.'
[2] Jer. Makkot 31d; Pesikta ed. Buber f. 158 b; Midrash Tehillim ed. Buber f. 107a.   See Note 127.
[3] Tanḥuma ed. Buber, Niṣṣabim § 5.   [4] Ibid. Noah § 7 (f. 17a).
[5] Ibid. Bereshit § 22; Shemini § 1; Aḥarè § 8, cf. § 13, etc.
[6] Ibid. Beshallaḥ § 11; Bemidbar § 10; Aḥarè § 18.

Lord upholdeth all that fall, and raiseth up those that are bowed
down' (Psalm 145, 14); it does not say, 'those that stand,' but
'those that are bowed down'—even the wicked.[1] These illustrations from a single compilation of 'sermon-stuff' suffice. The
humanity of God is, indeed, written all over the revelation as it
was read by philosophically unsophisticated men; the preachers
at most did no more than seek to improve less obvious texts.
Often they also held up this side of God's character as an example for man's imitation and a motive to it.[2]

One point in which they go beyond the explicit teaching of the
Old Testament deserves particular mention. We shall see that
in its moral teaching Judaism is peculiarly sensitive to the injuries
to the honor of a fellow-man or to his good name; these are
graver wrongs than injuries to his person or property. In this
also God sets man the example. Even in the infliction of merited
punishment he spares the honor of the transgressor. Ezek. 29,
16 —by a contorted exegesis, it must be admitted — is made to
teach that God does not allow anything that might serve as a
memorial and reminder of a sin committed by an individual or
the community. In the ordeal of the adulteress, for example,
she is not allowed to drink the potion from a cup belonging to
another woman, lest the latter should be able to say, This is
the cup from which so-and-so drank the potion and died; the
law says '*bull* or sheep' not '*calf* or sheep,' in order not to
recall the sin of the golden calf; God did not reveal, nor will he
reveal, the name of the tree whose fruit Adam ate with such
disastrous consequences, lest whenever men saw a tree of the kind
they might think, That is the tree that brought death into the
world.[3]

All this is the communicative aspect of the goodness of God,
an inexhaustible theme in the Scriptures, especially in the later
writings, and equally in Jewish literature. This goodness is

[1] Ibid. Wayyeṣè § 10. In the sequel, the impartiality of God's love, compared with man's.
[2] See below, p. 441.
[3] Pesiḳta ed. Buber f. 75b–76a; f. 142b; Gen. R. 15, 7, etc.

seen in the whole creation, with its adaptation to the well-being of all creatures; in the perpetual and unfailing provision not only for their needs but for their happiness; in protection and deliverance.[1] With God's goodness, or his loving-kindness, his truth is often coupled,[2] which is not only his fidelity to his word given, but his constancy in righteousness and grace. The goodness which he shows to all mankind is peculiarly manifested to his people, Israel; it extends to the unthankful and the evil, but embraces with peculiar graciousness the godly and upright. Here also Judaism is in full accord with the revelation of God in the Scriptures.

From an endless abundance in the rabbinical literature a few illustrative examples may be taken almost at random. In a touching anecdote about R. Meir at the grave of his apostate teacher R. Elisha bar Abuya, he finds in Ruth 3, 13 (cf. Psalm 145, 9) God, the absolutely good, who would deliver even such a sinner.[3] A contemporary, Jose ben Ḥalafta, contrasts man's way toward one who has angered him with God's. A man would seek the life of the offender; but God provides even the serpent he cursed with his food wherever it goes. The Canaanite, whom his curse made a slave, has the same food and drink as his master; he cursed the woman, but all men run after her; he cursed the ground, but all get their living from it.[4] Moses asked to be shown by what norm (attribute) God ruled the world; God answers, 'I will cause all my goodness to pass before thee' (Exod. 33, 19). I am under no obligation to the creature at all; but I give to them gratuitously, as it is written, 'I will be gracious to whom I will be gracious' (ibid.).[5] God has compassion like a father and comforts like a mother (Psalm 103, 13; Isa. 66, 13).[6] This side of God's character is naturally appealed to in the liturgy, especi-

---

[1] Psalm 36, 6–10; 136, 1–9; 145; Wisdom of Solomon 11, 23–26, etc.
[2] E. g. Psalm 25, 10; 57, 4; 61, 8; 69, 14.
[3] Jer. Ḥagigah 77c. Cf. Matt. 19, 17.
[4] Yoma 75a.
[5] Tanḥuma ed. Buber, Etḥannan § 3.
[6] Pesiḳta ed. Buber f. 139a.

ally in prayers for forgiveness. As has already been noted, God
himself is said to have taught Moses the liturgical use of the
thirteen norms of God's grace (Exod. 34, 6 f.), and promised to
accept the prayer and pardon the sinner.[1] The oldest prayers
for forgiveness [2] seem to have consisted chiefly of Biblical passages of similar tenor, largely from the Psalms.[3] One of the two
ancient benedictions before reciting the Shema' in the morning[4]
begins, "With abounding love thou hast loved us, O Lord our
God, with great and exceeding pity hast thou pitied us." In the
progressive amplification of the liturgy, more and more Psalms
of this tenor have been incorporated in the prayer-books.

More than one of the words generally translated 'mercy,'
'lovingkindness,' and the like, might in many contexts quite
as well be rendered 'love,' with the active forthputting of love
more in mind than the affection itself.[5] But the latter is often
expressed by the commonest and by the strongest terms in the
Hebrew language.[6] God's love for his people Israel is a frequent
topic in the Old Testament, especially in the prophets from the
seventh century on. Thus Hosea: 'When Israel was young I
loved him, and out of Egypt I called my son' (11, 1). The inextinguishable love of God for his people, like the love of a husband for the wife of his youth in spite of her unfaithfulness, is
the subject with which the Book of Hosea begins (chaps. 1–3),
and the ruling idea throughout his prophecies. Love is the power
which shall at last reclaim the erring people, bringing it to repentance and reviving its early love. The gifts of the reunion
are set forth in one of the most significant verses of Scripture:
'I will espouse thee unto me forever. I will espouse thee unto
me in rightousness and in justice, and in loving-kindness and in

---

[1] Rosh ha-Shanah 17b; Tanḥuma ed. Buber, Wayyera § 9.
[2] Seliḥot, Dan. 9, 9; for mercy and forgiveness.
[3] See Elbogen, Der jüdische Gottesdienst, pp. 221 f.
[4] אהבה רבה; cf. the counterpart אהבת עולם ('with eternal love'), Berakot
11b. Elbogen, op. cit. pp. 20, 100.
[5] See Note 128.
[6] See Note 129.

compassion; and I will espouse thee unto me in faithfulness, and thou shalt know the Lord.' An echo of this is heard in Jer. 31, 1 ff. with its climax: 'With everlasting love have I loved thee, therefore with affection I have drawn thee' (31, 3).[1] The peculiar love of God to the patriarchs, especially to Abraham, is emphasized;[2] it is the confidence of their descendants that the same love is continued to them.[3] It is in accordance with the whole tenor of prophecy, whose warnings and exhortations as well as its promises and consolations are addressed directly to the nation in its religious character, that the love of God should be usually his love for the people collectively; and the Jews of later times understood it similarly as embracing all members of the people. But the same individualizing process which translated the prophetic doctrine of national retribution and national return to allegiance and obedience into individual retribution and individual repentance, appropriated for the individual, not only the mercy and lovingkindness of God, but its origin, the personal love of God. The most striking proof of this is acceptance of the afflictive providences of God by the sufferer as 'chastisements of love,' the discipline of a father prompted by love for his child, to correct faults and develop character.[4]

Akiba deduced God's love to all mankind from the divine image in man: "Beloved is man, because he was created in the image (of God); still more beloved that it was made known to him that he was created in the image, as it is said, 'In the image of God he made the man.' Beloved are the Israelites, because they are called sons of God; still greater love that it was made known to them that they are called sons of God, as it is said, 'Ye are sons of the Lord your God' (Deut. 14, 1). Beloved are the Israelites, because to them was given the precious instrument; still greater love that it was made known to them that to them was

---

[1] See also Deut. 7, 8; 23, 6; 1 Kings 10, 9; Hos. 3, 1; Isa. 43, 4; Mal. 1, 2, etc.

[2] Deut. 4, 37; 10, 15; Isa. 41, 8.

[3] See below, pp. 536 ff.

[4] See Vol. II, pp. 254 ff.

given the precious instrument with which the world was created
(sc. the Torah-revelation). 'For good doctrine have I given to
you, do not forsake my Torah.'" [1] More pregnant expression of
the Jewish conception of God's relation to men could hardly be
given: God's love for mankind in making man alone of all
creatures in the image of God; his peculiar love to Israel in calling them his sons; the immensity of his love in giving to them
the religion which was both instrumental and final cause in the
creation of the world; and all these proofs of his love known not
by inference or reasoning, but by revelation direct from God himself. It is not irrelevant to add that the same Akiba found the
comprehensive commandment of the Law, we might say the
essence of religion on its manward side, in the sentence, 'Thou
shalt love thy neighbor (fellow man) as thyself.' [2]

That the greatest gift of God's love is the revelation of the
true religion is the burden of the very ancient benediction before
the Shema', Ahabah Rabbah, or Ahabat 'Olam, of which mention has already been made; for this reason it is called the
'Blessing of the Law.' [3]

The peculiar love of God for Israel is the ground of his choice
of Israel to be their God and they his people. In the Scriptures
the doctrine of an election which had its motive, not in any excellence in them, but solely in unmerited favor, is pressed to under-
mine the presumption of the intrinsic superiority of Israel to the
other nations, with its fruits in the pride of self-righteousness on
the one hand and contempt of the heathen on the other. But
God's partiality for Israel is manifested and explicitly affirmed
in the Old Testament in a way that might have quite the opposite effect. God is Israel's lover; and when, moved by Israel's
praises of his beauty, the nations say, We will come with you,
as it is written, Whither has thy lover gone, thou fairest among
women? (Cant. 6, 1), the Israelites reply, You have no part in

---

[1] Abot 3, 14. (Prov. 4, 2).
[2] See Vol. II, pp. 85 f.
[3] Elbogen, Der jüdische Gottesdienst, p. 20. See also Jewish Encyclopedia s.v. 'Ahabah Rabbah,' I, 281.

him, as it is written, 'I am my lover's and my lover is mine' (Cant. 6, 3).[1]

More serious than such allegorizing are utterances like this: 'I have loved you, saith the Lord. Yet ye say, Wherein hast thou loved us? Was not Esau Jacob's brother? saith the Lord; yet I loved Jacob and hated Esau.'[2] The execution of God's hatred upon 'the people with whom the Lord is wroth forever' is vividly depicted in the following verses. The predictions of the doom of the heathen nations in the prophetic books are in fact the expression of a vindictive hatred, and those against Edom are among the most sanguinary.[3] The modern reader may explain such prophecies as the projection of the hatred the Jews felt towards the nations that wronged and oppressed them and their demand for divine vengeance, and he may describe such too human outbreaks of passion as a lapse from the higher teaching and spirit of the religion; but he will do well to remind himself that his rationalizing explanation and his discrimination of superior and inferior were not accessible to the Jews, who, consistently with the principle of revealed religion as they apprehended it, could do nothing but take such prophecies as the literal word of God, true expression of God's feeling, and predictions to the fulfilment of which his truth was engaged. The furthest they could go was to emphasize the enormity of the crimes against God and man which deserved such an enormous doom.

Over against these oracles, however, stand the prophecies of the conversion of all nations to the true religion, and the time to come when the Lord shall reign alone in all the earth with the allegiance and obedience of all men. The incongruities of Jewish notions in this sphere were thus given in Scripture itself, with the same authority of revelation. They come out most strongly, as we shall see hereafter, in the effort to combine them in a picture

---

[1] Sifrè Deut. § 343 (ed. Friedmann, p. 143a).
[2] Mal. 1, 2 f. See Note 130.
[3] See Isa. 13, 13–22 (Babylon); 34, 1–15; 63, 1–6; Jer. 49, 7–22; Obad. 1–21 (Edom); and in general Isa. 13–23; Jer. 46–51; Ezek. 25–32.

of the great crisis with which the present chapter of the world's history ends, and of what the next age is to be like.[1]

The Jews would have been singularly unlike the rest of mankind if in the generation after the destruction of Jerusalem by the Romans, and even more after the disastrous end of the war under Hadrian, they had not found a bitter satisfaction in calling to mind the prophecies of God's signal vengeance on the Babylonian destroyers, such as Isa. 13 and Jer. 50 f., with an application to modern Nebuchadnezzars and Antiochuses, and dwelt on the predictions of the doom of Edom (Rome) in Isa. 34, Jer. 49, 7–23, Isa. 63, 1–6. But, considering how much room the destruction of the heathen nations fills in the prophets and the fierce exultation over their fate that breathes in the prophecies, the vindictive aspect of God's dealing with the oppressors of his people is far from being as prominent in rabbinical utterances, even from that dreadful century, as we should expect. The same may be said of the apocalypses that reflect the fall of Jerusalem, Fourth Esdras and the Syriac Baruch; for the tragedy of Israel, which itself was but an act in the tragedy of mankind, vengeance was no solution.

That within his people, God, who is righteous and loves righteousness (Psalm 11, 7), has an especial affection for the righteous is taught in the Scripture both by word (e.g. Psalm 146, 8) and example. On the former verse a teacher of the second century remarked: "You will not find a man who loves one of the same calling. The scholar, however, loves one of his calling, as, for example, R. Ḥiyya loved R. Hoshaya, and R. Hoshaya, R. Ḥiyya; and God loves one of his calling, as it is said, The Lord is righteous, he loves righteousness, his countenance beholds the upright.' This refers to Noah, for it is said, 'And the Lord said unto Noah, 'Come thou and all thy house into the ark; for thee have I seen righteous before me in this generation.'[2] (Gen. 7, 1).

[1] See Part VII.
[2] Gen. R. 32, 2; cf. Midrash Tehillim on Psalm 11, 7 (ed. Buber f. 51a).

CHAPTER III

MINISTERS OF GOD

THE title 'king' was probably first applied to God in his peculiar relation to Israel;[1] but as the horizon of history widened and monotheism became more conscious of its implications, God was king as ruler of the nations, eternally sovereign in the whole world he had created.[2] The religious interest in the sovereignty of God, as in monotheism itself, is altogether in the unity of the moral government of the world; and, like the interest in his omnipotence,[3] it is above all in the certain fulfilment of that great purpose which he has revealed by his prophets, the good world that is to be. The sovereignty of God in Judaism is, therefore, inseparable from the teleology of religion. The most expressive name for this ideal is *malkut Shamaim*;[4] all the hopes of humanity are in the coming of that day when 'The Lord shall be king in all the earth,' the day when His will is done on earth as it is in heaven.[5] But meanwhile God is king, though men acknowledge him not, know it not. We shall see hereafter how vital these ideas are in Jewish piety.

Jewish imagination pictured God in a royal palace seated upon a lofty throne, as Isaiah saw it in his vision (Isa. 6), surrounded by his ministers and an innumerable celestial court of many ranks and functions.[6] A similar vision is found in 1 Kings 22, 19ff., where Micaiah ben Imlah sees the Lord sitting upon his throne, and all the host of heaven standing by him on his right hand and on his left, in council with him; while in Job they present them-

---

[1] E. g. Isa. 43, 15; 44, 6; Zeph. 3, 15; Psalm 5, 2; 84, 4, etc.
[2] Jer. 10, 7, 10; 46, 18; 48, 15; Zech. 14, 9, 16, 17; Mal. 1, 14; Psalm 47, 3; 95, 3; 145, 13, etc.
[3] Above, p. 375.   [4] Pp. 432–434 ; II, 371 ff.   [5] Matt. 6, 10.
[6] It is probable that the organization and ceremonial of the Persian court and of the orientalized Macedonian monarchies contributed to the concrete detail of this imagery. On God's palace and throne in the heavens see also Psalm 11, 4; 103, 19; 123, 1.

selves before him at stated times, as officials of an empire or
inspectors of the provinces might come up to court to give account of what was going on in the world.[1] In Job they are called
bene elohim, 'divine beings.' [2] This expression was later avoided
because of its liability to misunderstanding or cavil; the Greek
versions substitute 'angels.' Another word for the members of
God's celestial court is *ḳedoshim*, which also originally at least
connoted 'divine beings,' [3] but was understood 'holy beings' in
the later senses of holiness.[4]

The general name for these beings is derived from their
principal function as seen from man's side; they are God's messengers, or envoys, whom he employs in the world on various
missions.[5] Jacob in his dream at Bethel sees them in numbers
going up and down between heaven and earth (Gen. 28, 12).
They are the Lord's army, under a general (Josh. 5, 14 f.), 'the
host of heaven.' On their errands they are usually sent singly;
they appear to men in human form, are taken for men, and sometimes simply called so in the narrative, as in Gen. 18. They
present themselves unexpectedly, deliver their message or accomplish their task, disclosing in doing so their true character,
and sometimes vanish miraculously.[6] In all the older narratives
of the appearance of such divine messengers they are anonymous;
and so they remain in the prophets, particularly in Ezekiel and
Zechariah, where an angel is assigned to the prophet as the
medium or interpreter of revelation. Names of individual angels
are found within the canon first in Daniel; in succeeding apocalypses they multiply.[7]

[1] Cf. also Zech. 1, 8 ff.
[2] Job. 1, 6; 2, 1; cf. 38, 7. Compare also Gen. 6, 2; Dan. 3, 25; *bene
elim*, Psalm 29, 1; 89, 7. See Note 131.
[3] See Psalm 89, 6, 8; Job 5, 1; 15, 15; Deut. 33, 2; Zech. 14, 5; and frequently in the later literature.
[4] Lev. R. 24, 8. Other names, Note 132.
[5] *Mal'akim*, ἄγγελοι, angels; i.e. 'messengers.' Note 133.
[6] E. g. Judges 13, 20.
[7] Jer. Rosh ha-Shanah 56d, below: The names of the angels were brought
up from Babylon. Before the exile the seraphim are spoken of as a class (Isa.
6); after it appear (in Daniel) the names Gabriel and Michael.

The giving of personal names to angels is a very significant step. Whereas the divine messenger formerly had individuality in men's apprehension only *ad hoc*, and in the errand upon which he was for the occasion employed, and even the *angelus comes et interpres* of Ezekiel has no other, Gabriel and Michael, though they do no other things than their anonymous prototypes, acquire a permanent function and a distinct personality: Gabriel is the angel of revelation,[1] Michael is the champion of the Jews; other nations have their own angelic princes as champions.[2] In Tobit the angel who plays so important a part is Raphael (5, 4 *et alibi*). The author of the Book of Daniel does not introduce the names of Gabriel and Michael as if they were something new; on the contrary he assumes that both the names and the functions of these angels were familiar, and it is evident from the approximately contemporary parts of Enoch that the Jews by that time had a much more extensive angelic lore.

God's will in the world was executed by a multitude of such deputies. Not only is his revelation communicated through them, not only are they his instruments in providence and history, but the realm of nature is administered by them. The movements of the heavenly bodies are regulated by an angel who is appointed over all the luminaries of heaven.[3] There are regents of the seasons, of months, and of days, who ensure the regularity of the calendar; the sea is controlled by a mighty prince;[4] rain and dew, frost and snow and hail, thunder and lightning, have

---

[1] Dan. 8, 16; 9, 21; cf. Luke 1, 19 f. Revelation, it should be added, is not his only employment.

[2] Dan. 10, 13–21. Other nations, Ecclus. 17, 17 (Deut. 32, 8, above, pp. 226 f.); Jubilees 15, 31 f.: God gave the spirits power over the nations to lead them astray from Him, but over Israel neither angel nor spirit was given power; He himself alone is its ruler and protector, etc. According to R. Ḥama bar Ḥanina, the angel with whom Jacob wrestled was the champion of Esau. Gen. R. 78, 3.

[3] Enoch 75, 3. In the Slavonic Enoch 4 the angels who rule the stars are two hundred in number; cf. Enoch 80, 6; 4 Esdras 6, 3. More commonly the heavenly bodies were conceived to be themselves living and intelligent beings. Compare the δυνάμεις τῶν οὐρανῶν, Matt. 24, 29.

[4] שר של ים, Baba Batra 74b; Tanḥuma ed. Buber, Ḥuḳḳat § 1; Pesaḥim 118b. שר של ארץ, Jer. Sanhedrin 28d, middle.

their own presiding spirits.[1] There are angel warders of hell and
tormentors of the damned;[2] champions of nations and guardians
of individuals,[3] recording angels[4] — in short, angels for everything. As the divine king, God received a worship that was more
than royal homage; his palace was a temple in which angelic
choirs perpetually intoned his praises and incense was burned
upon the altar by a celestial priesthood.[5] The angels thus constitute a hierarchy in numerous orders Cherubim, Seraphim,
Ofannim, and so on.[6]

How much of this development is indigenous; how far it was
promoted or accelerated by acquaintance with other religions,
particularly with that of the Persians, is an inquiry into which
it is needless to enter here. However they came by it, an angelic
mythology of this kind was widely current among the Jews in
the centuries with which we are concerned. It is much more
abundant and extravagant in popular writings, especially the
apocalypses,[7] than in the early rabbinical sources, and in the latter
often seems to be an exhibition of homiletic ingenuity rather than
serious opinion. There was nothing approaching a 'doctrine of
angels.' The Synoptic Gospels and the first half of Acts are the
best witnesses to the popular notions of the time; the Epistles
of Paul are in the same vein; while the Revelation of John is
exuberant in its use of the angelic stage machinery of the Jewish
apocalypses.

In relation to the idea of God, which is our present interest in
it, what I have called the angelic mythology of Judaism is a
naïve way of imagining the mediation of God's word and will in

---

[1] See in general Enoch 72–82; cf. Jubilees 2, 2. Princes of fire and of
hail, שר של אש, שר של ברד, Pesaḥim 118a, below.

[2] Enoch 53 f.; 63, 1; 66, 1. שר של גיהנום, 'Arakin 15b.

[3] Matt. 18, 10; Acts 12, 14 f.; Palestinian Targum on Gen. 33, 10; cf.
Ḥagigah 16a; Ta'anit 11a.

[4] Tanḥuma ed. Buber, Meṣora' § 2 (Eccles. 5, 5): Every word that issues
from a man's mouth is written down in a book. See Note 134.

[5] Ḥagigah 12b; Ḥullin 91b; etc.

[6] See below, pp. 408 f.

[7] In the books we call the Apocrypha (except Tobit) references to angels
are infrequent, and do not go beyond the Old Testament.

the universe by personal agents. They are not, like the good
demons in the later phases of Neoplatonism, the product of an
abstract or transcendent idea of God, but of one naïvely personal;
and they do not consciously infringe upon the belief in his
omnipresence or omniscience.

The angels — using this familiar word comprehensively for the
whole hierarchy — are spirits, not immaterial, but of an ethereal,
fiery substance, blazing light.[1] Or those which are employed on
God's errands are winds; while those which form the heavenly
choir are fire.[2] They were created, as we have seen, together
with the world, on the second day or the fifth.[3] They do not eat
and drink; therefore in Tobit, Raphael is at pains to explain that
he did not really partake of food when he sat at meat with
them, but only seemed to them to do so.[4] Genesis 18, 8, where
Abraham's guests eat the sumptuous meal his hospitality set
before them (cf. also 19, 3), is interpreted in the same way in
the Palestinian Targum — "they seemed to him to eat" — and
in the Midrash.[5]

But whatever angels may do or seem to do in their visits to
earth, there is general agreement that in heaven there is neither
eating nor drinking.[6] R. Akiba was sharply taken to task for
interpreting Psalm 78, 25, 'Man did eat angels food' (the
manna). "Bread of the mighty ones" (lehem abbirim), is the
bread which the ministering angels eat. When this exegesis was
reported to Rabbi Ishmael he bade the reporters tell Akiba that
he erred — "Do the ministering angels eat bread!" — arguing
that Moses, all the forty days he spent on the mount of revelation, neither ate nor drank (Deut. 9, 9, 18).[7] A fortiori the angels.

[1] Psalm 104, 4. See Note 135.
[2] Midrash Tehillim on Psalm 104, 4 (ed. Buber f. 221b).
[3] Above, p. 381.
[4] Tobit 12, 19. The oldest precedent is Manoah's angel, Judges 13, 16;
cf. 6, 18 ff.
[5] Gen. R. 48, 14; Lev. R. 34, 8; Eccles. R. on 3, 14. See Note 136.
[6] Pesikta ed. Buber f. 57a.
[7] Yoma 75b. See Bacher, Tannaiten, I, 245 f. and Note 137.

In another respect angels are unlike men, they do not propagate their kind. Inasmuch as they are ever-living spirits there was no need to renew the generations, as mortals must do.[1]

That angels, although created, do not die, is the universal belief; but of course they can be annihilated by God.[2] The miscegenation of the 'divine beings' with fair women, as narrated in Gen. 6, 1–4 — a fragment of an old myth which was evolved into a whole romance[3] — made it impossible to affirm impeccability of the angelic nature; but it seems to have been assumed that the angels were sorted out in that crisis, and those who did not fall then were in no danger of falling similarly thereafter. The 'evil impulse'[4] which prompts men to sin has no dominion over the angels,[5] as it will have none over men in the Age to Come.

The angels are not impassive spectators or disinterested messengers in the drama of life and history. The angel champions of the nations contend for their cause against the champion of the Jews;[6] an adversary (saṭan) among the angels appears as accuser of the high priest Joshua, and argues the nullity of the institutes of atonement which he administers;[7] the angelic adversary in Job has a cynical skepticism about disinterested goodness and unmistakable jealousy of Job's reputation with God.[8] Judaism followed the Bible, therefore, in imagining the angelic princes of the heathen nations appearing before God as accusers,

---

[1] Enoch 15, 4–7; Matt. 22, 30; Gen. R. 8, 11; Ḥagigah 16a; Pesiḳta Rabbati ed. Friedmann, f. 179b.

[2] A whole troop of them was burned up for opposing the creation of Adam, Sanhedrin 38b.

[3] Enoch 6–11; Jubilees 5, cf. 4, 15; Testaments of the Twelve Patriarchs, Reuben 5; Syriac Baruch, 56, 10–13, etc. For other references see Charles, The Book of Enoch, 2 ed. p. 14; Flemming, Das Buch Henoch, p. 24. See also Midrash Abḳir in Yalḳuṭ Gen. § 44; with Theodor's note on Gen. R. 26, 2 (p. 247).

[4] יצר הרע. See below, pp. 479 ff.

[5] Gen. R. 48, 11 (R. Ḥiyya); Lev. R. 28, 8. Hence the Ten Commandments are not for them, Shabbat 89a.

[6] Dan. 10, 13, 20 f. It was the angelic champions of Babylon, Media, Greece, and Rome that Jacob saw ascending and descending the ladder. Pesiḳta ed. Buber f. 151a (Meir). Bacher, Tannaiten, II, 28 f.

[7] Zech. 3, 1 ff.   [8] Job 1 f.

charging the Israelites with the same sins and vices as the heathen;[1] Satan accuses them every day of the year except on the Day of Atonement.[2] The destroying angels, or angels of punishment, execute God's sentence; but it is a work to which they are nothing loth.[3]

Thus there are different dispositions, partialities and antipathies, among angels as in human society; there is no monotony of universal benevolence on high, nor is even justice dispassionate. And though there are no enmity, strife, hatred, or foes, in that place, still it is necessary for God to 'make peace in his high places' (Job 25, 2).[4]

The various ranks of angels constitute the *familia* on high,[5] with whom God consults as a master with his household servants.[6] It was to the angels, according to a common opinion, that he said, 'Let us make man in our image, after our likeness' (Gen. 1, 26). They often take the liberty of familiar servants, and raise objections or remonstrate with their master, as they did when he proposed to create man.[7] Similarly the angels opposed the giving of the law at Sinai.[8] Frequently questions or objections which men might raise to something in God's conduct of affairs in the world are thus put into the mouth of the angels, to give God, so to speak occasion to explain or justify his ways — a transparent homiletical device which modern writers have not always recognized.[9]

[1] Pesikta ed. Buber f. 176a.
[2] Ibid. He accuses them 364 days in the year (ha-Saṭan, by Gematria =364); Yoma 20a.   [3] See Note 138.
[4] Sifrè Num. § 42 (ed. Friedmann f. 13a, l. 12 ff.).
[5] The Latin word *familia* is usually employed; e.g. Berakot 16b–17a (prayer of R. Safra): "May it be thy will, O God, to make peace in the household above and in the household below." Other occurrences, Sifrè Num. § 42 (f. 13a); Sanhedrin 98b, 99b; Ḥagigah 13b, below, etc. See Note 139.
[6] God confers about everything with the household above. Sanhedrin 38b.
[7] Gen. R. 8, 3 ff.; 17, 4. They quote Psalm 8, 5, 'What is man that Thou art mindful of him?'
[8] Shabbat 88b; Cant. R. on Cant. 8, 11.
[9] See Blau, Jewish Encyclopedia, I, 585 A–B.

The angels are also represented as forming a kind of heavenly senate or high court (*bet din*) over which God presides. God, it is said, judges no cause alone, but with his court (*bet din*) ; but he alone seals the decision with his seal, which is truth. 1 Kings 22, 19 is adduced: the host of heaven on God's right and left are inclining the scales in Ahab's favor or against him; the seal is found in Dan. 10, 1 and 21. Nor are they his assessors in judicial cases alone; he does nothing in his world without consulting his council.[1]

Gen. 1, 26 has already been referred to; in Isa. 6, 8 God seems to associate the Seraphim with himself: 'Whom shall I send and who shall go for us.'[2] The Jews had thus sufficient example in revelation for their notions about the relations between God and the members of the 'upper household' or the 'upper council.'

The angels have greater knowledge than men — as indeed demons have also — especially knowledge of the future, which they impart to the prophets;[3] but their knowledge is derivative, and is even described as a kind of eaves-dropping — "what they hear from behind the curtain"[4] — and is limited; they do not know the year of God's vengeance and the deliverance of Israel, for he has not revealed it to them; it is a secret in his own mind (Isa. 63, 4).[5]

There are millions upon millions of angels, an innumerable host.[6] Among these celestial beings are some who abide continually in the proximity of God, and are not, like the ministering angels, employed in various services. The seraphim, fiery natures as

[1] Jer. Sanhedrin 18a; Gen. R. 12, 1; Cant. R. on Cant. 1, 9. In the last passage Isa. 6 is taken as a judgment scene. It was a common belief that man's life and fortune were determined from year to year by a judicial procedure in the supreme court above; see below, p. 533. Cf. also the places cited p. 407, notes 5 and 6.

[2] Cf. also Gen. 11, 7.

[3] In the later prophets and the apocalypses, angels are the usual medium of revelation.

[4] Ḥagigah 16a.

[5] Sanhedrin 99a; Matt. 24, 36.

[6] Dan. 7, 10; Job. 25, 3; cf. Sifrè Num. § 42; Ḥagigah 13b. See also Rev. 5, 11; Deut. 33, 2.

their name imports, come from Isa. 6, where their form and office are described. The cherubim, of whom there is mention in several places in the Old Testament, were imagined chiefly as they are represented by Ezekiel [1] in his description of the living car surmounted by a throne, on which God is conveyed away from the doomed sanctuary. From the corresponding description in Ezekiel 1 (where the name cherub does not occur) come the four 'beasts,' [2] the ḥayyot (Ezek. 1, 5–14), who constitute a distinct class of celestials, the supporters of God's throne. The wheels of the car which were full of eyes, and in which was the spirit of the 'beasts' (Ezek. 1, 15–22), form another class, the ofannim ('wheels'). [3] In the Parables of Enoch where Enoch is translated in spirit to the heaven of heavens, he sees round about the house which was girt by streams of fire, "cherubim and seraphim and ofannim, never-sleeping beings, [4] who keep watch over his glorious throne; and countless angels, a thousand thousands, a myriad myriads," etc. [5] In the Revelation of John the 'four beasts' take the place of the cherubim; they are described severally, with some variations from Ezekiel 1, and regularly appear with the throne of God. [6] Through this book the four beasts attained a celebrity in the church which they had not in Judaism. They were early associated with the Four Evangelists, [7] and were commonly represented in art as their attributes, whereas Judaism forbade any imaging of angels. [8]

Of the angels in the narrower sense the most important class

---

[1] Ezek. 10, 1–22; 11, 22 f.

[2] Our versions, more respectfully, 'living creatures'; cf. Rev. 4, 6 ff.

[3] Ḥagigah 12b. In the highest story of heaven ('arabot) are the ofannim and serafim and ḥayyot ha-ḳodesh. The ḥayyot beneath the throne, see below, pp. 412 f.

[4] The 'watchers' ('wakeful') cf. Dan. 4, 10, 14, 20; frequent in Enoch.

[5] Enoch 71, 7 f.; cf. 61, 10.

[6] Rev. 4, 6: ἐν μέσῳ τοῦ θρόνου καὶ κύκλῳ τοῦ θρόνου—a position difficult to visualize. See also 5, 6 ff.; 6, 1 ff.; 7, 11 ff.; 14, 3; 15, 7; 19, 4.

[7] The prevailing symbolism of the Latin Church assigns the man to Matthew, the lion to Mark, the bull to Luke, the eagle to John.

[8] Mekilta on Exod. 20, 23, Baḥodesh 10 init. (ed. Friedmann f. 72b; ed. Weiss f. 79b); cf. Rosh ha-Shanah 24b.

are the 'ministering angels,' [1] those whom God employs in various
services, or who await his commands.   Among these the angels
whose names we have already met, Gabriel, Michael, Raphael,
maintain their precedence.   Uriel is often mentioned in Enoch.
Enoch 9, 1, groups the four together, seemingly as the chief
angels.[2]   Elsewhere in the book the four are Michael, Raphael,
Gabriel, and Phanuel; while in 20, 1–8, seven are named, including the last four.[3]   In Tobit, when Raphael unmasks, he
describes himself as "one of the seven holy angels who present
the prayers of the holy ones (angels), and enter into the presence
of the glory of the Holy One."[4]   These principal angels are
called 'angels of the presence,'[5] מלאכי הפנים, that is, those who,
like the chief ministers of a king, have immediate access to his
presence.   These are the seven meant in the Revelation of John
8, 2; as princes among the angels they are called also arch-
angels.[6]

An angel who sooner or later visits every man is the Angel of
Death, who, consequently, filled a larger place in men's thoughts
than the rest, and is the subject of many stories.   He comes only
on an order from God, and executes his commission impartially
on the righteous and the wicked; no plea or remonstrance avails.[7]

The religious importance of Jewish notions and imaginations
about the angelic hierarchy, its occupations in heaven, and its
commissions on earth, is in small proportion to their abundance.
Doubtless the belief in the attendance of a guardian angel helped
the pious to realize God's constant providential care, and the
recording angel, keeping a memorandum of all a man's words

[1] מלאכי השרת.
[2] Michael, Uriel, Gabriel, Raphael, together, with their stations and the
significance of their names, etc., Num. R. 2, 10; Pesiḳta Rabbati ed. Friedmann f. 188a; Pirḳè de R. Eliezer c. 4.
[3] Enoch 40, 9; 71, 8–13. Seven is the number also in Enoch 81, 5; 90,
21; Revelation of John 8, 2.
[4] So in the longer text, Tobit 12, 14 f.
[5] The name comes from Isa. 63, 9. Enoch 40, 2; Testaments of the Twelve
Patriarchs, Levi 3; Jubilees 1, 27, 29; 2, 2; 15, 27.
[6] 1 Thess. 4, 16; Jude 9 (Michael). See further Note 140.
[7] See Blau, Jewish Encyclopedia, IV, 480–482.

and deeds to be reported to God, may sometimes have steadied
a vacillating conscience; but for the rest, angels, whether in ser-
mons or folklore, hardly belonged to religion at all:[1] they were
not objects of veneration, much less of adoration; and in orthodox Judaism they were not intermediaries between man and God.[2]
An unsophisticated biblical Protestantism takes them much in
the same way, without the wealth of legend which surrounded
them in the older churches.

As the first chapter of Genesis gave rise to an esoteric cosmological speculation, the Ma'aseh Bereshit, of which mention has
been made above,[3] so the description of the cherubic car and
throne, with the 'four beasts' (ḥayyot) and the living 'wheels'
(ofannim), in Ezekiel was the starting point for speculations
on the mysteries of the godhead which led into theosophy. This
esoteric tradition was even more carefully guarded than the
mysteries of cosmology,[4] and of its content very little is known.
The fountain head of the tradition, as it appears in second century accounts of the matter, was R. Johanan ben Zakkai, in the
generation after the fall of Jerusalem; he imparted it to R.
Joshua (ben Hananiah); Joshua to R. Akiba; Akiba to Hananiah
ben Ḥakinai.[5] Another disciple of Johanan who left a name for
his attainments in this sphere was R. Eleazar ben 'Arak. A story
in which he has a leading part illustrates the manner of this
secret teaching, if not the matter. One day as Eleazar ben 'Arak
was accompanying his master Johanan ben Zakkai on a journey,
he said to him, Rabbi, expound to me one section of the doctrine
of the chariot. The master replied, Have I not told you that
the chariot is not expounded to a single hearer unless he be a

[1] It has been observed that the Mishnah makes no mention of angels; but
the character of the work gives no occasion to do so. They occur often
enough in the second century Midrash.
[2] They communicate God's message to men; but they do not convey
men's prayers to God. See Note 141.
[3] Pages 383 f.
[4] See Note 142.
[5] Tos. Ḥagigah, 2, 2. The last named was a fellow-student and associate
of Simeon ben Yoḥai, whom the Cabala claims as its great authority.

scholar of penetrating intelligence.[1] Eleazar said, Give me permission, and I will recite to you. Forthwith R. Johanan dismounted from the ass he was riding, and they both wrapped up their heads and sat on a rock under an olive tree while Eleazar recited to him. When he had finished, Johanan stood up and kissed him on the head, saying "Blessed is the Lord God of Israel who has given to our father Abraham a son who knows how to expound and to have insight into the glory of our Father who is in heaven. One excels in teaching but not in preaching, and another in practicing but not in teaching; but Eleazar ben 'Arak is excellent in both. Blessed art thou, our father Abraham, that from thy loins is sprung Eleazar ben 'Arak, who knows how to expound and to have insight into the glory of our Father who is in heaven." [2]

A mediaeval Midrash enumerates a great variety of questions to which the study of the 'chariot' alone could find an answer,[3] but whether they really represent its topics, especially in our centuries, may well be doubted.

A theory of the nature of angels differing widely from the common notions described above is set forth by Joshua ben Hananiah, already named as a disciple of Johanan ben Zakkai, and is probably a specimen of the esoteric angelology of the mystical school. It is in the form of a dialogue between the rabbi and Hadrian, who frequently figures in the rôle of interlocutor in discussions of Jewish law or theology. Hadrian asked R. Joshua ben Hananiah: "You say that no company of angels on high praises God more than once; but that God every day creates a company of new angels, who utter a song before him and are gone. The rabbi answered, Yes. — Whither do they go? — To that whence they were created. — And whence were they created? — From the river of fire.[4] — What does that river of

---

[1] See Note 143.

[2] Tos. Ḥagigah 2, 1. An embellished version in Ḥagigah 14b, top; and especially in Jer. Ḥagigah 77a, where other examples may be found.

[3] Midrash Mishlè 10 (ed. Buber f. 34a). See Note 144.

[4] נהר דינור, Dan. 7, 10.

fire do? — It is like the Jordan here, which flows unremittingly day and night. — Whence does it come? — From the sweat of the beasts (*ḥayyot*) which they sweat under the weight of the throne of God." [1]

The last words may be meant in some occult sense, intelligible only to the initiated, or else the rabbi ends the colloquy, as is often done, in a kind of irony, with an answer that is as good as the questioner deserves. The angels who spring out of the stream of fire and sink back into the perennial stream again probably come from the esoteric tradition; [2] though the notion that a new chorus of angels is created daily to sing but one song, is taken up by homilists who do not belong to the circle.[3]

The adepts of the chariot did not confine themselves to speculations on these high mysteries, they sought immediate knowledge of them. Their theosophy, like others, had a practical as well as a theoretical side, and had its methods of inducing the mystic rapture. Their visions of Paradise were soon — if not from the first — taken for real ascents to heaven.[4] The most famous of these adventures was that of four of the most eminent schoolmen of the early second century, Simeon ben Azzai, Simeon ben Zoma, Elisha ben Abuya, and R. Akiba. To all but Akiba the consequences were disastrous: Ben Azzai looked and died; Ben Zoma looked and lost his mind; Elisha ('Aḥer') cut down the plants (of Paradise); Akiba made his exit in safety.[5] The perils of theosophy to reason and faith were never more concisely exposed. It may perhaps be surmised that the isolation and eclipse of Eleazar ben 'Arak [6] is to be accounted for by his preoccupation with theosophy as much as by the comforts of life at Emmaus.[7]

---

[1] Gen. R. 78, 1; Lam. R. 3, 8; cf. Ḥagigah 14a.
[2] Bacher, Tannaiten, I, 172.
[3] Samuel ben Naḥman, Gen. R. 78, 1, and others; cf. Ḥagigah 14a.
[4] Ḥagigah 14b, end. See Bacher, Tannaiten, I, 332 f..
[5] Tos. Ḥagigah 2, 3 f.; Ḥagigah 14b; Jer. Ḥagigah 77b.
[6] See Bacher, l. c. pp. 71 f.   [7] See Note 145.

CHAPTER IV

THE WORD OF GOD. THE SPIRIT

GOD's will is made known or effectuated in the world not only through personal agents (angels), but directly by his word or by his spirit. To the realism of the natural mind, the spoken word is not a mere articulate sound conveying a meaning; it is a thing, and it does things. A blessing or a curse, for example, is not the expression of a benevolent or malevolent, but impotent, wish; it *is* a blessing or a curse. Once uttered, it is beyond the speaker's power to revoke or reverse it. When blind old Isaac, deceived by Rebecca's ruse and Jacob's falsehoods, bestows on Jacob the blessing he thought he was giving Esau, he cannot undo what he has done; the best he can do is to invent a second-best blessing for his firstborn and best loved son (Gen. 27). So when Micah's mother curses the unknown thief who had stolen her eleven hundred pieces of silver, and her son, alarmed by the curse he overheard, confesses and makes restitution, she cannot take off the curse; she can only try to divert it by dedicating the silver to Jehovah to make an idol for her son to have in his house (Judges 17). Similarly the prophetic word is not a mere prediction that something will come to pass; it brings to pass what it foretells. God touches Jeremiah's mouth with his hand, and says: 'Lo, I have put my words in thy mouth. See, I have commissioned thee this day over the nations and over the kingdoms to root out and pull down and destroy and overthrow; to build and to plant' (Jer. 1, 9 f.). The oracles of doom or of restoration he pronounces in God's name are real forces working destruction or reconstruction. The efficacy of charms and incantations inhered in the formula itself, whether it worked of itself or constrained demons to do the magician's bidding. It is unnecessary to multiply illustrations of the belief that the word is a concrete reality, a veritable cause.

What was true of the words of men was true in an eminent degree of the words of God. The fiats of God in the first chapter of Genesis are creative forces: 'God said, Let there be light, and light came into being,' and so throughout. 'By the word of the Lord the heavens were made, and by the breath of his mouth all their host. . . . For he spake, and it came into being; he commanded and there it stood' (Psalm 33, 6, 9).[1] As has been noted in a former connection, the significance which the rabbis found in creation by a word was the bringing the end to pass instantly, without the toil and pains by which men make things.[2] All other words of God are similarly effective. Like the rain and snow which come down from heaven and do not return thither till they have accomplished their mission by refreshing and fertilizing the earth, 'So shall it be with my word which issues from my mouth: it will not return to me unaccomplished, but will do what I please and succeed in what I sent it for' (Isa. 55, 11). The word of God is sometimes vividly personified, as in Wisdom 18, 15 f.: "Thine all-powerful word, from heaven, from out the royal thrones, a fierce warrior, leaped into the midst of the doomed land (Egypt), bearing as a sharp sword thine irrevocable command, and, standing, filled all things with death; its head touched the sky, it stood firm on the earth." [3] But it is an error to see in such personification an approach to personalization. Nowhere either in the Bible or in the extra-canonical literature of the Jews is the word of God a personal agent or on the way to become such.

It is with the word precisely as it is with 'wisdom,' which is so vividly personified in Prov. 8 and elsewhere. The Jews identified the divine wisdom with the Torah, which also is sometimes

---

[1] Cf. also Wisdom 9, 1 f.; Ecclus. 42, 15 (λόγοις κυρίου); 4 Esdras 6, 38: O domine, loquens locutus es ab initio creaturae in primo die dicens, Fiat caelum et terra! et tuum verbum opus perfecit.

[2] See Note 146.

[3] Like an enormously tall angel, such as Sandalfon is in the chariot mysteries, Ḥagigah 13b. Cf. Gospel of Peter c. 10, the two angels at the resurrection of Jesus.

personified. Wisdom and Torah, like the word, were for them realities, not mere names or concepts; but they never gave them personal existence. Cherubim and seraphim, the four 'beasts,' and even the 'wheels' with their rims full of eyes in Ezekiel's vision, stand ever in God's presence in heaven; but neither 'wisdom' nor 'word' is there. Philo, indeed, finds his Logos in both the wisdom and the word of God, and interprets what the Scriptures say about them in this sense, thus conferring upon them whatever of personality belongs to that 'secondary deity'; but his notion of the Logos was not derived from them.

The God of the Bible is in its own expressive phrase a 'live God,' a God that does things; Philo's God is pure Being, of which nothing can be predicated but that It *is*, abstract static Unity, eternally, unchangeably the same; pure immaterial intellect.[1] Between the transcendent deity and the material world of multiplicity and change, of becoming and dissolution, is a gulf that must somehow be spanned. The Neoplatonists in their time endeavored to overcome the dualism of the system by interposing in descending order Nous, the universal active intelligence; Psyche, the universe soul; and primordial matter; remaining thus, so far as terms went, in the Platonic tradition. Philo's intermediary is the Logos. Stoic influence is manifest in the name and the functions of the Logos, as it is in many other features of Philo's system; but in making it a 'secondary deity,' above which is a transcendent God, he has made of it something widely different from the immanent energetic Reason of the universe which is the only God of Stoicism.

In his theology the Logos is the manifest and active deity; and in his interpretation of the Scriptures, where God appears to men, converses with them, reveals his will and purpose, it is, according to Philo, of the Logos that all this should be understood. The twofold meaning of the Greek word (reason, utterance) made it natural to appropriate for the Logos what was said of the divine wisdom (σοφία) and of the word of God (λόγος, ῥῆμα);

[1] See Note 147.

and allegorical ingenuity enabled Philo to find the Logos in many other places and associations.[1]

That the idea of a divine intermediary, whether derived from Philo or the independent product of a similar Platonizing theory of the nature of Deity, had some currency in Hellenistic Jewish circles may be inferred from the adoption and adaptation of it in certain New Testament writings,[2] and from Gnosticism as well as from Catholic Christianity. But that this philosophy deeply or widely influenced Jewish thought there is no evidence. In the Palestinian schools there is no trace of it. Their idea of God has been set forth in a previous chapter.[3] He is the living God of the Old Testament, not the impersonal Being of Greek metaphysics. He employs upon occasion agents like the angels, and instrumentalities of various kinds such as his word or spirit, to reveal his will and purpose or to effect his ends; but a God who by definition did not himself do anything would have seemed to them to contradict the very idea of God, as much as a God who was personally active in the world contradicted Philo's definition of godhead *in se*.

The erroneous opinion widely entertained that Palestinian Judaism made of the word of God a personal intermediary comparable to Philo's Logos and, as many think, in some way connected with it,[4] is based primarily on the use of *memra* in the Targums. *Memra* is properly what is said, 'saying, utterance,' 'word' in this sense. It is, however, not employed in the Targums in the rendering of such Hebrew phrases as 'the word (*dabar*) of the Lord,' the 'word of God,' 'My word,' 'Thy word,' etc. They translate the Hebrew *dabar* in all senses and uses, not by *memra* but regularly by *pitgama* (rarely by *milla*). Where the 'word of God' in the Hebrew Scriptures is the medium or

[1] See Note 148.

[2] Hebrews, Colossians, the Gospel of John. In John alone the intermediary is named Logos.

[3] See above, Part II, chap. 1; see also immediately below (*memra*, etc.).

[4] Gfroerer, Das Jahrhundert des Heils (1838), and many since him. See Harvard Theological Review, XIV (1921), 222 ff.

instrumentality of revelation or of communication with men, it is not in the Targums his *memra;* nor is the creative word of God his *memra.* This is really the most important thing to be said about *memra* in the Targums—it is *not* the equivalent of the 'word of God' in the Old Testament corresponding to λόγος or ῥῆμα in the Greek versions; and in so far as Philo's Logos is an intermediary in creation and revelation — two of its principal functions — it is in contrast instead of correspondence with the *memra* of the Targums.[1]

Memra is frequently a word of command, as in translation of the idiomatic *peh,* 'command' (lit., 'mouth'), of men or of God.[2] In the same sense it is used in such circumlocutions as, "Ye have contemned the command (*memra*) of the Lord whose presence abides among you," for 'Ye have contemned the Lord who is among you' (Num. 11, 20). To hearken to God, or to his voice, is regularly 'to receive (implying 'obey') the command (*memra*) of the Lord.'[3] The protection or support of God is extended to men through his word; the effective command suffices. The motive of reverence is evident when Onkelos paraphrases, 'The Lord your God, he it is that fights for you' (Deut. 3, 22), "his word fights for you" — he commands the victory. When Abraham believed in the *memra* of the Lord (Heb. 'believed in the Lord,' Gen. 15, 6), and it was reckoned to him for righteousness, *memra* is the promise of the preceding verses.[4] For 'God came to Abimelech in a dream of the night and said to him,' etc., the same Targum has, "A word (*memar*) from before the Lord came," etc. When God says that he will meet the Israel-

---

[1] On *memra* in the Targums see Moore, 'Intermediaries in Jewish Theology,' Harvard Theological Review, XV (1922), 41–61, and Strack–Billerbeck, Kommentar zum Neuen Testament aus Talmud und Midrasch, on John 1, 1 (Exkurs über den Memra Jahves), II (1924), 302–333. An exhaustive exhibition of the usage, with the result that the Memra is not an intermediary, to say nothing of a hypostasis, but "ein inhaltsloser, rein formalhafter Ersatz für das Tetragramm," and that the Logos of the Gospel of John is not derived from it or connected with it.

[2] E. g. Gen. 45, 21; Deut. 1, 26; Num. 14, 41.

[3] E. g. Lev. 26, 14; Deut. 28, 15.

[4] Cf. Exod. 14, 31.

ites at the Tabernacle (Exod. 25, 22), the Targum paraphrases, "I will cause my word (*memri*) to meet thee, and I will speak with thee." [1]

In many other contexts *memra* is introduced as a buffer-word — sometimes in very awkward circumlocutions — where the literal interpretation seemed to bring God into too close contact with his creatures.[2] But nowhere in the Targums is *memra* a 'being' of any kind or in any sense, much less a personal being. The appearance of personality which in some places attaches to the word is due solely to the fact that the *memra* of the Lord and similar phrases are reverent circumlocutions for 'God,' introduced precisely where in the original God is personally active in the affairs of men; and the personal character of the activity necessarily adheres to the periphrasis. It is to be observed, finally, that *memra* is purely a phenomenon of translation, not a figment of speculation; it never gets outside the Targums.

Various other circumlocutions in the Targums have the same motive, namely, to avoid expressions that literally rendered in the vernacular did not beseem the dignity of God. Thus in Hos. 1, 2 ('The beginning of the word of the Lord by (in) Hosea'), "The word (*pitgam*) of prophecy from before the Lord which was with Hosea." [3] When God is said to be, or abide, in a place, to come to a place, or to depart from a place, the Targums generally paraphrase, 'the Presence' (*shekinta*) abode there; God caused his presence to abide there; his presence ascended thence, and the like.[4] Unlike *memra* which is found exclusively in the Targums, 'the Presence' (Hebrew, *shekinah*) is very common in the literature of the school and the

---

[1] Cf. Exod. 29, 42 f.; 19, 17.

[2] Various other devices are employed to the same intent, such as the substitution of a passive voice for the active, the interruption of the connection of a noun with a following genitive ('construct state'), the frequent introduction of קדם, מקדם, etc.

[3] ‏פתגם נבואה מן קדם יהוה דהוה עם הושע‎.

[4] E. g. Exod. 25, 8; 34, 6; Deut. 12, 5, 11, 21; 32, 20; Hos. 5, 6.

synagogue.[1]   It also frequently has a semblance of personality simply because it is a more reverent way of saying 'God,' not because it is a personal divine being that takes the place of God. The notion of such a double of God would have been regarded by the rabbis as a palpable case of the heresy of 'two powers.'

When the Scripture speaks of men's seeing God, or of God's manifesting himself to men, the Targum interprets, 'The *glory* of God.'   In Exod. 24, 10, Moses and his companions, with the seventy elders of Israel, 'saw the God of Israel'; Onkelos renders, "saw the glory (*yeḳara*) of the God of Israel."   So in Isa. 6, 1, the prophet saw "the glory of the Lord," sitting upon his lofty throne.   The same circumlocution is used in other connections; thus e.g., Gen. 17, 22 ('God ascended from Abraham'), it was 'the glory of the Lord' that ascended; Exod. 20, 17 ('God has come to prove you'), "The glory of the Lord was revealed to you."   *Yeḳara* is the Aramaic equivalent of the Hebrew *kabod*, which it regularly translates; and in introducing it in such contexts as have just been quoted the Targums interpret in conformity with many passages of Scripture in which the presence of God is manifested by his 'glory,' the splendor of impenetrable light by which he is at once revealed and concealed.[2]

In such paraphrases the Targums interpret what the historian would call more primitive notions of God by the higher conceptions of deity to which religion had advanced in later parts of the Scriptures and which prevailed in Judaism.

It was of especial importance to do this in the translation of the synagogue lessons, that the unlearned, naturally inclined to a naïve imagination of God, might not seem to be confirmed by the Scripture itself in conceptions inconsistent with the implicit or explicit teaching of Scripture elsewhere — as for example that God cannot be seen by mortal eyes.   It is, however, an egregious error to think that the Targums attempt to dispose of all the anthropomorphisms of Scripture.   They do not scruple

[1] See below, pp. 434 ff.
[2] Exod. 29, 43; 40, 34; Kings 8, 11, etc. Compare the use of δόξα in LXX and the New Testament.

to render literally the hands and feet, the eyes and ears of God, in which even the prosaic mind might recognize natural metaphors for his power or his knowledge; they reproduce faithfully the whole range of human emotions attributed to him. And any one who will read the Targums on such chapters as Gen. 2–4 or Gen. 18 will see how little they are concerned to tone down narratives in which God appears and behaves most like a man. If he will then compare Philo's treatment of such narratives with the Targums and the Midrash, he will discover how innocent the Palestinian masters were of an 'abstract' or 'transcendent' — or any other sort of a philosophical — idea of God.

In the Old Testament superhuman strength, courage, skill, judgment, wisdom, and the like, are attributed to 'the spirit of God,' or of 'the Lord,' which suddenly comes upon a man for the time being and possesses him, or more permanently rests upon him and endows him. In old narratives it is more common of physical power and prowess and the gift of leadership;[1] in the Prophets it is occasionally used of prophetic inspiration.[2] The equivalent phrase 'the holy spirit' is very rare,[3] and is never associated with prophecy. In Judaism, on the contrary, the holy spirit is specifically the spirit of prophecy. When the holy spirit was withdrawn from Israel, the age of revelation by prophetic agency was at an end. The scribes, interpreters of the word of God written and custodians of the unwritten law, succeed. But though God no longer spoke by the holy spirit through the mouth of prophets, he still upon occasion spoke by a mysterious voice. So the Tosefta: "When the last prophets, Haggai, Zechariah, and Malachi, died, the holy spirit ceased out of Israel; but nevertheless it was granted them to hear (communications from God) by means of a mysterious voice."[4]

---

[1] Num. 11, 16 f.; Judges 6, 34; 11, 29; 13, 25; 14, 6, 19; 15, 14; 1 Sam. 11, 6; 16, 3, etc.; Exod. 31, 3; 36, 1; 1 Sam. 10, 10; 2 Sam. 23, 2, etc. In the older narratives the spirit is often a physical force, and is in general a way of conceiving God acting at a distance. It is nowhere a personal agent.

[2] E. g. Ezek. 3, 24.   [3] Isa. 63, 10, 11; Psalm 51, 13.

[4] Tos. Soṭah 13, 2; cf. Soṭah 48b; Yoma 9b; Sanhedrin 11a.

The phrase I have thus translated (*bat ḳol*,) means properly, 'resonance, echo,' for example, of the human voice.[1] In the use we are discussing it is an articulate and intelligible sound proceeding from an invisible source, generally from the sky, or out of the adytum of the temple. An example of such an utterance is Dan. 4, 28 (English versions 4, 31): 'A voice came down from heaven, To thee it is said, O king Nebuchadnezzar, the kingdom is passed away from thee.' Similarly in The New Testament: 'And, lo, a voice from heaven, saying,' etc. (Matt. 3, 17).[2]

The preference for *bat ḳol* instead of the simple *ḳol*, 'voice,' is doubtless to avoid saying that men heard the actual voice of God. Numerous instances are reported in which such a mysterious voice was heard by individuals or by numbers together in the later centuries. The most important occasion was when the learned were assembled at Jamnia in the endeavor to settle certain questions on which the schools of Hillel and Shammai were at strife. The voice is reported to have said, "The dicta of both are words of the living God, but that of the school of Hillel is the norm (*halakah*)."[3] Once, when the learned were gathered in the house of Gorion in Jericho, a mysterious voice said: "There is here a man who is worthy that the holy spirit should rest upon him, but that his generation is not worthy." All eyes turned to the elder Hillel. The same words were spoken at another time at a meeting in Jamnia, and everybody saw that Samuel the Little was meant.[4] John Hyrcanus heard such a voice out of the inner sanctuary announcing that his sons, who were on a military expedition to Antioch (really, against Antiochus Cyzicenus), had gained the victory; note was made of the time, and it proved to be the very hour at which the battle was won.[5]

[1] In the meaning 'echo,' Exod. R. 29, 9, end: "If a man calls to his fellow, his voice has an echo (*bat ḳol*), but the voice which issued from the mouth of God (at Sinai) had no echo" — lest it should be thought that another than He uttered the words, 'I am the Lord thy God.'

[2] See Blau, 'Bat Ḳol,' Jewish Encyclopedia, II, 588–592.

[3] Jer. Berakot 3b, below.

[4] Tos. Soṭah 13, 3 f.; Soṭah 48b; Sanhedrin 11a. Instead of 'the holy spirit,' the Talmud has, 'the *shekinah*.'

[5] Josephus, Antt. xiii. 10, 3 § 282; Tos. Soṭah 13, 5; Soṭah 33a.

CHAPTER V

MAJESTY AND ACCESSIBILITY OF GOD

In the preceding chapters Jewish conceptions of God and his relations to the world of nature and men, as they were developed from the Scriptures in the teaching of the school and the synagogue, have been discussed. We have seen that the idea of God was eminently personal. He was supramundane but not extramundane; exalted but not remote. He was the sole ruler of the world he had created, and he ordered all things in it in accordance with his character, in which justice and mercy were complementary, not conflicting, attributes. His will for men was righteousness and goodness; and that they might know what He required, He had defined his will in two-fold law. His far-reaching and all-embracing plan had for its end the universality of the true religion in an age of universal uprightness, peace, and prosperity — the goal to which all history tended — "the reign of God." The influence of these conceptions in practical religion will be further considered when we come to treat of Jewish piety.

There are, however, phenomena from which it has been inferred that the conception of God which dominated Jewish thought and feeling was radically at variance with that which appears in the explicit and consentient testimony we have adduced. In the endeavor to exalt God uniquely above the world, Judaism, it is said, had in fact exiled him from the world in lonely majesty, thus sacrificing the immediacy of the religious relation, the intimate communion of the soul with God. In exaggerated forms of this theory, philosophical terminology is abused, and the God of Judaism is qualified as 'absolute' or 'transcendent.'[1] It is necessary, therefore, to examine more closely the grounds on which this opinion is based.

[1] See 'Christian Writers on Judaism,' Harvard Theological Review, XIV (1921), 197–254, especially pp. 226 ff.

One of the arguments put in the foreground is the names and titles of God which prevail in the literature of the period, particularly those which express his exaltation, majesty and supremacy, and the circumlocutions which displace the simple appellative.

The proper name of the national God, יהוה, now become universal God, had long since ceased to be commonly used. No date can be fixed for either the beginning or the consummation of this disuse. In the later books of the Old Testament it occurs with declining frequency.[1] In one of the collections of Psalms incorporated in the Psalter, an editor substituted the appellative, God, for the proper name.[2] The Greek version represents the name by 'the Lord' (ὁ κύριος), and subsequent translators did the same. Where the synagogue lessons were read in Hebrew, the reader substituted *Adonai*, 'the Lord,' for the proper name, both in the original and in the vernacular translation (Targum),[3] and doubtless a similar evasion was customary in the schools.[4] Neither Philo nor Josephus had any inkling that it had ever been otherwise.[5]

According to Philo the proper name might be uttered only in the temple. There, down to the destruction of Jerusalem, it was

---

[1] In some of the latest, however, the Tetragrammaton is used freely. When once the principle was established that it was not to be pronounced, but a substitute such as 'the (ineffable) Name,' 'God,' 'the Lord,' read in its place, there was no reason for not writing it. In the Targums it is written even where the Hebrew has *Elohim*, 'God.'

[2] Psalms 42–83. Cases in which the editorial change is especially evident are 43, 4; 44, 5; 45, 8; 50, 7; 51, 16, etc. Compare also Psalm 53 with Psalm 14. See Note 153.

[3] See Dalman, Der Gottesname Adonaj (1889), especially pp. 43–62, 62–79; cf. Worte Jesu, 146–155.

[4] In quotations of Scripture, השם, 'the Name'; Dalman Worte Jesu, 149 f.

[5] Philo, Vita Mosis ii. 11 § 114 (ed. Mangey II, 152): On the gold plate on the front of the high priest's mitre were incised the four letters of the Name, "which it is lawful only for those whose ear and tongue are purified by wisdom (the priests) to hear and utter in the sanctuary; for no other whomsoever anywhere." Josephus, Antt. ii. 12, 4: Moses asked God to tell him His name, that when he offered sacrifice he might invoke Him by name to be present at the sacrificial rites. And God indicated to him his own name, which theretofore had not been communicated to men; about which it is not lawful for me to say anything.

spoken in the benediction pronounced by the priest over the people (Num. 6, 23–27). In the synagogue a substitute was used.[1] The temple benediction was said at the daily public sacrifice, with the name 'as it is written.'[2] In the special ritual of the Day of Atonement the high priest pronounced the name ten times. The priests who stood near him fell upon their faces, the more remote said, Blessed be His name whose glorious kingdom is for ever and ever. And before either of them moved from the spot the name was hidden from them (passed from their knowledge). In former times they used to utter it with raised voice; after the unruly multiplied, they spoke it in a soft voice. Rabbi Tarfon, who as a young man had assisted at the service, testified that he tried to hear it, but the high priest uttered it so that it was drowned in the singing of the other priests. In earlier times the pronunciation of the name was taught to any man; after the multiplication of the unruly, only to proper persons.[3][4] After the destruction of the temple the tradition of the name was scrupulously guarded, and in the end it seems to have been lost altogether; in later times we hear of it only in mystical theurgic circles.[5]

There were divers motives for the disuse of the proper name, and they probably worked in the main without the clear consciousness of those who were influenced by them. Something must be allowed for an instinctive feeling that the only God has no need to be thus distinguished. So long as monotheism was still contending for supremacy it was necessary to affirm with emphasis that Jehovah is the only God; but the very emblem of its triumph was that it sufficed to say 'God.' A motive that was

---

[1] Sifrè Num. § 43 (on 6, 27) and § 39 (on 6, 22; ed. Friedmann f. 12a).

[2] M. Tamid 7, 2; M. Soṭah 7, 6. See Note 154.

[3] Jer. Yoma 40d, near end. The 'unruly' (פרוצים) are such as 'break through' the fence of the Law, disregarding all restraints and regulations. Compare Ḳiddushin 71a; Eccles. R. on 3, 11. Bacher, 'Shem ha-Meforash,' Jewish Encyclopedia, XI, 262 ff.

[4] According to Ḳiddushin 71a, only to pious members of the priesthood. Examples of the tradition of the (twelve-letter) name, ibid.

[5] See Note 155.

more on the surface was to guard the sacred name not only from abuse and profanation but from the disrespect of trivial use. An even stronger motive, perhaps, was the concern about the misuse of the name in magic. It was a universal belief in the age that the *names* of gods in incantations and adjurations put the power of these gods at the command of the magician, and no name could be more potent than that of the God of the whole world. If this was the motive for secrecy, the means defeated the end; for the *secret* name of a god is a vastly more powerful spell than that which everybody knows. The Greek magical papyri show that the adepts were alive to this fact. They knew also that the barbarous names of foreign gods are more efficacious than familiar ones; and they took full advantage of the prestige of antiquity and the mystery that surrounded the Jewish Scriptures. It is no surprise, therefore, that we find the authors of magic books acquainted with the pronunciation of the tetragrammaton, which they concealed in an abracadabra of variations.[1] The Jews similarly believed that all manner of miracles could be wrought by one who knew the secret of 'the Name.'[2] It can hardly be doubted that the use of the name had an important place in the secrets of theosophy, and that it figured among the means by which the adepts accomplished their visits to paradise.

In the Mishnah, Abba Saul contributes to the catalogue of Israelites who have no share in the Age to Come, "the man who mutters the name as it is spelled."[3] A teacher of the third century adds to these words the explanation, "as the Samaritans do when they take an oath."[4] That the Samaritans, though

---

[1] It may be conjectured that the names of God of 12 and 42, and of 72, letters (Ḳiddushin 71a; Lev. R. 23, 2), were mystifications of a similar nature and purpose. On these names see L. Blau, Das altjüdische Zauberwesen, pp. 137 ff.; also Bacher, Jewish Encyclopedia, XI, 264.

[2] Bacher, ibid. It was said that Moses killed the Egyptian (Exod. 2, 14), by pronouncing the Name over him (Exod. R. 1, 30). A Babylonian rabbi heard a Persian woman cursing her son by the Name, and instantly he died. Jer. Yoma 40d, below.

[3] M. Sanhedrin 10, 1; Sanhedrin 90a; Tos. Sanhedrin 12, 9. See Note 154.

[4] Jer. Sanhedrin 28b, top.

they substituted 'the Name' in reading the Scriptures, did pronounce it in certain circumstances is confirmed by the fact that Theodoret in the fifth century learned from them a pronunciation which agrees with what modern scholars for grammatical reasons believe to be the original sound of the name, namely Ιαβε.[1]

At the end of M. Berakot, along with other rabbinical decrees given in the face of prevalent heresies, it is said that it was ordained that a man should salute his fellow "with the Name," after Biblical examples (Ruth 2, 4; Judges 6, 12), "Ihvh be with you," with the response, "Ihvh bless thee." That this ordinance was recognized as a suspension of the law justified by exceptional circumstances is clear from the following words: 'It is a time to act for the Lord; they have made void Thy law' (Psalm 119, 126);[2] or as R. Nathan transposes it, "They have made void Thy law, it is a time to act for the Lord." What the date or occasion was is unknown. The ordinance must have been temporary, if, indeed, it actually affected the general custom. To homilists of the third century is attributed the saying that two generations used the *shem ha-meforash*, the men of the Great Assembly, and the generation that suffered the persecution of Hadrian; but there is every presumption that this is midrash, not tradition.[3]

It is frequently said by Christian scholars that the prohibition of the use of the proper name Ihvh was based on an erroneous interpretation of Lev. 24, 16, which the Jews, it is said, took to forbid on pain of death the mere utterance of the name of God.[4] There is, in fact, no evidence at all that the Jews either misunderstood or misapplied the verse in this sense; they interpreted it of cursing God by name (cf. vs. 11), and use it as authority only for the rule, "The blasphemer is not liable (to the penalty

---

[1] Quaest. xv in Exod.
[2] See above, p. 259.
[3] Midrash Tehillim on Psalm 36, 11 (ed. Buber f. 126a). See Note 155.
[4] E.g. Bousset, Die Religion des Judentums, 2 ed. p. 354, with a long list of predecessors.

of death) until he distinctly pronounces the Name."[1] The law
in Lev. 24, 16, exemplified by vs. 11 ff., is not cited as authority
for the prohibition of the enunciation of the proper name, nor in
illustration of it. The only Biblical support given to it is what
seems to us a far-fetched fancy, but was in the method of Akiba's
school a valid deduction. In Exod. 3, 15 ('This is my name forever'), the word *le'olam* ('forever') is written, not, as regularly,
לעולם but לעלם. That no such peculiarity in the letter of divine
revelation is without significance was the first principle of their
hermeneutics, and in this case, if לעלם be pronounced *le'allem*,
the significance would be, "this is my name *to conceal*."[2] It
should be needless to say that this exegetical subtlety was not
cause but consequence of the suppression of the name. The
important thing is that it never occurred to the rabbis to justify
the custom by appeal to Lev. 24. Nor was the utterance of the
name Ihvh judged by the courts as prescribed in Lev. 24, 16;
the penalty is exclusion by divine judgment from a part in the
Age to Come.[3]

Exodus 20, 7 (Deut. 5, 11). 'Thou shalt not take the name
of the Lord thy God in vain,' was rightly understood by the
Jews of oaths.[4] The words are also quoted, however, against the
unnecessary use of the name of God even in prayers.[5] The
reason for such periphrastic benedictions as "Blessed be His
name whose glorious kingdom is for ever and ever" is "that the
name of Heaven (God) be not mentioned idly."[6] If a rabbi (who

---

[1] M. Sanhedrin 7, 5; cf. Sifra on Lev. 24, 11 and 16 (ed. Weiss f. 104c, d);
Mekilta on Exod. 21, 17 (ed. Friedmann f. 82a; ed. Weiss f. 89a); Mekilta de-
R. Simeon ben Yoḥai, p. 127; Sanhedrin 55b–56a; Jer. Sanhedrin 25a. See
Dalman, Der Gottesname Adonaj, pp. 43 ff. Cf. Philo, Vita Mosis ii. 25
§ 203 f. Note 156.

[2] Jer. Yoma 40d, below (see above, p. 425); Ḳiddushin 71a; Pesaḥim
50a. See Note 157.

[3] Above, p. 426.

[4] LXX: Οὐ λήμψῃ τὸ ὄνομα Κυρίου τοῦ θεοῦ σου ἐπὶ ματαίῳ. Josephus,
Antt. iii. 5, 5: ἐπὶ μηδενὶ φαύλῳ τὸν θεὸν ὀμνύναι. Philo, De decalogo, c. 19 § 92:
ὀμνύουσι ἐπὶ τοῖς τυχοῦσιν. So also the Targums, etc. Cf. Temurah 3a. See
further, Note 158.

[5] Berakot 33a, end, and parallels.

[6] Jer. Berakot 10a, below.

has authority to do so) hears a man using the name of Heaven idly, he must excommunicate him, upon pain of a like sentence on himself.[1]

The disuse of the proper name IHVH was, thus, not the consequence of a changed idea of God or his relation to the world. It was, however, a principal cause of the introduction of many substitutionary words and phrases in which recent writers see evidence that in the Jewish thought of this period God occupied a remote supramundane sphere, too great to be immediately active in the world, and too exalted in majesty and holiness to be immediately accessible to humble piety, and that religion suffered the consequences of having to do with an absentee God.

The first of these substitutes was probably the appellative *Elohim*, God, as in the editing of Psalms 42–83; but precisely because it was the common appellative, used of heathen gods as well as of the God of Israel, it was an unsatisfactory equivalent for the proper name; and conspicuously infelicitous when, as often happens, the proper name and the appellative stood side by side in the text, as, for example, "JHVH, the God of Israel," where the result was "God, the God of Israel." We have seen that in the reading of the Scriptures *Adonai*,[2] 'Lord,' was regularly substituted, and probably the drawling pronunciation which distinguished *Adonāi* as vice-proper name from *adonai*, 'my master, my lord,' in address to a man, early established itself. But by the very fact that *Adonai* was the regular surrogate for the ineffable name it contracted something of the sacredness which belonged by nature to the latter and the same scruple attached to *Elohim* when it became a virtual proper name, 'God.'

The Bible itself is, however, much more richly provided with names, titles, appropriated epithets, of God. 'The Holy One of Israel' for example, is so common throughout the Book of Isaiah that it may be called a preferred synonym for 'the God of Israel.'

[1] Nedarim 7b. 'The Name' in these passages is not the ineffable Name, but any of the names or titles of God. See Note 159.
[2] On this substitution see Ḳiddushin 71a and Note 160.

In Jewish use the limitation, 'of Israel,' is dropped, and 'the Holy One,' usually with the appended eulogy, 'blessed is He,' is one of the commonest substitutes for the name of God or the word 'God.'

Another name, more widely distributed in the Old Testament is 'Elyon,' 'Most High,' sometimes as an attributive (El 'Elyon), more frequently as a proper noun, chiefly in poetical or elevated style.[1] By the side of El 'Elyon may be put the phrase Elohè Marom, 'God of (the) Height' (High Heaven) (Mic. 6, 6).[2] It is therefore not a new idea but a more prosaic expression when in later books he is called Elohè ha-shamaim, 'God of heaven'; and from this again it is but a step to the use of Heaven itself as a metonymy for God, as in Dan. 4, 23 (שמיא Aramaic); 1 Macc. 4, 10, 40, etc.[3]

Names or epithets of God significant of his abode in the height of heaven are no novelty in later Jewish writings; they go back at least as far as the age of the kingdoms. Their increased frequency is partly explained, as suggested above, by the disuse of the proper name, for which these old poetical words or phrases furnished welcome surrogates. Unquestionably, however, the preference for terms expressive of God's exaltation falls in with a marked tendency in the religions of the times, and notably in the religions of Syria.[4] No one, so far as I know, has been tempted to explain the Phoenician parallels by the prevalence of 'abstract' notions of deity, or to find in them a feeling of the remoteness of the gods.

There is a more general observation to be made. Whatever reflection or intent there may have been in the selection or invention of a significant title for God, as soon as it is established in

---

[1] Num. 24, 16; Deut. 32, 8; Isa. 14, 14; Gen. 14; and frequently in the Psalms. Aramaic, ע אלהא, Dan. 3, 26, 32; 5, 18, 21; עלאה alone, Dan. 4, 14, 21, 22, 29, 31; 7, 25. 'Most High' is not 'the highest god,' but the God on High. See Note 161.

[2] Marom, 'height, high heaven,' as the abode of God, Isa. 57, 15; cf. 58, 4; 24, 21.

[3] See above, p. 367. Note 162.

[4] Ibid.

use it becomes interchangeable with 'God,' and is read and heard
or said without recalling its etymology or history. The Jews who
called God 'the Most High,' or 'the Holy One,' or even 'the
Place,' meant by them all just 'God'; precisely as we call him
'the Lord' without thinking of the meaning of the word 'lord'
at all. The French Protestant, in whose Bible the name Iʜvʜ
is represented by 'l'Eternel,' does not think of God's eternity
when he hears or utters the word, more than of any of the other
attributes. We call him 'the Almighty' without emphasizing in
our minds his omnipotence above, say, his goodness.

Stress is also laid on the frequency with which in Jewish use the
title 'king' is applied to God. He is 'king of the universe' (or 'of
the ages,' τῶν αἰώνων); 'king of the world' (τοῦ κόσμου); 'king of
heaven' (or 'the heavens'); 'king of all Thy creation'; 'the great
king'; 'king of kings,'[1] etc. An example of a heaping up of titles
of royalty in a rhetorical prayer is 3 Macc. 2, 2: "Lord, Lord,
king of the heavens and ruler (δεσπότης) of all the creation, holy
among the holy, monarch, all-powerful ruler (παντοκράτωρ)," etc.
From the New Testament we may quote 1 Timothy 1, 17, in the
familiar version: "Now unto the king, eternal, immortal, invisible, the only wise God, be honor and glory forever and ever,
Amen," or from the same Epistle: "The blessed and only poten-
tate, king of kings and lord of lords, alone possessing immortality,
dwelling in unapproachable light, whom no man hath seen or
can see; to whom be honor and eternal might." Corresponding
expressions are common in the rabbinical literature.[2]

In the frequency of such phrases some modern writers find
further evidence of the inferiority of the Jewish idea of God.
"'King,' it is said, has for the Oriental an entirely different meaning from what it has for us; the word suggests the arbitrariness of

[1] Examples from the Apocrypha: Tobit 13, 6, 10; 2 Macc. 7, 9; Tobit 13,
7, 11; Judith 9, 12; Tobit 13, 15; 2 Macc. 13, 4. For other references, see
Bousset, Religion des Judentums, 2 ed. p. 431 n. 2. In the New Testament,
Matt. 5, 35; 1 Tim. 1, 17; 6, 15; Rev. 15, 3.

[2] See Note 163. It is needless to say that Christian liturgies abound in
similar ascriptions.

the tyrant and the unapproachableness of the despot. As an
oriental prince is surrounded by a hierarchy of officials in sharply
distinguished classes, so God also has his heavenly court. Access
to him is not easy. If a man wishes to approach him with a petition, he has to engage the mediation of subordinate officials." [1]

It must, I fear, be confessed that the Jews had never thought
of the advantages of a limited monarchy as a form of divine
government,[2] to say nothing of the democracy which some modern
theologians are proclaiming as the next advance in religion. But
it is only fair to say for them that they held to the revelation in
their hands, in which the royalty of God was the confidence of
the present and the assurance of the future.[3] The prophets and
psalmists would have been surprised to hear that when they
called God 'king,' the word connoted the arbitrariness of a tyrant
and the jealously guarded seclusion of a despot. And the Jews
of later times who repeated or imitated the language of Scripture
would have had no less reason to be astonished at the imputation.
That God did rule the world with almighty power directed by
perfect wisdom and perfect goodness; that its history was a
whole divine plan, the end of which was the good world to be,
when the Lord should be king over all the earth, his sovereignty
acknowledged and his righteous and beneficent will obeyed by
all creatures—this is the very essence of religious monotheism. It
was this vision and this faith ἐλπιζομένων ὑπόστασις πραγμάτων
ἔλεγχος οὐ βλεπομένων,[4] which alone sustained the Jews through
catastrophe after catastrophe, as it has so often since sustained
those who inherited it from Judaism when experience and reason
threw all their weight into the scale of despair.

It is not strange that the faith that the King of Israel, who
was king of the universe, would in the end make right prevail
over wrong in his world, vindicate his people, overthrow the

---

[1] Bousset, l. c., p. 431 f.
[2] The autocracy of God is in fact their rejection of the limited monarchy
of the supreme god in organized polytheisms.
[3] See above, p. 375.
[4] Hebrews 11, 1.

proud empire, bring in a new age, an age of uprightness and goodness, of peace and happiness, when true religion and pure morals were universal — that this faith, I say, should be kept ever before men's minds in an age that seemed to the pious Jew to be the antipodes of all this.   In such a time, as we ourselves have experienced, men either give up the very idea of a divine government of the world, or they cling with all their souls to the inscrutable sovereignty of God.   There were many Jews to whom experience seemed to prove that there is 'no judgment and no judge' in the world,[1] while others put their trust in the almighty ruler and his revealed purpose of good; and these too found confirmations in experience.

For illustration of the latter attitude we may take a verse or two from the Psalms of Solomon.   The author of the second of these hymns described the profanation of the temple by Pompey as a punishment of the sins of the Asmonaean rulers and the people of Jerusalem; he pictured the inglorious death of Pompey, his unburied body tossing neglected on the waves of the Egyptian shore: — "He never reflected that he was a man, nor thought of his end.   He said to himself, I will be lord of the land and the sea, and did not know that God is great, strong in his great might.   He is king over the heavens, judging kings and rulers. . . .   Now see, ye potentates of the earth, the judgment of the Lord, that he is a great king and just, judging all under heaven." [2]   The seventeenth Psalm, the subject of which is the future kingdom of the Messiah, the son of David, begins: "O Lord, thou art our king for ever and ever. . . .   We will hope in God our deliverer, for the might of our God is forever with mercy; and the reign of our God is forever over the nations"; and ends with the corresponding refrain, "The Lord himself is our king for ever and ever."   The hope and assurance of the messianic kingdom is God, the almighty King.

[1] Cf. Wisdom of Solomon 1, 16–2, 20.

[2] Psalms of Solomon 2, 32–36. Note the sequel: "Bless the Lord, ye that fear the Lord with intelligence, for the mercy of the Lord is upon those that fear him, with judgment," etc.

The core of the preaching and teaching of Jesus is the 'kingdom of God,' the coming time in which He shall be owned and obeyed by all men as king, and there is no equivocation in his use of the phrase. The prayer he taught his disciples, "Thy kingdom come, thy will be done on earth as it is done in heaven,' is illustrated by such a Jewish prayer as this: "We therefore trust in thee, O Lord our God, that we may soon behold the glory of thy power, to cause the idols to pass away from the earth, and the false gods shall be utterly cut off; to perfect the world in the reign (kingdom) of the Almighty, and all the children of flesh shall call upon thy name; to turn unto thyself all the wicked of the earth. All the inhabitants of the globe shall perceive and know that unto thee every knee shall bow and every tongue confess. Before thee, O Lord, our God, they shall bend the knee, and prostrate themselves; and give honor to thy glorious name. They shall take on them the yoke of thy sovereignty (kingdom),[1] and do thou reign (be king) over them soon, for ever and ever. For thine is the kingdom, and forever thou wilt reign in glory, as it is written in thy Law, 'The Lord shall reign (be king) for ever and ever.' And it is said, 'And the Lord shall be king over all the earth: in that day shall the Lord be one and his name one.'"[2] It is the prevailing opinion that this prayer was formulated in the first half of the third century, though in substance it may be much earlier. That it expresses the conception of the kingdom of God at the beginning of our era there is no question. It will be observed that there is no mention in it of the restoration of the Jewish kingdom or of the coming of the Messiah.

Somewhat has been said above of the use of the term 'the presence' (*shekinta*) in the Targums as a circumlocution when the text speaks of God's dwelling in a place or removing from one, and the like.[3] While the other buffer-words discussed in that

---

[1] Which the Jew does when he recites the Shema'.

[2] Singer, Authorised Daily Prayer Book, p. 76 f. See Elbogen, Der jüdische Gottesdienst, p. 143; Kohler, 'Alenu,' Jewish Encyclopedia, I, 336 ff.

[3] Pages 419 f.

connection (*yekara, memra*) are peculiar to the synagogue translations, 'the Presence' is frequent in the Talmud and Midrash.
Often it is a mere metonymy for 'God,' as when R. Jose ben
Ḥalafta says: "Never did the Presence descend to earth, nor did
Moses and Elijah ascend to heaven; for it is written, The heavens
are the Lord's heavens, and the earth he has given to the children
of men" (Psalm 115, 16).[1] In the passages cited above on the
omnipresence of God, the word in the texts is 'the Presence.' The
Lord was revealed in the thornbush to teach that there is no
place on earth void of the Presence; it is the Presence which,
like the sea flooding the cave, filled the tabernacle with its radiance, while the world outside was no less full of it.[2] In a much
later work ten descents of the Presence to the world are enumerated, from the first in the Garden of Eden to the last, still future,
in the days of Gog and Magog; the Scripture proofs alleged are
all verses in which God (or the Lord) comes down to earth (Gen.
11, 5, etc.), or is upon the earth, as in Gen. 3, 8; Zech. 14, 4.[3]
In a special sense God dwelt in the tabernacle, and later in the
temple. When he took up his abode in them a cloud enveloped
the tabernacle, or filled the temple, and thus veiled the glory of
the Lord, too deadly bright for mortal eyes.[4] This association of
the Presence with the manifestation of his glory in depths of
light, led, as has been remarked above, to the conception of the
Presence (*shekinah*) itself, in such connections, as light.[5]

It is, however, ordinarily perceived by faith, not by sight. All
worship demands a *praesens numen*, and however men may enter-
tain the idea of the omnipresence of God, they find it difficult to
realize his specific presence in the particular place where they
gather for religious service without some aid to faith or imagination. This is the origin and meaning of the teaching that wherever

[1] Sukkah 5a, top; cf. Mekilta on Exod. 19, 20 (ed. Friedmann f. 65b; ed.
Weiss f. 73a). where *kabod* is read in place of *shekinah*. See Note 164.
[2] Above, p. 370.
[3] Abot de-R. Nathan 34, 5. — Tannaite sources, see Note 164a.
[4] Exod. 40, 34 f.; 1 Kings 8, 10 f.; cf. Isa. 6, 1–4.
[5] More intense than that of the midsummer sun, Ḥullin 59b–60a.

ten men (the quorum of the synagogue) are met for prayer, there is the Presence. How many 'Presences' are there then? a caviller asked. R. Gamaliel (II) answered by asking an attendant, 'How does the sun get into that man's house? The sun shines, he replied, on all the world. — If the sun, one of the millions of servants that are before the blessed God, shines on all the earth, how much more the Presence (of God)! [1]

R. Isaac, a pupil of Johanan and a favorite homilist of the third century, says: "Whenever Israelites prolong their stay in the synagogues and schools, God makes his Presence tarry with them." [2] The following midrash also is handed down in the name of Isaac: "Whence do we learn that God is found in the synagogue (building)? Because it is said, 'God standeth in the congregation of God' (Psalm 82, 1). And whence that when ten are praying together the Presence is with them? Because it is said, 'God standeth in the congregation of God' (ibid.). [3] And whence that when three are sitting as judges the Presence is with them? Because it is written, 'In the midst of the judges he will judge' (Psalm 82, 1b). [4] And whence that when two are sitting and studying the Law the Presence is with them? Because it is written, 'Then those who fear the Lord spoke to each other, and the Lord hearkened and heard,' etc. (Mal. 3, 16). And whence that even when *one* is sitting and studying the Law, the Presence is with him? Because it is written, 'In every place where I cause mention to be made of my name, I will come unto thee and bless thee'" (Exod. 20, 21; E. V. 24). [5]

In all these cases the Presence is not something else than God, but a reverent equivalent for 'God,' as the beginning of the passage just quoted shows: The Holy One, Blessed is He, — a com-

---

[1] Sanhedrin 39a. The anecdote has no earlier attestation, and the form is that of the Babylonian Talmud.

[2] Pesiḳta ed. Buber f. 193a–b. See Note 165.

[3] See Note 166.

[4] *Elohim*, 'judges,' as according to Jewish interpretation in Exod. 21, 6 and elsewhere.

[5] Berakot 6a. On Exod. l. c. cf. Onkelos: "In every place where I make my Presence to rest, I will send my blessing unto thee and will bless thee."

mon metonymy—is found in the synagogue; the Presence is with the congregation gathered for prayer, etc. Similarly Christians speak of God's being in their churches, and of the presence of the Holy Spirit in their religious assemblies or with the individual in secret prayer, without meaning anything different.

In Jewish literature also the 'holy spirit' frequently occurs in connections in which 'the Presence' (*shekinah*) is elsewhere employed, without any apparent difference of meaning;[1] but the fact that within a certain range the terms are interchangeable is far from warranting the inference that *shekinah* and *ruḥ hakodesh* were identified in conception. In the Jewish thought of the time the specific function of the holy spirit was the inspiration of prophecy or of Scripture, differing in this respect from the Old Testament as well as from Christian usage.

Some older Protestant theologians, in their misdirected search for Christian dogmas in Jewish disguises found the *Shekinah*, as well as the *Memra* — always the question-begging proper name with a capital! — to their purpose, and recognized in them the same 'hypostasis.' So far as making the Presence something distinct from God goes, they had an eminent Jewish precursor in Maimonides. His Arab-Aristotelian metaphysics made of God simple Unity in so rigorous a sense as to exclude all attributes, whether defined as essential, accessory, or relative, and he regarded the ascription of attributes to God as merely a subtler kind of anthropomorphism. He was constrained, therefore, like Philo, to interpret much of the Bible as metaphor or allegory. Assuming that Onkelos was actuated by similar ideas in his endeavor to render the anthropomorphic expressions in the Pentateuch innocuous by paraphrase,[2] he held that the Glory, the Word, the Presence, in the Targum mean created (physical) things, distinct from God; the Glory and the Presence being of the nature of light.[3] It does not follow that Maimonides con-

---

[1] See Note 167.

[2] Expressions implying motion were peculiarly objectionable: a God who is not in space cannot change place.

[3] Moreh Nebukim i. 21; cf. also chapters 10, 25, 28, and 64.

sidered these things as permanently existent, still less that he ascribed to them personality; and in expressly making them *created* beings he excludes the idea of any participation in divine nature or 'essence.' The philosophical horror of 'anthropomorphisms' which Philo and Maimonides entertained was unknown to the Palestinian schools. They endeavored to think of God worthily and to speak of him reverently; but their criterion was the Scripture and the instinct of piety, not an alien metaphysics. More recently, with no better reason, these 'intermediaries' have had to do duty again for the remoteness of God.[1]

The agencies which God employs to manifest his presence or convey his revelation, or execute his will, whether personal or impersonal, may in this function be called intermediaries, as Moses is called an intermediary in the giving of the Law;[2] but not 'mediators' in the sense which we commonly attach to the word.[3]

That the angels intercede for men, and particularly for Israel, is a notion frequently found in apocalypses and popular writings. Especially in parts of Enoch and in the Testaments of the Twelve Patriarchs, they bring before God the cause of those who have been wronged, and invoke his intervention; and they present to him the prayers of the righteous.[4] Biblical precedent for the unsolicited intercession of angels may be found in Zech. 1, 12, where the angel of the Lord pleads for God's compassion on Jerusalem that had so long lain in ruins; and especially in Job 33, 23; (when a man is pining away to his death) 'If there be for

---

[1] See 'Christian Writers on Judaism,' Harvard Theological Review, XIV (1921), pp. 222 ff.

[2] Gal. 3, 19; Heb. 8, 6; Pesiḳta ed. Buber f. 45a; Jer. Megillah 74d, above, and elsewhere. In Philo, Moses takes the part of μεσίτης καὶ διαλλακτής after the sin of the golden calf. Vita Mosis ii. 19 § 166 (ed. Mangey II, 160). Assumption of Moses 1, 14 (arbiter testamenti illius); 3, 12.

[3] On the Logos in Philo see Note 168.

[4] Enoch 9; 15, 2; 40, 6; 99, 3; 104, 1; Testaments of the Twelve Patriarchs, Levi, 3, 5, with Charles' note *in loc.*; Revelation of John 8, 3 f.; Tobit 12, 12, 15. In the Talmud, Michael offers upon the heavenly altar, Ḥagigah 12b. See Note 169.

him an angel, an intercessor, one of a thousand, to vouch for man's uprightness, then is He gracious unto him and saith, Deliver him from going down to the pit,' etc.[1]

But man is not dependent on angelic intercession. The attitude of orthodox Judaism is represented by R. Judan [2] in the following often quoted utterance: "If a man has a patron, when a time of trouble comes upon him, he does not at once enter into his patron's presence, but comes and stands at the door of his house and calls one of the servants or a member of his family, who brings word to him, 'So and so is standing at the entrance of your court.' [3] Perhaps the patron will let him in, perhaps he will make him wait. Not so is God. If trouble comes upon a man, let him not cry to Michael or to Gabriel; but let him cry unto Me, and I will answer him forthwith, as the Scripture says, 'Whosoever shall call on the name of the Lord shall be delivered' (Joel 3, 5 = E. V. 2, 32).[4]

That imagination pictured the sovereign of the universe throned above the highest heaven, surrounded by a countless host of worshipping and ministering spirits, did not hinder the Jews from believing him near when they called upon him; nor did they think him so preoccupied with the great affairs of the world as to have no interest in their very small affairs. Reverence might dictate a phraseology which seems to us artificial or turgid. Precautions might be taken where they seemed necessary against the tendency of the common mind to image God as an unnaturally magnified man; but, on the other hand, the teachers are fond of dwelling on what we may call the humanity of God, and that not merely as an example to men, but as a revelation of his own character. They do not even allow the dignity of God to check a kind of playfulness in their speech of him, which readers unfamiliar with the ways of the Midrash sometimes decry as fatuous. A lady [5] once asked Jose ben Ḥalafta:

---

[1] Cf. also 5, 1.　　[2] A favorite homilist of the fourth century.
[3] The outside door.　　[4] Jer. Berakot 13a below. See Note 170.
[5] מטרונה (matrona), a Gentile lady of rank.

What has your God been doing since he finished making the
world? He has been matching couples in marriage, was the
reply, the daughter of so and so for so and so, so and so's wife
for so and so. The lady declared that she could do as much as
that herself; nothing easier than to couple any number of slaves
with as many slave girls. You may think it easy, he said, but
for God it is as difficult as the dividing of the Red Sea. The lady
accordingly tried the experiment with a thousand male and as
many female slaves, setting them in rows and bidding this man
take this woman, and so on. Next morning they came to her,
one with a broken head, another with gouged out eyes, a third
with a broken leg; one man saying, I don't want her, and a girl
saying, I don't want him. So that the lady was constrained to
admit that the mating of men and women was a task not unworthy of the attention or beneath the intelligence of God.[1]

A topic not infrequently adverted to in rabbinic teaching is
the humility of God. Idea and word come from Psalm 18, 36,
'Thy humility has made me great.' [2] Modern translators have
balked at the word. The Authorized English version turns
humility into 'gentleness' (margin, 'meekness'), others say
'condescension.' The Jews seem to have seen no impropriety
in God's being humble, or lowly. The quality is illustrated by
comparing God's demeanor towards men with that of a master to
his disciple, or that of an earthly king, showing how regardless
God is of the precedence due his rank, on which men so strenu-
ously insist for themselves.[3]

R. Johanan said: "Wherever (in the Scripture) you find the
almighty power of God, you will find in the context his lowly
deeds. This is taught in the Pentateuch, and repeated in the
Prophets, and again in the Hagiographa. In the Pentateuch:

---

[1] Pesiḳta ed. Buber f. 11b–12a; Gen. R. 68, 4, and elsewhere. See Note
171.

[2] ענותך תרבני. A different interpretation would have been possible without changing the text.

[3] Tanḥuma ed. Buber, Bereshit 4; cf. Midrash Tehillim on Psalm 18, 36
(ed. Buber f. 78a–79b).

'The Lord your God is the God of gods and the Lord of lords [the mighty and the awful,' etc.]; and in the sequel it is written, 'He doth execute justice for the fatherless and the widow [and loveth the stranger, giving him food and raiment'] (Deut. 10, 17 f.). In the Prophets, 'Thus saith the high and lofty one that inhabiteth eternity, whose name is Holy, [I dwell in the high and holy place']; and in the sequel, 'with him also that is of a contrite and humble spirit,' etc. (Isa. 57, 15). In the Hagiographa, 'Extol him that rideth upon the skies by Jah, his name,' [1] and in the sequel, 'A father of the fatherless, and a judge of the widows [is God in his holy habitation'] (Psalm 68, 5 f.)." [2]

A later homilist, Eleazar ben Pedat, adds to the three verses cited by Johanan four others in which God puts himself on a level with the lowly, namely, Psalm 138, 6; Isa. 66, 1 f.; Psalm 10, 16–18; Psalm 146, 6–10. [3] In these also the point is the juxtaposition of the greatness of God with his personal concern for the humble, the needy, the distressed. God's interest in the common joys and sorrows of men is illustrated by R. Simlai in words that are often repeated: "We find that God pronounces a benediction on bridegrooms, and adorns brides, and visits the sick, and buries the dead, and comforts mourners." [4] These offices of humanity are evidences not merely of the general goodness of God, but of that highest kind of charity which involves personal sympathy and service. [5] In such deeds of kindness God is a pattern for man's imitation; this is what is meant when it is said, 'Walk after the Lord thy God,' that is, imitate these traits of God's character and conduct. As he clothed the naked, visited the sick, comforted the mourners, so do thou also. [6]

---

[1] See Note 172.

[2] Megillah 31a.

[3] Tanḥuma ed. Buber, Wayyera 3 (f. 42b). Buber reads, "with the hearts of the lowly." See his note in loc.

[4] Gen. R. 8, 13; Eccles. R. on Eccles. 7, 2; Tanḥuma ed. Buber, Wayyera 1 (f. 42a), and ibid. 4 (f. 43b); Soṭah 14a. For the Scriptures see Gen. 1, 28; 2, 22; 3, 21; 18, 1; Deut. 34, 6; Gen. 35, 9.

[5] גמילות חסדים. Vol. II, pp. 171 ff.

[6] Soṭah 14a.

It would be easy to multiply utterances of this kind, for which the Scriptures furnish abundant occasion. Those which have been quoted suffice to show that the exaltation of God was not his exile. He who dwells in the high and holy place, dwells no less with him that is of a contrite and humble spirit. His almighty power and his humility go together; he is lofty enough to think nothing beneath him, great enough to count nothing too small to be his concern. The conclusive proof of this is the whole character of Jewish piety in those centuries, and the intimacy of the religious relation which is expressed by the thought of God as Father, which will be discussed in later chapters.[1]

[1] See Vol. II. pp. 201 ff.

PART III

MAN, SIN, ATONEMENT

CHAPTER I

THE NATURE OF MAN

THE unity of mankind was too plainly written in the Scriptures to leave room for any question. All the races of men are descended from a single pair, to whom with their posterity God gave the generic name Man (Heb. *adam*).[1] That God made from one (ancestor) every race of men to settle all over the face of the earth in times and bounds of his appointment,[2] was universal Jewish doctrine. The reason Paul gives is that men of all nations might feel their way to the one true God who is not far from every one of us, and find him. In the Mishnah, in the solemn admonition to witnesses in a capital case, not by false testimony to be the cause of the death of a man and of his (potential) offspring, we read, "For this reason a single man only was created, to teach you that if one destroys a single person,[3] the Scripture imputes it to him as though he had destroyed the whole (population of the) world, and if he saves the life of a single person, the Scripture imputes it to him as though he had saved the whole world." [4] This gives occasion to introduce various other reasons why only one man was created. All men, notwithstanding their different appearance, were stamped by God with one seal, the seal of Adam. "Therefore every man is bound to say, On account of *me* the world was created." That is, every man is to feel himself individually responsible, as though the whole human race depended on his conduct. Other reasons of a more obvious character are added in the Mishnah and the

---

[1] Gen. 1, 26 f.; 5, 2 f.; 9, 5–7. See Philo, De opificio mundi c. 24 § 76 (ed. Mangey, I, 17); De Abrahamo c. 12 § 56 (II, 9).

[2] Acts 17, 26.

[3] The words 'of Israel' found in some editions here and in the corresponding place below are modern interpolations.

[4] M. Sanhedrin 4, 5. See also Note 173.

parallel Tosefta. It was to keep one man from saying to
another, My forefather was greater than yours — to exclude
pride of ancestry; or to prevent families from quarreling, and
men from assaulting and robbing one another, by the reflection
that they are all of one stock.[1]

Not only are all the races of men derived in the genealogies
of Genesis from one common ancestor, whose name Adam (Man)
is only the appropriation of the appellative by which all his kind
are named, and again after the flood from one man Noah through
his three sons,[2] but the whole conception of history as a divine
plan, from the point of view of the unity of God, assumes the
unity of mankind.

Man was made in the image and likeness of God.[3] R. Akiba,
in a sentence already quoted in another connection, said: "Dear
(to God) is man, in that he was created in the (divine) image;
still more dear in that it is known to him that he was created
in the image, as it is said, In the image of God he made the man"
(Gen. 5, 1).[4] In the last words Akiba's younger contemporary,
Simeon ben 'Azzai, finds the most comprehensive principle of the
law governing man's dealings with his fellow — the image of
God must be reverenced in our common humanity.[5] In the law
itself this principle is applied to manslaughter: 'Whoso shed-
deth man's blood, by man shall his blood be shed; for in the
image of God made He man' (Gen. 9, 6);[6] even a beast that
kills a man is under the same condemnation (Gen. 9, 5; cf.
Exod. 21, 28 ff.) A wide extension is given to the principle in a
Midrash: "See that thou do not say, Inasmuch as I have been

---

[1] M. Sanhedrin l. c.; Tos. Sanhedrin 8, 4 f.; Sanhedrin 38a.

[2] Gen. 10.

[3] Gen. 1, 27, cf. vs. 26; 5, 1; 9, 6; Psalm 8, 5 ff.

[4] Abot 3, 14. In Abot de-R. Natan c. 39 attributed in abbreviated form
to R. Meir, the disciple of Akiba. See Bacher, Tannaiten, I, 279.

[5] Sifra, Ķedoshim Perek 4, 12 (on Lev. 19, 18; ed. Weiss f. 89b); Jer.
Nedạrim 41c; Gen. R. 24, 7, with Theodor's note there. See Note 174, and
below, Vol. II, p. 85.

[6] Mekilta, Baḥodesh 8 (ed. Friedmann f. 70b; ed. Weiss f. 78a).

despised, my fellow shall be despised with me; inasmuch as I have been cursed, my fellow shall be cursed with me. R. Tanḥuma said, If thou doest thus, reflect whom thou dost despise — 'In the image of God He made him.'" [1]

In Leviticus Rabbah (34, 3) it is narrated of Hillel that in one of his last conversations with his disciples he found in the words of Genesis the obligation to keep the body clean by bathing: Those who are in charge of the images of kings which are set up in their theatres and circuses scour them and wash them off, and are rewarded and honored for so doing; how much more I, who was created in the image and likeness (of God), as it is written, 'In the image of God He created man' (Gen. 5, 1).[2]

The divine likeness was the common inheritance of mankind — that was the point on which Jewish thought seized to draw from it a moral consequence, a universal principle of conduct Wherein more specifically the resemblance lay, does not seem to have been a subject of speculation in the Palestinian schools. When the question was raised, with whom God was talking when he said, 'Let us make man in our image after our likeness,' [3] the most natural answer was, With the angels, who are called in the Bible *bene elohim*, 'divine beings,' or simply *elohim*, 'divinities,' the 'household above,' with which God habitually consulted.[4] The divine image could thus be conceived as a likeness to the angels, the more easily as in Bible story angels always appear in the form of men. The words of God in Gen. 3, 22, 'Behold the man is become as one of us in knowing good and evil,' were taken by R. Pappos, a contemporary of Akiba, to mean that he was become in this respect like one of the ministering angels;

[1] Gen. R. 24, 7. See Theodor's note *ad loc.*

[2] It is to be remarked that this is immediately followed by another saying, the point of which is the attention to be paid to the soul, the transient guest in the body, which is here today, and tomorrow is gone.

[3] Gen. 1, 26 f. and 3, 22 were early brought into the field by Christian apologists; e.g. Justin, Trypho, c. 62.

[4] See above, pp. 392, 407 f. The angels protested against the creation of man, quoting Psalm 8, 5.

whilst Akiba interpreted, "God set before him two ways, one of death and the other of life, and he chose the way of death." [1]

In Psalm 8, 6–9, with obvious reminiscence of Gen. 1, 26–28, the poet says of man: 'Thou madest him scarcely inferior to divine beings,[2] and didst crown him with glory and honor; thou gavest him dominion over the works of thy hand, everything thou didst put under his feet,' etc. The amplified paraphrase in Ecclus. 17, beginning, "After his own image He made them, and put the fear of him upon all flesh, and (gave him) to have dominion over beasts and birds" (17, 3 f.), dwells in the sequel on man's intellectual endowment, but does not bring it into any closer connection with the divine image.[3]

It was natural that Jews whose notions of human nature had been formed under the influence of Greek thought should put more definitely the question wherein the image of God in man consisted. And in accord with Greek ideas the author of the Wisdom of Solomon answers, In immortality: "For God created man for immortality, and made him the image of his own peculiar nature; but by the envy of the devil death entered into the world," etc. (2, 23 f.).[4] A blessed immortality is the essential nature of deity; participation in it, or the potentiality of it, is that wherein God made man like himself.

Philo, from his Platonic premises, finds the image of God in the soul of man, more specifically in the intellectual soul.

"Moses did not liken the form of the rational soul to any created thing, but spoke of it as a tested and approved coin (bearing the figure) of that divine and invisible spirit, marked and stamped by the seal of God, whose impression is the eternal Logos. For he says, 'God breathed into his face a breath of life,' so that necessarily he who receives (this breath) represents

---

[1] Mekilta, Beshallaḥ 6, on Exod. 14, 28 (ed. Friedmann f. 33a; ed. Weiss f. 40a). See Bacher, Tannaiten, I, 317 f. On the Two Ways see Note 175.

[2] מאלהים. The versions unanimously, "than angels," doubtless in the sense of the author.   [3] See Note 176.

[4] With the variant, ἀϊδιότητος, 'eternity.' The same variant in Philo, De aeternitate mundi § 75 (ed. Cohn).

Him who sends it forth; wherefore also it is said that the man was created after the image of God, not, of a truth, after the image of any created thing."[1]

With the likeness of God was given to man dominion over the living creatures, the fish of the sea and the fowls of the air, domestic cattle and wild beasts,[2] and all the smaller animals (Gen. 1, 26), with the commission: 'Increase and multiply and fill the earth and subdue it, and subject the fish of the sea,' etc. (vs. 28; cf. also Psalm 8, 7 f.).[3]

The Syriac Apocalypse of Baruch expresses the Jewish understanding of man's place in the creation thus: "Long ago when the world with its inhabitants was not yet in being, thou didst conceive the thought, and command with a word, and at once the works of creation stood before thee. And thou saidst that thou wouldst make for thy world man an administrator of thy works, that it might be known that he was not made for the sake of the world, but the world for his sake." [4] That the world and everything in it was made for man is in fact a natural conclusion from the place given him in the story of creation, as well as from his own valuation of himself as the summit of creation. Cicero argues it from the latter point of view, and it is frequently asserted by Christian Apologists.[5]

In Jewish sources it is commoner to find that the world was made for Israel, a view which need not be taken as a piece of national vanity.[6] To Israel had been given the revelation of

---

[1] De plantatione Noe c. 5 (ed. Mangey, I, 332); cf. Quis rerum divinarum heres c. 48 (I, 505); De opificio mundi c. 23 § 69 (I, 15 f.); c. 51 (I, 35). For Philo it is a likeness at the third remove: God, Logos, Ideal Man, actual individual man. See Note 177.

[2] Emending וכל חית הארץ; cf. vs. 30.

[3] See also Wisdom 9, 2 f.

[4] Syriac Baruch 14, 17 f.; cf. 21, 24.

[5] Cicero, Natura deorum ii. 53 § 133; Justin Martyr, Apology ii. 4, 2; cf. i. 10, 2; Trypho 41, 1; Apology of Aristides, c. 1; Ep. to Diognetus c. 10, etc.; Origen, Contra Celsum iv. 23.

[6] Cf. Hermas, Vis. i. 1, 6: "God, who dwells in heaven, and created the things that are out of what was not, and increased and multiplied them for the

the true religion (for which it is elsewhere said that the world was created), which is one day to be the universal religion. It is indeed frequently not Israel but the righteous in whose favor the inference is drawn. Thus in Sifrè Deut. § 47 (on Deut. 11, 21): "As the heavens and the earth which were created only for the honor of Israel live and abide for eternal ages, how much more the righteous for whose sake the world was created."[1] In the same context, R. Joshua ben Ḳarḥa, a disciple of Akiba, quotes Eccles. 1, 4, 'A generation goes and a generation comes, while the earth lasts for ever.' "It ought to be, The earth goes and the earth comes, and the generation (of men) lasts for ever. For which was created for the sake of which? Was the earth created for the sake of the generation, or the generation for the sake of the earth? Was it not the earth for the sake of the generation? But the generation, because it does not abide by the commands of God, passes away, while the earth, because it abides by the commands of God, does not pass away."[2]

The question why man should be created at all, which was raised by the ministering angels when they learned God's purpose, is answered by Him, Who then shall fulfil my law and commandments? The angels themselves could not do it, for it supposed conditions which did not exist among them, for example, in rites connected with death or birth, permitted and prohibited food, or sacrificial worship.[3] That is, man was made that there might be creatures to fulfil the Law, or, in other words, to practise a human religion. On the other hand, in Ecclesiastes Rabbah on 1, 4, in the sequel of the passage quoted above,

---

sake of his holy church," etc. The world made for Israel, 4 Esdras 6, 55, 59; 7, 11; Assumption of Moses 1, 12; Pesiḳta Rabbati ed. Friedmann f. 135a–b.

[1] Cf. Syriac Baruch 15, 7; cf. 21, 24. The world created only for him who fears God (the religious man), Berakot 6b, end.

[2] More fully in Eccles. R. on Eccles. 1, 4, from which this translation is made; see Bacher, Tannaiten, II, 319.

[3] Tanḥuma ed. Buber, Beḥuḳḳotai § 6 (f. 56b). There seems to be no earlier trace of this anonymous midrash, which stands in a group of more or less ingenious twists of Psalm 89, 7.

the Law was created for the sake of Israel, not Israel for the Law.[1]

The dual nature of man is a frequent subject of remark. Rabbi Simai said:[2] "All the creatures that were created from the heaven, their soul and their body was from heaven (of celestial substance); and all the creatures that were created from the earth, their soul and their body was of the earth, except man, whose soul is from heaven, his body from the earth.[3] Therefore if a man keeps the law and does the will of his Father who is in heaven, he is like the creatures above, as it is written, 'I said ye are divine beings, and sons of the Most High, all of you'; but if he does not keep the law and do the will of his Father who is in heaven, he is like the creatures below, as it is written, 'Surely like man ye shall die'" (Psalm 82, 6 and 7).[4]

God created man with four characteristics of the creatures above and four of those below; he eats and drinks like the cattle, like them he multiplies, voids excrement, and dies; he stands erect like the ministering angels, like them also he has speech, and reason, and sees like them (not like cattle whose eyes are in the side of their head).[5] In a Baraita in Ḥagigah 16a only three characteristics on each side are enumerated (dying and seeing not being specified), and instead of merely possessing speech, men like the ministering angels talk the sacred language (Hebrew).[6] Man is thus on one side of his nature akin to the angels, on the other to the brutes, and takes rank in the creation above

[1] It cannot be said too often that such variations are not differences of opinion, still less conflicting teachings, but casual exegetical or homiletical conceits. See also Gen. R. 1, 4.

[2] Probably in the latter part of the second century. Bacher, Tannaiten, II, 543 ff.

[3] Cf. Tanḥuma ed. Buber, Bereshit § 15 (R. Simeon ben Laḳish): He created man's body from (the earth) below and his soul from (heaven) above. Bacher, Pal. Amoräer, I, 412 f.

[4] Sifrè Deut. § 306 (on Deut. 32, 2; f. 132a, near end).

[5] Gen. R. 8, 11; 14, 3. Bacher, Pal. Amoräer, II, 22 f.

[6] See Note 178.

the one or below the other according to his character. This is
the sense of a midrash found in several places, attributed to R.
Simeon ben Laḳish: If a man is worthy (וכה), they say to him,
Thou didst precede the ministering angels (or, as another source
has it, the whole creative work); if not, they say to him, Insects
and worms preceded thee.[1]

The dual nature of man is the subject of a fine passage in
Philo. Man, according to Moses, is composite of earthy matter
and divine spirit; for the artist took clay and moulded out of
it a human form, and thus the body was made; but the soul is
not derived from any originated thing whatever, but from the
father and ruler of the universe. For what He breathed in was
nothing else than a divine breath (spirit) which from that blessed
and happy nature is sent to sojourn hither for the good of our
race, in order that, though in respect to its visible part it be
mortal, in respect to its invisible part it is made immortal. So
we may properly say that man is intermediate between mortal
and immortal nature, sharing in each so far as needs be, and that
he is at once mortal and immortal — mortal as to his body, immortal as to his intellect.[2] Greek philosophy, however, has
here contributed everything but the text (Gen. 2, 7). The
'breath of life' ($\pi\nu o\grave{\eta}\ \zeta\omega\hat{\eta}s$) which God breathed into Adam's
nostrils, thus making him 'a living soul' (person), turns into a
$\pi\nu\epsilon\hat{v}\mu a$-soul of obvious Stoic extraction, for which, as the immortal in man, Philo in the end substitutes 'intellect' ($\delta\iota\acute{a}\nu o\iota a$),
like a true Platonist.

There are various fantasies in the Midrash about the creation
of Adam on which it would be idle to dwell here. One, repeated
in several places, attributes to him enormous dimensions: he
was a huge mass that filled the whole world to all the points of

[1] Gen. R. 8, 1; Lev. R. 14, 1; Tanḥuma ed. Buber, Tazri'a § 2. The
soul of Adam was created before the works of the sixth day (or on the first
day); his body after the creeping things on the sixth day. (The angels were
created on the second day or on the fifth; see above, p. 381.) See Note 179.

[2] Philo, De opificio mundi c. 46 § 135 (ed. Mangey, I, 32).

the compass.[1] The dust of which his body was formed was gathered from every part of the world,[2] or from the site of the future altar.[3] Of greater interest is the notion that man was created androgynous, because it is probably a bit of foreign lore adapted to the first pair in Genesis. R. Samuel bar Naḥman (third century), said, When God created Adam, he created him facing both ways (דיו פרצופים); then he sawed him in two and made two backs, one for each figure.[4] In the same paragraph of Genesis Rabbah a homilist of the fourth century says, When God created Adam he created him androgynous (אנדרוגינוס): this is what is written, 'Male and female he created them.'[5]

In the Bible it is affirmed, or consistently assumed, that God has taught men what is right and what is wrong, set before them the consequences of the alternatives, and left them to choose between them. So God did with Adam in the Garden; so he did with Noah for himself and his posterity of all races (Gen. 9), of which Judaism made the so-called Noachian precepts, a law binding on all mankind. At Sinai again, God offered the whole Law to all the seventy nations, and as a whole they refused it.[6] A fundamental passage for the Jewish apprehension of man's relation to God's revealed will is Deut. 11, 26–28: 'Behold I have set before you this day a blessing and a curse; the blessing in case ye shall hearken unto the commandments of the Lord your God which I command you this day, and the curse if ye shall not hearken unto the commandments of the Lord your God, but turn aside out of the way which I command you this

---

[1] Lev. R. 18, 2 (Joshua ben Levi); Gen. R. 8, 1, and elsewhere.

[2] Sanhedrin 38 a, end.

[3] The earth for the body of the first man was taken from the place where in future atonement should be made (the altar of earth, Exod. 20, 21); Gen. R. 14, 8; Jer. Nazir 56b, below. See Note 180.

[4] Gen. R. 8, 1, דיו פרצופין, דיפרוסופן. Bacher, Pal. Amoräer, I, 547 and n. 3, cites the parallels and various attributions. — Plato, Symposium 189D–190A. See Note 181.

[5] Jeremiah ben Eleazar.

[6] See above, pp. 227, 278.

day,' etc.[1] Similarly Deut. 30, 15–20: 'See, I have set before thee this day life and good, and death and evil, in that I command thee this day to love the Lord thy God, to walk in his ways, to keep his commandments and his statutes and his ordinances. . . . I call heaven and earth to witness against you this day that I have set before thee life and death, the blessing and the curse; therefore choose life, that thou mayest live, thou and thy posterity,' etc. The choice is left to man; but lest Israel should say, Inasmuch as God has set before us two ways, we may go in whichever we please, the Scripture adds, 'Choose life, that thou mayst live, and thy posterity.'[2] In the sequel is a comparison of the two ways, one of which is at the outset a thicket of thorns but after a little distance emerges into an open plain, while the other is at first a plain, but presently runs out into thorns. So it is with the way of the righteous and the way of the wicked.[3]

That man is capable of choosing between right and wrong and of carrying the decision into action was not questioned, nor was any conflict discovered between this freedom of choice with its consequences and the belief that all things are ordained and brought to pass by God in accordance with his wisdom and his righteous and benevolent will. The theological problem of the freedom of the will in relation to the doctrine of divine providence and the omniscience of God did not emerge until the tenth century, when Jewish thinkers like Saadia (d. 942) heard around them on every hand the Moslem controversies over predestination.[4] Long before there was any theologizing on this point, it had been necessary to assert emphatically the responsibility of man for what he does and is, against such as were inclined to put off on God the responsibility for their misdeeds, just as it was

---

[1] On this passage see Sifrè Deut. § 53–54.

[2] Sifrè on Deut. 11, 26 (§ 53).

[3] Ibid. Bacher, Tannaiten, II, 302 f.

[4] The mediaeval Jewish philosophers almost without exception maintained the freedom of the will.

necessary to affirm the doctrine of retribution against those who thought that God let things in the world go their own gait, and that there was no such thing as a moral providence.

Thus Sirach: "Say not, It was the Lord's fault that I fell away . . . say not, He led me astray. . . . He made man from the beginning, and left him to his own counsel.[1] If thou willst, thou wilt keep the commandments, and to deal faithfully is a matter of choice.[2] He has set before thee fire and water, thou canst stretch out thy hand to whichever thou willst. Before man are life and death, and whichever he chooses will be given him."[3] The same freedom is asserted in the Psalms of Solomon (9, 4): "Our deeds are in the choice and power of our soul, to do righteousness and iniquity in the works of our hands."[4] The author of Fourth Esdras, agonizing over the problem how the perdition of the mass of mankind, Gentile and Jew, can consist with the character of God, does not impugn God's justice in condemning them. "Ask no more about the multitude of those who perish," the angel answers, "for they themselves, having freedom given them, spurned the Most High, and despised his law and abandoned his ways."[5]

The rabbinical teaching is in complete accord with this, as appears in the passage from Sifrè Deut. §§53–54 cited above.[6] The sententious words of Akiba are familiar: "Everything is foreseen (by God), and freedom of choice is given (to man), and the world is judged with goodness, and all depends on the preponderance of (good or ill) doing."[7] Simeon ben ʿAzzai, Akiba's younger contemporary, quotes the phrase, 'freedom of choice

---

[1] καὶ ἀφῆκεν αὐτὸν ἐν χειρὶ διαβουλίου αὐτοῦ. See Note 182.

[2] Text and translation of this hemistich are very doubtful. See Note 183.

[3] Ecclus. 15, 11–17.

[4] Note the sequel (vs. 9): He who does righteousness treasures up life for himself with the Lord, and he who does unrighteousness is himself responsible for his life in its destruction.

[5] 4 Esdras 8, 55 f.; note also the following verses, and see further 7, 19–24.

[6] Sifrè Deut. § 54 adduces also the words of God to Cain, Gen. 4, 7, to the same intent.

[7] Abot 3, 15. Bacher, Tannaiten, I, 275. With the last clause, cf. above, p. 379.

is given,' in a context which attaches decisive importance to man's primary choice to attend to the words of God or not.[1] If a man of his own accord resolves to hearken (to the command of God), he will be helped to do so without his endeavor; if to forget (ignore) them, he will be made to do so when he does not wish to. 'Freedom of choice is given' — as in Proverbs 3, 34, 'If it is with the scorners, He scorns them, but unto the humble He gives favor.' Others preferred for a proof-text Exod. 22, 25.[2]

In the same sense, a later homilist, brings verses from the Law, the Prophets, and the Hagiographa to prove that a man is led (by God) in the way in which he chooses to go (Num. 22, 13 and 20; Isa. 48, 17; Prov. 3, 34).[3] R. Simeon ben Laḳish, quoting Prov. 3, 34, comments: "If a man comes to defile himself, the opportunity is given him (by God); if to purify himself, he is helped to do it."[4] Well known is also the saying of R. Ḥanina (bar Ḥama, early in the third century): "Everything is in the power of Heaven except the fear of Heaven; 'Now, O Israel, what doth the Lord thy God require of thee but to revere the Lord thy God, to walk in all his ways, to love him,'" etc. (Deut. 10, 12).[5] God in his providence determines beforehand what a man shall be and what shall befall him, but not whether he shall be godly or godless, righteous or wicked.[6] As the proof-text says, religion is the one thing that God *requires* of man; He does not *constrain* him to it. It is unnecessary to multiply examples further; there are no dissentient voices.

From Josephus, on the other hand, we should get the impression that determinism was one of the subjects chiefly in dispute between the Pharisees and the other sects. In one place, indeed, this is the only specific difference he names,[7] referring the

---

[1] Man's initial choice determines his subsequent particular choices.
[2] Mekilta on Exod. 15, 26 (ed. Friedmann f. 46a–b; ed. Weiss f. 54b). Bacher, Tannaiten, I, 412; cf. Pal. Amoräer, II, 81.
[3] Makkot 10b.
[4] Shabbat 104a and parallels.
[5] Berakot 33b; Megillah 25a; Niddah 16b.
[6] Niddah 16b.   [7] Antt. xiii. 5, 9.

reader for the rest to the fuller account in the second book of the Jewish War. As he describes it in the passage cited they were divided over destiny (εἱμαρμένη): the Essenes exempted nothing from its sway; the Sadducees denied that there was any such thing; while the Pharisees held the middle ground — some things, but not all, are the work of destiny; some are in man's own power to determine whether they shall come to pass or not.

In the account in the War (ii. 8, 14) to which Josephus refers he says that the Pharisees ascribe everything to destiny and to God; to do right or not lies principally in man's power, but destiny also is auxiliary in every action. An explanation of this is intended in Antt. xviii. 1, 3: While the Pharisees hold that all things are brought about by destiny, they do not deprive the human will of its own impulse to do them, it having pleased God that there should be a concurrence (?), and that to the deliberation of destiny that of men, in the case of one who wills, should assent, with (the concomitant of) virtue or wickedness.[1] The Sadducees deny destiny altogether, and make God incapable of doing or looking (with complacency) upon anything evil. They say that good and evil lie open to men's choice, and that according to each man's own inclination he takes to one or the other.

It suited the author to describe the Jewish sects as so many philosophies.[2] He remarks that the Essenes follow the Pythagorean mode of life;[3] and the Pharisees are very much like the Stoics.[4] Different notions about the immortality of the soul divided Greek schools of philosophy also; the problem of determinism was a subject of acute controversy among them in his time, and if the issue were to be defined in a word it would be εἱμαρμένη, 'destiny,'[5] which in Josephus occurs in all the descriptions of the Jewish sects. It seems to be generally assumed that

[1] See Note 184.
[2] Bell. Jud. ii. 8, 2 § 119; cf. Antt. xviii. 1, 2; ibid. 6 § 23.
[3] Antt. xv. 10, 4 § 371.
[4] Vita, c. 2, end.
[5] On εἱμαρμένη see Note 185.

what Josephus means is that the sects were divided over the relation of divine providence to human freedom, and that he used εἱμαρμένη for what we might call the decrees of God. It is certain, however, that no contemporary reader could have understood him in any such sense, since not only was that not the current conception of εἱμαρμένη, but he himself expressly makes 'destiny' a determining factor distinct from God, even though subordinate to him.[1]

Philo, as might be expected from his philosophical affinities, consistently maintains man's self-determination. Intelligence is the only imperishable thing in us.[2] "For it alone, the Father who begat it deemed worthy of liberty, and having loosed the bonds of necessity let it range at large, having gifted it with a portion such as it was able to receive of His own most proper and distinctive possession, the faculty of volition." Other living things, in whose souls mind, the thing for which liberty is specially claimed, does not exist, are handed over, yoked and bridled, to the service of men, as menial slaves to masters; but man, endowed with a free and self-controlled judgment and volition and acting for the most part purposefully, naturally incurs blame for the wrong he does premeditatedly, and praise for what he voluntarily does right. Plants and animals are not praiseworthy when they bear abundantly nor blamable for their failure; the motion and change that lead to one or the other was imparted to them without any preference or volition on their part. The soul of man alone, having received from God the power of moving voluntarily, and therein being made most like Him, and being liberated as far as possible from that stern and harsh tyrant, Necessity, is rightly accused, when[3] he does not give all due regard to Him who made him free; wherefore it will most justly pay the inexorable penalty visited on emancipated slaves who prove ungrateful. . . . God made man unrestrained and free, acting voluntarily and of his own choice, to the end

---

[1] Bell. Jud. ii. 8, 14; Antt. xviii. 1, 3.
[2] Διάνοια.   [3] ὅτε conj. Cohn.

that, being acquainted with bad things as well as good, and acquiring conceptions of honorable and shameful conduct, and thinking clearly about right and wrong and all that has to do with virtue and vice, he may habitually choose the better and avoid the contrary. For this reason the divine word is written in Deuteronomy, Behold, I have put before thy face life and death, good and evil; choose life!" [1]

To man alone this alternative, with its consequences, is presented. The creatures higher than he in the scale of being have no such dual nature; they are pure immaterial souls. The irrational creatures beneath him, precisely because they lack discourse of reason, cannot be guilty of the voluntary wrong-doing which comes of calculation. "Man is practically the only one of all, who, knowing the difference between good and bad, often chooses the worse and avoids what he ought to endeavor after, so that he is condemned for sins committed purposely." [2] Knowledge and freedom are the conditions of accountability. This was one of the motives God had in breathing into man the breath of life whereby he became a living soul, otherwise a man when punished for his sins might say that he was punished unjustly, and that the one really to blame was He who had not breathed into him intelligence; or that he had not sinned at all, since some say that deeds done involuntarily or in ignorance are not to be classed as wrong-doing. [3]

[1] Quod deus sit immutabilis c. 10 § 46–50 (ed. Mangey, I, 279 f.).
[2] De confusione linguarum c. 35 § 177 f. (I, 432).
[3] Legum allegor. i. 13 § 35, on Gen. 2, 7 (I, 50). Reference may also be made to De victimis c. 7 § 214 (II, 243) and the similar language in De sacrificiis Abelis et Caini c. 40 (I, 190).

CHAPTER II

SIN AND ITS CONSEQUENCES

WHERE it is believed that religion was given to men by revelation, and that it is a divinely ordained regulative for man's whole life, practical religion resolves itself into living accordingly. Duty will be defined in effect as it is in a classic Protestant symbol: "The duty which God requireth of man is obedience to his revealed will," and sin, as in the same symbol: "Sin is any want of conformity unto, or transgression of, the law of God." These succinct definitions of duty and of sin are what necessarily follow from the conceptions of revealed religion and of Sacred Scripture entertained by the Puritan and Presbyterian divines who framed them; conceptions identical with those of the Jewish doctors of the Law. If the Scribes and Pharisees of New Testament times had possessed the skill in the art of definition which Christian theologians developed in centuries of scholastic exercise, they might have put the Jewish conception in precisely the same way. They also, as we shall see, distinguished between sins of commission and of omission, transgressions of the 'Thou shalt not's' of the Law, neglect of its 'Thou shalt's.' They too recognized that "Some sins in themselves, and by reasons of several aggravations, are more heinous in the sight of God than others." [1] In short, it would be impossible to find a better formulation for the Jewish conception of sin than these definitions of the doctrine of the Reformed Churches. These Christian theologians, indeed, taught that only what they called the moral law was of perpetual obligation; [2] the ritual, ceremonial, and civil law were done away in the new dispensa-

[1] Westminster Shorter Catechism, Questions 39, 14, 83.
[2] They thought they were following Paul, but he makes no such distinction; and they included in the moral law the obligation of worship, the observance of the sabbath, etc.

It is a consequence of the fundamentally religious (i.e. non-moral) idea of sin that to constitute a sin it is not necessary that a man should know the rule of the law nor be aware that he is infringing it, still less that the intention to do an unlawful act should be present. Protestants in particular are so habituated to associate the word sin exclusively with the so-called moral law, and to regard knowledge and intention as of the essence of sin, that it requires some effort to put themselves at the point of view of the Old Testament, consistently maintained by Judaism, of which none of these things is true.[1]

With the multitudinous and minute regulations of the laws, it was inevitable that they should often be infringed in ignorance, or mistake, or pure accident. For such cases the law itself creates a special category of sins committed 'unwittingly' (בשגגה), or through inadvertence. For various sins of this class special forms of ritual expiation are prescribed.[2] The opposite is sinning 'with a high hand' (ביד רמה), wilfully and defiantly,[3] or arrogantly, insolently (בזדון).[4] For such sins no expiation is provided:[5] 'The person who does anything wilfully, whether he be native born or foreign, blasphemes the Lord, and that person shall be cut off out of the midst of his people;[6] for he despised the word of the Lord, and nullified his commandment; that person shall be utterly cut off, his guilt is upon him.'[7]

These principles are the foundation of the rabbinic teaching on the subject. In the Mishnah Shebu'ot 1, 2-2, 5, is a long casuistical discussion among teachers of the middle of the second century, further elaborated in the Talmud, concerning the respective specific and general piacula, and their efficacy in the

[1] See Note 187.
[2] Lev. 4; 5; Num. 15, 22-31; Psalm 19, 13.
[3] Num. 15, 30 f.; Psalm 19, 14.
[4] Deut. 17, 12.
[5] The same principle in the old Roman religion, see Note 188.
[6] Not by human justice but by the act of God.
[7] Num. 15, 30 f. The laws in Num. 15,1-21 to which this sanction is attached are purely ritual. See Sifrè Num. § 111 ff. (ed. Friedmann f. 31b-33b.

various conceivable cases of ignorance or forgetfulness. The
details of the casuistry are nothing to our purpose;[1] the important thing is that the offenses contemplated all have to do
with such things as eating food religiously unclean or consecrated food while the man is himself unclean, or being present
within the precincts of the temple in a state of uncleanness.[2] It
is for such sins, according to Lev. 16, 16 f., that the high priest
on the Day of Atonement with the blood of the goat of the sin-
offering makes expiation for the holy place, 'from the uncleannesses of the children of Israel and from their transgressions —
even all their sins,' and similarly for the tabernacle 'that dwells
with them in the midst of their uncleannesses.'[3]

The distinction between unwitting and wilful sins is also observed by the rabbis. Thus in Sifra on Lev. 16, 6 (the high
priest's confession over the bullock of his sin-offering, corresponding to the confession of the sins of the people over the
scapegoat), the words 'all the iniquities of the children of Israel,
and all their transgressions, even all their sins' (Lev. 16, 21) are
thus interpreted in the name of the learned (the consensus of
authority): "'Iniquities' are the 'insolent' misdeeds; 'transgressions' are 'rebellious' acts; 'sins' are the 'unwitting' offenses."[4] For the first two classes the law provides no sacrificial
atonement; Judaism found their guilt borne away by the scapegoat, on condition of repentance.[5]

Learning in the Law is naturally an aggravation.[6] The saying
of R. Judah ben Ila'i in Abot 4, 13, "Be attentive in learned

---

[1] Only those will regard this casuistry as futile who do not know the religion of the Old Testament.

[2] M. Shebu'ot 1, 4 and 1, 5, end; Tos. Shebu'ot 1, 3. See Note 189.

[3] See also Sifra, Aḥarè Pereḳ 4 (ed. Weiss f. 81c). Compare the semi-
annual riddance of sin from the sanctuary in Ezek. 45, 18–20, on account of
erring and sinful men. The words 'expiate,' 'remove sin,' and 'make clean,'
are interchangeable.

[4] Sifra, Aḥarè Pereḳ 1 (ed. Weiss f. 80d); cf. ibid. Pereḳ 4, f. 82a). Tos.
Yom ha-Kippurim 2, 1; Yoma 36b (with the passages from which the
equivalences are deduced).

[5] See below, pp. 498, 500.

[6] Luke 12, 47 f.

as defined in the law (נילוי עריות), and homicide (שפיכת דמים).[1]
In the time of persecution under Hadrian a conference of rabbis
at Lydda laid down the rule that under duress, to save his life,
a Jew might yield on any point of the law except these three.[2]
There was, however, a natural disposition, at least for hortatory
purposes, to treat all deliberate and wilful transgression as a
constructive rejection of God and his Law,[3] and this was favored
by the fact that the word פשע is used liberally in the Scriptures
for sins which do not in the very fact involve 'rebellion.' Enum-
erations of kinds of sinners who have no portion in the World to
Come are made on different grounds; we shall return to them
further on.

Another phrase by which the sinner who rejects God is described is כופר בעיקר, which we might render, 'the radical infidel,' literally, 'one who denies (or disbelieves in) the root' (the
author of all things, God).' A 'philosopher' is said to have asked
R. Reuben in Tiberias, Who is the most hateful man in the
world? The rabbi replied, 'He who denies his Creator.' To the
question how that was, he answered by reciting the commandments, Honor thy father and thy mother, Thou shalt not kill,
Thou shalt not commit adultery, and so on to the end of the
Decalogue, continuing, No man denies the obligation of one of
these commandments until he denies the root (God, who gave
them), and no man goes and commits a transgression unless he
has first denied Him who laid the command upon him.[4]

That no man is without sin is the teaching of Scripture as of
all experience. In Solomon's prayer at the dedication of the
temple we read: 'When they sin against Thee — for there is no
man that does not sin,' — etc. (1 Kings 8, 46); similarly in

---

[1] Sifra, Aḥarè Perek 4 (ed. Weiss f. 81c); Jer. Peah f. 15d.
[2] Jer. Sanhedrin 21b, above; Sanhedrin 74a. Graetz, Geschichte der
Juden, IV (1853), 185 and 524 f.
[3] See Schechter, Aspects of Rabbinic Theology, c. 14 ('Sin as Rebellion').
[4] Tos. Shebu'ot 3, 6. Bacher, Tannaiten, II, 384. See Note 194. On the
distinction between heinous and venial sins see Note 195.

Eccles. 7, 20: 'For there is no righteous man on the earth whose deeds are good and who does not sin'; Prov. 20, 9: 'Who can say, I have made my heart clean, I am pure from my sin.'[1] Indeed, where the idea of sin had so wide an extension as in Judaism, taking in not only grave moral offenses, but every infraction or neglect of the minutiae of ritual and observance, sinlessness was inconceivable. The fact is too plain to need frequent assertion in Jewish literature any more than in the Old Testament. The sentence of Ecclesiastes, 'There is no righteous man on earth whose deeds are good and who does not sin,' were impressed by R. Eliezer ben Hyrcanus on his disciples.[2] Expressions of the consciousness of personal sin are attributed to some of the teachers who stood in the highest repute among their contemporaries for godliness and uprightness.[3] Even the patriarchs and other worthies of the olden times such as Moses and David were not morally blameless. As long as a man lives, his conflict with the evil impulses of his nature continues, and he is never secure.[4] In a late Midrash the words of Job 15, 15, 'He putteth no trust in his saints,' are applied to the righteous of the Old Testament, and it is deduced from the verse that God does not call a righteous man 'saint' till he is dead; even of the patriarchs this holds good.[5] The strongest assertions of universal sinfulness are in the apocalypses of Esdras and Baruch, written in the deep depression — almost despair — that followed the destruction of Jerusalem. "What is man that Thou shouldst be wroth with him, or the mortal race that Thou shouldst be bitter against it? For of a truth there is no man that is born who has not done

---

[1] See also Job 4, 17 ff.; 15, 14–16; 25, 5 f. Philo, Vita Mosis ii. 17 § 147 (ed. Mangey, II, 157). The consecration of priests (Lev. 8) required sin offerings, "intimating that to sin is innate in every one that is born, even if he be virtuous, by the very fact that he is born."

[2] Sanhedrin 101a.

[3] See e. g. the words of Johanan ben Zakkai, Berakot 28b.

[4] Enoch 5, 8 f. Only after the renewal of the world will sin disappear.

[5] Midrash Tehillim on Psalm 16, 2 (ed. Buber f. 60b); Eccles. R. on Eccles. 4, 3 (R. Joshua ben Levi). Bacher, Pal. Amoräer, I, 162 f. There were some, however, who attributed sinlessness to the patriarchs: Mekilta, Wayyassa' 2 (ed. Friedmann f. 48a; ed. Weiss f. 56b). See below, p. 516.

wickedly, and none of those that exist (?) who has not sinned. (4 Esdras 8, 34 f.).[1]

Independent of its penal consequences, the effect of sin itself on the sinner is often remarked. It makes men afraid. R. Simeon ben Yoḥai said: "See how grave is the power of a transgression. Before the Israelites put forth their hand to transgression (the making of the golden calf), it is said of them, 'The appearance of the glory of the Lord was like devouring fire (on the top of the mount in the eyes of the children of Israel' — Exod. 24, 17). They were not afraid, neither did they tremble. After they put forth their hand to transgression, it is said, 'And Aaron and all the children of Israel saw Moses (when he came down from the mountain)and behold the skin of his face was a beam of light, and they were afraid to come near him'" (Exod. 34, 30).[2]

Parallels in later Midrashim adduce other examples. R. Ishmael generalizes, "So long as a man does not sin he is feared, as soon as he sins he himself is in fear." Thus it was with Adam in the Garden (Gen. 3, 8), the Israelites at Sinai (Exod. 34, 30, as above), David (2 Sam. 17, 2), Solomon (Cant. 3, 7 f.), Saul (1 Sam. 28, 5).[3]

The worst consequence of sin is its growing power over the sinner. Seemingly trivial sins lead to great ones; the unrestrained outbreak of rage in which a man rends his garments and smashes his furniture and throws his money about is to be looked on as heathen. "For this is the art of evil impulse (יצר הרע). Today it says to a man, Do this! and tomorrow, Do that! until at last it says, Worship other gods, and he goes and does it."[4] Nay, yielding to evil impulse is *ipso facto* idolatry. 'There shall be *in thee* no strange god and thou shalt not worship a foreign god' (Psalm 81, 10). What is the 'foreign god' within a man's

---

[1] See also 7, 46 and 68.
[2] Sifrè Num. § 1, on Num. 5, 3.
[3] Pesikta ed. Buber f. 44b–45a. Bacher, Tannaiten, II, 337.
[4] Shabbat 105b (attributed to Johanan ben Nuri; in Abot de-R. Nathan to his contemporary Akiba); Tos. Baba Ḳamma 9, 31.

body? It is evil impulse.[1] Schechter quotes from Sifrè: "He who transgresses a light commandment will end in violating the weightier one. If he neglect (the injunction) 'Thou shalt love thy neighbor as thy self' (Lev. 19, 18), he will soon transgress the commandment, 'Thou shalt not hate thy brother in thy heart' (ibid. vs. 17), and 'Thou shalt not avenge nor bear a grudge against the children of thy people' (ibid. vs. 18), which resulting in transgressing 'And thy brother shall live with thee' (Lev. 25, 36), will lead to the shedding of blood."[2] An ancient Midrash derives from Isaiah 5, 18 ('Woe to those who draw iniquity with cords of recklessness and sin as it were with a cart rope') the lesson: In its beginning sin is like a thread of a spider's web, but it ends by becoming stout as a cart rope.[3] In Genesis Rabbah, where the saying is attributed to Akiba, it runs: "At the beginning it (sin) is like a thread of a spider's web, but in the end it becomes like this ship's cable. This is what the Scripture says (Isa. 5, 18)."[4] In another figure, At the beginning it is weak as a woman: afterwards it grows strong as a man.[5]

There is a whole philosophy of conduct in the aphorism of Simeon ben 'Azzai: "Spring to fulfil the smallest duty, and flee from sin; for a duty draws another in its train, and a sin draws after it another sin. The reward of a duty done is another duty, and the reward of a sin is another sin."[6] The same thought is expressed by R. Judah the Patriarch: "A man who has fulfilled one duty for its own sake[7] should not rejoice over that duty (by itself), for in the end it brings many duties in its train; nor should a man who has committed one transgression grieve over it (by itself), for in the end it draws in its train many transgressions; for a duty draws a duty after it, and a transgression draws

---

[1] Shabbat 105b; cf. Jer. Nedarim 41b.

[2] (Deut. § 187). Aspects of Rabbinic Theology, pp. 226 f. (with erroneous reference to Sifra).

[3] Sifrè Num. § 112, on Num. 15, 30; cf. Sanhedrin 99b; Sukkah 52a.

[4] Gen. R. 22, 6. Bacher, Tannaiten, I, 276 f.

[5] Gen. R. l.c.

[6] Abot 4, 2. See Bacher, Tannaiten, I, 409.

[7] I.e. because it is a duty set him by God, not in prospect of reward, or any other extraneous motive.

a transgression." [1] Strack, in his edition of Abot, aptly quotes Schiller,

> Das eben ist der Fluch der bösen That,
> Dass sie fortzeugend Böses muss gebären.

(Piccolomini v. 1)

No man can confine the effect of his sins to himself. The Bible abounds in examples of the calamitous consequences to the people of the sins of individuals. A striking instance is the insurrection of Korah and his company against the authority of Moses in Num. 16: 'The Lord spoke to Moses and Aaron, saying, Separate yourselves from among this congregation, that I may consume them in a moment. And they fell upon their faces, and said, O God, the God of the spirits of all flesh, shall one man sin and will thou be wroth with all the congregation?' [2] Upon these verses R. Simeon ben Yoḥai employs a striking figure to illustrate the truth that no man can sin for himself alone. A number of men were sitting in a boat when one of them took an auger and began boring a hole beneath him. His companions said to him, What are you sitting there and doing! He replied, What business is it of yours? Am I not boring under myself? They answered, It is our business, because the water will come in and swamp the boat with us in it. So Job said, 'If in truth I have erred, my error remains my own' (Job 19, 4); but his companions answered him, He adds to his sin rebellion, in the midst of us he slaps his hands [3] (and multiplies his words against God)" (Job 34, 37). [4]

Nor is the worst that in the social organism if one sins all the rest suffer, but that a sinner leads others into sin and so does them the greatest harm one man can do another. R. Simeon ben

---

[1] Sifrè Num. § 112, on Num. 15, 30.   Bacher, Tannaiten, I, 409 f.; II, 460 f. Cf. Tanḥuma ed. Buber, Teṣè § 1.

[2] Num. 16, 20–22.

[3] A gesture of disrespectful impatience.

[4] Lev. R. 4, 6. See also the preceding context (Israel compared to lost sheep, Jer. 50, 6). So are Israel; one sins and all of them suffer from it. 'One sinner destroys much good' (Eccles. 9, 18).

Yoḥai taught: One who causes another to sin does a worse thing to him than one who kills him; for he who kills him only puts him out of this world, while he who causes him to sin puts him out of this world and the world to come both.[1]   The Egyptians who killed Israelites, and the Edomites who met them sword in hand, are excluded (from admission into the congregation of Israel) for only three generations; the Ammonites and Moabites, because they took counsel to cause Israel to sin (at Baal Peor, Num. 25), are excluded for all time.[2]   A somewhat similar thought is found in the Testaments of the Twelve Patriarchs, Gad 6, 4: If one who has wronged you denies his fault, do not contend about it with him, lest he swear to it, and thus you sin doubly (by having pressed him into perjury).

Sin thwarts God's purpose of grace.   "Whenever I seek to do you good, you enfeeble the supernal power.[3]   You stood at the Red Sea and said, 'This is my God and I will glorify him' (Exod. 15, 2), and I sought to do you good; then you changed your mind, and said, 'Let us make us a leader and return to Egypt' (Num. 14, 4).   You stood at Mt. Sinai and said, 'All that the Lord says, we will do and obey' (Exod. 24, 7), and I sought to do you good, but you changed your mind, and said to the calf, 'These are thy gods, O Israel' (Exod. 32, 4).   Thus whenever I seek to do you good you enfeeble the supernal power."[4]   Sin separates men from God (Isa. 59, 2).

That sin causes the withdrawal of God's presence is the motive of a homiletic conceit (on Gen. 3, 8) repeated in various places, and attributed, as such popular turns often are, to more than

---

[1] Sifrè Deut. § 252, on Deut. 23, 8; Tanḥuma ed. Buber, Phineas § 4. Bacher, Tannaiten, II, 82.

[2] Ibid. Cf. Sanhedrin 107b, mid.: One who sins and causes the multitude to sin, to him no opportunity of repentance is given (by God). See also Matt. 5, 19.

[3] Reverent periphrasis for 'the power of God.'

[4] Sifrè Deut. § 319; cf. Pesiḳta ed. Buber f. 166a–b: Whenever the righteous do the will of God they add power to might (גבורה, the Almighty; Lam. R. on Lam. 1, 6, 'to the Might above'). Schechter, Aspects of Rabbinic Theology, p. 239, cf. p. 34.

one author. Originally the Presence of God (*shekinah*) was here below. When Adam sinned it mounted aloft to the nearest firmament; when Cain sinned, to the second; and so on through the generations of Enosh,[1] of the Flood, of the dispersion of nations (Tower of Babel), and the men of Sodom, until the wickedness of the Egyptians in the days of Abraham caused it to retreat to the seventh and most remote heaven.[2] The righteous patriarchs and their successors in the line of Moses, and ending with him, brought God's Presence down again through the same seven stages.

[1] In the generation of Enosh, according to the Jewish interpretation of Gen. 4, 26 (אז הוחל לקרא בשם יהוה), idolatry began. Mekilta, Baḥodesh 6 (ed. Friedmann f. 67b; ed. Weiss 74b); Sifrè Deut. § 43, on Deut. 11, 16 (ed. Friedmann f. 81b); Gen. R. 23, 7.

[2] Gen. R. 19, 7; Pesiḳta ed. Buber f. 1b; and elsewhere. Bacher, Pal. Amoräer, II, 489.

CHAPTER III

THE ORIGIN OF SIN

Sin began with Adam. Only a single commandment — a prohibition — was laid upon him, and he transgressed it. See how many deaths were the penalty for him and his descendants through all generations to the end of the world.[1] "Thou didst lay upon him thy one commandment and he transgressed it and forthwith thou didst decree against him death and against his posterity. From him were born nations and tribes, peoples and kindreds, that cannot be numbered; and every nation walked according to its own will, and they did wickedly before thee and contemned thee, and thou didst not prevent them."[2] R. Judah (ben Ila'i) interpreted Deut. 32, 32 of Israel: 'The grapes are grapes of gall.' "Ye are the sons of Adam the first man, who brought the sentence of death upon you and on all the generations of his descendants who come after him until the end of all the generations."[3] The same Rabbi said: "Should a man ask you, If Adam had not sinned, and had eaten of that tree, would he have lived and endured forever? answer him, There was Elijah, who did not sin; he lives and endures forever."[4]

A late Midrash uses the consequence of Adam's sin to illustrate that God himself cannot correct the evil men have done. When God created Adam he showed him all his admirable works — all created for man's sake — and warned him: "Take good heed not to spoil and destroy my world, for once thou hast spoiled

[1] Sifra, Wayyiḳra Pereḳ 20 (ed. Weiss f. 27a). The quotation of this passage in Raymund Martini, Pugio Fidei p. 674 f. (ed. Carpzov p. 866 f.) has messianic additions, bringing in Isa. 53. See Note 196.

[2] 4 Esdras 3, 7. Mandasti diligentiam unam tuam. For *diligentia* in the sense of 'commandment, ordinance' see 4 Esdras 3, 19; 7, 37.

[3] Sifrè Deut. § 323.

[4] Pesiḳta ed. Buber f. 76a; Tanḥuma ed. Buber, Emor § 12. Bacher, Tannaiten, II, 264. ('That tree' is the tree of life.)

it, who is there to correct it after thee? Not only so but thou wilt cause the death of that righteous man (Moses)."[1] The passage continues with a parable. A woman who had transgressed the law was confined in prison. There she gave birth to a son and brought him up, and there she died. After a time, as the king was walking past the door of the prison, the son cried, O my lord the king, here I was born, here I grew up; for what sin I was put here I do not know. The king answered, For the sin of thy mother. So it was with Moses (Gen. 3, 22–24, combined with Deut. 31, 14). Adam was driven out of the garden, and access to the tree of life was shut off by the cherubim and the flaming sword; for his sin all his descendants are in bondage to death, even so righteous a man as Moses.

That without sin there would be no death is a natural inference from the story of the fall in Genesis. Thus, in the Wisdom of Solomon: "God did not make death, and has no pleasure in the destruction of the living" (1, 13); "God created man for immortality, and made him the image of his own peculiar nature; but by the envy of the devil death entered into the world, and they who are of his party make experience of it" (2, 23 f.).[2] That Adam's sin involved all his posterity, the righteous as well as the wicked, in death, is the consistent teaching of the rabbis, e.g. Genesis Rabbah 16, 6 (end): "'Thou shalt surely die.' Death to Eve; death to him and to his posterity."[3] The Scripture really makes Eve the first transgressor, and Jesus son of Sirach, in a chapter on bad women, carries this badness back to the mother of the race: "From a woman was the beginning of sin, and because of her we all die."[4]

Death is thus the damage that all men suffer from Adam's sin. To ancient conceptions of the solidarity of the family, clan, nation, race, and the liability of all for one, this raised no ques-

---

[1] Eccles. R. on Eccles. 7, 13 ('Consider the work of God, for who can make straight what he has made crooked').

[2] See above, p. 448. On the envy of the devil, below, pp. 478 f.

[3] Cf. Tanḥuma ed. Buber, Bereshit § 23.

[4] Ecclus. 25, 24.

tion of divine justice; that the sins of the fathers are visited upon the children was the doctrine of experience as well as of Scripture. But resentment against the forefather who had entailed this liability on all his descendants was a natural sentiment. In an old homiletic Midrash we read: "God caused all the generations of men, the righteous and the wicked, down to the resurrection, to pass before Adam, and said to him, See wherefore thou hast brought death upon the righteous. When Adam heard, he was troubled, and said, Lord of the world, have I done this in thy world? I am not concerned that the wicked die, but about the righteous, lest they murmur against me. I pray thee do not write of me that I brought death upon them. God answered, This is what I will do; when a man comes to depart out of the world, God will appear to him and say, Write down thy deeds that thou hast done, for thou diest because of thy deeds that thou hast done. When he has written them down, I will say, Set your seal to it! and he will do so, as it is written, 'By the hand of every man he will seal' (Job 37, 7). In the future, when God sits to judge his creatures, he will bring all the books of the children of men, and will exhibit to them their deeds. Wherefore it is written, 'By the hand of every man he will seal.'" [1] In another place in the same Midrash, the righteous descendants of Adam upon whom death was decreed reproach Adam, saying, Thou art the cause of our death. He replies, I was guilty of one sin, but there is not a single one among you who is not guilty of many iniquities.[2] Death came in with Adam, but every man has deserved it for himself; his descendants die in consequence of his sin, but not for the guilt of it. It is substantially what Paul says: δι' ἑνὸς ἀνθρώπου ἡ ἁμαρτία εἰς τὸν κόσμον εἰσῆλθεν καὶ διὰ τῆς ἁμαρτίας ὁ θάνατος, καὶ οὕτως εἰς πάντας ἀνθρώπους ὁ θάνατος διῆλθεν ἐφ' ᾧ πάντες ἥμαρτον (Rom. 5, 12).[3]

The problem becomes oppressive when the doom of sin is not alone the miseries of this life and death at the end of them, but

---

[1] Tanḥuma ed. Buber, Bereshit § 29. [3] For that all have sinned.
[2] Ibid., Ḥuḳḳat § 39.

the pains of hell. It is thus, as the tragic fate of mankind, only
deepened by the contrast to the salvation of a few among whom
no man can with assurance count himself, that it presents itself
to the authors of Fourth Esdras and of the Syriac Apocalypse of
Baruch. That sentence of death was pronounced on Adam and
his descendants for the transgression of one commandment we
have already seen in 4 Esdras.[1] Similar is 7, 11: "For their
sake (Israel) I made the world, and when Adam transgressed my
ordinances what was made was judged."[2] "This is my first and
last word: It were better that the earth had not produced Adam,
or having produced him, constrained him not to sin. For what
advantage is it to men to live the present life in sadness, and
look forward to perdition when they are dead. O Adam! what
hast thou done. For if thou didst sin, what resulted was not
thy disaster alone, but ours who are come from thee. For what
does it profit us that a deathless age is promised us, but we do
works of death," etc.[3] Again (4, 30–32): "A grain of evil seed
was sown in the heart of Adam from the beginning, and how
much ungodliness has it produced and will continue to produce
until the threshing-floor comes!"[4] If there were any inclination
to infer from this language that not only the penalty of death
but the infection of sin descended from Adam to his posterity,
the author elsewhere excludes such an inference. In accord with
the rabbinical teaching, he ascribes Adam's first sin to the fact
that he 'was possessed by an evil heart.' "Cor enim malignum
baiulans, primus Adam transgressus et victus est, sed et omnes
qui de eo nati sunt. Et facta est permanens infirmitas et lex
cum corde populi, cum malignitate radicis; et discessit quod
bonum est, et mansit malignum" (3, 21 f.). Later generations,
after the building of Jerusalem, "in omnibus facientes sicut fecit

---

[1] Above, p. 474.

[2] See Note 197.

[3] 4 Esdras 7, 116 ff. See Note 198.

[4] On the 'grain of evil seed,' the 'evil heart' in Adam and his posterity, see
below, p. 486. Men's life-long conflict is with the 'cum eis plasmatum cogita-
mentum malum, ut non eos seducat a vita ad mortem' (7, 92).

Adam et omnes generationes eius, utebantur enim et ipsi cor malignum (3, 26).[1]

The Syriac Apocalypse of Baruch, contemporary with 4 Esdras, expresses the same ideas. "When Adam sinned and death was decreed upon those that are born, then enumeration was made of those who should be born, and for this number a place was prepared where the living should dwell and where the dead should be kept" (23, 4).

In evident imitation of Fourth Esdras: "O what hast thou done, Adam, to all those that are begotten of thee. And what shall be said to the primal Eve who hearkened to the serpent? For this whole vast multitude goes to destruction, and those whom the fire devours are innumerable. And again I will speak before Thee. Thou, O Lord God, knowest how it is with thy creation. For Thou at the beginning didst command the dust to produce Adam, and Thou knowest the number of those who are begotten of him, and Thou knowest how greatly those have sinned against Thee who have lived (hitherto), and (that they) did not confess Thee as their Maker" (48, 42–46). It is explicitly asserted, as if against some who would put all the blame on the first parents: "If Adam first sinned and brought death on all who in his time did not exist, yet those also who were born of him, every one of them individually prepared for himself future torment, or again every one of them individually chose for himself future glories" (54, 15). And a few verses later: "Adam was therefore not the cause except to himelf alone; each man of us all became individually Adam to himself" (54, 19).

The tempter in Genesis is the serpent. In the Wisdom of Solomon, as we have seen, it was the envy of the devil that introduced death into the world. Whether the author imagined that the devil employed the serpent as an instrument, or himself assumed the form of a serpent cannot be decided — perhaps the author did not put the alternative to himself.[2] In the Reve-

[1] On the passages in 4 Esdras see Note 199.
[2] Cf. Pirḳè de-R. Eliezer c. 13; Greek Apocalypse of Baruch c. 9.

lation of John, however, the identification is explicitly made. The great dragon is ὁ ὄφις ὁ ἀρχαῖος,[1] ὁ καλούμενος Διάβολος καὶ ὁ Σατανᾶς, ὁ πλανῶν τὴν οἰκουμένην ὅλην. The tempter appealed to desires and ambitions inherent in human nature (Gen. 3, 5 f.), and yielding to this impulse man transgressed the commandment of God. This is the uniform doctrine of Judaism, as it is, indeed, the meaning of the story in Genesis. Adam's eating the forbidden fruit was like the sin of every other man, a following of the promptings of human nature where they ran counter to divine law.

Jewish imagination, increasingly in later times, invested Adam before the fall with many extraordinary physical qualities — lofty stature, radiant skin, and the like [2] — but he was not conceived as being mentally and morally otherwise constituted than his posterity. That he possessed free will in another sense than they, or that in his nature as it came from the hand of God with its *integerrimae vires* there were no desires that could incline his uncorrupted good will to disobedience — to such speculations, which have been rife in the Christian theology of the West since Augustine, there is no parallel in Judaism. Correspondingly, there is no notion that the original constitution of Adam underwent any change in consequence of the fall, so that he transmitted to his descendants a vitiated nature in which the appetites and passions necessarily prevail over reason and virtue, while the will to good is enfeebled or wholly impotent.[3]

The impulses which prompt a man to do or say or think things contrary to the revealed will of God are comprehensively named *yeṣer ha-ra‘* (יצר הרע).[4] The phrase comes from Gen. 8, 21, 'The

[1] The primal serpent, נחש הקדמוני.
[2] Gen. R. 12, 6; Tanḥuma ed. Buber, Bereshit § 18. Six things that Adam lost are enumerated. There is nowhere a suggestion that the image of God was among them.
[3] It may not be superfluous to remark that the Augustinian doctrines on these points had no influence in the Eastern Church, and were variously mitigated in the West.
[4] It is the *cor malignum* of 4 Esdras in the passages quoted above (p. 477). See Note 200.

imagination of man's heart is evil from his youth,' and 6, 5,
'Every imagination of the thoughts of his heart was only evil
continually.' In this familiar translation 'imagination' has the
sense of 'device, scheme,' and includes not only the conception
but a purpose to realize it; while 'heart,' as generally in Hebrew,
is the organ of mind and will, rather than the seat of the affections. In modern terms we might paraphrase the former passage, 'Every thing that man devises in his mind is evil, from his
youth on.' In Deut. 31, 21, the noun *yeṣer* is used without the
explicit adjective, but in a context of apostasy where its evil
character needs no expression.[1] In rabbinical literature the
name is used in a variety of connections and applications into
which no single rendering fits. 'Evil impulse' perhaps comes
nearest to being a common equivalent; but it must be remarked
that the impulses to which this title applies are not, as will be
shown below, intrinsically evil, much less in themselves sin, but
evil from their effect when man yields himself to be impelled by
them to consciously unlawful acts.[2]

Man was created with this impulse, to use the word collectively; or in the Jewish way of expressing it, God created the
evil impulse in man. R. Abahu, about the beginning of the
fourth century, is reported to have interpreted Gen. 6, 6 ('The
Lord regretted that he had made man on the earth, and he was
grieved at[3] his heart'). "He mourned only over the heart of
man, as one does who has made something bad, and knows that
he has not made a good thing, and says, What have I made? So
God: It was I that put the bad leaven in the dough,[4] for 'the
devising of man's heart is evil from his youth.' So the words
are to be understood: He grieved over the heart (disposition)
of man."[5] In the same way an earlier Rabbi, Phineas ben Jair,

[1] Psalm 103, 14 is not parallel, though it is sometimes taken so in the
Midrash (Yalḳuṭ, Midrash Tehillim in loc., Targum).
[2] See below, pp. 482 f.   [3] אל.
[4] A frequent metaphor; e.g. Gen. R. 34, 10; Berakot 17a; Jer. Berakot
7d. See Note 200.
[5] Tanḥuma ed. Buber, Noah § 4. 'His heart' in Gen. 6, 6 is man's heart,
not God's (Bacher, Pal. Amoräer, II, 141).

contemporary of the Patriarch Judah, enumerated three things that God regretted having created, one of which was the evil impulse.[1] That the impulse is created by God is the constant assertion or assumption. Thus in Sifrè God says: "My sons, I created for you the evil impulse; I created for you the Law as an antiseptic.[2] The evil impulse must be very evil since its creator himself testifies against it. 'The devising of the heart of man is evil from his youth'" (Gen. 8, 21).[3] The meaning of Jesus son of Sirach is the same in the passage quoted above:[4] "He at the beginning made man, and left him to the power of his own counsel," where διαβούλιον is probably equivalent to יצר (Ecclus. 15, 14).[5]

The evil impulse is present in the child from the earliest infancy. Among the questions which the legendary 'Antoninus'[6] puts to Rabbi Judah the Patriarch is, From what time does the evil impulse bear sway over a man, from the formation of the embryo in the womb or from the moment of birth? Rabbi at first answered, From the formation of the embryo; but owned himself convinced by Antoninus' argument that if so the child would kick in the womb and break a way out, and found a text of Scripture to confirm his revised opinion, 'Sin croucheth at the door' (the exit from the womb; Gen. 4, 7).[7]

The opportunity or the invitation to sin may come from without, but it is the response of the evil impulse in man to it that converts it into a temptation. It pictures in imagination the

[1] Jer. Ta'anit 66c, below; Sukkah 52b. Deduced from Mic. 4, 6, אשר הרעתי, as if, 'that which I have made evil.' Bacher, Tannaiten, II, 498 f.

[2] Sifrè Deut. § 45, on Deut. 11, 18; Ķiddushin 30b; Baba Batra 16a. Occupation with the Law a preventive of the evil impulse. See below, pp. 489 ff., and Note 201.

[3] Sifrè ibid. (f. 83a); Ķiddushin l.c. See Note 201a.

[4] Page 455.

[5] See Note 202.

[6] On 'Antoninus' in the Talmud see L. Ginzberg, Jewish Encyclopedia, I, 656 f.; a convenient list of his questions, Bacher, Tannaiten, II, 458 f.

[7] Sanhedrin 91b; cf. Gen. R. 34, 10 (with Gen. 8, 21 for Scripture proof). See also Midrash Tehillim on Psalm 9, 2 (ed. Buber f. 41b); Jer. Berakot 6d, above (verbal association with Job 38, 13).

pleasures of sin, conceives the plan, seduces the will, incites to the act. It is thus primarily as the subjective origin of temptation, or more correctly as the tempter within, that the *yeṣer ha-ra'* is represented in Jewish literature. Since it compasses man's undoing by leading him into sin, it is thought of as maliciously seeking his ruin — a kind of malevolent second personality. Throughout his life, from infancy to old age, it pursues its deadly purpose, patiently biding its time. If it can bring about his fall in the first twenty years it does it, or in forty, or sixty, or eighty — to the very day of his death; as it was with John (Hyrcanus) the high priest, who filled the office for eighty years and at last became a Sadducee![1] It is man's implacable enemy.[2] Only in the world to come will it be extirpated by God.[3] There is no kind of sin to which it does not instigate men; it leads them not only to transgress the commandments of God but to cavil at them.[4] Hence it is not strange that in parallel passages in the Midrash 'evil impulse' may be found in one and 'sin' in another, with the same things said about them. It is hardly necessary to say that the interchangeableness of the terms does not imply that the impulse is identified with sin. It is, to use the language of the Schoolmen about the surviving *concupiscentia* in the baptized, *fomes peccati*, not *peccatum* as Luther would have it.

Yet, as has been said above, the impulses natural to man are not in themselves evil. When God looked upon the finished creation and saw that it was all very good (Gen. 1, 31), the whole nature of man is included in this judgment, as R. Samuel ben Naḥman observes: "'And behold it was very good.' This is the evil impulse. Is then the evil impulse good! Yet were it not for the evil impulse no man would build a house, nor marry a wife, nor beget children, nor engage in trade. Solomon said 'All

[1] Pesiḳta ed. Buber f. 80a–b; Tanḥuma ed. Buber, Beshallaḥ § 3; cf. Gen. R. 54, 1.
[2] Tanḥuma l.c.; ibid. Wayyigash § 1.
[3] Ezek. 36, 26. See below, p. 493.
[4] Pesiḳta ed. Buber f. 38b–39a; cf. Yoma 67b. In the latter it is Satan who raises the same objections. See below, p. 492.

labor and all excelling in work is a man's rivalry with his neighbor' (Eccles. 4, 4)." [1] The appetites and passions are an essential
element in the constitution of human nature, and necessary to
the perpetuation of the race and to the existence of civilization.
In this aspect they are therefore not to be eradicated or suppressed, but directed and controlled. [2] Considered from the other
side, as the tempter within that draws men away from the commandments and leads them into sin, the impulses are to be
combated and subdued. [3]

From the two *yods* in וייצר in Gen. 2, 7 it is deduced, as we
shall see, that God created in man two impulses, respectively
good and bad; and from the fact that no similar expression occurs in the creation of the domestic animals it is inferred that
they have neither the good nor the evil impulse. A Babylonian
rabbi forcibly objects that any one can see how they wound,
and bite, and kick — plain signs of bad impulse. [4] The reflection
that, since the evil of evil impulse is not merely that it does harm
but that it does wrong, running counter to the commandment of
God, only moral agents are capable of it, does not seem to have
suggested itself to Jewish teachers, who indeed manifest no interest in the impulses of animals. Those who interpreted 'the
sons of God' in Gen. 6, 2 of angels who sinned through lust [5] must
logically have endowed them with evil impulse, as is done explicitly in Midrash Abkir. [6] This interpretation was, however,
emphatically rejected by the Palestinian authorities at least in
the second century. R. Simeon ben Yoḥai explained, 'sons of
the judges,' and launched an imprecation at those who were
audacious enough to understand the words of celestial beings. [7]

---

[1] Gen. R. 9, 7; Eccles. R. on Eccles. 3, 11.
[2] Sanhedrin 107b; Soṭah 47a.
[3] Pesiḳta ed. Buber f. 158a (on Psalm 4, 5).
[4] Gen. R. 14, 4; Berakot 61a.
[5] Enoch 6, 1 ff.; Jubilees 5, 1 ff.; Philo, De gigantibus c. 2 (ed. Mangey,
I, 263); Josephus, Antt. i. 3, 1.
[6] Quoted in Yalḳuṭ on Gen. 6, 2 (§ 44); cf. Jellinek, Bet ha-Midrasch, IV,
127. It was only when they descended to dwell in this world that the evil
impulse had dominion over them.　　　[7] Gen. R. 26, 5.　　**See Note 203.**

That the evil impulse has not dominion over the angels is deduced by R. Aḥa (fourth century) from Gen. 18, 5.[1] As in many
such cases the exegetical inference is not the source of the opinion, but only an ingenious support for it.

Philo holds that neither the beings above man in the scale nor
those below him are capable of sin; the former because they are
pure immaterial souls, not bound fast in that seat of endless
chance and change, a body; the latter, because, lacking intelligence, they are not guilty of voluntary and deliberate wrong-
doing. Man alone, having clear knowledge of right and wrong
often chooses the worst course and shuns what he ought to
strive for, so that he particularly is condemned for sins committed with forethought.[2]

The Scripture unqualifiedly declared man's native impulse to
be evil;[3] and apart from this it is natural that, as the focus of
temptation, the root of sin, the evil impulse should first engage
Jewish thought. But man's experience is of a contrariety of
impulses, such as is described by R. Alexander and R. Tanḥum
in the prayers quoted elsewhere;[4] or as Paul expresses it in Christianized Hellenistic form in the seventh chapter of Romans.
What gives poignancy to such plaints is that man is conscious of
a better self which does not complacently acquiesce in the courses
which his evil impulse impels him to, even though it fails to
thwart them. He has good impulses as well as bad, and this
also is of God's creation. Accordingly we find the doctrine of
the two impulses early established. It attaches itself exegetically, as we have seen, to the anomalous spelling of the verb
וייצר יהוה אלהים את האדם, Gen. 2, 7, with two *yods*, which signify
the two *yeṣers*, יצר טוב and יצר הרע,[5] or to the use of לבב, 'heart,'

---

[1] Gen. R. 48, 11. See above, p. 406.
[2] De confusione linguarum c. 35 §§ 176–177 (ed. Mangey, I, 432). Philo
conceives 'sin' morally, the deliberate wrong-doing of a being endowed with
reason and in the exercise of freedom, as in Greek and Roman jurisprudence.
See also De opificio mundi c. 24 § 73 (I, 17).
[3] Gen. 6, 5; 8, 21. Above, pp. 479 f.
[4] Note 200.   [5] Gen. R. 14, 4. See pp. 479 f.

whose two *bets* indicate doublemindedness, while לב is single-minded. Thus in Sifrè the command, 'Thou shalt love the Lord thy God, with all they heart' (בכל לבבך) is interpreted, "with both thine impulses, the good impulse and the evil impulse." [1] These associations with the letter of Scripture, it need hardly be repeated, are not the origin of the distinction. R. Jose the Galilean in the early second century, applies it as if it were generally familiar to the judgment of the three classes, the righteous, the wicked, and the 'middling.' [2] That in the conflict of impulses on even terms the evil is stronger than the good is taken to be too plain to need proof. Man should always rouse his good impulse against the evil (Psalm 4, 5a), and may thus succeed in overcoming it; but if not, more potent means are at his command, such as immersing himself in the study of the Law. [3]

This duality of impulses does not correspond to the duality of man's natural constitution, so that the evil impulse resides in the body while the good impulse proceeds from the soul. That the physical organism, as material, is evil *per se*, sense the origin of error, the appetites and passions the source of moral evil — these ideas, which through prevalent philosophies had gained wide currency in the Hellenistic world, have no counterpart in Palestinian Judaism. It is in the ideas and expressions of Greek philosophy that the author of Fourth Maccabees writes: "When God made man he implanted in him his affections and dispositions; and then over all he enthroned the sacred ruling mind." [4] From the same premises he develops his thesis that the rational faculty (λογισμός) in proper exercise, while it cannot eradicate appetite and passion and evil disposition, is capable of dominating them with an authoritative sway. [5] In more popular form

---

[1] Sifrè Deut. § 32, on Deut. 6, 5 (ed. Friedmann f. 73a); M. Berakot 9, 5; Tos. Berakot 7, 7.

[2] Berakot 61b. Bacher, Tannaiten, I, 368. See also Note 204.

[3] R. Simeon ben Laḳish, Berakot 5a, top; see below, pp. 490 f.

[4] 4 Macc. 2, 21 f.   [5] This is the thesis of the book (1, 1).

Paul represents the dualism of Hellenistic thought when he describes the tragedy of man as a losing struggle between the aspirations of the mind and the impulses of the body: "I see another law in my members, warring against the law of my mind and making me captive to the law of sin that is in my members" (Rom. 7, 23).

A similar way of conceiving the conflict of impulses in man — without the pessimistic note — may have been common among Jews who lived in a Hellenistic atmosphere; it was not the psychology of the rabbis. For them, on the contrary, it is 'the heart,' that is the mind and will, with which the Scripture associates the evil impulse (Gen. 6, 5; 8, 21); it is the יצר לב האדם, 'the devising of man's heart,' or יצר מחשבות לבו, 'the devising of the thoughts of his heart,' that is, of his mind.[1] It is the mind which generates the thoughts and devices, the promptings and purposes, of evil. Thus the word 'heart' itself is often used in a sense entirely equivalent to yeṣer,[2] especially when the text of Scripture suggests a bad connotation. Thus, for example, in Sifrè on Num. 15, 39 ('Do not roam, following your own heart and your eyes which ye go a-whoring after'). The heart and the eyes lead men into sin; but the eyes merely follow the heart, for there are blind men who are guilty of all abominable deeds in the world.[3] In 4 Esdras, as we have seen the *cor malignum*, or the *granum seminis mali* in the heart, is used in connections in which the rabbinical texts say *yeṣer ha-ra'*.

But while it is thus the mind that devises evil and wills it, the body is not a mere involuntary instrument in its accomplishment. Sin, however it may be analyzed, is the sin of the *man*,

---

[1] See also Jer. 17, 9 f.

[2] Gen. R. 34, 10: The wicked are in the power of their heart (Psalm 14, 1; Gen. 27, 41; 1 Kings 12, 26; Esther 6, 6), but the righteous have their heart in their power (1 Sam. 1, 13; 27, 1; Dan. 1,8); cf. ibid. 67, 8. On the two hearts see above, p. 485.

[3] Sifrè Num. § 115, on Num. 15, 39; applied literally to the commandment against adultery in Jer. Berakot 3c. Cf. also Midrash Tehillim on Psalm 14, 1. On the heart in rabbinical literature see especially Schechter, Some Aspects of Rabbinic Theology, pp. 255–261; and Note 205.

not of either half of his nature. This is the point of the parable
of the two keepers of the king's garden, who conspired to rob it
and were punished together, which is found, with variations that
do not affect the sense, in several places.[1]

> In time to come God will bring the soul and say to it,
> Why didst thou trangress the commandments? and it will
> say, The body transgressed the commandments; from the
> day that I departed from it, did I ever sin? Then God turns
> and says to the body, Why didst thou transgress the com-
> mandments? It replies, The soul sinned; from the time
> when the soul departed from me, did I ever sin? And what
> does God do? He brings both of them and judges them
> together. It is like a king who had a park in which were
> grapes and figs and pomegranates, first ripe fruits. The
> king said, If I station there a man who can see and walk he
> will eat the first ripe fruit himself. So he stationed there
> two keepers, one lame and the other blind, and they sat
> there and guarded the park. They smelled the odor of first
> ripe fruit. The lame man said to the blind man, Fine first
> fruits I see in the park. Come let me ride on your shoulders
> and we will fetch and eat them. So the lame man rode on
> the back of the blind man and they got the fruits and ate
> them. After a while the king came seeking for the first ripe
> fruit and found none. He said to the blind man, You ate
> them. He replied, Have I then any eyes? He said to the
> lame man, You ate them. He replied, Have I then any legs?
> So the king made the lame man mount on the back of the
> blind man and judged them together." [2]

Another version is found in the Talmud:

> Antoninus said to Rabbi: Body and soul can escape from
> the judgment. How? The body says, It was the soul that
> sinned, for since the day that I separated from it, here
> I lie like a stone, silent in the tomb. And the soul says, It
> was the body that sinned, for from the day that I separated
> from it I am soaring in the air like a bird. Rabbi replied,
> I will give you a parable for it. A human king had a

---

[1] The parable is ultimately of Indian origin; see Note 206.
[2] Tanḥuma ed. Buber, Wayyiḳra § 12.

fine park in which were fine new fruits, and he stationed
in it two keepers, one lame and the other blind. The lame
man said to the blind man, Fine early fruits I see in the
park; let me mount you and we will get them and eat them.
So the lame man rode on the back of the blind man and they
got the fruits and ate them. After a while the owner of the
park came and said to them, Where are the fine early fruits?
The lame man said, Have I then any legs to get to them?
The blind man said to him, Have I then any eyes to see?
What did he do? He made the lame man mount on the
back of the blind man and judged them together. So God
will bring the soul and inject it into the body and judge
them together.[1]

In this joint responsibility the guilt of the soul is the greater
because it is, so to speak, better bred, as is also illustrated by
a parable.[2] Two men (jointly) committed the same offense
against the king, one of them a simple villager, the other a man
brought up in the palace. He let the villager go and pronounced
sentence on the other. His courtiers said to him, Both of them
committed the same offence; you have let the villager go and
sentenced the courtier! He replied, I let the villager go because he did not know the laws of the government, but the
courtier was continually with me and knew what the laws of the
government are, and what judgment is pronounced against one
who offends against me. So the body is a villager — 'God
fashioned man out of dust from the ground'; but the soul is a
courtier from above — 'He breathed into his nostrils a soul of
life.' And they both sin; for the body cannot exist without soul,
for if there is no soul there is no body, and if no body, no soul.
And they both sin — 'The soul that sinneth, it shall die' (Ezek.
18, 20).[3]

---

[1] Sanhedrin 91a–b. In Mekilta, Beshallaḥ Shirah 2 (end), where only the
incipit of the parable is quoted, and in Mekilta de-R. Simeon ben Yoḥai ed.
Hoffmann, p. 59, as in the Talmud, the parable is attributed to Rabbi in
reply to Antoninus; in Lev. R. 4, 5, to R. Ishmael.

[2] Cf. Philo, De spec. legg. i. 7 § 214 (ed. Mangey, II, 243); cf. De sacrif.
Abelis et Caini c. 40 § 136 ff. (I, 190.)

[3] Tanḥuma ed. Buber, Wayyiḳra § 11.

Notwithstanding the strength and the deceitfulness of the evil impulse, it is in man's power to defeat and subdue it. To achieve this victory he must combat it from its first motions, and persistently, in the use of the means that God has appointed. If he yields to it, it acquires the mastery of him by habit; the cob-web grows into a cable,[1] the passing stranger becomes the master of the house. As Paul puts it: "Do you not know that to whichever you yield yourself to obey as slaves, his slaves you are whom you obey, whether of sin ending in death or of obedience leading to righteousness?"[2] This is the very difference between the wicked and the righteous: the wicked are in the power of their evil impulses, the righteous have power over them.

There are various ways in which a man may resist evil impulse. One of the chief themes of the Hebrew sages in the Proverbs of Solomon and in Sirach is the part of wisdom in controlling the appetites and passions by keeping the consequences in mind and dwelling on the folly of wrong-doing. In the Hellenistic literature this naturally takes the form of the supremacy of reason over the senses and their promptings.[3] In the teaching of the rabbis the role of eudaemonistic prudence and of reason in itself is less marked; their ethic is more distinctly religious. That man should incite his good impulse to contend with the evil is self-evident but not always sufficient. Another method to which all the righteous of ancient times resorted, and which is commended to their successors, was to adjure their impulse by an oath in the name of the Lord; so Abraham did (Gen. 14, 22), Boaz (Ruth 3, 13), David (1 Sam. 26, 10), Elisha (2 Kings 5, 16); whereas the wicked, like Gehazi (2 Kings 5, 20), adjure their impulse with an oath to do wrong.[4] But the most potent antidote for evil impulse is to occupy one's self with the word of God. In a passage from which a quotation has already been

---

[1] Above, p. 470.   [2] Rom. 6, 16.
[3] Note also the thesis of 4 Macc.
[4] R. Josiah, Sifrè Deut. § 33, on Deut. 6, 6.   Bacher, Tannaiten, II, 360.

made in another connection,[1] it is said that the words of the Law are compared to a medicine that preserves life.[2] The parable with which the saying is illustrated shows that the medicine is thought of primarily as a prophylactic.

"A king had smitten his son a grievous blow. He bound a bandage upon the wound and said, My son, so long as this bandage is upon your wound you may eat and drink whatever you like, and bathe in warm water or in cold, and you will take no harm. But if you remove the bandage from it a deep ulcer will result. So God said to the Israelites, my children, I have created for you the evil impulse, and I have created for you the Law as an antiseptic. So long as you occupy yourselves with it, the evil impulse will not have dominion over you, as it is said, 'If thou doest well is there not uplifting?' (Gen. 4, 7);[3] but if you do not occupy yourselves with the Law, you will be delivered into its power, as it is said, 'And if thou doest not well, sin crouches at the door' (ibid.). Not only so, but his business will be with you, as it is said, 'And unto thee is his desire.' And if you will, you shall rule over it, as it is said, 'And thou shalt rule over it.' And it says, 'If thy enemy hunger feed him bread' (Prov. 25, 21), i.e. feed him the bread of the Law; 'and if he thirst give him water to drink, for burning coals thou dost heap upon his head'"[4]

In the school of R. Ishmael it was taught: If that ugly one (evil impulse) encounters thee, drag him to the school;[5] if he is stone he will be worn away (as by water), if he is iron he will be shattered to pieces (as by fire and a sledge hammer).[6]

R. Simeon ben Laḳish gives a prescription for the treatment of evil impulse, as follows: "A man should always stir up his good impulse against the evil impulse, for it is said, 'Be stirred

[1] Above, p. 481.
[2] סם חיים. Cf. Prov. 4, 20–22; ʿErubin 54a. See also Ecclus. 21, 11: ὁ φυλάσσων νόμον κατακρατεῖ τοῦ ἐννοήματος αὐτοῦ.
[3] Rashi (on Ḳiddushin 30b) interprets: "You will be raised above your evil impulse." On Gen. 4, 7 he adopts the interpretation of the Targum 'forgiveness.
[4] Sifrè Deut. § 45; Ḳiddushin 30b.
[5] Bet ha-Midrash.
[6] Isa. 55, 1 combined with Job 14, 19; Jer. 23, 29. Ḳiddushin 30b; Sukkah 52b. Bacher, Tannaiten, II, 336 f.

up, and sin not' (Psalm 4, 5).[1] If he conquers it, well; if not, let him occupy his mind with the Law, for it is said, 'Think in your heart' (ibid.). If he conquer it, well; if not, let him recite the Shema', for it is said, 'Upon your bed' (ibid.). If he conquer it, well; if not, let him be mindful of the day of his death, for it is written, 'And be silent. Selah'" (ibid.).[2] To stimulate the better self to contend against the worse; occupy one's self intensely with the word of God; confess one's faith in the one true God, and the duty of loving him with all one's being, renewing thus the assumption of the yoke of the kingdom of Heaven; meditate on the hour of death (and the judgment of God) — these are the weapons with which victory may be won in this battle that man wages for the freedom of his soul.[3]

Application to the study of the Word of God (the Law) is thus effective, not solely because in it the will of God for man's life is set forth, with the blessings promised to conformity and the penalties of transgression, but because the mind thus preoccupied with religion excludes temptations from without and evil devisings within. This way of thinking is akin to ours when we speak of the Word of God in itself as a means of grace; devout attention to it makes men better.

By such means finally the end may be achieved which is set before man, to love God with all his heart, the evil impulse now subdued to His service, as well as the native good impulse. In a late collection, which is here quite in the spirit of the older time, the figure is used of iron, out of which when it is made hot in the forge, man can make whatever implements he pleases. So it is with the evil impulse, with which nothing can be done except by means of the words of the Law, which is like a fire. The same verse from Proverbs (25, 21 f.) follows which is quoted above.[4] If a man has yielded to the evil impulse, there

---

[1] רגזו ואל תחטאו.

[2] Berakot 5a.

[3] For many other sayings about the *yeṣer ha-ra'* see Ḳiddushin 30; Sukkah 52.

[4] Abot de-R. Nathan c. 16.

is still a remedy—repentance. "There is no malady in the world for which there is not a cure. What is the cure for evil impulse? Repentance." Even the generation of the Flood, it is said in the sequel, would have been spared, if they had used the respite God gave them, to repent of their evil ways.[1]

The evil impulse is frequently personified. The something within that seduces man into doing what is repugnant to his better judgment and purpose, drugs his conscience, overmasters his will to good, or blinds him to the consequences of his acts, has always seemed to his introspective imagination to be a demonic power, other than his conscious self, that maliciously plots and compasses his undoing. Such an imagination is implied when R. Jonathan (reported by R. Samuel bar Naḥman) says: "The evil impulse seduces a man in this world and bears witness against him in the world to come; as it is written, If a man pampers his slave from childhood, it will end by the slave's becoming a witness" (Prov. 29, 21).[2]

Personified as the tempter, evil impulse may be identified with Satan; and since by their arts they cause the death of the sinner, they can by a further association become the angel of death. Thus R. Simeon ben Laḳish could say: Satan and evil impulse and the angel of death are the same.[3] For, as it is said by an anonymous Tannaite authority in the preceding context (with reference to Job): "Satan comes down and misleads a man, then goes up and stirs up God's wrath, and obtains permission and takes away his soul." It is nothing strange, therefore, that in parallel passages Satan and evil impulse interchange,[4] as elsewhere do evil impulse and sin. It is a similar personification

---

[1] See below, pp. 520 f.
[2] Sukkah 52b. The ἀπ. λεγ. מנון is by permutation of letters in a kind of cipher made equivalent to סהדה. Cf. Gen. R. 22, 6; Whoever fosters his evil impulse in youth, it will end by being his master (?) in his old age (Prov. 29, 21). See Note 206.
[3] Baba Batra 16a. Schechter, Aspects of Rabbinic Theology, pp. 244 f.
[4] E.g. Sifra, Aḥarè Pereḳ 13 (ed. Weiss, f. 86a), יצר הרע משיב עליהן, compared with Yoma 67b השטן משיב עליהן.

when it is asserted that on the judgment day God will slaughter
the evil impulse before the eyes of righteous and wicked.[1] The
usual expression, however, is impersonal: in the world to come
God will eradicate it, or it will be eradicated. So for example in
the Tanḥuma, where Moses is remonstrating against God's declared purpose to destroy Israel for the sin of the golden calf,
R. Simeon ben Yoḥai said: "Moses never left off praying until
God yielded to him. And God said, In this world, because the
evil impulse exists in you, ye have sinned against me; but in
the world to come I will eradicate it from you, as it is said, 'I
will take away the heart of stone out of your flesh and give you
a heart of flesh'" (Ezek. 36, 26).[2] This verse is the standing
proof text, and is the origin of the comparison of the evil impulse with stone; in a catalogue of the names and epithets applied to 'evil impulse' in the Scriptures, 'stone' is for this reason
included.[3]

The conception of sin in Judaism has already been discussed.[4]
It is fundamentally any departure from the divinely revealed
rule of life, whether in the sphere of morals or of religious observance, whether deliberate or unwitting. But, as we have seen,
the element of intention, which brings into the moral realm even
acts which in and of themselves have no moral quality, is clearly
recognized; and although, in the Jewish use of the word, a man
may 'sin' without meaning to and even without knowing it,[5] the
'sinner' in our sense of the word is only the man who knowingly
and wilfully transgresses or ignores the revealed will of God, and
that persistently or habitually. Not only so, but Judaism had
so fully absorbed the teaching of the prophets that for it, next
to apostasy and practical irreligion, the intrinsically heinous

---

[1] Sukkah 52a. See Note 207.
[2] Tanḥuma ed. Buber, Ki tissa § 13, end; ibid. Wayyiḳra § 12 end. In
some manuscripts Jer. 31, 33 is also quoted.
[3] Seven names of 'evil impulse' are enumerated in Sukkah 52a. Schechter, Aspects of Rabbinic Theology, p. 243 f.
[4] Above, pp. 460 ff.
[5] See Note 208.

offenses are violations of what we call the moral law, and particularly the wrongs a man does to his fellows.[1] It is such sins that as the habit of life define the character of the 'wicked man' (רשע). The Psalms give specifications in multitude both of the attitude of the wicked to God and his law and of their vices and crimes.

The critical historian may see in the composite portraits of the wicked — often thrown into darker shade by the pendent pictures the godly, or righteous, paint of themselves — monuments of the long and embittered conflict between puritans and worldlings in the later Persian and the Greek centuries, and he may make his subtractions accordingly on both sides; but for the Jews in the age which concerns us they were divinely revealed descriptions of the two classes into which mankind divides itself, and are accepted in all the subsequent literature as definitions.[2]

The antithetic idea of righteousness is in like manner determined by the axioms of revealed religion. The righteous man is not one who follows the suggestions of his individual conscience, nor one who conforms his conduct to the fluctuating and elastic standards of custom and public opinion, nor one who is guided by the principles of a rational ethics, but he alone who strives to regulate his whole life by the rules God has given in his twofold law. The sincerity and supremacy of this purpose and the strenuous endeavor to accomplish it are the marks of the righteous man. Such a man shares in the universality of sin; judged by the ideal, 'there is no righteous man . . . who does not sin' (Eccles. 7, 20); but he is not for that denied the character and name of a righteous man, much less must he be called a 'sinner.'

Righteousness, in the conception of it which Judaism got from the Scriptures, had no suggestion of sinless perfection. Nor are the sins of the righteous all venial; the gravest moral lapses may

[1] See Part V., Morals.
[2] For an example in Hellenistic literature, see Wisdom of Solomon 1–2.

befall them, as they did David. What distinguishes the righteous man who has fallen into sin is his repentance — a remedy which God, in knowledge of man's frailty and foresight of his sin, mercifully created before the world. Paul's definition of righteousness as perfect conformity to the law of God would never have been conceded by a Jewish opponent, to whom it would have been equivalent to admitting that God had mocked man by offering to him salvation on terms they both knew to be impossible — God, because he had made man a creature of the dust with all his human frailties (Psalm 103, 14) and implanted in him the 'evil impulse'; man, above all the conscientious man, through his daily experience. God was too good, too reasonable, to demand a perfection of which he had created man incapable.[1] In the rabbinical literature, as in the Old Testament, the righteous and the wicked are in standing contrast; their whole character and their relations to God and men are contradictory. Every man is either in the one category or the other, though he can change sides.[2] Common observation shows, however, that there are men whose character is not positive or consistent enough for either company, and so a 'middling class' was recognized, especially where the context is of a divine judgment. R. Jose the Galilean distinguished the righteous, who are ruled by their good impulse; the wicked, ruled by their evil impulse; and the middle class, who are ruled now by the one, now by the other [3] So on New Years Day, according to R. Johanan (toward the close of the third century), three kinds of record books are opened: those for the completely righteous and for the completely wicked are at once written up and sealed, the one to life, the other to death; but the books of the middling class are kept open for ten days (till the Day of Atonement) that they may repent in them.[4] The schools of Shammai and Hillel, before the fall of

[1] On Paul's argument see Note 209.
[2] See especially Ezek. 18.
[3] Berakot 61b.
[4] Rosh ha-Shanah 16b; cf. Jer. Rosh ha-Shanah 57a; Pesiḳta ed. Buber f. 157b–158a.

Jerusalem, differed about the fate of these religious and moral mediocrities at the last judgment; according to the former they went down to Gehenna and were there purified in purgatorial fires, and then came up; the school of Hillel had it that God graciously inclined the balance to the good side.[1]

[1] Tos. Sanhedrin 13, 3; Rosh ha-Shanah 16b–17a. Bacher, Tannaiten, I, 18.

CHAPTER IV

RITUAL ATONEMENT

As has been remarked above, the specific purifications and expiations of the Law apply almost solely to cases which have intrinsically no moral quality, and, considered as of positive obligation created by the revealed will of God, to accidental or unwitting infringement of such rules.[1] In many such cases a sacrifice is required, which is remedial since it removes the contamination and restores the state of religious purity or holiness, and in relation to God is regarded as piacular. Such sacrifices were prescribed for the individual in various specified cases and circumstances, and similar piacula formed a regular or occasional part of the *sacra publica*. It was believed, moreover, that all kinds of sacrifice, public and private, propitiated God and worked the remission of sins.[2] In the schools the attempt was made to classify them all, and to define the kinds of sin for which the species respectively atoned.[3] What, for instance, was the peculiar efficacy of the whole burnt offering, which in the Old Testament is given no specific application?[4] Later we find the theory that the perpetual morning and evening holocausts in the temple atoned for the residents of Jerusalem; the evening sacrifice for transgressions committed during the day, the morning sacrifice for those of the night.[5]

---

[1] Above, p. 461. See e.g. Sifra on Lev. 4, 2 (ed. Weiss f. 15b): Sin offerings are brought for unwitting sins, not for presumptuous sins.

[2] Ezek. 45, 13–17. The prophet is speaking of the public cultus, but the same thing is said of the private burnt offering, Lev. 1, 4, etc.

[3] See Note 210.

[4] Tos. Menaḥot 10, 12. The most favored opinion was that it atones for thoughts of sin entertained in the mind; cf. Tanḥuma ed. Buber, Ṣau § 9; ibid. Lek leka § 13; Lev. R. 7, 3.

[5] So that no man lodged in Jerusalem with unexpiated sin (Isa. 1, 21). Tanḥuma ed. Buber, Phineas § 12; Pesiḳta ed. Buber 55b, 61b.

An authoritative deliverance on the whole subject is M. She-bu'ot 1, 6. After reciting the specific expiations: "For the rest of the transgressions defined in the Law, venial or heinous, presumptuous or inadvertent, witting or unwitting, of omission or of commission, including those the penalty of which is, to be exterminated (by the act of God) or to be put to death by the sentence of a court, the scapegoat expiates." [1] This Mishnah is solely concerned with the particular application of the several piacula, not with the conditions of their effectiveness. In a corresponding passage in the Mishnah on the Day of Atonement it is made clear that the effect of the piacula is not *ex opere operato:* Sin offering and prescribed trespass offering expiate; [2] death and the Day of Atonement expiate when conjoined with repentance; repentance alone expiates for venial sins of omission and (some) sins of commission. For grave offenses, repentance suspends the sentence till the Day of Atonement comes and expiates. [3] Repentance is thus the *conditio sine qua non* of the remission of sins.

Cases were constantly arising in which a man was in doubt whether he had broken the law or not, and some of the things about which such uncertainties might most easily arise were among those which exposed the transgressor to be exterminated by the hand of God. In such a case the traditional law, in conformity, as it was understood, with Lev. 5, 17 f., provided for a 'suspensive trespass offering' (אשם תלוי), in distinction from the prescribed trespass offering (אשם ודאי), of which four varieties were distinguished. [4] Such a sacrifice was properly a voluntary offering (נדבה), [5] and extra-scrupulous persons made fre-

---

[1] Lev. 16, 21.

[2] In the particular cases in which they are prescribed. Repentance is presumed from the bringing of the sacrifice.

[3] M. Yoma 8, 8. See Note 210.

[4] The *asham wadai* ('sure, certain') is offered in cases where the offerer knows that he has committed one of the offenses for which the law prescribes an *asham;* the *asham talui* when he is in doubt whether he has done something that demands expiation. See Note 211.

[5] Keritot 25a.

quent sacrifices of this kind.   R. Eliezer [1] taught that a man may
volunteer an *asham talui* at any time that he pleases; this is
called the trespass offering of the pious (*asham ḥasidim*).[2]   It is
related of Baba ben Buṭa [3] that he did this every day in the year
except alone the Day of Atonement, and asseverated that he
would have done so on that day also if he had been allowed,
but they told him to wait until a case of doubt arose.   The consensus is that a man should make such a sacrifice only for an
offense which if deliberate would be liable to extermination and
if inadvertent would require a sin offering.[4]   The story of Baba
ben Buṭa, apparently narrated by R. Eliezer, carries the *asham
ḥasidim* back to Herodian times, from which it would be inferred
that in its original extension only to cases of actual doubt it
was older — how much older no one can say.

Offerings of this kind, and indeed private piacula universally,
were ordinarily practicable only for residents of Jerusalem and
its vicinity.   The vast majority of the Jews, dispersed as they
were over the face of the earth, never had opportunity to make
such sacrifices, even by proxy; while the inhabitants of the more
distant parts of Palestine, who resorted in numbers to the Holy
City at the festivals, could make but infrequent use of all the
sacrificial purifications and expiations provided in the Law.[5]
For the great mass of Jewry, therefore, the public piacula, maintained, like the rest of the cultus, for the benefit of all by the half-
shekel poll-tax, alone had expiatory significance; and of these
again, the rites of the Day of Atonement, in which, through the
universal fast and the special services of the synagogues, all
religiously-minded Jews made themselves participants in spirit,
overshadowed all the rest.   The Mishnah quoted above from

[1] Disciple of Johanan ben Zakkai, in the generation after the fall of Jerusalem.

[2] M. Keritot 6, 3.   The pious did not wait till an actual doubt arose, but
had themselves perpetually in suspicion.

[3] Contemporary of Herod the Great.

[4] M. Keritot 6, 3; Tos. Keritot 4, 4.

[5] In some cases cumulation was permissible.

Shebuʻot shows how upon the scapegoat the real burden of expiation for what we should denominate sins rests. Nor is it insignificant that in the passage from M. Yoma quoted in the same connection [1] it is the Day of Atonement itself that expiates; [2] for the Day of Atonement, of fasting and humiliation before God, of confession of sins, and contrition for them, and of fervent prayer for forgiveness,[3] was, even before the destruction of the temple, the reality, of which the rites of the day in Jerusalem, whatever objective efficacy was attributed to them, were only a dramatic symbol.

A theory of the way in which sacrifices and other rites expiate sin is in a revealed religion a superfluous speculation. God has attached to certain cases certain conditions on which he promises to remit sins. The essential condition is the use of the means he has appointed, whatever they are. To neglect them because a man does not see how they can be of any effect, is itself deliberate and wilful sin, vastly graver than the original offense. Judaism had, therefore, no motive for discussing the *modus operandi* of sacrificial atonement, and never even raised the question.[4] The attitude of religion to the whole matter will come before us in another connection.

The Mishnah quoted above makes repentance the indispensable condition of the remission of every kind of sin, and this, with the other side of it, namely, that God freely and fully remits the sins of the penitent, is a cardinal doctrine of Judaism; it may properly be called the Jewish doctrine of salvation. This is the message of the prophets to the nation. Its sins draw down upon it, as they deserve, the dire judgments of God; it seeks in vain to move him to condone its faults by sacrifice and magnificent liturgies; equally vain are fasting and clamorous supplication without amendment. There is but one way of forgiveness

---

[1] Page 498.

[2] The biblical text for this is Lev. 16, 30. See Note 212.

[3] Note the accumulation of terms in Dan. 9, 3 ff., most of which are technical in the liturgy.

[4] See Note 213.

and restoration — turn from your evil ways, turn again to the Lord your God—but that is a sure way. If they heed the warning and return to undivided allegiance to their God and let justice and loving kindness prevail among men, the doom will be revoked; if they disregard all monitions, and the judgment falls, even then, when in ruin and exile they turn to him again, he will take them back into his favor and restore them to welfare in their own land. This is the burden of Hosea and his successors, to the end of prophecy.[1] In the Law it fills some of the most impressive chapters in Deuteronomy;[2] the national history from the exodus to the fall of Jerusalem was presented, especially in Judges and Kings, with the express purpose of exemplifying this as the first law of history. These teachings sank deep into the hearts of religiously-minded Jews under foreign rule: national sin was the cause of their distress, national repentance the sole hope of better days — witness the penitential outpourings in prayer such as Neh. 9, Dan. 9, Baruch 1, 15 ff., and in many of the Psalms.

In Judaism the principle was applied to the individual as well as to the people collectively. Ezekiel had individualized the prophetic doctrine of retribution with unflinching logic, and with it the counterpart, the doctrine of repentance: 'If the wicked man turn from all his sins that he hath committed, and keep all my statutes, and do that which is lawful and right, he shall surely live, he shall not die. None of his transgressions that he hath committed shall be remembered against him; for his righteousness that he hath done he shall live' (Exek. 18, 21 f.). Many of the penitent confessions and supplications in the Psalms are personal,[3] and furnish pattern and phrase for the Jewish liturgy. Thus the whole great prophetic doctrine of collective repentance

---

[1] That Hosea is the great exponent of the doctrine of repentance was recognized by the rabbis. See Note 213a.

[2] E.g. Deut. 4, 25–40; cc. 29–30; Lev. 26.

[3] So, e.g., Psalm 51. — The question of the plural 'I' in the Psalms (the worshipping community or the people) does not concern us here; the Jews interpreted them individually.

and reformation was translated into personal religion; it became the condition of salvation for the individual as it had been originally for the nation. When the old notion of a common fate for all men in the universal gathering place of the dead in Sheol gave place to the belief in a separation of righteous and wicked at death, and a destiny beyond death accordant with their diverse character, and particularly when more concrete form was given to the imagination of the hereafter by the belief in a reunion of body and soul for the life of the World to Come, in which wickedness had no place, and participation in the blessedness of that world became the *summum bonum*, repentance and the remission of sins, as the indispensable condition, gained a new significance in association with ideas which we are accustomed to comprehend in the word 'salvation.'[1]

The belief in the moral government of this world, and in retribution as a principle of God's dealing with individuals in this life, was too firmly established to be displaced by the new doctrine, which came as an extension and welcome complement of the old, not as a substitute for it. Nor did the essential 'healthy-mindedness' of Judaism ever succumb to an extravagant 'other-worldliness' such as finds the meaning and end of this life only in another. For that, the Jews would not only have had to ignore the greater part of their Scriptures, but to be infected with the prevalent pessimistic dualism, which, in one form or another, was the fundamental philosophy of the other-worldly religions of the age. That such dualism had found entrance into certain circles is evident from the frequent mention of the heresy of 'Two Powers';[2] but the religious leaders never failed to condemn it as incompatible with the corner-stone of Judaism.

The destruction of the temple in 70 A.D. made an end of the whole system of sacrificial expiation, public and private, and of the universal piaculum, the scapegoat of the Day of Atonement.

---

[1] See Vol. II, pp. 94 f.
[2] This is at least one of the variety of heresies comprised under that name. See above, pp. 364 ff.

The loss was keenly felt. It is narrated that R. Johanan ben Zakkai was one day going out of Jerusalem accompanied by his disciple, R. Joshua (ben Hananiah). At the sight of the temple in ruins, Joshua exclaimed, "Woe to us, for the place where the iniquities of Israel were atoned for is destroyed!" Johanan replied, "Do not grieve, my son, for we have an atonement which is just as good, namely, deeds of mercy,[1] as the Scripture says, 'For I desire mercy and not sacrifice'" (Hos. 6, 6).[2] The story comes to us in a late source, but it illustrates the dismay with which the cessation of sacrifice must have filled many hearts,[3] and the better insight of men like Johanan to whom the condition of God's forgiveness and his favor is essentially moral, not ritual. This was no new doctrine. The prophets of the eighth century, and among their successors most emphatically Jeremiah, had combated the prevalent notion that God can be propitiated by gifts and offerings, and that sin can be expiated by multitudinous and costly sacrifices. The ostentatious worship of unjust men, God resents as an imputation on his character; the only way to avert his wrath is sincere and thorough-going amendment.[4] Such a transformation not only of conduct but of character is the moral aspect of repentance, that 'return' to God in love and obedience which from Hosea on is the one way of salvation for the sinful nation.

The prophetic teaching about sacrifice becomes in many of the Psalms an article of personal religion: God has no delight in sacrifice and oblation, he does not demand burnt-offering and sin-offering; what he wants is that men should do his will with

---

[1] גמילות חסדים, the charity that has a personal character. See Vol. II, pp. 171 ff.

[2] Abot de R. Nathan 4, 5. Bacher, Tannaiten, I, 39; cf. Pal. Amoräer, I, 225. — Hos. 6, 6 is quoted in Matt. 9, 13; 12, 7, in deflected application.

[3] See also Sifrè Deut. § 43, on Deut. 11, 15 (ed. Friedmann f. 81a), the tears of Gamaliel, Joshua, and Eleazar ben Azariah, and Akiba's cheerfulness. Note 214.

[4] Amos 4, 4 f.; 5, 21 ff.; Hos. 4, 8, 13; 5, 6; 8, 11 ff.; 14, 3 ff.; Isa. 1, 11 ff.; 22, 12 f.; 28, 7 f.; Jer. 6, 20; 7, 21 ff., etc. See Encyclopaedia Biblica, IV, col. 4222.

delight and have his law in their hearts (Psalm 40, 6 ff.). God
does not complain of Israel for any lack of sacrifices — as though
he, to whom the world and all the creatures in it belong, needed
their offerings, or fed on the flesh of bulls and goats and drank
their blood! 'Let thanksgiving to God be thy sacrifice, and thy
vows a'peace-offering; invoke me (in prayer) in the day of distress, and I will rescue thee and thou wilt honor me' (Psalm 50,
8–15). He desires not sacrifice, nor is he pleased with holocausts: 'The sacrifices of God are a broken spirit; a broken
and contrite heart God does not spurn' (Psalm 51, 18 f.). The
great lesson of the psalm is that the remedy for sin, the condition
of restoration to God's favor, is not expiation but contrite confession, with prayer for an inward purification and a better mind.
The Jewish sages teach the same truth: see Prov. 21, 3; 15, 8;
21, 27; 16, 6; Ecclus. 7, 8 ff.; and especially 31, 21–32, 26. It
is frequently emphasized by Philo; see e. g. De plantatione Noe
c. 25 §§ 107 f.[1]

The sacrificial institutions were an integral part of revealed
religion, and had the obligation of statutory law. It was not
for the interpreters of the law to narrow their scope or subtract
from their authority. Nor was it of any practical concern to inquire why the divine law-giver had ordained thus and not otherwise, or, indeed, ordained them at all. It was enough that he
had enjoined upon Israel the observance of them.[2] A false re-
liance on the efficacy of sacrifice of itself is condemned in the
spirit of the Scriptures. The 'fool's sacrifice' in Eccles. 4, 17 is
interpreted of such as sin and offer sacrifice, but do not repent,[3]
and consequently do not secure the remission of sins. The
magnitude of the offering does not count with God; the burnt-
offering may be taken from large cattle or small; it may be only

[1] Ed. Mangey, I, 345. Encyclopaedia Biblica, IV, 4223. See Note 215.
[2] On Israel alone. The rest of mankind (descendants of Noah) do not
bring sin offerings even for the violation of the commandments of God that
were given to them. Sifra, Wayyikra Ḥobah, init., on Lev. 4, 2 (ed. Weiss
f. 15b).
[3] Berakot 23a. Bacher, Pal. Amoräer, I, 75.

a bird, "to teach that whether a man bring a large offering or a small one does not matter, provided only he directs his mind intently to Heaven (God)."[1] From certain differences in the phraseology of the ritual for the burnt-offering of the ram and the bullock respectively in Lev. 1, 9 and 13, the lesson is drawn: "Let no man say within himself, I will go and do ugly and improper things; then I will bring a bullock, which has a great deal of meat, and offer it as a burnt-offering on the altar, and I shall obtain mercy with Him, and He will accept me in repentance.[2] God does not eat and drink (Psalm 50, 12 f.). Why then did he bid man sacrifice to him? To do his good pleasure.[3]

The important thing is that while the temple was still standing the principle had been established that the efficacy of every species of expiation was morally conditioned — without repentance no rites availed. With the cessation of the cultus repentance itself[4] was left the sole condition of the remission of sins.[5] It was of no small moment that the cessation of the sacrificial cultus was believed to be but a temporary suspension. In the two generations between the destruction of the temple by Titus and the erection of a temple of Jupiter on its site in Hadrian's new Aelia Capitolina which no Jew was allowed to set foot in, the Jews of Palestine had become wonted to a religion without a sacrificial cultus. For the cultus itself the learned found, as we shall see, a surrogate in the study of the ritual laws,[6] the kinds of sacrifice, their respective modes, applications and signifi-

---

[1] Sifra, Wayyiḳra Nedabah Pereḳ 9, on Lev. 1, 17 (ed. Weiss f. 9b); cf. Sifrè Num. § 143, on Num. 28, 6 (ed. Friedmann f. 54a, top); Menaḥot 110a, below.

[2] Lev. R. 2, end. But let him do good works and study the Law, and bring but a lean ram . . . and offer it on the altar, and He will be with him in mercy and receive him in repentance (Seder Eliahu Rabbah ed. Friedmann, p. 36, below.

[3] Sifrè Num. § 143. See Note 216.

[4] Including the fruits of repentance (Matt. 3, 8; Luke 3, 8 and 3, 10–14; Acts 26, 20), good works.

[5] So explicitly, Maimonides, Hilkot Teshubah 1, 3. See Note 217.

[6] Sifrè Deut. § 306, on Deut. 32, 2 (ed. Friedmann f. 131b, below). See Note 218.

cance, the whole cultus being thus perpetuated in thought and feeling when the fulfilment in act was made impossible by God himself, who for the sins of his people had again given over his holy house to be desecrated by the heathen. For the sacrificial expiations of the Law, repentance, with its fruit, good works, was the equivalent.

CHAPTER V

REPENTANCE

WHERE so much is attributed to repentance, our estimate of the religion will be largely determined by what it means by repentance. The foundation of the doctrine in the Law and the Prophets, and the appropriation of it, national and individual, has been exhibited above.[1] It remains to set forth the teaching of the school and synagogue concerning the nature and efficacy of true repentance, and inasmuch as in the current Christian representations of Judaism neither the character of this teaching nor the central significance of the doctrine of repentance in the Jewish conception of the religious life and of the way of salvation is adequately recognized, no apology need be made for treating the subject at what might otherwise seem disproportionate length.

Notwithstanding the importance of the idea of repentance in the Old Testament, the language has no specific name for it. The fundamental conception in the prophets is turning back to the allegiance and obedience of God, corresponding to their conviction that moral as well as religious evils are in their essence a falling away from God and his righteous will. They use for such a turning back from wrong-doing and return to God the every-day Hebrew word for 'turn about, go back' (שוב) leaving it to the context of their indictment to make the application plain. By this association the transparent primary sense of repentance in Judaism is always a change in man's attitude toward God and in the conduct of life, a religious and moral reformation of the people or the individual.[2]

The Hebrew of the schools found need of a noun for 'repentance,' and took תשובה, which in the Bible is used only for 're-

---

[1] Pages 500 ff.   [2] See Note 219.

turn' in the literal sense, or for a return of speech in an argument, 'reply'; while for the verb 'repent' to distinguish it from 're-turn' in its ordinary sense, they coined the phrase עשה חשובה, 'do repentance.'[1]

The Mishnah Yoma 8, 8 has been quoted above (page 498). Repentance is there the condition *sine qua non* of the efficacy of all the ritual expiations, including those of the Day of Atonement. But that none might imagine that thereby an indulgence to sin was established, the Mishnah proceeds (8, 9): "If any one says to himself, I will sin, and repent, (and again) I will sin and repent (and thus escape the consequences), no opportunity is given him to repent.[2] If he says, I will sin, and the Day of Atonement will expiate it, the Day of Atonement does not expiate it." The man who so presumes on the remission of sins through the goodness of God does not know the meaning of repentance, and annuls in himself the very potentiality of it.[3]

> What then?   What rests?
> Try what repentance can; what can it not?
> Yet what can it when one cannot repent?

Against such presumption on the mercy of God, Jesus son of Sirach gives warning: "Say not, I sinned, and what happened to me? For the Lord is long-suffering. Do not become rashly confident about expiation, and go on adding sin to sins; and do not say, His compassion is great, he will forgive (ἐξιλάσεται) the multitude of my sins; for mercy and wrath are with him, and upon sinners his anger will rest. Delay not to turn to the Lord (repent), and do not put it off from day to day" (Ecclus. 5, 4–7).

In a late Midrash, the question is raised, why power to repent is denied to such a sinner, and it is replied: "If a man repents

---

[1] See Note 220.

[2] Literally, "They do not put it in his power to repent." The indefinite plural subject, as frequently, is a reverent way of saying, "God does not put it in his power."

[3] A psychological explanation is given in the Talmud: By repetition a sin comes to seem to the sinner licit. Yoma 87a (Rab).

and goes back to his sins, that is no repentance. If one goes
down to take a bath of purification, holding some unclean reptile
in his hand, he gets no purification. He must cast away what
he has in his hand; after that he can take his bath and be
purified."[1] Centuries before, Sirach used a similar figure: A man
who bathes (to purify himself) from (contact with) a dead body,
and touches it again, what profit was there in his bath? So a
man who fasts for his sins and goes again and does the same
things — who will listen to his prayer, and what profit was there
in his afflicting himself? (Ecclus. 31, 30 f.).

"Scripture says: 'Let the wicked man forsake his way and the
bad man his plans, and let him return to the Lord (repent), and
He will have mercy upon him' (Isa. 55, 7). For God desires
repentance; he does not desire to put any creature to death,
as it is said: ('As I live saith the Lord Jehovah) I do not desire
the death of the wicked man, but that the wicked man turn
from his evil way and live'" (Ezek. 33, 11).[2]

The substance of repentance is the abandonment of evil deeds
and evil intentions, a radical change of conduct and motive.
The essentially moral character of repentance is exemplified
by the 'nine norms' of repentance (corresponding to the nine
days intervening between New Years and the Day of Atonement),
which are found in the nine exhortations God utters in Isa. 1,
16 f.: 'Wash you, make you pure, remove the evil of your misdeeds from before my eyes, cease doing evil, learn to do well,
seek after justice, relieve the oppressed, do justice to the orphan,
take up the cause of the widow.' "What is written after this?
'Come now, let us argue the matter, saith the Lord: if your sins
be like scarlet, they shall become white as snow.'"[3] The moral
reformation which the prophet demands of the people is individualized, and the promise appropriated to the individual sinner.

---

[1] Pesiḳta Rabbati c. 44 (ed. Friedmann f. 182b). The simile comes from
Tos. Taʻanit 1, 8. Other occurrences, see Schechter, Aspects of Rabbinic
Theology, p. 335, n. 1. See Note 221.

[2] Pesiḳta Rabbati l. c.; cf. Pesiḳta ed. Buber, Shubah, f. 157 a.

[3] Pesiḳta Rabbati ed. Friedmann f. 169 a. Cf. Jer. Rosh ha-Shanah 59c.

The touchstone of genuine repentance is that, every opportunity being given to repeat the misdeed, the man escapes the snare; for example, in case of adultery, under identical conditions.[1]

Repentance, as a turning from sin unto God, involves not only desisting from the sinful act, but the resolve not to commit it again, the abandonment of an evil way of life with the stedfast purpose no longer to walk in it. Maimonides formulates the consistent teaching of Judaism when he says: "What is repentance? Repentance is that the sinner forsakes his sin and puts it away out of his thoughts [2] and fully resolves in his mind that he will not do it again; as it is written, 'Let the wicked man forsake his way and the bad man his thoughts (plans),'" etc. (Isa. 55, 7).[3]

There is in the Old Testament another word, נחם, commonly translated 'repent,' which properly means 'be sorry' for something, or for having done something. Thus God was sorry that he had made man (Gen. 6, 6 f.); [4] he was sorry that he had made Saul king (I Sam. 15, 11, 35). Such regret frequently involves a change of mind regarding the future as well as the past, and this, rather than the feeling by which it is prompted, is often the principal import of the word. So it is in various places where it is said that God will not repent (change his mind),[5] or that if men change their conduct, turning from their evil ways, God will change his mind and not inflict on them the evils he had purposed,[6] or in the contrary case, will withold the good he had promised.[7] The corresponding Greek is μετανοεῖν, or (less frequently) μεταμέλεσθαι.[8] But however the notion of a change of purpose may predominate in many uses of the verb, the primary sense, 'be sorry,' is always present. Thus in Jer. 8, 5 f.: 'Why does this people, Jerusalem, apostatize with an unending apostasy? They cling to deceit; they refuse to return (repent). . . .

[1] Yoma 86b. See Note 222.   [2] That is, 'intentions, plans.'
[3] Hilkot Teshubah 2, 2; cf. ibid. 2, 1.
[4] Note the poignancy of the feeling in the second clause of verse 6.
[5] Num. 23, 19; I Sam. 15, 29; cf. Ezek. 24, 14.
[6] Jer. 18, 8; 3, 13.   [7] Jer. 18, 10; 26, 19; 42, 10.   [8] See Note 223.

Not a man is sorry for his wickedness, and says, What have I done!'

In Jer. 31, 18 f. God says: 'I have heard Ephraim [1] bemoaning himself: Thou didst chastise me and I have been chastised. . . . Turn me that I may turn, for thou art the Lord my God. For after I turned, I was sorry, and after I was taught the lesson, I smote upon my thigh; I was ashamed, yea, covered with disgrace, for I bore the opprobrium of my youth.' The words 'after I turned, I was sorry' (אחרי שובי נחמתי), were understood, as we might render it, 'after my conversion, I sorrowed for my sin.' [2] In this sense they are quoted by Maimonides as biblical authority for including sorrow for sin in the definition of repentance.[3] Specific proof-texts were indeed unnecessary; sorrow for sin is a constant motive in the penitential prayers of which there are so many examples in the Scriptures.[4]

The obligation to confess to God one's sins is explicit in the Law: 'When a man or a woman has committed any of all the sins of men . . . they shall confess their sins that they have committed' (Num. 5, 6 f.).[5] The model introductory formulas for private confession were found in Psalm 106, 6; 1 Kings 8, 47; Dan. 9, 5; and in the prescription Lev. 16, 21. They were framed in the first instance for the confession of the high priest over the bullock which he offered as a sin offering for himself and his house (Lev. 16, 6, 11);[6] but inasmuch as they were derived for that purpose from the confessions of laymen (David, Solomon, Daniel), they were found appropriate for private individuals also.

---

[1] The tribes of Israel in exile.

[2] Vulgate: Converte me, et convertar . . . Postquam convertisti me, egi poenitentiam.

[3] Hilkot Teshubah 2, 2.

[4] See above, p. 501. On the cultivation of the spirit of penitence, see below, p. 516. See further Note 224.

[5] Cf. also Lev. 5, 5. Sifra in loc. (ed. Weiss f. 24b); Sifrè Num. §§ 2–3 on Num. 5, 7.

[6] Sifra, Aḥarè Pereḳ 1 (ed. Weiss f. 80d); M. Yoma 4, 2; Tos. Yom ha-Kippurim 2, 1; Yoma 36b.

Maimonides gives such a formula: "O God, I have sinned, I have done iniquity, I have transgressed before thee, and have done thus and so. I am sorry and ashamed for my deed, and I will never do it again." [1] This is the essential part of confession; but if a man amplifies his confession and goes on longer in this vein, it is laudable. He adds that neither obligatory sin offerings and trespass offerings have any effect until the offerer repents and makes confession in words; nor do capital punishment or stripes expiate the offense, except on the same condition. Similarly, if a man has injured his fellow and seized his property, even though he have made restitution, his fault is not atoned for until he has made confession and turned from ever doing anything of the kind in the future. [2]

The public confession of the high-priest on the Day of Atonement was in similar form, but without specification: "O Lord, thy people Israel have sinned, done iniquity, transgressed before thee. O Lord, forgive (כפר) the sins, iniquities, and the transgressions which thy people Israel have sinned, done, and transgressed before thee, as it is written in the law of Moses, thy servant, On this day shall atonement be made," etc. (Lev. 16, 30). The people responded: "Blessed be His name whose glorious kingdom is forever and ever." [3]

That the confession of sins is a condition of the divine forgiveness is declared or implied in numerous places in the Scriptures: 'He who conceals his transgressions shall not succeed; but he who confesses and forsakes them shall obtain mercy" (Prov. 28, 13); [4] 'I acquaint Thee with my sin and do not con-

---

[1] Hilkot Teshubah 1, 1. Cf. Sifrè Zuṭa in Yalḳuṭ I § 701. See Schechter, Aspects of Rabbinic Theology, 337–338 n.

[2] See Note 225.

[3] I.e. the name of the Lord, the universal and eternal king (Psalm 145, 12 f.). Sifra, Aḥarè Pereḳ 4, on Lev. 16, 21 (ed. Weiss f. 82 a). This benediction accompanies each stage in the special ritual of the Day of Atonement (M. Yoma 4, 1, etc.).

[4] On Prov. 28, 13 see Pesiḳta ed. Buber f. 159a (one who confesses obtains mercy on condition of 'and forsakes'); Tanḥuma ed. Buber, Wayyesheb § 11. — Cf. 1 John 1, 8 f.

ceal my guilt. I say, I will confess on my part my transgressions
to the Lord, and thou dost pardon the guilt of my sin' (Psalm
32, 5).[1] In the eyes of Job's friends it is the hopeless symptom
of his case that he will not confess his sin even under chastisement. In Jeremiah (2, 35) God says to Judah, after a grave
indictment: 'Thou sayest, I am innocent . . . I will enter into
judgment with thee because thou sayest, I have not sinned.'[2]
God's ways are not like men's (Isa. 55, 7 f.): In the administration of human justice a criminal is tortured till he confesses, and
then the penalty is inflicted; God punishes until the sinner confesses and then lets him go.[3]

An important text for penitential prayer is Hos. 14, 2–4:[4]
'Take with you words and return to the Lord, say to him, Altogether forgive guilt, and accept good, and let us pay (in place
of) bullocks (the utterance) of our lips. We will never again call
the work of our hands our gods.' The last clause quoted is cited
for the principle that repentance involves the resolve not to
repeat the offense.[5] The preceding verse is thus enlarged on in
a late Midrash: God says to Israel: "My sons, I will not receive from you burnt-offerings nor sin offerings nor trespass
offerings nor oblations; but I would have you propitiate me by
prayer and supplication and by fixing your thoughts. Lest one
should imagine that empty words suffice, we are taught, 'For
Thou art not a God that likes wickedness, evil cannot abide with
thee' (Psalm 5, 5); but with confession and with pleas for mercy
and with tears. This is what is meant when it says, Take with
you words." [6]

That confession of sins belongs to repentance and is a condition of the divine forgiveness, and that when the Israelites thus

[1] See also Psalm 38, 19.
[2] Jer. Ta'anit 65d, middle; cf. Midrash Tehillim on Psalm 80, 1. See
Note 226.
[3] See Pesiḳta ed. Buber f. 159a, and the editor's note.
[4] Maimonides, Hilkot Teshubah 2, 2.
[5] See its teaching developed in Yoma 86a–b.
[6] Pesiḳta Rabbati ed. Friedmann f. 198b. (See the editor's note.) Perhaps the reference should extend to Psalm 5, 5–7.

confess their iniquities, God at once turns and has mercy on them, is authoritatively taught also on the ground of Lev. 26,40ff.[1]

Numerous examples of collective penitential prayers have been referred to above.[2] Confession of national sin, acknowledgment of the justice of God's judgments upon the sinful people, and appeal to his promises of forgiveness and restoration on condition of repentance, are the regular preamble to the prayer for deliverance. In purely individual form, Psalm 51 is the typical prayer of the penitent sinner in the canon. The Prayer of Manasses, found in some manuscripts of the Greek Bible and in the Apostolic Constitutions,[3] composed to fit the situation supposed in 2 Chron. 33, 18 f. and supply the prayer there twice referred to, well represents the kind of prayer which that archsinner ought to have made according to Jewish notions. Some extracts from it have been already given, but the whole should be read. It is a well-ordered composition, following familiar models, and made peculiarly appropriate to the king only by the specific confession of the sin of setting up idols (vs. 10 end) [4] and the reference to his imprisonment in vs. 10 (2 Chron. 33, 11).

Repentance, in the rabbinical definition of it, includes both the *contritio cordis* and the *confessio oris* of the Christian analysis. Nor is the element of *satisfactio operis* lacking. We shall see that in the case of a wrong done to a fellow man by deed or word, in his person, property, or honor, reparation is the indispensable condition of the divine forgiveness; and that for offenses against God, good works, especially charity (צדקה), is one of the things that cause the revocation of a dire decree.[5]

Men may be moved to repentance by the warnings of God in his word and providence, by experience of the consequences of

---

[1] Sifra in loc., Beḥukkotai Perek 8 (ed. Weiss f. 112b).

[2] In form, the prayer of an individual in behalf of the people (Ezra 9; Dan. 9), or recited in the presence of the assembly (Neh.9; Baruch 1, 15—3, 8).

[3] Const. App. ii. 22.   Swete, The O. T. in Greek, ed. 2, II, 824–826.

[4] στήσας βδελύγματα καὶ πληθύνας προσοχθίσματα (cf. 2 Chron. 33, 19).

[5] See Vol. II, p. 67 n; also Note 227.

sin and apprehension of worse consequences in this world and another — repentance induced by fear. But there is a repentance that springs from a nobler motive — love to God; and this is more highly esteemed by God and brings a larger grace. The former causes wilful sins to be treated as unwitting (Hos. 14, 2); the latter causes wilful sins to be treated as righteous deeds. (Ezek. 33, 14 f.).[1] A similar distinction is made between serving God out of love and serving him out of fear.[2]

The Westminster Shorter Catechism, the most widely known and accepted of the doctrinal standards of the Reformed Churches, thus defines repentance:

> "Repentance unto life is a saving grace, whereby a sinner, out of a true sense of his sin, and apprehension of the mercy of God in Christ, doth, with grief and hatred of his sin, turn from it unto God, with full purpose of, and endeavor after, new obedience."

With the omission of the words *in Christ*, this definition completely embodies the rabbinical teaching. And naturally so, for the Puritan theologians who framed the catechism drew their conception of the nature of repentance from the same source as the rabbis, the Jewish Scriptures, just as we have already seen in their definition of sin.[3]

The same doctrine of repentance which we find in the rabbinical sources is attested elsewhere. An instructive passage from Sirach has been quoted above.[4] The Psalms of Solomon (9, 11–15): "To whom shouldst thou show favor, O God, if not to those who call upon the Lord?[5] Thou wilt purge from sins one who confesses and pleads for exculpation. For shame is upon us and on our countenances for all (our misdeeds); and to whom wilt thou remit sins if not to them who have sinned? Righteous men thou dost bless, and dost not correct (punish) them for the things

---

[1] Yoma 86b (R. Simeon ben Laḳish); cf. 36b.

[2] E.g. Sifrè Deut. § 32, on Deut. 6, 5. See Vol. II, pp. 98 ff. See further Note 228.

[3] Above, p. 460.   [4] Pages 508, 509.   [5] Joel 3, 5 (2, 32).

in which they have sinned; and thy goodness is (shown) in dealing with sinners when they repent." Similarly, Ecclus. 17, 13 ff.: God said to men, Abstain from everything wrong, and enjoined them how each should treat his neighbor. "Their ways are continually before him, nor can they be hidden from his eyes. . . . All their works are as the sun before him, and his eyes are perpetually on their ways. Their unrighteous acts are not hidden from him, and all their sins are before the Lord. . . . After this he will arise and requite them, and inflict the retribution they deserve on their heads. Yet to those that repent he gave opportunity to return,[1] and encouraged those who despaired to hold out." And Ecclus. 17, 29: "How great is the mercy of the Lord, and his forgiveness (ἐξιλασμός) to those who return to him!" 18, 20 f.: "Before judgment examine thyself, and in the hour of visitation thou wilt find forgiveness. Before thou fallest ill, humble thyself, and in a time of sins show repentance (ἐπιστροφήν)." For Sirach, as for Philo, Enoch is ὑπόδειγμα μετανοίας ταῖς γενεαῖς.[2] The Prayer of Manasses, vs. 7: "Thou art the Lord Most High, compassionate, long-suffering, and abundant in mercy, repenting (μετανοῶν) over the ills of men. Thou, O Lord, according to the abundance of thy goodness, hast promised repentance and remission[3] to those who have sinned against thee, and by the abundance of thy compassion thou hast appointed repentance for sinners that they may be delivered. Thou, therefore, O Lord, the God of the righteous, didst not impose repentance on righteous men, on Abraham and Isaac and Jacob, who did not sin against thee;[4] but thou didst impose repentance on me, who am a sinner," etc. There follows a confession of his sins, and petition for forgiveness and deliverance, concluding: "Do not condemn me to a fate in the nethermost parts of the earth, for thou art God, God of those who are

---

[1] See Note **229**.

[2] Ecclus. 44, 16; Philo, De Abrahamo c. 3 §§ 17–19 (ed. Mangey, II, 3).

[3] Cf. Luke 24, 47; Acts 5, 31.

[4] Cf. Luke 15, 7 (righteous men who have no need of repentance). On the question of the sinlessness of the patriarchs see p. 468.

penitent. And thou wilt display in my case all thy goodness, in that thou savest me, unworthy as I am, according to thy great mercy." [1]

In Jubilees 5, 17 f. it is said: "Concerning the Israelites it is written and ordained, If they turn to Him in righteousness, he will forgive all their transgressions and pardon all their sins. It is written and ordained, He will be merciful towards all who once in the year turn from all their iniquity." [2]

In popular moralizing literature like the Testaments of the Twelve Patriarchs greater prominence is given to the manifestation of grief for sin by long continued fasting, especially by abstinence from flesh and wine. Thus Reuben, after seven months grave illness sent upon him for fornication with his father's concubine (Gen. 35, 22), of his own resolve repented before the Lord for seven years, during which he drank no wine or other intoxicating drink, and ate no flesh nor any food that tempts the appetite, but continued mourning over his great and unexampled sin (Test. Reuben 1, 9 f.).[3] In the cases of Reuben and Judah the ascetic motive in the specific form of the self-imposed penance is obvious; Joseph practises similar abstinence for seven years as a prophylactic against the seductions of Potiphar's wife.[4]

It is noticeable, and not insignificant, that the Apocalypses have relatively little about repentance.

The Hellenistic literature is here in full accord with the Palestinian. Thus, in Wisdom 11, 23: "Thou hast mercy on all men, because all things are in thy power; and dost overlook the sins of men to the end that they may repent." [5] So God dealt with the Canaanites: "Sending judgments upon them for a

---

[1] See Note 230.

[2] On the Day of Atonement (Lev. 16, 30). Cf. Pesiḳta ed. Buber f. 15b, f. 174b, etc.

[3] See also Test. of Simeon, 3, 4; Judah 15, 4; 19, 2 (in Judah 19, 2 some MSS. read μετάνοια τῆς σαρκός).

[4] Compare also the 'great penance' of Adam and Eve (Life of Adam and Eve, init.); cf. Pirḳè de-R. Eliezer c. 20.

[5] εἰς μετάνοιαν, Rom. 2, 4; cf. Acts. 17, 30.

short time, thou didst give them place for repentance, being not ignorant that their origin was evil and their badness inbred" (ibid. 12, 10). By such lessons God taught his own people that the righteous man must be humane,[1] and made his children of good hope that He would grant repentance in case of sins (12, 19; see the sequel).[2]

Among the witnesses to the Jewish doctrine of repentance in the first century of our era the Gospels and the first part of the Book of Acts are of peculiar importance. Repentance is the burden of John's mission; with the same words Jesus took up his work — Repent, for the reign of God is at hand! It is a μετάνοια εἰς ἄφεσιν τῶν ἁμαρτιῶν,[3] and the remission of sins is the condition of deliverance in the imminent crisis and of participation in the blessings of the reign of God or of the messianic age (Acts 2, 38; 3, 19 ff.). The significant thing is that in this insistent demand for repentance no definition or explanation is given. John, Jesus, the Apostles, all assume that their hearers know well enough what repentance is,[4] and how the forgiveness of sins depends upon it; and have no more need to be told that the impenitent sinner has no right in the good things of the Days of the Messiah or the World to Come.[5] If we ask where the masses got these notions and beliefs, the only possible answer is, In the popular religious instruction of the synagogue, through which the teaching of the students of Scripture in their schools was disseminated among all classes. That the common people had their religious conceptions directly from the Scriptures themselves is unimaginable; all the more where, as in this case, these conceptions form a complex which as such is nowhere explicit in the Old Testament. It is to be observed, further, that the conceptions of the necessity, nature, and effects of repentance entertained by John or by Jesus and his disciples

[1] φιλάνθρωπος.
[2] On Philo's doctrine of repentance see Note 231.
[3] Mark 1, 4.
[4] E.g. Luke 3, 10.
[5] On the last point see Vol. II, pp. 362 f.

differ in no respect from those of their countrymen to whom they addressed their appeal; and naturally, since they were derived from the same source, the liturgy and the homilies of the synagogue.

The new thing is the motive of urgency in the appeal — the day of doom is at hand. With John the association of repentance for the remission of sins with baptism is distinctive; in the apostolic preaching the characteristic thing is the added demand of the belief that Jesus of Nazareth, rejected, crucified, risen and ascended to heaven, whence he was presently to come to judgment, was the Messiah foretold by the prophets.[1] From their point of view it would be more exact to describe this, not as an additional demand, but as a necessary part of the repentance required — repentance for the guilt which as members of the Jewish people their hearers shared in the rejection of God's servant whom he sent 'to bless you, in turning every one of you from your iniquities' (Acts 3, 26).

When the gospel came to be preached to Gentiles, the premises of the Jewish doctrine of repentance were lacking; but the ground was prepared in more than one way for an understanding of the demand. On the one hand, there were the efforts of the Jews to convert the Gentiles from polytheism and idolatry to the worship of the one true God, and from vices which, following their Scriptures, they regarded as peculiarly heathen. For such conversion they employed the same terms that were used of the repentance or conversion of Israelites.[2] On the other hand, Cynics and Stoics had long preached conversion in the market places, exhorting their hearers to an immediate and complete change of conduct and character, and had given literary form to this demand in the diatribe.[3]

---

[1] Acts 2, 22 ff. (vs. 38 f.); 3, 12–26, etc.
[2] See Note 232.
[3] P. Wendland, Die hellenistisch-römische Kultur, 2–3 ed. (1912), pp. 75–96. (Literature, p. 75.)

CHAPTER VI

THE EFFICACY OF REPENTANCE

REPENTANCE is the sole, but inexorable, condition of God's forgiveness and the restoration of his favor, and the divine forgiveness and favor are never refused to genuine repentance. This was the promise of God through his prophets to the sinful nation from Hosea on, and accordingly the rabbis also taught that the deliverance of the people from the yoke of heathen rule was conditioned on national repentance.[1] "Great is repentance, said R. Jonathan, for it brings the deliverance, as it is said, 'A deliverer will come to Zion and to those who turn from transgression in Jacob' (Isa. 59, 20). How is this? — A deliverer will come to Zion *because of those* who turn from transgression in Jacob."[2] A saying of Johanan recorded in the same context runs: "Great is repentance, for it supersedes a prohibition in the law;[3] for it is said, 'If a man put away his wife, and she go from him and become another man's, may he return unto her again? Would not that land be grossly polluted? Thou hast played the harlot with many lovers, Yet return to me, saith the Lord'" (Jer. 3, 1).[4] To this aspect of the doctrine we shall return in a later chapter. Here we are concerned with individual repentance.

The exhortations and assurances to the nation were translated into an individual application by Ezekiel as the counterpart of his individualized doctrine of retribution, and he proclaimed in the name of the Lord the efficacy of repentance in terms as categoric and unqualified as those in which he set forth the dire

[1] Sanhedrin 97b–98a. R. Eliezer (ben Hyrcanus), against R. Joshua, who held that the deliverance would come in God's time without this condition. See Bacher, Tannaiten, I, 138, and below, Vol. II, p. 351.

[2] Yoma 86b. Note other eulogies of repentance there.

[3] Deut. 24, 1–4.

[4] Johanan takes ושוב as an exhortation, as does the Vulgate, "tamen revertere ad me, dicit Dominus, et ego accipiam te."

consequences of a lapse from righteousness.[1] No less positive
are other utterances of the prophets, such as Isa. 55, 7. Upon
the word of God himself in such scriptures the Jewish doctrine
of the unlimited efficacy of repentance is based.

R. Simeon ben Yoḥai formulates it thus: "If a man has been
completely righteous all his days and rebels at the end, he destroys it all, for it is said, 'The righteousness of the righteous
man will not save him in the day when he transgresses' (Ezek.
33, 12). If a man has been completely wicked all his days and
repents at the end, God receives him, for it is said, 'And as for
the wickedness of the wicked, he shall not stumble by it in the
day when he turns from his wickedness'" (ibid.).[2]

In accordance with this, later authorities teach that even those
sins which *ipso facto* exclude the sinner from a share in the World
to Come,[3] do so only in case he dies without repentance.[4] If he
turn from his wickedness and die in a state of repentance, he is
one of the children of the World to Come, for there is nothing
that can stand before repentance. Even if a man has been all
his days one who denied God (כפר בעיקר),[5] and at the last repents,
he has a share in the World to Come, for it is said: 'Peace,
peace, to him that is afar off and to him that is near, saith the
Lord . . . and I will heal him' (Isa. 57, 19). All these wicked
men, and the apostates and the like, if they turn in repentance,
whether openly or in secret, are received, as it is said, 'Return,
ye backsliding children.'[6] Even though he be still (outwardly)
a backslider, and repent only in secret and not openly, he is received in repentance."[7]

---

[1] See especially Ezek. 18; 33, 7–20.
[2] Tos. Ḳiddushin 1, 14 f.; cf. Ḳiddushin 40b; Jer. Peah 16b (with different proof-texts).
[3] On these sins see below, pp. 525 f.
[4] The extension to death-bed repentance results from the application of
Ezekiel's doctrine to the belief in a future life.
[5] See above, p. 467.
[6] Jer. 3, 14; 3, 22. The sequel of the words quoted must be taken with
them.
[7] Maimonides, Hilkot Teshubah 3, 14.

It is not improbable that the emphasis on the possibility of repentance for apostates, even though their return be in secret and not publicly announced, has a particular motive in the conditions of the author's time; but the doctrine itself is ancient. Thus R. Judah bar Simon quotes Hosea 14, 2 ('Return, O Israel, to the Lord thy God'):[1] "Even though you have been guilty of denying God (אפילו כפרת בעיקר)."[2] R. Eleazar said: "It is the way of the world, when a man has insulted his fellow in public and after a time seeks to be reconciled to him, that the other says: You insult me publicly and now you would be reconciled to me between us two alone! Go bring the men in whose presence you insulted me, and I will be reconciled to you. But God is not so. A man may stand and rail and blaspheme in the market place, and the Holy One says, Repent between us two alone, and I will receive you."[3]

That repentance is possible even in the very article of death was argued by R. Meir to his former teacher, the apostate Elisha ben Abuya, in his last illness. To Meir's exhortation to repent, Elisha replied, Would I be received even now? Meir answered by quoting Psalm 90, 3, to which he gave the turn, 'Thou lettest man return (repent) even unto crushing — that is until life is crushed out of him — and sayest repent, ye children of men.'[4]

There is danger, however, in presuming on this possibility. In Sifrè on Num. 6, 26 (§ 42) a series of unqualified expressions of God's readiness to hear prayer and forgive sin are paired with utterances of a directly opposite tenor. For example, Jer. 3, 14, 'Repent, ye backsliding children,' with the words of the same prophet in 8, 4, 'If a man repent, He will not repent';[5] similarly, Isa. 55, 6, 'Seek the Lord while he may be found,' with

---

[1] Here also the point is in the sequel of the quotation: 'I will heal their backsliding, I will love them freely; for mine anger is turned away from him.'

[2] Pesiḳta ed. Buber f. 163 b.

[3] Ibid.

[4] Jer. Ḥagigah 77c, top; Eccles. R. on Eccles. 7, 8. See Note 233.

[5] In this sense the clause, אם ישוב ולא ישוב, detached from its context, is here taken. In all cases the sequel must be recalled (Jer. 3, 14–18; 8, 4–6).

Ezek. 20, 31, 'As I live, saith the Lord God, I will not be sought by you.' The contradiction is reconciled in every case by the same formula: the invitation or promise holds until the sentence[1] is sealed; the contrary after it is sealed. And the doom of the impenitent sinner may be sealed long before his death.[2] The specific application to repentance is made in the Tanḥuma. In the sacerdotal benediction Num. 6, 26, 'The Lord will show thee favor and give thee peace,' and another Scripture says, 'who will not show favor' (Deut. 10, 17). How so? If a man repents before the sentence is sealed, the Lord will show him favor; when once it is sealed, the words apply, 'who will not show favor.'[3]

That God accepts the repentance of the worst of sinners is proved by king Manasseh. No figure in the whole history is painted so black. He had erected altars of the Baals throughout the land, and installed foreign gods and an idol in the very temple of Jehovah; he offered his children to 'the King' (Moloch) in the fires of the Tophet in the Valley of Hinnom; he practised nefarious augury, necromancy, and sorcery. In these ways he led his people astray till they outdid in evil the nations of Canaan that the Lord had exterminated when the Israelites came into the land.[4] To the warning of the Lord, king and people gave no heed. The Chronicler adds that the Assyrians came and carried Manasseh off to Babylon in chains; there in his distress he humbled himself before the God of his fathers and prayed, and God yielded to his entreaty and heard his supplication and restored him to Jerusalem and to his throne. 'Then Manasseh knew that Jehovah is (the true) God' (2 Chron. 33, 11–13). His prayer is said to be recorded in the Chronicles of the Kings of Israel.[5]

[1] גזר דין.
[2] Cf. Rosh ha-Shanah 17b–18a.
[3] Tanḥuma ed. Buber, Naso § 18 (f. 17a–b); Num. R. 11, 15. See Note 234.
[4] 2 Chron. 33, 1–9; cf. 2 Kings 21, 1–15.
[5] In Sifrè Deut. § 32, on Deut. 6, 5 (ed. Friedmann f. 73b, below) Manasseh is adduced as an example of the effect of chastisement in leading to repentance. — On the Prayer of Manasseh see above, p. 514.

The inference was plain: if one who, in spite of the law (Deut. 13, 6 ff.) and the warnings of the prophets, had sinned so flagrantly and wilfully, and caused the whole people to sin, could be forgiven and restored to God's favor upon his penitent prayer, there was no one whose repentance could not be accepted.

The divine justice (מדת הדין) would have hindered the reception of Manasseh's supplication; but God made a kind of loop-hole in the firmament in order to receive him in repentance.[1] A more expansive version is found in the Palestinian sources. In his distress Manasseh called on every heathen deity by name to rescue him. When he got no help from them at all, he remembered the words of Deut. 4, 30 f., 'In thy distress, when all these things are come upon thee in the latter days, thou shalt return to the Lord thy God, and hearken unto his voice; for the Lord thy God is a merciful God; he will not fail thee, nor destroy thee,' etc., and said, I call upon him; if he answer me, well, and if not, all ways are alike.[2] The ministering angels stopped up the windows of the firmament to keep Manasseh's prayer from coming up to God, and said to God, Is there repentance for a man who set up an idol in thy temple? God answered, If I do not receive him in repentance, I shall bolt the door in the face of all penitents. What did God do? He made a kind of loop-hole beneath the glorious throne and heard his supplication (2 Chron. 33, 13).[3]

The Scriptures furnished other examples of great sinners the acceptance of whose repentance was evident from the fact that dire sentence against them was revoked or remitted.[4] In the chapter on repentance in the Pesiḳta from which the case of Manasseh has just been quoted, Israel is supposed to ask; "Lord of the worlds, if we repent, wilt thou receive us? God answers,

---

[1] Sanhedrin 103a.

[2] One religion is as unprofitable as another.

[3] Jer. Sanhedrin 28c; Pesiḳta ed. Buber f. 162a–b; Lev. R. 30, 3, etc. See Note 235.

[4] Even the Israelites who worshipped the golden calf at the foot of Sinai. Tanḥuma ed. Buber, Balak § 21, end. See Note 236.

I accepted the repentance of Cain, and will I not accept your repentance?"[1] Among the kings, besides Manasseh, Ahab and Jeconiah are adduced; and of nations the men of Nineveh, with a recital of their repentance and the proof of its acceptance.[2] Other biblical examples elsewhere cited are Enoch, Reuben, Judah.[3]

The repentance of Manasseh led to his restoration to the throne, as the Scripture says; but when the sphere of retribution was extended beyond this world, the question could still be raised whether such as he would have a part in the World to Come. In the Mishnah Sanhedrin 10, 2, among the exceptions to the rule that all Israel has a share in the World to Come, it is said: "Three kings[4] and four private persons have no share in the World to Come." The three kings are Jeroboam, Ahab, and Manasseh. R. Judah (ben Ila'i) contended on the ground of 2 Chron. 33, 13 that Manasseh would have a place in the World to Come, but the others replied (the text says), God restored him to his kingdom, not to the life of the World to Come.[5] Nevertheless, Johanan, the most influential of the Palestinian teachers of the third century and head of the school of Tiberias, not only held to the opinion of R. Judah, but declared: Whoever says that Manasseh has no share in the World to Come discourages all penitents.[6]

There are also whole classes of sinners who are denied a share in the World to Come — heretics, 'epicureans,' various kinds of unbelievers, apostates, delators, etc.[7] Besides these the rabbinical authorities denounced the same doom on other sins of a

[1] Pesiḳta ed. Buber f. 160a.
[2] Ibid., ff. 160–163.
[3] On Enoch, see above, p. 516. Reuben, Judah, Test. of Twelve Patriarchs, above, p. 517. In the Midrash, Sifrè Deut. § 31 (ed. Friedmann f. 72b), and § 347; Judah and Reuben, Tanḥuma ed. Buber, Wayyesheb § 17.
[4] Tos. Sanhedrin 12, 11 adds Ahaz, making *four* kings.
[5] M. Sanhedrin 10, 2; Sanhedrin 102b–103a.
[6] Ibid. 103a. מרפה ידיהן של בעלי תשובה.
[7] On the classes or individuals thus excluded see Maimonides, Hilkot Teshubah 3, 6 ff., and below, Vol. II, pp. 388 f.

less radical nature;[1] but this fate befalls those only who die impenitent.[2]

Several post-talmudic sources have a catalogue of twenty-four sins that render repentance difficult or altogether impossible.[3] Four of them fall under the former category — God does not put it in the sinner's power to repent;[4] the rest are obstacles to repentance, but do not wholly prevent it. "If a man repent of them, he is a penitent, and has a share in the World to Come."[5] The hindrances, as Maimonides explains, are in man himself — the effect of sin upon his conscience, or, in the case of sins against his fellows, circumstances which make it difficult to fulfil the conditions of reparation and reconciliation.[6]

Repentance was included in the plan of God before the creation of the world, or, as it is expressed, was created before the world. The proof-text is Psalm 90, 2 f.: 'Before the mountains were brought forth. . . . Thou turnest men to contrition, and sayest, Return (repent), ye children of men.' The seven things thus created are the Law (the future revelation), repentance, paradise, hell, the glorious throne (of God), the (celestial) temple, and the name of the Messiah.[7] The reflection which thus gives repentance a premundane existence in the plan of God is obvious from the other members of the group — the Law, paradise, hell. God knew that the man he purposed to create, with his freedom and his native evil impulse, would sin against the revealed will of God in his law and incur not only its temporal penalties in

----

[1] Abot 3, 11 (Eleazar of Modiim); Sanhedrin 99a. Even one who puts his fellow to shame publicly (cf. Baba Meṣi'a 58b, below.

[2] Maimonides, l. c. 3, 14.

[3] Ibid. 4, 1 ff., with comment showing in what ways they hinder repentance; the list is probably derived from a lost minor tractate. (Schechter, Aspects of Rabbinic Theology, p. 331 n. 2).

[4] Cf. ibid. 6, 3.

[5] Ibid. 4, 6.

[6] Ibid. 4, 3; 6, 3. Isa. 6, 10 is quoted, as in Matt. 13, 14 f. and parallels; Acts 28, 26 f.

[7] Pesaḥim 54a and Nedarim 39b; Gen. R. 1, 4; Tanḥuma ed. Buber, Naso § 19 init. See above, p. 266, and Notes 33 and 34.

this life but the pains of hell.   He must therefore have provided
beforehand the remedy for sin, repentance.

God not only provided repentance as the sovereign remedy
for sin, but continually sets forth its efficacy and urges men to
avail themselves of it.   By the repeated warnings of his providence and by the temporal punishments he inflicts, he endeavors
to bring them to repent.[1]   God's dealing with transgressors is
contrasted with the administration of human (Roman) justice.
When a robber is brought up before the criminal court, the judge
reads the charges, then pronounces sentence, and forthwith the
man is led off to execution.   God's way is different: first he reads
the charges—'And now they sin still more and have made them
a molten image' (Hos. 13, 2); then he smites them — 'Ephraim
is smitten, their root is dried up' (Hos. 9, 16); then he imposes
upon them, as it were a burden—'The guilt of Ephraim is bound
up in a bundle, its sin is laid in store' (Hos. 13, 12); and after
that he passes sentence upon them — 'Samaria shall pay the
penalty, because it has rebelled against its God' (Hos. 14, 1);
and finally he brings them back in repentance — 'Repent, O
Israel' (Hos. 14, 2).[2]

God bade Jeremiah, Go, say to Israel, Repent!   He went and
delivered the message.   They replied, Master, how can we repent?   With what face can we come into the presence of God?
Have we not provoked him to wrath and outraged him?   Those
very mountains and hills on which we worshipped strange gods,
are they not standing there?   'Upon the tops of the mountains
they sacrifice' (Hos. 4, 13).   'Let us lie in our shame and let our
disgrace cover us' (Jer. 3, 25).   When the prophet returned to
God and reported their words, God bade him say to them, If
ye come to me, is it not to your Father in heaven that ye come?
'For I have been a father to Israel, and Ephraim is my firstborn' (Jer. 31, 9).[3]

To similar intent another rabbi lets God answer the same de-
spairing response of the people to the prophet's summons: "Did

---

[1] See below, pp. 528 f.   [2] Pesiḳta ed. Buber f. 159b.   [3] Ibid. f. 165 a.

I not write in my law, 'I will set my face against that soul and cut him off from the midst of his people' (Lev. 20, 6). Have I then done so? Nay, but ('Repent, thou backsliding Israel, saith the Lord), I will not frown upon you, for I am merciful, saith the Lord, I will not bear a grudge forever' (Jer. 3, 12).[1]

It is unnecessary to multiply illustrations of a doctrine which lies so plainly on the face of the Scriptures and is everywhere assumed in the teaching of the school and the synagogue. Some expressions to the same effect have already been quoted from the extra-canonical literature,[2] in which, however, the theme is not nearly so prominent as in the rabbinical sources.

God's efforts to lead men to repent and so to avert the doom impending over them for their sins are not confined to Israel. Numerous instances are adduced in Midrash Tanḥuma. God hoped that the generation of the Flood would repent and he might receive them; for this reason he had Noah build the ark under their eyes and explain to them what it was for.[3] Notwithstanding their rebellion he stretched out his hand[4] to the builders of the Tower of Babel and bade them repent, promising to receive them, repentance being the one thing he requires (Deut. 10, 12).[5] The Scripture says: 'As I live, saith the Lord, I do not desire the death of the wicked' (Ezek. 33, 11).[6] Why? Because he may perhaps repent. So also (from Gen. 18, 20 f.) it is inferred that God opened to the people of Sodom and Gomorrah a door of repentance;[7] and when God communicated to Abra-

[1] Pesiḳta ed Buber, f. 165a. The following verses in Jer. 3 are to be recalled by the quotation. ('Only acknowledge thine iniquity, 'etc.)
[2] Above, pp. 515 ff.
[3] Tanḥuma ed. Buber, Bereshit § 37.
[4] On this phrase see Sifrè Num. § 134 (ed. Friedmann f. 50b, middle); Mekilta, Shirah 5 (ed. Friedmann f. 38b; ed. Weiss f. 46a). God's hand is held out to all who come into the world.
[5] Tanḥuma ed. Buber, Noah § 28, applying a verse specifically addressed to Israel.
[6] The heathen are 'the wicked' in an eminent sense.
[7] Gen. R. 49, 6 and elsewhere. So also to the Egyptians, before the catastrophe at the Red Sea, Mekilta, Shirah 5 (on Exod. 15, 5). See Note 237.

ham his purpose to destroy the cities of the plain, Abraham began at once to make a plea for them, thinking that perhaps they might repent.[1] Most conclusive is the repentance of the Ninevites at Jonah's preaching, and God's annulment of the doom pronounced upon them,[2] to the profound dissatisfaction of the prophet whose attempted flight had been prompted by a presentiment that the heathen were near repentance and that his soft-hearted God would forgive them.[3]

On the other hand the particularistic note is sometimes struck. Thus, on Num. 6, 26, 'The Lord will show favor to thee,' and the contrary in Deut. 10, 17, we find the usual reconciliation: If a man repent, God shows him favor, with the supplement: It might be inferred that this applies to all men (including the heathen), but this inference is not admissible, for the text says, 'to *thee*,' and not to another people (thus restricting the promise to Israel).[4] The exhortations to repentance in the Scriptures and the promises of forgiveness and restoration are in the nature of the case addressed almost exclusively to Israel, and are correctly so interpreted. For the Gentile to participate in this promise, as in all others, the indispensable condition is the repentance, or conversion, in which he abandons his false religion for the true, the heathenish freedom of his way of life for obedience to the revealed will of God in his Law; in a word, becomes a proselyte to Judaism, a Jew by naturalization.[5] This is the logical attitude of a revealed religion, and has always been maintained by the Christian church: repentance avails nothing — or, more exactly, repentance in the proper sense is impossible — outside the church. The 'gate of repentance' which is open to those outside is the gate of entrance into the true religion, to whose professors alone God's promises of grace, and first of all the forgiveness of sins, belong. Moslem doctrine is the same.

[1] Tanḥuma ed. Buber, Wayyera § 9; cf. § 16.   [2] Jonah cc. 3–4.
[3] Mekilta, Bo, Introduction (ed. Friedmann f. 1b–2a; ed. Weiss f. 1b–2a).
[4] Pesiḳta ed. Buber f. 156a–b.
[5] It is such a conversion that Philo oftenest has in mind when he writes of repentance. See above, pp. 327 f.

God is ever waiting to receive the confession and supplication of the penitent sinner. The figure of a gate, or door, of access to God frequently occurs. God makes or opens this door for individuals, as he did for Adam.[1] The gates of prayer (petition) are sometimes closed; but the gates of repentance are always open.[2] Repentance is like the sea, in which nothing hinders any man from purifying himself at any time; while prayer is compared to a bath, access to which may for various reasons be prevented.[3] In the story of Manasseh's repentance quoted above there are open windows in the firmament through which the confession and supplication of the penitent rise to the ears of God; and when the angels try to stop them, God himself makes a new opening beneath his very throne (whither the angels dare not venture). "If ye repent, I will receive you and judge you favorably, for the gates of Heaven (God) are open, and I am listening to your prayer; for I am looking out of the windows, peering out through the crevices, until the sentence is sealed on the Day of Atonement. Therefore Isaiah says, 'Seek the Lord while he may be found.'"[4]

The purport of all this imagery is plain: the repenting sinner may be sure that at all times and under all circumstances God takes note at once of his repentance. An arrow carries the width of a field; but repentance carries to the very throne of God.[5] In a later Midrash this is ascribed, in an amplified form, to the Patriarch Judah: "Great is the power of repentance, for as soon as a man meditates in his heart to repent, instantly it (his repentance) rises, not ten miles, nor twenty, nor a hundred, but a journey of five hundred years; and not to the first firmament but

---

[1] Gen. R. 21, 6. According to this, Adam did not take the opportunity; hence Cain appears as the first penitent, ibid. 22, 12 f.

[2] Ibid. The comparison to the sea is suggested by Psalm 65, 6.

[3] Pesiḳta ed. Buber f. 157a–b.

[4] Ibid. f. 156b. The reference to the ten Penitential Days, see below, p. 532; Vol. II, pp. 62 f.

[5] Ibid. f. 163b; cf. Yoma 86a, end; from Hosea 14, 2, שובה ישראל עד ה' אלהיך (see above p. 387). Bacher, Pal. Amoräer, I, 534.

to the seventh; and not to the seventh firmament only — it stands before the glorious throne" (Hos. 14, 2).[1]

God encourages and assists every movement of man's heart towards him. The words of the lover in the Song of Songs (5, 2), 'Open to me, my sister,' are thus applied: God says, "Open to me an entrance no larger than the eye of a needle, and I will open to you an entrance through which tents and great timbers can pass."[2]

In view of several passages in the Old Testament, e.g. Jer. 31, 18 f., the question could be raised whether the initiative in repentance, conceived as a reciprocal 'return,' is on God's side or man's. In the Midrash on Lam. 5, 21, 'Turn thou us unto thee, O Lord, and we shall be turned,' the Israelite church[3] says to God: "Lord of the World, it is for Thee to do—'Turn us (and we shall be turned).' God replies, It is for you to do, as it is said, 'Turn unto me and I will turn unto you' (Mal. 3, 7). Israel answers, It is for Thee, as it is written, 'Turn us, O God of our salvation' (Psalm 85, 5).[4] The Midrash on Psalms combines the two. The children of Korah said: How long will ye say, 'Turn, O backsliding children' (Jer. 3, 14), whilst Israel said, 'Return, O God, how long?' (Psalm 90, 13). . . . But neither Thou (God) wilt return by thyself, nor will we return by ourselves, but we will return both together, as it is said, 'Turn us, O God of our salvation. . . . Wilt Thou not come back and revive us' (Psalm 85, 5–7). As Ezekiel said, 'Behold, O my people, I will open your grave. . . and will put my spirit in you, and ye shall live' (Ezek. 37, 12–14).[5]

The Scripture thus gives authority and example to prayers, that God may give repentance.[6]

---

[1] Pesikta Rabbati ed. Friedmann f. 185a. See Note 238.

[2] Pesikta ed. Buber f. 163b; cf. ibid. 46b and the editor's note there. Schechter, Aspects of Rabbinic Theology, p. 327.

[3] כנסת ישראל.

[4] Lam. R. on Lam. 5, 21. The Midrash operates with the unusual שובנו (instead of the causative), see the commentaries.

[5] Midrash Tehillim on Psalm 85, 5. The condensed translation is Schechter's.

[6] E.g. Shemoneh 'Esreh, 5. See above, pp. 293 f.

The sin of the repentant sinner is not only forgiven, the memory of it is expunged. Among the 'sweetest' words of God to mankind (Cant. 5, 16) R. Levi names Ezek. 18, 21 f.: If the wicked man turns from all his sins, etc., God says, 'None of his transgressions that he has committed shall be remembered against him; by his righteousness that he has done he shall live.'[1] The same verse from Ezekiel is similarly used elsewhere: "See how excellent repentance is! God says, 'Return unto me and I will return unto you' (Mal. 3, 7). For no matter how many wicked deeds a man has to his charge, if he repent before God, God imputes it to him as if he had not sinned, as it is said, 'None of his transgressions that he has committed shall be remembered' (Ezek. 18, 22).[2]

There is no forgetfulness with God, but, if one might venture to say so, for Israel's sake he is made forgetful; 'Who is a God like thee that forgets iniquity[3] and passes over the transgressions of the remnant of his inheritance' (Mic. 7, 18). So David says: 'Thou hast forgotten the iniquity of thy people, thou hast covered all their sin' (Psalm 85, 3).[4]

God, says Philo, esteems repentance as highly as sinlessness.[5] Repentance is a purification of the inner man: 'O Jerusalem, wash thy heart from wickedness, that thou mayest be saved. How long shall thy wicked thoughts abide within thee?' (Jer. 4, 14). Nothing else can purify from sin. To the unrepentant God says, 'For if thou wash thee with lye and use exceeding much soap, yet thy guilt remains a spot before me' (Jer. 2, 22).[6]

To the exhortation of Hos. 14, 2, Israel responds with the question, Lord of the World, what wilt thou do with all our

---

[1] Tanḥuma ed. Buber, Wayyeṣè § 22.

[2] Ibid. Wayyera § 16. From the same passage in Ezekiel, Justin Martyr learns that God holds the penitent sinner ὡς δίκαιον καὶ ἀναμάρτητον.

[3] נשא עון, 'forgiving,' read as נשה, 'forgetting.' Similarly in Psalm 85, 3.

[4] Jer. Sanhedrin 27c, and elsewhere; Pesiḳta ed. Buber f. 167a. Bacher, Pal. Amoräer, II, 112 f.

[5] De spec. legg. i. 3 § 187 (ed. Mangey, II, 240). See Note 239.

[6] Pesiḳta ed. Buber f. 156b; cf. also Sifrè Num. § 42 (ed. Friedmann f. 12b, middle).

iniquities? He answers, Repent, and they will be swallowed up out of the world, as it is said, 'He will turn and have mercy upon us, He will submerge our iniquities, and Thou wilt cast into the depths of the sea all our sins' (Mic. 7, 19).[1]

The complete annulment of the sinner's past is expressed in an even more forcible way by the figure of a new creation. God says, when you are gathered to judgment before me on New Years Day and go forth in peace (acquitted), I impute it to you as if you were created a new creation (or creature).[2] Another version, ascribed to R. Isaac, is found in the Pesiḳta Rabbati: God says to Israel, Repent in these ten days between New Years and the Day of Atonement, and I will justify[3] you on the Day of Atonement and create you a new creation.[4] The same figure is used by Paul: 'If any man is in Christ (it is) a new creation; the old has passed away, all has become new.'[5]

The pre-eminence of repentance is expressed in the following passage: "Men asked Wisdom, What is the doom of the sinner? It answered, 'Evil pursues sinners' (Prov. 13, 21); they asked Prophecy the same question, and it answered, 'The soul (the individual) that sins shall die' (Ezek. 18, 4); they asked the Law, and it answered, 'Let him bring a trespass offering (asham) and it shall be forgiven him,' as it is said, 'And it shall be accepted for him to make atonement for him' (Lev. 1, 4). They asked the Holy One, blessed is He, and he answered, 'Let him repent, and it shall be forgiven him.' This is the meaning of the text, 'Good and right is the Lord, therefore will he instruct sinners in the way' (Psalm 25, 8)."[6] That is, he shows them the way that they may repent. As Schechter observes, this is not meant to put the three parts of Scripture in contradiction to one

---

[1] Pesiḳta Rabbati ed. Friedmann f. 185b. Cf. Targum Micah 7, 19.

[2] Jer. Rosh ha-Shanah 59c, below (R. Eleazar ben Jose); Pesiḳta ed. Buber f. 155b; Lev. R. 29, end. Bacher, Pal. Amoräer, II, 261.

[3] מזכה, 'acquit, declare guiltless,' corresponding to Paul's use of δικαιόω.

[4] Pesiḳta Rabbati ed. Friedmann f. 169a.

[5] 2 Cor. 5, 17; cf. Gal. 6, 15.

[6] Pesiḳta ed. Buber f. 158b; Jer. Makkot 31d, below.

another and to the words of the Lord himself, but to indicate the pre-eminence of repentance above all other expiations.[1]   In fact, Jewish doctrine finds a place for expiation by suffering the consequences of sin, and by death, as well as by sacrifice; but all are conditional upon repentance.

[1] Aspects of Rabbinic Theology, p. 294.

CHAPTER VII

MOTIVES OF FORGIVENESS

FORGIVENESS is a prerogative of God which he shares with no other and deputes to none. The angels, as we have seen, are more jealous of God's honor, more insistent on strict justice, less inclined to let mercy have the final word, than their Master. The Israelites are warned that the angel whom God sends to lead them through the desert will not pardon their transgression (Exod. 23, 21).[1] David says to God: "Lord of the World, to an angel wilt thou hand me over, who shows no favor? Who can stand before him? 'If thou, O Lord, shouldst keep note of iniquities, O Lord, who could stand?' If Thou sayst that forgiveness is not in Thy power, it *is* in Thy power, as it is said, 'For with Thee is forgiveness, that Thou mayst be revered' (Psalm 130, 3 f.)."[2]

God is moved to forgive sin by his own character. Mercy is the attribute which best expresses his nature,[3] and it is shown to all his creatures. 'Gracious and merciful is the Lord, long-suffering and of great loving-kindness. Good is the Lord to all, and his mercies are over all his works' (Psalm 145, 8 f.). The words are often quoted and applied. God's goodness and mercy embrace man and beast, Jew and Gentile, righteous and wicked.[4]

The Jew had not only the general uncovenanted mercy of God to appeal to like the Gentiles. He had in the Scriptures the assurance of God's peculiar love to Israel, and here again what the prophets declared of his love for his people collectively was appropriated individually by the members of the people.

---

[1] Tanḥuma ed. Buber, Mishpaṭim § 11. It is neither in the angel's nature to pardon sin, nor is he commissioned to do so.

[2] Ibid.

[3] See above, pp. 389 f., 393 f.

[4] See Note 240.

God's love for Israel had its origin and ground in his love for its forefathers, Abraham, Isaac, and Jacob. So Moses declares: 'Behold, unto the Lord thy God belongeth the heaven and the heaven of heavens, the earth with all that therein is. Only the Lord ardently loved thy fathers, and chose their seed after them, even you, in preference to all the nations, as is now the case' (Deut. 10, 15; cf. 4, 37).[1] On their part the character and conduct of the patriarchs were peculiarly well-pleasing to God. They fulfilled and exemplified the fundamental law, 'Thou shalt love the Lord thy God with all thy heart, and with all thy soul, and with all thy might.' R. Meir quotes his master Akiba: "'Thou shalt love the Lord thy God with all thy heart,' like our father Abraham, as it is said, 'For I know him, that he will command his sons and his household after him' (Gen. 18, 19); and with all thy soul (life), like Isaac, who bound himself upon the altar; 'and with all thy gratitude,' that is, give thanks to him like Jacob, as it is said, 'I am not worthy of all the mercies and of all the faithfulness that thou hast shown unto thy servant,'" etc. (Gen. 32, 11).[2]

It was natural to believe that God would show especial favor or indulgence to their descendants for the sake of the affection and esteem in which he held their fathers, and for this expectation there was good warrant in the Scriptures.[3] When the prophet in Isa. 41, 8 ff. would inspire his fellow exiles to faith in the signal deliverance their God was about to work for them, he addresses them: 'But thou, Israel, my servant, Jacob whom I have chosen, the seed of Abraham, my friend, . . . fear not, for I am with thee, be not dismayed, for I am thy God,' etc. The people that bears the name of Israel and of Jacob, the posterity of Abraham, God's 'friend,' has in that very fact the assurance that the God of their fathers will not desert them in their distress.

---

[1] Also and especially 7, 6–10.

[2] Sifrè Deut. § 32, on Deut. 6, 5. מאדך is taken as if from הודה, 'confess, give thanks.' Bacher, Tannaiten, II, 49 f.; cf. p. 38, n. 3. On Isaac, see below, pp. 539 ff.

[3] See also Lev. 26, 44 f.; an example 2 Kings 13, 23.

The appeal to the memory of the patriarchs and God's sworn promises to them has its most striking and conclusive precedent in the intercession of Moses for the people after the sin of the golden calf (Exod. 32, 11–13; cf. Deut. 9, 27). All his pleas, it is observed, did not persuade God to relent in his purpose to destroy the faithless and insensate people which at the very foot of Sinai had broken the first commandment of the Decalogue, until Moses urged, 'Remember Abraham, Isaac, and Israel, thy servants, to whom thou didst swear by thine own self, and saidst unto them, I will multiply your seed as the stars of heaven, and all this land that I have spoken of will I give unto your seed, and they shall inherit it forever. Then the Lord repented of the evil which he said he would do unto his people.'[1] R. Hezekiah ben Ḥiyya (3d cent.) expressly draws the inference: Moses' intercession was not accepted by God until he made mention of the good desert of the forefathers. God said to him, Moses, if it were not for the good desert of their forefathers, I would destroy them; you cannot adduce any good desert in the people itself (as a reason for sparing them).[2] "When Israel sinned in the desert, Moses stood before God and uttered ever so many prayers and intercessions before him, and was not answered. But when he said, 'Remember Abraham and Isaac and Israel, thy servants,' he was answered at once."[3]

In fact the prominence given in the words of God himself to this peculiar relation to the patriarchs, to his covenant with them or oath to them,[4] and the appeal to this relation by their posterity in pleading for God's help,[5] or in expressions of confidence in his

---

[1] On the intercession of Moses see Berakot 32a; Soṭah 14a. Moses did not rely on his own merit, but the merit was ascribed to him, Berakot 10b (Psalm 106, 23). See Note 241.

[2] Tanḥuma ed. Buber, Wayyera § 9. Cf. Bacher, Pal. Amoräer, I, 55. See Note 242.

[3] Shabbat 30a. — God advises Israel to appeal to the merit of the patriarchs, in order to gain their cause before Him. Pesiḳta ed. Buber f. 153b; Lev. R. 29, 7. — See also the Musaf for New Years (Singer, Daily Prayer Book, p. 251 f.).

[4] See e.g. Lev. 26, 40–45; Deut. 9, 5.

[5] E.g. Deut. 9, 26–29; cf. Gen. 32, 9–12.

deliverance,[1] gave sufficient ground for the Jewish belief that because of the fathers God blessed their descendants.

Among the patriarchs Abraham is pre-eminent.   In Gen. 26, 3–5, God says to Isaac: 'I will perform the oath which I swore to Abraham thy father, and will multiply thy posterity like the stars of heaven, and will give to thy posterity all these lands . . . because Abraham listened to my voice and kept the charge I gave him and my commandments, my statutes, and my law.'[2] An ancient homiletical Midrash has a parable of a king who planned building a palace. He dug in several places seeking proper ground for a foundation; at last he struck rock beneath, and said, Here I will build, so he laid the foundations and built. Just so when God sought to create the world, he examined the generation of Enosh[3] and the generation of the Flood, and said, How can I create the world when these wicked people will rise up and provoke me to anger? When he saw Abraham who was to arise, he said, Now I have found a rock ($\pi\acute{\epsilon}\tau\rho\alpha$) on which to build and establish the world. For this reason he calls Abraham a rock (צור, Isa. 51, 1 f.).[4] Abraham obtained possession of both worlds; for his sake this world and the world to come were created.[5]   In another Midrash we even find the statement that "for all the idle and false things that Israelites do in this world, Abraham is sufficient to atone."[6] But it is only necessary to read the context to see how far this is from a doctrinal valuation of the patriarch's merit.

An ancient Midrash runs: "You will find that all the signal interventions (נסים, 'miracles') that were wrought for Israel were for Abraham's sake (בזכותו של אברהם). The exodus from Egypt was for his sake, for it is written, 'He remembered his holy word unto Abraham his servant, and brought out his

---

[1] E.g. Micah 7, 18–20.   [2] See also Neh. 9, 7 f.
[3] On the sin of the generation of Enosh (Gen. 4, 26), see above, p. 473.
[4] Yelammedenu in Yalḳuṭ, I, § 766 (on Num. 23, 9); cf. Matthew 16, 18.
[5] Tanḥuma ed. Buber, Ḥayyè Sarah § 6 (by metathesis of בהבראם, Gen. 2, 4, באברהם).
[6] Pesiḳta ed. Buber f. 154a.

people with joy,' etc. (Psalm 105, 42 f.); the cleaving of the Red Sea was for his sake, for it is written, 'To him who parted the Red Sea into parts' (Psalm 136, 13); [1] . . . the cleaving of the Jordan (Josh. 3, 14 f.); . . . the giving of the Law was for his sake, for it is written, 'Thou hast ascended on high, thou hast led captivity captive, thou hast taken gifts among men'" (Psalm 68, 19). [2] Such homiletic ingenuities, as we have often occasion to observe, had no authority; in the same context in the Yalkuṭ R. Johanan is quoted as saying: We find in the Law and the Prophets and the Scriptures that Israel crossed the Jordan only for the sake of Jacob (Gen. 32, 11; Josh. 4, 22 f.; Psalm 114, 5–7).

In the passage quoted above (p. 536) from Sifrè Deut. § 32 the characteristic virtue of Isaac is found in that "he bound himself upon the altar" as a willing sacrifice, a proof that he loved God with his whole soul (life), which he thus surrendered to fulfil God's command. In Genesis it is Abraham's faith and his obedience to God's will even to the offering of his only son, the child of promise, that constitutes the whole significance of the story; Isaac is a purely passive figure. In the rabbinical literature, however, the voluntariness of the sacrifice on Isaac's part is strongly emphasized. Instead of a child he is a man in the fulness of his strength (according to the rabbinical chronology, [3] thirty-seven years old), whom, plainly, the aged father could not have bound against his will. The text in Sifrè is even stronger — "he bound himself." In a dispute with Ishmael, who claimed superior merit because he had been circumcised at thirteen, when he could have refused, while Isaac was but an infant and unable to object, Isaac declares: "You taunt me about one member of the body. If God were to say to me now, Sacrifice thyself! I would make the sacrifice forthwith." [4] According to

---

[1] See Note 243.

[2] Yelammedenu in Yalkuṭ on Josh. 13, 16 (II, § 15).

[3] Seder 'Olam R. c. 1 (ed. Ratner f. 3 f.), with Ratner's note. The opposite view, Ibn Ezra on Gen. 22, 4.

[4] Sanhedrin 89b; cf. Tanḥuma ed. Buber, Wayyera § 42; Gen. R. 55, 4.

the Midrash this immediately preceded the command to Abraham to sacrifice his son, which thus appears as a test of Isaac's sincerity in the assertion. The willingness of Isaac to be offered in sacrifice is much earlier made a part of the story in Josephus, according to whom he was twenty-five years old.[1]

Rabbi Jonathan (ben Eleazar), in a homiletic exposition of Isaiah 63, 16 ('Abraham acknowledges us not and Israel does not recognize us') infers that Abraham and Jacob both refused to intercede for sinful Israel. When God said to them, Thy children have sinned, they replied, Let them be wiped out, that thy name may be hallowed; but Isaac pleaded for them: they are God's children, as much as his. He reduces the time of man's accountability by subtracting his minority, the half of his life spent in sleeping, the hours occupied by praying, eating, and other necessary doings, from seventy to twelve and a half. If God will bear the whole of man's sins, well and good; if not, let him bear half and Isaac will take half. "And if Thou sayest that I must bear the whole, lo, I sacrificed myself to Thee," thus making expiation for his people. Thereupon the Israelites exclaim, Thou art our father! But Isaac admonished them to praise God rather than him, and revealed God to their eyes. Then they lifted their eyes on high, saying: "Thou, O Lord, art our father, our Redeemer from eternity is Thy name!"[2]

On the ancient petition on public fasts, "He who answered Abraham our father on Mount Moriah shall answer you and hearken to the voice of your crying in that day," the Talmud lets Abraham remind God how, when he was bidden to offer his only son, he made no reply, as he might have done and was at first inclined to do, but suppressed his impulse and did God's will, and he asks, as in requital, that, when Isaac's sons are in tribulation and have none to undertake their defense, God himself shall undertake their defense, and let the binding of Isaac their

---

[1] Antt. i. 13, 2 § 227; cf. ibid. 13, 3 § 232. Philo makes him a young lad. De Abrahamo c. 32 § 176. See Note 244.

[2] Shabbat 89b. Bacher, Pal. Amoräer, I, 72.

father be remembered in their behalf, and mercy in full measure be shown them.[1]

The 'Binding of Isaac' found a place in the Liturgy of the synagogue. Thus, in the Additional Prayers (Musaf) for New Years: "Remember unto us, O Lord our God, the covenant and the loving-kindness, and the oath that thou swarest unto Abraham our father on Mount Moriah;[2] and may the binding with which Abraham our father bound Isaac his son on the altar be before thine eyes, how he suppressed his compassion in order to do thy will with a perfect heart. So may thy compassion suppress thine anger against us," etc.[3] In the later liturgy, as well as in the Palestinian Targum and the younger Midrashim,[4] the 'Akedah has a much larger place.

The appeal to God's mercy for the sake of the forefathers is frequent in writings of divers kinds. Thus, in the prayer of Azarias (Greek Daniel 3, 34 ff.): "Do not withdraw thy mercy from us, for the sake of Abraham thy beloved, and of Isaac thy servant, and of Jacob thy saint, to whom thou didst promise to make their posterity as numerous as the stars of heaven and as the sand on the sea-shore."[5] Similarly in 2 Macc. 8, 15, before a battle with a Syrian army, the Jews pray to God to deliver them from Nicanor, who purposed to sell them into slavery: "If not for their own sake, yet for the sake of the covenants with their fathers, and because God's reverend and glorious name had been named upon them." In the Testaments of the Twelve Patriarchs, Levi, predicting the laying waste of the temple and the dispersion of his descendants in captivity among all nations, abominated, reviled, and hated, by the righteous judgment of God, concludes: "And but for the sake of Abraham and Isaac

---

[1] Jer. Ta'anit 65d, top; Pesikta ed. Buber f. 154a–b. See Note 245.

[2] Cf. M. Ta'anit 2, 4.

[3] Note that the merit here is solely Abraham's. — Elbogen gives good reason for thinking that the passage was not an original part of the prayer; see Der jüdische Gottesdienst, p. 143.

[4] See Note 246.

[5] Exod. 32, 11–13.

and Jacob your fathers, not one of my posterity would be left
on the earth" (c. 15).   Asher makes a similar prediction concerning the dispersion of his descendants, but ends: "But the
Lord will gather you together again in (his) fidelity through his
mercy, for the sake of Abraham, Isaac, and Jacob" (c. 7).

In the letter to the nine tribes and a half, appended to the
Syriac Apocalypse of Baruch, Baruch urges his readers to pray
continually with their whole souls that the Almighty may be
reconciled to them, and not reckon to their charge their many
sins, but be mindful of the uprightness of their fathers (84, 10).[1]
They are warned that when the Day of Judgement comes, there
will be no intercession of the fathers.

Paul's confidence that God will not finally leave the Jews in
the alienation in which they now are through disobedience, but
that in his plan of grace all Israel will eventually be saved, rests
on the same premises: 'Considered from the point of view of
the gospel, the Jews are hateful to God for your (Gentiles) sake;
but considered from the point of view of the election, beloved
of God for the sake of the patriarchs; for the favors of God and
his call (to a mission and destiny) are unalterable' (Rom. 11,
28 f.).[2]

The three patriarchs, who are called by eminence 'the
fathers,'[3] are, of course, not the only ones among the ancestors
of Israel who deserved well of God and for whose sake he bestows
benefits on the people.   "Three excellent leaders and adminis-
trators (פרנסים) arose for Israel, Moses and Aaron and Miriam,
and for their sake three excellent gifts were given to Israel, the
well, the pillar of cloud, and the manna.   The well was for
Miriam's sake, and when she died the well was taken away, but
returned for the sake of Moses and Aaron.   When Aaron died
the pillar of cloud was taken away, but both of them returned for
Moses' sake.   When Moses died all three of them were taken

[1] 85, 12; cf. 4 Esdras 7, 105.
[2] ἀμεταμέλητα, things about which He does not change His mind.
[3] Berakot 16b: The name 'fathers' is given to three and the name 'moth-
ers' to four (Sarah, Rebecca, Leah, Rachel).

away, and did not return" (Zech. 11, 8).[1] Solomon, in difficulty about the installation of the ark in the temple, was
answered at once when he made mention of the good desert
of his father David.[2] It is unnecessary to multiply instances
further.

That God's favor is extended to the descendants of virtuous
ancestry even to remote generations had the solemn warrant of
the Decalogue: 'He visits the iniquities of the fathers upon the
children to the third and fourth generation of those that hate
him, but shows mercy unto the thousandth generation of those
that love him and keep his commandments,' that is, to countless
generations of their descendants.[3]

It is to be noted that in several of the passages quoted above,
the appeal is in reality to the covenant with the patriarchs or
the oath to them, rather than to the piety and virtue that commended them to God.

It is further to be observed that, in accordance with the Scripture precedents, the good desert of the fathers is generally
thought of as a ground of God's favor to their posterity collectively, rather than individually. It is in the national aspect that
the question is raised among the rabbis of the first half of the
third century at what point in the history this desert ceased to
influence God's dealings with the people. Various limits are set,
ranging from the days of Elijah to those of Hezekiah.[4] The texts
adduced for the diverse opinions are not to the point; the significant thing is the common assumption implied in the question
and the attempt to answer it. Against a vain confidence that
Abraham's lineage of itself will avail his unworthy descendants

[1] Tos. Soṭah 11, 10; more fully, Taʿanit 9a; cf. Sifrè Deut. § 305 (ed.
Friedmann f. 129a–b). Bacher, Tannaiten, II, 420.
[2] Tanḥuma ed. Buber, Waʾera § 6. For the good desert of David, God
promises to deliver Jerusalem from Sennacherib, Berakot 10b.
[3] Exod. 20, 6 f.; cf. Deut. 7, 9. Mekilta, Baḥodesh 6 (ed. Friedmann
f. 68b; ed. Weiss f. 75b).
[4] Shabbat 55a; cf. Jer. Sanhedrin 27d; Lev. R. 36, 6. In the two last R.
Aḥa concludes that it endures forever, and is appealed to in prayer, deducing
from Deut. 4, 31. Note 247.

in the approaching crisis, John the Baptist warns the crowds that resorted to his preaching: 'Offspring of vipers! who suggested to you to flee from the coming wrath? Bear fruit befitting repentance, and do not presume to say to yourselves, We have Abraham for father; for I tell you, God can, of these stones, raise up children for Abraham.'[1]

That the righteousness of a godly father will not save a degenerate son is too plainly and emphatically asserted by Ezekiel not to have found a place in the teaching of the schools.[2] On Deut. 32, 39, 'There is none that can save out of my hand,' the Sifrè enlarges: Fathers do not save their sons; Abraham did not save Ishmael, nor did Isaac save Esau. Nor can brother save brother; Isaac did not save Ishmael nor Jacob, Esau; even if men should give all the wealth of the earth, they could not give a ransom for him, as it is written, 'A man can by no means redeem his brother, nor give to God his ransom; for too costly is the redemption of their life, that it should live for ever.'[3]

The customary rendering of זכות אבות by 'merit of the fathers' has led some scholars erroneously to attribute to the rabbis a doctrine corresponding to the Roman Catholic doctrine of the treasury of merits. In the first place, there is no rabbinical *doctrine* on the subject, as the foregoing exposition should suffice to make evident. Second, the notion of the efficacy of the merit of the fathers has not the remotest affinity to Catholic doctrine. The *thesaurus meritorum Jesu Christi et sanctorum* is a fund, so to speak, deposited to the credit of the Church, on which the Pope, as the successor of Peter and the vicar of Christ, draws when he grants indulgences to the faithful.[4] The 'merit of the fathers' is no treasury of supererogatory and superabundant

---

[1] Matt. 3, 7–9; Luke 3, 7–8; cf. John 8, 33, 39.
[2] On the efforts to reconcile Exod. 20, 5 with Deut. 24, 16, Ezek. 18, 20, see Schechter, Aspects of Rabbinic Theology, pp. 185–189.
[3] Sifrè Deut. § 329 (ed. Friedmann f. 139b); cf. Sanhedrin 104a. See Note 248.
[4] See the Bull of Leo X, Cum postquam circumspecta tua (1518), defining the doctrine of indulgences, and the Catholic Encyclopedia.

good works; and, above all, there was no Church, and no Pope to dispense it upon his own conditions. That God, having regard to the character of the patriarchs, his relations to them and his promises to them, in his good pleasure shows special favor or undeserved lenience to their posterity, is a wholly different thing. Men may seek of God the forgiveness of sins 'for the sake of the fathers'; but they cannot claim to have their demerit offset by the merit of the fathers.[1]

[1] On the merit of the Fathers see Note 249.

CHAPTER VIII

EXPIATORY SUFFERING

HOWEVER full and free the divine forgiveness of the penitent sinner be conceived to be, experience shows that it does not annul all that we call the consequences of sin, whether we think of them as natural or penal. In the doctrine of the Catholic Church, the penitent, in the absolution, is relieved of the eternal, but not of the temporal, penalty of sin; hence the necessity of the *satisfactio pro peccatis* [1] which is an integral part of true repentance. Judaism also recognizes sins for which expiation remained to be made by the sinner after his repentance had been accepted. Rabbi Ishmael distinguishes four cases: For the neglect of a commandment requiring a man to do something, repentance itself at once secures forgiveness for the sin of omission (Jer. 3, 22); for the transgression of a prohibition (sin of commission), repentance suspends the sentence and the Day of Atonement atones (Lev. 16, 30); for transgressions the penalty of which is to be cut off (from the people by the act of God) or capital punishment by the sentence of a court, repentance and the Day of Atonement suspend the sentence, and sufferings atone (Psalm 89, 33); but if a man gives occasion for profaning the name of Heaven (God), though he repent, there is no power in repentance to suspend sentence, nor in the Day of Atonement to atone, but repentance and the Day of Atonement atone for a third, and bodily sufferings throughout the rest of the year for a third, and the day of death wipes out the rest (Isa. 22, 14).[2] The Mekilta on Exod. 20, 7, in which we have the tradition of the school of Ishmael, exhibits the genesis of these distinctions, which have their origin, not in reflections on the varieties and

---

[1] The inflictions are *satisfactoriae poenae*.

[2] Tos. Yom ha-Kippurim 5, 6–8; Yoma 86a. See Bacher, Tannaiten, I, 258 and note.

relative heinousness of sins, but in the endeavor to harmonize apparently discrepant utterances of scriptures by applying them to different cases.[1]   It is, however, the general teaching that sins are expiated by sufferings: "Chastisements wipe out all a man's wickednesses."[2]   Sufferings propitiate God as much as sacrifices; nay, more than sacrifices, for sacrifices are offered of a man's property, while suffering is borne in his person.[3] But they have this effect only when they are received in the spirit of penitence and submission. To this subject we shall revert in treating of Jewish piety.

That a criminal expiates his offence by his death is a mode of expression familiar to us. So in Jewish law, when a criminal drew near the place of execution he was exhorted to confess in the formula, "May my death be an expiation for all my wickednesses."[4]   Those who thus confess have a share in the World to Come. As we have seen, death finally wipes out the guilt even of those who have caused the name of God to be profaned — always supposing that they have repented of their sin. The general principle is formulated in Sifrè Num. § 112: All who die are expiated by death (except the man who despises the word of the Lord).[5]

The sufferings and death of the righteous have a propitiatory or piacular value for others than themselves. The death of Miriam is narrated (Num. 20) in the immediate sequel of the ritual of the red heifer (Num. 19), to teach that as the red heifer expiates, so does the death of the righteous; the context of the death of Aaron (Num. 20, 27–29) teaches a similar lesson.[6]

---

[1] Mekilta, Baḥodesh 7, on Exod. 20, 7 (ed. Friedmann f. 68b–69a; ed. Weiss f. 76a); cf. Mekilta de-R. Simeon ben Yoḥai on the same verse (ed. Hoffmann, pp. 106 f.).

[2] Berakot 5a, end; cf. Sifrè Deut. § 32 (ed. Friedmann f. 73b, near top). See the whole context, and Vol. II, pp. 253 f.

[3] Sifrè, l.c.

[4] M. Sanhedrin 6, 2; Tos. Sanhedrin 9, 5. Confession of the particular offense is not exacted.

[5] Sifrè on Num. 15, 31.

[6] Mo'ed Ḳaton 28a; Jer. Yoma 38b; Tanḥuma ed. Buber, Aḥare § 10. See Note 250.

Elsewhere we read: "In a time when there are righteous men in a generation, the righteous are seized for the generation; if there are no righteous men in the generation the school children are seized for the generation."[1] That the suffering and death of innocent children is for the transgression or neglect of the law of God on the part of their parents is often dwelt upon. According to an ingenious piece of Haggadah spun out of Psalm 8, 3, 'Out of the mouth of babes and sucklings hast thou founded strength' (i.e. the Law), the children of the Israelites at Sinai, including those still in their mother's womb, voluntarily became surety for their fathers' observance of the law of God, with full cognizance of the risk.[2]

In the Second Book of Maccabees, which, though written in Greek, is in general accord with Palestinian teaching, the martyr brothers declare to their tormentor that they suffer on their own account, having sinned against their God (7, 18). "We suffer on account of our own sins; but if, for the sake of punishment and chastisement, the Living One, our Lord, is for a brief time wroth with us, he will yet again be reconciled to his servants" (7, 32 f.). "I, like my brothers, give up my body and my lot in life for the laws of our fathers, and I beseech God speedily to become gracious to his people . . . and that with me and my brothers the wrath of the Almighty may cease, which has justly fallen upon our whole race" (7, 37, 38). The martyrs suffer as members of a sinful people; and they pray that God, having so signally punished its sins, may let them be the last to suffer, and restore his favor to the nation. It is the old conception of the solidarity of the nation.

In Fourth Maccabees, on the other hand, the aged Eleazar, in the extremity of his torments prays: "Thou knowest, O God, that when I might be saved, I am dying in fiery tortures on account of thy law. Be gracious to thy people, being satisfied

---

[1] Shabbat 33b.
[2] Cant. R. on Cant. 1, 4; Midrash Tehillim on Psalm 8, 3; Tanḥuma Wayyigash, init. See Schechter, Aspects of Rabbinic Theology, p. 311, and Note 251.

with our punishment in their behalf. Make my blood a sacrifice for their purification, and take my life as a substitute (ἀντίψυχον) for theirs (6, 27–29). The author, in the conclusion, puts it thus: "These, therefore, being sanctified for God's sake, were honored not only with this honor,[1] but also in that for their sake the enemies did not have power over our nation, and the tyrant was punished, and the fatherland purified,[2] they having become, as it were, a substitute, dying for the sin of the nation; and through the blood of those godly men and their propitiatory death, divine Providence saved Israel, which was before in an ill plight" (17, 20–22). Here the sufferings and death of the righteous martyrs are a vicarious expiation for the sins of their people.

As we have seen in the case of Isaac, his willingness to lay down life at God's bidding is reckoned by God as though the sacrifice had been accomplished,[3] and was pleaded by his descendants as a ground for the remission of their sins. In Num. 25, 10–13 the priesthood is bestowed by a covenant in perpetuity on Phineas and his descendants because 'he was zealous for his God and made atonement for the Israelites,' thus averting God's wrath from the people and saving them from complete destruction for the apostasy at Baal Peor. In the sense of the biblical narrative he made this atonement, or expiation, by killing two conspicuous and defiant sinners in the very act (Num. 25, 6–8; cf. Psalm 106, 30). The Haggadah, however, represents Phineas as having exposed himself by this act not only to obloquy but to peril. Sifrè on Num. 25, 13 ('Because he was zealous for his God and made atonement for the Israelites,') applies to him Isa. 53, 12, 'Because he exposed his life to death.'[4] "It is not said, 'to make atonement for the Israelites,' but, 'and he made atonement for the Israelites'; for even to the present time he has not ceased, but stands and makes atonement, and will do so till the time when the dead shall come to life."[5]

---

[1] Namely, of standing by the throne of God and enjoying a blessed eternity.
[2] Cf. 1, 11.
[3] Above, pp. 539 ff.
[4] See Note 252.
[5] See Note 253.

R. Simlai applied the same verse (Isa. 53, 12) more specifically to Moses. 'I will divide him a portion with the great, and he shall divide the spoil with the mighty': "Like Abraham, Isaac, and Jacob, who were mighty in the law and commandments. 'Because he exposed his life to death': Because he gave himself over to death, as it is written, 'And if not (if thou wilt not forgive their sin), blot me out, I pray, of the book which thou hast written' (Exod. 32, 32). 'And was numbered with the transgressors': He was numbered with those who died in the wilderness. 'And he took away the sin of many': Because he made atonement in the matter of the golden calf (Exod. 32). 'And made intercession for the transgressors': Because he sought mercy for the transgressors of Israel, that they might turn again in repentance." [1] In the Mekilta on Exod. 12, 1 [2] this is enounced as a general principle. "You will find that the patriarchs and the prophets gave themselves for Israel. What does it say of Moses? 'And now if Thou wilt forgive their sin, well; but if not, blot me out, I pray, from the book Thou hast written' (Exod. 32, 32); and again, 'If Thou deal thus with me, kill me outright, I pray, if I have found favor in Thy sight; and let me not behold the evil that has befallen me' (Num. 11, 15). And what does it say of David? 'Lo, it is I that have sinned and done wickedly, but these sheep, what have they done? Let Thy hand, I pray, be upon me and upon my father's house' (2 Sam. 24, 17). Everywhere you will find that the fathers and the prophets gave their life for Israel."

An example of the voluntary acceptance by a prophet of contumely and maltreatment at the hands of the people, and of the exceptional honor God bestowed on him on this account, is found by the Midrash in Isa. 6, 8. God warns Isaiah of what he has to expect, reciting what befell Amos and Micah, and asks whether he will take upon him to be beaten and insulted. The prophet replies: 'For this I gave my back to the smiters and

[1] Soṭah 14a. See Note 254.
[2] Ed. Friedmann f. 2a; ed. Weiss f. 2a.

my cheeks to those who pluck out the beard' (Isa. 50, 6), and God praises him in the words of Psalm 45, 8, and gives him rank among the prophets with the highest.[1]

Many Christian scholars have labored to prove that Isaiah 53 and cognate passages, expecially Psalm 22, were applied by ancient Jewish interpreters to the Messiah.[2] Raimundus Martini in his Pugio Fidei adduced some testimonies to this effect, the most explicit of which, however, are not extant in our texts.[3] In view of such utterances as have been quoted above about the fathers and the prophets, it would be neither strange nor especially significant, if among the many and diverse homiletical applications of scripture to the Messiah, something of a similar kind should have been said about him. Such application, would, however, be no evidence that the Jews had a doctrine of a suffering Messiah.

The acceptance by Isaiah of the hardships of his calling which has been quoted above, has in fact a counterpart in a mediaeval Midrash, in a compact between God and the Messiah at the creation, in which the Messiah agrees to endure the sufferings that are set before him on condition that no Israelite of all the generations to come shall perish.[4] The work is late, and it is not certain that the messianic homilies were originally a part of it. To take its testimony for authentic rabbinic Judaism would be like taking that of a Carolingian author for primitive Christianity. Moreover, the passage in question is palpably an appropriation of Christian doctrine for a Jewish Messiah. The same imitation appears also in the following homily (37), when it is said that in the days of the Messiah, when God pours out floods of blessing on Israel (Psalm 31, 20), the patriarchs will

---

[1] Pesiḳta ed. Buber f. 125b–126a; Lev. R. 10, 2.

[2] See Note 255.

[3] Compare especially the quotation from "Sifrè," Pugio f. 674 f. (ed. Carpzov pp. 866 f.) with Sifra on Lev. 5, 17.

[4] Pesiḳta Rabbati 36, ed. Friedmann f. 161b–162a, quoted in extenso in Yalḳuṭ on Isaiah 60 (§ 499). The Messiah is addressed as 'Ephraim.' See Vol. II, pp. 370 f.

stand and say to him, "Ephraim, Messiah our Righteousness, although we are thy forefathers, thou art greater than we, because thou hast borne the iniquities [1] of our children, and there have passed over thee hardships such as have not passed upon men of earlier or later times, and thou wast an object of derision and contumely to the nations of the world for Israel's sake."

[1] The phrase of Isa. 53, 11.